HARDBOILED
MYSTERY
WRITERS

HARDBOILED
MYSTERY
WRITERS

Raymond Chandler
Dashiell Hammett
Ross Macdonald

A Literary Reference

EDITED BY
MATTHEW J. BRUCCOLI
AND RICHARD LAYMAN

A Bruccoli Clark Layman Book

CARROLL & GRAF PUBLISHERS
NEW YORK

Hardboiled Mystery Writers
Raymond Chandler, Dashiell Hammett, Ross Macdonald

Carroll & Graf Publishers
An Imprint of Avalon Publishing Group Incorporated
161 William Street, 16th Floor
New York, NY 10038

Copyright © 1989 by The Gale Group

First Carroll & Graf trade paperback edition 2002

Library of Congress Cataloging-in-Publication Data is available.

ISBN: 0-7867-1029-2

Printed in the United States of America
Distributed by Publishers Group West

PERMISSIONS

RAYMOND CHANDLER

TEXT: Excerpts from letters by Raymond Chandler reprinted from *Selected Letters of Raymond Chandler*, ed. Frank MacShane, copyright © 1981 by the Estate of Raymond Chandler. Published by permission of the Estate of Raymond Chandler. Excerpts from *Raymond Chandler Speaking*, ed. Dorothy Gardiner and Katherine Sorley Walker, reprinted by permission of Ed Victor Ltd. Copyright © 1962. P. 21, "Raymond Chandler and Hollywood," courtesy of Southern Illinois University Press. P. 26, "A Cato of the Cruelties," courtesy of *Partisan Review*. P. 37, "Philip Marlowe Speaking," courtesy of *Kenyon Review*. P. 63, "The Decline and Fall of the Detective Story," by permission of Doubleday, Inc. Copyright © 1981 by the Estate of W. Somerset Maugham. P. 56, "Twelve Notes on the Mystery Story," courtesy of *Antaeus*. P. 77, "Raymond Chandler, Private Eye," courtesy of *Commentary*. P. 81, "Trouble in Mind," by permission of George V. Higgins. Copyright © 1988 by George V. Higgins. Articles from the *New York Times* and the *Times Literary Supplement* used by permission.

PHOTOS: P. 38, courtesy of Kent State University Library.

DASHIELL HAMMETT

TEXT: P. 114, "Introduction" to *The Maltese Falcon*, by permission of Alfred A. Knopf, Publisher. Copyright © 1962 by the Modern Library. P. 126, excerpt from *Memo From David O. Selznick*, ed. by Rudy Behlmer, by permission of Viking Press. Copyright © 1972. P. 132, "Oh, Look—Two Good Books," by permission of the *New Yorker*. P. 142, "Our Literary Nudism," by permission of *Esquire Magazine*. P. 179, "With Corporal Hammett on Adak," by permission of E. E. Spitzer. P. 206, "The Strange Case of Dashiell Hammett," by permission of the *New York Post*. P. 228, "Hammett: Profiler of Hard-Boiled Yeggs," by permission of the *Los Angeles Times*. P. 235, "Homage to Dashiell Hammett," courtesy of the Mystery Writers of America. P. 237, "Mystery Writer was Enigmatic Throughout Life," by permission of the *Baltimore News-American*. P. 238, "Books and Authors," by permission of the *Baltimore Sun*. Excerpts from the *New York Times* and the *Times Literary Supplement* used by permission.

PHOTOS: Pp. 94-95 from *Dashiell Hammett Tour*, courtesy of Don Herron. P. 129, New York Public Library at Lincoln Center, the Astor, Lenox and Tilden Foundations.

ROSS MACDONALD

TEXT: Material by Kenneth Millar used by permission of the Estate of Kenneth Millar, courtesy of Margaret Millar. P. 244, reprinted by permission of Harold Ober Associates, Inc. Copyright © 1971 by Matthew J. Bruccoli and C.E. Frazer Clark, Jr. P. 248, 252, excerpts from *Ross Macdonald*, by permission of Harcourt, Brace Jovanovich. Copyright © 1984 by Matthew J. Bruccoli. P. 269, "Murder in the Library," courtesy of the Mystery Writers of America. P. 282, "An Interview with Ross Macdonald," by permission of *Concept*. P. 288, "Ross Macdonald: At the Edge," courtesy of the *Journal of Popular Culture*. P. 295, "A Conversation with Ross Macdonald," courtesy of the *Tamarack Review*. P. 309, "Down These Streets a Mean Man Must Go," courtesy of *Antaeus*. P. 312, *A Collection of Reviews by Ross Macdonald*, courtesy of Herb Yellin, Lord John Press. P. 314, "A Slightly Stylized Conversation with Ross Macdonald," from *Writer's Yearbook*, courtesy of *Writer's Digest*. Excerpts from the *New York Times* used by permission.

PHOTOS: P. 257, by permission of Hal Boucher. Pp. 270, 273, 304, courtesy of University of California, Irvine.

CONTENTS

PREFACE   ix

ACKNOWLEDGMENTS   xi

RAYMOND CHANDLER   3
    1888-1959

DASHIELL HAMMETT   85
    1894-1961

ROSS MACDONALD   243
[KENNETH MILLAR]
    1915-1983

INDEX   319

PREFACE

The *Literary Reference* series is a reference source with a twofold purpose: 1) it makes significant literary documents accessible to students and to scholars, as well as to nonacademic readers; and 2) it supplements the *Dictionary of Literary Biography* (1978-   ). The *Literary Reference* series has been conceived to provide access to a range of material that many students never have the opportunity to see. By itself it is a portable archive. Used with *DLB*, it expands the biographical and critical coverage of the essays by presenting key documents on which these essays are based. *DLB* places authors' lives and works in the perspective of literary history; the *Literary Reference* series chronicles evolving literary history.

Each volume in the *Literary Reference* series concentrates on the major figures of a particular literary period, movement, or genre; this volume is restricted to three masters of the hardboiled movement: Raymond Chandler, Dashiell Hammett, and Ross Macdonald (Kenneth Millar). These figures have been selected for their influence on American literary history and because their careers generated documents of enduring interest. Wherever possible, letters, notebooks and diary entries, interviews, and book reviews are included in *Literary Reference* entries. Each document is chosen to illuminate a notable event in a writer's personal or professional life or to reveal the development of his reputation. Entries vary in length and content according to the author's writing habits, the availability of his papers, and the amount of attention given him and his works in the literary press. In this volume the Hammett entry is substantially longer than either the Chandler or the Macdonald because more materials are available. During his long public life Hammett attracted an unusual amount of attention because of his flamboyant life-style and political activism; as a result, the Hammett entry is swelled by significant materials of an unusual nature, such as his editorials in an army newspaper, legal depositions about his literary works, and public testimony about his Communist party affiliations.

Although *hard-boiled* is freely and inappropriately applied to a range of books and writers, there have been few satisfactory definitions of it as a literary term. (See page 248 in this volume.) Critics have agreed that it is a characteristically American way of writing. The hard-boiled style has been called the authentic voice of American literature, and it has even been claimed that the hard-boiled style is the only endemically American prose. Certainly, its influence has been world-wide. The French existentialists made a cult of it; and British writers have imitated it with indifferent results.

Attempts to identify a hard-boiled school are misleading because *school* implies adherence to a common artistic doctrine or the influence of a teacher figure; but the American hard-boiled writers have been too independent and disparate to fit convenient classification. Nonetheless, there are certain recognizable background elements in what has been called the golden era of hard-boiled fiction commencing in the late Twenties. Many of the writers appeared in the pulp magazines (of which *Black Mask* was the outstanding incubator of talent), and almost all of them wrote detective-mystery-crime fiction. The dominant figure during this period was Dashiell Hammett, but he was not a schoolmaster. Raymond Chandler, who emerged a decade after Hammett, did not imitate him. Ross Macdonald acknowledged his admiration for both Hammett and Chandler, but he did not write like either one—although the tone of Macdonald's work is closer to Chandler than to Hammett.

Yet, if the concept of a hard-boiled literary school is a distortion, there is clearly a hard-boiled tradition in American literature extending from the frontier writers and the vernacular humorists. There one finds the elements of self-reliance and anti-authoritarianism that form the codes of individual conduct in Sam Spade, Philip Marlowe, and Lew Archer. Hard-boiled writing is more than a literary technique: it is an American response to life.

Literary documents often convey messages beyond the words they employ. Dashiell Hammett's holograph explanation of the circumstances that caused him to abandon the first draft of *The Thin Man* provides insights into the world of professional authorship while indicating significant facts about the development of literary ideas. The draft was discarded because Hammett's agent made the mistake of attempting to sell it in violation of contract. As a result, Hammett's last novel was drastically different from the book that first occurred to him.

A writer's career aspirations or his private observations about his work are frequently best revealed in his correspondence. For Raymond Chandler, letters were a substitute for writing fiction, and his epistolary comments on his work and that of other writers enlarge the reader's appreciation of the novels. Chandler's letters also reveal the complexity of character and deep literary intelligence in this writer of mere detective stories.

Book reviews by influential critics, contemporaries of the author, evoke the literary atmosphere of an era. They are invaluable for the understanding of a writer's reputation, providing the groundwork upon which subsequent assessments of his work depend. Reviews influence public opinion as they chart the course of an author's critical reception. Critics and fellow writers have at times been instrumental in directing a writer's career; thus two articles in the *New York Times Book Review*—one of which was by Eudora Welty—initiated a reappraisal of the entire Ross Macdonald canon. Movie reviews are also included for Hammett and Chandler. Both worked in Hollywood, and both had novels made into classic movies—albeit by other hands.

Interviews contribute to the formation of an author's public image, as he publicly addresses his readers and often attempts to establish his position in literature. Of the three writers included in this volume, Ross Macdonald was the most generous provider of interviews, for which he took great pains to be truthful. A full understanding of Ross Macdonald's work is impossible without access to certain of his interviews.

Fiction, as F. Scott Fitzgerald observed, is transmuted autobiography. In addition to the letters and interviews, personal photographs may explicate an author's life and work. Reproductions of dust jackets and advertisements—a book's packaging for the public—reveal the publisher's attempt to define an author's audience and establish impressions of his works. For detective or crime or suspense fiction, dust jackets and paperback covers typically present a progression from the garish to the respectable as the author's reputation escalated. These illustrations in the *Literary Reference* series present in the most direct way the stages of an author's publishing history, illustrating the taste of his era as well.

Each author entry in the *Literary Reference* series is therefore a concise illustrated biography as well as a sampling of the diverse materials that have heretofore been accessible only to a limited group of researchers. Too often readers see only the results of an author's painstaking toil and hear only the conclusions of others about the merits of his work. They rarely have the opportunity to glimpse a writer's work in progress, to consider firsthand the judgments of his contemporaries, and to examine extracts from his personal papers. The *Literary Reference* series offers these opportunities, facilitating the study of an author's life and career from a variety of perspectives, each of which enriches the appreciation and understanding of his enduring achievements.

ACKNOWLEDGMENTS

This book was produced by Bruccoli Clark Layman, Inc. Karen L. Rood is senior editor for the *Dictionary of Literary Biography* series. Matthew J. Bruccoli and Richard Layman were the in-house editors.

Production coordinator is Kimberly Casey. Art supervisor is Cheryl A. Crombie. Copyediting supervisor is Joan M. Prince. Typesetting supervisor is Kathleen M. Flanagan. William Adams, Laura Ingram, and Michael D. Senecal are editorial associates. The production staff includes Brandy H. Barefoot, Rowena Betts, Charles D. Brower, Joseph M. Bruccoli, Amanda Caulley, Teresa Chaney, Patricia Coate, Sarah A. Estes, Cynthia Hallman, Judith K. Ingle, Warren McInnis, Kathy S. Merlette, Sheri Beckett Neal, Virginia Smith, and Mark Van Gunten. Jean W. Ross is permissions editor. Susan Todd is photography editor. Penney L. Haughton did photographic copy work for the volume.

Walter W. Ross and Jennifer Toth did the library research with the assistance of the reference staff at the Thomas Cooper Library of the University of South Carolina: Daniel Boice, Cathy Eckman, Gary Geer, Cathie Gottlieb, David L. Haggard, Jens Holley, Dennis Isbell, Jackie Kinder, Marcia Martin, Jean Rhyne, Beverly Steele, Ellen Tillett, Carol Tobin, and Virginia Weathers.

This volume would not have been possible without the assistance of able librarians and bookmen. We are grateful to Roger Berry, University of California–Irvine; Dean Keller, Kent State University Library; R. N. Slythe, Dulwich College Library, London; Otto Penzler, The Mysterious Press; Ralph B. Sipper, Joseph the Provider Books; and Fred Zentner, Cinema Bookshop, London.

Special thanks are due William Blackbeard, San Francisco Academy of Comic Art. His expertise and generosity have been essential.

RAYMOND CHANDLER

(23 July 1888–26 March 1959)

MAJOR BOOKS:

The Big Sleep (New York: Knopf, 1939; London: Hamish Hamilton, 1939);

Farewell, My Lovely (New York: Knopf, 1940; London: Hamish Hamilton, 1940);

The High Window (New York: Knopf, 1942; London: Hamish Hamilton, 1943);

The Lady in the Lake (New York: Knopf, 1943; London: Hamish Hamilton, 1944);

Five Murderers (New York: Avon, 1944);

Five Sinister Characters (New York: Avon, 1945);

Finger Man (New York: Avon, 1947);

The Little Sister (London: Hamish Hamilton, 1949; Boston: Houghton Mifflin, 1949);

The Simple Art of Murder (Boston: Houghton Mifflin, 1950; London: Hamish Hamilton, 1950:

The Long Good-Bye (London: Hamish Hamilton, 1953; Boston: Houghton Mifflin, 1954);

Playback (London: Hamish Hamilton, 1958; Boston: Houghton Mifflin, 1958);

Killer in the Rain (London: Hamish Hamilton, 1964; Boston: Houghton Mifflin, 1964);

Chandler Before Marlowe, edited by Matthew J. Bruccoli (Columbia: University of South Carolina Press, 1973);

The Blue Dahlia, edited by Bruccoli (Carbondale & Edwardsville: Southern Illinois University Press, 1976; London: Hamish Hamilton, 1976);

Raymond Chandler's Unknown Thriller: The Screenplay of Playback (New York: Mysterious Press, 1985; London: Harrap, 1985);

Poodle Springs, by Chandler and Robert B. Parker (New York: Putnam, 1989; London: Macdonald, 1990).

BIOGRAPHIES:

Alan Close, *The Australian Love Letters of Raymond Chandler* (Ringwood, Victoria: McPhee Gribble, 1995);

Frank MacShane, *The Life of Raymond Chandler* (New York: Dutton, 1976).

BIBLIOGRAPHY:

Matthew J. Bruccoli, *Raymond Chandler: A Descriptive Bibliography* (Pittsburgh: University of Pittsburgh Press, 1979).

LETTERS:

Selected Letters of Raymond Chandler, edited by Frank MacShane (New York: Columbia University Press, 1981; London: Cape, 1981).

NOTEBOOKS:

Raymond Chandler Speaking, edited by Dorothy Gardiner and Kathrine Sorley Walker (London: Hamish Hamilton, 1962; Boston: Houghton Mifflin, 1962);

The Notebooks of Raymond Chandler & English Summer, edited by Frank MacShane (New York: Ecco Press, 1976; London: Weidenfeld & Nicolson, 1977).

Chandler entered Dulwich College, a public school (private preparatory school) in a London suburb, in 1900.

ARCHIVES:

The principal collections of Chandler's manuscripts and papers are at the University of California, Los Angeles, Library and at the Bodleian Library, Oxford University.

* * * * *

The people whom God or nature intended to be writers find their own answers, and those who have to ask are impossible to help. They are merely people who want to be writers.

To Mrs. Robert J. Hogan, 27 December 1946 [excerpt] (*Selected Letters of Raymond Chandler,* edited by Frank MacShane)

* * * * *

LETTER:

To Hamish Hamilton, 10 November 1950, *Selected Letters of Raymond Chandler,* edited by Frank MacShane, pp. 235-238.

Chandler responded to a request from his English publisher with a detailed autobiographical statement.

6005 Camino de la Costa
La Jolla, California
November 10, 1950

Dear Jamie:

Why do people want biographical material? Why does it matter? And why does a writer have to talk about himself as a person? It's all such a bore. I was born in Chicago, Illinois, so damned long ago that I wish I had never told anybody when. Both my parents were of Quaker descent. Neither was a practicing Quaker. My mother was born in Waterford, Ireland, where there was a very famous Quaker school, and perhaps still is. My father came of a Pennsylvania farming family, probably one of the batch that settled with William Penn. At the age of seven I had scarlet fever in a hotel, and I understand this is a very rare accomplishment. I remember principally the ice cream and the pleasure of pulling the loose skin

Chandler as a student at Dulwich College

did book reviews, essays, etc., for the old *Academy*, sketches and verses for the *Westminster Gazette*, odd paragraphs here and there, etc. I served in the First Division of the Canadian Expeditionary Force in what used to be called the Great War, and was later attached to the R.A.F., but had not completed flight training when the Armistice came. So far I had shown very little talent for writing, and that little was riddled with intellectual snobbery. I arrived in California with a beautiful wardrobe, a public school accent, no practical gifts for earning a living, and a contempt for the natives which, I am sorry to say, has in some measure persisted to this day. I had a pretty hard time trying to make a living. Once I worked on an apricot ranch ten hours a day, twenty cents an hour. Another time I worked for a sporting goods house, stringing tennis rackets for $12.50 a week, 54 hours a week. I taught myself bookkeeping and from there on my rise was as rapid as the growth of a sequoia. I detested business life, but in spite of that I finally became an officer or director of half a dozen independent oil corporations. The depression finished that. I was much too expensive a luxury for those days. Wandering up and down the Pacific Coast in an automobile, I began to read pulp magazines, because they were cheap enough to throw away and because I never had any taste at any time for the kind of thing which is known as women's magazines. This was in the great days of the *Black Mask* (if I may call them great days) and it struck me that some of the writing was pretty forceful and honest, even though it had its crude aspect. I decided that this might be a good way to try to learn to write fiction and get paid a small amount of money at the same time. I spent five months over an 18,000 word novelette and sold it for $180. After that I never looked back, although I had a good many uneasy periods looking forward. I wrote *The Big Sleep* in three months, but a lot of the material in it was revamped from a couple of novelettes. This gave it body but didn't make it any easier to write. I was always a slow worker. In the best month I ever had, I wrote two 18,000 word novelettes and a short story which was sold to the *Post*. For Gardner this would be the work of a couple of days, but for me it was a terrific production and I have never approached it since. I went to Hollywood in 1943 to work with

off during convalescence. I spent five years in Dulwich and thereafter lived in France and Germany for a couple more years. At that time I was thought to be a British subject, since my mother had regained her British nationality while I was still a minor. So that when I returned to the United States, the record shows that I was admitted as a British subject. It took a long, long struggle, and finally a law suit against the Attorney General of the United States to get it changed. The point of law was that a minor cannot be expatriated, and I don't know why they found it so hard to accept this. It cost me quite a lot of money to force it on them. I had done several years free lancing in London in a rather undistinguished way. I

Billy Wilder on *Double Indemnity*. This was an agonizing experience and has probably shortened my life; but I learned from it as much about screen writing as I am capable of learning, which is not very much. I was under contract to Paramount after that and did several pictures for them, including one original screen play, *The Blue Dahlia*, which was written from scratch (that is without any basic story) and shot complete in twenty weeks. I was told at the time that this was some sort of a record for a high budget picture. All my books, except *The Little Sister*, have been made into pictures, two of them twice. Like every writer, or almost every writer, who goes to Hollywood, I was convinced in the beginning that there must be some discoverable method of working in pictures which would not be completely stultifying to whatever creative talent one might happen to possess. But like others before me I discovered that this was a dream. It's nobody's fault; it's part of the structure of the industry. Too many people have too much to say about a writer's work. It ceases to be his own. And after a while he ceases to care about it. He has brief enthusiasms, but they are destroyed before they can flower. People who can't write tell him how to write. He meets clever and interesting people and may even form lasting friendships, but all this is incidental to his proper business of writing. The wise screen writer is he who wears his second-best suit, artistically speaking, and doesn't take things too much to heart. He should have a touch of cynicism, but only a touch. The complete cynic is as useless to Hollywood as he is to himself. He should do the best he can without straining at it. He should be scrupulously honest about his work, but he should not expect scrupulous honesty in return. He won't get in. And when he has had enough, he should say good-bye with a smile, because for all he knows he may want to go back.

By the end of 1946 I had had enough. I moved to La Jolla. Since then I have written two screen plays, one of them with only occasional visits to a studio to talk over the story, and one without any visits to the studio at all. I shall probably do others, and if so I shall do them as well as I know how; but I shall keep my heart to myself.

I have been married since 1924 and have no children. I am supposed to be a hard-boiled writer, but that means nothing. It is merely a

Chandler enlisted in the Gordon Highlanders of Canada in World War I: "Once you have had to lead a platoon into direct machine-gun fire, nothing is ever the same again."

method of projection. Personally I am sensitive and even diffident. At times I am extremely caustic and pugnacious; at other times very sentimental. I am not a good mixer because I am very easily bored, and to me the average never seems good enough, in people or in anything else. I am a spasmodic worker with no regular hours, which is to say I only write when I feel like it. I am always surprised at how very easy it seems at the time, and at how very tired one feels afterwards. As a mystery writer, I think I am a bit of an anomaly, since most mystery writers of the American school are only semi-literate; and I am not only literate but intellectual, much as I dislike the term. It would seem that a classical education might be rather a poor basis for writing novels in a hard-boiled vernacular. I happen to think otherwise. A classical education saves you from being fooled by pretentiousness, which is what most current fiction is too full of. In this country the mystery writer is looked down on as sub-literary merely because he is a mystery writer, rather than for instance a writer of social significance twaddle. To a classicist—even a very rusty one—such an attitude is merely a parvenu insecurity. When people ask me, as occasionally they do, why I don't try my hand at a serious novel, I don't argue with them; I don't even ask them what they mean by a serious novel. It would be useless. They wouldn't know. The question is parrot-talk. The problem of what is significant literature I leave to fat bores like Edmund Wilson—a man of many distinctions—among which personally I revere most highly (in the *Chronicles of Hecate County*) that of having made fornication as dull as a railroad time table.

Reading over some of the above, I seem to detect a rather supercilious tone here and there. I am afraid this is not altogether admirable, but unfortunately it is true. It belongs. I am, as a matter of fact, rather a supercilious person in many ways. I shouldn't be at all surprised if it shows in what I write. And it may well be this which arouses such flailing anger in pip-squeaks like John Dickson Carr and Anthony Boucher.

Yours ever,
Ray

POEM:
"The Unknown Love," *Chambers's Journal*, 12 (19 December 1908): 48.

Chandler in the 1920s

After resigning from the British Admiralty, Chandler attempted to support himself as a free-lance writer in London. This poem is his earliest located publication.

When the evening sun is slanting,
When the crickets raise their chanting,
And the dewdrops lie a-twinkling on the grass,
As I climb the pathway slowly,
With a mien half proud, half lowly,
O'er the ground your feet have trod I gently pass.

Round the empty house I wander,
Where the ivy now is fonder
Of your memory than those long gone away;
And I feel a sweet affection
For the plant that lends protection

To the window whence you looked on me that day.

Was it love or recognition,
When you stormed my weak position
And made prisoner my heart for evermore?
For I felt I long had known you,
That I'd knelt before the throne you
Graced in Pharaoh's days or centuries before.

Though your face from me was hidden,
Yet the balm was not forbidden
On your coffin just to see the wreath I sent.
Though no word had passed between us,
Yet I felt that God had seen us
And had joined your heart to mine e'en as you went.

Let them talk of love and marriage,
Honeymoon and bridal carriage,
And the glitter of a wedding à la mode!
Could they understand the union
Of two hearts in dear communion
Who were strangers in the world of flesh and blood?

In my eyes the tears are welling
As I stand before your dwelling,
In my pilgrimage to where you lived, my fair.
And ere I return to duty
In this world of weary beauty,
To the stillness of the night I breathe my prayer:

When the latest great trump has sounded,
When life's barque the point has rounded,
When the wheel of human progress is at rest,
My belovèd, may I meet you,
With a lover's kiss to greet you,
Where you wait me in the gardens of the blest!

POEM:

"The Perfect Knight," *Westminster Gazette*, 34 (30
September 1909): 2.

*This poem from Chandler's apprenticeship period intro-
duces the theme of knighthood that critics have identified
in his novels.*

He hath a sword of altar fire,
He hath a shield of shimmering air,
The one to slay his base desire,
The one to guard him from despair.

He hath a burnished helm of laughter,
He hath a lance of righteous wrath,
To gild the smoke-stain on his rafter,
To dash the foul thing from his path.

He hath a gauntlet of emotion,

He hath a prancing steed of love,
He hath a banner of devotion
To lead wherever he may rove.

He hath a mind to see and wonder,
A soul to answer to his sight,
A heart of song and mighty thunder,
A voice of endless pure delight.

He hath a vast and sunny garden
To tend through unexhausted time,
With Israfil to be its warden,
With flowers meet for every clime.

His strength is higher than the mountain,
And older than the universe,
Why doth he thirst beside his fountain
And seek for nothing with a curse?

E'en in his fury is he craven,
Glaring he wails he cannot see;
He hides his head and prays for Heaven,
Who hath all Heaven in his fee.

LETTER:

To James Howard, 26 March 1957 [excerpt], *Selected
Letters of Raymond Chandler*, edited by Frank
MacShane, pp. 432-433.

*In this letter to an official of the Mystery Writers of Amer-
ica Chandler discusses his apprenticeship as a mystery
writer and contrasts it with the attitude of unteachable
writers.*

6925 Neptune Place
La Jolla, California
March 26, 1957

Dear Mr. Howard:

. . . In 1931 my wife and I used to cruise up
and down the Pacific Coast, in a very leisurely
way, and at night, just to have something to read,
I would pick a pulp magazine off a rack. It suddenly struck me that I might be able to write this
stuff and get paid while I was learning. I spent
five months on my first novelette, but I did something I have never been able to persuade any
other writer to do. Writers who asked me for help
or advice later on. I made a detailed synopsis of
some story–say by Gardner, he was one of them,
and he is a good friend of mine–and then tried to
write the story. Then I compared it with professional work and saw where I had failed to make
an effect, or had the pace wrong, or some other mis-

zine and get a lift out of it and start banging the typewriter on borrowed energy. They get a certain distance and then they fade. They don't know why, so they come to someone like me, or perhaps someone like you, and ask what is wrong. You try to tell them, but you never get it home. They think all they need is some little twist; they never get it into their heads that writing is like an iceberg, for every foot that shows above water there are eight below.

Yours very truly,
Raymond Chandler

CHANDLER'S PULP STORIES:

Between 1933 and 1941 Chandler published twenty-one stories in pulp magazines, or dime novels, as they were called (but Black Mask *cost fifteen cents). In addition to documenting his apprenticeship before* The Big Sleep, *these stories are of particular interest because he re-cycled some of them for his early novels. Material from "Killer in the Rain" and "The Curtain" was incorporated in* The Big Sleep; *material from "The Man Who Liked Dogs," "Try the Girl," and "Mandarin's Jade" was incorporated in* Farewell, My Lovely; *material from "Big City Blues," "The Lady in the Lake," and "No Crime in the Mountains" was incorporated in* The Lady in the Lake.

Chandler in Black Mask
"Blackmailers Don't Shoot" (December 1933)
"Smart-Aleck Kill" (July 1934)
"Finger Man" (October 1934)
"Killer in the Rain" (January 1935)
"Nevada Gas" (June 1935)
"Spanish Blood" (November 1935)
"Guns at Cyrano's" (January 1936)
"The Man Who Liked Dogs" (March 1936)
"Goldfish" (June 1936)
"The Curtain" (September 1936)
"Try the Girl" (January 1937)

Other Chandler Pulp Publications
"Noon Street Nemesis," *Detective Fiction Weekly* (30 May 1936)
"Mandarin's Jade," *Dime Detective* (November 1937)
"Red Wind," *Dime Detective* (January 1938)
"The King in Yellow," *Dime Detective* (March 1938)
"Bay City Blues," *Dime Detective* (June 1938)

Chandler married Pearl Eugenie Hurlburt (Cissy) in 1924 when she was fifty-three and he was thirty-five

take. Then I did it over and over again. But the boys who want you to show them how to write won't do that. Everything they do has to be, they hope, for publication. They won't sacrifice anything to learn their trade. They never get it into their heads that what a man wants to do and what he can do are entirely separate things, that no writer worth the powder to blow him through a barbed wire fence into hell is ever in his own mind anything but starting from scratch. No matter what he may have done in the past, what he is trying to do now makes him a boy again, that however much skill in routine technical things he may have acquired, nothing will help him now but passion and humility. They read some story in a maga-

"The Lady in the Lake," *Dime Detective* (January 1939)

"Pearls Are a Nuisance," *Dime Detective* (1 April 1939)

"Trouble Is My Business," *Dime Detective* (August 1939)

"The Bronze Door," *Unknown* (November 1939)

"No Crime in the Mountains," *Detective Story* (September 1941)

LETTER:

To Alfred A. Knopf, 19 February 1939, *Selected Letters of Raymond Chandler*, edited by Frank MacShane, pp. 3-5.

When The Big Sleep *was accepted in 1939 Knopf was one of the most respected literary imprints in America. Alfred Knopf published Chandler's first four novels through 1943.*

> Route 1, Box 421
> Riverside, Calif
> Feb. 19th. 1939

Dear Mr. Knopf:–

Please accept my thanks for your friendly letter and please believe that, whether you wrote to me or not, I should have written to thank you for the splendid send-off you are trying to give me. Having been more or less in business a great part of my life, I have some appreciation of what this involves, even though I know nothing of the publishing business.

Mr. Conroy wrote to me twice that you had said something about my getting to work on another book and I answered him that I wanted to put it off until I had an idea what kind of reception this one would get. I have only seen four notices, but two of them seemed more occupied with the depravity and unpleasantness of the book than with anything else. In fact the notice from the *New York Times*, which a clipping agency sent me as a come-on, deflated me pretty thoroughly. I do not want to write depraved books. I was aware that this yarn had some fairly unpleasant citizens in it, but my fiction was learned in a rough school, and I probably didn't notice them much. I was more intrigued by a situation where the mystery is solved by the exposition and understanding of a single character, always well in evidence,

rather than by the slow and sometimes long-winded concatenation of circumstances. That's a point which may not interest reviewers of first novels, but it interested me very much. However, there's a very good notice in today's *Los Angeles Times* and I don't feel quite such a connoisseur of moral decay as I did yesterday. They have Humphrey Bogart playing the lead, which I am in favor of also. It only remains to convince Warner Brothers.

As to the next job of work for your consideration, I should like, if you approve, to try to jack it up a few more notches. It must be kept sharp, swift and racy, of course, but I think it could be a little less harsh–or do you not agree? I should like to do something which would not be automatically out for pictures and which yet would not let down whatever public I may acquire. *The Big Sleep* is very unequally written. There are scenes that are all right, but there are other scenes still much too pulpy. Insofar as I am able I want to develop an objective method–but slowly–to the point where I can carry an audience over into a genuine dramatic, even melodramatic novel, written in a very vivid and pungent style, but not slangy or overly vernacular. I realize that this must be done cautiously and little by little, but I think it can be done. To acquire delicacy without losing power, that's the problem. But I should probably do a minimum of three mystery novels before I try anything else.

Thank you again and I do hope that when the returns are in, you will be not too disappointed.

> Very sincerely,
> Raymond Chandler

NOTEBOOK ENTRY:

From *Raymond Chandler Speaking*, edited by Dorothy Gardner & Kathrine Sorley Walker, pp. 207-209.

This plan for future work was made after Chandler had written The Big Sleep. *He did not write* Zone of Twilight, English Summer, *or the series of "fantastic stories." Parenthetical notes were added in April 1942.*

Chandler's first detective story, in the December 1933 Black Mask

Los Angeles dinner meeting of Black Mask *contributors, the only time Chandler and Hammett met. Standing, left to right: Raymond J. Moffatt, Chandler, Herbert Stinson, Dwight Babcock, Eric Tayler, Hammett. Seated: Arthur Barnes, John K. Butler, W. T. Ballard, Horace McCoy, Norbert Davis.*

Since all plans are foolish and those written down are never fulfilled, let us make a plan, this 16th day of March, 1939, at Riverside, California.

For the rest of 1939, all of 1940, spring of 1941, and then if there is no war and if there is any money to go to England for material.

Detective Novels
Law is Where You Buy It
Based on *Jade, the Man Who Liked Dogs, Bay City Blues*. Theme, the corrupt alliance of police and racketeers in a small California town, outwardly as fair as the dawn.
(Farewell, My Lovely)

The Brasher Doubloon
A burlesque on the pulp novelette, with Walter and Henry. Some stuff from *Pearls Are a Nuisance* but mostly new plot.
(Written 1942 but as a novel with Phil Marlowe, to be published under the title *The High Window*)

Zone of Twilight
A grim witty story of the boss politician's son and the girl and the blending of the upper and under-worlds. Material, *Guns at Cyrano's, Nevada Gas*

(Dated, I'm afraid, by events)
If advisable, try *Goldfish* for material for a fourth

Dramatic Novel
English Summer
A short, swift, tense, gorgeously written story verging on melodrama, based on my short story. The surface theme is the American in England, the dramatic decay of the refined character and its contrast with the ingenuous, honest, utterly fearless and generous American of the best type
(Still hoping to do this, April 1942)

Short-long stories
A set of six or seven fantastic stories, some written, some thought of, perhaps one brand new. Each a little different in tone and effect from the other. The ironic gem *The Bronze Door*, [*Seven from the Stars*], the perfect fantastic atmosphere story *The Edge of the West* [*Seven from Nowhere*], the spooky story *Grandma's Boy*, the farcical story *The*

Disappearing Duke, the Allegory Ironic *The Four Gods of Bloon*, the pure fairytale *The Rubies of Marmelon* [*Seven Tales from Nowhere*]. The three mystery stories should be finished in the next two years, by end of 1940. If they make enough for me to move to England and to forget mystery writing and try *English Summer* and the Fantastic Stories, without worrying about whether these make money, I tackle them. [(And still praying I may someday do these)] But I must have two years' money ahead, and a sure market with the detective story when I come back to it, if I do. If *English Stories* is a smash hit, which it should be, properly written, written up to the hilt but not overwritten, I'm set for life. From then on I'll alternate the fantastic and the dramatic until I think of a new type. Or may do a suave detective just for the fun.

To this Cissy added:
Dear Raymio, you'll have fun looking at this maybe, and seeing what useless dreams you had. Or perhaps it will not be fun.

LETTER:
To Charles Morton, 18 December 1944 [excerpt], *Selected Letters of Raymond Chandler*, edited by Frank MacShane, pp. 35-39.

In this letter to the associate editor of the Atlantic Monthly *Chandler discusses his mixed feelings about writing for the movies. He later wrote "Oscar Night in Hollywood" for the* Atlantic (*March 1948*).

. . . I cannot complete my piece about screenwriters and screenwriting for the simple reason that I have no honesty about it. I may wake up with a different notion, but you cannot bully me into sending you something I am so deadly unsure about. There are points like these to make, but when you make them you get in a mess. E.g., 1. There is no mature art of the screenplay, and by mature I don't mean intellectual or postgraduate or intelligentsia-little magazine writing. I mean an art which knows what it is doing and has the techniques necessary to do it. 2. An adult, that is dirty or plain-spoken art of the screen, could exist at any moment the Hays Office (Title for an Essay on same: *Dirtymindedness As a Career*) and the local censorship boards would let it, but it would be no

IN JANUARY

RAYMOND CHANDLER leads off with one of the most powerful stories we've seen in a half dozen years—a story so real and life-like that the characters seem to step right out of the printed text, walk and talk and act before you, play their drama of petty greed, of love and lust and murderous impulse, of tense conflict and mad sacrifice.

You won't soon forget the huge Dravec whom a pistol-full of bullets couldn't stop; the sleek Joe Marty, the slimy Steiner, the beautiful, erratic girl Carmen, or the silent detective who faces guns from either side.

Everyone knows that crime is sordid, for crime springs from the worst of human impulses and thrives on the evil passions of mankind. A story, therefore, of all-criminals is depressing, leaving you with an impression of repulsion and disgust. But when characters of good intention who are the prey of evil purposes, set out to break the toils of crime thrown about them and rescue a victim through honest love and sacrifice of self, then you have a setting where the most powerful of human emotions clash, and the fight, whether won or lost, is a tonic in itself.

Such is "**Killer in the Rain**," by **Raymond Chandler**, in the January issue.

And altogether, this January number, coming up, is, we believe, one of the very best we have been fortunate enough to get together for you, and an eminently fitting one with which to start the new year toward better and even better things.

In addition to Mr. Chandler's great story, **Frederick Nebel**, in "**He Was a Swell Guy**," gives you one of the choicest of all Cap. Steve MacBride stories; **Erle Stanley Gardner**, who makes you read so fast and so easily that you are unconscious of the passing words, brings back an old **Black Mask** favorite in the swiftest of gun-action; **George Harmon Coxe** presents hard headed, scrapping Flash ___ in a nerve wracker, called "Mur__ ___ure"; Roger Torrey introduces a new one to you in "**Beginner's Luck**," but with the same old Torrey dynamic punch.

IN JANUARY

"Killer in the Rain"
By Raymond Chandler
A powerful story of crime and love and sacrifice.

"He Was a Swell Guy"
By Frederick Nebel
Kennedy gives MacBride a tip —and it's murder.

"Winged Lead"
By Erle Stanley Gardner
It's the man behind the guns that counts.

"Murder Picture"
By George Harmon Coxe
Flash Casey finds that there are times when killers object to having their pictures taken.

"Beginner's Luck"
By Roger Torrey
It might have been luck but it was also a case of just plain guts.

There's the line-up. You know all the names, and the stories are every one **Black Mask** quality. Not a dud in a carload.

JANUARY BLACK MASK
On ALL Newsstands December 7th

127

Announcement for Chandler's fourth detective story, published in January 1935

[13]

more *mature* than *Going My Way* is. 3. There is no available body of screenplay literature, because it belongs to the studios, not to the writers, and they won't show it. For instance, I tried to borrow a script of *The Maltese Falcon* from Warners; they would not lend it to me. All the writer can do is look at pictures. If he is working in a studio, he can get the scripts of that studio, but his time is not his own. He can make no leisurely study and reconstruction of the problems. 4. There is no *teaching* in the art of the screenplay because there is nothing to teach; if you do not know how pictures are made, you cannot possibly know how to write them. No outsider knows that, and no writer would be bothered, unless he was an out-of-work or manqué writer. 5. The screenplay as it exists is the result of a bitter and prolonged struggle between the writer (or writers) and the people whose aim is to exploit his talent without giving it the freedom to be a talent. 6. It is only a little over 3 years since the major (and only this very year the minor) studios were forced after prolonged and bitter struggle to agree to treat the writer with a reasonable standard of business ethics. In this struggle the writers were not really fighting the motion picture industry at all; they were fighting those powerful elements in it that had hitherto glommed off all the glory and prestige and who could only continue to do so by selling themselves to the world as the makers of pictures. This struggle is still going on, and the writers are winning it, and they are winning it in the wrong way: by becoming producers and directors, that is, by becoming showmen instead of creative artists. This will do nothing for the art of the screenplay and will actually harm those writers who are temperamentally unfitted for showmanship (and this will include always the best of them). 7. The writer is still very far from winning the right to create a screenplay without interference from his studio. Why? Because he does not know how, and it is to the interest of the producers and directors to prevent him from learning how. If even a quarter of the *highly-paid* screenwriters of Hollywood (leaving out all the people who work on program pictures) could produce a completely integrated and thoroughly photographable screenplay, with only the amount of interference and discussion necessary to protect the studio's investment in actors and free-

dom from libel and censorship troubles, then the producer would become a business co-ordinator and the director would become the interpreter of a completed work, instead of, as at present, the maker of the picture. They will fight to the death against it.

I have a three year contract with Paramount, for 26 weeks work a year, at a vast sum of money (by my standards). Nothing of the above would give particular offense to the studio, but much of it would be deeply resented by many individuals and would involve me in constant arguments which would wear me out. But there is still more to be said, and it is worse yet. A system like this, prolonged over a long period of time, produces a class of kept writers without initiative, independence or fighting spirit; they exist only by conforming to Hollywood standards, but they can produce art only by defying them. Few, very few, of them are capable of earning a living as independent writers, but you will always have to have them, because you will never find enough talent in all Hollywood to make more than one tenth of its pictures even fairly good. Granted that there are too many made; they are going to be made, or the theaters will be dark. Enormous vested interests and the livelihoods of countless thousands of people are involved. Granted again that ninety per cent of Hollywood's pictures are not really worth making; I say that ninety percent of the books and plays and short stories they were made from are not worth seeing or reading, by the same standards. And you and I know those standards are not going to change in our time.

Yet a writer, like me, who has little experience in Hollywood, and presumes to discuss the writers of Hollywood, must either lie, or say that they are largely over-dressed, overpaid, servile and incompetent hacks. All progress in the art of the screenplay depends on a very few people who are in a position (and have the temperament and toughness) to fight for excellence. Hollywood loves them for it and is only too anxious to reward them by making them something else than writers. Hollywood's attitude to writers is necessarily conditioned by the mass of its writers, not by the few who have what it calls integrity. It loves the word, having so little of the quality. Yet it is not fair for me to say in print that the writers of Holly-

A "WHITE" ISSUE IN JUNE

HOLD everything!

Believe it or not we are reluctant to express our own, editorial feeling toward a given story, even one by any of the tried-and-true favorite writers of the magazine. Once on a time we did say that we had never seen a better detective story in print or manuscript form than "MALTESE FALCON," and the fame and wealth that came to **Dashiell Hammett** seem to have justified our enthusiasm.

In the case of a comparatively new writer, however, it is possible to speak without suspicion of favorable prejudice. But in place of telling it ourselves, we will let two writers, unacquainted with each other, contributors to other markets, tell it for us. These two writers called at widely separated intervals. The first spoke of "the best story he had ever seen published in America." The second mentioned "the best story he had ever read in **BLACK MASK**." And both referred to identically the same story, one by **Raymond Chandler**, published in **BLACK MASK** some months ago.

The point is that "NEVADA GAS," by **Raymond Chandler**, is the lead novelette in the June issue, and it is our humble opinion that "NEVADA GAS" is the best work, by and large, that **Mr. Chandler** has yet given us. Just let us say, mildly, that you are going to get one great kick out of "NEVADA GAS" next month, and we won't be accused of overstatement.

Why, you know **Hugh Candless**, you have seen and listened to his perfect type; and **George Dial** and **Johnny De Ruse**, maybe. And **Francine Ley**? Well, we won't say anything about **Francine**; she has a way of speaking for herself. And we doubt if **Zaparty** or **Mops Parisi** is on your calling list.

It's dollars to doughnuts that you'll read "NEVADA GAS" more than the once and find something which the excitement and the rush of action made you miss the first time over. And that, by the way, was an old trick in the work of **Dash Hammett,** wasn't it?

*With Chandler's fifth story–published in the 1935 issue–*Black Mask *began grooming him as Hammett's successor.*

wood are what they are; they have a guild and it may be that in so large an industry they must fight as a group; it is obvious that I have done nothing to help them achieve what they have achieved, and am not likely to, except indirectly, by helping to get out a few pictures a bit above the ruck. It is not even fair to call them overpaid; because other writers as a group are shockingly underpaid; Hollywood is the only industry in the world that pays its workers the kind of money only capitalists and big executives make in other industries. If it is something less than ideal, it is the only industry that even tries for idealism; if it makes bad art, no other makes any art, except as a by-product of money-making. If it makes money out of poor pictures, it could make more money out of good ones, and it knows it and tries to make them. There is simply not enough talent in the world to

do it with, on any such scale. Its pictures cost too much and therefore must be safe and bring in big returns; but why do they cost too much? Because it pays the people who do the work, not the people who cut coupons. If it drains off all the writing talent in the world and then proceeds to destroy it by the way it treats it, then why is it able to drain off that talent? Because it knows how to pay for talent. The man who publishes my books has made more out of me than I have out of him, and he has not made it by selling the books, but by cutting himself in on radio and motion picture and reprint rights, which did not cost him a cent. Did he venture anything on the books? Of course not, not a dime. He was insured against loss by the rental libraries. He does not even know how to sell my kind of books, or how to promote them or how to get them reviewed. He just sits there and waits for

Chandler's first novel was published when he was fifty-one, after a five-year apprenticeship in the pulp magazines.

something to happen, and when it happens, he rubs his hands and cuts himself a nice fat slice of it. But Hollywood pays me a large salary merely to try to write something it can perhaps use. And when I write something that pays, then it tears up my contract and writes a better one. I cannot despise an industry that does this and I cannot say the men in it are bad artists because they do not produce better art. Yet, if I am honest about art, that is the only thing I can say. It is better to say something, is it not? At least, for the present.

* * * * *

But James Cain–faugh! Everything he touches smells like a billygoat. He is every kind of writer I detest, a faux naif, a Proust in greasy overalls, a dirty little boy with a piece of chalk and a board fence and nobody looking. Such people are the offal of literature, not because they write about dirty things, but because they do it in a dirty way. Nothing hard and clean and cold and ventilated. A brothel with a smell of cheap scent in the front parlor and a bucket of slops at the back door. Do I, for God's sake, sound like that? Hemingway with his eternal sleeping bag got to be pretty damn tiresome, but at least Hemingway sees it all, not just the flies on the garbage can.

To Blanche Knopf, 22 October 1942 [excerpt] (*Selected Letters of Raymond Chandler*, edited by Frank MacShane).

* * * * *

Phew! I'm exhausted. And what do I know about art anyway? Thank heaven that when I tried to write fiction I had the sense to do it in a language that was not all steamed up with rhetoric. In spite of all your kindness and understanding I am beginning to hate you. It took me twenty years to get over writing this sort of twaddle and look at me now!

ARTICLE:
Irving Wallace, "He Makes Murder Pay," *Pageant*, 2 (July 1946): 126-129.

This article by the future best-selling novelist was apparently based on an interview. At this point in his career Chandler had published four novels and had written four produced screenplays.

No other living writer can bring to gat-and-gore fiction quite the same degree of mayhem as Raymond Chandler. The literary cocktail he dispenses has a savage kick and a tart flavor all its own. Critics agree that he is one of the most skillful operators in the business since Conan Doyle invented Sherlock Holmes. Hollywood also agrees. Chandler's annual income from murder on the screen and between covers is around $100,000.

His career of fictional crime began one summer night 12 years ago, the way literary careers begin in romantic novels. On a vacation in California, oil executive Chandler picked up a detective magazine just before going to bed. By page 50 he was fretful. "Hell's bells," he said to his wife. "I can write better stuff than this." "Well, why don't you?" she mumbled, and went soundly to sleep. At dawn she found him furiously writing.

For five months he wrestled with the same story, an 18,000-word shocker titled *Blackmailers Don't Shoot*. *Black Mask* magazine, a pulp whose graduates include Dashiell Hammett and Erle Stanley Gardner, bought it for $180. Chandler quit the oil business for murder at one cent a word.

Selling every story he wrote, he averaged $50 a week for six years. Then, in 1939, he clicked with his first Phillip Marlowe novel, *The Big Sleep*. It's still his favorite because, he says, "It's my ambition to write a mystery story without one word of explanation at the end. In *The Big Sleep* I almost succeeded."

In 1940 came his biggest seller, *Farewell My Lovely*; in 1942 *The High Window*; in 1943 *Lady in the Lake*. First issued by publisher Alfred A. Knopf, each of these sold 10,000 copies, a big figure for detective fiction, which in the $2 edition is bought mostly by rental libraries. But the 25-cent reprints of all four Chandler books are flirting with the million mark.

Public and publishers have one complaint against Chandler: there isn't enough to go around. Three hundred crime novels are published annually in the United States. Erle Stanley Gardner has written 44 in a decade. Leslie Charteris has piloted the Saint through 30. Of Chandler's there are only four. But whereas most whodunits are hastily read and promptly forgotten, the Chandler spell lingers on.

Contrary to publishing custom, his murder fiction has been reissued for connoisseurs in a handsome $2 edition. It has been published in England, France, Denmark, Spain, Portugal and Latin America. It has been dramatized on the radio and sold to the movies. RKO fashioned *Farewell My Lovely* into a taut and distinctive melodrama with the title *Murder, My Sweet*. First filmed as a dismal quickie, *The High Window* is being expensively remade by 20th Century-Fox, starring Fred MacMurray. MGM expects to assign Spencer Tracy and a fat budget to *Lady in the Lake*. Lauren Bacall and Humphrey Bogart star in Warners' *The Big Sleep*.

Chandler's most recent movie was a one-man job, *The Blue Dahlia*. While writing it he carried tension, suspense and mounting terror right into the studio and established a solid Hollywood reputation for eccentricity. He turned in the script piece by piece and prowled around muttering at schedule-crazed executives, "What do you think ought to happen next?" With only a few scenes left to shoot, no one in the studio knew the ending. Front-office nerves were snapping when Chandler, at the last minute, delivered the killer to the camera.

Except for such pleasures, Chandler thinks the lot of the screen writer is a foul one: "He's treated like a cow–something to milk dry and send out to graze." Yet Chandler loves Hollywood: "Anyone who doesn't is either crazy or sober."

He has his own home there, a modest bungalow. When he takes a walk, the neighbors look up from their newspapers and lawn mowers to nod. The bemused passer-by with the baggy tweeds, horn-rimmed spectacles, fat brown pipe and slight stoop looks like a graying professor with something on his mind. But there's probably nothing on his mind–nothing but a murder and a sexy redhead sitting in his detective's lap and a butler silently offering doped cigarets.

Everyday reality is Chandler's refuge from the exotic world of his fancy. His close friends are plain people; he avoids the Hollywood crowd. "I dislike actors," he says flatly. He also "loathes" drunks, bridge and golf. He doesn't care for children: "I love to hear the patter of little feet going *away* from me." His likes extend to tea and travel,

music, reading, walking and an 18-pound Persian cat.

Chandler was born in Chicago. His mother was Anglo-Irish, his father American. A divorce sent Chandler to England with his mother. He grew up there, now claims he is American and has a long-standing argument with the State Department which claims he is British.

After a classical education at Dulwich College, London, Chandler tried reporting. He failed dismally. The creator of a master sleuth could never track down a news lead: "I always got lost."

Chandler was placing essays and book reviews and collecting rejection slips on his short stories when World War I projected him into the Canadian infantry and later into the Royal Flying Corps.

Back in America in the '20s, he strung tennis rackets, was in turn accountant and tax expert, then landed a handsome job in oil. In 1924 he married Pearl Hulburt, a New Yorker. They're still very much married.

When Chandler moved in on murder, he set out to raise the mystery story to the level of genuine literature. He has succeeded in producing action-filled narratives distinctive for good writing. His dialogue is low American–brash, unsentimental, crackling with wit. His characterizations, often in Marlowe's words, are studded with electric images: "eyes like strange sins"; "a smile I could feel in my hip pocket"; a voice "that grew icicles."

On almost every page there are phrases a poet might envy: "old men with faces like lost battles"; "the surf curled and creamed, almost without sound, like a thought trying to form itself on the edge of consciousness."

Every character who steps into Chandler's lurid world is unforgettably described.

The cigaret girl "wore an egret-plume in her hair, enough clothes to hide behind a tooth pick, one of her long beautiful naked legs was silver and one was gold. She had the utterly disdainful expression of a dame who makes her dates by long distance."

The crooked cop: "a windblown blossom of some two hundred pounds with freckled teeth and the mellow voice of a circus barker . . . the kind of cop who spits on his blackjack at night instead of saying his prayers . . ."

[18]

Chandler's first crime story appeared in Black Mask *in 1933; he became a star contributor (courtesy of Otto Penzler).*

[19]

Chandler has injected into the world of detective fiction a shot of vibrant life. He has tried, he says, "to get murder away from the upper classes, the week-end house party and the vicar's rose garden and back to the people who are really good at it." His terrain is the seamy underworld of Los Angeles and surrounding California. His people are real people: a few of them honest; many of them shabby, cruel, depraved; some of them with a streak of good in the bad.

These people hate and kill because violence is their norm, not (as in the conventional mystery) just a secret vice masked by blameless years on the stock exchange. They kill, not with the studied refinement of amateurs, but with the impromptu skill of professionals using the tools of their trade: pistols, knives, blackjacks and poisons. Their everyday business is dope and pornography and crooked gambling joints, and if they have a hobby it is blackmail.

It is a sordid world, the world of Raymond Chandler. But down these mean streets there goes a man, Chandler avers, who is not himself mean— the 33-year-old private detective Marlowe, college graduate and bachelor who gets bedeviled by aphrodisiacs, blondes and his clients' daughters. Chandler has this to say of him:

"He is neither tarnished nor afraid. He must be a complete man and yet an unusual man. He must be, to use a rather weathered phrase, a man of honor . . . I think he might seduce a duchess and I am quite sure he would not spoil a virgin.

"He is a relatively poor man, or he would not be a detective at all. . . . He will take no man's money dishonestly and no man's insolence without a due and dispassionate revenge. He is a lonely man . . ."

In creating situations and drama for Marlowe, Chandler often starts from a true story he happens to overhear. "I learn something too hot for the papers to publish," he says, "and it starts me thinking and then my imagination takes over." It is said that his first novel, revolving about a fat homosexual who ran a rental library of pornography, had its basis in unprintable fact.

Chandler's adverse critics—who are few— complain that Marlowe is a one-syllable man; that his tales are twice-told, never varying from a pat formula; that his prose is one part slang, one part suspense and one part sex; that even Einstein couldn't follow his plots with any degree of comfort.

Chandler fans concede only the fourth charge. It is all too true that in the Master's inventive hand the skeins of crime become tangled, that there is more of sound and fury than logic in Marlowe's probings into human depravity. But, they would add, Chandler has pace and drive; he is honest and colorful and supremely entertaining. And what more can you ask?

Chandler himself has no delusions of grandeur but he's sure he'll stay in business. "People will continue to read mysteries," he predicts. "Maybe because regular novels are no longer satisfying as stories. Or maybe it's the inner sadism in people. Or maybe Somerset Maugham is right— that everyone is fascinated by mysteries because murder is the one irrevocable crime. Murder is final. You can get back the jewels, but never a human being's life."

* * * * *

F. Scott Fitzgerald had one of the rarest qualities in all literature, and it's a great shame that the word for it has been thoroughly debased by the cosmetic racketeers, so that one is almost ashamed to use it to describe a real distinction. Nevertheless, the word is charm–charm as Keats would have used it. Who has it today? It's not a matter of pretty writing or clear style. It's a kind of subdued magic, controlled and exquisite, the sort of thing you get from good string quartettes. Yes, where would you find it today?

To Dale Warren, 13 November 1910 [excerpt] (*Selected Letters of Raymond Chandler*, edited by Frank MacShane)

* * * * *

MOVIE REVIEW:

Bosley Crowther, review of *The Blue Dahlia*, *New York Times*, 9 May 1946, p. 27.

The Blue Dahlia was the only produced screenplay Chandler wrote without a collaborator. He wrote it on alcohol in order to meet Paramount's deadline.

THE BLUE DAHLIA, an original screen play by Raymond Chandler; directed by George Marshall; produced by John Houseman for Paramount Pictures. At the Paramount.

Johnny Morrison	Alan Ladd
Joyce Harwood	Veronica Lake
Buzz Wanchek	William Bendix
Eddie Harwood	Howard da Silva
Helen Morrison	Doris Dowling
Captain Hendirckson	Tom Powers
George Copeland	Hugh Beaumont
Corelli	Howard Freeman
Leo	Don Costello
Dad Newell	Will Wright
The Man	Frank Faylen
Heath	Walter Sande

To the present expanding cycle of hard-boiled and cynical films, Paramount has contributed a honey of a rough-'em up romance which goes by the name of "The Blue Dahlia" and which came to the Paramount yesterday. And in this floral fracas it has starred its leading tough guy, Alan Ladd, and its equally dangerous and dynamic lady V-bomb, Veronica Lake. What with that combination in this Raymond Chandler tale, it wouldn't be simply blasting that you will hear in Times Square for weeks to come.

For bones are being crushed with cold abandon, teeth are being callously kicked in and shocks are being blandly detonated at close and regular intervals on the Paramount screen. Also an air of deepening mystery overhangs this tempestuous tale which shall render it none the less intriguing to those lovers of the brutal and bizarre

In manner of previous Ladd pictures, the rough stuff begins at the start, when our hero returns from the Pacific and finds his wife something less than true. A clip on the jaw for her boyfriend and a passing twist upon her shapely arms are sufficient to register the displeasure of the husband before he walks out. But the facts of his presence and anger make him the suspected one when, a few hours later, the gay wife is found in her bungalow—slain!

And so it is that the hero is launched on a catch-as-catch-can chase, trying to spot the killer before he himself is caught. En route, he falls in with a lady of considerable nerve (Miss Lake, of course) who insists upon rendering assistance which she is peculiarly qualified to give. He also has the rooting interest of a couple of ex-Navy pals who do very little to aid him but inject grimly comical twists. Thus confused, the perilous rat-race runs in and out of gaudy Hollywood dives,

fancy hotels and police chambers until the inevitable rat is caught.

Mr. Ladd, through it all, is his usual (as they say) imperturbable self, displaying a frigid economy in his movement of lips and limbs—except, of course, in those moments when it is essential that he protect himself. Then he goes into action like a hawser that has suddenly snapped. One adversary is nothing. Two thugs make a fair and equal match. The low art of knuckle-duster fighting is elaborately displayed in this film.

As for Miss Lake, her contribution is essentially that of playing slightly starved for a good man's honest affection, to which she manifests an eagerness to respond. And it is indeed remarkable how obvious she makes this look without doing very much. Howard da Silva is considerably more dramatic as a high-powered night club proprietor, and William Bendix looks and acts brutely eccentric as Mr. Ladd's slug-nutty pal. Doris Dowling as the faithless wife, Tom Powers as a nerveless detective chief and Will Wright as a crooked gunshow worker give able performances.

George Marshall has tautly directed from Mr. Chandler's crafty script. The tact of all this may be severely questioned, but it does make a brisk, exciting show.

ARTICLE:

Matthew J. Bruccoli, "Raymond Chandler and Hollywood," *The Blue Dahlia* (1976).

This afterword to the published screenplay reconstructs Chandler's work in The Blue Dahlia *and surveys his uneasy relationship with Hollywood.*

A pre-occupation with words for their own sake is fatal to good film making. It's not what films are. It's not my cup of tea, but it could have been if I'd started it twenty years earlier.–Chandler to Dale Warren (7 November 1951).

I am not interested in why the Hollywood system exists . . . I am interested only in the fact that as a result of it there is no such thing as an art of the screenplay, and there never will be as long as the system lasts, for it is the essence of this system that it seeks to exploit a talent without permitting it the right to be a talent. It cannot be done; you can only destroy the talent, which is ex-

actly what happens–when there is any talent to destroy.– Chandler, "Writers in Hollywood" (1945).

. . . most writers in Hollywood are employees. . . . As an individual I refuse to be an employee, but of course I am only an individual.–Chandler, "Critical Notes" (1947).

Raymond Chandler occupies a canonized position among twentieth-century detective novelists. Along with Dashiell Hammett and Ross Macdonald, he was one of the big three of hard-boiled fiction; but Chandler has always enjoyed special attention. His style has been justly admired, and he has been accorded considerable serious critical consideration. Indeed, he has been regarded as almost a major writer in some quarters–especially in Europe. Such a judgment is not an absolute distortion, for Chandler clearly merits respect. He, as much as anyone else, took a sub-literary American genre and made it into literature. Hammett did it first, but Chandler did it better.

The genre he worked in was the hard-boiled detective story, which flourished in the late twenties and thirties in the pulp magazines or "dime novels"–especially in *Black Mask* under the editorship of Capt. Joseph Shaw. Here Chandler began publishing in 1933 as a forty-five-year-old unemployed oil company executive. These detective stories as written by Hammett, Cornell Woolrich, Carroll John Daly, George Harmon Coxe, Frank Gruber, Horace McCoy, and Erle Stanley Gardner had certain common elements in addition to the detective hero (sometimes a policeman, sometimes a private eye, sometimes a civilian): a great deal of violence and an attempt to write tough dialogue. Frequently the results were close to self-parody. The heroes absorbed endless beatings, and were often too hard-boiled to believe. The most serious flaw of the school was the tendency of the speech to exaggerate toughness into something unrealistic. How much of the eat-nickels-and-spit-dimes dialogue can be blamed on the influence of Hemingway remains a moot point. Chandler not only made his dialogue believable, he even gave it style. As a writer who had failed as a poet before World War I, he possessed a concern with words, a feeling for good writing, and an obvious pleasure in striking metaphors or similes. But, more

than any other element, it was his conception of his hero that distinguished his work from that of the other "Boys in the Black Mask." Chandler's Philip Marlowe is not a thug; he is complex and highly intelligent. Marlowe is the Los Angeles knight imposing a little justice on a corrupt world, handling problems that the agents of the law are too busy, too dumb, or too crooked to deal with.[1] A loner, he makes a bare living while serving his personal code of honor and duty. Philip Marlowe is not greatly different from Hammett's Sam Spade, who appeared in *The Maltese Falcon* (1930), nine years before *The Big Sleep*. Nevertheless, there is the difference that Marlowe is more idealistic and less cynical than Spade, acutely sensitive beneath his tough manner: the anti-romantic hero. It has become a critical commonplace that the private-eye figure–particularly Marlowe–was a response to the corruption of the twenties and the social injustice of the thirties. However, it is not necessary to seek politico-socio causes for Marlowe's concern with honor and justice, which were moral concerns for Raymond Chandler. He was not political, and his work included no political ideas apart from his distrust of power. Remember, Chandler lived in England from age eight to age twenty-four (1896-1912) and received a public school education at Dulwich College. Chandler/Marlowe's code is that of the Edwardian-Georgian gentleman. His hero is an English gentleman transplanted to one of the bizarre colonies, setting an example for the natives.

Raymond Chandler published his first novel *The Big Sleep* in 1939, when he was fifty-one years old. In 1944–at age fifty-six–he commenced as a screenwriter at Paramount for $1,750 per week. Between 1944 and 1951 he worked on at least seven screenplays for Paramount, Warner Brothers, MGM, and Universal. Chandler was most closely involved with Paramount; and in 1945 signed a three-year contract with that studio calling for two scripts a year, for which he received a $50,000 annual guarantee whether or not he delivered the scripts. His Hollywood agent was H. N. "Swanie" Swanson (who also represented F. Scott Fitzgerald, William Faulkner, and John O'Hara). In addition to handling Chandler's services, Swanson also sold six of his novels to the movies–only one of which Chandler worked on.

Chandler's seven years on the payrolls of the studios were largely unsatisfactory, although he earned a great deal of money. In 1947, for example, Universal paid him $100,000 for writing the screenplay version of *Playback*–which was never produced. Although Chandler respected the potential of the movies, he was unable to work comfortably under the mandatory collaborative system. As late as 1948 Chandler called the movies "the only original art the modern world has conceived,"[2] but he disliked most of the people he had to work with, and feuded with his collaborators. He was further annoyed to see his own books butchered by other screenwriters. The only classic movie made from his work, Howard Hawks' *The Big Sleep*, did not involve Chandler.[3]

The earliest movie versions of Chandler's novels were strange attempts to superimpose characters created by other writers on Chandler's plots: *The Falcon Takes Over* (1941) combined *Farewell, My Lovely* with Michael Arlen's "Falcon"; and *Time to Kill* (1942) combined *The High Window* with Brett Halliday's Michael Shayne. Chandler's first screenwriting job at Paramount teamed him with Billy Wilder on James M. Cain's *Double Indemnity* (1944). He disliked both Wilder and the finished product, although the movie was a great success and received an Academy Award nomination for best screenplay. Chandler then collaborated on a pair of undistinguished projects: *And Now Tomorrow* (1944), a sentimental movie about a deaf girl and her doctor; and *The Unseen* (1945), a spooky suspense job. Meanwhile RKO remade *Farewell, My Lovely* as *Murder, My Sweet* (1945) without Chandler, a superior movie directed by Edward Dmytryk, in which Dick Powell was the first Philip Marlowe.

Late in 1944 Paramount had a crisis: Alan Ladd was about to be recalled by the army, and there was no script ready for him.[4] John Houseman's account of how *The Blue Dahlia* was written includes the characteristic elements of Raymond Chandler's personality and work, which may be summarized by the concept of *honor*. In completing this screenplay he did the honorable thing, and honor is what *The Blue Dahlia* is about. Johnny Morrison lives by the code of the hard-boiled Los Angeles knight ("Down these mean streets a man must go who is not himself mean, who is neither tarnished nor afraid . . . if he is a man of honor in one thing, he is that in all things"), the agent of justice functioning apart from the law. It does not occur to Johnny Morrison/Alan Ladd to seek police assistance. His wife has been murdered, and he is obligated to do something about it. She was unfaithful and was responsible for the death of their child in a drunken car accident; nevertheless she was his wife. This sense of honor is even shared by Eddie Harwood, Helen Morrison's lover. A fugitive murderer, Harwood–well played by Howard da Silva–now an elegant quasiracketeer, is troubled with guilt over his broken marriage to Joyce (Veronica Lake) and recognizes Johnny Morrison's moral superiority. Harwood's gangster partner, Leo, sees these conflicts in him and warns: "Just don't get too complicated, Eddie. . . ."

Houseman's account of the evolution of the plot can be supplemented from Chandler's letters. Chandler did in fact know at the start who the murderer of Helen Morrison was supposed to be: Buzz Wanchek. But at that time the conduct of servicemen in movies had to be cleared with Washington; and the Navy Department ruled that Wanchek, a wounded hero, could not be the murderer. Bad for morale; disrespect for the service. Therefore Chandler was required to abandon the plot rationale of his screenplay. In June 1946 he complained to James Sandoe, a crime literature specialist:

> Yes, I'm through with The Blue Dahlia, it dates even now. What the Navy Department did to the story was a little thing like making me change the murderer and hence make a routine whodunit out of a fairly original idea. What I wrote was a story of a man who killed (executed would be a better word) his pal's wife under the stress of a great and legitimate anger, then blanked out and forgot all about it; then with perfect honesty did his best to help the pal get out of a jam, then found himself in a set of circumstances which brought about partial recall. The poor guy remembered enough to make it clear who the murderer was to others, but never realized it himself. He just did and said things he couldn't have done or said unless he was the killer; but he never knew he did them or said them and never interpreted them.[5]

Hence the absurd trick-shooting scene– supposedly proving that Buzz could not have shot

Helen Morrison. Another departure from Chandler's original intention comes at the close of *The Blue Dahlia*. The script ends with the three war buddies looking for a bar after Joyce Harwood drives away: "Did somebody say something about a drink of bourbon?" But in the print of the movie that was released, Buzz and George walk away leaving Johnny with Joyce in a promissory happy-ever-after finish.

Director George Marshall has responded to John Houseman's memoir—mostly substantiating it, but challenging Houseman's statement that he tried to rewrite the screenplay as he shot it:

> When the treatment was handed to me exactly as written on yellow foolscap paper, I was so impressed by the material and the quality of writing I remarked to an associate (maybe John himself), that in all the years I had been making films, I had finally found a story which was so beautifully written I could shoot it right from the treatment. . . . Why would I want to re-write something which I had thought so perfect at the beginning? Surely because the material had been put into the script form would be no reason for destroying its inherent value.[6]

The only piece of rewriting that Marshall claims is the scene in which Leo and his thug have kidnapped Johnny Morrison. In the movie version—but not in the screenplay—Leo's toe is broken during the brawl. The injury actually occurred to actor Don Costello while the scene was being shot, so Marshall had to revise the rest of the scene to accommodate Costello/Leo's broken toe. Chandler was not available for this chore because he was at home completing the screenplay. Marshall fully endorsed Chandler's complaints about the Navy Department tampering with the plot.

Although Marshall denies that he tampered with the dialogue, Chandler reported otherwise in a letter to Sandoe:

> . . . it is ludicrous to suggest that any writer in Hollywood, however obstreperous, has a "free hand" with a script; he may have a free hand with the first draft, but after that they start moving in on him. Also what happens on the set is beyond the writer's control. In this case I threatened to walk off the picture, not yet finished, unless they stopped the director putting in fresh dialogue out of his own head. As to the scenes of violence, I did not write them that way at all. . . . The bro-

ken toe incident was an accident. The man actually did break his toe, so the director immediately capitalized on it.[7]

Whatever else Marshall may or may not have done to the screenplay, this letter goes a good way toward putting Chandler's complaints against Marshall in perspective. The rights of the matter seem to be that the director had an injured actor and an incommunicado writer, so he improvised lines and action to accommodate the accident and kept shooting. Nevertheless, Chandler objected to even this emergency revision. It appears, then, that what disturbed him was the place of the writer in the movie-making system—which was subservient to the director. Once the camera starts rolling, the movie becomes the director's movie. Chandler understood this and resented it: "There is no such thing as an art of the screenplay."[8]

George Marshall's assessment of the responsibilities of a movie director are instructive for outsiders who tend to lament what this director or that director does to a screenplay by an admired author:

> A director's function is to make as good a film as possible. He must be the guiding force on the stage. He must be able to translate the words as written in the script into a visually entertaining painting; always hoping that it will be the best thing he has ever done. Unfortunately, there are times when the words as written do not fit the people who are to say them. Casting problems have forced the producer to use artists of lesser ability than the ones originally chosen. There are also times when the set does not fit the action called for in the script, so new words are written to overcome the problem; or an injury, as described in the Blue Dahlia. A director must be a master of all trades and he had better well have an answer, and a damn good one, when problems arise.[9]

Chandler was not proud of *The Blue Dahlia*, feeling that the plot change and the incompetent performance of "Miss Moronica Lake" had damaged it. He complained to Sandoe: "The only times she's good is when she keeps her mouth shut and looks mysterious. The moment she tries to behave as if she had a brain she falls flat on her face. The scenes we had to cut out because she loused them up! And there are three godawful close shots of her looking perturbed that make me want to throw my lunch over the fence"[10] (30 May

1946). Nevertheless *The Blue Dahlia* was a success. It grossed over $2,750,000–a lot of money in those days. Chandler received his second Academy Award nomination for the screenplay, but the Award went to Muriel and Sydney Box for *The Seventh Veil*. The critical reception was predictably mixed. Bosley Crowther of the *New York Times* praised it as entertainment ("a honey of a rough-'em-up-romance"); John McCarten ridiculed it in *The New Yorker;* and John McManus of *PM* found it wanting in relevance. The best review came from James Agee in *The Nation* (3 June 1946): "The picture is as neatly stylized and synchronized, and as uninterested in moral excitement, as a good ballet; it knows its own weight and size perfectly and carries them gracefully and without self-importance; it is, barring occasional victories and noble accidents, about as good a movie as can be expected from the big factories."

The Blue Dahlia is a good–but not a great–movie; certainly not in the same class with *The Big Sleep*. Probably the chief problem is in the casting. Alan Ladd and Veronica Lake are unconvincing, although Ladd's work later improved. But some of the blame for the weakness of the movie belongs to Raymond Chandler. Apart from the problem of the Navy-dictated plot change, the plotting is still weak. Joyce Harwood is not integrated into the action. She picks up Johnny Morrison in her car on a rainy night for no reason and feels an instantaneous commitment to him for no reason. There is no explanation for her behavior toward him before she learns of the murder of Helen Morrison–except, possibly, elective affinity. She is the mandatory Hollywood love interest. Boy must find Girl, whether he needs her or not; and Chandler did not show any originality in handling this requirement.

Chandler never returned to his novel after he converted it into this screenplay. Since the working draft of the novel has not been found, we can only speculate about whether *The Blue Dahlia* was originally conceived as a Philip Marlowe vehicle.

While Chandler was working on *The Blue Dahlia, The Big Sleep* was made at Warner Brothers with Humphrey Bogart as a superb Marlowe. In 1946 Chandler had his first opportunity to work on one of his novels, when MGM teamed him with Steve Fisher on *The Lady in the Lake*. Chandler disliked everything about the project–especially his collaborator–and withdrew, refusing screen credit. This experimental "camera eye" movie was directed by Robert Montgomery who also played the offscreen Marlowe. The idea was that the camera would serve as the narrator and would therefore photograph only what Marlowe could see. Then in 1947 Fox remade *The High Window*–again without Chandler's participation–as *The Brasher Dubloon* with George Montgomery as the fourth Marlowe.

After abortive jobs on *The Innocent Mrs. Duff* (Paramount, 1946) and *Playback* (Universal, 1947?)–both unproduced–Chandler received a choice assignment in 1950 to work with Alfred Hitchcock at Warner Brothers on Patricia Highsmith's *Strangers on a Train,* but this project turned into another failure from Chandler's point of view. Here is Hitchcock's report of the collaboration:

> . . . our association didn't work out at all. We'd sit together and I would say, "Why not do it this way?" and he'd answer, "Well, if you can puzzle it out, what do you need me for?" The work he did was no good and I ended up with Czenzi Ormonde, a woman writer who was one of Ben Hecht's assistants. When I completed the treatment, the head of Warner's tried to get someone to do the dialogue, and very few writers would touch it. None of them thought it was any good.[11]

Chandler reluctantly accepted joint screen credit with Ormonde. *Strangers on a Train* was Chandler's last Hollywood writing job. After his death in 1959, four more movies were made from his novels. *The Little Sister* became *Marlowe* in 1969, with James Garner playing a quizzical Philip Marlowe. An atrocious parody of *The Long Goodbye* was written by Leigh Brackett and directed by Robert Altman; Elliot Gould was the transmogrification of Marlowe in this offense. Robert Mitchum reincarnated Marlowe twice: *Farewell My Lovely* (sans comma, 1975) and *The Big Sleep* inexplicably reset in England (1978).

"There's always some lousy condition," Monroe Stahr says in *The Last Tycoon*. That Raymond Chandler worked to little purpose in Hollywood can in large part be blamed on the conditions of movie-making. But blame also attaches to Chandler, whose contempt for the professionals rendered him incapable of collaborating with them comfortably, even when he was assigned to work with the best in the business. Indeed, this contempt was hardly distinguishable from self-contempt. When he was in the position to write *The Blue Dahlia* alone, he had to anesthetize himself.

Notes:

1. This view of Chandler's work has been developed by Philip Durham in *Down These Mean Streets a Man Must Go* (Chapel Hill: University of North Carolina Press, [1963]).
2. "Oscar Night in Hollywood," *Atlantic Monthly* (March 1948).
3. The screenplay for *The Big Sleep* was by William Faulkner, Leigh Brackett, and Jules Furthman. There is an undocumented anecdote that at one point Faulkner sent a message to Chandler asking whether the Sternwood chauffeur had committed suicide or had been murdered, and Chandler replied that he didn't know.
4. "In less than two weeks I wrote an original story of 90 pages. All dictated and never looked at until finished. It was an experiment and for one subject from early childhood to plot-constipation, it was rather a revelation. Some of the stuff is good, some very much not."–Chandler to Charles W. Morton, 15 January 1945, in Kathrine S. Walker and Dorothy Gardiner (Eds.), *Raymond Chandler Speaking* (Boston: Houghton Mifflin, 1962).
5. Chandler Collection, UCLA Library.
6. Letter to Matthew J. Bruccoli, 16 December 1974.
7. 2 October 1947, Chandler Collection, UCLA Library.
8. "Writers in Hollywood," *Atlantic Monthly* (November 1945).
9. To Matthew J. Bruccoli, 16 December 1974.
10. Chandler Collection, UCLA Library.
11. François Truffaut, *Hitchcock* (New York: Simon & Schuster, 1967), pp. 142-143.

Screenplays Written By Chandler

Double Indemnity. Paramount, 1944. Screenplay by Chandler and Billy Wilder from the novel by James M. Cain. Screenplay received Academy Award nomination. Directed by Billy Wilder; produced by Joseph Sistrom.

And Now Tomorrow. Paramount, 1944. Screenplay by Chandler and Frank Partos from the novel by Rachel Field. Directed by Irving Pichel; produced by Fred Kohlmar.

The Unseen. Paramount, 1945. Screenplay by Chandler and Hagar Wilde; adapted by Wilde and Ken Englund from *Her Heart in Her Throat* by Ethel Lina White. Directed by Lewis Allen.

The Blue Dahlia. Paramount, 1946. Screenplay by Chandler from his original screen story. Screenplay received Academy Award nomination. Directed by George Marshall; produced by John Houseman.

Strangers on a Train. Warner Brothers, 1951. Screenplay by Chandler and Czenzi Ormonde; adapted from the Patricia Highsmith novel by Whitfield Cook. Directed and produced by Alfred Hitchcock.

Unproduced Chandler Screenplay Assignments

The Innocent Mrs. Duff. Paramount, 1946. From the novel by Elisabeth Sanxay Holding.

Playback. Universal, 1947-48. From Chandler's original story. Converted into novel.

ARTICLE:

R. W. Flint, "A Cato of the Cruelties," *Partisan Review*, 14 (May-June 1947): 328-330.

This article in an influential Marxist journal attempted to detect a concealed political message in Chandler's work.

Raymond Chandler has, in the past, written for the *Atlantic* on the ethics of Hollywood, just as the late Wendell Willkie once wrote on ethics in general for *The American Scholar*. There has been enough respectability in the wares of these two successful specialists in the American ethos to suit the upper-middlebrow market, and enough authenticity in their attitudes to cover the objections of litterateurs.

Philip Marlowe, private dick, is our myth, the closest thing to flesh and blood that Hollywood has recently seen fit to apotheosize. Who, then, is this Marlowe and what is his mighty line? To be solemn first, Philip Marlowe is as much of the existentialist hero as modern America has stomach for. We've become used to the French version, but the term, like pragmatism, means a *way* of philosophizing rather than a body of doctrine. It's a fruitful term, and we should try to salvage it from the purely cultic interpretation that is threatening, through fear more than anything else, to discredit its legitimate use. Marlowe is the American middle-class Existentialist, the People's Existentialist, you might say, insofar as his function cuts across class lines. The marks of his integrity are a searing doubt as to the motives of his fellow countrymen–popularized by Bogart with literary antecedents in Lardner and many others–and a profound awareness of fate. But the red badge that sets him apart is an almost Biblical faith in the value of decision. He is forever rolling the stone uphill–a little too sentimental and self-pitying for a true Stoic, but an existentialist nonetheless. Whatever the alternatives, Marlowe acts and acts alone: his life is all decision–a blind inevitable moral energy plowing through the wildest ambiguities always into the heart of insecurity and danger.

Marlowe's world is the laissez-faire liberal world turned inside-out–a jungle of predatory creatures making amusing patterns out of their guilt and boredom, and desperately lonely. On the surface, nothing happens for obvious reasons. If external amiability isn't faked, it's at least better to assume so until told otherwise. Underneath this casual cruelty–the convention set by Cain, Hammett, et al.–move the tides of human destiny and decision, as crude as the surface is intricate and ambiguous.

The Marlowe epics screen better than they read, and I suspect it's because Chandler strains too much in the books to be arty, although he is often brilliantly successful in patches. His conventions admirably suit the movies where the camera, if it's alert, establishes the proper sense of desolation–that miasmic, Dantesque background of California roadways, police stations, office buildings, and fake interiors in which Chandler specializes.

We have come a long way from Holmes to here. The plot is complex and we are still thrown a few clues from time to time, but suspense grows now out of a human rather than a literary situation; it is continuous rather than cumulative, like life in a Camus novel or in modern "crisis" theology. Our hero is no longer the wizard, the mental giant, the latter-day Paracelsus: he is not even the intellectual master of the situation. Where Holmes needed all the glamor he could muster to make Victorian respectability seem worth an elaborate defense, Marlowe lives by the light of his sentimental but genuine humanity: he's the fall-guy, *der reine Narr*, Parsifal-Cassandra whom nobody believes because he has no aces up his sleeve.

In another of his functions, that of father-confessor, he departs radically from the fiction detective tradition. His goodness is obvious enough to become a catalyst in a corrupt society–the great strength that is intended to compensate for his lack of subtlety and the conventional insouciance. Everyone confesses his basic sickness as well as his immediate troubles to Marlowe. In the current Chandler film, *Lady in the Lake*, for example, the weak capitalist, in Marlowe's healing presence, is strong enough to throw over his vicious secretary and confess his loneliness; the crooked cop can't look at Marlowe without a self-revealing yen to "work him over"; the old people confess their utter exhaustion and fear; the sick playboy knocks Marlowe cold for telling the truth, but is soon recompensed by being shot full of holes in his shower by a former sin; and finally, we have the vicious secretary herself, still the superb, capable American Girl whom we have come to know so well from the tradition that starts, perhaps, in Henry James and enters the crime milieu in Nora of *The Thin Man*, but is omnipresent in such creatures as the wooden young lady in *All the King's Men*, and Isabel Bolton's final hypostatization as the "European" paragon of *Do I Wake or Sleep*. The Girl is Marlowe's greatest challenge and his greatest conquest; to her, like Hamlet to his mother, Marlowe "must be cruel, only to be kind"–the therapy of harshness which Marx also prescribes for our bourgeois ills.

A comparison of Marlowe's state of mind and that of the follower of Marx would be suggestive. Both have the attitude of a Jewish prophet toward a bad world: both are proximately tough to counter a degenerate laissez-faire that has learned to use sham-morality brilliantly, but both are ultimately tender and apocalyptic. I don't claim to find any political sophistication in Chandler: I merely suggest the implications of his theory of man, which he would doubtless deny. Leftism in general, insofar as it has popular attributes in America, seems to have settled temporarily on the *PM* level of pervasive general "concern" mixed with a folksy, sexy assertion of man's finiteness and dependence on nature. It's a mixture too usually dismissed by the exacerbated intellectual who, however, welcomes the image of Marlowe as a sign of "vitality" in the movies.

Cover art for paperbacks of The Big Sleep, 1942-1971

LETTER:

To Bernice Baumgarten, 11 March 1949 [excerpt], *Selected Letters of Raymond Chandler*, edited by Frank MacShane, pp. 150-151.

Chandler reacted to Flint's article in this letter to his agent at Brandt & Brandt.

. . . Another writer in an avant garde magazine referred to me as a "Cato of the Cruelties." Apart from the obvious compliment of being noticed at all by the rarified intellectuals who write for these publications–and I should understand them well, because I was one of them for many years–I cannot grasp what they do with their sense of humor. Or let me put it in a better way: Why is it that the Americans–of all people the quickest to reverse their moods–do not see the strong element of burlesque in my kind of writing? Or is it only the intellectuals who miss that? It is as though the public, most inconstant in its own emotions, expected a writer to be utterly constant in his. And as for true-to-life I don't think these cloud-dwellers can have much understanding of the kind of world they live in and the kind of world Dickens lived in. There is a strong element of fantasy in the mystery story; there is in any kind of writing that moves within an accepted formula. The mystery writer's material is melodrama, which is an exaggeration of violence and fear beyond what one normally experiences in life. (I said normally; no writer ever approximated the life of the Nazi concentration camps.) The means he uses are realistic in the sense that such things happen to people like these and in places like these. But this realism is superficial; the potential of emotion is overcharged, the compression of time and event is a violation of probability, and although such things happen, they do not happen so fast and in such a tight frame of logic to so closely knit a group of people.

Yours,
Ray

FROM LETTERS ON WRITING:

These excerpts from Selected Letters of Raymond Chandler, *edited by Frank MacShane, reveal Chandler's hard-headed approach to the literary profession.*

Whether it is possible to write a strictly honest mystery of the classic type. It isn't. To get the complication you fake the clues, the timing, the play of coincidence, assume certainties where only 50 per cent chances exist at most. To get the surprise murderer you fake character, which hits me hardest of all, because I have a sense of character. If people want to play this game, it's all right by me. But for Christ's sake let's not talk about honest mysteries. They don't exist.

–To George Harmon Coxe, 27 June 1940

But I think most critical writing is drivel and half of it is dishonest (that is, conditioned by information about advance sales), and there is no point in my adding to it. It is a short cut to oblivion, anyway. Thinking in terms of ideas destroys the power to think in terms of emotions and sensations. I suppose, like other people, I have at times a futile urge to explain to whoever will listen why it is that the whole apparatus of intellectualism bores me. But you have to use the language of intellectualism to do it. Which is the bunk. The business of a fiction writer is to recreate the illusion of life. How he does it, if he can do it, it does not in the least help him to know.

–To James Sandoe, 17 December 1944

Can I do a piece for you entitled *The Insignificance of Significance*, in which I will demonstrate in my usual whorehouse style that it doesn't matter a damn what a novel is about, that the only fiction of any moment in any age is that which does magic with words, and that the subject matter is merely the springboard for the writer's imagination; that the art of fiction, if it can any longer be called that, has grown from nothing to an artificial synthesis in a mere matter of 300 years, and has now reached such a degree of mechanical perfection that the only way you can tell the novelists apart is by whether they write about miners in Butte, coolies in China, Jews in the Bronx, or stockbrokers on Long Island, or whatever it is; that all the women and most of the men write exactly the same, or at least choose one of half a dozen thoroughly standardized procedures; and that in spite of certain inevitable slight differences (very slight indeed on the long view) the whole damn business could be turned out by a machine just as

THE VIOLENCE-SCREEN'S
ALL-TIME ROCKER-SHOCKER!

HUMPHREY **BOGART** AND LAUREN **BACALL**

Bogy'n Baby
paired off for
a hot time-and
the big thrill in
cold, cold crime!

"THE **BIG SLEEP**"

WITH MARTHA VICKERS A HOWARD HAWKS PRODUCTION
DOROTHY MALONE
A WARNER BROS. RE-RELEASE

·When it came to be re-issued. The Big Sleep (1946) had mysteriously become·

The poster for the classic 1946 movie version of The Big Sleep, *written by William Faulkner, Leigh Brackett, and Jules Furthman*

well, and will be almost any day now; and that the only writers left who have *anything* to say are those who write about practically nothing and monkey around with odd ways of doing it.

–To Charles Morton, 12 December 1945

A good story cannot be devised; it has to be distilled. In the long run, however little you talk or even think about it, the most durable thing in writing is style, and style is the most valuable investment a writer can make with his time. It pays off slowly, your agent will sneer at it, your publisher will misunderstand it, and it will take people you never heard of to convince them by slow degrees that the writer who puts his individual mark on the way he writes will always pay off. He can't do

it by trying, because the kind of style I am thinking about is a projection of personality and you have to have a personality before you can project it. But granted that you have one, you can only project it on paper by thinking of someone else. This is ironical in a way; it is the reason, I suppose, why in a generation of "made" writers I still say you can't make a writer. Preoccupation with style will not produce it. No amount of editing and polishing will have any appreciable effect on the flavor of how a man writes. It is the product of the quality of his emotion and perception; it is the ability to transfer these to paper which makes him a writer, in contrast to the great number of people who have just as good emotions and just as keen perceptions, but cannot come within a googol of miles of putting them on paper. I know several made writers. Hollywood, of course, is full of them; their stuff often has an immediate impact of competence and sophistication, but it is hollow underneath, and you never go back to it. I don't anyway.

–To Mrs. Robert Hogan, 8 March 1947

A long time ago when I was writing for pulps I put into a story a line like "he got out of the car and walked across the sun-drenched sidewalk until the shadow of the awning over the entrance fell across his face like the touch of cool water." They took it out when they published the story. Their readers didn't appreciate this sort of thing: just held up the action. And I set out to prove them wrong. My theory was they just *thought* they cared nothing about anything but the action; that really, although they didn't know it, they cared very little about the action. The things they really cared about, and that I cared about, were the creation of emotion through dialogue and description; the things they remembered, that haunted them, were not for example that a man got killed, but that in the moment of his death he was trying to pick a paper clip up off the polished surface of a desk, and it kept slipping away from him, so that there was a look of strain on his face and his mouth was half open in a kind of tormented grin, and the last thing in the world he thought about was death. He didn't even hear death knock on the door. That damn little paper clip kept slipping away from his fingers and he just wouldn't push it to the edge of the desk and catch it as it fell.

—To Frederick Lewis Allen, 7 May 1948

I begin at last to realize that I have a very unorthodox attitude to plots. Most writers think up a plot with an intriguing situation and then proceed to fit characters into it. With me a plot, if you could call it that, is an organic thing. It grows and often it overgrows. I am continually finding myself with scenes that I won't discard and that don't want to fit in. So that my plot problem invariably ends up as a desperate attempt to justify a lot of material that, for me at least, has come alive and insists on staying alive. It's probably a silly way to write, but I seem to know no other way. The mere idea of being committed in advance to a certain pattern appalls me.

—To James Sandoe, 23 September 1948

To say little and convey much, to break the mood of the scene with some completely irrelevant wisecrack without entirely losing the mood—these small things for me stand in lieu of accomplishment. My theory of fiction writing (which is probably not worth serious discussion) is that the objective method has hardly been scratched, that if you know how to use it you can tell more in a paragraph than the probing writers can tell in a chapter.

—To Hamish Hamilton, 22 June 1949

When I started out to write fiction I had the great disadvantage of having absolutely no talent for it. I couldn't get characters in and out of rooms. They lost their hats and so did I. If more than two people were on scene I couldn't keep one of them alive. This failing is still with me, of course, to some extent. Give me two people snotting each other across a desk and I am happy. A crowded canvas just bewilders me. (I could say the same of some rather distinguished writers, only they don't know it and I do.) I don't know who was the original idiot who advised a writer, "Don't bother about the public. Just write what you want to write." No writer ever wants to write anything. He wants to reproduce or render certain effects and in the beginning he hasn't the faintest idea how to do it.

—To Paul Brooks, 19 July 1949

REVIEW:
Anthony Boucher, "Chandler Revalued," *New York Times Book Review*, 27 September 1949, p. 24.

An influential mystery critic, as well as a novelist, Boucher reacted against what he regarded as Chandler's misanthropy.

After a long and notable career in the pulp magazines, Raymond Chandler made his mark in books with four novels published between 1939 and 1943. Most critics and almost all readers recognized in him the legitimate successor of Dashiell Hammett. It's been six years since his last novel, "The Lady in the Lake." In that time his early short stories have been gathered into books; he has written numerous films and one important, if idiosyncratic, critical essay on the detective story; his detective Philip Marlowe has become a starring radio character; and the Chandler name has become an evocative symbol of American hardboiled writing at its best.

His new novel, "The Little Sister," has been awaited with as much eagerness as Hammett's ten-year-promised novel—especially by those critics and readers who have felt that Hammett and Chandler are significant exponents not merely of the detective story but of the American novel. It is partly, of course, this heightened expectation which makes "The Little Sister" seem unsatisfactory. But partly, too, dissatisfaction comes from the revelation of an abyss of emptiness.

Plot and characters are the stuff of any run-of-the-mill toughie. Chandler's treatment differs from the routine in his prose, which is still vigorous, clean, distinctive. It differs, too, in a tautly cryptic method of narration which lets you decide just who killed whom—but only by an extreme effort of will which you are not markedly inclined to make.

But the great distinction dividing this from all other detective stories is its scathing hatred of the human race. The characters, aside from the little sister, are reasonably well-painted cardboard, brought to life only by the sheer force of their viciousness. An honorable motive, a decent impulse would be as out of place in these pages as a coarse word in the mouth of an Eberhart heroine.

Lauren Bacall with Humphrey Bogart, as the definitive Marlowe in The Big Sleep

Mr. Chandler's publishers, quoting from his dedication in "Five Murderers," describe him as "the brave man who rescued murder from the vicar's garden and gave it back to the people who are really good at it." Students of murder would, I think, doubt that glamour gals and gang-leaders provide murders of any marked psychological (or novelistic) interest. Certainly in the present case they provide simply the spectacle of a prose writer of high attainments wasting his talents in a pretentious attempt to make bricks without straw—or much clay, either.

* * * * *

From now on I am going to write what I want to write as I want to write it. Some of it may flop. There are always going to be people who will say I have lost

the pace I had once, that I take too long to say things now, and don't care enough about tight active plots. But I'm not writing for those people now. I'm writing for the people who understand about writing as an art and are able to separate what a man does with words and ideas from what he thinks about Truman or the United Nations.

To Carl Brandt, 21 December 1950 [excerpt] (*Selected Letters of Raymond Chandler*, edited by Frank MacShane).

* * * * *

LETTER:

To D. J. Ibberson, 19 April 1951, *Selected Letters of Raymond Chandler*, edited by Frank MacShane, pp. 270-274.

RAYMOND CHANDLER

This letter to an English correspondent provides Chandler's fullest profile of Philip Marlowe.

April 19, 1951

Dear Mr. Ibberson:

It is very kind of you to take such an interest in the facts of Philip Marlowe's life. The date of his birth is uncertain. I think he said somewhere that he was thirty-eight years old, but that was quite awhile ago and he is no older today. This is just something you will have to face. He was not born in a Midwestern town but in a small California town called Santa Rosa, which your map will show you to be about fifty miles north of San Francisco. Santa Rosa is famous as the home of Luther Burbank, a fruit and vegetable horticulturist, once of considerable renown. It is perhaps less widely known as the background of Hitchcock's picture *Shadow of a Doubt*, most of which was shot right in Santa Rosa. Marlowe has never spoken of his parents, and apparently he has no living relatives. This could be remedied if necessary. He had a couple of years of college, either at the University of Oregon at Eugene, or Oregon State University at Corvallis, Oregon. I don't know why he came to Southern California, except that eventually most people do, although not all of them remain. He seems to have had some experience as an investigator for an insurance company and later as investigator for the district attorney of Los Angeles county. This would not necessarily make him a police officer nor give him the right to make an arrest. The circumstances in which he lost that job are well known to me but I cannot be very specific about them. You'll have to be satisfied with the information that he got a little too efficient at a time and in a place where efficiency was the last thing desired by the persons in charge. He is slightly over six feet tall and weighs about thirteen stone eight. He has dark brown hair, brown eyes, and the expression "passably good looking" would not satisfy him in the least. I don't think he looks tough. He can be tough. If I had ever had an opportunity of selecting the movie actor who could best represent him to my mind, I think it would have been Cary Grant. I think he dresses as well as can be expected. Obviously he hasn't very much money to spend on clothes, or on anything else for that matter. The horn-rimmed sunglasses do not make him distinctive. Practically everyone in Southern California wears sunglasses at some time or other. When you say he wears 'pyjamas' even in summer, I don't know what you mean. Who doesn't? Were you under the impression that he wore a night-shirt? Or did you mean that he might sleep raw in hot weather? The last is possible, although our weather here is very seldom hot at night. You are quite right about his smoking habits, although I don't think he insists on Camels. Almost any sort of cigarette will satisfy him. The use of cigarette cases is not as common here as in England. He definitely does not use bookmatches which are always safety matches. He uses either large wooden matches, which we call kitchen matches, or a smaller match of the same type which comes in small boxes and can be struck anywhere, including on the thumbnail if the weather is dry enough. In the desert or in the mountains it is quite easy to strike a match on your thumbnail, but the humidity around Los Angeles is pretty high. Marlowe's drinking habits are much as you state. I don't think he prefers rye to bourbon, however. He will drink practically anything that is not sweet. Certain drinks, such as Pink Ladies, Honolulu cocktails and crème de menthe highballs, he would regard as an insult. Yes, he makes good coffee. Anyone can make good coffee in this country, although it seems quite impossible in England. He takes cream, and sugar with his coffee, not milk. He will also drink it black without sugar. He cooks his own breakfast, which is a simple matter, but not any other meal. He is a late riser by inclination, but occasionally an early riser by necessity. Aren't we all? I would not say that his chess comes up to tournament standard. I don't know where he got the little paper-bound book of tournament games published in Leipzig, but he likes it because he prefers the continental method of designating the squares on the chess board. Nor do I know that he is something of a card player. This has slipped my mind. What do you mean he is "moderately fond of animals"? If you live in an apartment house, moderately is about as fond of them as you can get. It seems to me that you have an inclination to interpret any chance remark as an indication of a fixed taste. As to his interest in women as "frankly carnal," these are your words, not mine.

Marlowe cannot recognize a Bryn Mawr accent, because there is no such thing. All he implies by that expression is a toplofty way of speaking. I doubt very much that he can tell genuine old furniture from fakes. And I also beg leave to doubt that many experts can do it either, if the fakes are good enough. I pass the Edwardian furniture and pre-Raphaeline art. I just don't recall where you get your facts. I would not say that Marlowe's knowledge of perfume stops at Chanel Number 5. That again is merely a symbol of something that is expensive and at the same time reasonably restrained. He likes all the slightly acrid perfumes, but not the cloying or overspiced type. He is, as you may have noticed, a slightly acrid person. Of course he knows what the Sorbonne is, and he also knows where it is. Of course he knows the difference between a tango and a rumba, and also between a conga and a samba, and he knows the difference between a samba and a mamba, although he does not believe that the mamba can overtake a galloping horse. I doubt if he knows the new dance called a mambo, because it seems to be only recently discovered or developed.

Now let's see, how far does that take us? Fairly regular filmgoer, you say, dislikes musicals. Check. May be an admirer of Orson Welles. Possibly, especially when Orson is directed by someone other than himself. Marlowe's reading habits and musical tastes are just as much a mystery to me as they are to you, and if I tried to improvise, I'm afraid I would get him confused with my own tastes. If you ask me why he is a private detective, I can't answer you. Obviously there are times when he wishes he were not, just as there are times when I would rather be almost anything than a writer. The private detective of fiction is a fantastic creation who acts and speaks like a real man. He can be completely realistic in every sense but one, that one sense being that in life as we know it such a man would not be a private detective. The things which happen to him might still happen to him, but they would happen as the result of a peculiar set of chances. By making him a private detective, you skip the necessity for justifying his adventures.

Where he lives: in *The Big Sleep* and some earlier stories he apparently lived in a single apartment with a pull-down bed, a bed that folds up into the wall and it has a mirror on the under side of it. Then he moved into an apartment similar to that occupied by a character named Joe Brody in *The Big Sleep*. It may have been the same apartment, he may have got it cheap because a murder had taken place in it. I think, but I'm not sure, that this apartment is on the fourth floor. It contains a living room which you enter directly from the hallway, and opposite are French windows opening on an ornamental balcony, which is just something to look at, certainly not anything to sit out on. Against the right-hand wall as you stand in the doorway is a davenport. In the left-hand wall, nearest to the hallway of the apartment house, there is a door that leads to an interior hall. Beyond that, against the left-hand wall, there is this oak drop leaf desk, an easy chair, etc; beyond that, an archway entrance to the dinette and kitchen. The dinette, as known in American apartment houses or at any rate in California apartment houses, is simply a space divided off from the kitchen proper by an archway or a built-in china closet. It would be very small, and the kitchen would also be very small. As you enter the hallway from the living room (the interior hallway) you would come on your right to the bathroom door and continuing straight on you would come to the bedroom. The bedroom would contain a walk-in closet. The bathroom in a building of this type would contain a shower in the tub and a shower curtain. None of the rooms is very large. The rent of the apartment furnished, would have been about sixty dollars a month when Marlowe moved into it. God knows what it would be now. I shudder to think. I should guess not less than ninety dollars a month, probably more.

As to Marlowe's office, I'll have to take another look at it sometime to refresh my memory. It seems to me it's on the sixth floor in a building which faces north, and that his office window faces east. But I'm not certain about this. As you say, there is a reception room which is a half-office, perhaps half the space of a corner office, converted into two reception rooms with separate entrances and communicating doors right and left respectively. Marlowe has a private office which communicates with his reception room, and there is a connection which causes a buzzer to ring in

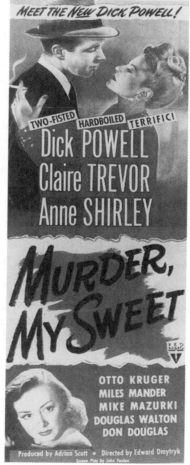

Dust jacket for the first printing of Chandler's second novel. The 1945 movie was retitled
Murder, My Sweet

his private office when the door of the reception room is opened. But this buzzer can be switched off by a toggle switch. He has not, and never has had, a secretary. He could very easily subscribe to a telephone answering service, but I don't recall mentioning that anywhere. And I do not recall that his desk has a glass top, but I may have said so. The office bottle is kept in the filing drawer of the desk,—a drawer, standard in American office desks (perhaps also in England) which is the depth of two ordinary drawers, and is intended to contain file folders, but very seldom does, since most people keep their file folders in filing cases. It seems to me that some of these details flit about a good deal. His guns have also been rather various. He started out with a German Luger automatic pistol. He seems to have had Colt automatics of various calibers, but not larger than .38, and when last I heard he has a Smith & Wesson .38 special, probably with a four-inch barrel. This is a very powerful gun, although not the most powerful made, and has the advantage over an automatic of using a lead cartridge. It will not jam or discharge accidentally, even if dropped on a hard surface, and is probably just as effective a weapon at short range as a .45 caliber automatic. It would be better with a six-inch barrel, but that would make it much more awkward to carry. Even a four-inch barrel is not too convenient, and the detective branch of the police usually carries a gun with only a two and a half-inch barrel. This is about all I have for you now, but if there is anything else you want to know, please write to me again. The trouble is, you really seem to know a good deal more about Philip Marlowe than I do, and perhaps I shall have to ask you questions instead of your asking me.

With kindest regards,
Yours ever,

* * * * *

I have the attitude that film work is too valuable a connection to discard completely but not valuable enough to let it dominate your life. Hack work is all right in small doses, but they must be kept small. I know that mystery writers are regarded as hacks in certain quarters simply because they are mystery writers. This is a confusion of thought, to my mind. A writer who accepts a certain formula and works within it is no more a hack than Shakespeare was because to hold his audience he had to in- clude a certain amount of violence and a certain amount of low comedy, no more a hack than the Renaissance painters were because they had to exploit the religious motives which were pleasing to the church. My definition of a hack is a man who lets someone else tell him how and what to write, who writes, if he is a writer, not to an accepted formula, but to some editor's definition of it. But the frontier is always vague.*

To Hamish Hamilton, 28 September 1950 [excerpt] (*Selected Letters of Raymond Chandler,* edited by Frank MacShane)

* * * * *

FROM LETTERS ON PHILIP MARLOWE:

These excerpts from Selected Letters of Raymond Chandler, *edited by Frank MacShane, provide insights into his hero's system of values.*

Time this week calls Philip Marlowe "amoral." This is pure nonsense. Assuming that his intelligence is as high as mine (it could hardly be higher), assuming his chances in life to promote his own interest are as numerous as they must be, why does he work for such pittance? For the answer to that is the whole story, the story that is always being written by indirection and yet never is written completely or even clearly. It is the struggle of all fundamentally honest men to make a decent living in a corrupt society. It is an impossible struggle; he can't win. He can be poor and bitter and take it out in wisecracks and casual amours, or he can be corrupt and amiable and rude like a Hollywood producer. Because the bitter fact is that outside of two or three technical professions which require long years of preparation, there is absolutely no way for a man of this age to acquire a decent affluence in life without to some degree corrupting himself, without accepting the cold, clear fact that success is always and everywhere a racket.

–To John Houseman, October 1949

I don't think my friend Philip Marlowe is very much concerned about whether or no he has a mature mind. I will admit to an equal lack of concern about myself. But it is very natural that you, being what you term a "shabby twenty-three," and having had apparently a fairly hard time of it should be more concerned than I am with what the boys in their sweet lingo call the social orientation of the individual. Don't take it too hard. Very few people are capable of straight thinking on any subject. If being in revolt against a corrupt society constitutes being immature, then Philip Marlowe is extremely immature. If seeing dirt where there is dirt constitutes an inadequate social adjustment, then Philip Marlowe has an inadequate social adjustment. Of course Marlowe is a failure and he knows it. He is a failure because he hasn't any money. A man who without physical handicaps cannot make a decent living is always a failure and usually a moral failure. But a lot of very good men have been failures because their particular talents did not suit their time and place. In the long run I guess we are all failures or we wouldn't have the kind of world we have. But you must remember that Marlowe is not a real person. He is a creature of fantasy. He is in a false position because I have put him there. In real life a man of his type would no more be a private detective than he would be a university don. Your private detective in real life is usually either an ex-policeman with a lot of hard practical experience and the brains of a turtle or else a shabby little hack who runs around trying to find out where people have moved to. It is obvious that the more highly organized police work becomes, the leaner are the pickings left for the private operator. I think I resent your suggestion that Philip Marlowe has contempt for other people's physical weakness. I don't know where you get the idea, and I don't think it's so. I am also a little tired of the numerous suggestions that have been made that he is always full of whiskey. The only point I can see in justification of that is that when he wants a drink he takes it openly and doesn't hesitate to remark on it. I don't know how it is in your part of the country, but compared with the country-club set in my part of the country, he is as sober as a deacon.

–To Mr. Inglis, October 1951

ARTICLE:

R. W. Lid, "Philip Marlowe Speaking," *Kenyon Review*, 31 (1969): 153-178.

Ross Macdonald wrote that Chandler "invested the sun-blinded streets of Los Angeles with a romantic presence." Professor Lid moves from an examination of Chandler's terrain to an analysis of Marlowe's value system and code of conduct.

"You know something, Marlowe? I could get to like you. You're a bit of a bastard–like me."–*The Long Goodbye*

Raymond Chandler wrote about Los Angeles during its period of kooky architecture. Chateaus and villas and castles, all redolent of other lands, dominated the lush hillsides of Beverly Hills and Bel Air. Down below, in Hollywood, could be found the gingerbread counterpart to this not quite real world of the very rich and the very exclusive–restaurants, drive-ins, commercial buildings, even conservative establishments like banks which took on the shapes of stuffed animals and items of headdress, or of recognizable physical objects, or bore broad resemblance to sugar-frosted palaces of desert sheiks. The casual observer of this sun-drenched land, faced with the imagination gone rampant, might wonder if perhaps it would all suddenly disappear in a cataclysm, or somehow turn back into a pumpkin; but Raymond Chandler was an intimate of the scene, and he mapped its contours, including the grandeur of its physical landscape, backed by mountains and edged by the Pacific Ocean, with an eye for detail equalled only by Ernest Hemingway. Chandler was an extraordinary cultural historian, and, while time and circumstance have somewhat lessened the immediacy of his Los Angeles of the '30s and '40s, they have not rendered it obsolete.

It was the period when Fred Allen cracked that Southern California was a fine place to live–if you were an orange. Los Angeles was by and large a cultural desert situated in an oasis. Religious faddists and health cultists were common, and dreams of all kinds seemingly came true: the obscure car-hop in a drive-in might, next week, be a starlet posing for publicity stills at Warner Bros. Or so legend had it. Hollywood itself was the land of perpetual youth, of ever-hopefuls, and also of wistful, aging Ponce de Leóns. To be an "extra" was to be precisely that, a supernumerary waiting for a bit role in life from the casting office. Chandler's fiction overwhelmingly captures the sense of missed opportunity, the lost .chance, the closed door. At some remove from the events of his fic-

[37]

Inscription to a Chicago bookseller in Farewell, My Lovely *(Kent State University Library)*

tion, he obviously felt these things himself, including a sense of personal wreckage.

It was Chandler's seriousness which set him, like Dashiell Hammett, apart from the *Black Mask* school of hard-boiled writers out of which they emerged. The extraordinary colloquial quality of Chandler's prose was an aspect of this seriousness; it made available the expression of his vision. Chandler's sun-bleached landscape, for all the Hollywood glitter, is in part a fallen paradise, a Garden of Eden after the serpent has done his work.

As Chandler so often reminds us, his demiparadise is a land of drifters, grafters, and minor hoodlums; of lone women on the make or on the downhill; of sad drunks and mean drunks, and just drunks: people with better days behind them. In this world cops, as often as not, are crooked, politicians corrupt, and businessmen walk the narrow line between legitimate and illegitimate enterprise. "There ain't no clean way to make a hundred million bucks," says Bernie Ohls, a tough and honest cop, to Philip Marlowe, Chandler's private detective, in *The Long Goodbye*. Some 60 pages later, in the same novel, Chandler's private detective says to Ohls: "We're a big rough rich wild people and crime is the price we pay for it, and organized crime is the price we pay for organization. We'll have it with us a long time. Organized crime is just the dirty side of the sharp dollar." In both instances the voice speaking is the thinly disguised voice of the author. It is almost as if Chandler, making his own goodbye in his last serious novel, wanted to state directly what the plots of his earlier novels had failed fully to convey. For it was part of Chandler's originality that he saw the American psyche as criminally obsessed with the dollar, and, perhaps without being fully aware of it, society itself as criminal. In the end Chandler's romantic sensibility recoiled from the vision of evil which his art insisted upon.

Something of the same sense of a lost paradise which haunts the last page of *The Great Gatsby* pervades Chandler's Pacific Eden. I have in mind Nick Carraway's evocation of "the fresh, green breast of the new world" and his vision of its trees, which "had once pandered in whispers to the last and greatest of all human dreams." Chandler similarly poses through the juxtaposition of landscape and people the imaginative possibilities of the American continent, and also suggests some reasons for the failure to realize them. But unlike Fitzgerald in *Gatsby*, Chandler in his fiction was mainly concerned with the aftermath of the dream, the fallen state of the world after the dream has not merely become tawdry and tarnished but exists only as a debased passion.

Chandler's Marlowe drives north, out of Los Angeles, on the inland route some forty miles. It's a bad night for him. He is in a sardonic mood, commenting on the scene before him. He eats dinner in a restaurant. ("Bad but quick. Feed 'em and throw 'em out. Lots of business. We can't bother with you sitting over your second cup of coffee, mister. You're using money space.") Then he stops in a bar for a brandy and comes out to drive home. ("I stepped out into the night air that nobody had yet found out how to option. But a lot of people were probably trying. They'd get around to it.") He turns toward the ocean and the coastal route back to Los Angeles.

> The big eight-wheelers and sixteen-wheelers were streaming north, all hung over with orange lights. On the right the great fat solid Pacific trudging into shore like a scrubwoman going home. No moon, no fuss, hardly a sound of surf. No smell. None of the harsh wild smell of the sea. A Califor-

nia ocean. California, the department-store state. The most of everything and the best of nothing. Here we go again. You're not human tonight, Marlowe.

> Malibu. More movie stars. More pink and blue bathtubs. More tufted beds. More Chanel No. 5. More Lincoln Continentals and Cadillacs. More windblown hair and sunglasses and attitudes and pseudo-refined voices and waterfront morals. Now, wait a minute. Lots of nice people work in pictures. You've got the wrong attitude, Marlowe. You're not human tonight.
>
> I smelled Los Angeles before I got to it. It smelled stale and old like a living room that had been closed too long. But the colored lights fooled you. The lights were wonderful. There ought to be a monument to the man who invented neon lights. Fifteen stories high, solid marble. There's a boy who really made something out of nothing.

> *(The Little Sister)*

Landscape in Chandler directly reflects the half-insubstantial quality of American life—the sense of people exploiting things to make their lives real and meaningful: to be better people than they are. But the ground base is always there. It is themselves they have exploited in their search for the equivalents of class and station, position, genealogy, tradition.

Chandler was a master at portraying the schizoid aspects of American culture and the ways in which the base and ideal and their manifestations are so closely intertwined as to be inseparable, if not indistinguishable. The lives of his characters reveal this split in motive and intention and conduct, just as the patterns of his novels reveal the cohesiveness of American life which underlies and makes a whole of this self-perpetuating opposition.

Marlowe crosses and crisscrosses the landscape of greater Los Angeles, which provides almost infinite variety of background, moving from terrain to terrain, locale to locale, setting to setting. Chandler bears down so heavily on landscape in his novels that physical property almost takes on a value and meaning of its own; one is reminded of the motion pictures and the way in which the camera invests physical props with significance by panning back and forth over them, by lingering with them. But, while the vastly different places Chandler's Marlowe visits, and the people

Dust jacket for the first printing of Chandler's third novel

he encounters, are seemingly held together by a thread of meaning solely of Marlowe's making, a pattern gradually emerges, a meaningful arrangement and sequence of events; and behind this pattern lies, broadly speaking, the pattern of American society as Chandler sees it: mobile, fluid, a reticulated crisscrossing of people through time and circumstance. One begins to see why, in Chandler's fiction, the world of Los Angeles' Bunker Hill, with its decayed buildings and decaying people, is just a stone's throw away from the deep lawns and private driveways and stately mansions of Santa Monica; why, in other words, all segments of society are inextricably linked in Chandler's sun-filled but nightmarish landscape.

In *Farewell, My Lovely*, Marlowe tries to help the police find Moose Malloy, an ex-con who had negligently killed a man in Marlowe's presence. Malloy was bent on finding "little Velma," once a singer in a dance hall which changed hands and clientele some eight years earlier. Because Velma may lead to Malloy, Marlowe looks for clues to her whereabouts. He begins by locating the deceased dance hall owner's wife, Jessie Florian:

1644 West 54th Place was a dried-out brown house with a dried-out brown lawn in front of it. There was a large bare patch around a tough-looking palm tree. On the porch stood one lonely wooden rocker, and the afternoon breeze made the unpruned shoots of last year's poinsettias tap-tap against the cracked stucco wall. A line of stiff yellowish half-washed clothes jittered on a rusty wire in the side yard.

The woman he meets inside will be just as burnt out, an alcoholic with a face gray and puffy, dressed in "a shapeless flannel bathrobe many moons past color and design." Eventually, Marlowe will connect Mrs. Florian with Lindsay Marriott, who later the same day hires him to act as a bodyguard in a transaction involving the buying back of a stolen jade necklace. The worlds of the drunken Jessie Florian and Marriott, who lives off rich women, are vastly different. He lives in a house overlooking the Pacific, with carpeting in the living room so thick it almost tickles Marlowe's ankles when he goes to see him. "It was the kind of room where people sit with their feet in their laps and sip absinthe through lumps of sugar." Jessie Florian and Marriott become linked when Marlowe learns that Marriott not only put up the money to refinance Mrs. Florian's home but also sends her a monthly check, supposedly because she was once a servant in his family. They also become linked in death. First Marriott, then Mrs. Florian, is murdered. But only near the end of the novel does Marlowe connect both to Velma.

In the course of *Farewell, My Lovely*, Marlowe is led by events to Aster Drive, where there are "great silent estates, with twelve-foot walls and wrought iron gates and ornamental hedges; and inside, if you could get inside, a special brand of sunshine, very quiet, put up in noise-proof containers just for the upper classes." Here, without realizing it at first, he finds Moose Malloy's "little Velma" in the person of Helen Grayle, the wife of a millionaire. Marlowe has gone to Aster Drive because Mrs. Grayle possessed the jade necklace which Marriott was supposedly redeeming when he was killed. Hence Marlowe's discovery of the identity of Velma is far from direct, almost accidental in one sense, and involves people who seemingly have no relation to each other until Marlowe, digging into the past and beneath the surface of events, demonstrates those relations.

In his best novels Chandler gave a high gloss of reality to these intricate alignments of people and events. In most he kept the artificiality of the form at bay. In one or two he lost control, for reasons too various to concern us here But, in general, it could be fairly said that Chandler extended the form by making available to writers who came after him a more complex understanding of the fabric of society and a more serious and sensitive view of its dynamics. This is no small achievement in itself.

Along with Hammett, Chandler gave the detective story back its inherent realism. But he also added a personal dimension to the form–and here Marlowe played a less traditional role than the one described above, in which his function was to search out and make visible the links between people and events and reveal the developing pattern of significance.

Chandler once said that "Marlowe just grew out of the pulps. He was no one person." In the sense in which he meant it, his statement is true enough. Marlowe (who was to have been called Mallory, perhaps in Chandler's mind a link with

Poster for the 1946 movie version of The High Window

the author of *Morte D'Arthur*; the name involvement would be in keeping with Chandler's intense literary sense) had his antecedents in the various heroes of Chandler's *Black Mask* stories. Significantly enough, he appeared under his own name at just the time Chandler turned from shorter fiction to the novel. In part Marlowe seems to have made possible this shift to the longer form, as he did the emergence of a highly personal voice, one that seemed to speak directly to readers everywhere in the authentic rhythms of American speech. Precisely how Marlowe made these developments possible for his British-educated author is a somewhat complex matter, as is the whole question of Chandler's relationship with his narrator-hero and its meaning for his art.

Like some other famous detective-heroes, including Poe's Dupin and Conan Doyle's Sherlock

Holmes, Marlowe is to a certain extent an obvious projection of his author. Chandler gave Marlowe his own wit. He gave him an education which allowed Marlowe to make use of Chandler's own, which was classical and literary. He imbued him with his own romanticism. "I'm a romantic," Marlowe says. "I hear voices crying in the night and I go see what's the matter. You don't make a dime that way. You got sense, you shut your windows and turn up more sound on the TV set." Marlowe's self-derision is intended by his author to redound to his credit, and to belie the sentimentalism in his voice. There is also irony here, at least for the author, in the fact that as a private detective Marlowe has no status, no authority, no assured place in society. Like his author, Marlowe as detective is an idealist hiding behind cynicism and wise talk, and, while he never fully articulates his reason for remaining a private detective, his actions suggest some, as his author intended. Basically they are old-fashioned reasons, for Marlowe in certain ways is, like his author, an old-fashioned sort of person. He is Chandler's knight, righting the balance in a wronged and fallen universe. He corrects injustices, stands up for the underdog, speaks out for the little guy. As Chandler put it in "The Simple Art of Murder," "Down these mean streets a man must go who is not himself mean, who is neither tarnished nor afraid. . . . He is the hero; he is everything." Marlowe as a projection of Chandler's romantic ego satisfied some imaginative need of his sedentary author directly to intervene in the violence of the world, to propitiate and ameliorate those brute aspects of life which his hurt sensibility found it difficult to accept. But, as Chandler's knight said in *The Big Sleep*, looking down at a wrong move he had made in a chess game, "knights had no meaning in this game. It wasn't a game for knights."

Marlowe is the wholly honest man, a saint in a world of sinners. For all his wisecracking and whiskey drinking, he has a rather narrow and somewhat puritanical code. He is loyal to his clients, hard-working, more interested in justice than in his fee, impervious to bribery, or a roughing-up by police or hoodlums. He takes the threats against his life as they come. He is impossible to impress; he sees through sham and hypocrisy. He is also a bit too good to be true–and Chandler under-

stood this limitation, particularly in his later years, when his relationship with his hero underwent a subtle transformation. But this is the Marlowe we remember from Chandler's fiction. We are apt to overlook the other Marlowe, a sadder, wiser Marlowe, a lonelier man than his earlier self, who lived alone and seemed to like it.

This other Marlowe is not a new figure on the scene. He represents a deepening of those aspects of his author's personality which were held in check by dint of will and by the very art which Marlowe made possible. The appearance of this disenchanted Marlowe late in Chandler's writing career suggests that from the first Marlowe's presence in Chandler's fiction involved a more serious displacement of personality than his identity as mere fictional alter ego would imply.

No matter how closely Chandler on occasion identified with his hero in his fiction, there are ways of telling them apart, and these have significance for Chandler's art. Marlowe was a native Californian, Chandler wasn't. In fact Chandler was a native American solely in the legal sense. He was born in Chicago in 1888. But then, while he was a child, his mother returned to England, and he grew up there, attending an established public school. It was not until 1912 that he arrived in California. He brought with him, as he put it, a beautiful wardrobe and a public school accent.

But while Chandler's wasn't a native American voice, Philip Marlowe's invented voice is. Commenting on the significance for his art of his British childhood in a letter published in the posthumous collection, *Raymond Chandler Speaking*, he said: "I had to learn American just like a foreign language. To learn it I had to study and analyze it. As a result, when I use slang, colloquialisms, snide talk or any kind of off-beat language I do it deliberately." In Chandler's hands the American language became racy and direct, occasionally colorful, always fast-paced. It was the language of the wisecrack and the sharp comeback. It had thought content without being muscle-bound by the formulas of language. It leveled people, took the stuffing out of them. It acted as a liberating force and gave Marlowe freedom of action to cross class and social barriers. Ultimately it was a means of dealing with the democratic experience, with American classlessness and rootlessness. The American language was Marlowe's invisible armor.

It is remarkable that Chandler's studied American-ness produced an authentic American voice; yet something like this happened. Confronted with his own feelings of deracination, with the sense of being caught between cultures, Chandler saw the potentialities of the American language from the multiple perspective of both outsider and insider. Elsewhere in his letters he reminds us of his alien-ness. As a young man he lived briefly in Paris. There he met a good many Americans. "Most of them seemed to have a lot of bounce and liveliness and to be thoroughly enjoying themselves in situations where the average Englishman of the same class would be stuffy or completely bored. But I wasn't one of them. I didn't even speak their language. I was, in effect, a man without a country." Chandler's sense of rootlessness followed him through his entire life. Perhaps it accounts for the way he made the loneliness of life in big city America one of his major themes. So insistent was this overmastering feeling that it hung on right through *The Long Goodbye*, in which Chandler tried to lay the ghost of his British self.

Chandler's alien voice can be heard quite clearly in the volume *Raymond Chandler Speaking*, particularly in his letters to his English publisher, Hamish Hamilton, and to Charles W. Morton, an editor for the *Atlantic Monthly*. Often he sounds like an exile from John Bull's island. He raises the old school tie, he adopts a somewhat patrician attitude toward writing, insisting on his amateur status. ("The English writer is a gentleman first and a writer second," he remarked in his "Notes on English and American Style," pointing to what he considered to be one of the defects of English style.) It is almost incredible to find him writing, in 1949: "I'm still an amateur, still, psychologically speaking, perfectly capable of chucking writing altogether and taking up the study of law or comparative philology." At this point in his career Chandler, who was sixty years old, had published his major fiction: *The Big Sleep* (1939), *Farewell, My Lovely* (1940), *The High Window* (1942), and *Lady in the Lake* (1943); in 1949 he published *The Little Sister*, which suggested a falling-off of his talent. Only *The Long Goodbye* remained to be written. (*Playback*, published after *The Long Goodbye*, had already

been written as a screenplay in 1947. It was never produced and Chandler later turned it into a book. Properly speaking, it is not part of the Chandler canon.)

It is hard at times to estimate the sincerity of the Chandler of the letters, for one thing because, without being a poseur, he is obviously posing to a certain extent. This Chandler is bent on justifying his career and propagating his reputation. And underneath, much of the time, he is feeling sorry for himself. He unjustly arraigns other writers. He makes mock modest comparisons between his achievements and those of others, denying that he is in their class as a writer but implying all the while that he is every bit their equal or better. He is seemingly humble while really prideful, his ironic sense of self dominating his feelings: "What greater prestige can a man like me (not too greatly gifted, but very understanding) have than to have taken a cheap, shoddy, and utterly lost kind of writing, and have made of it something that intellectuals claw each other about?" He is also neglecting Hammett, whose earlier achievement might be described in precisely the same terms.

He will knock the intellectuals, while being one himself. He harbors petty grievances. He sees himself in most situations as wronged. He is contentious. He indulges himself by answering letters from readers in which he argues in detail the personal habits of Marlowe, momentarily turning him into a real person. There is a certain self-laceration here, because he knows the reader is interested in Marlowe, not Chandler. And all the while, it strikes one, Chandler is strangely disaffected with Marlowe; or perhaps he is merely aware that in Marlowe he created a man more admirable than himself, forgetful that without Raymond Chandler there would be no Marlowe. In any case, he envisions Cary Grant as the movie actor who could best portray Marlowe as he conceives of him–a transplanted Englishman with inherently nice manners. One can't help but feel that Marlowe would be amused by this identification; but, I think he would also find it revealing of his author, and in keeping with his character.

The Raymond Chandler of these letters, which were written mainly during his sixties, is a man under considerable personal and psychological stress. He is preoccupied with himself in ways

Dust jacket for the first printing of Chandler's fourth novel

that are somewhat touching, and also pathetic. He shows a certain helplessness. He suffers mild paranoia. And he reveals, without intending to, something of the transformation of character, the rearrangement of personal experience, which went on in the creation of his fiction, as well as the role Marlowe played in this transmutation.

Essentially Marlowe released in Chandler a vein of self-criticism and self-knowledge. He tapped the secret resources, the reserves of his author's personality, those hidden forces which drove him to fiction, and made them available to the fiction writer as they weren't to the letter writer. All of Chandler's hostile emotions, his aggressive tendencies, all his anti-social feelings, his loneliness, his self-pity, which he never fully mastered, were transformed in fictional creations which not only bore a striking resemblance to the real world but revealed memorable truths about that world.

Marlowe gave Chandler someone to talk to, as well as speak through, so that the speaking voice we hear in Chandler's fiction is not an alien voice but that of a man purified in the fire of the human inferno.

In his book on Chandler, *Down These Mean Streets a Man Must Go*, Philip Durham accurately enough describes Chandler's art in terms of the "objective" tradition in fiction, though he unnecessarily limits the perspective of the author to the eyes of his first-person narrator:

> Theoretically, at least, the author tells us nothing; the only person in the novel from whom we can learn anything is Marlowe. If we receive knowledge of any other character it is only if and when Marlowe wants us to have it. What we know about Los Angeles is what Marlowe tells us or allows others to tell us. The detached author is not on the stage, and we are not even sure he is in the wings. The burden is always on the author never to let us know how he feels, never to give us any "dear reader" asides, and never to tell us how his characters feel; the characters must tell us everything we know about them by their own actions and expressions.

Durham's lengthy statement belabors the obvious point about the restrictions of point of view, while ignoring the equally obvious though more subtle point that all objectivity in fiction depends on a carefully preserved authorial attitude. The author is hidden from view–but he is also just around the corner; his felt presence in his work is not limited. It is dangerously misleading, in Chandler's case, to say that "we are not even sure" the detached author is "in the wings. The burden is always on the author never to let us know how he feels. . . ."

Chandler's novels are all written in the first person, with Marlowe as narrator; but Marlowe's voice, as I have tried to suggest, is not the only voice we hear in Chandler's fiction. Behind Marlowe stands the author, and sometimes we are aware of his subtle intrusion upon the seemingly objective account of events as offered us by his narrator-detective. An instance in point is chapter thirty-one of *Farewell, My Lovely*. The scene is a Los Angeles homicide bureau where Marlowe has gone to make a statement concerning the murder of Jessie Florian. Marlowe has only recently become aware of her connection with Lindsay Marriott, and this and other matters surrounding their deaths form the substance of the conversation between Marlowe and the homicide detective.

The chapter opens in the following manner, with the voice seemingly belonging to Marlowe, who at first sight merely appears to be setting the scene for the interview to follow between himself and Randall:

> A shiny black bug with a pink head and pink spots on it crawled slowly along the polished top of Randall's desk and waved a couple of feelers around, as if testing the breeze for a takeoff. It wobbled a little as it crawled, like an old woman carrying too many parcels. A nameless dick sat at another desk and kept talking into an old-fashioned hushaphone mouthpiece, so that his voice sounded like someone whispering in a tunnel. He talked with his eyes half closed, a big scarred hand on the desk in front of him holding a burning cigarette between the knuckles of the first and second fingers.

By the end of this paragraph, if not before, the reader is aware that more is going on here than the mere description of a homicide office at police headquarters. For one thing, the matter of the paragraph–the pink and black bug making its way across Randall's desk, the detective sitting at the other desk–has been arranged less as a sequence of fact than as two juxtaposed images (reinforced by parallel grammatical structures) which, taken together, provide commentary not only on the law

in our society but also on the individual, particularly the individual before the law. This is more obvious than it may at first appear, for midway through the passage occurs the arresting image by which the insignificant bug in its process across the desk is compared to an old woman carrying too many parcels–surely a reminder of the old woman, Jessie Florian, insignificant in the run of things, a peripheral figure even in the events which lead to her death. Jessie Florian had been wobbly not merely in her drunkenness but in the intent and purpose of her greed.

In his second paragraph, Chandler's art reinforces while it generalizes the suggestiveness of his Kafkaesque image:

> The bug reached the end of Randall's desk and marched straight off into the air. It fell on its back on the floor, waved a few thin worn legs in the air feebly and then played dead. Nobody cared, so it began waving the legs again and finally struggled over on its face. It trundled off into a corner, towards nothing, going nowhere.

At this point Chandler's bug has taken on broad symbolic overtones. It will continue its journey to nowhere through the pages of the chapter, to be rescued, significantly, by Marlowe, but only after it has served to suggest a dimension of meaning which it is impossible for Marlowe to relate directly.

Meanwhile, the nameless detective will abruptly leave the room at one point, his presence no longer required when Randall, a personalized representative of the law as opposed to this generalized figure, takes his place. The effect Chandler achieves in the first paragraph with the description of the nameless detective is, I think, harder to explain than that of the black bug with the pink head and pink spots. The detail is in part traditional, the category of image equally traditional. The "big scarred hand" of the detective, for example, conveys not only the idea of physical bigness but also of brute strength and physical violence, realities associated in the mind of the public with the police in general. The detective's repose and even the burning cigarette are suggestive of the patience and tired watchfulness of the law. But beyond this there is the detective's namelessness, his voice, which sounds like someone whispering in a

Robert Montgomery and Audrey Totter in the 1946 movie version of The Lady in the Lake, *which used an experimental camera-eye technique through which Marlowe (Montgomery) appeared on the screen only in reflections. Chandler worked on the screenplay, but withdrew and refused screen credit.*

tunnel (and hence is equally "nameless," unidentifiable, generalized), and his half-closed eyes–all in all the picture of an inscrutable figure which personifies the law as Chandler sees it.

In the first two paragraphs of chapter thirty-one we have been listening, largely without awareness, to the voice of the author. Chandler's art has been such that he has been speaking to us through Marlowe with relative directness undetermined by the needs of plot and character. As the chapter progresses the author is heard even more directly. After Randall has entered the room and Marlowe signed the prepared statement, the two men go on to discuss various aspects of the murders. Included in the discussion is Randall's slightly disguised threat that Marlowe should get out of the case and let the police handle things. ("We got friendly this morning. Let's stay that way. Go home and lie down and have a good rest.") Near the end of the chapter the talk turns to the Marriott-Florian relationship:

"I have a theory about that," he [Randall] said. . . . "I think Jessie Florian was Marriott's lucky piece. As long as he took care of her, nothing would happen to him."

I turned my head and looked for the pink-headed bug. He had tried two corners of the room now and was moving off disconsolately towards a third. I went over and picked him up in my handkerchief and carried him back to the desk.

"Look," I said. "This room is eighteen floors above ground. And this little bug climbs all the way up here just to make a friend. Me. *My* lucky piece." I folded the bug carefully into my pocket. Randall was pie-eyed. His mouth moved but nothing came out of it.

"I wonder whose lucky piece Marriott was," I said.

"Not yours, pal." His mouth was acid–cold acid.

"Perhaps not yours either." My voice was just a voice. I went out of the room and shut the door.

I rode the express elevator down to the Spring Street entrance and walked out on the front porch of City Hall and down some steps and over to the flower beds. I put the pink bug down carefully behind a bush.

I wondered, in the taxi going home, how long it would take him to make the homicide bureau again.

In Marlowe's voice–which is "just a voice"–we hear his recognition of not only the helplessness he feels and its source, which he acknowledges, but also his awareness of the aloneness of the individual in the big city. And beyond Marlowe's voice we hear the voice of the author. That is, we realize that something is being said beyond what the dialogue appears to be saying–and this something, I think, we take to be a statement by the author about American society. Chandler is commenting on the sheer puniness of the individual in America, his weakness before both the forces of corruption and the machinery of the law, which is not merely beyond his control but is seemingly beyond anyone's control, dispensing justice, and sometimes injustice, in the light of partial and imperfect truth. Society is the corrupter of the individual, the predator.

In Chandler's eyes, the breakdown in authority, which is part and parcel of the democratic process, is justification for Marlowe's attitude and temper of mind where the police are concerned:

"Until you guys [the police] own your own souls, you don't own mine. Until you guys can be trusted every time and always, in all times and conditions, to seek the truth out and find it and let the chips fall where they may–until that time comes, I have a right to listen to my conscience, and protect my client the best way I can. Until I'm sure you won't do him more harm than you'll do the truth good. Or until I'm hauled before somebody that can make me talk."

(The High Window)

Marlowe intervenes, intercedes; Marlowe runs afoul of the law: this partial pattern reappears in novel after novel. But Marlowe's combativeness, his slow-burning but explosive personality, is ultimately unable to cope with the hostility of the law and the oppressiveness of society in general. Per-haps this failure in part accounts for the habitual fatigue and weariness in Marlowe's voice, for the somber, almost dolorous ground tone against which he makes his wisecracks and smart retorts. In Chandler's fiction, much of the time Marlowe is a modern Sisyphus, a man forever pushing an unbearable burden uphill. In the end Marlowe, with his author, retreats to sentimentality as an antidote, a palliative to the brutalizing effects of society.

This turn toward sentimentality can be seen in chapter thirty-one of Farewell, My Lovely, where in the end Marlowe's pink bug is revealed as a sentimental symbol whose adventures fail to reveal any serious meaning. For all the Kafkaesque overtones, what is missing is something comparable to the terror and horror of the Metamorphosis. Kafka's bug, we are reminded, was a real person; Chandler's is merely a pink bug.

Chandler's uneasiness about the persistent sentimentality of this scene makes itself obvious. The author attempts to glide over any scrutiny of Marlowe's emotions by focusing on the reactions of the homicide detective, Randall. When, at one point, Marlowe says that the bug is his lucky piece and puts it carefully in his pocket, Randall becomes "pie-eyed. His mouth moved but nothing came out of it." The effect of such exaggerated language is to reduce Randall from the status of a real person to that of a stock character. He momentarily becomes the familiar dumb cop of the "B" grade movies.

In the last chapter of Farewell, My Lovely, Marlowe's pink bug again makes its appearance. Randall and Marlowe are discussing the suicide of Helen Grayle ("little Velma"), who, discovered in another city, shot herself rather than return to stand trial for the murders of Marriott and Moose Malloy. Randall finds her death unnecessary. With a clever lawyer, which her elderly millionaire husband could have easily supplied, she would never have been convicted of either murder. Marlowe, however, has an explanation for her conduct and suicide:

" . . . Who would that trial hurt most? Who would be least able to bear it? And win, lose or draw, who would pay the biggest price for the show? An old man who had loved wisely, but too well."

Barbara Stanwyck and Fred MacMurray in Double Indemnity

Randall said sharply: "That's just sentimental."

"Sure. It sounded like that when I said it. Probably all a mistake anyway. So long. Did my pink bug ever get back up here?"

He didn't know what I was talking about.

Both the allusion to Shakespear's *Othello* and the mention of the pink bug are intended to undercut Randall's "That's just sentimental," as is Marlowe's "It sounded like that when I said it." None of this attempt to make sentimentality a principle of structure seems to me fully satisfying, as well as it is done. For one thing, because structure is moral and causal. To manipulate structure as Chandler does at the end of *Farewell, My Lovely* by fantasying an explanation of events is to turn off the vision which has controlled the book's meaning. In the end one has to speak not merely of Chan-

dler's sentimentalism but of a more serious failure in his art: the dishonesty of a vision which failed to follow its own light at crucial points.

This lack of honesty infects, at various levels, both plot and character in Chandler's work. One sign of the moral juggling I am speaking of is reflected in the derivation of his novels–in the way he "cannibalized" his published stories for his novels, borrowing pieces and bits as they suited his purposes. There is nothing inherently wrong in a writer reusing the materials of his earlier fiction, but in Chandler what the reweaving of fragments ultimately suggests is an unsureness about the moral values he is attaching to people and events. Then, too, Marlowe on occasion invests in some of the figures he encounters a moral worth which nothing in either situation or character allows for. In *The Big Sleep* he speaks of Harry Jones, a small-

Chandler collaborated with director Billy Wilder on the screenplay for James M. Cain's Double Indemnity.

us nothing in the character of the movie star which would let us assume she would act this way. And the half-sister, Orfamay Quest, is an exceptionally unpleasant person, smug, hypocritical, a small-town puritan whose ethic has gone sour and become evil. Chandler uses Orfamay (and Manhattan, Kansas) to vent his anger against those aspects of middle-class American life which he finds offensive. In the end, "the little sister" is portrayed as a person worse than she would be in real life, just as Mavis Weld is seen as a better person than she would be. The moral confusion of *The Little Sister* reflects the confusion in plot in the novel. Marlowe, for example, takes the law into his own hands and rearranges the evidence at the scene of the murder. His action apparently stems from his conviction that Mavis Weld is innocent—though he never informs us of this, and he has little reason for believing it.

I am not here quarreling with Marlowe's role in Chandler's fiction nor with his author's conception of his hero, though both are open to question, but with Chandler's denial of his own vision, basically with his desire to improve upon and to soften the harsh quality of life which his own works reveal.

Over the years readers of Chandler's novels, as well as commentators on his art, have been struck by the heavy vein of gratuitous emotion in the Marlowe of *The Long Goodbye*, Chandler's last novel of importance, published in 1954. It was first pointed out by Chandler's agent, Bernice Baumgarten, when she received the manuscript of the novel in May 1952. She apparently made a number of specific objections to the book as it stood, and Chandler replied in part: "I knew the character of Marlowe had changed and I thought it had to because the hardboiled stuff was too much of a pose after all this time. But I did not realize that it had become Christlike, and sentimental, and that he ought to be deriding his own emotions. . . ." To his English publisher, who had apparently written Chandler to encourage and sympathize with him in the work at hand, he wrote: "Most of the points Bernice criticized in detail would have been changed automatically in revision and a great many that she did not criticize. . . . Be of good cheer. I don't mind Marlowe being a sentimentalist, because he always has been. His toughness

time grifter who is trying to sell him some information, as "A small man in a big man world. There was something I liked about him." Marlowe's vagueness here is particularly revealing, for there is nothing very likable about Harry Jones at this point except perhaps a certain stick-to-it-iveness. In the next chapter he will show a certain loyalty by refusing to reveal to Lash Canino the whereabouts of the woman Gladys, with whom he is in partnership. But his painful death by cyanide at Canino's hands in this chapter is gratuitous. It seems motivated as much by Chandler's desire to make the gangster worse than he is as to make Harry Jones better than he is.

Chandler's failure to sustain a morally dispassionate view of his characters can be seen throughout *The Little Sister*, in some ways the least successful of his novels. The sequence of events rather implausibly hinges on the movie star Mavis Weld wanting to take the blame for the murder of her gangster-lover by her "little sister" from Manhattan, Kansas. The trouble is that Chandler shows

has always been more or less a surface bluff. . . ." Seemingly the mask between author and hero had worn paper-thin. Marlowe's toughness, as we have maintained all along, had always been in part a mechanism of defense for his author.

The sentimentalism of Marlowe in *The Long Goodbye* has been variously attributed, sometimes to Chandler's age (he was now sixty-four), sometimes to the fact that his wife Cissy, who was eighteen years his senior, was seriously ill during the writing. Chandler was exceptionally close to his wife, who had been an invalid for many years, and he was clumsily to attempt suicide after her death in 1954. Both Chandler's age and his wife's illness undoubtedly contributed to the emotional tone of the book, but more relevant for his art is the discovery that, upon scrutiny, *The Long Goodbye* turns out to be a profoundly autobiographical novel in which the author on an imaginative level explores his own past and those aspects of his personality which continued to engage him. Ultimately the emotion that Marlowe expends in *The Long Goodbye* is for his author and the butt-end of his days.

In retrospect, even the minor figure of the writer in *The Long Goodbye* bears a broad resemblance to Raymond Chandler. Roger Wade is the author of a dozen best-selling historical novels; Chandler was the author of a half-dozen highly successful detective novels. Also, Chandler wanted to be a historical novelist but was talked out of it by his publisher. Wade drinks excessively, he has trouble finishing the book he is working on. He thinks little of himself and his talent. "You're looking at a small time operator in a small time business. . . . All writers are punks and I am one of the punkest." In discussing with Marlowe the possible reasons for Wade's drinking, his wife offers the suggestion that perhaps she's the cause. "Men fall out of love with their wives." Marlowe replies: "I'd say it's more likely he has fallen out of love with the kind of stuff he writes." In terms of the plot of *The Long Goodbye*, both Mrs. Wade and Marlowe are partly right.

The parallels to Chandler's life give one pause. His drinking was well-known; he had recently had trouble bringing to a conclusion *The Little Sister*, and he had a marked capacity for professional self-abasement which derived from much

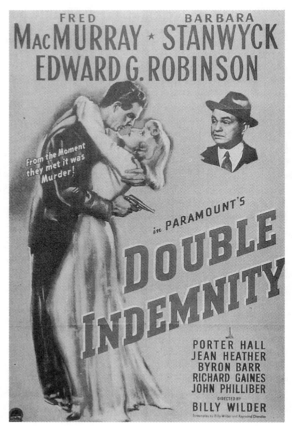

Poster for Double Indemnity *(1944), which received an Academy Award nomination for best screenplay*

the same source as Wade's: he wrote in a popular form. In the United States, unlike England, detective fiction has never been taken seriously by the critics. This irony was not lost on Chandler, as his letters make clear. The limited respect paid detective fiction undoubtedly contributed to his defensiveness about his art and also to the neglect, real or imaginary, which he intensely felt from time to time. One also has to remember that Chandler was far better educated than the mass of his readers; he had daily to face the fact that it *was* the tough talk, the violence, the glamor of crime that captured and held them. Most would never have a glimmering of the range of knowledge he displayed in his books or the art with which he wrote them.

It would of course be a dubious procedure to read Roger Wade's statements in *The Long Goodbye* as having a point-by-point application to Chandler personally, though it seems likely that on some level Chandler was working out the ambivalence he felt toward his own achievement as a writer in ways impossible to relate in his correspondence. In *The Long Goodbye* Roger Wade's wife and his publisher want to hire Marlowe to guard him from drinking and doing himself bodily harm so he can finish the book he is working on. Marlowe wants to refuse but never fully does so. He rescues Wade from the ranch of a doctor in Sepulveda Canyon who is drying him out, and he intervenes on other occasions. It is almost as if Marlowe were Roger Wade's guardian angel, and also as if, on another level, one part of Raymond Chandler were keeping watch over another. Not surprisingly, in terms of events in the novel Wade's compulsive drinking is only in a limited way connected with his writing: all the talk about writing is in point of fact irrelevant–except that it vitally concerns Raymond Chandler.

In the end Marlowe cannot save Roger Wade from suicide, or rather, from being murdered, for his wife kills him and makes it appear a suicide; but this event occurs only when the plot of Chandler's long novel demands his death–when, in effect, Chandler's new alter ego has said all that he wants him to say. By then, the essential parallel between Chandler's doubles has been directly sounded. At one point in the novel, the writer says to the detective: "You know something, Marlowe? I could get to like you. You're a bit of a bastard–like me." When, much later in the novel, Marlowe informs Wade's publisher, Harold Spencer, of his death, the words he uses echo this conversation: "Roger Wade is dead, Spencer. He was a bit of a bastard and maybe a genius too. That's over my head. He was an egotistical drunk and hated his own guts." Where in all this maze of romantically conceived self-criticism Raymond Chandler really stood is perhaps impossible to tell, and ultimately it is unimportant, for it is clear that Chandler was harder on himself than anyone else ever was–or will be.

What appears to have happened by the time Chandler wrote *The Long Goodbye* is that the paradox of his personality had largely resolved into new components. Chandler was no longer overly much interested in Marlowe as a projection of his own personality. Marlowe still went down mean streets in the service of his author, but now he was bent less on being the hero than on exploring the other selves of Raymond Chandler.

The main character in *The Long Goodbye* is Terry Lennox, an American with a British accent and British mannerisms. ("I lived there. I wasn't born there," he says of himself, much as Chandler speaks of himself in one of his published letters.) Lennox is in a number of ways a curious figure in the novel. He appears only in the opening pages and again at the end, yet his ghostly presence dominates the book, in part because of Marlowe's strong but irrational attachment to him. A minor but curious matter in the novel is that Terry Lennox's real name is Paul Marston; his initials are the same as Philip Marlowe's.

Marlowe first encounters Terry Lennox in the parking lot of a Sunset Strip nightclub. Lennox has drunkenly fallen out of a Rolls Royce. The woman with him (his ex-wife, the daughter of a millionaire) drives off in the Rolls, leaving him stranded. Marlowe feels sorry enough for Lennox to see him safely home to his Westwood apartment. "I'm supposed to be tough but there was something about the guy that got me. I didn't know what it was unless it was the white hair and the scarred face and the clear voice and politeness. Maybe that was enough." The prematurely white hair and the scarred face are both the result of Lennox's experiences in the British Commandos during World War II. The clear voice and the politeness are aspects of English-ness. Seemingly what Marlowe is in part admiring in Lennox is his British reticence, the stiff upper-lip, the code of the gentleman. For Lennox is in severe financial trouble here at the beginning of the book, and he is unable to bring himself to ask anyone for help–specifically, his ex-wife, or the two men whose lives he saved in the Commandos. The one, Mendy Menendez, is a Los Angeles gangster; the other, Randy Starr, is the operator of a Las Vegas gambling casino. Both feel under obligation to him.

Marlowe has no reason to see Lennox again, but by chance encounters him one day around Thanksgiving staggering along a row of shops on

RAYMOND CHANDLER

Once in a blue moon...

ONCE in a blue moon the public's estimate of a novelist crystallizes into the simple belief: Here. within his chosen field, or certain medium, is a truly great writer. Such a belief seems to be forming in regard to Raymond Chandler. author of *The Big Sleep*, *Farewell, My Lovely*, *The High Window*, and *The Lady in the Lake*. Mr. Chandler's four novels. together with his two volumes of novelettes. are usually classified as murder mysteries. But articles about them and their author in the *Atlantic Monthly*, *Harper's Bazaar* (forthcoming) , and elsewhere, and critical opinion generally, indicate beyond a doubt that they are much more than the usual murder mysteries whose chief function is ephemeral entertainment.

For example, here is what D. C. Russell (A's son) says about them, in part, in the March *Atlantic Monthly*:

I should like to record my gratitude to Raymond Chandler for what is, indeed, a new experience in mystery novels. It is a new experience because Chandler writes not out of habit and not with synthetic materials, as do so many mystery writers, but with an artistry of craftsmanship and a realism that can rank him with many a famous novelist. In his hands, words do become beautiful and wonderful things, operating with economy and precision. . . . Chandler writes the characteristic American speech and uses characteristic American humor. In doing this he comes closer to literature than other writers who disdain the native brand of thought and language. . . . He believes, and rightly I think, that most murder stories no longer have any relation to real life—that they have become a literary form and convention remote from realism. . . . Chandler in his works has returned to that world where murder is a commonplace: the world of racketeers in drugs and liquor, in gambling and prostitution; a world in which police and racketeers and politicians are often mixed up in sub-surface alliances. . . . It is strange to meet a murder novel writer who attacks his work with the earnest attention and serious sort of thought which are supposed to be the prerogative of eminent novelists. This is what Chandler does; and, so doing, he has removed his work from the realm of merely conventional entertainment to the point where it becomes a serious study of a certain kind of American society. This quality, and a grim sense of humor allied with an even grimmer sense of realism . . . plus a superb writing ability, have produced five novels which are worth the attention of more readers than just those

alone who are interested in the literature of murder.

Then, again, earlier this year Charles W. Morton (who has called Chandler "the top hot-shocker writer of recent years") writing in the *Boston Globe*, said:

The year [1943] brought me, also, the growing conviction that the best operator in the business, bar none, is Raymond Chandler. He had a small but ardent following for the past two or three years, but he is about to become a cult. When you can read a private detective yarn a dozen times, and when you find people in general who can quote long excerpts from the author and his characters, that author is obviously getting somewhere.

And Dale Warren, writing in the correspondence columns of the *Saturday Review of Literature*, said:

"Sir: I wish that critics who express themselves on the state of the detective story (Judge Lynch and Jaques Barzun in the *Saturday Review*, Edmund Wilson in the *New Yorker*, André Gide in the *New Republic*, etc.) would sample the collected and neglected works of Raymond Chandler. Some amateurs think of Chandler not only as the olive in the martini but the martini itself."

This is the author whom Erle Stanley Gardner has called "a star of the first magnitude in the constellation of modern mystery writers," and of whom the *Kansas City Star* said some time ago: "When the literary historians some years hence jot down the names of the Americans who developed a distinctive style of mystery story writing. Mr. Chandler will rank high on the list."

What does all this add up to? Certainly.

that Raymond Chandler is, first of all, a *writer*—one who uses words consciously as a literary medium—and as such a master of his craft. Second, that he is worth reading not only as an author of murder mysteries but as a *novelist*—whether you ordinarily read mystery stories or not. Third, that his novels may be considered a part of contemporary American *literature*, along with those of such writers as Hammett, Cain, O'Hara, Burnett.

Raymond Chandler has been writing now for about fifteen years. First he published novelettes in the *Black Mask*—novelettes which have recently been collected in the volumes *Five Murderers* and *Five Sinister Characters* (Avon Books). Then in 1939 he published *The Big Sleep*, the first book in which his famous character. Private Investigator Philip Marlowe, appeared. (the *Cleveland Plain Dealer's* reviewer said, "I hope it may be the first of a long series, for this fellow knows how to write"). Then followed *Farewell, My Lovely* ("The best hard-boiled mystery in ages"—Will Cuppy). *The High Window* ("A worthy successor to *The Big Sleep* and *Farewell, My Lovely*"—New Republic), and *The Lady in the Lake* ("Good news for Chandler fans. The new one is not only as good as, but actually better than his previous books—and that makes it downright superlative . . . If you don't read another mystery this year, read this one. Golly!"—Chicago News).

Meanwhile Private Investigator Marlowe had become "absolute tops among fiction sleuths of recent years," according to the *Boston Globe*.

All these novels, first published as Borzoi Books, enjoyed good sales. They have since been issued in various reprints, which together have sold many hundreds of thousands of copies. *The Big Sleep* was reprinted by Grosset & Dunlap and subsequently in Avon Books: *Farewell, My Lovely* by the World Publishing Company and Pocket Books: *The High Window* by Grosset & Dunlap (World Publishing Company and Pocket Books reprints are forthcoming) ; and *The Lady in the Lake* by Grosset & Dunlap (Pocket Books reprint forthcoming) . In addition. *The Big Sleep* and *Farewell, My Lovely* have been issued together in one volume by the World Publishing Company.

Chandler's books are published in England by Hamish Hamilton, and have been translated into Danish, French, Spanish, and Portuguese.

Many of the Chandler stories have been produced on the radio and are appearing in the movies. *The High Window* was released in January 1943, under the title *Time To Kill* with Lloyd Nolan, by Twentieth Century Fox. *Farewell, My Lovely* is currently being shown under the title *Murder, My Sweet*, with Dick Powell, Claire Trevor, and Anne Shirley. (RKO Radio Pictures). *The Big Sleep* is being filmed by Warners with Humphrey Bogart and Lauren Bacall and will be released later this year. MGM has just bought *The Lady in the Lake*. Also, Chandler has recently won recognition as a screen writer. For about two years he has been working for Paramount, and since his screen adaptation of James M. Cain's *Double Indemnity* he has been one of the most sought after writers in Hollywood.

IN SHORT, Raymond Chandler's career has followed a well-known pattern of success. It is no longer in the making; it is made. His position as an outstanding writer and an unusually successful one is well established.

In recognition of this fact, Chandler's four novels are being reissued in the new Black Widow Thrillers series. *The Big Sleep* has just been published and the others—*Farewell, My Lovely*, *The High Window*, and *The Lady in the Lake*—will be ready May 14. These are well-made books, bound in good cloth, stamped in gold.

They are available at all bookshops at $2.00 each.
They are Borzoi Books, published in New York by Alfred A. Knopf.

17

New York Times Book Review *ad for the 1945 Black Widow edition of Chandler's novels*

[52]

Hollywood Boulevard, disheveled and drunk. The police are about to pick him up as a vagrant but Marlowe gets to him first and takes him away in a taxi cab. He sobers him up and gives him $100; with that, Lennox sets off for Las Vegas and a job with Randy Starr. The next Marlowe hears of Terry Lennox is in the newspaper: he has remarried his ex-wife, Sylvia Potter, in Las Vegas at Christmas. And then, seemingly because Marlowe has been kind to him, Lennox begins occasionally to drop into his office late in the afternoon and take him off for a drink in a quiet bar. (Lennox now has his drinking under control.) The bar visits, including the gimlets they drink, become a ritual between the two. But finally Marlowe walks out on Lennox in disgust. Lennox has revealed the weak and unpleasant side of his personality. He married, and apparently remarried, Sylvia Potter for her money. His wife, he says, is a nymphomaniac; he regards himself as a highly paid pimp. Lennox carries on in this vein until Marlowe, disgusted, gets up to leave. "You talk too damn much," he says, "and it's too damn much about you."

A month later Marlowe is awakened at 5:00 in the morning by Lennox, gun in hand. He has apparently killed his wife–but Marlowe will not let him talk about it because Lennox wants him to drive him across the border to Tijuana, where he can catch a plane and disappear into the interior of Mexico. Knowingly to help Lennox escape the law would be to become an accessory to a crime. Yet Marlowe is prepared to violate the spirit, if not the letter, of the law; and this is only the first of several extraordinary actions Marlowe performs for this man whom he barely knows but feels strongly attached to. Upon his return from Tijuana, Marlowe is mercilessly grilled by the police about the disappearance of Terry Lennox; he is also subjected to a good deal of physical abuse–yet he refuses to talk, to reveal anything that will help the police find Lennox. Then Lennox is discovered dead in a Mexican village, an apparent suicide. Marlowe, who has had a letter from Lennox, does not think he has killed himself and insists on pursuing the matter, defying Sylvia Lennox's father, the millionaire publisher Harlan Potter, who wants the whole matter closed. Marlowe also does not think Lennox killed his wife. And, in the end, it turns out that Marlowe is right–she was killed by Eileen

Wade, who had been Paul Marston's wife in England during the war. In a suicide note, she writes:

> I have no regrets for Paul whom you have heard called Terry Lennox. He was the empty shell of the man I loved and married. He meant nothing to me. . . . He should have died young in the snow of Norway, my lover that I gave to death. He came back a friend of gamblers, the husband of a rich whore, a spoiled and ruined man, and probably some kind of crook in his past life. Time makes everything mean and shabby and wrinkled.

Eileen Wade has her own private fantasies, idealized and romantic, about the life she shared in wartime England with Paul Marston.

. . . Marston-Lennox is not dead. . . . His death was faked to free him from involvement with the police. At the end of the novel Lennox reappears in Marlowe's office, hair dyed, with a face altered by plastic surgery, and a Mexican accent. But Marlowe sees through the disguise, and, as they talk, he once more becomes disenchanted with Terry Lennox, who can mix with hoodlums as easily as with honest men, who, though a nice guy, has no morals at all. "You're a moral defeatist," Marlowe says to him. "I think maybe the war did it and again I think maybe you were born that way." Lennox has his own version of what changed him, as he reveals several pages later:

> "I was in the Commandos, bud. They don't take you if you're just a piece of fluff. I got badly hurt and it wasn't any fun with those Nazi doctors. It did something to me."

"I know all that," Marlowe replies. "You're a sweet guy in a lot of ways. I'm not judging you. I never did. It's just that you're not here any more. You're long gone." Marlowe sentimentally returns to Lennox a $5000 bill which Lennox, just as sentimentally, had sent him from Mexico; and then he says goodbye forever to his bogus Englishman.

It is likely that somewhere in Chandler's past, perhaps in the time he spent in the Canadian army in World War I, lie some milder but similar experiences to those Terry Lennox suffered in the Commandos. Seemingly he associated with people who were without moral fiber, who made him

For

JOSEPH THOMPSON SHAW

with affection and respect, and in memory of
the time when we were trying to get murder
away from the upper classes, the week-end house
party and the vicar's rose-garden, and back
to the people who are really good at it.

Chandler's first three short-story collections were published as paperback originals in 1944-1947.
Chandler dedicated his first collection of stories, Five Murderers, *to the editor of* Black Mask.

feel morally stained, much as Lennox makes Marlowe feel crummy, and he carried the scars of these experiences with him, much as Lennox did. It is unlikely that we will ever know what those experiences were, and, again, it is unnecessary to, as long as we realize that Chandler is burying some ghost of his former self in *The Long Goodbye*.

The ghostly British figure Marlowe takes his long farewell of had been a long time emerging in Chandler's fiction, though, rather surprisingly, he was announced as early as his first novel, *The Big Sleep*. I say "announced" because he is murdered before the novel begins and hence we never meet him, though a good deal of the novel is indirectly given over to searching for him. Ironically enough, everyone assumes Marlowe is searching for him, though he really isn't. But let me draw the parallels between the two novels which will make this development clear.

At the core of both *The Big Sleep* and *The Long Goodbye* lie precisely the same situation and some of the same characters, though the alignment of characters and their involvement in the plots of each novel are different. In each novel there is a millionaire with two daughters. One daughter is married to the figure who is in effect missing in the novel, Terry Lennox in *The Long Goodbye*, Rusty Regan in *The Big Sleep*. (It is just possible that "the big sleep" is the sleep of the men Chandler wanted to be.) In each case the men are British in background (Regan was an Irishman; Chandler, incidentally, was of Irish descent). In each case these men are liked by the millionaire in question, in part for having the basic masculine traits; they are good men, decent, kindly. Rusty Regan gave General Sternwood a kind of companionship in his old age which he found in no one else. Terry Lennox, as we have suggested, had about him many admirable things. Both men, incidentally, had been involved in fighting; Regan was in the Irish Rebellion.

In each novel one of the daughters is a nymphomaniac. In *The Big Sleep*, it is Carmen Sternwood, the unmarried daughter; at the end of the novel we learn that she insanely killed Regan. She also tries to murder Marlowe because, like Regan, he rejected her advances. At one point in the novel she takes off her clothes and climbs into Marlowe's bed, only to be thrown out of his apartment by him practically before she can get her clothes back on. In *The Long Goodbye*, the second daughter, Linda Loring, brings her suitcase and spends the night with Marlowe, who willingly accepts her. The sexual conduct of Marlowe here, it seems to me, represents less a shift in his moral code, as some critics are quick to suggest, than a deepening realism in his portrayal by his author. Throughout the earlier books Marlowe vacillated between the epicene and the hard-boiled.

The realignment of figures in *The Long Goodbye* is somewhat more complex than I have suggested here, but the significant point is that in this second and complementary version Chandler has come as close as he ever was to come to tapping those personal resources which motivated his art; he has come so close, in fact, that he all but takes his leave of the characters who fill his imaginative landscape.

But that farewell is only partly taken. There is, after all, a significance to Terry Lennox's reappearance which is extraneous to the novel; Chandler could not kill that part of himself, though he could do more than temporize with it, as he had done earlier. Marlowe's direct confrontation with his British counterpart involves a psychological reconciliation of some complexity for their creator.

It is obvious in his letters that Chandler's Americanization of self was never a fully accomplished fact. He was to some extent always a lonely stranger in the land of his birth. Even something which seems so typically American as Marlowe's love-hate relationship with the cops, which is carried on more or less elaborately from book to book, most probably goes back in part to the world of the British schoolboy. Chandler's authority fixation no doubt has other sources, including the seeming domination of his life by women. He lived with his mother until she died, then married a woman much older than himself. But what is most troubling and sometimes terrifying in the work of Raymond Chandler, who created an authentic American voice which still speaks to millions of readers, is that there hangs on about the world he created something of the inconsistency of nightmare. Perhaps for this reason he wrote what in the end must be considered screen versions of life, substituting the prismatic glamor of Hollywood and the West Coast for a closer look at

Beginning with The Little Sister *(1949), Chandler's novels were published in England before they appeared in America.*

those facts of life which in his awareness he found unbearable.

NOTES:
Chandler, "Twelve Notes on the Mystery Story," *Antaeus*, 25/26 (Spring/Summer 1977): 100-105.

Chandler's rules for mystery fiction reinforce his conviction that it should be judged by the same tests as "straight" or "mainstream" literature and that it must play fair with the reader.

1. It must be credibly motivated, both as to the original situation and the denouement; it must consist of the plausible actions of plausible people in plausible circumstances, it being remembered that plausibility is largely a matter of style. This requirement rules out most trick endings and a great many "closed circle" stories in which the least likely character is forcibly made over into the criminal, without convincing anybody. It also rules out such elaborate mises-en-scène as Christie's *Murder in a Calais Coach*, where the whole setup for the crime requires such a fluky set of happenings that it could never seem real.

2. It must be technically sound as to the methods of murder and detection. No fantastic poisons or improper effects from poison such as death from nonfatal doses, etc. No use of silencers on revolvers (they won't work) or snakes climbing bellropes ("The Speckled Bank"). Such things at once destroy the foundation of the story. If the detective is a trained policeman, he must act like one, and have the mental and physical equipment that go with the job. If he is a private investigator or amateur, he must at least know enough about police methods not to make an ass of himself. When a policeman is made out to be a fool, as he always was in the Sherlock Holmes stories, this not only deprecates the accomplishment of the detective but it makes the reader doubt the author's knowledge of his own field. Conan Doyle and Poe were primitives in this art and stand in relation to the

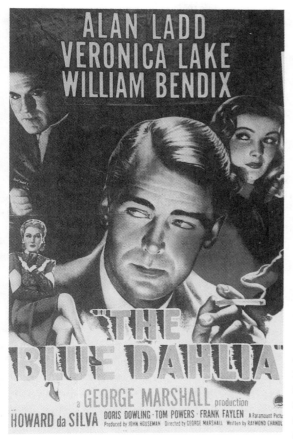

Chandler's original screenplay for The Blue Dahlia *received an Academy Award nomination in 1946.*

best modern writers as Giotto does to da Vinci. They did things which are no longer permissible and exposed ignorances that are no longer tolerated. Also, police art, itself, was rudimentary in their time. "The Purloined Letter" would not fool a modern cop for four minutes. Conan Doyle showed no knowledge whatever of the organization of Scotland Yard's men. Christie commits the same stupidities in our time, but that doesn't make them right. Contrast Austin Freeman, who wrote a story about a forged fingerprint ten years before police method realized such things could be done.

3. It must be honest with the reader. This is always said, but the implications are not realized. Important facts not only must not be concealed, they must not be distorted by false emphasis. Unimpor-

tant facts must not be projected in such a way as to make them portentous. (This creation of red herrings and false menace out of trick camera work and mood shots is the typical Hollywood mystery picture cheat.) Inferences from the facts are the detective's stock in trade; but he should disclose enough to keep the reader's mind working. It is arguable, although not certain, that inferences arising from special knowledge (e.g., Dr. Thorndyke) are a bit of a cheat, because the basic theory of all good mystery writing is that at some stage not too late in the story the reader did have the materials to solve the problem. If special scientific knowledge was necessary to interpret the facts, the reader did not have the solution unless he had the special knowledge. It may have been Austin Freeman's feeling about this that led him to the invention of the inverted detective story, in which the reader knows the solution from the beginning and takes his pleasure from watching the detective trace it out a step at a time.

4. It must be realistic as to character, setting, and atmosphere. It must be about real people in a real world. Very few mystery writers have any talent for character work, but that doesn't mean it is not necessary. It makes the difference between the story you reread and remember and the one you skim through and almost instantly forget. Those like Valentine Williams who say the problem overrides everything are merely trying to cover up their own inability to create character.

5. It must have a sound story value apart from the mystery element; i.e., the investigation itself must be an adventure worth reading.

6. To achieve this it must have some form of suspense, even if only intellectual. This does not mean menace and especially it does not mean that the detective must be menaced by grave personal danger. This last is a trend and like all trends will exhaust itself by overimitation. Nor need the reader be kept hanging onto the edge of his chair. The overplotted story can be dull too; too much shock may result in numbness to shock. But there must be conflict, physical, ethical or emotional, and there must be some element of danger in the broadest sense of the word.

7. It must have color, lift, and a reasonable amount of dash. It takes an awful lot of technical

adroitness to compensate for a dull style, although it has been done, especially in England.

8. It must have enough essential simplicity to be explained easily when the time comes. (This is possibly the most often violated of all the rules). The ideal denouement is one in which everything is revealed in a flash of action. This is rare because ideas that good are always rare. The explanation need not be very short (except on the screen), and often it cannot be short; but it must be interesting in itself, it must be something the reader is anxious to hear, and not a new story with a new set of characters, dragged in to justify an overcomplicated plot. Above all the explanation must not be merely a long-winded assembling of minute circumstances which no ordinary reader could possibly be expected to remember. To make the solution dependent on this is a kind of unfairness, since here again the reader did not have the solution within his grasp, in any practical sense. To expect him to remember a thousand trivialities and from them to select the three that are decisive is as unfair as to expect him to have a profound knowledge of chemistry, metallurgy, or the mating habits of the Patagonian anteater.

9. It must baffle a reasonably intelligent reader. This opens up a very difficult question. Some of the best detective stories ever written (those of Austin Freeman, for example) seldom baffle an intelligent reader to the end. But the reader does not guess the *complete solution* and could not himself have made a logical demonstration of it. Since readers are of many minds, some will guess a cleverly hidden murder and some will be fooled by the most transparent plot. (Could "The Red-Headed League" ever really fool a modern reader?) It is not necessary or even possible to fool to the hilt the real aficionado of mystery fiction. A mystery story that consistently did that and was honest would be unintelligible to the average fan; he simply would not know what the story was all about. But there must be some important elements of the story that elude the most penetrating reader.

10. The solution must seem inevitable once revealed. This is the least often emphasized element of a good mystery, but it is one of the important elements of all fiction. It is not enough merely to fool or elude or sidestep the reader; you must make

him feel that he ought not to have been fooled and that the fooling was honorable.

11. It must not try to do everything at once. If it is a puzzle story operating in a rather cool, reasonable atmosphere, it cannot also be a violent adventure or a passionate romance. An atmosphere of terror destroys logical thinking; if the story is about the intricate psychological pressures that lead apparently ordinary people to commit murder, it cannot then switch to the cool analysis of the police investigator. The detective cannot be hero and menace at the same time; the murderer cannot be a tormented victim of circumstance and also a heavy.

12. It must punish the criminal in one way or another, not necessarily by operation of the law. Contrary to popular (and Johnston Office) belief, this requirement has nothing much to do with morality. It is a part of the logic of detection. If the detective fails to resolve the consequences of the crime, the story is an unresolved chord and leaves irritation behind it.

Addenda

1. The perfect detective story cannot be written. The type of mind which can evolve the perfect problem is not the type of mind that can produce the artistic job of writing. It would be nice to have Dashiell Hammett and Austin Freeman in the same book, but it just isn't possible. Hammett couldn't have the plodding patience and Freeman couldn't have the verve for narrative. They don't go together. Even a fair compromise such as Dorothy Sayers is less satisfying then the two types taken separately.

2. The most effective way to conceal a simple mystery is behind another mystery. This is literary legerdemain. You do not fool the reader by hiding clues or faking character à la Christie but by making him solve the wrong problem.

3. It has been said that "nobody cares about the corpse." This is bunk. It is throwing away a valuable element. It is like saying the murder of your aunt means no more to you than the murder of an unknown man in an unknown part of a city you never visited.

4. Flip dialogue is not wit.

5. A mystery serial does not make a good mystery novel. The "curtains" depend for their effect

on your not having the next chapter to read at once. In book form these curtains give the effect of a false suspense and tend to be merely irritating. The magazines have begun to find that out.

6. Love interest nearly always weakens a mystery story because it creates a type of suspense that is antagonistic and not complementary to the detective's struggle to solve the problem. The kind of love interest that works is the one that complicates the problem by adding to the detective's troubles but which at the same time you instinctively feel will not survive the story. A really good detective never gets married. He would lose his detachment, and this detachment is part of his charm.

7. The fact that love interest is played up in the big magazines and on the screen doesn't make it artistic. Women are supposed to be the targets of magazine fiction and movies. The magazines are not interested in mystery writing as an art. They are not interested in any kind of writing as an art.

8. The hero of the mystery story is the detective. Everything hangs on his personality. If he hasn't one, you have very little. And you have *very few* really good mystery stories. Naturally.

9. The criminal cannot be the detective. This is an old rule and has once in a while been violated successfully, but it is sound as it ever was. For this reason: the detective by tradition and definition is the seeker after truth. He can't be that if he already knows the truth. There is an implied guarantee to the reader that the detective is on the level.

10. The same remark applies to the story where the first-person narrator is the criminal. I should personally have to qualify this by saying that for me the first-person narration can always be accused of subtle dishonesty because of its appearance of candor and its ability to suppress the detective's ratiocination while giving a clear account of his words and acts. Which opens up the much larger question of what honesty really is in this context; is it not a matter of degree rather than an absolute? I think it is and always will be. Regardless of the candor of the first-person narrative there comes a time when the detective has made up his mind and yet does not communicate this to the reader. He holds some of his thinking out for the denouement or explanation. He tells the facts but not the reaction in his mind to those facts. Is

Chandler with Taki in La Jolla, California, where he settled in 1946

this a permissible convention of deceit? It must be; otherwise the detective telling his own story could not have solved the problem in advance of the technical denouement. Once in a lifetime a story such as *The Big Sleep* holds almost nothing back; the denouement is an action which the reader meets as soon as the detective. The theorizing from that action follows immediately. There is only a momentary concealment of the fact that Marlowe loaded the gun with blanks when he gave it to Carmen down by the oil pump. But even this is tipped off to the reader when he says, "If she missed the can, which she was certain to do, she would probably hit the wheel. That would stop a small slug completely. However she wasn't going to hit even that." He doesn't say why, but the action follows

Poster for the 1951 movie made from Patricia High-smith's novel. Chandler did not enjoy working with Alfred Hitchcock, but the movie was well received.

Robert Walker revealing his reciprocal murder scheme to Farley Granger in Strangers on a Train

so quickly that you don't feel any real concealment.

11. The murderer must not be a loony. The murderer is not a murderer unless he commits murder in the legal sense.

12. There is, as has been said, no real possibility of absolute perfection [in writing a mystery story]. Why? For two main reasons, one of which has been stated above in Addenda Note 1. The second is the attitude of the reader himself. Readers are of too many kinds and too many levels of culture. The puzzle addict, for instance, regards the story as a contest of wits between himself and the writer; if he guesses the solution, he has won, even though he could not document his guess or justify it by solid reasoning. There is something of this competitive spirit in all readers, but the reader in whom it predominates sees no value beyond the game of guessing the solution. There is the reader, again, whose whole interest is in sensation, sadism, cruelty, blood, and the element of death. Again there is some in all of us, but the reader in whom it predominates will care nothing for the so-called deductive story, however meticulous. A third class of reader is the worrier-about-the-characters; this reader doesn't care so much about the solution; what really gets her upset is the chance that the silly little heroine will get her neck twisted on the spiral staircase. Fourth, and most important, there is the intellectual literate reader who reads mysteries because they are almost the only kind of fiction that does not get too big for its boots. This reader savors style, characterization, plot twists, all the virtuosities of the writing much more than he bothers about the solution. You cannot satisfy all these readers completely. To do so involves contradictory elements. I, in the role of reader, almost never try to guess the solution to a mystery. I simply don't regard the contest between the writer and myself as important. To be frank I regard it as the amusement of an inferior type of mind.

13. As has been suggested above, all fiction depends on some form of suspense. But the study of the mechanics of that extreme type called menace reveals the curious psychological duality of the mind of a reader or audience which makes it possible on the one hand to be terrified about what is hiding behind the door and at the same time to know that the heroine or leading lady is not going to be murdered once she is established as the heroine or leading lady. If the character played by Claudette Colbert is in awful danger, we also know absolutely that Miss Colbert is not going to be hurt for the simple reason that she is Miss Colbert. How does the audience's mind get upset by menace in view of this clear knowledge? Of the many possible reasons I suggest two. The intelligence and the emotions function on different levels. The emotional reaction to visual images and sounds, or their evocation in descriptive writing, is independent of reasonableness. The primitive element of fear is never far from the surface of our thoughts; anything that calls to it can defeat reason for the time being. Hence menace makes its appeal to a very ancient and very irrational emotion. Few men are beyond its influence. The other reason I suggest is that in any intense kind of literary or other projection the part is greater than the whole. The scene before the eyes dominates the thought of the audience; the normal individual makes no attempt to reconcile it with the pattern of the story. He is swayed by what is in the actual scene. When you have finished the book, it may, not necessarily will, fall into focus as a whole and be remembered by its merit so considered; but for the time of reading, the chapter is the dominating factor. The vision of the emotional imagination is very short but also very intense.

LETTER:

To Frederic Dannay, 10 July 1951, *Selected Letters of Raymond Chandler*, edited by Frank Mac-Shane, pp. 51-52.

In this letter to one of the two men who wrote under the pseudonym Ellery Queen, Chandler discusses his taste in mystery fiction.

Dear Frederic Dannay:

No, I would not care to nominate the ten best living detective-story writers. I don't mind sticking my neck out, but the point is, one has to agree on a few fundamentals before one starts picking lists of ten bests. For instance, does the category include writers of suspense stories in which there is little mystery, or none at all? If it does not, you eliminate some of the best performers,

Dust jackets for the English and American editions of Chandler's sixth novel, published in 1953. Many readers regard it as his best, but some critics complained that Marlowe had gone soft.

such as Elisabeth Sanxay Holding, certainly one of my favorites. And if it does, why call them detective stories? Charlotte Armstrong's *Mischief* contains no puzzle element whatever. On the other hand, some puzzle merchants, the people who have timetables and ground plans and pay the most meticulous attention to details, can't write a lick. There is a saying that a good plot will make a good detective story, but I personally question whether you can have a good plot if you can't create any believable characters or situations. My list, if I made it, would probably leave out some of those names which will inevitably appear on your ten best list. I just don't think they're any good, because by my standards they can't write. And it may also happen that single book, such as *The 31st of February* by Julian Symons, or *Walk the Dark Streets* by William Krasner, or the aforesaid *Mischief*, or *Mr. Bowling Buys a Newpaper* by Donald Henderson, will immediately put the writer above and beyond a whole host of writers who have written twenty or thirty books and are extremely well known and successful, and from a literary point of view entirely negligible. I don't particularly care for the hard-boiled babies, because most of them are traveling on borrowed gas, and I don't think you have any right to do that unless you can travel a little farther than the man from whom you borrowed the gas. I don't care about the had-I-but known girls, because I don't care whether dear little Lucille gets her neck stretched or not. But that's not quite honest. If I had a choice, I'd prefer that she did get it stretched. I don't care for the week-end chichi either here or in England. I don't seem to care who conked Sir Mortimer with the poker, nor why, nor who set the grandfather's clock twenty minutes slow. How did Frank Fustian come to be eating fly agaric in the locked room? I couldn't care less. It isn't that I don't like puzzles, because I like, for example, Austin Freeman. I like him very much. There is probably not one of his books that I haven't read at least twice, yet he bores a lot of people stiff. I even like his Victorian love scenes. And I have liked some very pedestrian stories, because they were unpretentious and because their mysteries were rooted in hard facts and not in false motivations cooked up for the purpose of mystifying a reader. I suppose the attraction of the pedestrian books is their documen-

tary quality and this, if at all authentic, is pretty rare, and any attempt to dish it up with chichi and glamour turns my stomach immediately. I think you are up against a difficult problem, because I think we may take it as granted that a mystery fan would rather read a bad mystery than none at all. You are bound to give some weight to volume of production, and strictly speaking volume of production means absolutely nothing. A writer discloses himself on a single page, sometimes in a single paragraph. An un-writer may fill a whole shelf, he may achieve fame of a sort and fortune of a sort, he may occasionally concoct a plot which will make him seem to be a little better than he really is, but in the end he fades away and is nothing. All good writers have a touch of magic. And unless we are to agree with Edmund Wilson that detective fiction is on the sub-literary level, and I personally do not agree with this, we demand that touch of magic; at least I do, although I am well aware that the public does not.

Yours very truly,

ESSAY:
W. Somerset Maugham, "The Decline and Fall of the Detective Story" [excerpt], *The Vagrant Mood* (Garden City, N.Y.: Doubleday, 1953), pp. 128-132.

Chandler wrote to London bookseller J. Francis: "As to Maugham's remarks about the decline and fall of the detective story, in spite of his flattering references to me, I do not agree with his thesis. People have been burying the detective story for at least two generations, and it is still very much alive, although I do admit that the term 'detective story' hardly covers the field any more, since a great deal of the best stuff written nowadays is only slightly if at all concerned with the elucidation of the mystery. What we have is more in the nature of the novel of suspense" (Selected letters of Raymond Chandler, edited by Frank MacShane, p. 322).

The social historian of the future may notice with surprise what is plainly a difference in American habits between the time when Dashiell Hammett wrote his stories and the time when Raymond Chandler wrote his. After an exhausting day passed in heavy drinking and hair-breadth escapes from violent death Ned Beaumont changes his collar and washes his hands and face, but Raymond Chandler's Marlowe, unless my memory deceives me, has a shower and puts on a clean shirt. It is evident that the habit of cleanliness had in the interval gained an increasing hold on the American male. Marlowe, unlike Sam Spade, is an honest man. He wants to make money, but will only earn it by lawful means, and he will not touch divorce. Marlowe is himself the narrator of the too few stories Raymond Chandler has written. Usually the narrator and protagonist of a novel remains a shadowy character, as for instance is David Copperfield, but Raymond Chandler has succeeded in making Marlowe a vivid human being. He is a hard, fierce, fearless man and a very likeable fellow.

To my mind the two best novelists of the hard-boiled school are Dashiell Hammett and Raymond Chandler. Raymond Chandler is the more accomplished. Sometimes Hammett's story is so complicated that you are not a trifle confused: Raymond Chandler maintains an unswerving line. His pace is swifter. He deals with a more varied assortment of persons. He has a greater sense of probability and his motivation is more plausible. Both write a nervous, colloquial English racy of the American soil. Raymond Chandler's dialogue seems to me better than Hammett's. He has an admirable aptitude for that typical product of the quick American mind, the wisecrack, and his sardonic humour has an engaging spontaneity.

The hard-boiled novel, as I have said, lays little stress on the detection of crime. It is concerned with the people, crooks, gamblers, thieves, blackmailers, corrupt policemen, dishonest politicians, who commit crimes. Incidents occur, but incidents derive their interest from the individuals who are concerned in them. If they are merely lay figures you do not care what they do or what happens to them. The result of this is that the writers of this school have had to pay more attention to characterisation than the old writers of the story of deduction found necessary. They have had to make their people not only credible, but convincing. Most of the older detectives were creatures of farce and the extravagant oddities their authors gave them succeeded only in making them grotesque. Such persons never existed but in their begetters' wrong-headedness. The other actors in their stories were stock characters without individuality. Dashiell Hammett and Raymond Chandler have created characters that we can believe in. They are only a little more heightened, a little more vivid, than people we have all come across.

Having been at one time a novelist myself, I have been interested in the way both these authors describe the appearance of the various persons they deal with. It is always difficult to give the reader an exact impression of what someone looks like and novelists have tried various methods to achieve it. Hammett and Raymond Chandler specify the appearance of their characters and the clothes they wear, though briefly, as exactly as do the police when they send to the papers a description of a wanted man. Raymond Chandler has effectively pursued the method further. When Marlowe, his detective, enters a room or an office we are told concisely, but in detail, precisely what furniture is in it, what pictures hang on the walls and what rugs lie on the floor. We are impressed by the detective's power of observation. It is done as neatly as a playwright (if he is not as verbose as Bernard Shaw) describes for his director the scene and the furnishings of each act of his play. The device clearly gives the perspicacious reader an indication of the sort of person and the circumstances the detective is likely to encounter. When you know a man's surroundings you already know something about the man.

But I think the enormous success these two writers have had, not only financial, for their books have sold by the million, but critical, has killed the genre. Dozens of imitators have sprung up. Like all imitators, they have thought by exaggeration to improve upon their models. They have been more slangy, so slangy that you need a glossary to know what they are talking about; their criminals have been more brutal, more violent, more sadistic; their female characters have been more blonde and more man-crazy; their detectives have been more unscrupulous and more alcoholic; and their policemen have been more inept and more corrupt. In fact they have been so outrageous that they have become preposterous. In their frantic search for sensationalism they have numbed their readers and instead of horrifying them have caused them to laugh with derision. There is only one of the many merits of the two authors I have been discussing that they do not seem to have thought worth copying. They have made no attempt to write good English.

I do not see who can succeed Raymond Chandler. I believe the detective story, both the story of pure detection and the hard-boiled story, is dead. But that will not prevent a multitude of authors from continuing to write such stories, nor will it prevent me from continuing to read them.

OBITUARY:
"Crime and the American Scene," *Times* (London), 28 March 1959, p. 10.

At the time of his death Chandler's work was more seriously regarded in England than in America. This assessment in the most respected London newspaper attempted to place him as a literary figure.

Raymond Thornton Chandler was an American citizen born in Chicago of Quaker parents on August 23, 1888. They sent him to school at Dulwich College and he completed his education in France and Germany. He then tried his hand at school-mastering, soldiering in a Canadian infantry regiment, accountancy, and the oil business. Finally he settled in America and began writing fiction. He served his apprenticeship in the "pulp" magazines of the late 1920s and early 1930s. "When in doubt," he said, "have a man come through the door with a gun in his hand"; and he retained considerable respect for the technical honesty of that kind of story.

His mature thrillers became something of a cult among intellectuals. They were praised by literary critics, who normally despise crime fiction. Their originality has been confirmed by a host of imitators; but it would be untrue to say he founded a school, rather he defined a school. Dashiell Hammett was his master. He admired Hammett's effect of realism, his sharp, aggressive attitude to life, and a style of writing which, Chandler insisted, was not personal to Hammett but inherent in the American language for him that can get it.

Chandler held strong views of what he called "the simple art of murder." He spoke disrespectfully of *The Hounds of the Baskervilles* and *The Purloined Letter*; he ridiculed *Trent's Last Case*; he had no patience with the classic detective story which depends on contriving a problem and deducing the answer. His dispute with Mr. John Dickson Carr on this subject split the upper echelons of crime writers.

Chandler's own success depended not so much on his plots or the shock value of their toughness as on the faceted irony of his style and his acridly atmospheric picture of Californian civilization. Modern crime, he believed, and therefore modern crime stories, belong to "a world gone wrong"; but "down these mean streets a man must go who is not himself mean, who is neither tarnished nor afraid." Such a man was Chandler's hero, Philip Marlowe, the lonely, sardonic, inflexibly honest private detective who provides the highly moral heart of all his books.

"Everything a writer learns about the art or craft of fiction," said Chandler, "takes just a little away from his need or drive to write at all. In the end he knows all the tricks and has nothing to say."

Raymond Chandler's fame rests on seven novels and a few relatively undistinguished short stories. *The Big Sleep*, which established his reputation on both sides of the Atlantic, was first published in 1939. His last book, *Playback*, appeared in 1958 after a long interval during which he wrote nothing. Gleams of the old brilliance were still there to confound his imitators: Philip Marlowe was still there, unfrightened and unstained; but the book was only the shadow of a shade. Raymond Chandler, having mastered his art, had nothing more to say.

He had already said a great deal in a very small compass. His name will certainly go down among the dozen or so mystery writers who were also innovators and stylists: who, working the common vein of crime fiction, mined the gold of literature.

ARTICLE:
George P. Elliott, "Country Full of Blondes," *Nation*, 190 (4 September 1960): 354-360.

A year after Chandler's death novelist Elliott attempted to position him in American literature, claiming that his sense of place shaped the way in which Southern California is perceived.

Covers for the first paperback editions of Chandler's novels

Raymond Chandler is dead, but he left behind five thrillers which still show every sign of life: *The Big Sleep* (1939), *The High Window* (1942), *The Lady in the Lake* (1943), *The Little Sister* (1949) and, most ambitious of them, *The Long Goodbye* (1953). There are also a dozen stories, an essay called "The Simple Art of Murder," and the last thriller, *Playback*, a sad hoked-up job that Chandler wrote during interludes in the lethal drinking bouts initiated by his wife's death. The five solid thrillers will probably be read by ordinary readers for a good while to come, so long, in fact, as the taste for violent thrillers endures and so long as Southern California has a place in people's imaginations.

Whether Chandler will ever be elected into literary history is another question. The odd thing is that he is known and enjoyed by those who have the power to vote him in–critics, writers, scholars, literary historians–and even so it begins to look as though his nomination for membership may not be seconded. To be sure, any comprehensive literary chronicle of the age will certainly list him along with Dashiell Hammett and Mickey Spillane as one of the chief practitioners of the "tough-guy mystery"; but this is indiscriminate and flattening, this has all the verve of a list of the most popular vaudeville comics in Texas during the reign of Hogg, this is pure chronicle. For, once out of his straight-back study and dropped into an aimless deck chair, this same chronicler knows well enough that Spillane has served up nothing but stews of slime and slop, whereas Hammett, the originator of the species, and Chandler, his chief descendant, are at least as good as any other mystery story writers whatever and probably better.

All this is well known to literary folk. I've asked around among my acquaintance and found scarcely anyone who does not know Chandler, and few who do not like him. Yet the stigma attaching to detective stories is great; they are recommended as Western movies are recommended, with uncritical guilelessness ("there's a terrific fight in it"); the type is viewed as being forbidden to serious discussion. One stalwart professor of American literature puts *The Long Goodbye* on a reading list of twenty or so modern novels; scarcely a student chooses to read it for the course; a student would rather read, say, *Studs Lonigan*, for there are serious essays telling him what to think about it and assuring him by their very existence that Farrell is *in*.

I would bet a good deal that right now (1) most of the literary folk of the country have read some of Chandler's best work with pleasure and profit but, ashamed of their pleasure, would deny it any literary value; and (2) these same people have read of Wallace Stevens' poems few more than the often-anthologized pieces, and those without anything like full comprehension or pleasure, and yet would grant high value to the body of his poetry. Well, I do not mean to suggest that I think Stevens is less than excellent or that Chandler is more than pretty good. But I do suggest that it is time we publicly honor Chandler (and Hammett his master). I suggest that, if literary history is going seriously to scrutinize bores with a vein of silver (Frank Norris, say, or James Fenimore Cooper), then it isn't too delicate to take a good look at master entertainers who are also silverstreaked.

There is no use pretending that the detective story has much to recommend it as a form. In fact, I should imagine that no novel written within its conventions could be first-rate, just as no opera written within the conventions of the Broadway musical could be first-rate. (The words of a musical may not be complex or strong, and the music may be neither refined to simplicity nor developed in sustaining patterns which justify its pretentiousness; the performances might be virtuoso except that we have no schools from which coherent ensemble virtuosity of theatrical performance is likely to develop; the best we can expect is a *Porgy and Bess*, good but no more than good, well done but no more than well done.) The detective story damagingly interferes in what is of the very essence of a novel; it manipulates the motives and relationships of its characters for an artificial and trivial end. Even in those rare detective stories where the motives are credible enough and the relationships are reasonably subtle and valid, the reader is kept from apprehending them in a way that is really serious. Knowledge of motive and relationship is parceled out to him for reasons of plot excitement–a matter of some, but low, value–and this very excitement works against a profound or thoughtful or complexly moving appreciation of the characters' essential natures.

Dorothy Sayers, who was bright and only bright, tried to give her mode of fiction merit-by-association: she called *King Oedipus* a great detective story. But this, even though she may have meant it half-facetiously, is not cute; it blurs distinctions. What I discover when seeing *King Oedipus* is not whodunit nor why; like Sophocles' original audience, I already know this. What I discover and rediscover is the full significance of what Oedipus discovers–its significance to himself, to those about him, to his society–and I, who am neither king, Greek, parricide, nor mother-lover, I can experience this man's fate as man's fate, as my fate. That is the way of greatness. And the way of detective story discovery?

> I guess you and Orrin belong to that class of people that can convince themselves that everything they do is right. He can blackmail his sister and then when a couple of small-time crooks get wise to his racket and take it away from him, he can sneak up on them and knock them off with an ice pick in the back of the neck. Probably didn't even keep him awake that night. You can do much the same (*The Little Sister*).

Too bad, honey. That's *your* problem.

Chandler's novels are a good deal more successful as thrillers than as detective stories, and a thriller, as demonstrated by the example of Graham Greene (he's respectable), need not distort motive or relationship very much. It forbids that contemplation which is essential to reading great fiction, the movement of which is most of the time quite slow. But a thriller can do a good many things of literary value, and some of these things Chandler does admirably.

The obvious accomplishment of his thrillers is to generate a sort of nervous tension which is the literary analogue to the tension generated just by being an American citizen. Tension alone is not so much: one can induce it by chain-smoking a couple of packs of cigarettes and slugging down a fair amount of liquor, driving eighty miles an hour to a juke box joint where one drinks black coffee and plays a slot machine, then driving home again chortling every so often, "We sure had a good time, didn't we?" In fact this sort of tension-making is an unexceptional way to spend the evening in Southern California, and if Philip Marlowe did not do things like it we would not believe in him. "I didn't do more than ninety back to Los Angeles. Well, perhaps I hit a hundred for a few seconds now and then" (*Playback*).

But, as I think, these tension-making actions are only externalizings of deep and chronic and ill-conceived trouble within the actor-reader. (There is something drastically wrong with the world and with me as part of it; I don't know what it is, it isn't what they tell me it is. I don't think I could figure it out if I tried; anyhow I am afraid to look too closely.) One temporary relief from this malaise, and I think many suffer from it much of the time, is to read a story which produces in the reader a safe version of the same thing and which purges this induced tension by showing a Marlowe who figures out what's wrong with at least part of the world and then remedies it.

Good enough. This is a considerable endeavor for a novelist to undertake. To accomplish it adequately, he must have, and make us share, a clarifying and steady vision of the evil which infects the world he shows, and he must persuade us that the hero's action is more than a simple wish-fulfillment, is a possible and dignified deed however bitterly limited it may be.

Hammett's vision was of a society so corrupt that it corrupts all individual relationships; it is not surprising that he turned to left-wing politics. Spillane's murked vision was of a human nature so corrupt that no clean action is possible; it is fitting that he turned for solace to the wet-mud notions and dry-mud practices of the Jehovah's Witnesses. Chandler's vision was of a world which is no less violent, ugly, unjust, or loveless than theirs; yet it is not exactly corrupt. Moral corruption implies a prior innocent nature, whether Christian or Rousseauistic, to be corrupted. Chandler's attitude is to look at what's there in the expectation that good and evil are all mixed together; consequently he does not suffer such rage as do the other two. It is a stoic vision. In his novels Chandler did not quite sustain it, being much too romantic and not quite courageous enough to bear the full bitterness of that vision: Marlowe's solutions are morally too easy; they promise, dreamily, to remedy more than they ever could, as he recognizes, despairingly, at the end of each novel.

What did it matter where you lay once you were dead? In a dirty sump or in a marble tower on top of a high hill? You were dead, you were sleeping the big sleep, you were not bothered by things like that. Oil and water were the same as wind and air to you. You just slept the big sleep, not caring about the nastiness of how you died or where you fell. Me, I was part of the nastiness now (*The Big Sleep*).

It is fitting that, when life afflicted him, Chandler turned to heavy drinking and despair. According to a reminiscence by Ian Fleming in *London Magazine* for December, 1959, when the police arrived at Chandler's house in La Jolla after the death of his wife, "they found him in the sitting room firing his revolver through the ceiling." A strange, appropriate gesture.

Chandler has a good many of the lesser virtues and vices of a romancer. Two of the locations for these are his style and the way he treats blondes.

Some of the style is of the genre–Marlowe's hyper-aggressive truth-telling, for instance. "You don't care who murdered your daughter, Mr. Potter. You wrote her off as a bad job long ago. Even if Terry Lennox didn't kill her, and the real murderer is still walking around free, you don't care." But what is special about the style is Chandler's own rhinestone brilliance. Of a masters' chess game he is reconstructing by book, Marlowe says: "a prize specimen of the irresistible force meeting the immovable object, a battle without armor, a war without blood, and as elaborate a waste of human intelligence as you could find anywhere outside an advertising agency" (*The Long Goodbye*). Surely no American since Mark Twain has invented so many wisecracks as this British-educated classicist: "as gaudy as a chiropractor's chart," "he looked like a man who could be trusted with a secret–if it was his own secret." The dialogue, when it is not hobbled by plot work, is fast, glittering and tough; sometimes it includes a tawdriness that is appropriate only to the character:

"A half smart guy," she said with a tired sniff. "That's all I ever draw. Never once a guy that's smart all the way around the course. Never once."

I grinned at her. "Did I hurt your head much?"

"You and every other man I've ever met" (*The Big Sleep*).

But sometimes in the narrative the tawdriness becomes Chandler's:

In the cove the waves don't break, they slide in politely, like floorwalkers. There would be a bright moon later, but it hadn't checked in yet (*Playback*).

The famous language of his style is a fabrication based only in part on the argots of police and criminals. For this is the world of romance and the style is a romantic style. "Her hair was the pale gold of a fairy princess. There was a small hat on it into which the pale gold hair nestled like a bird in its nest. Her eyes were cornflower blue, a rare color, and the lashes were long and almost too pale."

That is the blonde of blondes, Eileen Wade in *The Long Goodbye*, and her entrance in chapter thirteen sets off three paragraphs of quite dazzling toughguy dithyramb on blondes:

There is the blonde who gives you the up-from-under look and smells lovely and shimmers and hangs on your arm and is always very very tired when you take her home. . . . There is the soft and willing and alcoholic blonde who doesn't care what she wears as long as it is mink or where she goes as long as it is the Starlight Roof and there is plenty of dry champagne. . . . And lastly there is the gorgeous show piece who will outlast three kingpin racketeers and then marry a couple of millionaires at a million a head and end up with a pale rose villa at Cap Antibes, an Alfa-Romeo town car complete with pilot and co-pilot, and a stable of shopworn aristocrats.

The endless come-on to the certain cheat, that is the sort of women Marlowe dreamily desires. They arouse in him lust's nervous equivalent of infatuation. They are sex appellant and they do not promise love; yet it is never the pleasures of sensuality they want. They want to use him for some other end of their own. Each time, he escapes; each next time, he forgets they are all traps. Just as he courts in each novel the dangers which brutally get him beaten up, so he succumbs each time to the glitter girls. If he wants a woman he cannot trust her.

If you say that all this provides somewhat meager fare for romance, I must agree. But if you say that this distorts life beyond recognition, I must object that you do not know that meager region, Southern California, as well as Chandler did.

His chief accomplishment, it seems to me, is to create for the place a fictional image which corresponds to the actuality more vividly and more accurately than anything written by anyone else. Southern California has occasioned novels by solemn natives, the thrillers of James M. Cain who nearly makes it but not quite, satires by pukka sahibs and *The Day of the Locust* which contains fragments of splendid phantasmagoria. But Chandler is the authentic jinn of the place: he comes from a higher realm yet is of a rank inferior to the angels; he knows the place well and in its own terms and, as a jinn must, he influences it in turn.

If you want the feel and aspect of Los Angeles and vicinity during the thirties, forties and early fifties, you could hardly do better than to read his fictions. There is a considerable change in this fictional world between *The Big Sleep* and *The Long Goodbye;* part of this change was a deepening in Chandler as a writer and part of it was, no doubt, a result of his greater acquaintance with the region; but part of it too took place in Southern California itself. As it has grown in population, wealth and importance, its appearance has become less macabre and its vileness has turned inward, hidden behind solider false fronts.

I knew Southern California pretty well during those years, and his props are all genuine. If I made a list of places, people and events I have known, and mixed in with it such like from his novels, you wouldn't be able to tell fact from fantasy; for in this respect his fantasy is factual.

The desiccated old folks are there on the front porch in "wood and cane rockers . . . held together with wire and the moisture of the beach air" (*The Little Sister*), refugees from Kansas and Protestantism; they have lost their centers; they have not controlled their children or had much of anything to pass on to them; they no longer believe in the old faith or ways and have turned to cultism, avarice, distraction, despair; they are bitter, suckers, and sort of decent. Young people of

striking appearances are indeed floating around all over Los Angeles, pumping gas, frying hamburgers, strutting along the beaches, projecting their personalities furiously–waiting like the old folks but waiting to be discovered. The strapless blondes with cold come-on eyes are in Chasen's restaurant, all right (as they are in Chandler's The Dancers), escorted by the middle-aged joyboys with exactly perfect suntans and blasted eyes.

There used to be a lion farm near Los Angeles, an ostrich farm, an alligator ranch; now there is Disneyland with animal dolls. Myself, I lived on a carob plantation not far from Riverside. (Riverside, so we were spieled at any rate, is where the Easter sunrise vigil took root in this country, and where Carrie Jacobs Bond was supposed to have written "The End of a Perfect Day" after the first sunrise service on Mt. Rubidoux–Resurrection sundae topped with canned whipped cream.) Carobs are Eastern Mediterranean trees which yield dry brown pods "used for feeding animals and sometimes eaten by man"; they are the locusts that John the Baptist ate in the wilderness; the promoters of the plantation had in mind the Southern California market of quasi-religious health food addicts. (Have you ever visited the sub-society of vegewenies, glutenburgers and blackstrap molasses? There's one in every city.) Unfortunately, the plantation's soil was not suitable to carobs, and the dictionary definition should read "almost never eaten by man."

I once caught a glimpse of detecting; I must confess it resembled Marlowe's adventures less than the ennuis which Hammett reports from his own experience as a working detective. Back in the 1930s, when I was seventeen, a friend and I set out to see Boulder Dam. We hitched a ride to Las Vegas with a middle-aged, club-car Hoosier who said he would lend us his car to go see the dam if we would spend the next evening spying on his wife. She was there to divorce him and he suspected she was stepping out on him. At five in the afternoon she walked three blocks to a drugstore where she bought what appeared to be a pack of cigarettes and something else that appeared to be a bridge pad. At six she ate dinner with her parents, in whose bungalow she was staying. At 7:30 they began playing what appeared to be three-handed bridge, though it *might* have been gin rummy. At ten they paused for the Richfield reporter and iced tea. She and her father smoked cigarettes. Her mother chewed gum and fanned herself from time to time with a collapsible fan. They played another rubber and turned off the lights a little before midnight. No one emerged from either the front or the back door and no one entered. She was a decently dressed woman with a pleasant, low voice and brown hair, and she wore sensible shoes like a nurse. Our employer said she was a slut like all women, and regaled us with the story of a married woman he had seduced on a train a month before.

As for the violence which Chandler projects, I saw little of it except in fairly safe forms. There are the cohorts of hot rods and motorcycles; the roller skating derbies, which are formless, ungamelike contests the point of which is nothing but expert roller skating and mock-violent rudeness; the destruction derbies, at which old cars are smashed head-on, once two old locomotives. But most of all there is the chronic, self-exacerbated nervous tension, of the sort Chandler (a lapsed Quaker) both records and generates, which yearns toward violence for its relief.

Not the least source of this tension is the inflaming sexual provocation on every side; yet the provocation is not toward licentiousness but toward the fantasies of mere frustration. These folk are refugees from the Protestant Midwest, but they brought the forms with them. The titillation aims at marriage (the divorce rate in Hollywood is a bit lower than the national average) but not true marriage necessarily; when the form of marriage loses its content, what enters is not pretty–irascibility, for example, and sex for its own sake only it's inexpert sex, and the cold clutch of conjugal possessiveness. To be sure, there are the simply promiscuous: a film actor I know was accused by a world-famous 40-26-40 blonde of being a queer because he did not try to make her the second day of their acquaintance; when he objected that she was engaged to be married within the month, as every Hedda Hopper reader knew, and that he was faithful to his wife and had three children, she shrugged at him for being so square. And there are the very bizarre: a fellow I went to high school with was sent up for flagrant necrophilia with an officer's wife. But all such only sub-

stantiate Chandler's version: the sex is mostly in the nerves, very little in the heart. In the heart, if nothing else, there are cars.

Waiting in the grandstand one summer evening in 1950 for the auto races to start in San Bernardino, I watched the crowd as the little warm-up entertainments came along. Mostly there was M.C. patter alternating with popular records; some announcements; a local hillbilly in a Monkey Ward cowboy hat; the Indianapolis speedway winner of many years before to say a few words to us. The crowd rustled. Then the Orange Bowl Beauty Contest Queen (or some such) was crowned. She was a pink and tan girl in a short bare-shouldered pale blue organdy dress with a crimson silk sash; she was not quite used to high heels yet and wobbled; she had a Coca-Cola smile, and she sang a slinky night club song in a bouncy high school voice. The crowd scarcely paused in its restless chatter and not a wolf whistled. But then the '51 Dodge was driven about the track, and the '51 Chrysler, and the crowd fell silent; we were the first laymen to see them; and when the latest Jaguar slid out before our eyes, a rustle of sincere, abysmal reverence stirred among the people. The girl– the girl would turn into a starlet or a wife; but the Jag, now there was something one could trust.

And the architecture of that land: there are blue Dutch windmills selling pastries and handsome Mediterranean villas in Beverly Hills and– but why go on? There used to be lots of gimmicky developments: Venice, for example, which currently abounds with beatniks, was conceived as a stucco pleasure world with motorized gondolas on calm artificial canals, but it became a stucco-bungalow town with some dry, paved ditches in it and a rickety amusement park. If you object that such projects occur all over the nation, who's to deny you? Southern California is one of the dream centers of the world–though not of the best dreams maybe–and it's not only responsibilities that begin in dreams. Ten miles northwest of Times Square there is a hundred foot, decaying, stucco, pseudo-watch-tower proclaiming an undevelopment complete with artificial fishponds, unkempt plantings and a few lawned houses. It resembles nothing so much as a giants' seedy miniature golf course inhabited by commuting little ones. Marlowe could have followed up a lead there, one with dishwater blondes. . . . Nowadays in Southern California (as everywhere) the developments are mass-produced suburbias.

This whole hard-boiled, fantasy-sopped world which Chandler observed about him and which he suggests so sharply in his fiction, he takes pretty much at its own evaluation. Marlowe is the guy so wised up that he begins to think everything is rigged; desiring both love and justice, he settles (in the rigged society he sees) for ungratified lust and half-remedied injustices; and he provokes a violence which is not quite purging because it is not a punishment. This, however effective, is murky; yet I would maintain it expresses quite well the actual place—the people of those 666 developments that would like to be a city.

Still, Chandler's version is not *the* version of Southern California. He, rather more than is strategic in a writer, puts himself at the mercy of the place's notion of itself; for this notion is self-deceiving, somewhat inaccurate and confused. Marlowe sets some things straight and he sees through some of the shams, but finally he does not know what he wants; he learns over and over that he's not as smart as he thought he was and that what was most wrong has not been seen through at all; he goes through the forms but they are almost empty. Like the chess he turns to; for instance, at the end of *The High Window*:

> I went home and put my old house clothes on and set the chessmen out and mixed a drink and played over another Capablanca. It went fifty-nine moves. Beautiful cold remorseless chess, almost creepy in its silent implacability.

Chandler saw his region not just as it saw itself but in his own way too. And his version of it was so congenial and so strong that it affected his readers' versions. Chandler's fictions are one of the reasons Southern California now is seen as it is seen.

If you object that in the long view this is not so much for a writer to do, I cannot disagree. What I would maintain, though, is that he did as much as the J. F. Coopers of our literature ever did and that his novels are, for the time being, a lot more fun to read.

REVIEW:

"Marlowe's Victim," *Times Literary Supplement*, 23 March 1962, p. 200.

This unsigned review of Raymond Chandler Speaking *and* The Second Chandler Omnibus *appeared in the most influential British literary periodical when Chandler's work was undergoing a process of upward reevaluation.*

In the early 1930s a small group of English readers looked eagerly each month for the American magazine *Black Mask*, and compared the style of its contributors with that of Ernest Hemingway. The admiration they felt for the laconic severity of the fiction in this pulp magazine was no doubt exaggerated: but still, it is true that Captain Joseph T. Shaw, who edited *Black Mask* during its "golden decade" from 1926 to 1936, imposed upon his writers a stylistic pattern as firmly fixed as that of the *New Yorker* under Harold Ross. He believed that the work of his best writers would effect a revolution in American literature. What Captain Shaw wanted, as he told his writers, was stories of violent action directly told, and he eliminated everything unconnected with the physical excitement he demanded, as rigorously as Ezra Pound blue-pencilled the adjectives in the early work of Ernest Hemingway. He added, however, that "action is meaningless unless it involves recognizable human characters in three-dimensional form."

The stories in *Black Mask* had a corporate style. The men who wrote them were, with one exception, not easily distinguishable from one another, but their work was quite different from that appearing in any other magazine. The exception was Dashiell Hammett, who was almost immediately recognized by serious critics in England, although not in America, as a writer of high talent. Miss Laura Riding, writing in *Epilogue*, the periodical she edited with the assistance of Mr. Robert Graves, wrote about Hammett's *The Maltese Falcon* in 1936:

> The reader does not debate whether the girl was genuinely in love with Spade, or Spade with her; or stop to wonder whether Spade was an honest character or not. . . . There is no sentimental complexity, no architecture, no humour, no tragedy, no prepossession this way or that—and yet the writ-

The Marathon Street gate to the Paramount studios, where Chandler worked between 1943 and 1946

ing (writing of this kind), instead of being dull and careless, is impressive and definitive.

Among those who wrote for *Black Mask* during this period was Raymond Chandler, whose first story, "Blackmailers Don't Shoot," was published in the magazine in 1933. This crude story, and those that followed it in the next two or three years, seemed to be the work of a writer no more or less skilful than a dozen others who appeared in the magazine. It would have taken an extraordinary sensibility to discover in these stories the talent that was immediately evident when his first novel, *The Big Sleep*, was published in 1939. During the next five years Chandler wrote *Farewell, My Lovely*, *The High Window* and *The Lady in the Lake*. These four books made him famous. During the fifteen years of life left to him he wrote three

more crime novels, *The Little Sister*, *The Long Goodbye* and *Playback*. When he died he was probably, with the exception of Agatha Christie, the most famous crime writer in the world.

Raymond Chandler's literary career was a curious one. He was born in America but went to school in England, and as a young man lived in Bloomsbury and contributed occasionally to *The Westminster Gazette*, *The Spectator* and *The Academy*. After serving in the First World War with the Canadian Expeditionary Force he returned in 1919 to California, and there, by his own account, did a variety of jobs from working on an apricot ranch to stringing tennis rackets. He did a three-year bookkeeping course in six weeks, and became an officer or director of a number of small oil companies. In the depression these companies were ruined, and Chandler lost his job. It was after their collapse, he says in a letter to Mr. Hamish Hamilton included in *Raymond Chandler Speaking*, that: "Wandering up and down the Pacific Coast in an automobile, I began to read pulp magazines" and "decided that this might be a good way to try to learn to write fiction and get paid a small amount of money at the same time." It was a brave, and perhaps a desperate, decision by a man who was then in his forties. When his first novel was published he was fifty years old.

Such a background made Chandler exceptional among the *Black Mask* writers. They were professional craftsmen, doing a job for money: Chandler was an amateur, who brought to writing a zest and freshness that never left him, and a desire that what he wrote should be as good in its kind as he could possibly make it. Acknowledging Hammett as his early master Chandler aspired to make the crime story a work of art. Much of the criticism, of his own work and that of others, included in *Raymond Chandler Speaking*, is brilliantly intelligent. Nobody has said better things about the problems that must face any author who takes the writing of crime stories seriously:

> Dorothy Sayers tried to make the jump from the mystery to the novel of manners and take the mystery along with her. . . . She didn't really make it, because the novel of manners she aimed at was in itself too slight a thing to be important. It was just the substitution of one popular trivial kind of writing for another. I am not satisfied that the thing can't be done nor that sometime, somewhere, perhaps not now or by me, a novel cannot be written which, ostensibly a mystery and keeping the spice of mystery, will actually be a novel of character and atmosphere with an overtone of violence and fear.

Chandler's passionate concern with the sound and value of words is vividly illustrated in letters which express indignation about proof readers who were ready to improve his style, about novelists who used clichés by force of habit, about "the assumption on the part of some editorial hireling that he can write better than the man who sent the stuff in, that he knows more about phrase and cadence and the placing of words." He wished always to be judged by the standards of art, and was aware how often he fell short of them. Two

The Sunset Tower on Sunset Boulevard

years before his death he wrote, modestly enough, to his literary agent, Mrs. Helga Greene, that: "To accept a mediocre form and make something like literature out of it is in itself rather an accomplishment. . . . We [artists] are not always nice people, but essentially we have an ideal that transcends ourselves."

Chandler's distinctive marks as a writer were the depth and sharpness of his observation, his power to create atmosphere, and the crackling wisecracks which, either in dialogue or in the first person comments of his detective Philip Marlowe, enliven almost every page of his novels. "Did I hurt your head much?" Marlowe asks the blonde with silver fingernails in *The Big Sleep*, after he has hit her with his gun. Her reply has the exact tone and timing that mark Chandler's jokes: "You and every other man I ever met." It is impossible to convey in a single quotation Chandler's ear for dialogue, but no reader of *The Second Chandler Omnibus*, which contains his last three books, can fail to hear, in the conversations of film stars and publicity agents, rich men and gangsters, and policemen both honest and corrupt, an ear for the form of speech such as few writers are lucky enough to possess.

His power to create atmosphere can be found in the very first scenes of his first novel, the interview Marlowe has in *The Big Sleep* with the old general who sits shivering in his orchid-filled conservatory, or in the almost equally brilliant opening of *The High Window*, or in a dozen scenes from the later novels. The sharpness of his observation is inseparable from his gift for the telling phrase, and from the indignation always roused in him by meanness and corruption. If one had to choose a single paragraph that showed most of Chandler's gifts, the care for words, the attention to what people look like and the clothes they wear, and the basic seriousness that underlay his violent entertainments, his description of two policemen in *The Little Sister* would do as well as any:

> They had the calm weathered faces of healthy men in hard condition. They had the eyes they always have, cloudy and grey like freezing water. The firm set mouth, the hard little wrinkles at the corners of the eyes, the hard hollow meaningless stare, not quite cruel and a thousand miles from kind. The dull ready-made clothes, worn without style, with a sort-of contempt; the look of men who are poor and yet proud of their power, watching always for ways to make it felt, to shove it into you and twist it and grin and watch you squirm, ruthless without malice, cruel and yet not always unkind. What would you expect them to be? Civilization had no meaning for them. All they saw of it was the failures, the dirt, the dregs, the aberrations and the disgust.

The letters in *Raymond Chandler Speaking* show clearly, as Miss Dorothy Gardiner says, that he was a most prolific and original letter writer: but, editorially, this cannot be called a satisfactory book. Miss Gardiner and Miss Walker have filled nearly a quarter of it with bits and pieces from the workshop which we could have done without, including the opening of a new book which would certainly have been rewritten; and they have arranged the letters themselves in sections such as

"Chandler on Chandler," "Chandler on the Film World and Television," "Chandler on Cats," so that snippets of a single letter may appear in two or three parts of the book. The earliest of the letters goes back no farther than 1939, and the publication of *The Big Sleep*. They are the letters of an increasingly successful literary man, and inevitably fail to give us a clear or complete portrait of Chandler as a person. We are not told whether letters from an earlier period exist. For lack of them we learn nothing of how poor Chandler really was during the depression, or of his struggle to perfect a personal style in the early *Black Mask* stories: nor are we told how a photograph with the caption "A dinner of 'Black Mask' writers in the late twenties or early thirties" can refer to this period, when Chandler's first story in the magazine appeared in 1933. These omissions are important because Chandler's emotional life had a very great bearing upon his qualities and limitations as a writer.

From the four pages of biographical material printed before the letters it appears that Chandler's mother was divorced from his father when he was seven years old. He never saw his father again, but was brought up by his mother. After the First World War he accompanied her to California, and it was not until her death that he married, at the age of thirty-six, a woman who was seventeen years older than himself. They were married for thirty years, and during this time Chandler's devotion to her was unflawed. When she died he made an unsuccessful attempt to commit suicide.

It is not necessary to examine this background in detail to see that it must have played an important part in the development of Chandler's detective, Philip Marlowe. The crime novelist, Chandler said in his brilliant essay "The Simple Art of Murder," must be concerned with the sordid world of real crime and not with the country house murder beloved of lady detective story writers, yet to picture this world of real crime and criminals was not enough. "Down these mean streets a man must go who is not himself mean, who is neither tarnished nor afraid. The detective in this kind of story must be such a man. He is the hero, he is everything." This man was Philip Marlowe,

In the 1980s Chandler became the hero of two novels and a collection of short stories.

who rapidly became an idealized expression of the man Chandler would have liked to have been. Marlowe is tough, but he is strictly virtuous. He will not take more than his twenty-five (later forty) bucks a day. He is attracted to women, and immensely attractive to them, but not until *The Long Goodbye*, published in 1953, does he sleep with one. In fact, excessive sexuality in a woman often means that she is much worse than she should be. More than one woman eager to sleep with Marlowe, and denied that pleasure, has proved to be a murderess. He resists their wiles as easily as he resists attempts at bribery. His morality is as pure as his skull and teeth are insusceptible of damage. Perhaps it is not by accident that Chandler first called him Mallory, for he is at heart a perfect gentle knight.

How is it that Raymond Chandler, so intelligent and so sensitive, could not see that the figure of Marlowe was totally unreal, a concession to all that he had condemned in the orthodox detective story, a character deeply damaging to the artistic reality he set out to convey? He could not see it because this fragment of wish-fulfilment expressed the emotional weakness in his creator. Happily married to a woman old enough to be his mother, Chandler fulfilled in Marlowe dreams of violence and fabulous girls. There is an element of fantasy in all crime stories, but Marlowe is, when all allowances have been made, a disastrous piece of self-indulgence. Chandler is Marlowe's victim, much more than Conan Doyle was the victim of Sherlock Holmes. Under the spell of Marlowe even Chandler's dialogue becomes unreal, so that his women are liable to say things like "I wear black because I am beautiful and wicked–and lost," or "All these years I have kept myself for you." As time passed Chandler became more expert at constructing a plot, more clear about the sort of things he wanted to say, but when Marlowe took charge plot and reality moved farther and farther away. *Playback*, his last and weakest book, found Marlowe on the edge of marriage. In *The Poodle Springs Story* he was to have married Linda Loring, and there was to be a conflict between them because "She won't like it that he insists on sticking to his own business and modest way of life. . . . I am writing him married to a rich woman and swamped by money, but I don't think it will last." Marlowe

is Chandler's concession to himself and to the public, a measure of his inferiority to Hammett.

No doubt it is true that Hammett wrote just for the money, gave up when he thought he had enough, held no high opinion of his own books: yet there was in him a core of hardness which, combined with tact and taste, would have forbidden the creation of a Marlowe. The figure sketched in these brilliant, amusing, often touching letters (and one wishes very much that it was not a sketch merely, but a portrait done in the full colours of life) is that of a man on the surface contentious and strongly opinionated, beneath that surface basically shy, sentimental, longing to be loved. Yet in spite of the concessions to Marlowe, Chandler made out of this personality, with its considerable share of imbalance or maladjustment, a good deal of memorable fiction which is still not fully appreciated in his own country. "Over here [in England] I am not regarded as a mystery writer but as an American novelist of some importance," he wrote in 1955 to a fellow American crime writer, adding sadly: "I don't think somehow we shall ever reach that status in America." No doubt he was too pessimistic, but it is a pleasure to find ourselves, for once, in the vanguard of critical opinion.

REVIEW:

Richard Schikel, "Raymond Chandler, Private Eye," *Commentary*, 35 (Feburary 1963): 158-161.

This article in a politically conscious journal assesses Chandler as a social historian.

In reading *Raymond Chandler Speaking*, a collection of the late mystery writer's letters and literary fragments, one gets a sense of the peculiar loneliness of the writer of integrity who works in a popular genre that attracts few writers like himself and that the American literary culture tends to dismiss with easy, contemptuous generalizations. Chandler was a talented and devoted craftsman, one who spent his life either in spurts of hard work on his novels or in long periods of lying fallow and brooding about the lack of serious understanding and appreciation with which his work was received. Of non-literary topics, only cats–traditional companions of the lonely and disaffected–appear to have interested Chandler very deeply.

It is from the letters in this volume–about two hundred in all, addressed mainly to publishers, agents, and fellow writers of popular fiction–that one senses the kind of isolation that Chandler experienced during his career. In one letter he writes as follows:

> A thriller writer in England, if he is good enough, is just as good as anyone else. There is none of that snobbism which makes a fourth-rate serious novelist, without style or any real talent, superior to the mystery writer. . . . I don't think somehow we shall ever reach that status in America. . . . I'm afraid our instinct for classification is too strong.

At the same time, this feeling of being left out, or working at a vocation in which one's best and most conscientious efforts were underrated and misunderstood, can also be seen to have informed Chandler's fiction.

His great theme was not crime and punishment, though his letters reveal him to have had a sound technical knowledge of criminal history, psychology, and technique. His theme was, rather, an exploration of the belief that the moral man, who refuses to play the game of life in a conventionally immoral or amoral way, is doomed to the kind of loneliness Chandler himself suffered.

This understanding of Chandler and his theme provides, in turn, for speculation about the decline of a once promising figure in popular mythology, the private eye. As created by Dashiell Hammett and developed by Chandler, this figure offered a unique perspective on loneliness as a central condition of modern urban existence. Philip Marlowe, Chandler's detective, masked his feeling of emptiness behind a protective set of tough-guy mannerisms, and it is because Chandler's legion of imitators borrowed them, but not Marlowe's inner spirit, that the hard school is no longer interesting. The books are sometimes amusing as puzzles, but nothing about them catches in the mind. Marlowe did.

The successors to Marlowe lead lives of breathtaking excitement. One races headlong through the books, borne mindlessly along by a succession of cheap thrills. Marlowe, like his creator, was a plodder, the intensity of his dangerous moments heightened by the contrast with the lonely boredom of his normal life. This gave Chandler the opportunity to write about boredom, that great modern subject, without ultimately becoming boring himself. A quick turn of the plot always saved him and the reader from ennui.

Except for these flashes of excitement, Marlowe was very much the average unmarried lower-middle-class citizen of a great American city. There is genuine poignancy in the lot of these people. Their work has brought them to the city but does not reward them sufficiently to enjoy its pleasures. Barred from the fashionable world, yet given tantalizing glimpses of it, they bury their envy in the routine amusements of movies, television, and drinking in bars, and discover that these cannot completely deaden desire.

Chandler was a master of this milieu. Of today's serious writers, only Graham Greene has given us a comparable rendering of the habits and habitats of the individual at loose ends in a great city. Greene came, in time, to see the squalor of the bed-sitting room as a symbol of man's alienation from God. Chandler never went quite that far. A striving for faith becomes the moral imperative in Greene's later work. A gruff, typically American sentimentality is Chandler's equivalent to it. It is pragmatic and limited; it says no more than that everybody has the right to be left alone. So, with Chandler, mood become dominant, and response to it is everything in the appreciation of his work.

The atmosphere of cheap furnished apartments, of second-rate bars where one can always find a conversation and sometimes a woman, the very feel of an empty city street to the man who has just killed the evening alone in a second-run movie house, are done with wonderful rightness. So are the psychic defenses of the lonely man. Marlowe plays endless games of chess with himself, carefully setting up the classic problems, then spending the evening trying to solve them, sipping at a bourbon highball. He is persnickety, in an old-maidish way, about small things like coffee. The careful construction of an ideal cup of it occupies a lovingly written paragraph in almost every Marlowe novel. In fact, popular misapprehension to the contrary, Marlowe is more interested in good coffee than he is in booze, good or otherwise. Nor is Marlowe much of a boudoir athlete. He is rather offhand about women, perhaps a little defensive. Physically, of course, he needs them, but emotionally he knows they pose a threat to his independence. Consequently, he is wary, though gallant, in his treatment of them.

But why, since Marlowe is reasonably attractive, reasonably intelligent, does he do nothing to change his lot? Chandler answers this question in one of his letters, stating explicitly what is implict in the novels.

> If being in revolt against a corrupt society constitutes being immature, then Philip Marlowe is extremely immature. If seeing dirt where there is dirt constitutes an inadequate social adjustment, then Philip Marlowe has inadequate social adjustment. Of course Marlowe is a failure and usually he knows it. He is a failure because he hasn't any money. A man who without physical handicaps cannot make a decent living is always a failure and usually a moral failure. But a lot of very good men have been failures because their particular talents did not suit their time and place.

The trouble with Marlowe's successors in fiction and in the mass media is that their talents all too well suit their time and place. The very presence of Marlowe in his shabby suit in his seedy office in unfashionable downtown Los Angeles was a criticism of the fast operators who were always trying to enlist his honesty in support of their crooked, but frequently respectable-seeming, schemes. One can only wonder what poor old Marlowe would have thought of well-groomed Efrem Zimbalist, Jr., and his fancy layout at "77 Sunset Strip." Probably he would have suspected him of fronting a number racket.

Where Chandler set out to record the experience of urban loneliness, his successors, for the most part, merely cater to that experience, offering ready-made daydreams to help the sufferer while away the lonely stretch from the end of dinner to bedtime. These detectives seem only accidentally to be on the side of morality; so shifty are their standards that one can as easily imagine them working for "the syndicate" (a fantasy creation in itself, and one that Chandler had no truck with) as against it. They live too fast and too well, they tum-

ble into bed too easily with the proliferation of unbelievably desirable women who people their books. They are insiders in an affluent society. Marlowe was always outside and his conflicts had a dimension beyond the simple one of cops *vs.* robbers.

When he finished the first draft of his most solid piece of work, *The Long Goodbye*, Chandler wrote:

> What is largely boring about mystery stories, at least on a literate plane, is that the characters get lost about a third of the way through. Often the opening, the *mise en scène*, the establishment of the background, is very good. Then the plot thickens and the people become mere names. Well, what can you do to avoid this? You can write constant action and that is fine if you really enjoy it. But alas, one grows up, one becomes complicated and unsure, one becomes interested in moral dilemmas, rather than in who cracked who on the head. . . . Anyhow I wrote [*The Long Goodbye*] as I wanted to because I can do that now. I don't care *whether the mystery was fairly obvious*, but I cared about the people, about this strange corrupt world we live in, and how any man who tried to be honest looks in the end either sentimental or plain foolish.

The two great private detectives of the hard school, Marlowe and Hammett's Sam Spade, were both code heroes, like those of Hemingway (whose style also had its influence on that school). As Leslie Fiedler has pointed out, Hemingway's heroes bear more than a superficial resemblance to the Western heroes of popular culture. Consciously or unconsciously, the classic private eye represents an attempt to transfer the man with a code from the lost Eden of the 19th-century American West to the modern Jungle of the Cities. Hammett was the first to make the attempt in the pulp magazines of the 20's. His original private eye, the Continental Op, discovered that his code of personal conduct, which consisted mostly of "doing the job," was inadequate to cope with the magnitude of the evil opposed to him. Hammett, a leftist, regarded moral evil as economically determined, and though his detective remained apolitical, his books, nevertheless, drew a political lesson. Since Hammett was a writer first and a political animal second, during the four years in which he wrote his novels he never tried to supply his heroes with social consciousness. Rather, they seemed to cling more and more desperately to the code of "the job." Sam Spade actually turns in his girl to the police rather than defile the code. Hammett himself, however, grew increasingly aware of the distance between the code and his political beliefs. He wrote *The Thin Man*, a slick crime comedy with no moral tow whatever, in 1934, and then fell silent, unable to bridge the gap between his special skills as a writer and his political beliefs. In 1939 Chandler published his first novel, *The Big Sleep*, and introduced Marlowe to the world. His tales would not be as bloody or as smoothly fast-moving as Hammett's, but Marlowe would prove to be a character of more depth than any Hammett ever created.

Marlowe rarely tangled with the kind of organized crime that the Continental Op encountered in *Red Harvest*. He was called upon only to pit his private morality against private immorality. Even so, the literary left tried to claim Marlowe for its own, tried to invest his struggle against evil with political significance. Chandler resented this deeply. As far as he was concerned, politics was merely an extension of ciminality by legal, but certainly not moral, means; he never fell victim to the kind of inner conflict that silenced Hammett.

Still, like it or not, Marlowe was a class figure. He was most believable when there were distinct differences between the styles of the rich, or at least upper middle class, and lower middle class. He began to seem a little out of place in the prosperous 50's, when even college professors were being cut in on the wealthiest society in human history. His stubborn refusal to join up with the rest of society seemed more eccentric than heroic, more adolescent than mature. Ian Fleming's James Bond, that cold, amoral, elegant killer, replaced Marlowe as our prime fictional detective. Curiously, in the fragment of the novel which Chandler left unfinished when he died in 1959, he had married Marlowe off—to an heiress, no less. The idea was not his; it was a friend's. But it is easy to see why it had a certain appeal to the writer. Besides giving him a new situation in which to place his man, it also made him seem less unnatural. Marlowe had begun to suffer from cultural lag.

Chandler was not happy with the marriage although he gave it a good try. "The contest be-

tween what she wants Marlowe to do and what he will insist on doing will make a good subplot," he insisted in one note. "I don't know how it will turn out, but she'll never tame him."

This was the first entirely new novel Chandler attempted after the death of his wife, an event which had sent him off on a monumental drunk and a bungled suicide attempt; and there is something touching about his attempt to give Marlowe the marital stability he had enjoyed but which he had now lost. The symbiotic relationship between a writer and an ongoing character has rarely been made more clear, and there is, obviously, a relationship between Chandler's dedication as a writer and Marlowe's as a detective. They are different manifestations of the same impulse to professionalism.

The last letter in the present collection is to the friend who had suggested marriage for Marlowe, and by now Chandler has strong reservations about the match. Chandler writes:

A fellow of Marlowe's type shouldn't get married, because he is a lonely man, a poor man, a dangerous man, and yet a sympathetic man, and somehow none of this goes with marriage. I think he will always have a fairly shabby office, a lonely house, a number of affairs, but no permanent connection. I think he will always be awakened at some inconvenient hour by some inconvenient person to do some inconvenient job. It seems to me that this is his destiny—possibly not the best destiny in the world, but it belongs to him. No one will ever beat him, because by his nature he is unbeatable. No one will ever make him rich, because he is destined to be poor. But somehow, I think he would not have it otherwise. . . . I see him always in a lonely street, in lonely rooms, puzzled but never quite defeated. . . .

It is a measure of the specific gravity of Chandler's creation that the writer's final summing up of the Marlowe character does not seem pretentious and that in his work there is ample evidence to support it. It is a measure of the private eye's decline that no fictional operative today could possibly elicit such a description. Chandler, in his concern with the real psychological issues of his time, and in his ability to focus these issues by his excellent anti-hero, was at least the equal of a middle rank "serious" novelist—perhaps the equal, on occasion, of a first-rate one.

ARTICLE:
George V. Higgins, "Trouble in Mind," *Guardian Review*, 17 June 1988, pp. 1-2.

This tribute by the leading American writer in the hard-boiled tradition was published in London to mark the centennial of Chandler's birth.

I guess God made Boston on a wet Sunday," Raymond Chandler wrote over three decades ago, wryly disparaging what he perceived in the fiction of John P. Marquand as failure to deliver substance commensurate to the elegance of his style. Perhaps he was right about Marquand's work; he was definitely wrong about God's. God made Boston late on a February evening, when He'd been chilled to the bone through the day by a 20-knot nor'-easter coming off the ocean like a runaway chainsaw going for the knees–His own fault, of course, since He'd made that as well–spitting fresh snow in diagonal sheets along the brick plaza on the western side of the city's New City Hall. God didn't look at that and see that it was good; God kids His creatures sometimes, but He doesn't kid Himself. He beat his hands together in the worn brown cotton gloves that He got cheap at the hardware store. He dropped the pick at 5:00, and said: "There's the quitting whistle. That'll do it for today," On His visits since then, He has not made repairs.

Seventeen years ago last February that saw-toothed wind and abrasive snow separately blew me and Ashbel Green into the Sea Grille at the Sears Crescent on the southern edge of that plaza for a dinner meeting. I knew three things about Ash Green, one more than he knew about me. I knew: he was senior editor at Alfred A. Knopf, Inc.; that unless someone had forged his name, his signature was as illegible as mine; and that after 14 years–and as many rejected novels–he had accepted *The Friends of Eddie Coyle*. I was right about all three. He knew three things about me: I had written the book; I had majored in English and American literature for my undergraduate and graduate degrees; and I must love Raymond Chandler's novels. Ash had two things right.

I had never read a novel by Raymond Chandler. I guess I thought Raymond Chandler was a screenwriter. If Ash Green had whipped an examination booklet from his pocket that evening and required me to list all the stories that I knew Raymond Chandler to have written, I most likely would have begun with *The Maltese Falcon* (Dashiell Hammett). I might, just might, have stumbled upon *The Big Sleep*–if you see a pattern here, it's because, in my ignorance, I thought that if Humphrey Bogart was in the movie, Raymond Chandler wrote it.

I bring all of this up on the centenary of Chandler's birth in Chicago, Illinois, because back in 1971, after I had taken immediate measures to remedy that particular area of my ignorance, I wondered then and wonder now why it is that writers of his quality are not routinely included in the university canons of modern literature. Rather late in life–a contemporary comforted me with the observation that it's nice, as one approaches 50, to discover what one wishes to be when one grows up–I have taken up contribution to the delinquency of minors, by teaching what I know cannot be taught, but only learned (Chandler knew this, too): creative writing. My students have found Chandler dark and forboding, but also compelling, and have candidly–and generously–admitted to precisely the same ignorance of his work that afflicted me in 1971. Last winter, at the State University of New York at Buffalo, we grappled with two major questions about Chandler (and also John O'Hara, among other masters of fiction). Why don't many people read them? Why don't those who do admit it? What follows is what I inferred from the discussions.

Chandler is fun to read. He's as bleak as tundra, and his dirtbag characters far outnumber his stellar citizens, but Philip Marlowe is a laconic tour-guide through a zoo of truly interesting animals. Evil characters are more intriguing than morally-upright characters. Recall how tedious it was to read Paradise Lost, and then, if you had the misfortune, how much worse it was to struggle through Paradise Regained. Once Lucifer got scragged, all joy was dissipated. Chandler had data. Data is what distinguishes the dilettante from the artist. We believe it when the real storyteller says that the biker was a snaggle-toothed killer because the real storyteller takes care to mention–just in passing, of course–that the fellow rode a Vincent Black Shadow. We believe it when Chandler writes about iterative public and private corruption in the Los Angeles of the post-Depression and post World War II period because Chandler knew the ways of that scabrous Los Angeles as well as he knew the orderly progression of the skin disease that forced him to wear cotton gloves when the skin peeled off his hands. He knew how the Signal Hill Oil Bonanza (at one point Los Angeles oil constituted 20 per cent of American production) had enriched South Basin Oil Company–one of the many Dabney Oil Syndicate subsidiaries that he autocratically managed as chief comptroller.

And he had, as well, the data of his personal history, which gave him no joy in the getting. His mother was Florence Thornton, an Irish girl who perceived no future in those parts and went to join her brother and his wife in the United States. Florence did not prosper, taking up with Maurice Chandler, a worker on the Union Pacific. He had a notable thirst, and pulled the scoot on his wife and his babe, Raymond. Florence divorced the sot and returned with the child, then seven, to Upper Norwood, where her brother maintained a house for his mother, Annie, and his spinster sister, Ethel, a safe distance from his law offices in Waterford and Dublin (J. Thornton & Sons, Solicitors & Notaries Public). I am indebted to Frank McShane, Chandler's American biographer, for most of the factual material here included–*The Life of Raymond Chandler*, Dutton, 1976–but not for my observations: Ernest Thornton seems to me to have been a most compassionate man, doing his level best, at considerable personal expense, to fit out the offspring of his feckless kin for worthwhile lives while taking the best care he could of those too old to learn trades (when James Michael Curley was governor of Massachusetts, he said he dreaded to appoint judges, because every time he did so, he created nine enemies and one ingrate).

Chandler grew up in a house of discontented and querulous women–his grandmother and his aunt pointedly excluded his mother from sherry, lest she forget her status as a humble mendicant. He had no male role model, as the current jargon has it, and in his childhood he was no great shakes at improvisation. His uncle saw to his enrolment at Dulwich College Preparatory School in 1900, where he (student 5724) completed his first year ranked second among 28 scholars. That performance subjected him to the close attention of Headmaster A. H. Gilkes, who supplemented the demanding curriculum by editing, line by line, the prose of his charges, and made them copy down, and read aloud, those books he had assigned. Chandler wasn't ranked in his class when he left Dulwich in April of 1905, probably because he was a sickly lad and also because he had shifted from Modern to Classical Side. Ernest Thornton underwrote his passage first to France and then to Germany, the purpose being to improve his language skills.

The effect was to intensify Chandler's perception of himself as an outsider. Since his father was an American, and he had been born in the United States, and his mother was a British subject, he had dual citizenship, but by himself in France he felt no kinship. He had but little truck with the English he met in Paris, and as for the Americans: "I wasn't one of them. I didn't even speak their language. I was in effect a man without a country." In his later life he expatiated on his arduous mastery of American dialect, with the same import: "I had to learn American just like a foreign language."

He learned life like a foreign language, too, but with far less facility or success. Returning to England in 1907, he finished third out of 600 taking the Civil Service Examinations, thus acquiring a position as an inventory clerk at the Admiralty. Naval Stores–and kowtowing to his superiors–proved not to his taste. After a few months, he quit. He was a flop as a reporter for the Daily Express, and the position he acquired at the Westminster Gazette paid him a pittance too small to support life. He wanted to be a writer, preferably a poet, but what poetry he turned out was Edwardian trash; and he thought Saki (H. H. Munro) was a splendid taleteller. He feared disclosure of his hopes to Ernest Thornton; he borrowed a grubstake of £500 from him to return to America and seek his fortune as a boy intended for business. On the steamer he struck up a friendship with an American family from Los Angeles firm enough to take him to the Wrong Coast (as we call it in Boston), establish him in business (first as bookkeeper for the Los Angeles Creamery, later as office manager for the Dabney Oil Syndicate), and finally as husband to Cissy Pascal, née Pearl Eugenie

RAYMOND CHANDLER

Hurlburt, October 29, 1870 (when and where she acquired the "Cecilia" shortened into "Cissy" is a story lost in time) who'd been married twice before (and, perhaps, divorced only once). MacShane doubts the inference that Chandler married his mother, but I don't: her divorce from concert artist/composer Julian Pascal (né Goodridge Brown) was final on October 4, 1920; she and Chandler were not joined in civil wedlock until February 6, 1924, about a month after his mother died (Cissy gave her age as 43). Until then they trysted in a pad he rented for her, which gave him some practice for the flings with secretaries that led–along with boozing–to his dismissal from his job (suspicions were aroused by his paramour's repeated failure to report for work on Monday, which led to detection of his failure to come in until Wednesday).

In 1932, Raymond Chandler discovered Ernest Hemingway. Chandler was 45 years old. He was out of work. He had always wanted to be a writer, and he was in such a mess that he had very little to lose by giving in to his baser instincts. It took him five months to write "Blackmailer's Don't Shoot," written in imitation of Dashiell Hammett for *Black Mask*. He got a penny a word. He was 50 when he started work on *The Big Sleep* (1939) which brought him $2,000 in hardcover sales. That and the other 10 stories that he published in *Black Mask* ranged from 15,000 to 18,000 words, somewhere around twenty per cent of the minimum wordage of novels published today. Raymond Chandler was an autodidact: he taught himself to write by remembering what A. H. Gilkes had taught him, and he taught himself to write novels by writing long stories.

The poor SOB was never happy, and that is the devil of it. He and Cissy paid $50,000 in USA income taxes in 1945 (chiefly attributable to his earnings from writing for the screen–work that he despised), but everyone persisted in calling him a crime novelist–which he was, but only at the beginning of his career, and he rightfully resented it as his work improved–and when she died at the end of 1954, he was permanently devastated.

When he repeatedly returned to England, where his popularity was much greater than in the USA, he was a burden to his admirers–he never did learn to handle the sauce. He never found a place where he felt at ease. Not even in death, March 26, 1959; he wanted to be cremated, and buried next to Cissy's remains, but no one thought about that when he hit the check-out counter, and he was buried intact in Mount Hope Cemetery in San Diego. By himself.

It is not necessary to survive a February nor'easter on City Hall Plaza in Boston to learn that Raymond Chandler was a rewarding writer. Neither is it necessary to read everything he wrote to perceive that he was an accomplished novelist.

Very few novelists can claim to have written two books as good as *Farewell, My Lovely*, and *The Long Goodbye*. He did not write about crime, or detection–as he insisted he did not. He wrote about the corruption of the human spirit, using Philip Marlowe as his disapproving angel, and he knew about it, down to the marrow. He was a chronically unhappy man, and he was as difficult as a hedge fence. But he was also one hell of a writer, and those are hard to find.

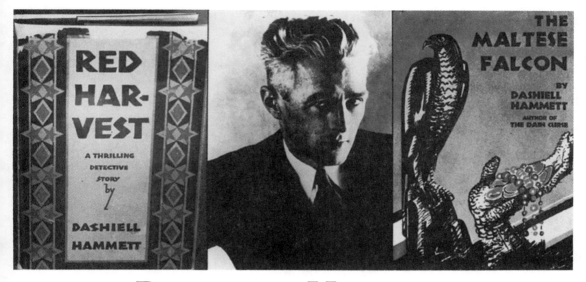

DASHIELL HAMMETT

(27 May 1894 – 10 January 1961)

BOOKS: *Red Harvest* (New York & London: Knopf, 1929);

The Dain Curse (New York: Knopf, 1929; New York & London: Knopf, 1930);

The Maltese Falcon (New York & London: Knopf, 1930; London & New York: Knopf, 1930);

The Glass Key (London: Knopf, 1931; New York: Knopf, 1931);

The Thin Man (New York: Knopf, 1934; London: Barker, 1934);

Secret Agent X-9, books 1 and 2 (Philadelphia: McKay, 1934);

$106,000 Blood Money (New York: Spivak, 1943);

The Battle of the Aleutians, by Hammett and Robert Colodny (Adak, Alaska: U.S. Army Intelligence Section, Field Force Headquarters, Adak, 1944);

The Adventures of Sam Spade (New York: Spivak, 1944); republished as *They Can Only Hang You Once* (New York: The American Mercury/Spivak, 1949);

The Continental Op (New York: Spivak, 1945);

The Return of the Continental Op (New York: Spivak, 1945);

Hammett Homicides (New York: Spivak, 1946);

Dead Yellow Women (New York: Spivak, 1947);

Nightmare Town (New York: The American Mercury/Spivak, 1948);

The Creeping Siamese (New York: Spivak, 1950);

Woman in the Dark (New York: Spivak, 1951);

A Man Named Thin (New York: Ferman, 1962);

The Big Knockover, edited by Lillian Hellman (New York: Random House, 1966); republished as *The Dashiell Hammett Story Omnibus* (London: Cassell, 1966);

The Continental Op, edited by Steven Marcus (New York: Random House, 1974);

Woman in the Dark (New York: Knopf, 1988).

MOTION PICTURES: *City Streets,* original story by Hammett, Paramount, 1931;

Mister Dynamite, original story by Hammett, Universal, 1935;

After the Thin Man, original story by Hammett, Metro-Goldwyn-Mayer, 1939;

Another Thin Man, original story by Hammett, Metro-Goldwyn-Mayer, 1939;

Watch on the Rhine, screenplay by Hammett, Warner Brothers, 1943.

OTHER: *Creeps by Night,* edited by Hammett (New York: Day, 1931; London: Gollancz, 1932);

Matthew J. Bruccoli and Richard Layman, eds., *New Black Mask 5 and 6,* includes Hammett's *After the Thin Man* in two parts (San Diego, New York & London: Harvest, 1986).

COLLECTIONS:

Nightmare Town, ed. Kirby McCauley, Martin H. Greenburg, and Ed Gorman (New York: Knopf, 1999);

Dashiell Hammett: Complete Novels (New York: Library of America, 1999);

Dashiell Hammett: Crime Stories and Other Writings (New York: Library of America, 2001).

BIOGRAPHIES:

Richard Layman, *Shadow Man* (New York: Harcourt Brace Jovanovich, 1981);

William F. Nolan, *Hammett: A Life on the Edge* (New York: Congdon & Weed, 1983);

Diane Johnson, *The Life of Dashiell Hammett* (New York: Random House, 1983);

Joan Mellen, *Hellman and Hammett* (New York: Harper-Collins, 1996);

Layman, *Dashiell Hammett* (Detroit: Gale Group, 2000);

Jo Hammett, *Dashiell Hammett: A Daughter Remembers,* ed. Layman with Julie M. Rivett (New York: Caroll & Graf, 2001).

BIBLIOGRAPHY:

Richard Layman, *Dashiell Hammett: A Descriptive Bibliography* (Pittsburgh: University of Pittsburgh Press, 1979).

LETTERS:

Selected Letters of Dashiell Hammett, ed. Richard Layman with Julie M. Rivett (Washington, D.C.: Counterpoint, 2001).

ARCHIVES:

Lillian Hellman donated a select collection of Hammett letters and manuscripts to the Harry Ransom Humanities Research Center, University of Texas, Austin. Other papers remain in private hands.

ARTICLE:

"Three Favorites," *Black Mask,* 7 (November 1924): 128.

Hammett provided the fullest account of his early life in response to a request from the editor of the pulp mystery magazine Black Mask. *Carroll John Daly, whose biography appears after Hammett's, was one of the earliest hard-boiled mystery writers.*

"I modestly announce that I am forty years old, somewhat flattered by the accompanying cut, married, that I have jacked through a number of trades before settling to my present one, and that I enjoy Prentice and his old mentor, Doc Shannon, better, probably, than any of the readers who have been so appreciative as to express kind words for us.

"Both of my heroes are built from life—with due allowances for circumstances. I know them both in the flesh. But I doubt that my actual acquaintance with these two—who, by the way, don't dream of the use I am putting them to—is as real to me as the adventures that their other selves live through in the pages that go to the BLACK MASK.

"That is, next to those most welcome of all works ever framed out of ink 'Pay to the order of'—what I enjoy most about the writing business. For the two or three more weeks that it takes to turn out a yarn, every character and action in it lives vividly for me."

Francis James.

"I was born in Maryland, between the Potomoc and Patuxent rivers, on May 27, 1894, and was raised in Baltimore.

"After a fraction of a year in high school—Baltimore Polytechnic Institute—I became the unsatisfactory and unsatisfied employee of various railroads, stock brokers, machine manufacturers, canners, and the like. Usually I was fired.

"An enigmatic want-ad took me into the employ of Pinkerton's National Detective Agency, and I stuck at that until early in 1922, when I chucked it to see what I could do with fiction writing.

"In between, I spent an uneventful while in the army during the war, becoming a sergeant; and acquired a wife and daughter.

"For the rest, I am long and lean and gray-headed, and very lazy. I have no ambition at all in the usual sense of the word; like to live as nearly as possible in the center of large cities, and have no recreations or hobbies."

Dashiell Hammett.

"I was born in Yonkers, Sept. 14, 1889; attended half the prep schools in the country with a fling at The American Academy of Dramatic Arts; a little known school devoted to the study of the human body; a short period at the study of law and a longer one in stenography.

My first business venture was the opening, with another chap, of the first moving picture show on the boardwalk at Atlantic City—came theatres at Asbury Park, Arverne, and a stock com-

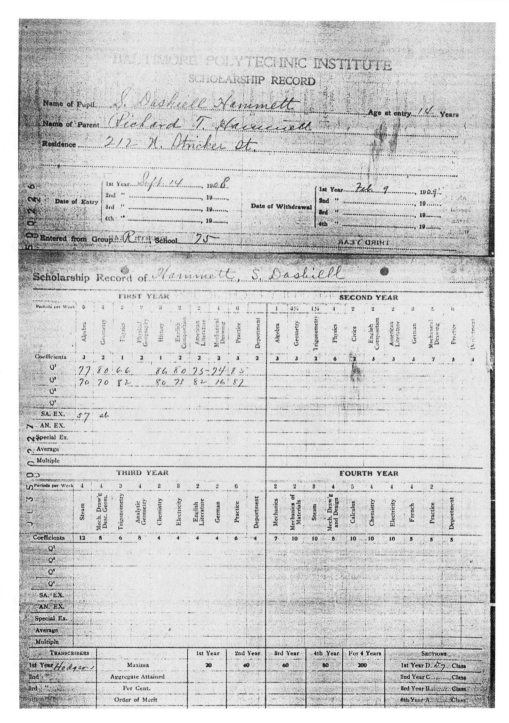

Hammett enrolled in Baltimore Polytechnic Institute in September 1908 and attended for one semester before he dropped out of high school for good in a failed attempt to rescue a family business from impending bankruptcy. His transcript shows him to have been an average student.

During World War I, when he served in the U. S. Army Motor Ambulance Corps at Camp Mead, Maryland, Hammett suffered from a bronchial ailment, which was later diagnosed as untreatable tuberculosis. He was honorably discharged in May 1929 with a medical disability and within a year moved to the West Coast. On 6 November 1920 he was admitted to the U.S. Public Health Service Hospital Number 59 in Tacoma, Washington, also called Cushman Hospital, for treatment of tuberculosis. He was hospitalized at Cushman and at a U.S. Public Health Service Hospital in San Diego, until 15 May 1921.

The nursing staff at Cushman Hospital in 1920. Hammett met his future wife, Josephine Dolan, at Cushman Hospital, where she was his nurse. Miss Dolan is at the far left.

On 7 July 1921 Hammett married Josephine Dolan in San Francisco. She was about six months pregnant with their first daughter, Mary.

Hammett, early 1920s

pany at Yonkers. After that the deluge–stock sales-man, real estate salesman, manager of a fire-alarm company, and a dozen or more other jobs.

"About Race Williams–he is a combination of fact and fiction; it is hard to tell where the one begins and the other leaves off. To my mind he is the hero of reality–not the proud fiction hero who shoots only when first wounded by an enemy.

"About letters; I welcome them, criticisms, suggestions for plots, and a friendly feeling toward my work. Race Williams is especially appreciative of his young admirer, Dorothy Suter, age twelve, of Youngstown, Ohio."

C. J. Daly.

ARTICLE:
"From the Memoirs of a Private Detective," *Smart Set*, 70 (March 1923): 88-90.

Among Hammett's earliest publications was this article consisting of recollections and observations about detection. Hammett had been a Pinkerton operative before and, briefly, after World War I, and he used his experiences as a private investigator in his fiction.

1. Wishing to get some information from members of the W.C.T.U. in an Oregon city, I introduced myself as the secretary of the Butte Civic Purity League. One of them read me a long discourse on the erotic effects of cigarettes upon young girls. Subsequent experiments proved this trip worthless.

2. A man whom I was shadowing went out into the country for a walk one Sunday afternoon and lost his bearings completely. I had to direct him back to the city.

3. House burglary is probably the poorest paid trade in the world; I have never known anyone to make a living at it. But for that matter few criminals of any class are self-supporting unless they toil at something legitimate between times. Most of them, however, live on their women.

4. I know an operative who while looking for pickpockets at the Havre de Grace race track had his wallet stolen. He later became an official in an Eastern detective agency.

5. Three times I have been mistaken for a Prohibition agent, but never had any trouble clearing myself.

6. Taking a prisoner from a ranch near Gilt Edge, Mont., to Lewistown one night, my machine broke down and we had to sit there until daylight. The prisoner, who stoutly affirmed his innocence, was clothed only in overalls and shirt. After shivering all night on the front seat his morale was low, and I had no difficulty in getting a complete confession from him while walking to the nearest ranch early the following morning.

7. Of all the men embezzling from their employers with whom I have had contact, I can't remember a dozen who smoked, drank, or had any of the vices in which bonding companies are so interested.

8. I was once falsely accused of perjury and had to perjure myself to escape arrest.

9. A detective agency official in San Francisco once substituted "truthful" for "voracious" in one of my reports on the grounds that the client might not understand the latter. A few days later in another report "simulate" became "quicken" for the same reason.

10. Of all the nationalities haled into the criminal courts, the Greek is the most difficult to convict. He simply denies everything, no matter how conclusive the proof may be; and nothing so impresses a jury as a bare statement of fact, regardless of the fact's inherent improbability or obvious absurdity in the face of overwhelming contrary evidence.

11. I know a man who will forge the impressions of any set of fingers in the world for $50.

12. I have never known a man capable of turning out first-rate work in a trade, a profession or an art, who was a professional criminal.

13. I know a detective who once attempted to disguise himself thoroughly. The first policeman he met took him into custody.

14. I know a deputy sheriff in Montana who, approaching the cabin of a homesteader for whose arrest he had a warrant, was confronted by the homesteader with a rifle in his hands. The deputy sheriff drew his revolver and tried to shoot over the homesteader's head to frighten him. The range was long and a strong wind was blowing. The bullet knocked the rifle from the homesteader's hands. As time went by the deputy sheriff came to accept as the truth the reputation for expertness that this incident gave him, and he not only

let his friends enter him in a shooting contest, but wagered everything he owned upon his skill. When the contest was held he missed the target completely with all six shots.

15. Once in Seattle the wife of a fugitive swindler offered to sell me a photograph of her husband for $15. I knew where I could get one free, so I didn't buy it.

16. I was once engaged to discharge a woman's housekeeper.

17. The slang in use among criminals is for the most part a conscious, artificial growth, designed more to confuse outsiders than for any other purpose, but sometimes it is singularly expressive: for instance, *two-time loser*–one who has been convicted twice; and the older *gone to read and write*–found it advisable to go away for a while.

18. Pocket-picking is the easiest to master of all the criminal trades. Anyone who is not crippled can become an adept in a day.

19. In 1917, in Washington, D.C., I met a young woman who did not remark that my work must be very interesting.

20. Even where the criminal makes no attempt to efface the prints of his fingers, but leaves them all over the scene of the crime, the chances are about one in ten of finding a print that is sufficiently clear to be of any value.

21. The chief of police of a Southern city once gave me a description of a man, complete even to a mole on his neck, but neglected to mention that he had only one arm.

22. I know a forger who left his wife because she had learned to smoke cigarettes while he was serving a term in prison.

23. Second only to "Dr. Jekyll and Mr. Hyde" is "Raffles" in the affections of the daily press. The phrase "gentleman crook" is used on the slightest provocation. A composite portrait of the gentry upon whom the newspapers have bestowed this title would show a laudanum-drinker, with a large rhinestone horseshoe aglow in the soiled bosom of his shirt below a bow tie, leering at his victim, and saying: "Now don't get scared, lady, I ain't gonna crack you on the bean. I ain't a rough-neck!"

24. The cleverest and most uniformly successful detective I have ever known is extremely myopic.

25. Going from the larger cities out into the remote rural communities, one finds a steadily decreasing percentage of crimes that have to do with money and a proportionate increase in the frequency of sex as a criminal motive.

26. While trying to peer into the upper story of a roadhouse in northern California one night– and the man I was looking for was in Seattle at the time–part of the porch roof crumbled under me and I fell, spraining an ankle. The proprietor of the roadhouse gave me water to bathe it in.

27. The chief difference between the exceptionally knotty problem confronting the detective of fiction and that facing the real detective is that in the former there is usually a paucity of clues, and in the latter altogether too many.

28. I know a man who once stole a Ferris-wheel.

29. That the law-breaker is invariably soon or late apprehended is probably the least challenged of extant myths. And yet the files of every detective bureau bulge with the records of unsolved mysteries and uncaught criminals.

NEWS ARTICLES:
"$125,000 in Gold Coin Stolen on S. F. Liner," *San Francisco Examiner*, 23 November 1921, pp. 1, 2.

It is reasonably certain that during his days as a private investigator in San Francisco Hammett worked on the Sonoma gold specie robbery described in this and the following newspaper stories. He claimed to have found the gold and thus to have cheated himself out of a trip to Hawaii, the ship's next port.

One of the biggest midocean robberies in Pacific Ocean annals was revealed on the arrival of the liner Sonoma in this port yesterday when the vessel's specie tanks were opened and $125,000 in English gold coin, put aboard at Sydney, was found to have vanished.

The loot comprised five steel money chests of the fifteen chests that were shipped. Only ten chests remained in the strong room.

The gold was consigned by the commonwealth of Australia to the International Banking Corporation of this city.

Weighing about 400 pounds, including the metal boxes, the whereabouts of the stolen treasure and the manner of its disappearance, after an all day search by police and private detectives, remained an inscrutable mystery.

Suspect "Inside Job."

An "inside job" involving several members of the Sonoma's crew is suspected. So thoroughly did the robbers plan their work that not the slightest clew has been discovered.

Three locks secured the door of the specie tank. Three different officers of the ship hold the keys and none of them can unlock the tank without the presence of the other two.

It was found that one of these locks had been sawed from the staple by a saw capable of cutting sheer steel. Another false lock had been put in its place.

The other two had been unlocked, evidently with keys. The work showed the hand of a master cracksman.

Evidence that the job had been carefully planned even before the liner touched at Sydney was seen in the sawing and replacing of one of the locks. This lock, the key to which is held by Captain J. H. Trask, had been removed and replaced at Sydney by the captain's orders, in view of the fact that the ship was to bear away an unusually large amount of treasure.

Had Keys Duplicated.

It was thought that impressions of the other two locks had been secured by the robbers aboard the liner from the keys as they hung on the racks in the quarters of First Officer Thomas McManus and Purser A. G. Conquest. It is believed that an impression of Captain Trask's key was similarly obtained, but that its use was defeated when he had the lock altered.

The stolen money was in English sovereigns, each box containing sovereigns to the value of 5,000 pounds, or approximately $25,000. The total value of the treasure shipped on the Sonoma was $375,000, of which a third was stolen.

An international ring of specie robbers, including either members of the crew or persons who frequently travel on the liners across the Pacific, is thought responsible for the crime.

The robbery was discovered after the liner had been moored to Pier 35. Officials of the International Banking Corporation immediately visited the ship, accompanied by armed guards and trucks to take the treasure to the vaults.

First Officer McManus and Purser Conquest accompanied them to the tanks, McManus securing Captain Trask's key. After the first two locks had been readily opened, Captain Trask's key failed to fit.

McManus immediately detected signs that the lock had been tampered with. A saw was procured and the staple cut. In the presence of the bank officials the strong-boxes were counted and the amazing robbery revealed.

Guards were immediately placed on the pier and aboard the liner. All members of the crew were searched before they had opportunity to land. Search of the large vessel was immediately begun by a special detail of customs officers, accompanied by police and detectives.

A careful study of the movements of the ship since the gold was taken aboard at Sydney was made by Captain Trask in an endeavor to ascertain precisely where the robbery had taken place.

It was thought likely that the crime had been consummated after the Sonoma left Honolulu and perhaps only a short time before arrival at this port. Captain Trask stated that he had regularly inspected the locks of the specie bank each day, and had seen nothing irregular.

Assuming that the plans of the robbers were temporarily frustrated by the substitution of a new lock at Sydney, it was argued that Honolulu was the first port at which a similar lock, for purposes of duplication, could have been secured.

Advices were immediately wired to Hawaii, requesting the island police to search for evidence that such a lock had been purchased and by whom.

By elimination two possibilities were left; namely, that the $125,000 in gold is still aboard the liner in some disguised form and will be found when the cargo is unloaded; or else that it was removed from the ship in some way in the two hours between entering the Heads and tying to pier 35. During a portion of this time the Sonoma was in quarantine.

Another theory entertained by the officials is that the gold was taken from the boxes, wrapped in small packages, and concealed in mailsacks in the hold. This, it was said, was a practicable means, as the mail is handled by machinery and the weight would not be noticed.

Fifteen years ago the liner Alameda was robbed of a single box of gold, through substitution of a box exactly similar. The last big specie robbery on the Pacific was that of the Nile, owned by the China Mail. In this crime $10,000 in bullion was taken, after the liner had left the port bound for the Orient.

"Dream Bares Hiding Place on S. F. Liner," *San Francisco Examiner*, 29 November 1921, p. 1.

Hours of close questioning of the members of the crew of the liner Sonoma yesterday led to the recovery of $102,300 of the $125,000 loot stolen from the specie tanks of the vessel as it neared this port last Tuesday on her homeward voyage from Sydney. Police officials and Pinkerton detectives are hopeful of finding the remainder of the gold coin.

Four members of the crew whom the police suspect as having figured in the sea robbery were taken to the Hall of Justice last night and further questioned as to their movements aboard the boat shortly before its arrival in port. No arrests have been made pending further investigation and the questioning of others of the crew who may have knowledge of the theft.

Seventy-five thousand dollars was recovered in three strongboxes found submerged in the bay by stout cords from the stern of the vessel as she lay moored at pier 35. Each box contained approximately 5,000 English pounds or $25,000 in gold.

Tucked away in a fire hose, which had been slipped down the ventilating pipe, running from the upper deck to the oil tanks, another small fortune in gold sovereigns was found estimated at more than $25,000.

With these disclosures at hand, detectives immediately instituted a rigid interrogation of the entire crew.

Finds Hidden Cache.

The discovery of the gold was made by First Assistant Engineer Carl Knudsen. He had been ordered to continue his search of the craft with the other officers of the ship. He explained that the hiding place of the gold had been revealed to him in a dream.

Down in the engine room, Knudsen noticed that the ventilating pipe to the oil tank had been tampered with by a wrench and that paint on the pipe had been marked by the tools. Reporting his find to F. S. Samuels, general manager of the Oceanic Steamship Company, he was ordered to open the pipe.

One of the joints was taken off, but nothing was found. Not satisfied, Knudsen began tapping the pipe with a hammer up between each deck, and shortly discovered that instead of a ring to his knocks he produced dull thuds.

Again unscrewing a joint, a fire hose was found suspended in the pipe. Assisted by detectives, Knudsen pulled the hose out and from it rolled $25,000 in gold coins.

Submerged in Bay.

News of the discovery spread quickly about the vessel and the clew was offered the officials to the hiding place of the three strong boxes submerged under the stern of the liner.

Grappling hooks were employed and with little effort the three weighty chests, each containing 5,000 pounds in English money, or nearly $75,000, were brought to the surface.

Officials of the International Banking Corporation to which institution the gold was consigned and who have been present at the ship since the robbery was first discovered, took charge of the gold as soon as it was found.

Under guard of detectives the specie was removed from the cabin of the liner where it was counted and deposited late yesterday in the vaults of the bank.

NEWS ARTICLE:
"Hammett Traps Gem Holdup Suspects," *San Francisco Call-Bulletin*, 26 January 1934, p. 7.

In 1934 when his syndicated comic strip "Secret Agent X-9" was published, King Features Syndicate promoted

2)620 Post Street (July 1921-October 1926)   *3)20 Monroe Street (October 1926-27)*

4)1309 Hyde Street

Hammett and his family lived in six different apartments in San Francisco during the time when he wrote most of his short stories and his first three novels. 1)120 Ellis Street (June-July 1921) [not shown],

5)891 Post Street (1927-Fall 1929)

6)1155 Leavenworth Avenue (Fall, 1929)

Hammett as a former detective who wrote from experience. To make the point, they ran accounts of the "Gloomy Gus" Schaefer jewel robbery, crediting Hammett with Schaeffer's arrest. Contemporary accounts of the case vary from the 1934 version syndicated by King Features.

In December, 1921, three thugs rifled the Shapiro Jewelry Company of St. Paul and escaped with $130,000 in gems and silver.

Two months later bay region police received the flash that the suspects were thought to be hiding somewhere near San Francisco.

Dashiell Hammett, author of "Secret Agent X-9," detective picture strip, which begins Monday on The Call-Bulletin comic page, was at that time a Pinkerton operative. He was assigned the case along with other investigators.

Hideout Near Vallejo

Weeks of searching revealed the gang headquarters at a roadhouse near Vallejo. Hammett, disguised as a wealthy business man in search of pleasure, frequented the hangout until he had his men well marked.

One night there was a meeting of the gang. To eavesdrop, Hammett went outside the house and climbed upon a side porch. Suddenly the porch, with a loud crash, gave way. Hammett, though badly bruised and shaken, managed to make a getaway before anyone could ask embarrassing questions.

The gang, convinced they were trailed, disappeared.

Hammett, after recovering, hopefully hung around Vallejo in various disguises. His efforts were soon rewarded. One day he saw "Gloomy Gus" Schaefer, one of the suspects.

Schaefer Shadowed

Schaefer was shadowed for weeks, the detective trying to get some tangible evidence with which to hold him after the arrest. Eternal vigilance brought results. Schaefer's wife was nabbed opening a safe deposit box in one of the Oakland banks. In the box were some of the stolen Shapiro jewels.

The whole gang was soon rounded up and sent back to St. Paul to stand trial. "Gloomy Gus"

was the only one convicted. He was sentenced, and a few years ago pardoned.

Schaefer is now on trial with the Touhy gang for the Jake Factor kidnaping. When through in Chicago, Schaefer will be brought to California to be tried for the Sacramento mail robbery pulled last year.

ARTICLE:
"Our Own Short Story Course," Black Mask, 7 (August 1924): 127-128.

In April 1924, Phil Cody succeeded George Sutton, Jr., as editor of Black Mask. *Five months later, he asserted himself publicly, rejecting two of Hammett's stories. By that time Hammett was a regular and popular contributor to the magazine, and Cody's action was bold, even though he published Hammett's response. "Women, Politics, and Murder" was published in the September* Black Mask. *"The Question Is One Answer" was not published under that title.*

We recently were obliged to reject two of Mr. Hammett's detective stories. We didn't like to do it, for Mr. Hammett and his Continental Detective Agency had become more or less fixtures in BLACK MASK. But in our opinion, the stories were not up to the standard of Mr. Hammett's own work–so they had to go back.

In returning the manuscripts, we inclosed the "Tragedy in One Act," referred to in the letter which follows. The "Tragedy" was simply a verbatim report of the discussion in this office, which led to the rejection of the stories.

We are printing Mr. Hammett's letter below; first, to show the difference between a good author and a poor one; and secondly, as a primary course in short story writing. We believe that authors–especially young authors, and also old authors who have fallen into the rut–can learn more about successful writing from the hundred or so words following, than they could possibly learn from several volumes of so-called short story instruction. Mr. Hammett has gone straight to the heart of the whole subject of writing–or of painting, singing, acting . . . or of just living for that matter. As the advertising gentry would say, here is the "Secret" of success.

I don't like that "tragedy in one act" at all; it's too damned true-to-life. The theater, to amuse me, must be a bit artificial.

I don't think I shall send "Women, Politics, and Murder" back to you–not in time for the July issue anyway. The trouble is that this sleuth of mine has degenerated into a meal-ticket. I liked him at first and used to enjoy putting him through his tricks; but recently I've fallen into the habit of bringing him out and running him around whenever the landlord, or the butcher, or the grocer shows signs of nervousness.

There are men who can write like that, but I am not one of them. If I stick to the stuff that I want to write–the stuff I enjoy writing–I can make a go of it, but when I try to grind out a yarn because I think there is a market for it, then I flop.

Whenever, from now on, I get hold of a story that fits my sleuth, I shall put him to work, but I'm through with trying to run him on a schedule.

Possibly I could patch up "The Question's One Answer" and "Women, Politics, and Murder" enough to get by with them, but my frank opinion of them is that neither is worth the trouble. I have a liking for honest work, and honest work as I see it is work that is done for the worker's enjoyment as much as for the profit it will bring him. And henceforth that's my work.

I want to thank both you and Mr. Cody for jolting me into wakefulness. There's no telling how much good this will do me. And you may be sure that whenever you get a story from me hereafter,– frequently, I hope,–it will be one that I enjoyed writing.

San Francisco, Cal.
DASHIELL HAMMETT

ARTICLE:
"Shall We Write Sex Stories?," *Writer's Digest*, 4 (June 1924): 17-18.

In June 1924 Canadian writer H. Bedford-Jones wrote a letter to Writer's Digest *attacking "sex stories." Asked to respond, Hammett took the opportunity to defend the seriousness of his writing.*

A discussion of an article by H. Bedford-Jones which appeared in the October *Writer's Digest*, enti-

tled "Sex Deftly Handled." Mr. Jones held that the writer could not afford to write them, as it affected both his reputation and his mental fibre.

In Defence of the Sex Story
By Dashiell Hammett

Just a voice in disagreement with nearly everything that Mr. Bedford-Jones says in "Sex, Deftly Handled."

Literature, as I see it, is good to the extent that it is art, and bad to the extent that it isn't; and I know of no other standard by which it may be judged. As Jim Tully, writing recently of another who held opinions somewhat similar to Mr. Bedford-Jones, said: "It would be well for him to remember that art knows no morals–art being a genuine something–while morals differ in all lands."

If you have a story that seems worth telling, and you think you can tell it worthily, then the thing for you to do it to tell it, regardless of whether it has to do with sex, sailors, or mounted policemen.

Sex has never made a poor story good, or a good one poor; but if Mr. Bedford-Jones will make a list of the stories that are still alive after several centuries, he'll find that many of the heartiest survivors have much to do with the relations between the sexes, and treat those relations with little of the proper Victorian delicacy.

Is Mr. Bedford-Jones in earnest, I wonder, when he places "The Exile of the Lariat" above "Casanova's Homecoming?"

Remembering, for instance, the meeting between Maurice and his mistress and Arcade in "The Revolt of the Angels," would he, I wonder, put Anatole France among his "mental prostitutes"?

Does he believe that Shakespeare's "Henry VIII" is, because of its comparative sexlessness, a better play than Shakespeare's "Measure for Measure"?

And the associates he gives the writer for sex magazines: "radicals . . . social perverts . . . moral lepers . . ." In Jack London's day, I understand, there were many good people who thought him a radical!

Now–that there may be no misunderstanding– here's exactly where Mr. Bedford-Jones' shoe pinches *me*, and where it doesn't. I've written altogether three stories that are what is sometimes called "sex stuff," and two–or possibly three–that might be so called if you stretched the term a bit. Against them, I've sold nine or ten stories in which not a single feminine name appeared; and half a dozen more in which the only female characters were very minor ones. Then quite a few stories with the ordinary "love interest" and so forth.

The "sex stuff" is about five per cent of what I have sold: and if figured upon what I have written the average would be much lower–

Surely not a large "pinch."

Reply to Mr. Hammett

By H. Bedford-Jones

Mr. Hammett is entitled to disagree; I like his honest opinion, and his argument is excellent. Unfortunately, it has nothing to do with the subject of my recent article, which was not "Sex," but "Sex, Deftly Handled."

A story worth telling, told worthily as possible–good gosh, Hammett, that's all any writer wants to do! The qualifier means a lot, however; that little "worthily" is the meat of the nut. Your letter itself shows that you're honest about your work, and you simply read too much into my article, which was no diatribe at all against sex in writing. Look at it this way. Suppose I let off a hot blast against smutty so-called "smoking room" stories: would you consider that I damned all after-dinner stories, which may be risqué and yet very witty? Not a bit of it. My argument is not against the story worth telling, but against the story deliberately written with a smutty pen to get the dinero. Your own record shows that you're not that sort of writer.

No, you can't lead me into that morass of morals and literature. I like a good sex story as well as anybody, if it's written with a clean mind. But, when it's written with a dirty mind, I don't like it– and you know perfectly well how much dirt is floating around in books and magazines, and how much of the stuff is put out deliberately as a mental aphrodisiac. Get my point better now?

ARTICLE:

"Vamping Samson," *Editor*, 69 (9 May 1925): 41-43.

In the column "Contemporary Writers and Their Work," the Editor *asked magazine writers to comment on recently published stories. Hammett provided commentary on his story "Ber-Bulu" (republished in* Dead Yellow Women *as "The Hairy One").*

This is my second attempt to respond to The Editor's inquiry concerning the "genesis, development and writing" of "Ber-Bulu" (Sunset Magazine, March, 1925). I tore up the first one: it was a nice clear account of every step in the story's construction, and that was what was the matter with it. It explained everything clearly if not truthfully, and was especially logical in dealing with things in the story that were done haphazardly, or, at best, intuitively. I shall try to avoid that sort of deceit now, but it is not likely that I shall be altogether successful: I can see too many things in the story now that I did not see when I was writing it. However:

"Ber-Bulu" grew out of wondering what sort of man was Samson if he was neither inspired Judge of Israel nor solar myth, if he was simply a rugged old warrior, nowise extra-human, whose peculiar adventures formed the nucleus of the familiar legend. Viewed thus, the final tragedy and much else of the story had to be pared off, disregarded as poetic interpolation, and the Samson who remained was the mighty hairy giant who lost his strength with his hair, and who was on the whole hardly an admirable figure.

To use Samson in fiction I had to find a natural link between his hair and his power, and to this end I shifted the stress from the seven locks of his head to his face. Some years ago James Montgomery Flagg decided that a beard was excusable on either of two grounds: that its owner had absent-mindedly signed someone else's name to a check in his smooth-faced days, or that he had a chin which bashfully tried to hide behind his larynx. The second excuse gave me my clue.

A giant could have so weakly ridiculous a face and head that, when the fierce bristles behind which he hid them were removed, he would be shamed into helplessness while his enemies were inspired with contempt for him.

I plucked this amended Samson out of Judges and christened him Levison: he was a bullying giant whose only strength lay in his muscles, and whose silly features were masked, from reader as well as from his own world, by bushels of dark hair.

Not wishing to set him among surroundings that would deprive him of any of the advantages of his physique, I selected the Sulu Archipelago shortly after the end of the Spanish-American War as the most suitable locale. It had the degree of modernity I needed, it had not been written out of reality, and I liked Moros. Further, the Bible story would be plausibly fresh in the minds of a folk newly acquainted with Christianity, and, with a missionary on hand, I could make that plausibility doubly sure. There need not have been any explicit connection between the older story and mine, but why ignore the value of so solid a stone in my story's foundation?

Neither did I need a Delilah, but why not hold a loose analogy with the Bible story? However, my Delilah must not take the center of the stage, as she would surely do if given an active part in the unmasking. I named her Dinihari (Dawn) and made her a complaisant Malay girl without great depth of character. But someone had to shave Levison! The simplest someone would be a rival for possession of the girl. I made him a Moro: a victorious white man would have been likely to take too much of the reader's interest.

I had, then (1) an island barely touched by civilization; (2) a giant whose weakness was hidden behind his hair; (3) a Moro, and Moros are, if a people may be put in a few words, superstitious pirates, fighters, gamblers, and lovers of rough humor; and (4) a shallow Malay girl who was desired by both men. The rest of the plotting was merely a matter of experimenting with these parts, fitting them this way and that, until they should click together in some sort of whole.

They came together in this shape: Jeffol, the Moro, brought the girl to the island from Borneo and installed her in his house with his several wives. Later, he lost his anting-anting or amulet, and, coincidentally, his money in a card game. Depressed, he was easily converted to Christianity by the missionary, who immediately ordered him to get rid of his harem, retaining his first wife as his legal wife. Jeffol was willing to scatter his harem, but he wanted to keep Dinihari. Compro-

mising, he set out for the seat of the white man's government to divorce his first wife so that the missionary could marry him to the girl. While Jeffol was gone Levison came to the island, built himself a house, and took Dinihari. Jeffol returned, fought Levison, and was beaten. The missionary, struggling to hold Jeffol to his new faith–which thus far had seemed an inadequate substitute for his anting-anting–and wishing to clear the island of Levison, suggested the Samson story to the Moro. (This angle was withheld from the reader until the last, of course, and even then I did not specify the extent to which the missionary had seen through Levison's mask of hair.) Jeffol, his old mother (whose hag's laughter I needed), and two friends overpowered Levison, shaved him from head to foot, and, with Dinihari joining in, laughed him off the island.

The action invented, nothing remained but the writing; that is, the clothing of this bald and, as you have discovered, quite hopelessly lifeless plot with words and phrases that would trick the reader, or at least the editor, into some sort of interest. How that was done–except in its cruder instances of planting a promise of things to come here, a hint there, pointing this character at one aspect of my desired result, that one at another–I can tell no more than anyone can about any story.

Because much of the preliminary action had to be condensed, and because the story as a whole had an anecdotal flavor, I wrote it in the first person, filtering it through the mind of the gambler to whom Jeffol lost his money, and using my gambler's affairs for bridges over which my story could pass smoothly and briskly from place to place and from one time to another. Also he let me set my stage quite thoroughly before introducing Levison, and kept the dialogue to a minimum. The story went off rather easily. I framed and wrote it in three days, an almost miraculous speed for me, who can seldom do anything in less than three weeks.

My earlier work is close enough for memory if hardly far enough away for perspective: it is not yet three years since I installed my first typewriter and picked out my first story, "The Barber and His Wife" (Brief Stories, December, 1922). My first sale and appearance in print was as one of the considerable company who came out in The Smart Set under the editorship of Messrs. Nathan and Mencken, though it is conceivable they don't boast of the discovery. (Since I have dragged them in, let me write down that no matter what faults they may have as critics–I've had a lot of Mencken's pointed out to me and have even noticed one or two on my own account–they have every possible editorial virtue that a writer–especially an obscure one–could wish to find at that point where manuscripts do or do not cast off their outer husks, submit to the cancellation stamp that is now a bust in the nose rather than an encouraging pat, and start home smaller, symbolically, than when they set out.)

Because I spent some years sleuthing around the country in the employ of Pinkerton's National Detective Agency, about half of the fiction I have written has had to do with crime, though, curiously, I was some time getting the hang of the detective story. And while, with the connivance of The Black Mask, that type of story has paid most of my rent and grocery bills during the past two years, I have sold at least one or two specimens of most of the other types to a list of magazines, varied enough if not so extensive, that includes Action Stories, Argosy-All Story, Black Mask, Brief Stories, Experience, Forum, Pearson's, Saucy Stories, Smart Set, Sunset, True Detective Mysteries, besides a few book-reviews, articles and short miscellaneous matter here and elsewhere.

PARODY:

"Another Perfect Crime," *Experience*, 3 (February 1925): 34.

Hammett wrote two pieces for the Chicago humor magazine Experience, *one of which remains unlocated but is known to exist from an inventory of his published work compiled by his secretary, Muriel Alexander, in the late 1940s. This piece is a parody of the "Golden Age" mystery, which Hammett deplored.*

Although convicted of Boardman Bowlby Bunce's murder, I did kill him. I forget why; I dare say there was something about the man I disliked. That is not important; but I feel that the attentiveness with which the public has read the interviews I did not give and looked at photographs of photographers' personal friends entitles that public to know why, here in the death cell, I have made a new will, giving my fortune to the fiction department of the Public Library. (Before starting that, however, I wish to state that while I do not object to having been born in any of the other houses pictured in various newspapers, I must, in justice to my parents, repudiate the ice-house shown in Wednesday's Examiner.)

To get on with my story: when I determined, for doubtless sufficient if not clearly remembered reasons, to kill Boardman Bowlby Bunce, I planned the murder with the most careful attention to every detail. A life-long reader of literature dealing with the gaudier illegalities, I flattered myself that I of all men was equipped to commit the perfect crime.

I went to his office in the middle of the afternoon, when I knew his employees would be all present. In the outer office I attracted their attention to my presence and to the exact time by arguing heatedly that the clock there was a minute fast. Then I went into Bunce's private office. He was alone. Out of my pockets I took the hammer and nails I had bought the day before from a hardware dealer who knew me and, paying no attention to the astonished Bunce, nailed every window and door securely shut.

That done, I spit out the lozenge with which I had prepared my voice, and yelled loudly at him: "I hate you! You should be killed! I shall injure you!"

The surprise on his face became even more complete.

"Sit still," I ordered in a low voice, taking a revolver from my pocket–a silver-mounted revolver with my initials engraved in it in four places.

Walking around behind him, carefully keeping the weapon too far away to leave the powder-marks that might make the wound seem self-inflicted, I shot him in the back of the head. While the door was being broken in I busied myself with the ink-pad on his desk, putting the prints of my fingers neatly and clearly on the butt of the revolver, the handle of the hammer, Bunce's white collar, and some convenient sheets of paper; and hurriedly stuffed the dead man's fountain pen, watch and handkerchief into my pockets just as the door burst open.

After a while a detective came. I refused to answer his questions. Searching me, he found Bunce's fountain pen, watch and handkerchief. He examined the room—doors and windows nailed on the inside with my hammer, my monogrammed revolver beside the dead man, my fingerprints everywhere. He questioned Bunce's employees. They told of my entrance, my passing into the office where Bunce was alone, the sound of hammering, my voice shouting threats, and the shot.

And then—then the detective arrested me!

It came out later that this would-be sleuth whose salary the property holders were paying had never read a detective story in his life, and so had not even suspected that the evidence had been too solidly against me for me to be anything but innocent.

ARTICLE:

"The Advertisement IS Literature," *Western Advertising* (October 1926): 35-36.

Between October 1926 and March 1928, Hammett wrote five articles about advertising for the trade journal Western Advertising, *which called itself "A magazine for the buyer and seller of advertising." In his first article, Hammett argued for the integrity of good ad copy.*

Advertising isn't literature, it's selling talk. Leave color and other literary embellishments to the essayist and fictionist. The best advertising copy talks to the man in the street in his own language. . . . How often is the wisdom of this much-repeated advice questioned? Not very often. The counsel itself is ignored as frequently as it is followed, but even those who most frequently ignore it seldom challenge its general truth. Yet little examination of the subject is required to show that advertising copy is literature—literature specifically applied—and that nothing but harm can come from the attempt to separate it from its parent stock.

Every writer who brings an idea to a blank sheet of paper is faced by the same primary task. He must set his idea on the paper in such form that it will have the effect he desires on those who read it. The more competent he is, the more stubbornly he will insist that the idea set down shall be his idea and not merely something like it, and

that the effect on the reader shall be the effect the writer desires and not an approximation of that effect. The selection and arrangement of words to accomplish effectively these twin purposes is a literary problem, no matter whether the work be a poem, a novel, a love letter or an advertisement. Whether he likes it or not, every man who works with words for effects is a literary worker. His only liberty is in deciding how adept he shall be.

The test by which advertising copy must stand or fall is the test by which we evaluate every branch of literature. Goethe, Carlyle, Croce, Spingarn, Mencken are a few of the many who have put it into words. "What has he tried to do? How well has he succeeded?" In the general literary field there is much quarreling over the correct answer to either question in any praticular case. Advertising's limitation, and its advantage, as applied literature, is that the answer to the first question is almost always unmistakably evident in the copy itself, and that the bookkeeping department can answer the second.

To write of washing machines in terms of yachts is not to be too literary. It is to be not sufficiently literary. The disproportionately florid, the gaudy, have worse reputation in literature than ever they have had in advertising. There are few literary points on which there is general agreement, but I know of no first-rate writer or critic who does not call that style most perfect which clothes ideas in the most appropriate words.

Clarity is First Objective

Another—perhaps the only other—point on which there is agreement is that clarity is the first and greatest of literary virtues. The needlessly involved sentence, the clouded image, are not literary. They are anti-literary. Joseph Conrad, whose work John Galsworthy pronounced "the only writing of the last twelve years that will enrich the English language to any extent," defined the writer's purpose as "above all else, to make you see." Anatole France, probably the tallest figure modern literature has raised, and the most bookish of men in the bargain, said: "The most beautiful sentence? The shortest!" He condemned the semicolon, a hangover from the days of lengthy sentences, as not suited to an age of telephones and airplanes. He insisted that all unnecessary

[101]

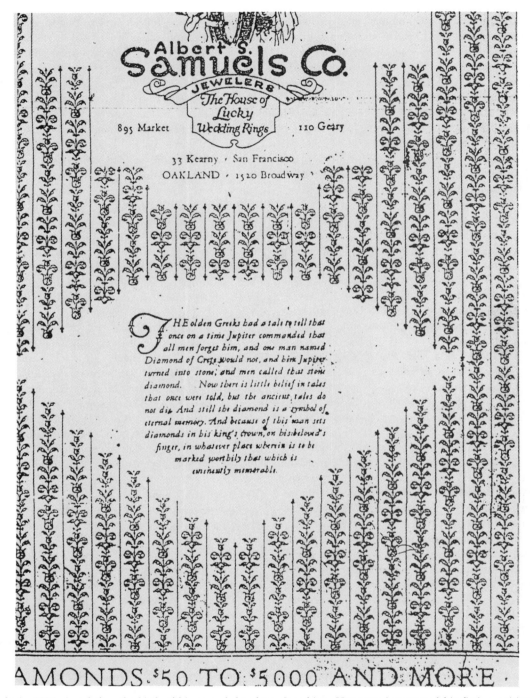

Early in 1926, just before the birth of his second daughter, Josephine, Hammett interrupted his fiction-writing career to take a job as the advertising manager for Albert S. Samuels Co., a jeweler in San Francisco. The ads in this format, which had run since January 1922, terminated in July 1926, the month a physical breakdown forced Hammett's resignation.

[102]

"which's" and "that's" must be carefully weeded out, as they would spoil the finest style. Is there anything in these extremely literary examples to be avoided by the copy writer?

Another, older, witness: Aristotle: "The excellence of Diction is to be clear and not common." Cannot language be both clear and common? It is doubtful. The language of the man in the street is seldom either clear or simple. If you think I exaggerate, have your stenographer eavesdrop a bit with notebook and pencil. You will find this common language, divorced from gesture and facial expression, not only excessively complicated and repetitious, but almost purposeless in its lack of coherence. Perhaps the plain man's speech is a little better. If you wish to learn how little, pick out half a dozen men at random, men whose daily work is not with words, and give them a piece of copy to write. The result will be interesting and instructive. It will be neither clear nor simple.

The favorite words of the plain man are those which enable him to talk without thinking. Those same words in an advertisement enable him to read without thinking, hardly a profitable aim for the copy writer. To say that our man in the street is never lucid, never apt in expression, would be absurd. But to trace back any ten of his expressive flashes is to find that at least nine of them originated in the mind of some professional worker with words, and reached the street by way of book, magazine, newspaper, pulpit, platform, theater or radio. And most of the nine will have at least one quality in common: they will be composed of simpler elements than the plain man is accustomed to use in his speech.

This, of course, is by no means a recent discovery. You may read tons of books and magazines without finding, even in fiction dialogue, any attempt faithfully to reproduce common speech. There are writers who do try it, but they seldom see print. Even such a specialist in the vernacular as Ring Lardner gets his effect of naturalness by skillfully editing, distorting, simplifying, coloring the national tongue, and not by reporting it verbatim.

Simplicity and clarity are not to be got from the man in the street. They are the most elusive and difficult of literary accomplishments, and a high degree of skill is necessary to any writer who

would win them. They are the most important qualities in securing the maximum desired effect on the reader. To secure that maximum desired effect is literature's chief goal. Can the copy writer find a better one? Does he want another?

PARODY:
"The Advertising Man Writes a Love Letter,"
   Judge (26 February 1927): 8.

In the national humor magazine Judge, *Hammett wrote a parody of the profession he briefly followed.*

Dear Maggie:
   I LOVE YOU!
   What is love? It is all in all, said Rossetti; it is the salt of life, said Sheffield; it is more than riches, said Lucas; it is like the measles, said Jerome. *Send for leaflet telling what these and other great men of all times have said about love!* It is FREE!
   WILL YOU MARRY ME?
   Will you be the grandmother of my grandchildren? Or will you, as thousands of others have done, put it off until too late–until you are doomed to the penalty of a lonely old age? Do not delay. *Grandchildren are permanent investments in companionship!*
   But simply to marry is not enough! You must ask yourself, *to whom?* Shall you marry a man just because you like his eyes, or his dancing? *Or will you insist on the best? IT COSTS NO MORE!*
   A man who is educated, brilliant, witty, thoughtful, handsome, affectionate, honorable and generous–a man who is made of the best moral, mental and physical materials obtainable–a man

In every way worthy, not only of being grandfather to your grandchildren, but great-great grandfather, to your great-great grandchildren.

All this can be yours if you act NOW!

Read what others have said (full names and addresses):

"He was one swell guy." Flora B****.

"In the four years we roomed together

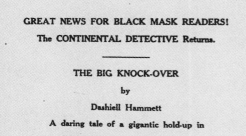

When Joseph Shaw took over the editorship of Black Mask *in November 1926, his first priority was to encourage the development of the best writers in the magazine's stable, as this statement indicates. At Shaw's urging, Hammett undertook his longest work to date, which was his first publication in the magazine in eleven months. Hammett's return was announced proudly.*

he never once left a ring in the bath tub." Paul G****.

"I laughed more the months I knew him than at any other time of my life." Fanny S****.

"He's one of those fellows who knows everything." Doris L****.

All this can be yours! Can you afford to be without it?

Mail the coupon TODAY!

Yours for prompt action,

FRANK

REVIEW COLUMN:
"Poor Scotland Yard!," *Saturday Review of Literature*, 3 (15 January 1927): 159.

From January 1927 until October 1929, Hammett reviewed over fifty books about crime for the Saturday Review of Literature.

False Face. By Sydney Horler. New York: George H. Doran Company. 1926. $2.

The Benson Murder Case. By S. S. Van Dine. New York: Charles Scribner's Sons, 1926. $2.

The Malaret Mystery. By Olga Hartley. Boston: Small, Maynard & Company. 1926. $2.

Sea Fog. By J. S. Fletcher. New York: Alfred A. Knopf. 1926. $2.

The Massingham Butterfly. J. S. Fletcher. Boston: Small, Maynard & Company. 1926. $2.

In some years of working for private detective agencies in various cities I came across only one fellow sleuth who would confess that he read detective stories. "I eat 'em up," this one said without shame. "When I'm through my day's gumshoeing I like to relax; I like to get my mind on something that's altogether different from the daily grind; so I read detective stories."

He would have liked "False Faces;" it is different from any imaginable sort of day's work. Scotland Yard promises to "safeguard the safety" (page 29, if you think I spoof) of an American inventive genius who has business with the British government. Arrayed against him and it is a medley of scoundrels–a "shuddersome" Communist with "a smile that revolted," a hyphenated "brute-beast" of a German, a Russian Baron who has "the air of a world cosmopolitan," and so on, including a nameless skeptic who doubts that a certain blueprint is an original drawing. Everybody moves around a good deal, using trains, motorcycles, automobiles, airplanes, submarines, secret passages, sewers, and suspended ropes. Most of the activity seems purposeless, but in the end dear old England is saved once more from the Bolshevists.

I don't think it will stay saved unless something is done to Scotland Yard. It is, if this evidence is to be believed, a scandalously rattle-brained organization: trivialities are carefully guarded while grave secrets are given out freely: no member ever knows what his coworkers are up to. But we aren't in a position to criticize our cousins: here in the same book is an American Secret Service operative occupied with stolen necklaces and red plots, when he should be home guarding presidents, or chasing counterfeiters, or performing some of the other duties of his department, and in "The Benson Murder Case" the New York police and district attorney are not a bit less haphazard.

Alvin Benson is found sitting in a wicker chair in his living room, a book still in his hand, his legs crossed, and his body comfortably relaxed

in a lifelike position. He is dead. A bullet from an Army model Colt .45 automatic pistol, held some six feet away when the trigger was pulled, has passed completely through his head. That his position should have been so slightly disturbed by the impact of such a bullet at such a range is preposterous, but the phenomenon hasn't anything to do with the plot, so don't, as I did, waste time trying to figure it out. The murderer's identity becomes obvious quite early in the story. The authorities, no matter how stupid the author chose to make them, would have cleared up the mystery promptly if they had been allowed to follow the most rudimentary police routine. But then what would there have been for the gifted Vance to do?

This Philo Vance is in the Sherlock Holmes tradition and his conversational manner is that of a high-school girl who has been studying the foreign words and phrases in the back of her dictionary. He is a bore when he discusses art and philosophy, but when he switches to criminal psychology he is delightful. There is a theory that any one who talks enough on any subject must, if only by chance, finally say something not altogether incorrect. Vance disproves this theory: he manages always, and usually ridiculously, to be wrong. His exposition of the technique employed by a gentleman shooting another gentleman who sits six feet in front of him deserves a place in a *How to be a detective by mail* course.

To supply this genius with a field for his operations the author has to treat his policemen abominably. He doesn't let them ask any questions that aren't wholly irrelevant. They can't make inquiries of anyone who might know anything. They aren't permitted to take any steps toward learning whether the dead man was robbed. Their fingerprint experts are excluded from the scene of the crime. When information concerning a mysterious box of jewelry accidentally bobs up everybody resolutely ignores it, since it would have led to a solution before the three-hundredth page.

Mr. Van Dine doesn't deprive his officials of every liberty, however: he generously lets them compete with Vance now and then in the expression of idiocies. Thus Heath, a police detective-sergeant, says that any pistol of less than .44 calibre is too small to stop a man, and the district attorney, Markham, displays an amazed disinclina-

The Stratford Magazine

Followed her over barren fell and down where
    the laurels grow.
Years went by with the days in train as slow
    as oxen-drawn
Wains in the hills —— But why such rain of
    grief for Eileen bawn?"
"I am Donald." He wept a spell — then turned
    and staggered slow
        Up the hill and down again.

Yes

By DASHIELL HAMMETT

All complaisant in love was she,
With never a can't or no for me;
    A smiling yes, a beguiling yes,
    A you-must-wait-a-whiling yes,
But always a yes; to every plea
She'll acquiesce most readily.
    Her sole defect in love is this:
    She's seldom kept these promises.

Page thirty

The Stratford Magazine

Submission to the posturings of steel.
To fool it all I have allowed the Law,
And given all its due, and turned a heel.

What is there now? Ah, have you never ripped
Asunder the deep reticence of spheres
That hold within their adamantine crypt
The images of endless rounded years?
Then neither can you comprehend the man
Who roams the valleys where the rivers ran.

Goodbye to a Lady

By DASHIELL HAMMETT

Ink is a stain, however gay
    It sing,
However saintlily it say
    Some holy thing.

Consummate sanctity, utter gayness,
    Neither'd requite
You for the loss of the dilute grayness
    Called white.

No word the hovering pen had learned
    Was ever traced
On a page that now is turned——
    Emptily chaste.

Page thirty-one

In their theme of sexual frustration, these two poems are typical of Hammett's half-dozen published poems. Strat-ford Magazine, published in Boston, called itself "A Periodical for Creative Readers."

Hammett's first novel was published serially in five parts in Black Mask. *Renamed* Red Harvest *for book publication, this work was considered by Shaw to be a sequence of related short stories, not a novel.*

Hammett's first novel was submitted over the transom (that is, unsolicited) to Alfred A. Knopf Publishers. Mrs. Knopf, who supervised the firm's mystery list, accepted the novel for publication. It appeared on 1 February 1929.

The Cleansing of Poisonville 11

was wanted at the phone. She excused herself and followed the maid out. She didn't go downstairs, but spoke over an extension within earshot of my seat.

I heard: "Mrs. Willsson speaking . . . Yes . . . I beg your pardon? . . . Who? . . . Can't you speak a little louder? . . . *What?* . . . Yes . . . Yes . . . Who is this? . . . Hello! Hello!" The telephone hook rattled. Then her quick steps sounded down the hallway.

I set fire to a cigarette and stared at it until I heard her going downstairs. Than I went to a window, lifted the edge of the blind, and looked out at Laurel Avenue and at the small white garage that stood in the rear of the house on that side. Presently a slender woman in dark coat and hat came into sight, hurrying from house to garage. She drove away in a Buick coupé. It was Mrs. Willsson. I went back to my chair and waited.

Three-quarters of an hour went by. At five minutes past eleven automobile brakes screeched outside. Two minutes later Mrs. Willsson came into the room. She had taken off hat and coat. Her face was white, her eyes almost black.

"I'm awfully sorry." Her little tight-lipped mouth moved jerkily. "You've had all this waiting for nothing. My husband won't be home tonight."

I said I would get in touch with him at the *Herald* in the morning and went away—wondering why the green toe of her left slipper was dark and damp with something that could have been blood.

II

I WALKED over to Broadway and got into a street car. Three blocks north of my hotel I got off to see what the crowd was doing around a side entrance of the City Hall. Thirty or forty men and a sprinkling of women stood on the sidewalk looking at a door marked *Police Department*—a mixed crowd—men from mines and smelters still in their working clothes, gaudy boys from poolrooms and dance-halls, sleek men with cunning pale faces, men with the dull look of respectable fathers of families, a few just as respectable and dull women, and some ladies of the night.

On the edge of this congregation I stopped beside a square-set man in rumpled gray clothes. His face was grayish, too, even to the thick lips, though he didn't look much more than thirty—a broad, thick-featured face with intelligence in it. For color he depended on a red Windsor tie that blossomed over his gray flannel shirt.

"What's the rumpus?" I asked this fellow.

He looked at me carefully before he answered, as if to make sure that the information was going into safe hands. His eyes were as gray as his shirt, but not so soft.

"Don Willsson's gone to sit on the right hand of God—if God don't mind looking at the bullet holes in him."

"Who put them there?"

The gray man scratched the side of his neck and said: "Somebody with a gun."

I would have tried to find a less witty informant in the crowd if the red tie hadn't interested me.

"Sure. I'm a stranger in town," I said. "Hang the Punch and Judy on me—That's what strangers are for."

"Mr. Donald Willsson, publisher of the *Morning* and *Evening Heralds,* son of the well-known Mr. Elihu Willsson," he recited in a rapid sing-song, "was found lying in Hurricane Street a little while ago, very dead, having been shot several places. Does that keep your feelings from being hurt?"

"Yeah. Thanks." I put out a finger and touched a loose end of his tie. "Mean anything? Or just wearing it?"

"I'm Bill Quint."

"The hell you are!" I exclaimed, trying to place the name. "By gad, I'm glad to meet you!"

I dug out my card case and ran through the collection of credentials I

Red Harvest *was edited heavily for book publication under the guidance of Knopf editor Harry C. Block. The extent of the revision is demonstrated by these excerpts from the* Black Mask *and Knopf publications of the work.*

had picked up here and there by one means or another. The red card was the one I wanted. It identified me as Henry F. Brannan (a lie), member in good standing of Industrial Workers of the World, Seaman's No.——. I passed it to Bill Quint. He read it carefully, front and back, returned it to me, and looked me over from hat to shoes—not trustfully.

"He's not going to die again," he said. "Which way are you going?"

"Any."

We walked down the street together, turned a corner, strolled along—aimlessly so far as I knew.

"What brought you in here, if you're a sailor?" he asked casually.

"Where'd you get that idea?"

"There's the card."

"Yeah. I got another that proves I'm a timber-beast. If you want me to be a miner I'll get one for that tomorrow."

"'No, you won't. I run 'em here."

"Suppose you got a wire from Chi?" I asked.

"To hell with Chi. I run 'em here. Drink?"

"Only when I can get it."

We went through a restaurant, up a flight of stairs, and into a narrow room with a long bar and a row of tables. Bill Quint nodded and said, "Hello," to some of the boys and girls at tables and bar and guided me into one of the booths that lined the opposite wall. We spent the next two hours drinking whiskey and talking.

The gray man didn't think I was a good Wobbly, didn't think I had any right to the red card I had shown him and the other one I had mentioned. As chief muckademuck of the I. W. W. in Personville he considered it his duty to find out how-come, and not to let himself be pumped about radical affairs while he was doing it. That was all right with me. I was more interested in Personville affairs. He didn't mind discussing them. They were something he could hide behind between casual pokings into my business with the red cards, my radical status.

What I got out of him amounted to this:

For forty years old Elihu Willsson had owned Personville heart, skin, guts and soul. He was president and majority stockholder of the Personville Mining Corporation, ditto of the First National Bank, owner of the *Morning Herald* and the *Evening Herald*, the city's only newspapers, and at least part owner of nearly every other enterprise of any importance in the city. Along with this other property he owned a United States Senator, a couple of Representatives and most of the State Legislature. Elihu Willsson was Personville, and he was almost the whole state.

Back in the war days, when the I. W. W. was blooming, they had lined up a lot of the Personville Mining Corporation's help. The help hadn't been pampered, and they used their new strength to demand the things they wanted. Old Elihu gave in to them and bided his time. In 1919 it came. Business was slack. He didn't care whether he had to shut down for a while or not. He cut wages, lengthened hours, generally kicked the help back into their old place.

Of course the help had yelled for action. Bill Quint had been sent out from Chicago to give it to them. He had been against a strike—a walk-out. What he advised was the old sabotage racket, staying on the job and gumming things up from the inside. But the Personville crew wouldn't listen to him. They wanted to put themselves on the map, make labor history. So they struck.

The strike lasted eight months. Both sides bled plenty. The Wobblies had to do their own bleeding. Old Elihu could hire strike-breakers, gunmen, National Guardsmen and even parts of the regular army to do his. When the last skull had been cracked, the last rib kicked in, organized labor in Personville was a used firecracker.

into safe hands. His eyes were gray as his clothes, but not so soft.

"Don Willsson's gone to sit on the right hand of God, if God don't mind looking at bullet holes."

"Who shot him?" I asked.

The gray man scratched the back of his neck and said:

"Somebody with a gun."

I wanted information, not wit. I would have tried my luck with some other member of the crowd if the red tie hadn't interested me. I said:

"I'm a stranger in town. Hang the Punch and Judy on me. That's what strangers are for."

"Donald Willsson, Esquire, publisher of the *Morning* and *Evening Heralds*, was found in Hurricane Street a little while ago, shot very dead by parties unknown," he recited in a rapid singsong. "Does that keep your feelings from being hurt?"

"Thanks." I put out a finger and touched a loose end of his tie. "Mean anything? Or just wearing it?"

"I'm Bill Quint."

"The hell you are!" I exclaimed, trying to place the name. "By God, I'm glad to meet you!"

I dug out my card case and ran through the collection of credentials I had picked up here and there by one means or another. The red card was the one I wanted. It identified me as Henry F. Neill, A. B. seaman, member in good standing of the Industrial Workers of the World. There wasn't a word of truth in it.

ing for nothing. My husband won't be home tonight."

I said I would get in touch with him at the *Herald* in the morning.

I went away wondering why the green toe of her left slipper was dark and damp with something that could have been blood.

·   ·   ·

I WALKED over to Broadway and caught a street car. Three blocks north of my hotel I got off to see what the crowd was doing around a side entrance of the City Hall.

Thirty or forty men and a sprinkling of women stood on the sidewalk looking at a door marked *Police Department*. There were men from mines and smelters still in their working clothes, gaudy boys from pool rooms and dance halls, sleek men with slick pale faces, men with the dull look of respectable husbands, a few just as respectable and dull women, and some ladies of the night.

On the edge of this congregation I stopped beside a square-set man in rumpled gray clothes. His face was grayish too, even the thick lips, though he wasn't much older than thirty. His face was broad, thick-featured and intelligent. For color he depended on a red windsor tie that blossomed over his gray flannel shirt.

"What's the rumpus?" I asked him.

He looked at me carefully before he replied, as if he wanted to be sure that the information was going

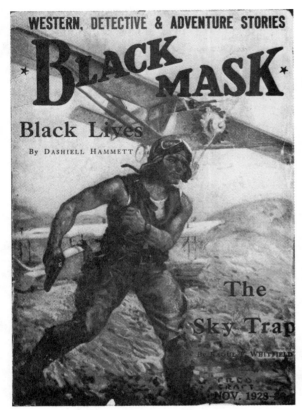

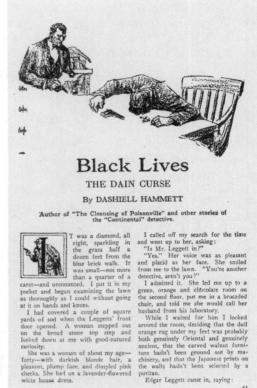

"Black Lives," Black Mask, November 1928. Three months before Red Harvest *was published, Black Mask began a four-part serialization of Hammett's second novel, again advertising it as a series of "adventures." The novel was published as* The Dain Curse.

Hammett's second novel was published by Knopf on 19 July 1929. Like Red Harvest, *it was retitled and substantially revised for book publication.*

tion to admit that a confession could actually be false. This Markham is an outrageously naïve person: the most credible statement in the tale is to the effect that Markham served only one term in this office. The book is written in the little-did-he-realize style.

"The Malaret Mystery" has to do with a death in Morocco. The reader is kept in rural England and the clues are brought to him through two or three or more hands. The result is a tiresomely slow and rambling story altogether without suspense, but this method does keep the solution concealed until the very last from those readers who have forgotten the plot, which is an old friend in not very new clothes. The motivation, if you are interested in that sort of thing, is pretty dizzy.

"Sea Fog," in spite of its rather free use of happenstance, is by far the best of this group. To the coast of Sussex comes a boy bound for the sea. In a deserted mill he spies on Kest and his map, in the morning fog he sees Kest killed, in the days that follow he sees more dead men. If toward the end these dead men turn up with almost mechanical regularity, Mr. Fletcher's skill keeps it from being too monotonous a process. But even that skill doesn't quite suffice to make the forced ending plausible. Poor old Scotland Yard is put up to silly tricks again. However, "Sea Fog" offers more than two hundred decidedly interesting pages.

Most of the fifteen stories in "The Massingham Butterfly" deal with crime in its milder forms. They are all mild stories, some of them obviously written long ago. There is no especial reason for anyone's reading them.

BOOK REVIEW:

Herbert Asbury, Review of *Red Harvest, Bookman,* (29 March 1929): 62

Herbert Asbury enjoyed a reputation as a novelist and journalist, but he was best known as the author of "Hatrack," the story which caused the April 1926 issue of H. L. Mencken's American Mercury *to be banned in Boston. Asbury was an unwavering advocate of Hammett's fiction.*

It is doubtful if even Ernest Hemingway has ever written more effective dialogue than may be found within the pages of this extraordinary tale of gunmen, gin and gangsters. The author displays a style of amazing clarity and compactness, devoid of literary frills and furbelows, and his characters, who race through the story with the rapidity and destructiveness of machine guns, speak the crisp, hard-boiled language of the underworld. Moreover, they speak it truly, without a single false or jarring note, for Mr. Hammett, himself an old-time Pinkerton detective, knows his crime and criminals through many years of personal contact. Those who begin to weary of the similarity of modern detective novels, with their clumsily involved plots and their artificial situations and conversations, will find their interest revived by this realistic, straightforward story, for it is concerned solely with fast and furious action and it introduces a detective who achieves his purposes without recourse to higher mathematics, necromancy or fanciful reasoning. It reads like the latest news from Chicago.

Mr. Hammett's hero, an operative of a private detective agency, who tells the story, is confronted by a mystery when he arrives in Personville, a western town so wicked that its citizens call it Poisonville, but it is a mystery of no particular consequence and he quickly gets to the bottom of it by simply employing common sense and his powers of observation.

Thereafter, he performs no miracles whatsoever. But in a moment of panic, soon regretted, Personville's big political and business boss hires him to rid the town of its gunmen and gangsters, and he proceeds to do the job by acting as a sort of *agent provocateur* among the criminal cliques, inciting one against the other by superb manoeuvering until in successive bursts of blazing fury they have destroyed themselves. He thus sets the local underworld by the ears and, in one way or another, he is concerned with no fewer than a score of killings. For a considerable period the detective is in doubt whether he may have committed one of the murders himself, for he awakens from a laudanum-and-gin debauch with the handle of an ice pick clutched in his hand and the steel sliver buried in a girl's breast. The chapter in which this excellent crime occurs is one of the high spots of the liveliest detective story that has been published in a decade.

BOOK REVIEW:

Walter R. Brooks, Review of *Red Harvest*, *Outlook and Independent*, 151 (13 February 1929): 274

Walter R. Brooks was a staff reviewer for the Outlook and Independent. *He was a short-story writer and author of a series of books for children.*

A thriller that lives up to the blurb on the jacket is unusual enough to command respect. When, in addition, it is written by a man who plainly knows his underworld and can make it come alive for his readers, when the action is exciting and the conversation racy and amusing–well, you'll want to read it. A detective from San Francisco goes to the city of Personville to break up the ring of thugs who control the town. He splits them into factions which turn the town into a battlefield. Knives and blackjacks and pistols and bombs and machine-guns have accounted for some twenty-five or thirty people by the time he finishes his job. And the book is full of vivid writing. The storming of Pete the Finn's stronghold in Whiskeytown is as real a fiction battle as we've ever attended.

We recommend this one without reservation. We gave it A plus before we'd finished the first chapter.

BOOK REVIEW:

E.S., Review of *Red Harvest*, *New Statesman*, 27 July 1929, p. 500.

In the beginning British readers had trouble accepting the verisimilitude of Hammett's novels, as this review demonstrates.

Red Harvest takes us to America again and to an almost inconceivable world. The English novelist who wants to write a story of peril and adventure has to go some distance from ordinary life. The municipal troubles of a small town would be of no service to him. The American novelist is luckier, for he can take train from New York or Chicago and, if Mr. Hammett is to be believed, find mediaeval violence and uncertainty co-existent with a good tram service. What troubles me about Mr. Hammett's book is that his hero is so often shot at without being hit. This, in the romantic stories which transport us to Ruritania or some such neighbourhood, seems reasonable enough. When we begin to read such a book we consent to being transported into a fairy-tale atmosphere, where the eventual safety and triumph of the hero are, as it were, certified on the title-page. But it is not easy to reconcile this convention with the realistic atmosphere of the modern American story of adventure. Mr. Hammett's hero seems to me to come alive out of page after page by sheer good luck, and if his luck had ever failed, then there would have been an end to Mr. Hammett's story. But the mere fact that an author of obvious intelligence can write such a tale and persuade an American publisher to print it throws a valuable light on American conditions. If there is anywhere on the North American continent a town even remotely like Personville, then it is a sociological phenomenon which we must take into our reckoning, and I cannot believe that Mr. Hammett has made up Personville purely out of his desire to have a background for sensational happenings.

INTRODUCTION:

Dashiell Hammett, Introduction to *The Maltese Falcon*, (New York: Modern Library, 1934).

The inclusion of The Maltese Falcon *in The Modern Library was a recognition of the book's enduring quality. In his introduction Hammett described how the novel was conceived.*

If this book had been written with the help of an outline or notes or even a clearly defined plot-idea in my head I might now be able to say how it came to be written and why it took the shape it did, but all I can remember about its invention is that somewhere I had read of the peculiar rental agreement between Charles V and the Order of the Hospital of St. John of Jerusalem, that in a short story called THE WHOSIS KID I had failed to make the most of a situation I liked, that in another called THE GUTTING OF COUFFIGNAL I had been equally unfortunate with an equally promising dénouement, and that I thought I might have better luck with these two failures if I combined them with the Maltese lease in a longer story.

I can remember more clearly where I got most of my characters.

The Maltese Falcon *was published in five monthly parts between September 1929 and January 1930. It was the first of Hammett's works Shaw promoted as a novel.*

On 14 June, before the novel began serialization in Black Mask, *Hammett sent* The Maltese Falcon *to Harry Block at Knopf, warning him in a letter mailed two days later to go easy on the editing. Knopf published Hammett's third novel on 14 February 1930 with only minor editorial changes made in response to Block's squeamishness about sexual content. The novel was reprinted seven times in its first year of publication.*

The World March 10, 1930

"BETTER THAN HEMINGWAY!

since it conceals not softness but hardness. He stands alone as an ace shocker... Even S. S. Van Dine must lower his monocle. It is everything you want."—Ted Shane, *Judge.*

"Mr. Hammett should turn out to be the great American Mystery Writer."—Will Cuppy

"He is raising the detective story to that plane to which Alexandre Dumas raised the historical novel." —Carl Van Vechten

"Probably the best detective story we have ever read."—Walter Brooks

"Consider an amalgamation of Hemingway, W. R. Burnett... Morley Callaghan and Ring Lardner... you would have a fair idea of the style and technique of Mr. Hammett."—William Curtis, *Town and Country.*

Merely a few quotations from the ecstatic press reception given THE MALTESE FALCON, by Dashiell Hammett. *At all bookshops, $2.50*

Alfred
A·Knopf   BORZOI BOOKS   730
Fifth Ave.

The World, March 11, 1930

"I FIND IT HARD TO FIGURE OUT

a way to tell you how good a book THE MALTESE FALCON is."

"The horsepower of Mr. Hammett's pen, especially in his brutal and very 'different' ending, must be sampled to be believed... *The Maltese Falcon* is the best one in Lord knows when."—Will Cuppy.

"Hammett writes with a lead pipe and poisoned arrows as coups-de-grace. He stands alone as an ace-shocker. *The Maltese Falcon* is the 'Broadway' of mysteries and should have been chosen by a bookclub... It's swell."—Ted Shane, *Judge.*

"He is raising the detective story to that plane to which Alexandre Dumas raised the historical novel."—Carl Van Vechten.

Just a few of the nice things that are being said about THE MALTESE FALCON by Dashiell Hammett. Still unconvinced? Read it and see.

At all bookshops, $2.50

Alfred
A·Knopf   BORZOI BOOKS   730
Fifth Ave.

These ads for Hammett's third novel appeared on 10 and 11 March 1930 in The New York World

Wilmer, the boy gun-man, was picked up in Stockton, California, where I had gone hunting a window-smasher who had robbed a San Jose jewelry store. Wilmer's original was not my window-smasher, unfortunately, but he was a fair pick-up. He was a neat small smooth-faced quiet boy of perhaps twenty-one. He said he was only seventeen, but that was probably an attempt to draw a reform school instead of a penitentiary sentence. He also said his father was a lieutenant of police in New York, which may or may not have been true, and he was serenely proud of the name the local newspapers gave him–The Midget Bandit. He had robbed a Stockton filling station the previous week. In Los Angeles a day or two later, reading a Stockton newspaper–there must be criminals who subscribe to clipping services–he had been annoyed by the description the filling-station proprietor had given of him and by the proprietor's statement of what he would do to that little runt if he ever laid eyes on him again. So The Midget Bandit had stolen an automobile and returned to Stockton to, in his words, stick that guy up again and see what he wanted to do about it.

Brigid O'Shaughnessy had two originals, one an artist, the other a woman who came to Pinkerton's San Francisco office to hire an operative to discharge her housekeeper, but neither of these women was a criminal.

Dundy's prototype I worked with in a North Carolina railroad yard; Cairo's I picked up on a forgery charge in Pasco, Washington, in 1920; Polhaus's was a former captain of detectives; I used to buy books from Iva's in Spokane; Effie's once asked me to go into the narcotic smuggling business with her in San Diego; Gutman's was suspected–foolishly, as most people were–of being a German secret agent in Washington, D.C., in the early days of the war, and I never remember shadowing a man who bored me as much.

Spade had no original. He is a dream man in the sense that he is what most of the private detectives I worked with would like to have been and what quite a few of them in their cockier moments thought they approached. For your private detective does not–or did not ten years ago when he was my colleague–want to be an erudite solver of riddles in the Sherlock Holmes manner; he wants to be a hard and shifty fellow, able to take care of himself in any situation, able to get the best of anybody he comes in contact with, whether criminal, innocent by-stander or client.

DASHIELL HAMMETT.
New York, January 24, 1934.

REVIEW ARTICLE:
William Curtis, "Some Recent Books," *Town & Country*, 15 February 1930.

The Maltese Falcon *marked a broadening of Hammett's reputation as he was discovered by reviewers who normally took little notice of mystery fiction. In the upper-middle-class slick magazine* Town & Country, *William Curtis favorably compared Hammett with Ernest Hemingway, among others.*

I believe I have discovered a new technique in the writing of murder-mystery stories and a new technician. His name is Dashiell Hammett and, in the last six months, Alfred A. Knopf has published three of his tales, "Red Harvest," "The Dain Curse" and "The Maltese Falcon." Of these, I have read the first and the last. First, as murder mysteries, they live up to the requirements of the type. There is an intricate, fast-moving plot in each of the two I have read. The so-called element of suspense is carefully appreciated by Mr. Hammett. But their significance to me goes much deeper than the question of plot structure. For the first time in my knowledge, the American policeman and police detective has been adequately represented in fiction. Now I have no personal knowledge of what the British police official is really like. There have, however, been such a number of British writers about the work of Scotland Yard and the various British Government Secret Service subsidiaries and they all agree so generally in their major outline, that all English-speaking peoples have a very fair idea of what the British policeman either is or would like to be considered as being. Until Mr. Hammett appeared, however, no American writer has taken the detective novel seriously enough to do more than ape the outstanding characteristics of the British school. Our most popular writer on this subject, the dangerously versatile Willard Huntington Wright, after he had tired of writing authoritatively on the ultra-modern art, set himself out to invent a super-eccentric detective to outdo the original Sherlock Holmes. He succeeded in his Philo Vance stories. With the single exception of Mr. Wright, alias S. S. Van Dine, we have no other one writer, American writer, that is, of murder mystery stories whose tales could possibly be considered as even a subsidiary of literature.

It is an ungracious act to compare one writer to another, but it is vastly time saving. With this apology made, if you were to consider an amalgamation of Mr. Hemingway, the Mr. Burnet who wrote "Little Cæsar" and "Iron Man," that other disciple of Hemingway, Morley Callaghan, and Ring Lardner in his prize-fighting aspect, you would have a fair idea of the style and technique of Mr. Hammett. His murder-mystery stories are not only plots, they are studies of character; and are as definite a contribution to our knowledge of the life of a modern gangster as is anything that has been written so far in this country. His first book, "Red Harvest," is the story of the cleaning up of a Western mining town which had fallen into the hands of four strong-armed bootleggers. The story is told in the first person by an operative of a private detective agency. Before taking to his typewriter, Mr. Hammett was for years with the Pinkertons. We are all the time hearing about the hard-boiled in literature. The first time I have actually seen it in print is in "Red Harvest." It perhaps seems stronger in that it is told in the first person. The operative who is the voice coming over the microphone describes his own actions and those of the people with whom he associates in a cold-blooded, matter-of-fact manner that, if it is meant to carry shock content, definitely succeeds. There is less beating about the bush, less mealy-mouthedness, more directness, more staccato action, in the pages of "Red Harvest" than in any other one publication I remember recently.

Also, there is a considerable quantity of very adroit writing. One thinks of Hemingway but, with the thought, one feels that Mr. Hammett is not imitating anybody but is writing in his own style and manner. Here is a typical piece of description: His employer has sent for him in the middle of the night; he comes in and finds that a man has tried to break in and has been shot. "A short, thick-set man in brown lay on his back with dead eyes staring at the ceiling from under the visor of a gray cap. A piece of his jaw had been knocked off. His chin was tilted to show where another bullet had gone through tie and collar to make a hole in his neck. One arm was bent under him. The other hand held a blackjack as big as a milk bottle. There was a lot of blood." He succeeds in cleaning up the town by the simple expedient of having the gangsters kill each other off. Here is his description of the final fight: "We waited a moment, and then Pete the Finn appeared in the dynamited doorway, his hands holding the top of his bald head. In the glare from the burning next-door house we could see that his face was cut, his clothes almost all torn off. Stepping over wreckage, the bootlegger came slowly down the steps to the sidewalk. Reno called him a lousy fish-eater and shot him four times in face and body. Pete went down. A man behind me laughed. . . . The other machine slowed up for us to climb aboard. It was already full. We packed it in layers, with the overflow hanging on the running boards. We bumped over dead Hank O'Marra's legs and headed for home. We covered one block of the distance with safety if not comfort. After that we had neither. A limousine turned into the street ahead of us, came half a block toward us, put its side to us, and stopped. Out of the side, gun-fire. Another car came around the limousine and charged us. Out of it, gun-fire. We did our best, but were too damned amalgamated for good fighting. You can't shoot straight holding a man in your lap, another hanging on your shoulder, while a third does his shooting from an inch behind your ear. . . . It was a sweet mess." There is about Mr. Hammett's writing, of which I have picked this out as perhaps the best purple patch, an air of being unstudied, of being his natural method of expression. About the Hemingway periods there is always an aroma of preoccupation, of having been studied a bit too long, of having been rewritten just once too often.

Mr. Hammett also has very considerable skill in his technique as a writer. Take these phrases from "The Maltese Falcon": "Spade said nothing in a blank-faced definite way. . . . 'He went like that, like a fist when you open your hand.' " He can do the rough humor and the brutal dialect of his gangsters and their women: " ' . . . Before he could go on with his shouting. 'And if you don't yell maybe I'll be able to hear you anyway. My deafness is a lot better since I've been eating yeast.'

He put a fist on top of each hump his thighs made in the covers and pushed his square chin at me. 'Old as I am and sick as I am,' he said very deliberately, 'I've a great mind to get up and kick your behind.' . . . 'Grease us twice!' His greenish eyes glittered happily. 'Are you telling me the Whisper was there? Yeah?' He threw his cigar on the floor, stood up, planted his fat hands on the desk top, and leaned over them toward me, oozing delight from every pore. 'Man, you've done something,' he purred. 'Dinah Brand is this Whisper's woman. Let's me and you just go out and kind of talk to the widow.' " And so on, and so on, and so on. One could go on quoting indefinitely. There is another thing Mr. Hammett does which, from the point of view of pure literature, is even more interesting. That is his introduction onto the printed page of words and expressions which we all use colloquially but which have not yet found their way into that formal English which still adheres to the academic traditions as formulated by Samuel Johnson. By this I mean such things as the following phrases: "As chief muckademuck of the I. W. W. in Personville. . . . She was strictly pay-as-you-enter. . . . I yes-yes'd her. . . . Max carries a .38, and anybody he sent to do the job would have had that much gun or more. . . . The next squirt of light. . . . I hit her door and asked how come. . . . Can I hide behind the sanctity of my clients' secrets and identities and whatnot, all the same priest or lawyer?" This is good writing, it's vigorous writing, it is personal writing. It has character. It has sincerity. It is essentially in the modern feeling.

It may surprise Mr. Hammett to be compared to the Hemingway-Burnet-Callaghan group. To my mind, however, speaking purely as one who has been following the progress of the novel for yahrs and yahrs and yahrs, I think Mr. Hammett has something quite as definite to say, quite as decided an impetus to give the course of newness in the development of the American tongue, as any man now writing. Of course, he's gone about it the wrong way to attract respectful attention from the proper sources. He's never been in Paris, has never played around with the Little Review group. He has not been picked up by any of the foghorn columnists. He's only a writer of murder mystery stories.

BOOK REVIEW:
Donald Douglas, "Not One Hoot for the Law," *New Republic*, 62 (9 April 1930): 226.

This review of The Maltese Falcon *in the self-conciously intellectual magazine* New Republic *is a further example of the critical opinion that Hammett's third novel achieved what Douglas calls "the absolute distinction of real art."*

Let's get down to brass knuckles and argue that no one has any business reading detective stories because they're read by tired presidents, or because they teach coppers how to have and hold a crook. In real life, the important thing is to catch the murderer in the quickest round-up. In fiction, the important thing is *not* to catch the murderer for two hundred pages. And if in real life, our jaded presidents and unemployed wives find "escape" in detective fiction, then so do all readers of Norse myths and the Scotch ballads and the exploits of romantic cowboys. The real, right detective story *is* and should be a myth wherein the demigod (disguised as a superman) pursues the demon-crook through the tangled maze of heart-shuddering adventure. For "real" murders, you have the dullness of courtroom scenes and the dull evidence given by two-fisted dicks.

Until the coming of Mr. Dashiell Hammett in "Red Harvest" and now in "The Maltese Falcon," the memorable detectives were gentlemen. The ever-delightful M. Lecoq and his copy, Mr. Sherlock Holmes, are fair gods against the gnomes. Their only worthy successor, Father Brown, is a priest. Scratch every other detective and you'll find a M. Lecoq. Now comes Mr. Hammett's tough guy in "Red Harvest" and his Sam Spade in "The Maltese Falcon," and you find the Pinkerton operative as a scoundrel without pity or remorse, taking his whiffs of drink and his casual amours between catching crooks, treating the police with a cynical contempt, always getting his crook by foul and fearless means, above the law like a satyr–and Mr. Hammett describing his deeds in a glistening and fascinating prose as "American" as Lardner's, and every bit as original in musical rhythm and bawdy humor.

There is nothing like these books in the whole range of detective fiction. The plots don't

Saturday, January 3, 1931.   THE EVENING STANDARD.

Something New in Detective Fiction.

THE MALTESE FALCON

By Dashiell Hammett,

WHO TELLS OF Samuel Spade, relentless sleuth; of medieval treasure of fabulous worth; of a beautiful and mysterious Irish girl; of a desperate gang of international criminals; of murder—of thrill after thrill.

On another page to-day we print the first instalment of a very rare literary phenomenon—a detective story by a real detective. The history of Mr. Dashiell Hammett's life has been, in its way, as strange and unexpected as the histories he writes of other people's lives. A Pinkerton's man to begin with, he found his health so much injured by war service that his return to his old profession did not last long. But, fortunately for him and for great numbers of readers, he found at the same time that he could write, and that so well that very shortly it became apparent that there was no further need for him to trouble himself about anything else.

Now in real life the profession of a detective is not as a rule a romantic one, nor are detectives usually at all romantic persons. The tasks they have to carry out, necessary as they may be, are generally humdrum and often sordid. It is not a life which stimulates the imagination, and those who follow it are very infrequently imaginative persons. In this, at least, the old type of detective story, in which the amateur always outshone the professional, was right enough. Where it was wrong was in postulating the brilliant amateur. The hunting out of crime is almost always, in practice, the accumulation of a great heap of uninteresting details.

The professional detective who turns novelist has a tendency to bring the prosaic nature of his training even into what he intends to be his wildest flights of fancy. Further, the expert in any subject has always a tendency, whatever his desire may be, to write for other experts rather than for the public at large. Where anything in the way of entertainment is involved too much knowledge is a very dangerous thing indeed. The expert supposes that technical points which interest him and his colleagues must interest everyone else: he is afraid of leaving unexplained some trivial detail on which a fellow expert will seek to trip him up.

Now in this sort of fiction the public does not want scientific accuracy, but it does want movement, and these two things are often in conflict. That conflict Mr. Hammett has known how to avoid. He is not muscle-bound with too much knowledge. He moves as freely as though he were in the realm of fairyland and free imagination—and it is an assured fact that the best of all detective stories take place in fairylands of their own. But he provides an atmosphere of realism evidently drawn from his own experience. He really has made the best of both worlds, and that is a very remarkable and unusual performance.

On another page the readers of the "Evening Standard" will be able to follow the adventures of Sam Spade and his associates in pursuit of the Maltese Falcon. It is not in our province now to tell them what the adventures are going to be, and we are quite sure tha̱ ... ̱anḵ us for doing so. ... ̱ are sure also of another thing, that when they come to the end of them they will realise that they have been for a time in another world, which, whether it exists or not, certainly ought to exist, so strange and varied and exciting are the things that can happen in this world the ex-detective has created. We might not, perhaps, care to live in it in the flesh: it is a little too exciting for that—but we must be grateful for this vivid glimpse of it.

Six months after its English book publication, Hammett's novel was serialized in a London newspaper.

matter so much. The art does; and there is an absolute distinction of real art. It is (in its small way) like Wagner writing about the gnomes in "Rheingold." The gnomes have an eloquence of speech and a fascinating mystery of disclosure. Don't get me wrong, bo. It's not the tawdry gumshoeing of the ten-cent magazine. It is the genuine presence of the myth. The *events* of "The Maltese Falcon" may have happened that way in "real" life. No one save Mr. Hammett could have woven them to such a silver-steely mesh.

BOOK REVIEW:
Will Cuppy, "Mystery and Adventure," *New York Herald Tribune*, 23 February 1930, p. 17.

Will Cuppy wrote one of the most prominent book-review columns in America. As he admits here, his enthusiasm for Hammett was late in developing.

This department announces a new and pretty huge enthusiasm, to wit: Dashiell Hammett. Moreover, it would not surprise us one whit if Mr. Hammett should turn out to be the Great American Mystery Writer. (The fact is, he may be that right now, and this department is merely hopping aboard the Hammett bandwagon ere it be too late–Herbert Asbury, Walter Brooks and Joseph Shaw have already discovered him.) The utterly convincing quality of Mr. Hammett's detective, Sam Spade, is the big news about "The Maltese Falcon"; Sam's 100 per cent authenticity is powerful enough to make one believe in the jeweled bird once presented by the Knights of Rhodes to the Emperor Charles V–a gadget which might turn up in almost any thriller. Add some most effective tricks of narrative and a satisfactory species of hard-boiled prose to his credit, too, not to mention a slick plot boasting of three murders incidental to a search for the rara avis in San Francisco. The horsepower of Mr. Hammett's pen, especially in his brutal and very "different" ending, must be sampled to be believed–of a mystery author. In short, "The Maltese Falcon" is the best one, outside the gay and polite classes, in Lord knows when. Read it and see.

BOOK REVIEW:
"Judging the Books," *Judge*, 1 March 1930.

The humor magazine Judge *was unequivocal in its praise for Hammett's work.*

Should you stumble on a frantic hundred-and-fifty pounder at Madison and Forty-eighth Street booing unheeding passersby; or if later in the day you should come on him pounding on bars, rudely accosting lady shoppers, insulting traffic cops and generally making himself painful around town, that would be us expressing ourself against him who hasn't read Dashiell Hammett. That twenty-minute hard-boiled boy has swept all the dilettante and drawing-room detecatiffs with their tiddledy-wink, card trick and cross-word puzzle mysteries out of Crime Hall and dragged in a free-for-all instead.

He writes with a lead-pipe and poisoned arrows as coups de grace. He stands alone as ace shocker. Hereafter even S. S. Van Dine must lower his monocle, cough up the encyclopedia and eat some humble pie.

We paeaned Hammett's "Red Harvest" till we went blue in the face and other publishers offered us bribes to lay off and give their tittivators a break. It was the pearl of underworld stories, and suggested the nice idea that the way to exterminate killers would be to let them slaughter themselves off. Then came "The Dain Curse," a love-cult mystery, overloaded with plot but 90 per cent pure bonanza. And now "The Maltese Falcon," a button-button-who's-got-the-falcon? of San Francisco.

It is everything you want. The conventional ingredients of the typical guess-who are there but so handled as to bring on maximum blood pressure. The characters are hard, hatable and out of police headquarters family albums. Sam Spade, the private dick, is harder than Hammett himself. The writing is better than Hemingway; since it conceals not softness but hardness. It is the "Broadway" of mysteries and should have been chosen by a book club. Still unconvinced? Well, it's swell.

BOOK REVIEW:
Review of *The Maltese Falcon, Times Literary Supplement*, 14 August 1930, p. 654.

The staid TLS *offered a more cautious assessment of Hammett's novel than American reviewers did.*

Newspaper advertisement

so the story goes, the bird disappeared, until at length it was traced to an antique dealer in Paris, and later to the home of a Russian general in Constantinople. Here Mr. Gutman, a wealthy American, gets news of the bird, which has been covered with a coat of black enamel to hide its value from curious eyes. He hires two members of a gang, a beautiful, unscrupulous young woman and an overdressed Greek, to steal the bird for him. They succeed in doing so, but each is suspicious of the other, so the girl sneaks the bird on board a ship at Hong-kong, with instructions that it is to await her arrival in San Francisco. A detective is hired by other members of the gang to secure possession of the falcon–though when he finally does so, and presents it to Mr. Gutman, it is discovered that——. A good "thriller."

MOVIE REVIEW:
Mordaunt Hall, Review of *Roadhouse Nights, New York Times*, 22 February 1930, p. 13.

With the success of The Maltese Falcon, *Hammett attracted the attention of major studios in Hollywood. The first movie made from his work was* Roadhouse Nights. *In fact, the movie has a tenuous connection with* Red Harvest, *on which it is ostensibly based.*

Roadhouse Nights, with Helen Morgan, Charles Ruggles, Fred Kohler, Jimmy Durante, Fuller Mellish Jr., Leo Donnelly, Tammany Young, Joe King, Lou Clayton and Eddie Jackson, based on a story by Ben Hecht, directed by Hobart Henley; "Hollywood on Broadway," staged by Jack Partington, with Charles Rogers, Paul Ash, Allen and Canfield, Harriett Lee, Paul Small, Worthy and Thompson and others; Jesse Crawford, organist. At the Paramount Theatre.

Helen Morgan, who was last seen in "Applause," is one of the featured players in "Roadhouse Nights," an audible film story of politics and bootlegging now at the Paramount. This picture has been produced with a sense of drama and also a sense of humor. There are moments when the impossible is accomplished, but as Hobart Henley has directed it so intelligently one is willing to accept them, together with convenient coincidences, as interesting imaginative feats.

After the Knights of Rhodes had been expelled by Suleiman the Magnificent in 1523 they settled in Crete, by the grace of the Emperor Charles V., and persuaded him to give them Malta. But as a condition the Emperor demanded every year a falcon in acknowledgment that Malta was still under Spanish rule. The Knights hit upon the idea of sending Charles not an insignificant stuffed bird, but a falcon of chaste workmanship, made of gold and encrusted with jewels. For more than seventy years,

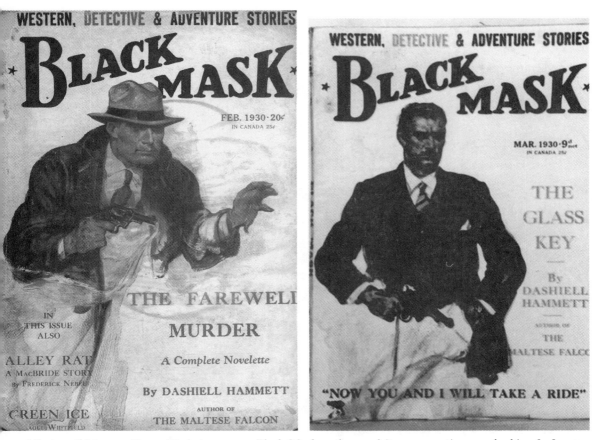

Nineteen thirty was Hammett's last year as a Black Mask *author, and it was an active year for him. In January the last installment of* The Maltese Falcon *was published; in February, his story "The Farewell Murder" was featured on the cover as "A Complete Novelette"; and in March the first of four monthly installments of Hammett's fourth novel,* The Glass Key, *was published.*

Ben Hecht, author of "Underworld," is responsible for the story, and his work is strong enough to withstand studio attacks. Perhaps it inspired Mr. Henley and the players, for one cannot point to a single disappointing performance in this film nor to a scene that does not hold the attention.

Charles Ruggles, well-known for his characterizations of inebriates, is perceived in this tale both drunk and sober. It falls to his lot to talk a lot of twaddle over the telephone to the city editor of a Chicago newspaper and at the same time to tick off by dots and dashes the story of a murder by rum-runners and the fact that a chief of police of a suburb of the Windy City is one of the leading figures in a liquor ring. One can't help thinking while Willie Bindbugel (Mr. Ruggles) stands in the telephone booth, with a desperate bootlegger a few yards away, and talks in one line and uses the Morse code in another, that he is straining his mighty brain. Be that as it may, the message is quite successful.

While this is going on, one also wonders why Sam Horner, the bootlegger, played by Fred Kohler, does not grasp what's happening, for he appears to be intelligent if lawless.

In a final episode of this narrative, Helen Morgan, as Lola Fagan, takes a leaf out of "Broadway" and saves her old-time sweetheart, Bindbugel, by putting a bullet through Horner's heart. This is accomplished with stirring effect and without the tried and trusted methods of old movie tactics.

Yes, that was Mr. Hammett . . . Started writing in *Black Mask* . . . Still writing for us . . . We know him . . . And thought he would be great . . . But it took the *Black Mask* stories published in book form . . . To wake up the country . . . As to how great he really is . . . We get 'em in *Black Mask* first . . . And the critics wait for them in books . . . And then say how good they are . . . Fair enough . . .

HAPSBURG LIEBE who wrote RED DICE . . . In this issue . . . Tells us . . . "We have an honest-to-goodness cow country . . . Here in Florida . . . One outfit runs 200,000 . . . Head of cattle . . . A round-up is a 'cow-hunt' . . . Earmarks are considered . . . More important than brands . . . The Florida cowpoke uses a twenty-odd foot stock whip . . . With which he can cut a snake's head off . . . And take a cigarette out of your mouth . . . (Not mine, thank you kindly) . . . And never touch hide." . . .

GEORGE C. KERN of Buffalo writes . . . "I'd walk ten miles if necessary to get my copy of *Black Mask*" . . . Edward W. Jewell, of Vancouver, writes . . . "Mr. Gardner is a gifted writer . . . I hope he will soon get out Black Barr and dust him off" . . . L. B. Kohnen, of Mt. Healthy, O., writes . . . "I wish *Black Mask* was published weekly instead of monthly" . . . (He should have a heart!) . . . Upton Meriwether, Box 505, Clovis, N. M. . . . Boosts the idea of Behind the Mask and says . . . "I'd like to get acquainted with some of the other *Black Mask* readers" . . . Bruce Griss, of Jersey, Channel Islands, Great Britain, writes . . . "We have not a magazine in Europe to equal *Black Mask*" . . . Mrs. Susie Murphy, of Charleston, West Va., asks . . . "Why can't we have some more stories of the Rev. MacGregor Daunt?" . . . (Attention of J. Paul Suter) . . . Well—Here's the music . . . Write your own words . . .

J. T. S.

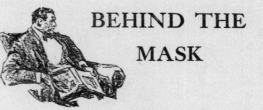

BEHIND THE MASK

YO-HO-HO . . . And a bottle of mucilage . . . And a pair of shears . . . We are busy . . . Cutting clippings . . . The papers are full of them . . . Also the mail . . . And here are a few . . . Will Cuppy says "He should turn out to be the great American mystery writer" . . . Carl Van Vechten says "He is raising the detective story to the plane Alexandre Dumas raised the historical novel" . . . Walter Brooks says "Probably the best detective story we have ever read" . . . Ted Shane says "Better than Hemingway. It is everything you want." . . . Eugene Cunningham says "The outstanding writer in the field of detective fiction." . . . Bruce Barton says "Thanks for the enjoyment you have given me." . . . There are lots more . . . But these are the best critics in America . . . Wait a moment . . . Perhaps we can get him over to the mike . . . Yes, here he comes . . . Ladies and gentlemen . . .

Dashiell   Hammett

"Hello Folks . . . Glad to be with you . . . Will tell you a story of an Agency Op very soon . . . Thanks a lot . . ."

119

Joseph Shaw was a tireless promoter of his authors, as this piece demonstrates. The Continental Op story Hammett promised was "Death and Company," his last appearance in the magazine.

[124]

In the beginning James Hanson, a reporter, is sent out by his city editor to look up a report on Horner's bootlegging activities. Hanson calls up to tell the result of his investigation to the newspaper and the city editor is seen listening at the telephone to Hanson, whose voice is heard. Suddenly the talking ceases. In another scene Horner is perceived putting his pistol back in his pocket and then taking a paper with penciled notes from Hanson, who is dead.

The city editor presumes that Hanson has been drinking, and so he sends Bindbugel out to follow up the story. Mr. Bindbugel has little knowledge of the den of iniquity run by Horner. He meets Lola, whom he recognizes as a girl from his home town. How he subsequently is sent away after being drugged and then returns is a mixture of comedy and drama. His persistence finally wins out, but he would have paid for it with his life had not Lola been ready with a pistol.

Horner's retreat is filmed impressively, for everybody in it, from the entertainers to the waiters and cook, have the appearance of desperadoes. Horner is a ruthless gunman, who expects to be obeyed or he will know the reason why.

Miss Morgan gives a human interpretation to the role of Lola. Mr. Ruggles is capital as the persistent reporter, and Fred Kohler lends to his part the necessary authority.

REVIEW COLUMN:

"The Crime Wave" [excerpts], *New York Evening Post*, 7 June 1930, p. 54; 3 July 1930, p. 55.

From April to October 1930 Hammett wrote a bi-weekly mystery book-review column for the New York Evening Post, *reviewing as many as thirteen books per column. In the columns of 7 June and 3 July, he expressed his dismay at the quality of the novels he was asked to read.*

. . . A fellow who takes detective stories seriously, I am annoyed by the stupid recurrence of these same blunders in book after book. It would be silly to insist that nobody who has not been a detective should write detective stories, but it is certainly not unreasonable to ask any one who is going to write a book of any sort to make some effort at least to learn something about his subject.

Most writers do. Only detective story writers seem to be free from a sense of obligation in this direction and, curiously, the more established and prolific detective story writers seem to be the worst offenders. Nearly all writers of Western tales at least get an occasional glimpse of their chosen territory from a car-window while en route to Hollywood, writers of sea stories have been seen on the waterfront; surely detective story writers could afford to speak to policemen now and then.

Meanwhile, a couple of months' labor in this arena has convinced me that the following suggestions might be of value to somebody:

(1) There was an automatic revolver, the Webley-Fosbery, made in England some years ago. The ordinary automatic pistol, however, is not a revolver. A pistol, to be a revolver, must have something on it that revolves.

(2) The Colt's .45 automatic pistol has no chambers. The cartridges are put in a magazine.

(3) A silencer may be attached to a revolver, but the effect will be altogether negligible. I have never seen a silencer used on an automatic pistol, but am told it would cause the pistol to jam. A silencer may be used on a single-shot target pistol or on a rifle, but both would still make quite a bit of noise. "Silencer" is a rather optimistic name for this device which has generally fallen into disuse.

(4) When a bullet from a Colt's .45, or any firearm of approximately the same size and power, hits you, even if not in a fatal spot, it usually knocks you over. It is quite upsetting at any reasonable range.

(5) A shot or stab wound is simply felt as a blow or push at first. It is some little time before any burning or other painful sensation begins.

(6) When you are knocked unconscious you do not feel the blow that does it.

(7) A wound made after death of the wounded is usually recognizable as such.

(8) Fingerprints of any value to the police are seldom found on anybody's skin.

(9) The pupils of many drug-addicts' eyes are apparently normal.

(10) It is impossible to see anything by the flash of an ordinary gun, though it is easy to imagine you have seen things.

(11) Not nearly so much can be seen by moonlight as you imagine. This is especially true of colors.

(12) All Federal snoopers are not members of the Secret Service. That branch is chiefly occupied with pursuing counterfeiters and guarding Presidents and prominent visitors to our shores.

(13) A sheriff is a county officer who usually has no official connection with city, town or state police.

(14) Federal prisoners convicted in Washington, D.C., are usually sent to the Atlanta prison and not to Leavenworth.

(15) The California State prison at San Quentin is used for convicts serving first terms. Two-time losers are usually sent to Folsom.

(16) Ventriloquists do not actually "throw" their voices and such doubtful illusions as they manage depend on their gestures. Nothing at all could be done by a ventriloquist standing behind his audience.

(17) Even detectives who drop their final g's should not be made to say "anythin' "–an oddity that calls for vocal acrobatics.

(18) "Youse" is the plural of "you."

(19) A trained detective shadowing a subject does not ordinarily leap from doorway to doorway and does not hide behind trees and poles. He knows no harm is done if the subject sees him now and then.

(20) The current practice in most places in the United States is to make the coroner's inquest an empty formality in which nothing much is brought out except that somebody has died.

(21) Fingerprints are fragile affairs. Wrapping a pistol or other small object up in a handkerchief is much more likely to obliterate than to preserve any prints it may have.

(22) When an automatic pistol is fired the empty cartridge-shell flies out the right-hand side. The empty cartridge-case remains in a revolver until ejected by hand.

(23) A lawyer cannot impeach his own witness.

(24) The length of time a corpse has been a corpse can be approximated by an experienced physician, but only approximated, and the longer it has been a corpse, the less accurate the approximation is likely to be.

LETTER:

Memo From David O. Selznick, edited by Rudy Behlmer (New York: Viking, 1972), pp. 26-27.

David O. Selznick, then executive assistant to Paramount Studio chief B. P. Schulberg (father of novelist Budd Schulberg), wrote this memo to his boss. The result was a contract for Hammett. In one weekend, Hammett wrote a seven-page manuscript titled "After School." After much revision, it was produced under director Rouben Mamoulian as City Streets. *The final screenplay credit was to "Oliver H. P. Garrett from an adaptation by Max Moran of Dashiell Hammett's original story." The movie starred Gary Cooper, Sylvia Sidney, Paul Lukas, and William Boyd. Hammett severed connections with Paramount at the end of 1930.*

To: Mr. B. P. Schulberg

July 18, 1930

We have an opportunity to secure Dashiell Hammett to do one story for us before he goes abroad in about three months.

Hammett has recently created quite a stir in literary circles by his creation of two books for Knopf, *The Maltese Falcon* and *Red Harvest*. I believe that he is another Van Dine–indeed, that he possesses more originality than Van Dine, and might very well prove to be the creator of something new and startlingly original for us.

I would recommend having him do a police story for Bancroft. . . . Hammett was a Pinkerton man for a good many years before becoming a writer. . . .

Hammett is unspoiled as to money, but on the other hand anxious not to tie himself up with a long-term contract. I was in hopes that we could get him for about $400 weekly, but he claims that this is only about half of his present earning capacity between books and magazine stories, and I am inclined to believe him inasmuch as his vogue is on the rise.

So far, I have tentatively discussed some such arrangement as the following: . . .

Four weeks at $300 weekly;
An option for eight weeks at the same salary;
And a bonus of $5000 for an original. . . .

David O. Selznick

DASHIELL HAMMETT

LETTER TO THE EDITOR:
Joseph Shaw, Letter to the editor, *Writer's Digest*, September 1930.

Shaw was sensitive to the charge that Black Mask *aggrandized criminal life. In this letter he defends* The Glass Key *against such attacks.*

Dear Editor:

. . . . . as far as I have any knowledge, *Black Mask* has published only one story in which the gangster was in any sense the "hero," and that story is the great novel by Dashiell Hammett, which recently was published by us serially under the title of *"The Glass Key."* This was a story of modern gangsters, a seriously written and highly dramatic presentation of the present day alliance between corrupt politicians and public officials and organized crime—which alliance is the sole reason for the profitableness of crime as a profession.

Even in this story, virtue comes out on top— the crook who has ruled a city is defeated, his gang is broken up, the corrupt politicians who have made his career possible are swept out of office by the voters. This novel, incidentally, will be published in book form by Alfred Knopf this Fall, as have all of Mr. Hammett's novels. If you have read this story, or will read it, you will agree with me, I am sure, that publication of it, and of all stories like it, is a public service. Not until the general public realizes that modern crime, modern gangs, cannot exist without the collusion of corrupt and equally criminal police and public officials, will it be possible to cure what is undoubtedly one of the most serious illnesses, to put it mildly, that our body police has ever suffered from.

Black Mask never has and never will make money or attempt to make money by appealing to the appetite for stories which present crime and criminals in a prepossessing and alluring light: our policy is and always will be the exact opposite—to appeal to those who hate crime and criminals and who get pleasure from reading stories in which they can identify themselves with the detective or other officers who are solving crimes and capturing criminals.

Joseph T. Shaw, Editor,
Black Mask

MOVIE REVIEW:
Mordaunt Hall, "Beer and Crime," *New York Times*, 18 April 1931, p. 17.

City Streets *was Hammett's first screenwriting credit.*

CITY STREETS, an adaptation of a story by Dashiell Hammett; directed by Rouben Mamoulian; produced by Paramount Publix. At the Times Square Paramount and the Brooklyn Paramount.

The Kid	Gary Cooper
Nan	Sylvia Sidney
Big Boy Maskal	Paul Lukas
McCoy	William Boyd
Pop Cooley	Guy Kibbee
Blackie	Stanley Fields
Agnes	Wynne Gibson
Pansy	Betty Sinclair

Another gangster film, called "City Streets," is holding the fort at the Paramount. It was directed by Rouben Mamoulian, who staged several plays for the Theatre Guild and who was also responsible for the picturization of "Applause." In this new work Mr. Mamoulian reveals some clever cinematic ideas, but more often than not he loses his interest in the story and dialogue through his zealousness for unusual camera stunts and angles. This production, however, is quite entertaining in spite of the hapless casting of Paul Lukas as the head of a gang of beer racketeers.

It has—what is rare at this time—those uncomfortable hushed periods between the players. Mr. Mamoulian atones for some of these desultory scenes by his photographic artistry. A prison is first seen from the gate, and a second later one beholds the high gray walls of the structure with birds flying in "that little patch of blue" the "prisoners call the sky." There are also adroit flashes of Gary Cooper, as the Kid, giving exhibitions of two-gun marksmanship at a Coney Island range. In other sections of this offering Mr. Mamoulian indulges his fancy for glimpses of the ocean, and in one sequence he permits the thoughts of a character to be heard, in much the same way as Alfred Hitchcock did in the British film "Blackmail."

Mr. Lukas is beheld here as Big Boy Maskal, who is presumed to be a smooth racketeer in his beer business and also in ordering the murder of

Sylvia Sidney and Gary Cooper in a scene from
City Streets.

Hammett met Lillian Hellman in Hollywood, probably in winter 1930-1931. She was a script reader for Samuel Goldwyn; he was working at Paramount. They became close companions, living together for much of the rest of their lives.

any one who opposes him. Considering that Guy Kibbee gives a sterling performance as a underling among the thugs, known as Pop Cooley, the miscasting of Mr. Lukas is all the more obvious. It is Pop Cooley who is instructed by Maskal to get rid of an individual known as Blackie, who resents the chief casting favoring eyes upon his girl, Agnes. Pop is rather gratified at being ordered to put an end to Blackie, not because he dislikes the man but because he looks upon it as a distinction in being singled out to do it by No. 1 of the slaughtering beer-makers.

But when Pop kills Blackie he gives his pistol to his daughter, Nan, and the girl is arrested by the police and eventually sent to prison, after every effort has been made to wring from her the name of the man who handed her the weapon.

While Nan is in jail, a young man known as the Kid, who is in love with her, becomes one of the beer racketeers. Soon after Nan's release Maskal flirts with her, and the Kid resents the chief's attentions. Thus the Kid is ordered to be put on the spot, but he is one too many for them and he sends the gunmen back home without their weapons. Eventually Lukas is shot by Agnes, and Nan is thought to be the slayer, which results in the decision of the racketeers that Nan must pay for killing Maskal by being "taken for a ride."

The Kid once again outwits the gangsters by taking them for the ride of their lives, across the railroad tracks in front of an oncoming express, which narrowly misses the automobile, then at breakneck speed over mountain roads. Finally, while still at the wheel, the Kid tells Nan to point her pistol at the three gangsters, and only when they have given up their firearms does he end the wild ride.

THE GLASS KEY

CHAPTER I

The Body in China Street

1

GREEN dice rolled across the green table, struck the rim together, and bounced back. One stopped short holding six white spots in two equal rows uppermost. The other tumbled out to the center of the table and came to rest with a single spot on top.

Ned Beaumont grunted softly—"Uhn!"—and the winners cleared the table of money.

Harry Sloss picked up the dice and rattled them in a pale broad hairy hand. "Shoot two bits." He dropped a twenty-dollar bill and a five-dollar bill on the table.

Ned Beaumont stepped back saying: "Get on him, gamblers, I've got to refuel." He crossed the billiard-room to the door. There he met Walter Ivans coming in. He said, "'Lo, Walt," and would have gone on, but Ivans caught his elbow as he passed, and turned to face him.

The manuscript for The Glass Key *was sold at auction by Christie's in London on 27 March 1985.*

The Glass Key *was published first in England, on 20 January 1931, and then in America on 24 April 1931. There were five American printings in the first month of publication.*

This clipping from Shaw's scrapbook identifies Hammett as the editorial voice responding to a
New Yorker *newsbreak.*

It is all melodramatic and incredible. Mr. Cooper gives a satisfactory showing as the Kid. Sylvia Sidney is excellent as Nan. William Boyd does capital work as one of the gangsters, but he would have been even better in the role played by Mr. Lukas.

Among the numbers in the stage contribution is a sketch in which a trained mule affords a great deal of genuine amusement.

BOOK REVIEW:
Dorothy Parker, "Oh, Look—Two Good Books!" *New Yorker* (25 April 1931): 91.

Dorothy Parker was a close friend of Lillian Hellman's known for her acid wit. Hammett reportedly found her annoying.

It seems to me that there is entirely too little screaming about the work of Dashiell Hammett. My own shrill yaps have been ascending ever since I first found "Red Harvest," and from that day the man has been, God help him, my hero; but I talked only yesterday, I forget why, with two of our leading booksy folk, and they had not heard of that volume, nor had they got around to reading its better, "The Maltese Falcon."

It is true that Mr. Hammett displays that touch of rare genius in his selection of undistinguished titles for his mystery stories–"The Maltese Falcon" and "The Glass Key," his new one, sound like something by Carolyn Wells. It is true that had the literary lads got past those names and cracked the pages, they would have found the plots to be so many nuisances; confusing to madness, as in "Red Harvest;" fanciful to nausea, as in "The Maltese Falcon;" or, as in the case of the newly-published "The Glass Key," so tired that even this reviewer, who in infancy was let drop by a nurse with the result that she has ever since been mystified by amateur coin-tricks, was able to guess the identity of the murderer from the middle of the book. It is true that he has all the mannerisms of Hemingway, with no inch of Hemingway's scope nor flicker of Hemingway's beauty. It is true that when he seeks to set down a swift, assured, well-bred young woman, he devises speeches for her such as are only equalled by the talk Mr. Theodore Dreiser compiled for his society flapper in "An American Tragedy." It is true that he is so hard-boiled you could roll him on the White House lawn. And it is also true that he is a good, hell-bent, cold-hearted writer, with a clear eye for the ways of hard women and a fine ear for the words of hard men, and his books are exciting and powerful and–if I may filch the word from the booksy ones–pulsing. It is difficult to conclude an outburst like this. All I can say is that anybody who doesn't read him misses much of modern America. And hot that sounds!

Dashiell Hammett is as American as a sawed-off shotgun. He is as immediate as a special extra. Brutal he is, but his brutality, for what he must write, is clean and necessary, and there is in his work none of the smirking and swaggering savageries of a Hecht or a Bodenheim. He does his readers the infinite courtesy of allowing them to sup-

Do you know this man?

He is the greatest living writer of detective stories. His last three stories have been published in book form by one of the greatest publishing houses and have been lavishly praised by the most competent critics. He is a true genius! His stories are like no others, but absolutely in a class by themselves. His name is Dashiell Hammett; and his latest story is called

THE GLASS KEY

It is a vivid and tremendous story of modern organized crime and politics, true to the facts of life in every detail; and it is the most powerful and stirring, and the finest, story of its kind we have ever seen. It will hold you gripped fast, tense with excitement and completely oblivious to your surroundings, from beginning to end. You will find it in the March issue of

BLACK MASK

BLACK MASK is a monthly magazine of detective, adventure and western stories of superior quality. If you do not know Black Mask get acquainted with it now. In addition to The Glass Key you will find six other stories that are miles above average in quality—hours, altogether, of the most enjoyable reading you have ever known. In this March issue, in addition to The Glass Key, you will find:

BOOM TOWN
Gambling, gunfighting and a manhunt in an oil town near the Mexican border.

THE BELL IN THE FOG
A brand new racket pulled on the New York police—for a while.

FROST RIDES ALONE
The air force of the Texas rangers vs. smugglers.

and three other great stories. Get a copy today from any news-dealer.

Knopf actively and successfully advertised The Glass Key, *concentrating on establishing the prominence of the author. The book has no series character and features no detective.*

A NEW WRAPPER AND A LOWER PRICE

The new Hammett for which the trade and public have been asking eagerly these many months will be published April 24th at $2.00

The GLASS KEY

By Dashiell Hammett

Woollcott has called THE MALTESE FALCON the best mystery story ever written by an American. ❴I won't call THE GLASS KEY even better—superlatives don't mean much these days—but I will promise it won't disappoint you and your readers. ❴The new wrapper will help and the reduction of the price to $2.00 should remove every last obstacle to your achieving for THE GLASS KEY the big sale you have told me the new Hammett ought to have. ❴If you will increase the order you have already placed at $2.50 by twenty-five percent, you'll be helping yourself, your customers, us, and Hammett. And I hope you'll agree that such an increase isn't unreasonable—even in times like these.

Alfred A. Knopf

ALFRED·A·KNOPF BORZOI BOOKS **730 FIFTH AVE·N·Y·**

After initially publishing The Glass Key *at $2.50, which was twenty-five percent more than mystery novels commonly sold for at the time, Knopf reduced the price to $2.00 in an effort to stimulate sales.*

EX-DETECTIVE HAMMETT

by Elizabeth Sanderson

A CRITIC once said of Dashiell Hammett's work: "The writing is better than Hemingway, since it conceals not softness but hardness". If hardness consists of writing about criminals as though they were human, of looking on detectives with an unbiased eye and setting them down as less than paragons of shrewdness and integrity, of admitting corruption, human frailty and occasional pleasant qualities in both his man-hunters and their quarry, Dashiell Hammett's hardness is the main reason for his success. He writes of people he knows, people with whom he has worked professionally, and his characters, instead of being the stock marionettes of the usual detective story, are the flesh-and-blood figures of any good novel. As a consequence the usual detective story formulas are not enough to carry them, and Mr. Hammett disregards the old rules. The result is that he has written, in *Red Harvest, The Dain Curse, The Maltese Falcon* and *The Glass Key*, four of the best detective stories ever published. He is, in addition, a master of terse, abrupt prose, and he can tell more in one sentence of it than many an earlier mystery novel writer managed to convey in a chapter.

It was with a great deal of interest, then, that I set out to interview this man who had contributed a new form of fiction to contemporary literature.

Dashiell Hammett is tall, slim, sophisticated, with prematurely white hair above a young face. He was born in Maryland in 1894, and he holds that the only remarkable thing about his family is that there were, on his mother's side, sixteen army men of France who never saw a battle. The family name was De Chiel, and "Dashiell" is its Americanized version. (He will impress upon you that the accent falls on the second syllable.) He grew tired of school at the age of thirteen, and started on years of diverse jobs by working as a newsboy. Before the war broke out he had been a freight-clerk, a general worker around railroads, and a copy-writer for a small San Francisco jewel-ler. The World War broke the De Chiel curse: Dashiell Hammett saw fighting, and when he left the army he left it with tuberculosis. During his recuperation he met and married a hospital nurse, who is now the mother of his two daughters, aged ten and five. The next job he found he held eight years; it was as a detective for the Pinkerton Detective Agency.

To Mr. Hammett being a detective was just another job; it was no fulfilment of a long-stifled boyish ambition born of reading Nick Carter. He admits that the first four years were full of interest and stimulation: he helped to send Nicky Arnstein to jail; he spent three months on a hospital cot trying to coax evidence from a suspect in the next bed; disguised as an ardent I.W.W. he was sent to Minnesota to follow another suspicious character; he worked on the Arbuckle case, which, he says, was a frame-up by some newspaper boys, who saw a big scoop in Arbuckle's guilt. (And politics in California, he asserts, are the most corrupt in the world.)

His Pinkerton career was interrupted for a time by another prolonged rest, and in his leisure he began to write. But he went back to Pinkerton's, and when I asked why he had finally left that profession he answered: "I suppose because they wouldn't let me go to Australia after some stolen gold. It sounded romantic. Later they found some of the gold in a San Francisco fire-hose". So Dashiell Hammett settled down to write for a living, and has written in some form or other—as often for the movies as for the bookstores—ever since.

Mr. Hammett says that the detective in *Red Harvest* and *The Dain Curse* was drawn from a real man. Spade, in *The Maltese Falcon*, is half real and half imaginary, and all the rest of Hammett's characters were made by combining the traits and experiences of people he really knew as a detective. A detective is not actually a romantic figure, and few thieves or murderers are ever pure "criminal types". So Dashiell Hammett left the Philo Vances to Mr. Van Dine and wrote of what he had seen as a hard-working man among men of very little culture or nobility. With all his experience to draw on, and in spite of the remarkable success that has come to him from his detective stories, Mr. Hammett does not want to go on writing them. He wants to write a play. Later he will write straight novels, but not until he has written his play.

He ought to be successful as a playwright. His dialogue is dramatic, accurate and economical. He can inject qualities into commonplace scenes that turn them into extraordinary situations. His characters are living ordinary persons, compounded of good and evil qualities. He can portray ruthlessness and greed

Bookman, *January 1932*

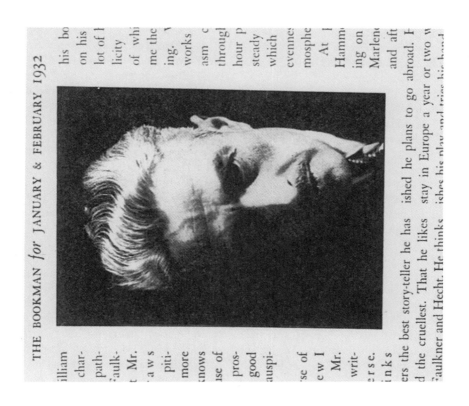

ply descriptions and analyses for themselves. He sets down only what his characters say, and what they do. It is not, I suppose, any too safe a recipe for those who cannot create characters; but Dashiell Hammett can and does and has and, I hope, will. On gentle ladies he is, in a word, rotten; but maybe sometime he will do a novel without a mystery plot, and so no doggy girls need come into it. But it is denied us who read to have everything, and it is little enough to let him have his ladies and his mysteries, if he will give us such characters as Sam Spade, in "The Maltese Falcon," and such scenes as the beating-up of Ned Beaumont in "The Glass Key."

His new book, "The Glass Key," seems to me nowhere to touch its predecessor. Surely it is that Beaumont, the amateur detective of the later story, a man given perhaps a shade too much to stroking his moustache with a thumbnail, can in no way stack up against the magnificent Spade, with whom, after reading "The Maltese Falcon," I went mooning about in a daze of love such as I had not known for any character in literature since I encountered Sir Launcelot when I hit the age of nine. (Launcelot and Spade–ah well, they're pretty far apart, yet I played Elaine to both of them, and in that lies a life-story.) The new book, or, indeed, any new book, has no figure to stand near Sam Spade, but maybe all the matter is not there. For I thought that in "The Glass Key" Mr. Hammett seemed a little weary, a little short of spontaneous, a little dogged about his simplicity of style, a little determined to make startling the ordering of his brief sentences, a little concerned with having his conclusion approach the toughness of the superb last scene of "The Maltese Falcon." But all that is not to say that "The Glass Key" is not a good book and an enthralling one, and the best you have read since "The Maltese Falcon." And if you didn't read that, this is the swiftest book you've ever read in your life.

BOOK REVIEW:

Will Cuppy, Review of *The Glass Key*, *New York Herald Tribune*, 26 April 1931, p. 13.

Get your copy of "The Glass Key," the best of the spring mysteries by quite some margin. This department believes and can prove that Mr.

Hammett's new volume is about twice as good as his "The Maltese Falcon," hitherto regarded by the better fans as about the last word in hard-boiled detectivism. Since you'll have to take sides in this argument, don't delay learning about the strange, brutal and fairly enigmatic career of Ned Beaumont, his gambling luck, his doings in dirty civic politics, his solution of a murder and maybe his great love for Janet Henry, daughter of Senator Ralph Bancroft Henry, and sister of the corpse.

It seems that Ned is lieutenant and buddy to Paul Madvig, a city boss, who is trying to elect Senator Henry and wipe out Shad O'Rory, another boss, when somebody up and murders the senator's son on China Street–it might have been Paul Madvig, some of Shad's anthropoid gangsters or a lot of other people. The secret is well kept and expertly spilled at the proper second. More and greater mysteries reside in the mental and emotional make-up of Mr. Hammett's characters, who provide fascinating problems in all directions. What one reader wants to know, just out of idle curiosity, is this: Are there people like that? And is life like that? And if so, can anything be done? Meanwhile you get a story positively without rubber stamps, a brilliant study in the ugly and abysmal which should be read by authors of all kinds and distributed as tracts to the mystery mongers.

Mr. Hammett's is plain, blunt writing, and it is most effective. "The Kid yelped and fell down on the hallway floor," says he, when he wishes to indicate that the Kid yelped and fell down on the hallway floor, and the occasional lapses with dictionary words needn't be worried about. Moreover, he belongs to the "he said" and "she said" school of dialogue–instead of "he jibbed" and "she guzzled"–and that, too, is effective, if it doesn't absorb all your attention with its simplicity. In other words, "The Glass Key" is a whiz of an opus.

BOOK REVIEW:

Bruce Rae, Review of *The Glass Key*, *New York Times*, 3 May 1931, IV: 23.

There can be no doubt of Mr. Hammett's gifts in this special field, and there can be no question of the success of his latest book. Municipal politics at its lowest is his theme and he has done the subject justice with a score of convincing under-

SAMUEL DASHIELL HAMMETT, former newsboy, stevedore, detective and advertising man, today acknowledged the smartest, liveliest and most literate detective story author in America, is one of several first rank writers now in Hollywood, improving scenarios for the cinema

LAURENCE STALLINGS, modestly listed in *Who's Who* as a "newspaper man", won for himself the evergreen perpetuity of laurel with his war novel, *Plumes*. He was one of the first of the literary Titans to join the movie ranks and was responsible for *The Big Parade*

SIDNEY HOWARD, the distinguished playwright whose *They Knew What They Wanted* won the Pulitzer prize in 1925, has written and adapted a number of successful films for Ronald Colman, beginning with *Raffles* and including *Arrowsmith*. His own plays will soon be filmed

PAUL GREEN, formerly a philosophy professor at the University of North Carolina, won the Pulitzer prize for the best American play in 1927 with his Negro drama, *In Abraham's Bosom*. His first cinema effort was the adaptation of *The Cabin in the Cotton*; his latest, *State Fair*

GLADYS BRONWYN STERN, more generally known as "G.B.", is the widely read English author, whose best known book is *The Matriarch*—the saga of a Jewish family. Her latest novel, *Long Lost Father*, will be published next month. She is now in Hollywood, under contract

BEN HECHT, sometimes considered l'enfant terrible of American letters, has been writing for the movies for some time now. His first great cinema success was the gangster film, *Underworld*, with George Bancroft. He and Gene Fowler have just sold *The Great Magoo* to the films

CLEMENCE DANE, the British playwright and novelist, is another newcomer within Hollywood's gaudy gates, imported for the purpose of mental uplift. As the author of *A Bill of Divorcement*, Katharine Hepburn's first picture, she is already sure of cinema success

CHARLES MACARTHUR is the ex-Chicago reporter whose name, coupled with that of Ben Hecht, has adorned a number of successful Broadway plays, including *The Front Page* and *Twentieth Century*. He is also among the more erudite of the Hollywood scenario writer ensemble

ROSAMOND LEHMANN is the third of the trio of literary ladies who have temporarily forsaken England for Hollywood. Like Miss Stern and Miss Dane, she has signed a cinema contract to write for the screen. As author of *Invitation to the Waltz*, she won high critical kudos

THEODORE DREISER, Americana's war-horse, made his first venture into cinema-land with *An American Tragedy*. The harrowing details of that encounter are well known to the public-at-large. Now, however, Mr. Dreiser will permit another novel to be filmed—*Jennie Gerhardt*

ERNEST HEMINGWAY, like Mr. Dreiser, was not wholly in accord with Hollywood's rendering of his novel, *A Farewell to Arms*. In fact, Mr. Hemingway's quoted comment on it is practically unprintable. Now he, too, has relented, and will permit *The Sun Also Rises* to be filmed

WILLIAM FAULKNER is one of the last authors on earth whom we should expect to find writing for the movies, but here he is, with a Hollywood contract tucked away in his pocket and two films already practically finished, *Today We Live*, and *Sanctuary*. More are forthcoming

Lifting the Hollywood fog

Hammett was identified by the trendy Vanity Fair *as a celebrity seven months before his last book was published.*

In 1930 I started writing a book entitled "The Thin Man." By the time I had written these 65 pages my publisher and I agreed that it might be wise to postpone the publication of "The Glass Key" — scheduled for that fall — until the following spring. This meant that "The Thin Man" could not be published until the fall of 1931. So — having plenty of time — I put these 65 pages aside and went to Hollywood for a year. One thing and/or another intervening after that, I didn't return to work on the story until a couple of more years had passed — and then I found it easier, or at least generally more satisfactory, to keep only the basic idea of the plot and otherwise to start anew. Some of the

Hammett made a false start on his fifth novel in 1931. Dissatisfied with the advance he received for The Glass Key, *Hammett took on a new agent, Ben Wasson (also William Faulkner's agent), who advised Hammett to have a new novel ready for circulation to publishers while the success of* The Glass Key *was fresh. Wasson was overly aggressive and sold the fragment in violation of Hammett's contract with Knopf. As a result, Hammett abandoned the draft. He donated the typescript for auction to support a war-bonds drive in 1942, appending this note.*

incidents in this original version
I later used in "After The Thin
Man," a motion picture sequel,
but — except for that and for the
use of the characters' names Guild
and Wynant — this unfinished
manuscript has a clear claim
to virginity.

Dashiell Hammett

Hardscrabble Farm
Pleasantville, N.Y.
January 14, 1942

CREEPS
BY
NIGHT

CHILLS AND THRILLS

SELECTED BY

DASHIELL HAMMETT

THE JOHN DAY COMPANY

NEW YORK

CONTENTS

	PAGE
INTRODUCTION	7
Dashiell Hammett	
A ROSE FOR EMILY	15
William Faulkner	
GREEN THOUGHTS	33
John Collier	
THE GHOST OF ALEXANDER PERKS, A.B.	65
Robert Dean Frisbie	
THE HOUSE	87
André Maurois	
THE KILL	91
Peter Fleming	
TEN O'CLOCK	113
Philip MacDonald	
THE SPIDER	143
Hanns Heinz Ewers	
BREAKDOWN	187
L. A. G. Strong	
THE WITCH'S VENGEANCE	211
W. B. Seabrook	

5

	PAGE
THE RAT	231
S. Fowler Wright	
FAITH, HOPE AND CHARITY	273
Irvin S. Cobb	
MR. ARCULARIS	311
Conrad Aiken	
THE MUSIC OF ERICH ZANN	347
H. P. Lovecraft	
THE STRANGE CASE OF MRS. ARKWRIGHT	365
Harold Dearden	
THE KING OF THE CATS	395
Stephen Vincent Benét	
THE RED BRAIN	423
Donald Wandrei	
THE PHANTOM BUS	441
W. Elwyn Backus	
BEYOND THE DOOR	453
Paul Suter	
PERCHANCE TO DREAM	483
Michael Joyce	
A VISITOR FROM EGYPT	505
Frank Belknap Long	

6

As a money-making scheme, Ben Wasson arranged for Hammett to "edit" an anthology of horror and thriller stories. In fact, the collection was compiled by Wasson and included works by several of his clients. Hammett contributed an introduction.

The Thin Man was first published in its entirety, though in bowdlerized form, in Redbook Magazine. The sheets of the magazine publication were then bound, along with sheets for five other novels, and offered as a subscription premium for the magazine.

world characters and their satellites. Senator Ralph Bancroft Henry is up for re-election, with the backing of the unsavory Paul Madvig, when the Senator's son, Taylor Henry, is murdered. Ned Beaumont, Madvig's lieutenant, apparently knows something about the crime, and so do half a dozen others, including a gambler's girl and a couple of gunmen. The Senator has a daughter, of course, and Beaumont, who strikes one as a cheap honky-tonker, falls in love. Plenty of authentic and coarse dialogue gives realism to the story. Mr. Hammett's new book is bound to find favor, although probably not as much as was accorded his earlier work, "The Maltese Falcon."

BOOK REVIEW:

Walter R. Brooks, Review of *The Glass Key*, *Outlook* (29 April 1931): 601.

Another of Dashiell Hammett's grand detective stories is out. In *The Glass Key*, Ned Beaumont, gambler and political hanger-on, tries to protect his friend, Madvig, a political boss, from a murder charge that is hanging over him. The suave and deadly opposition boss, Shad O'Rory, Senator Henry and his daughter Janet, Madvig's daughter, Opal, the killer, Jeff, and the various other guerillas, gangsters, politicians and their women, stand out clearly and sharply, softened by no romantic haze. Mr. Hammett does not show you their thoughts, only their actions, and the story is amazingly swift, harsh and thrilling. Be you high-, low- or middle-brow, don't miss this item by a man who has now written the three best detective stories ever published.

INTERVIEW ARTICLE:

Marguerite Tazelaar, "Film Personalities: A Private Detective Does His Stuff in Hollywood," *New York Herald Tribune*, 12 November 1933, V: 3.

"I liked Hollywood. I went out for four months and stayed almost two years, and I'd go back again, for a time, if I had the chance."

Dashiell Hammett was speaking in a slow drawl, a glint of amusement in his eye, yet with a kind of shy, lazy seriousness, too. A tall, thin man with a pale, sensitive face and quiet voice, he is the last person in the world you would think of as a former Pinkerton detective or the creator of those sinister underworld types, so curiously alive, who peopled "The Glass Key" and "The Maltese Falcon."

The former mystery story is now in the hands of a picture company, pending production, and the latter was filmed last season. The criticism Hammett made of its screening was that he thought the producers had stuck too closely to his book. "You need to simplify a story as much as possible when you're going to make a picture of it," he said. "If you don't you'll have too many lines and so lose your full effect. No, I didn't work on the thing at all. I was doing originals most of the time. I believe it's better to have somebody else than the author do adaptations, because the story isn't so rigid in the mind of the man who hasn't written it."

For eight years Mr. Hammett was a Pinkerton detective. . . . "The first three or four years were fun. Then it got tedious. . . . For excitement the Anaconda strike, back in 1920-'21, tops the list. That was when they finally broke the I. W. W. The funniest case I ever worked on was the Arbuckle affair in San Francisco. In trying to convict him everybody framed everybody else."

Hammett is working on a book now and some short stories. His latest complete novel, "The Thin Man," will be published this winter. In his short pieces, he says, he has handled other than the mystery plots, and the novel he is working on now is not a mystery story. He says virtually every character he has written about he has known in person.

Detective stories can be done much better in books than on the screen, Mr. Hammett believes. The difficulty in filming them comes in handling the clews, for if you plant them so that the audience doesn't notice they have forgotten them by the time the big surprise unfolds, and if you point them up in the beginning, they catch on right away.

ARTICLE:

Edwin Balmer, "Our Literary Nudism," *Esquire* (September 1934): 30, 89

We were not in the least surprised to receive from a friend of ours the letter just below.

He edits a high brow magazine which is not only extremely smart but in the better senses, a wholly "modern" magazine.

He wrote to me and, I believe, to other editors whom he deemed to be confronting the same contemporary trend:

"I am afraid that you will think this is a somewhat preposterous sort of letter.

"I am writing it because we are a little in a quandary here as to how far it is wise for us to go in the direction of tabooed words. I often feel that I am more than a generation behind the trend of the day when I read the manuscripts that are sent to us, go to the movies, glance at the tabloids, or read the novels of Faulkner *et al.*

"Would you, as a favor, tell me whether or not you permit, in your pages, such words as *Christ* (used as an expletive), *bitch, bastard,* or *Lesbian*?

"I find an increasing insistence on these words in the manuscripts that are sent me by young and often really promising writers. Before deciding how brave we are to be as apostles of the new candor, I thought it best to drop you this line. I confess to feeling a little silly in writing it."

Because some discussion of the sort suggested was certainly due and overdue, we were not surprised.

You who are not in the editing trade, and therefore may judge of the "new candor" only from what reaches you in print, you do not know the half of it. We still save you from something. Not from much, I agree; yet from something.

Now the question seems to be, should we continue to do it?

My reply to my friend was in part:

"I am very glad you brought this matter up for discussion, because it is not only the words but the subjects which require the use of such words that give us difficulty.

"It has been amazing to me to see, in recent years, the apparently unashamed increase of perverted subjects. I have had to read many stories that were for the most part excellent and well done, but under which lay an unpublishable idea."

At least it seemed to me an unpublishable idea. But what idea is today "unpublishable" or

fails of publication, if not in magazine, then in book form?

Not long ago a young lady authoress appeared in my office with a manuscript which she was submitting for serial publication; and as she came recommended by a literary agent of standing, and also already had obtained a book contract for her manuscript, and as she was in haste to have a decision before sailing for Europe, I set to the reading of her novel without first putting it through "the mill."

The "mill," in our shop, involves a first reading by younger members of our staff–who, I must confess, occasionally startle me by the calmness of their comments upon some of the manuscripts they read; but this one topped anything they have yet reported. Its candor was complete and plus; there was no situation which even by inadvertence grazed any of the decencies.

I could not believe that anyone would bring it out even between book covers; but some one did. The book contract which the lady authoress proudly produced in reply to my expressed doubts was genuine.

"I was told to write it raw," she observed, "and I am sure to sell ten thousand. Why don't you climb aboard the bandwagon?"

I find, that, as to our present position in regard to printing profane and obscene expressions, I replied to my friend that we permit on our pages *damn* when it is a characterizing bit of dialogue, but that we prefer to draw a pencil through the *God* in the proffered *God damns* indigenous to modern American manuscripts.

Further, we feel it well to substitute another expletive for the "*Jesus Christ*" liberally offered by contemporary authors as exclamations or comments when other words run low. Also we are reluctant to encourage writers to habituate their characters to labeling each other as bitches and bastards, playfully or otherwise. And we like to avoid Lesbianism.

I recall the comment of one of my manuscript readers who spared herself–and me–the synopsizing of a novel sent by an agent, and in respect to which I had not had the fortune to act as shock absorber.

"I tell you, Mr. Balmer," she replied to my first question as to the subject of this particular *tour-*

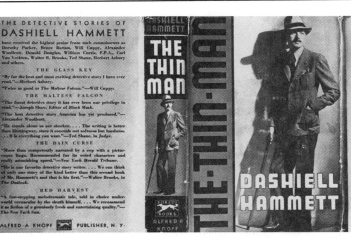

Hammett posed for the American dust jacket of The Thin Man, *a circumstance that has caused confusion about the title. The Thin Man of the novel is the murdered inventor Clyde Wynant, but it became commonplace for people who had not read the novel to assume that Hammett himself was The Thin Man.*

de-force, "it makes those novels of ordinary adultery seem just nice."

Such are the subjects offered, as my friend notes, and by young and often really promising writers, and with ever-increasing insistence.

Closing my manuscript portfolio, I open some of the buckram-bound best-sellers of some of my own friends, I go to the movies and glance at the tabloids, and I wonder whether the reaction of distaste is silly.

Let us leave out any debate as to the absolute rightness or wrongness of anything. Let us leave it merely to taste, good or bad; for that, at least, is left us.

There is probably nothing more moral or "right" in employing Latin-derived euphemisms rather than the crude Anglo-Saxon vulgarities now affected, but it is certainly better manners.

The stage at some spots in New York, has gone the limit; and some books also have arrived at the place where there is nothing beyond. The literary "strip-act" has at last removed even the loin-cloth. As to vocabulary, the writers not only have exhausted the dictionary, but have tapped, for fresher obscenities, the treasures of the back-fence thesaurus. No word so low but some one, today, finds it essential to his literary life.

Do most of us really like that?

It appears to me, as an editor, that there is at least reasonable doubt as to the persisting pleasure produced by some of the words and ideas so freely scattered upon published pages.

There is a distinct difference in usage, even between book-publishers, as there is between magazines; and while the best book-publishers undoubtedly would have refused the volumes previously referred to, yet their own present code of candor certainly is more emancipated–to put it lightly–than the code of magazines of similar standing.

As editor of the Redbook Magazine, I had the privilege of first publication of that very modern mystery story, "The Thin Man." Mr. Alexander Woollcott, a most competent critic, believes and declares it "the best detective story yet written in America."

Before buying it, I read it with the greatest appreciation, but in the manuscript as it came to me, were lines which did not seem to enhance the story. In fact, upon one of the pages was a phrase–

put in the form of a five-word question–which had never before reached my desk as part of a literary production.

I have not asked my distinguished friend, but I feel that it would have been a rare phrase in the manuscripts reaching him, or he surely would have queried it in his list of debatable words. At any rate, I confess that I drew a pencil through those five words.

"The Thin Man," after its magazine appearance, was brought out in book form, and promptly became a very best seller; its publisher is a firm famous for its excellent selection of fiction and for its maintenance of high literary standards.

Being somewhat curious, I wanted to see what editing–if any–was done to certain passages distinguished for the new candor. I could have spared myself the trouble. The book-publisher not only preserved the phrase, but referred to it in large type in advertisements.

We find in the New York Times of January 30th, 1934, this announcement over the facsimile signature of the publisher.

"I don't believe the question on page 192 of Dashiell Hammett's 'The Thin Man' has had the slightest influence upon the sale of the book. It takes more than that to make a best-seller these days. Twenty thousand people don't buy a book within three weeks to read a five-word question."

Let us credit that statement with 100% sincerity.

I don't believe that "the five-word question" did make "The Thin Man" a best seller. It had conspicuous qualities far above it. But the famous question, taken in connection with the advertisement, certainly celebrates a degree of candor which few magazines have attained.

To be fair, however, let me add that I have since encountered the word, which made memorable this question, in "Anthony Adverse." There it occurs quite casually; but so much occurs, and quite casually, in that remarkable volume which has reached a crest of popularity attained, in recent years, only by miniature golf!

We seem to be welcoming a common condition of literary nudism. It is an artistic loss. Upon the pages of novels, as in nudist camps, we find too many people whose sole claim to attention is that they have their clothes off.

It is a cheap way to stir up excitement. It is far easier to provide oneself with the "courage" to copy the alley fence than to think up something really distinguished to say. It is far, far easier, that it, to be "courageous" than creative.

"Some book-sellers are afraid to recommend this book," reads an advertisement just out as I am writing this. It continues:

"Be sure to ask for it. It's the year's sensation."

"Vigorous, original, bawdy and beautiful."

A very good friend of mine wrote this novel, which, with its "bawdy" pages, has chapters of great interest and beauty.

"I didn't show it to you," he told me. "No magazine could possibly have printed it."

Now, are the magazines wrong? Should we let down the bars further and faster than we are doing?

My own magazine cannot be accused of being crinoline-minded. We gave first publication not only to "The Thin Man" but to Sinclair Lewis' frank and realistic account of a modern feminist in love, "Ann Vickers."

Do you want the periodical publishers to follow the book-publishers and the theatrical producers, to the camps of the literary nudists?

BOOK REVIEW:

Herschel Brickell, "The Literary Landscape," *North American Review* (March 1934): 283.

The discovery of Hammett by mainstream reviewers continued with the publication of his fifth novel.

Detective stories do not often make their way into this department, but the Landscaper would be failing in his duty if he did not report that one of the recent books that gave him the greatest amount of pleasure was Dashiell Hammett's *The Thin Man* (Knopf, $2), Mr. Hammett being the distinguished author of *The Maltese Falcon*, among other books, and generally recognized as the top of the heap in his field. *The Maltese Falcon*, by the way, is now available in the Modern Library edition, a recognition it heartily deserves, since it is one of the finest thrillers ever to be put between covers.

The Thin Man is a murder-mystery, cut more or less according to pattern, with the difference that the detective seems entirely credible and all the people talk and act as if they had wandered in off the streets, or right out of the first pages of your favorite newspaper. They are a mad lot, most of them, but real. And the punch of Mr. Hammett's stream-lined dialogue, which is like nobody else's, never fails. There is a good deal more to be said on this subject, as the author in question is unique in his field, but other books are waiting, and the Landscaper closes the matter by recommending *The Thin Man* as ace writing, much too good to be missed, whether you ordinarily like detective stories or not.

BOOK REVIEW:

Isaac Anderson, "New Mystery Stories," *New York Times Book Review*, 7 January 1934, p. 18.

Dashiell Hammett is in a class by himself. His detectives are not patterned after those of any other writer. Quite probably they are drawn from life. This creator should know his types, for he was at one time a Pinkerton operative. At any rate, they impress one as being real. They are rough in their manners and in their methods, and they are not at all particular as to how they get results so long as they get them. Their language is forcible, but it is not the sort that was used in drawing-rooms in the good old days that grandmother so fondly remembers. In this new story Mr. Hammett is at the top of his form.

The central figure is Nick Charles, a former private detective who has come into money and has retired in order, apparently, to devote himself to an intensive study of the liquor problem from the consumer's standpoint. While in New York on a visit he is more or less dragged into a murder investigation. A woman named Julia Wolf has been murdered in her apartment. She was, or had been, secretary to Clyde Wynant, a former client of Nick Charles. Wynant is missing, and the police are looking for him. According to Charles, Wynant is "a good guy, but screwy." The second part of that description might equally well be applied to the other members of the Wynant family: Dorothy, the daughter, who drinks far too much, tells lies and explains them away with other lies; Gilbert, the son, whose mind is cluttered up with undigested Freud, and Mimi, the divorced wife, now married to a man who calls himself Chris Jorgenson.

Charles is asked to investigate the murder on behalf of Wynant, whose whereabouts are still unknown, but he is by no means eager to take a hand, even though his wife, Nora, hints that she would like to have him prove that he is still a good detective. The police, in the meantime, suspect that he is working on the case and try their best to worm information out of him. While Charles never does formally take up the investigation, he cannot avoid frequent contacts with the various members of the Wynant family and with others who are, in one way or another, involved in the affairs of Wynant or of his secretary. Neither can he avoid drawing his own conclusion from the bits of information that come his way. When he finally solves the mystery, his wife finds the solution "pretty unsatisfactory," but that is because she has been expecting something in the jig-saw puzzle manner, with every piece in place before an arrest is made. The trouble with this method, according to Charles, is that the murderer has plenty of time to escape while the last few pieces are being fitted in.

The story is told by Charles himself, and there is nothing highbrow in his manner of telling it, any more than there is in his methods of detection. Those who want that sort of thing must look elsewhere, but those who enjoy a good story, racily told in the sort of language that a roughneck detective might be expected to use will find in this story a welcome relief from the neatly patterned solutions of the miracle men of detection fiction.

BOOK REVIEW:

John Chamberlain, Review of *The Thin Man*, *New York Times*, 9 January 1934.

Dashiell Hammett has been praised to the skies for his manner of writing mystery stories, for his hard-boiled lingo, for the speed and execution of his plots, for the realism of his characters, for his Hemingwayese and his Little Caesaritis, for his ability to knock 'em all dead. So we can omit the references to his hard, athletic prose, to his im-

plied refutation of Philo Vance, and to his various other much-belauded qualities, and concentrate instead upon the amazing laziness of Nick Charles, the detective of "The Thin Man" (Knopf, $2).

Really, this Nick Charles is a dream of a man. Detectives usually work so hard, burn up so much energy, wear down so many gumshoes to the inner soles, that we are worn out reading of them. But Nick Charles is a magnet, and the iron fillings group themselves around him with no seeking on his part. He should have been a psychoanalyst. In any case, he has the bedside manner. People run up to him on the street to confess. They buttonhole him in speakeasies to make known their hidden terrors. Gunmen blast their way to his hotel room to assure him of their innocence. Mulrooney's men take him into easy confidence. The culprit pals around with him, offering plausible explanations and alibis, even though Nick Charles has said repeatedly that he is not working on the case of the murder of Julia Wolf, who has been the stenographer of the mad and missing inventor, Clyde Wynant. And, in the end, Nick Charles puts the puzzle together with all the nonchalance of a man who is sitting for a cigarette advertisement picture. Nick Charles reminds one of Sidney Lenz performing a card trick, so deft and easy does he make it all appear.

Those Cute Little Thugs.

Of course, the easiness is all on the surface; Nick merely knows when to listen, where to go, whom to see. He has come, with his wife, Nora, who thinks thugs are cute, like Pekingese or bunny rabbits, to have a week's drinking in New York around Christmas time. Sleuthing is far behind Nick; he has all he can do to take care of his wife's property. But no sooner has he adorned a bar with his capable elbow than Dorothy Wynant has blown up to him. "Aren't you Nick Charles?" she asked. The minute Nick says "yes" his fate is foreordained. He will solve the mystery.

Personally, we wish he had been more interested in psychoanalysis than in the identity of the murderer. For the Wynant family–from Mimi, the mother, whose long nails can scratch, to Gilbert, the boy who experiments with morphine grains on sister Dorothy–is a family of latter day cards; one would like to see how far they can go. Incidentally, they have charm; but so had Lucrezia and Cesare Borgis. Nick walks among them with aplomb where a lesser man would have taken to the woods; his life is just so much bullet-proof chain mail. Between Mimi and Studsy Burke, proprietor of the Pigiron Club, we had rather beard Studsy. He, at least, would cleanly bump you off, where Mimi would leave your face hanging in picturesque ribbons.

We are very sorry to have committed the major blunder of being a day late with a review of "The Thin Man," but we live in a family of Hammett fiends, most of whom have been waiting since 1931 (the date of publication of the last Hammett mystery) with their tongues hanging out. And we really had no desire to be trampled on in an unconvincing effort to prove that possession is still nine points of the law. We are, of course, no Caspar Milquetoast, but bravery has its limits. We are sure the Hammett fiends of the nation will understand.

Mr. Hammett's detective *malgré lui*, Nick Charles, may be part of the art that influences life. Debonaire, sometimes disagreeable in a candid and paradoxically agreeable way, cautious, noncommittal, he makes a perfect man-about-town to imitate. His cool way of saying the most outrageous things should commend itself to the sherry-party-goer. Nick Charles can insult you and make you like it. Incidentally, Mr. Hammett has been reading "The Grand Manner." Maybe he has been passing it on to his detectives.

BOOK REVIEW:

Will Cuppy, Review of *The Thin Man*, *New York Herald Tribune*, 7 January 1934, p. 11.

We're another if Dashiell Hammett hasn't done it again. This most unusual author, darling of brows both high and low, has come through with a new hard-boiled opus worthy to stand beside the best of his other works, which (if you don't know) are "The Dain Curse," "Red Harvest," "The Maltese Falcon" and "The Glass Key."

In fact, "The Thin Man" is better than we fans had a right to hope for. "The Glass Key" (1931), if memory serves, was hardly up to "The Maltese Falcon" (1930), which also suffered in spots from a little too much falcon. Well, there are

no jewelled gadgets in this one, and there's plenty of that peculiar Hammett quality. For our part, the Hammett gift resides especially in the natural dialogue, or maybe in the natural characters who speak it.

Our sleuth this time turns out to be Nick Charles, who seems to be of Greek extraction–anyway, his wife, Nora, often calls him "a Greek louse." And he suddenly gets involved in the murder of Julia Wolf, confidential secretary to Clyde Wynant, the missing inventor; corpse discovered by Mrs. Mimi Jorgensen, ex-wife of same. So what about Shep Morelli, a homicidal dope? Who worked the badger game in Cleveland under the name of Rhoda Stewart? And where is Victor Rosewater, who made trouble about the invention? And so forth, but the main thing is to savor the Hammett lingo as you go along. Says Morelli, when told to ask the police: "Me that a police captain's been in a hospital for three weeks on account of we had an argument?" That isn't grammar, but it's literature.

You'll also take to Dorothy, the inventor's beautiful daughter, who has few inhibitions. Says she: "He's my father. I never liked him. I never liked Mamma. I don't like Gilbert." Gilbert's her brother. Dorothy shows up drunk at one point, with a revolver she got from a gunman in a Tenth Avenue joint. They all seem to drink a bit too much: which prevents one from following their psychology very closely, unless there's a psychology of tipsy people. And where this department got the idea that folks in books should be sober, so that you can check up on their mentality, we don't know, unless it was from Louisa M. Alcott. Three deaders in all. Required reading.

BOOK REVIEW:

T. S. Matthews, "Mr. Hammett Goes Coasting," *New Republic* (24 January 1934): 316.

A respected critic, Matthews pointed out that Hammett's fifth novel showed signs of artistic laziness.

Now that Dashiell Hammett is beginning to be taken seriously by the highbrows, my first enthusiasm for him is beginning to cool a little. Not that "The Thin Man" is not a first-rate murder story, and one that only Dashiell Hammett could have written. But, perhaps because he has turned the trick so easily before that he is now getting a little tired of it, perhaps because we are beginning to notice that he sometimes repeats his effects, "The Thin Man" seems a less excitingly fresh performance than, say, "The Maltese Falcon." It is still head-and-shoulders above any other murder story published since his last one. His hero this time is Nick Charles, a retired detective, whose holiday in New York with his rich young wife is threatened by the disappearance of Clyde Winant, an eccentric inventor, an old client of Nick's—in Nick's own words, "a good guy, but screwy." When it comes to that, the whole Winant family are pretty screwy, and Nick quite pardonably wants to have nothing to do with the case. He gets dragged in, willy-nilly, however, and in spite of his apparent laziness and an obvious addiction to liquor in a harsh and frequent form (his first remark to his wife in the mornings is usually a request for a drink "to cut the phlegm"), he bestirs himself sufficiently to get his man.

One reason why Hammett's books have been so outstanding, aside from the naturalism of his style, the careless humanity of his characters, is that his murders are gangster-political affairs, they come naturally out of his tough backgrounds, instead of being the kind of academic and farfetched bridge problems in a vacuum of the ordinary detective-story writer. In "The Thin Man," though his New York setting is authentic, and contains some very lifelike policemen, speakeasy proprietors and "rats," the crime and the criminal are in the orthodox tradition. Perhaps Mr. Hammett is coasting, or perhaps a little blue eagle has whispered something in his ear.

INTERVIEW ARTICLE:

Hammett, "Author of Stories Is Sorry He Killed His Book Character, *San Francisco Call-Bulletin*, 3 November 1934.

The MGM publicity department was almost certainly responsible for this article.

I was sitting in David O. Selznick's private projection room, squirming in my seat as the ghosts of my past paraded before my eyes, when a shot from a darkened doorway and my good friend,

Nunheim, crumpled to the sidewalk.

I am extremely sorry that I killed Nunheim, but I did not realize my friendship for him until after I had killed him. He was a rat, it is true, but he was a likable rat. He had pulled me out of many difficult places while I was writing "The Thin Man" and now that I have killed him he has been haunting my footsteps all the way from Florida to Hollywood.

This is only one example of what detective novelists must suffer. They create characters and work with them so long that the characters appear as living beings. Then we kill them, because it happens to be the easiest way to solve the labyrinthine problems of writing a detective story.

I could have used Nunheim to great advantage in the sequel to "The Thin Man," which I happened to be writing right now. I should have saved him so I could kill him in the sequel. I have devised a marvelous method of terminating his career in the sequel—but it remains a method without a Nunheim. Once a man's life is in jeopardy he cannot be executed a second time.

Wire-Haired Pooch Gets Another Role

This seems to be the trouble with all of the characters in "The Thin Man." I have viewed the picture three times, and every one of them appeals to me as a lovely character and a living personality, thanks to Producer Hunt Stromberg, Director W. S. Van Dyke and the cast.

The sequel is to be a continuance of the "Thin Man" mystery, picking up the story where the other ended and using the same characters—even to Asta, the wire-haired fox terrier.

Nunheim's passing causes me more anguish today than ever before. In the sequel, somebody must be killed—but I am at logger-heads to determine which character shall die. It would not be a mystery if somebody does not pay the supreme sacrifice.

Of course, I'm sure I will spare William Powell and Myrna Loy. None but a Frankenstein could eliminate either of these fine people. Yet the dilemma still haunts me.

Shall it be Minna Gombell, or Maureen O'Sullivan, or Henry Wadsworth, or William Henry, or Edward Brophy—or poor little Asta?

God forbid! It shall not be Asta!

I don't believe the question on page 192 of Dashiell Hammett's The Thin Man has had the slightest influence upon the sale of the book. It takes more than that to make a best seller these days. Twenty thousand people don't buy a book within three weeks to read a five word question.

Knopf chose to promote The Thin Man *as a bold book setting new standards for candid fiction. The five-word question referred to in this ad was posed by Nora Charles to her husband after he had wrestled with Mimi Jorgensen, the ex-wife of the inventor whose disappearance provides the mystery of the novel. Nora asks, "Didn't you have an erection?" "Oh, a little," he replies. "If you aren't a disgusting old lecher," she retorts. Largely as a result of this exchange the novel was banned in Canada.* Redbook *editor Edwin Balmer had excised the passage when he published the novel.*

Hence, the detective novelist's nightmare. The weapons are oiled, the knives are sharpened—awaiting the next victim. Little wonder that detective novelists never live to enjoy old age. They do not enjoy any age. They are constantly hounded by the crimes of their past . . . future.

* * * * *

INTERVIEW ARTICLE:

Joseph Harrington, "Hammett Solves Big Crime; Finds Ferris Wheel," *New York Evening Journal,* 28? January 1934.

Dashiell Hammett knows about crime from experience. In the days before he wrote about it, he solved, single-handedly, perhaps the biggest theft ever committed. He hates to hear the case brought

In a promotion arranged by King Features Syndicate, Hammett posed with King Features columnist Bugs Baer

"Bugs" Baer, famous columnist, proudly holds up "Bugs," Jr., who has just been made a member of the Secret Agent X-9 Club by Dashiell Hammett (right), famous detective story writer and author of "The Thin Man" and the thrilling detective strip, both of which are appearing currently in the Evening Journal. Picture by Evening Journal Staff Photographer.

From 29 January 1934 until 27 April 1935, Hammett lent his name as the writer of continuity for a syndicated daily (except Sunday) comic strip about the adventures of a super-hero crime fighter. The strip was drawn by Alex Raymond, who continued it after Hammett was fired for missing deadlines.

Division of Investigation

U. S. Department of Justice
318 Hewes Building
San Francisco, California

HRP:OHP   May 5, 1934

MR. NATHAN
MR. TOLSON
MR. CLEGG
MR. COWLEY
MR. EDWARDS
MR. EGAN
MR. QUINN
MR. LESTER
CHIEF CLERK
MR. ROOER

Director
Division of Investigation
U. S. Department of Justice
Washington, D. C.

Dear Sir:

In response to your letter of May 2, 1934 concerning a series of illustrated stories which is currently appearing in several papers on the West Coast dealing with the activities of Special Agent K-9.

Please be advised that undoubtedly the series of articles referred to is an illustrated story written by Dashiell Hammett, captioned "Secret Agent X-9". Attached hereto is today's illustration appearing in today's San Francisco Call-Bulletin and which, I am advised, appears in other affiliated Hearst papers on the West Coast. I am also attaching hereto a memorandum submitted by Special Agent ████████████ in this matter.

Discussing the matter with Agent ████████████ it does not appear that Hammett has made any representation to the effect that he is a former Special Agent of the Division of Investigation, or the Department of Justice.

Very truly yours,

R. E. Vetterli
R. E. Vetterli
Special Agent in Charge

Encl. 2.
c.c. Los Angeles

RECORDED
&
INDEXED
MAY 16 1934

62-31619-2

DIVISION OF INVESTIGATION
MAY 14 1934 A.M.
U. S. DEPARTMENT OF JUSTICE

DE-INDEXED
DATE 3/5/57
13

Hammett's comic strip prompted FBI director J. Edgar Hoover, who had misunderstood the hero's name, to inquire whether Hammett ought to be investigated for ridiculing the service. This response to Hoover's inquiry is the first item in Hammett's 278-page FBI file that covers twenty-seven years.

[152]

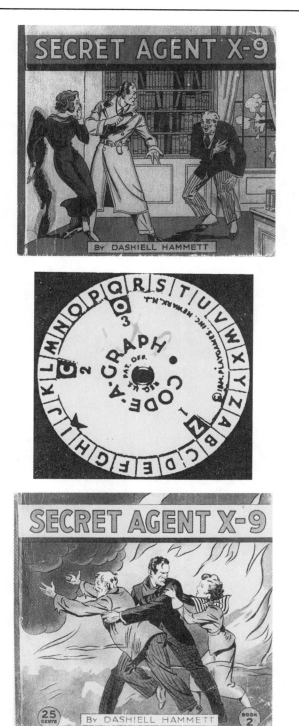

Secret Agent X-9 *was sold with a decoder to decipher coded messages displayed in the strip*

Hammett and his sister Reba at the Hotel Lombard, January 1934.

The movie of Hammett's novel The Thin Man, *which starred William Powell and Myrna Loy as Nick and Nora Charles, was very successful, prompting MGM to hire Hammett to write sequels*

In addition to Secret Agent X-9, in 1934 and 1935 King Features Syndicate distributed a series of Hammett's short stories and, four months after the book publication, the entire text of The Thin Man *to newspapers all over the country. Hammett's works were aggressively advertised, as in this full-page ad in the San Francisco Call-Bulletin. The stories were edited for newspaper publication; for example, the Continental Op is referred to as Continental Op Number 7, apparently to identify him with Secret Agent X-9.*

up, though, seeing that he's taken enough ribbing about it.

It was the theft of a full-grown ferris wheel from a client of the Pinkertons. Hammett, a Pinkerton then, solved it by process of elimination. He eliminated everybody right away, except carnival owners. He just tracked down carnivals with ferris wheels until he found one for which the company had no receipted bill, he said.

"Those are the facts. Sometimes the story, in certain circles, gets garbled. So much so that I am called The Man Who Stole A Ferris Wheel. There's no truth to that."

Takes Charge Lightly

The author of "The Thin Man" and "The Maltese Falcon" whose comic strip "Secret Agent X-9" begins in the New York Journal Monday was not particularly outraged by the libel. He isn't as [ ] or grim as the detectives he writes about. The incorrect identification of the ferris wheel mystery undoubtedly had its origin in Hammett's reputation for mischievousness, which, in certain quarters, exceeds his fame for shocking drama. He declared:

"I do take most of my characters from real life. Nick's wife in 'The Thin Man' is real, for instance. Nick himself is a composite of two or three detectives."

Appearance Striking.

None of his detectives ever look like himself, probably because he is too much like a fictionized detective in appearance. Very tall, very lean, with a dark moustache, a brown face and a shock of snow white hair sweeping back from his forehead, any description of himself would be unconvincing. He is meticulous in his dress, is very lazy, and proud of it. He explained:

"I'm a two-fisted loafer. I can loaf longer and better than anybody I know. I did not acquire this genius. I was born with it. I quit school when I was thirteen because I wanted to loaf. I sold newspapers for a while, loafed, became a stevedore, loafed, worked in a machine shop, loafed, became a stock broker, loafed, went into the advertising business, loafed, tried hoboing in earnest, loafed, became a Pinkerton detective for seven years and went into the army.

Newspaper advertisement

"I was a sergeant during the war, but–please get this straight–not in the war. The war and my service in the army were contemporary, that's all you can say about it."

After the war, in which he took no part, Hammett became ill. He spent a year in a hospital, then tried to go back to work, but found it didn't agree with him. He remarked:

"That's how I came to take up writing, and I've been at it ever since.

"Hobbies? Let's see, I drink a lot. Also play poker. That's all. I had a dog once, but he died.

Summers I live down at Port Washington; Winters here in Manhattan. I'm married; two children."

Hammett never works at regular hours and hasn't slept at nights for years. When he does work, he gets at his typewriter between midnight and 2 A.M. and stays there until daybreak; if his inspiration is strong, or he is being hounded for copy, he may stay at it until noon, then go to bed, getting up at sundown.

MOVIE REVIEW:
Frank S. Nugent, Review of *Mister Dynamite, New York Times*, 25 May 1935, p. 12.

In September 1934 Universal bought Hammett's screen story "On the Make," which had been rejected by Paramount. The movie that resulted, called Mister Dynamite, *was released in May 1935 and starred Edmund Lowe in the title role.*

MR. DYNAMITE, from Dashiell Hammett's story, "On the Make"; screen play by Doris Malloy and Harry Clork; directed by Alan Crosland; a Universal production.

Mr. Dynamite	Edmund Lowe
Lynn	Jean Dixon
Charmion	Esther Ralston
Dvorjak	Victor Varconi
Mona	Verna Hillie
Lewis	Minor Watson
King	Robert Gleckler
Williams	Jameson Thomas
Sunshine	Matt McHugh
Rod	G. Pat Collins
Jans	Greta Meyer
Felix	Bradley Page
Joe	James Burtis

Much as we hesitate to spread the tidings, the evidence points this morning to the birth of a new screen detective. His name is T. N. Thompson, private operative who concludes each case in a blaze of glory and a burst of profanity from the San Francisco detective squad. In the fast and furious person of Edmund Lowe, the newest of the Vance-Chan-Mason line is making his bow to Times Square in an amiable excursion into homicide called "Mr. Dynamite," at the Roxy.

Mr. Dynamite—you might as well get used to the name, because no one calls T. N. Thompson

anything else—is the creation of Dashiell Hammett, who wrote "The Thin Man." Mr. Hammett's distinction among mystery tale spinners is that he never takes his corpse as seriously as his detective; and he never lets his detective take himself seriously at all.

The three or four corpses in the picture and Mr. Lowe lend themselves agreeably to this technique. When Dynamite meets a body he doesn't go prowling around looking for fingerprints; instead he steals the clues and uses them later to show up his pet foe, the chief of detectives. He regards his clients as fair game and bills them heavily for office supplies, such being a handy term for ermine wraps for his feminine stooge and accomplice. Reprehensible—as some one has said—is the word for Mr. Dynamite's private detecting.

At any rate, there's no cause to complain about the death rate in the new picture. The first to go is a young unknown who has won $10,000 in a gambling casino. He is machine-gunned on the casino grounds, which is no end embarrassing to the proprietor, one Mr. Lewis. Next to depart is Jari Dvorjak, concert pianist, whose demise occurs in the presence of Mr. Lewis's attractive daughter. The Lewis family now is completely embarrassed, particularly since the police are inclined to be unpleasant about it, too.

In desperation—it had to be that—Lewis calls in Mr. Dynamite to prove to the world that even a gambler draws the line somewhere—specifically at murder. Dynamite uses his wits and his tongue, in about a 50-50 proportion, and cracks the case. But not until two other whiteskins have bitten the dust.

A racy, toughly written tale, the picture has all the advantages of swift pace, a capable cast and a compact story. Mr. Lowe proves again that, given the lines, he can play them with any man. Jean Dixon is excellent as his verbally hard-hitting assistant. Verna Hillie, Minor Watson, Victor Varconi, Esther Ralston and the others must share a collective bow.

MOVIE REVIEW:
Frank S. Nugent, Review of *After the Thin Man, New York Times*, 26 December 1936, p. 19.
To capitalize on the success of The Thin Man, *MGM produced a series of sequels starring William Powell and*

Dashiell Hammett Confesses!

Ace detective writer breaks down under third degree and bares secrets of his exciting 'Girl Hunt'

He wrote "The Thin Man," which (l. to r.) William Powell, Maureen O'Sullivan and Myrna Loy made into a motion picture classic.

Next week, in this magazine, Dashiell Hammett, above, will smash through with another thrilling story, "Girl Hunt."

By JAMES H. S. MOYNAHAN,
Author of "Blowoff," "The House That Death Built," "The Corpse of the Nude Girl."

THERE'S as much jealousy between authors as between actresses and sopranos, but ask professional detective-story writers who their own favorite is, and they'll cast all their votes for Dashiell Hammett. Here one of Hammett's competitors as a crime novelist provides a vivid closeup of the author of "The Thin Man," "The Glass Key," "The Maltese Falcon" and "Girl Hunt," the mystery story beginning in this magazine next week.

HAMMETT—his full name is Samuel Dashiell Hammett—talks like "Continental Op No. 7," the character he has made as famous as Sherlock Holmes and who reappears in "Girl Hunt," beginning next week in this magazine.

When I arrived for this interview, I told him: "This will be practically painless."

"Dash," in coarse yellow lounging robe, nodded at the pantry: "Do yourself a drink, maybe it won't hurt you so much!"

I brought the brandy and soda out into a living room so filled with books that I had to move a couple of novels and the current London Mercury off the coffee table to set down my drink. These books are characteristic of the Hammett menage. A glance over their titles would tell Sam Spade, one of his famous detective characters, that here, undoubtedly, was the library of a college professor.

"How'd you come to write this yarn, 'Girl Hunt'?" I asked him when we were settled.

He bent his straight brows together and explained that there had been two famous cases of flypaper poisoning, and they had suggested a basic idea for a story. Just the idea, for as "Girl Hunt"

emerged from his typewriter it did not parallel the actual crimes in any detail.

I went on. "This McCloor, the big gangster in the 'Girl Hunt,' did he have a prototype in real life?"

I found that he did. The real Babe McCloor was a member of Jimmie the Riveter's mob—they were a bunch of boys that the Pinkertons, Mr. Hammett's former employers, ran down in the Winter of 1921-22. They'd been pulling stickups up and down the Pacific coast and knocking over various commercial enterprises until Jimmie was taken into custody coming out of the postoffice in Seattle. An army of deputies rushed the mob to the station in handcuffs. Just outside the station, the yegg who was McCloor's original made a dive, handcuffs and all, for a deputy's gun and shot it out right there in the street.

He knew another mobster as tough as Jimmie. "Once I was sitting with this Detroit mug when a fight started across the room. He tossed a .45 Colt into my lap. 'Will you hold that gun for me,' he asked. 'I wanna get into this fight.'"

In writing a story Hammett decides on his characters, he told me, and when he knows them thoroughly, and their relations to each other, he sits down and lets them work the story out for him. "If I don't like the way a character behaves," he told me, "I kill him off in the next paragraph." He spread his hands. "Why not? If somebody works for you and you don't like him you fire him, don't you?"

"Ever shot at yourself?" I asked.

"That's one thing you never get to like," he said. "It even gets worse every time." He didn't care much for the time he and other Pinkerton men went to a house to arrest a gang of negroes who had been stealing dynamite back during the war days. "Everybody thought it was the Germans," he explained, "and there was quite a scare. When I got inside this house men were being knocked around in fine shape. In the excitement I had a feeling something was wrong but I could

not figure what it was till I happened to look down and saw this negro whittling away at my leg." He bears the scar to this day.

"How do you go about getting a confession?" I asked him, still on his years as a detective.

He laughed. "I'll tell you a hot one," he said. "I once knew a man who used to be an ace at that stuff and what do you think he used to do? He'd talk to these mugs about their mothers until he had them weeping. I've even known him to go down and pray with them. Then he'd get the confession and turn 'em in. He saw nothing inconsistent in it, either. But that's a funny thing—the way people confess. I used to think it'd be hard, but you'd be surprised how eager people seem to be to get put away.

"The best way, I've found, is to see their side. Why, we know you didn't mean any harm when you cut up these three gals in the bathtub, but if you start acting ashamed and secretive, the District Attorney may think there was something criminal about it. They go for it every time."

HAMMETT was born in St. Mary's County, Md., May 27, 1894, and was educated in public schools and the Polytechnic Institute of Baltimore. Successively clerk, stevedore and private detective, he turned to writing in 1922, while an invalid from war injuries he suffered in an ambulance corps.

His first stories appeared in Smart Set and Black Mask when those magazines were edited by Henry L. Mencken, Baltimore's other most distinguished citizen. He works on a typewriter and never rewrites; his first draft is his last, hence he produces slowly and laboriously the stories that established a new school of detective fiction and made him the most imitated writer of the time. His machine-gun style and sharp dialogue marked a new era in smartly-done thrillers.

He is married and has two daughters. He likes dogs, music and table tennis, and is a connoisseur of fine liqueurs. He reads endlessly of everything except detective stories. His favorite bedtime tale is Spengler's "Decline of the West."

14

Copyright, 1936, King Features Syndicate, Inc.

This syndicated interview/article was written to promote the newspaper syndication of Hammett's story "Girl Hunt," one of a series of his stories syndicated by King Features.

Myrna Loy. After the Thin Man *was the second of six* Thin Man *movies.*

AFTER THE THIN MAN, from a story by Dashiell Hammett; screen play by Frances Goodrich and Albert Hackett; music and lyrics by Nacio Herb Brown and Arthur Freed, Walter Donaldson, Chet Forrest and Bob Wright; directed by W. S. Van Dyke; produced by Hunt Stromberg for Metro-Goldwyn-Mayer. At the Capitol.

Nick Charles	William Powell
Nora	Myrna Loy
David	James Stewart
Selma	Elissa Landi
"Dancer"	Joseph Calleia
Aunt Katherine	Jessie Ralph
Robert	Alan Marshall
Casper	Teddy Hart
Abrams	Sam Levene
Polly	Dorothy McNulty
Lum Kee	William Law
Dr. Kammer	George Zucco
Phil	Paul Fix

If "After the Thin Man" is not quite the delight "The Thin Man" was, it is, at the very least, one of the most urbane comedies of the season and an enterprise so agreeable that we are convinced that the Capitol (where it begins its engagement today) is one of Santa Claus's favorite Broadway children. Sequels commonly are disappointing and Metro-Goldwyn-Mayer was borrowing trouble when it dared advance a companion piece to one of the best pictures of 1934. But Dashiell Hammett's sense of humor has endured, W. S. Van Dyke retains his directorial facility and William Powell and Myrna Loy still persuade us that Mr. and Mrs. Nick Charles are exactly the sort of people we should like to have on our calling list on New Year's Day and for all the rest of the year.

In a changing age it is completely heartening to discover that the Charles family–Nick, the amateur sleuth, Nora, his understanding but frequently underfoot wife, and Asta, the hydrant fancier–has weathered successfully the well-known vicissitudes of time. They have managed to retain their liking (Asta excepted) for alcoholic beverages and they continue to immerse themselves in mur-

der mysteries in a spirit of good fellowship, clean fun and malice toward none, the murderer included. If Asta has reason to suspect the faithfulness of Mrs. Asta, there being a black scotty in the offing, and if Nora happens to stem from an atrocious line of Nob Hill relics, these are essentially minor revelations and revolutions: the Charleses carry on.

And they really do carry on, with Nick–the democratic–taking up with all kinds of disreputable characters and Nora, eyebrows only slightly raised, meeting them with dignity and a twinkle in her eye. The picture bruises that dignity slightly by placing its murder right in the midst of her Nob Hill relatives, as stuffy a group of chromos as the screen has assembled on a mauve set. It is the worthless husband of Nora's favorite cousin who gets himself dispatched on a New Year's Eve with a packet of negotiable bonds in his pocket and a few score suspects lurking about to baffle Detective Abrams and us, the public.

Nick's ultimate solution of the case–which we could not reveal if we would–is about the most thoroughly upsetting dénouement of the year and is practically enough to drive the second-guessers in the audience to the nearest soda fountain for a sedative or a rhubarb and soda. Anyway, it proves that this Mr. Charles is a fairly superior detective, considerably less elementary than Sherlock Holmes and much more enigmatic than Charlie Chan. But who cares about the mystery story plot when you have such matters as that welcome-home party for Nick and Nora at which the guests, strangers all, fail to recognize their involuntary hosts; or that scene in which Nora tells her sleepy husband she really would not think of asking him to prepare some scrambled eggs? But of course she is terribly fond of his cooking or that baby-bootie knitting scene at the end. . . . We won't mention the other details. It will be better for you to enjoy them for yourselves. We warn you that you will.

INTERVIEW:

Henry Dan Piper, "Dashiel [sic] Hammett flees Night Club Round Succumbing to Rustication in New Jersey," *Daily Princetonian,* 11 November 1936, pp. 1, 4.

In the fall of 1936 Hammett rented a house in Princeton, New Jersey, where he stayed through the winter until his rowdy parties prompted neighbors to ask him to leave. Princeton student Henry Dan Piper interviewed Hammett for the university newspaper.

Wearied of New York's sophisticated clatter, the tall, prematurely greying Dashiell Hammett, author of "The Thin Man" and "The Glass Key," has escaped to the privacy of a rambling, white clapboard farmhouse perched on a hillside outside of Princeton.

"This is the life" he sighed, seated in his armchair before a roaring fire, and succumbing to the inquisition of a PRINCETONIAN interviewer. "You can get fed plenty cooped up in a three-room apartment, making the same rounds every night—Stork Club, 21, Dempsey's—seeing the same old faces and hearing the same damned chatter. Nuts."

"There isn't much to tell about me," he said. "Baltimore as a kid . . . school for a coupla of years . . . stevedore . . . newsboy . . . Golly, I've seen lots of things, but I never seemed to stick long at 'em.

"When the Armistice came along, all I could boast was a pair of weak lungs contracted in the Ambulance Corps. I did some private detective work for Pinkerton's, but all the time I was getting sicker, and found myself shortly in a California hospital.

"Then it was a case of turning to something to keep the butcher away from the door while I tried to bluff along the baker. So I rented a second-hand typewriter and pounded out my first novel. It was just a case of lucky breaks after that.

"Yes, I'm working on a book here, but it's not a mystery, and it's not about Princeton. I really don't like detective stories, anyway. I get too tangled up in the plots. This one is just about a family of a dozen children out on an island. You see, all I do in a story is just get some characters together, and then let them get in each other's way. And let me tell you, 12 kids can sure get in each other's way!"

Asked if he were indulging in any more stories about the liquor-swilling, sophisticated penthouse dwellers of "The Thin Man," Hammett wrinkled his brow and exclaimed, "I can't understand why people get the idea all I ever write is artificial, with tinseled-and-ginned up characters. They're just like lots of people I know, neurotics and what have you.

"You know, ideas float around that New York and Hollywood people are all nuts. I've just come back from working on a new Powell-Loy film and I admit lots of those guys out there are screwy. But, hell, they've got tons of money to be screwy with. And anyhow, they're no more bats than a lot of over-stuffed executives I've had the misfortune to meet.

"Yes, it's going to be like the others," he said, returning to the new movie. "They say they're going to call it 'After the Thin Man.' Heaven only knows why. Before Hollywood started monkeying with the plot it was something like 'The Thin Man,' but its own mother wouldn't recognize it now."

MOVIE REVIEW:

Frank S. Nugent, Review of *Another Thin Man*, *New York Times*, 24 November 1939, p. 39.

Despite Hammett's lack of cooperation MGM released the third of the Thin Man movies, Another Thin Man, *based on Hammett's sketchy screen story, in November 1939. Hammett was released permanently from his MGM contract on 14 July 1939.*

ANOTHER THIN MAN, screen play by Frances Goodrich and Albert Hackett based on a story by Dashiell Hammett; directed by W. S. Van Dyke 2d; produced by Hunt Stromberg for Metro-Goldwyn-Mayer. At the Capitol.

Nick Charles	William Powell
Nora	Myrna Loy
Jan Stack	Otto Kruger
Colonel Macfay	C. Aubrey Smith
Lois Macfay	Virginia Gray
Dorothy Waters	Ruth Hussey
Lieutenant Guild	Nat Pendleton
Dudley Horn	Patric Knowles
Freddie	Tom Neal
Mrs. Bellam	Phyllis Gordon
Phil Church	Sheldon Leonard
"Diamond Back" Vogel	Don Costello
"Creeps"	Harry Bellaver
Nickie Jr.	William A. Poulsen
Smitty	Muriel Hutchison
"Dum-Dum"	Abner Biberman
Mrs. Dolley	Marjorie Main
and Asta.	

Hammett was bound by contract to deliver his sixth novel to Alfred A. Knopf Publishers in 1936. When he failed, Knopf angrily released him from the contract, which was picked up for a $5,000 advance by Bennett Cerf at Random House. The novel, titled "There Was a Young Man," was announced for publication in 1939, but Hammett did not deliver. Two years later, he returned the advance to Cerf, telling him "I'm afraid I'll never write it. I'm petering out."

Hammett speaking at an anti-Nazi rally, late 1930s

An Open Letter to All People of Good Will

The overwhelming majority of the American people, reared in the tradition of liberty and democracy, are revolted by Nazism and Fascism.

Hitler agents and fascist-minded persons in America, however, are trying to undermine the foundations of American democracy. Most of them dare not appeal openly to the American people with a fascist program because of America's great democratic traditions. While paying lip service to democracy, the fascists and the fascist-minded organizations are spreading anti-Semitism (the weapon of all fascist movements), in order to weaken democracy and destroy the principles of the Declaration of Independence and the Bill of Rights.

The tide of anti-Semitism which has engulfed Nazi Germany, Italy, Poland, Rumania, Czechoslovakia and Hungary, has not only destroyed whole Jewish communities but democracy as well. The crisis of the Jewish people is part and parcel of the crisis of democracy.

June, 1939

TO HELP US ACCOMPLISH THESE AIMS,

TO SPREAD THESE IDEAS,

TO DO SOMETHING PRACTICAL TOWARDS

STAMPING OUT ANTI-SEMITISM —

SUPPORT AND SUBSCRIBE TO EQUALITY

- - - - - - - - - (Please detach here) - - - - - - - - -

EQUALITY
220 Fifth Avenue
New York City

Gentlemen:

Please enter my subscription for one year of EQUALITY for which I am enclosing $1.50.

Name _____

Address _____

City_____ State_____

By the end of the 1930s Hammett was active in left-wing politics, and if he had not joined the Communist Party USA, he was certainly a sympathetic with the party's aims. In the summer of 1939 Hammett headed the seven-person group that formed Equality Publishers, which dedicated itself to "an uncompromising fight against the enemies of humanity." The group published Equality *magazine, which had its own editorial board, from May 1939 to October/November 1940 and then faded from existence.*

We, the editors of *Equality*, recognizing that the forces of anti-Semitism and Fascism are inseparable, know that they can be destroyed.

Equality appeals to all people of good will, regardless of race, color or creed, to defend democratic rights. Where anti-Semitism and Fascism exist, there you find not only persecution of Jews but also of Catholics and Protestants. Fascism makes war upon labor, upon all liberal thought, upon culture, upon science, upon the Negro people and all minority groups. Under a Hitler, Mussolini, or a Franco, human dignity is degraded, while barbarism, national oppression and wars of invasion are made state worship.

Equality calls upon the Jews to whom the threat of anti-Semitism and Fascism is most directly apparent, to affirm this truth: *To survive, a people must be willing to fight in its own defense.*

We believe that silence on the part of certain Jews in the face of persecution of their fellows abroad or in the face of discrimination and slander against Jews here, is a criminal abdication of their human right to life, liberty and the pursuit of happiness.

The fight against anti-Semitism and the defense of democracy are one. It is in the immediate self-interest of the American people to combat the threat of anti-Semitism and racial intolerance to America. It is in the especial self-interest of the Jewish people to resist anti-Semitism and take a leading part in the defense of American democracy!

To arouse the American people to an active fight against anti-Semitism, and to unite the Jewish people in the defense of their rights and of democracy, we are launching *Equality*, a new progressive monthly, which will pursue the following policies:

Program of Equality

We will work for united action by all peoples, all religious groups and all nationalities, to defend democracy and combat anti-Semitism and Fascism.

We will expose Fascist tendencies and anti-Semitic organizations and activities wherever they assert themselves, and we will name names.

We will urge cooperation with all movements which are fighting honestly and unequivocally against Fascism and anti-Semitism.

We will support adequate legislation and will encourage militant action for the outlawing of discrimination. We will expose and combat social and economic discrimination wherever it appears and will defend the rights of labor as an integral part of the defense of democratic rights.

We will present up-to-the-minute news, comment and analyses by competent authorities on the status and problems of the Jews in the United States and the Americas, Germany, Poland, Rumania, Palestine and the Soviet Union.

We will present articles on Jewish history with particular emphasis on the rich, dramatic but insufficiently known contributions and traditions of the Jewish people to American culture and democracy.

We will present translations of the best of Jewish literature in all languages and will encourage the growth of a contemporary American-Jewish culture in English.

We set as our goal a united American people acting in the defense of its own democracy.

We dedicate ourselves to an uncompromising fight against the enemies of humanity.

Editorial Council

RABBI MICHAEL ALPER
NATHAN AUSUBEL
BENNETT A. CERF
ABRAHAM CHAPMAN
DASHIELL HAMMETT
MOSS HART
LILLIAN HELLMAN
ARTHUR KOBER
LOUIS KRONENBERGER
PRINCE HUBERTUS ZU LOEWENSTEIN
ALBERT MALTZ
DUDLEY NICHOLS
DOROTHY PARKER
BERTRAND E. POLLANS
DONALD OGDEN STEWART
LEANE ZUGSMITH

NATIONAL FEDERATION
for
CONSTITUTIONAL LIBERTIES
Washington, D. C.

CHAIRMAN
REV. OWEN A. KNOX
Detroit, Mich.

BENJAMIN ALLEN
Treasurer

MILTON N. KEMNITZ
Executive Secretary

VICE-CHAIRMEN
JOSEPHINE TRUSLOW ADAMS
Philadelphia, Pa.

MALCOLM COTTON DOBBS
Chattanooga, Tenn.

HON. VITO MARCANTONIO
Congressman from New York

CARRY MCWILLIA
Los Angeles, Cali.

ALFRED K. STEAR
New York, N. Y

MAX YERGAN
New York, N. Y

Committee on Election Rights — 1940
100 Fifth Ave., New York, N.Y.   GRamercy 3-6322
DASHIELL HAMMETT Chairman   HELEN R. BRYAN Executive Secretary

September 7, 1940.

Dear Friend:

Your right to vote as you please is being violated in many States, and is being threatened with violation in many more.

Enclosed is a brief outline of what the enemies of democracy are doing in this field, and of what may be done -- and must be done -- to combat them. Read it.

THE NATIONAL FEDERATION, through its COMMITTEE ON ELECTION RIGHTS - 1940, is already at work. Legal action, the arousing of public opinion, the organization of widespread protest, is being undertaken in Massachusetts -- where election officials have denied the Prohibition, Socialist, Socialist Labor and Communist Parties a place on the ballot -- and in West Virginia, Pennsylvania and Arizona, where terrorism, official violation of State and National laws, and the courts have combined to deny minority parties their constitutional rights.

The COMMITTEE must plan and carry out similar campaigns in other States. This is a fight that must be made NOW. It is a fight that will be won or lost in the two short months between now and election day.

The COMMITTEE needs your help.

It needs money -- whatever you can give.

It needs you as a member of the NATIONAL FEDERATION FOR CONSTITUTIONAL LIBERTIES -- either as an individual or as a member of an affiliated organization.

It needs your help in sending protests to public officials and newspapers wherever the rights of minority parties are violated, and to the U. S. Attorney General and members of Congress.

It needs any information you have about the violation of minority rights in your locality.

And it needs all this NOW.

Sincerely yours,

Dashiell Hammett
Chairman

In 1940 Hammett served as national chairman of the Committee on Election Rights–1940, a group that promoted members of the Communist Party in the elections of that year.

[164]

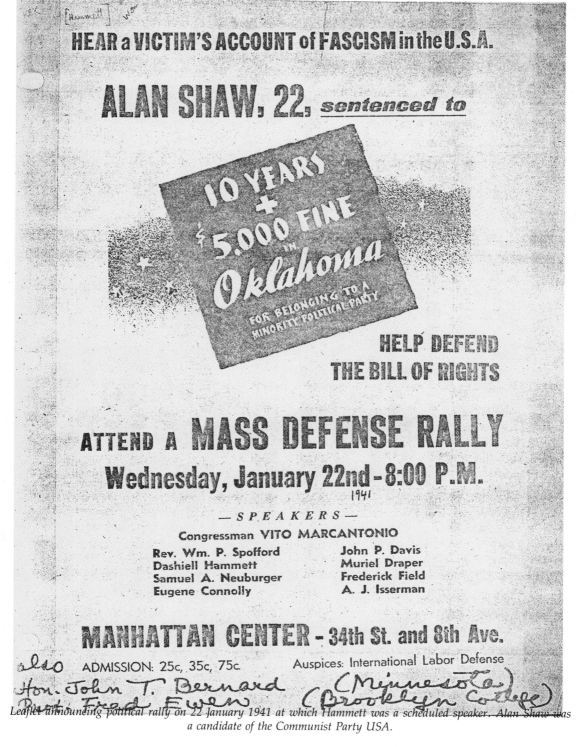

Leaflet announcing political rally on 22 January 1941 at which Hammett was a scheduled speaker. Alan Shaw was a candidate of the Communist Party USA.

Two years after the 1941 hit Broadway production of Lillian Hellman's play Watch on the Rhine, *Warner Brothers released a movie version adapted by Hammett. The movie edition of the play published in 1943 is illustrated with scenes from the film, including this frontispiece showing Paul Lukas and Bette Davis in the climactic scene.*

[166]

Defend Your Right to Vote!

What to Do

RIGHT NOW, Mail the post card below to Governor Lehman.

Wire or write to YOUR OWN ASSEMBLYMAN AND YOUR OWN STATE SENATOR urging defeat of the Dunnigan and Devany Election Bills.

Ask your union or other organization to pass resolutions against the Dunnigan and Devany Bills and send copies to Assemblymen and State Senators.

Contribute to the working fund of the Committee on Free Elections.

The Committee on Free Elections was established by the National Federation for Constitutional Liberties. It stands for the right of minority parties, regardless of their platforms, to place their candidates on the ballot, and the right of citizens to vote as they please.

For more copies of this folder, or additional information, address:

DASHIELL HAMMETT, Chairman
COMMITTEE ON FREE ELECTIONS
100 FIFTH AVENUE
NEW YORK CITY

HONORABLE HERBERT H. LEHMAN
EXECUTIVE MANSION
ALBANY, NEW YORK

DEAR SIR:

You proclaimed the week of February 16th to 23 as "Bill of Rights Week." In your proclamation you said:

"We know that the safeguards of our freedom, guaranteed in our basic Law, will remain strong only if we are vigilant in their protection and if our faith in the democratic processes is unshaken."

I believe that the Dunnigan and Devany Election Bills violate the principles of the Bill of Rights of the United States Constitution. They would destroy the very foundations of representative government and deny Americans the right to vote as they please.

I urge you to use all your influence to prevent the enactment of these undemocratic measures.

Name ....

Address ....

MAR 8 1941

"Defend Your Right to Vote!" promotional leaflet for Committee on Free Elections

The Dunnigan and Devany Bills Endanger Your Right to Vote as You Please

In Albany today, attempts to amend the election law threaten "Ja" elections for New York State. These bills ban one political party by name. They could be used to outlaw all parties except the one in power.

- These bills are Senate Introductory numbers 2 and 3 introduced by Senator John J. Dunnigan, and Assembly Introductory number 201 introduced by Assemblyman John A. Devany, Jr., to bar certain persons from public office or employment, and ban political parties from the ballot.
- Americans who advocated such laws as the Child Labor Amendment or the popular election of the President of the United States could be included under these laws.
- Such citizens would become ineligible for public office and the political parties they belong to can be outlawed, under these bills.

Your Party Could Be Snatched Off the Ballot

Your party, even if it is not named in the bills, could be killed on the basis of these and similar questions:

- Most trade unions, many church societies, some lodges and business men's organizations have international affiliations. Do you belong to such an organization?
- Mere criticism of the party in power might be interpreted as "antagonism to our form of government." Do you ever criticize the party in power?
- Today peaceful strikes for a living wage are branded as violent attempts to sabotage national defence. Would you give up your right to strike peacefully for a living wage?

One Man Alone Could Take Away Your Vote

The Secretary of State, a political appointee, would decide which parties to exclude from the ballot. Representing the party in power, he could prohibit any opposition parties or candidates.

These bills which attempt to define persons antagonistic to our form of government are in themselves antagonistic to democracy. You have a voice in government only so long as you can exercise your choice unhampered, without limitation on the number or political opinions of the candidates and parties.

"In the maintenance of free elections rests the complete and enduring safety of our form of government."
President Franklin D. Roosevelt
Philadelphia, September 20, 1940.

Threat to Free Elections Sweeps Across the Nation

The Dunnigan and Devany Bills represent more than a narrow, isolated threat to a free ballot.

- In Pennsylvania, Oklahoma, South Dakota, Colorado, Washington, Wyoming, Wisconsin, Vermont, California, and Oregon, similar legislation is pending.
- In California a state law passed last year bars the Communist Party by name from primary elections.
- In West Virginia an amendment to the State Election Law, making it virtually impossible for any new or minority party to qualify for a place on the ballot has just been enacted.
- These attacks on free elections are part of the vast plan to stifle civil liberties and repeal the Bill of Rights through anti-strike legislation, criminal syndicalism laws and similar measures.

Place One Cent Stamp Here

THE HONORABLE HERBERT H. LEHMAN

EXECUTIVE MANSION

ALBANY, NEW YORK

On 17 September 1942 Hammett, age forty-eight, entered the U.S. Army as a private, despite poor eyesight, bad teeth, and a questionable political record. After being briefly stationed at Camp Shenango in Transfer, Pennsylvania, a facility designed to house suspected subversives, he was sent to Adak, Alaska, in the Aleutians.

THE BATTLE OF THE ALEUTIANS

In honor and memory of the men of the North Pacific Theater who died

so that a continent might be free

★   ★   ★

A chain of unsinkable aircraft carriers now stretches
across the North Pacific — from the shores of Alaska to
the threshold of Japan. This small book is a partial record
of the men who fought for these Aleutian bases, and the
men who built them into impregnable fortresses that history
will remember as the Northern Highway to Victory.

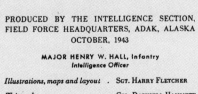

★   ★   ★   ★   ★

PRODUCED BY THE INTELLIGENCE SECTION,
FIELD FORCE HEADQUARTERS, ADAK, ALASKA
OCTOBER, 1943

MAJOR HENRY W. HALL, Infantry
Intelligence Officer

Illustrations, maps and layout .   SGT. HARRY FLETCHER

Written by . . . .   CPL. DASHIELL HAMMETT
CPL. ROBERT COLODNY

Reproduction by detachment 29th Engineers stationed
with Headquarters Western Defense Command
1944

Hammett was instructed to write a history of the war in the Aleutians in 1942 and 1943. He enlisted the help of Corporal Robert Colodny, a historian and a veteran of the Abraham Lincoln Brigade. Colodny wrote the text; Hammett wrote the captions for photos.

[169]

In the gay tradition of its predecessors, howbeit a trifle more forced in its gayety, is "Another Thin Man," latest of the Dashiell Hammett series to reach the Capitol's screen. With William Powell back in domestic harness as Nick Charles, with Myrna Loy as the almost too-perfect helpmeet, and with–of all people–a Nick Jr. to guarantee the continuance of the series, this third of the trademarked Thin Men takes its murders as jauntily as ever, confirms our impression that matrimony need not be too serious a business and provides as light an entertainment as any holiday-amusement seeker is likely to find.

This still does not mean that we are willing to surrender to it completely. Some of the bloom is off the rose. A few of the running gags are beginning to show signs of pulling up lame. All this is bound to happen when a "Thin Man" leads to "After the Thin Man" and develops "Another Thin Man." The law of diminishing returns tends to put any comedy on a reducing diet and it may, unless his next script is considerably brighter, confound us with a Thin Man thinned to the point of emaciation. It hasn't happened yet, mark! We're merely getting in our warning early, notifying Metro-Goldwyn-Mayer that there's a limit to everything–including the charm of the delightful Mr. and Mrs. Charles.

It's murder again, of course, that Nick and Nora are up against when they run out to Long Island to spend a quite week-end with Colonel Macfay–murder and an unpleasant chap named Phil Church, who has the anti-social habit of dreaming that people are dead. (And when he wakes up, sure enough: they're dead.) Mr. Church dreams about the Colonel. Exit Colonel. Later on he dreams about Nick. Exit Mr. Church. (Seems there's a law at Metro against killing detective heroes.) Anyway that leaves two murders to be unriddled and a likely passel of suspects, including such picturesquely named gentlemen as Diamond-Back Vogel, Creeps and Dum-Dum.

Frances Goodrich and Albert Hackett have spun their who-dunnit into a thoroughly mystifying tangle, but one of the rules of the Thin Man is that the corpses be kept from crowding the comedy. That is why the two most amusing sequences concern Nora's rhumba with a loving Latin in a night club, Nick's invasion of a frankly unrespectable rooming house run by our favorite biddy, Marjorie Mains. If all of it had been up to their standard, our report this morning should have been unqualifiedly thankful. We're still appreciative, but we found too many chestnuts in the dressing.

EDITORIALS:

The Adakian

Because of Army regulations prohibiting the mailing of camp newspapers during the war, copies of The Adakian *are rare. Between 19 January 1944 and 1 April 1945, Hammett occassionally contributed most of thirteen signed articles which are reproduced here.*

[21 January 1944, p. 3]
CHICAGO MURDER MYSTERY

Here's one for the E. Phillips Oppenheim fans, just as it comes to us from the Army News Service:

Mrs. Adele Born Williams, 54, wife of Frank Starr Williams, State Department Attache, is in a critical condition with a gunshot wound in her head, following a shooting in an apartment in the exclusive Drake Hotel on Lakeside Drive.

Before lapsing into unconsciousness, the socially prominent Mrs. Williams told authorities "a well-dressed" woman stepped from behind the door and opened fire on her and her daughter, Mrs. Patricia Wodbody, 28.

The daughter, who escaped unharmed, described the assailant as about 50 years old, wearing a black Persian lamb coat, and with a flower in her gray hair.

Williams, who was formerly commercial attache at the US Legation in Tokyo, arrived from Washington by plane and was questioned along with his daughter.

Investigators found the weapon in a service elevator shaft, but it bears no fingerprints.

(The Adakian's crime expert is a Hammett fan. He says this is not up this alley and refuses to make any guesses.)

[23 January 1944, p. 2]
STRICTLY POLITICAL

AP despatch [*sic*] from Washington:

In Adak, Hammett was given a staff of six men (which later grew to nine) and asked to start a camp newspaper. Because Gen. Harry Thompson, commander of field forces in the area, was a fan of Hammett's work, The Adakian, *as the newspaper was called, enjoyed full support and editorial freedom.*

The Democratic Nat'l. Committee, giving a powerful shove to the draft Roosevelt movement within the party, called on FDR to "continue as the great world humanitarian leader," in both war and peace.

After selecting Chicago as the site of the national convention and installing youthful Robert E. Hannegan–hailed as a 2d Jim Farley–as Nat'l Chairman, the committee members roared approval of a resolution declaring that the liberal spirit and far-sighted idealism of Roosevelt must be impinged in the peace.

(Listen, chum. This is no time to be starting that. I'm writing it down just as we got it from AP. So you don't understand what that means. So what? So I don't either. So I'll give you six, two and even that FDR doesn't understand it. Can he help it if politicians talk like that? Can I help it if I do not always know what's going on in civilian heads? Anyhow, they're going to have a hundred-bucks-a-plate dinner tonight while I'm eating Spam.)

[29 January 1944, p. 4]
EDITORIAL NOTE

After a few dry-run issues to get our hands in, here we go with the first regular edition of a daily newspaper.

Our job is to give you–every morning–a newspaper that you'll like to read and that will keep you as up-to-date as possible on what's happening here, back at home and in the rest of the world.

We've got a lot of problems–space, equipment, and God knows what all–but we're not going to bother you with them and we're not going to use them as excuses when we fall down on the job.

On the other hand, we can use all the help you can give us. We haven't got as full a staff as we need. If you think you'd fill a spot on it, come up and see us. We need news of what's going on in organizations on the Post. We'll always need small sharp material, in word or picture. If you've got any–let's see it.

This is your newspaper. If we ever forget it– lower the boom on us.

[15 February 1944, p. 4]
— AND HERE

Up to Saturday, personnel of this Post had bought less than half of their 4th War Loan Drive quota.

The quota was set at $613,325. Only $297,300 has been subscribed. This figures out to 48.47 per cent. God knows what you people are doing with your money.

One answer might be that a lot of you are tired of being urged to buy 'em and are showing how you feel about it by *not* buying them.

Another answer might be that the sales campaign up here has been none too hot. For instance, there are a couple of pieces of War Bond campaign literature on my desk now–both urging you to put your savings in War Bonds so you can afford to come back to Alaska for a vacation after the war.

Me, I like Alaska and probably will come back some day–but as bond salesmanship here and now that appeal seems to me as weak as USO fruit punch.

Well, it's your money and you do what you want with it. But if you're saving any, War Bonds are the best bet I know–unless somebody's selling you Dupont stock at half-rates.

The 3 local outfits with the best bond sales records are the 38th Special Service Co., well over its quota with a mark of nearly 115 per cent; the 42d CA Brigade, with more than 97 per cent of its quota; and the Air Force, with nearly 90 per cent.

[18 February 1944, p. 4]
EDITORIAL NOTE

The Adakian plans to run a series of brief histories of the organizations that make up this military community.

Organization Orientation Officers can help us greatly by sending us the following information:
1. Name of organization.
2. When and where activated.
3. Outline of history before coming to Adak.
4. Last station before coming here.
5. Date of arrival.
6. Outline of activities here.
7. Commanding officer's name.
8. Date he took command.
9. Brief biographical note on CO.

You can make these histories short as you like, or you can go into detail. Either way, we'll be grateful.

[21 February 1944, p. 4]
EM MAIL

One of the uncomfortable parts of an EM's life in a place like this is the unit censor system.

It's not easy to write even the most impersonal letter when you know it has to be read by an officer with whom you probably have day to day contact.

But it's a necessary system, so most of us learn to push the thought of it pretty far back in our heads when we sit down to write. Except, of course, those cut-ups who write for the censoring officer's amusement.

Once in a while, however–in spite of the strictness of the regulations laid down for unit censors– we are unpleasantly reminded of our lack of privacy.

At times this goes so far–at many posts, not only here–that excerpts from letters become the bases for Orderly Room jokes.

It is doubtful that anything else so deeply humiliating can happen to an EM.

A soldier I know told me about such a case yesterday. He probably couldn't prove anything and, in any event, he is like most of us–not a guardhouse lawyer.

But he was thoroughly upset and said it was now impossible for him to write at all. He hoped he'd forget about it in a little while and be able to write home again.

[19 December 1944, p. 3]
DON'T LET 'EM KID YOU INTO BUYING WAR BONDS

War Bonds aren't for fun.

They are good solid investments for people

who want to save money. And they ought to be thought of that way.

I suppose comic posters and snap slogans– "You'll be fond of your bond"–must sell *some* bonds, or they would not be used so much, but don't try to tell me that anybody's sucking money out of the U S Steel Corporation with gags!

And it's the U S Steel Corporation and its brothers in big business who buy the bulk of the War Bonds–many times the amount bought by individuals.

Why do you suppose that is, chum?

Oh, because they're patriotic! Well, maybe, but if you're going to be so damned patriotic why not just give the government your money?

On the other hand, if you're like most of us and the U S Steel Corporation and are trying to put a dollar or two aside now and then–

And if you want it to earn you a little something while you're sweating out the end of the war–

And if–most important of all–you want to be sure you can get your hands on it when you want it–

Then War Bonds are what you want.

And don't be a chump and pass them up just because you don't like the way somebody tries to sell them to you.

[18 March 1945, p. 1]
MR. & MRS. CIVILIAN

One of the worries that bedevil our world just now is how ex-soldiers are going to get along with civilians when this war is over.

On the soldier side you often find the feeling that civilians have been living at the top of the bottle where the cream is thickest.

And in some civilian circles you can find fear that the returning service man will think of himself as strictly a hero who has made his life-time contribution to the world and now–for the rest of his life–wants nothing but ease and fat pickings.

With a couple of cross-purpose viewpoints like these, somebody's bound to get bruised. But, on the other hand, it's not necessary to be too fearful of the outcome. Life has a way of jarring us loose from most of our exaggerated notions.

It's happened after all our wars; it'll happen after this one.

But this time it should not take so long for our difficulties to be ironed out, for civilian and ex-soldier to meet on common ground.

There are some ten millions of us in the service, which means practically every civilian is related–at least by marriage–to one or more of us. And these family rows blow over quickly.

You may not like Uncle Ed and you may know all Aunt Emmy's faults, but it's easier to understand them than if they were a pair of strangers labeled Mr. and Mrs. Civilian.

And easier for them to understand you.

[25 March 1945, p. 1]
THE WWLA

Yesterday we carried a story from Detroit about a new organization–the War Workers' League of America–which seems to have been born in a Buick plant, claims a membership of 2500, and advocates "a bill of rights for war workers" and "equal rights with war veterans" in the reconversion period.

It's easy to see why this should have stirred up a good deal of interest on the island, but, unfortunately, we haven't the answers to all the questions that have been asked.

All we know is what the ANS Wire said, which is what we printed, and the chances are we'll never know much more.

There's hardly a day that some new organization doesn't spring up somewhere, and start advocating or opposing something or other.

Many of them are simply crackpot, others are some bright boy's idea of how to make a living; a few fill a need and survive–the rest are seldom heard of again.

This one–the WWLA–can hardly be expected to do anything for its members that existing workers' organizations can't do and its chance of celebrating any anniversaries doesn't seem too hot.

Many of us are prone to pick up a stray news item of this sort and pretend to ourselves that it's really representative of what's going on back home and how people back there look at things.

That's just about as sensible as if folks back there judged us by some of our "characters."

[31 March 1945, p. 3]
THIS MONTH'S PAYDAY SPECIAL

Today's the last day of the Red Cross drive–and it's payday.

Add 'em together and they spell *give*.

You're never going to buy anything better with your money.

How many lives did you personally save last year? How many people did you personally lift out of dispair [*sic*]?

You don't have to count on your fingers if you've got the Red Cross working for you.

You can just say, "Plenty," and let it go at that.

Put the Red Cross to work for you.

Give.

[1 April 1945, p. 1]
RUMORS, RUMORS, RUMORS

This past week has been busy as a bird dog with rumor and fuel for rumor.

Germany's final collapse and peace in Europe have seemed no more than an hour or two away.

A non-com playing with a walkie-talkie on Iwo, a radio operator picking up orphan flashes at Hickam Field in Hawaii, an Army and Navy Register report that Eisenhower is about to relieve Marshall for duty in the Pacific–anything could pin our ears to the radio.

Back in the States people were even jumpier.

The New York Stock Market was scared into a decline on Monday.

A couple of days later the Chicago grain market had its cash-in-while-you-may nervous spell.

On the same day a murder trial in the same city was adjourned and stores shut down for the day all over the country–expecting an armistice announcement, that never came.

Later there was more fuel for these hopeful if short-lived fires–the statement of an unnamed German prisoner of "high rank" that Germany no longer has an organized defense or an organized central government; the British PM's warning to Cabinet and Commons members to stay where they could be reached should Germany fold during the Easter holidays.

Rumors will come thicker and thicker from now on out.

If we try to believe all of them we're going to have nothing left to believe with when peace actually comes.

That happened to a lot of people last time.

ARTICLE:
Cpl. Sid Kross, "Let's Face 'Em," *G. I. Galley*, July 1945, p. 6.

It's fast becoming standing operating procedure in the Alaskan Department that if you want to start a publication get T/4 Samuel Dashiell Hammett to do it.

Shipped to one of the windswept, bleak islands of the Aleutians with a Signal Corps outfit 2 years back, he was assigned as message center clerk. This lasted only as long as it took to translate Samuel to Dashiell, the author of *The Thin Man* series, the *Maltese Falcon* and *Red Harvest*.

With B/Gen Harry B. Thompson, APO 980 post commander, wanting a daily news sheet it was only the aforementioned matter of time before Dashiell and the paper were synonymous.

Hammett did not rush into publication immediately upon receiving the assignment. Instead, he combed the special service units for the best talent available and before Vol. 1, No 1, ever appeared he had a capable 10 man staff ready for the assignment.

Another prepublication must was a personal survey of the reader's desires in the way of a daily new sheet. This survey produced the decision to refrain from pinups and comics and give the news hungry enlisted men of the island as complete a news coverage as possible.

As space is limited to 4 legal size Mimeographed pages the staff takes advantage of the news items from the press associations, ANS, and monitoring the short wave broadcasts. From these sources are rewritten the news stories for the paper as concisely as possible thereby giving the readers as complete a war and home front picture as is done in some stateside daily papers.

Three members of the staff are artists and at least one up to the minute map is used in every issue in connection with war front news. Besides this the artists submit daily cartoons from which 2 are selected by a conference of the entire staff. These cartoons deal with life on the "rock," as the island is often known, and are usually so good that they are reprinted by almost every post paper in the command.

Through all this Hammett has been the directing force. Actually, his job has been in an editing capacity and he does very little writing himself. But his plan for publication has been so good and so well managed that the APO 980 *Daily News* is the most sought reading matter on the island.

With the daily going so well, Hammett answered an I and E call to go on an orientation tour with 4 other GI's. On this trip Hammett and his team talked on major morale subjects to the troops at every post and station in the command.

Ending up on the Alaska mainland, Hammett was retained by the I and E office to help inaugurate a new monthly magazine publication which is called the "Army Up North" and which is being used as the orientation guide for the command. With the first publication off the press last January, Hammett headed back to his "own stomping grounds," the APO 980 *News* office.

Hammett, now 50, had to wait until 2 years ago before age restrictions were lifted which allowed him to enlist. He had been a bitter and active foe of Fascism since 1936 and wanted to follow up this public attitude by getting back into uniform. He first wore GI in World War I.

His first assignment was with the Eastern Signal Corps Training Center at Ft Monmouth, N J, a short hop from his New York home. But he was constantly fretting for an overseas assignment and at last his chance arrived with the APO 980 assignment.

Hammett is well liked by all the doggies who have come in contact with him and often his gray, thatched head is propped in a reflective mood as he ponders problems his fellow GI's bring to him.

His brother GI's have become reconciled to the fact that he wanted to enlist, that he wanted overseas service, and every other unusual factor connected with his present assignment—save one. They know he is sincere when he says he likes the bleakness and williwaws and storms of "the rock" but they still can't figure out how any sane man can feel that way.

* * * * *

ARTICLE:
Sgt. Al Weisman, "The Thin Man Returns from the Wars," *In Short*, May 1946, pp. 50-52.

Shortly after Samuel Dashiell Hammett exchanged his ODs for tweeds, he told New York newspapermen that the Aleutian islands, where he had served two years as a GI, were actually beautiful and not hell holes. "The trouble is that the men up there don't lift their heads up long enough to see how nice the islands look," he was quoted as saying.

Civilians who read this were surprised, to say the least. They had come to believe, from servicemen's letters and magazine and newspaper articles, that the Aleutian islands were the most forbidding in the world–foggy, windswept, stormbound lava piles that ought to be given back to the natives as quickly as possible.

But Aleutian GI's, when they heard of Hammett's remarks, only laughed. They realized that readjustment for the 51-year-old author of *The Thin Man* and other mysteries wasn't going to be any problem. As an ex-GI, he sounded as screwy as when he was a non-com up in the Aleutians and Alaska.

Hammett was on Adak for 18 months and distinguished himself on two counts: He was unlike other enlisted men in that he was always in good humor and maintained a genial disposition, and he seriously liked the Aleutian weather. In fact, he insists that his health improved in the Aleutians. Other men say they have lost weight, teeth, hair and humor.

Hammett came to Adak a member of the Signal Corps. But fame caught up with him shortly after he hit the island, and the commanding general summoned him one day and asked him to put out a daily newspaper. Hammett agreed, if enough men were assigned to help him. "I got into the Army to get away from writing," he said.

"How many men will you need?" the general asked.

"At least ten," Hammett said.

This unprecedented number of men for an Army newspaper was granted and so began one of the Army's most extraordinary publishing ventures. The four-page paper published chiefly world news and cartoons by three artists. Hammett, as editor, wrote occasional editorials, but

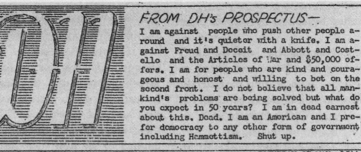

FROM DH's PROSPECTUS—

I am against people who push other people around and it's quieter with a knife. I am against Freud and Deceit and Abbott and Costello and the Articles of War and $50,000 offers. I am for people who are kind and courageous and honest and willing to bet on the second front. I do not believe that all mankind's problems are being solved but what do you expect in 50 years? I am in dead earnest about this. Dead. I am an American and I prefer democracy to any other form of government including Hammettism. Shut up.

VOL I Number 50   SATURDAY 27 MAY 1944

HAMMET HITS HALF CENTURY

50 YEARS AGO TODAY
By R. Harvey Jack

At the same time that the wireless was born in Italy a little bundle of joy? was born in St. Mary's County, Md. named Dashiell Hammett. Many renowned personages call it pre-destination that these 2 "live wires" should occur at the same time. Since then "Sam" has attained great heights in the field of writing his greatest, perhaps, being editor of the local island newspaper.

MOUNTBATTEN RESIGNS
Kandy, Ceylon, May 27 (AP) —Admiral Lord Louis Mountbatten resigned today "as a protest against the unsportsmanlike criticism" of Dashiell Hammett, Aleutian editor.
When asked for comment, Hammett laughed heartily.

L GREEN'S DRUG

DASHIELL HAMMETT'S AUTOGRAPH

FREE WITH EACH SUNDAE

— OLIVER PEDIGO

NEW WALGREEN'S FOR HAMMETT
Pittsburgh, May 27 (AP)— Pittsburgh marked the 50th birthday of Dashiell Hammett, protege of R. Harvey Jack, local composer, musician, bookkeeper, typist and gambler, by opening a new Walgreen's today in his honor.

Whose honor?

Jack wired from the Aleutians that he had broken a champagne bottle over Hammett's head.

HALF-CENTURY CLAIMS FOUL
Somewhere in the Aleutians, May 27 (AP)—T/5 Dashiell Hammett is 50 today.

The author of "Blood Money" and former war correspondent for Godey's Lady's Book observed the occasion with a quiet scream and a light repast with his Aleutian haunt.

A few Friends (few people know that Hammett is a Quaker) joined him in a simple birthday feast of AP dispatches garnished with the heads of old mimeograph operators. Correction fluid and blood were served.

Congratulatory wires poured in from all corners of Four Corners, Idaho.

The regular Russian communique reported no important changes on the land front.

CRACK

CPL BERNARD ANASTASIA 44

On Hammett's fiftieth birthday, the Adakian *staff published a commemorative issue of the paper*

VOL I Number 50   DH   **SATURDAY 27 MAY 1944**

In the Aleutians, he was made editor of the daily DH or You'll Do It This Way. He's always got a good word for his staff at the usual $10 per word. Never, on any occasion, has Hammett upbraided his staff except on the nights of January 29th, 1944 to May 27th, 1944 inclusive.

When we spoke to Hammett this afternoon, he was reclining on his staff, speculating about the second front. He was on the phone, mumbling:"Hello, Ike? Listen, I think you ought to do it this way..."

NOTES:
(1) His exact age is a military secret and if revealed, would switch the odds on the betting.
(2) It was in 743,896 installments.
(3) Even Spade and Archer couldn't find out why.
(4) Hammett lost $100,000 on this film.
--BK

DASHIELL HAMMETT

Don L. Miller

Sam Hammett, nee Hashiell Dammett, was born as a mister approximately (1) 50 years ago today only it was a Wednesday, according to figures released by Commonwealth and Southern.

He spent his post-natal youth as an athletic instructor for the Baltimore & Ohio Railroad, and proof reading requisitions at Camp Meade, Maryland.

It wasn't until he was 7 that people began to pay attention to Sam. At the turn of the century, Sam was published in Argosy (2) and True Story under the fictitious names of Dash Iell and Pamela Hammette. Two years later, Red Harvest followed. The Thin Man followed Red. They met in a men's room 3 weeks later and have never conversed since(3).

His most famous work, written when he was 17, was The Gefulte Fish which has since been made into a movie (4). The book sales were beyond the publisher's expectations, despite the economic depression of the era.

When Pearl Harbor broke, everyone was surprised but Hammett. Inspired by the attire of Lord Morris Mountbatinthehead, Hammett enlisted in the Army after the Navy, Coast Guard, Merchant Marine, and Dogs for Democracy, Inc., said no.

Hammett got overseas by smuggling himself into a general's portfolio; Hammett had nothing to read on the way.

Movies

HUSKIE
Today:THE THIN MAN;A good thing the theater is aired daily;spindly's a word for this one.The main stink is the script by Dashiell Hammett and the liquid-dated characters effulging from his non-compassed mentis. Whoever heard of sleuths substituting scotch for the Holmes' needle, and how could Wm. Powell and Myrna Loy do anything but look guilty in this Hammett ham-stringing? This Thin Man has a bad case of rickets.

CASTLE
Today: THE MALTESE FALCON;Something not-kosher about this bird. Ample proof that Hackheel Spam-mitt will get nowhere as a writer, and fast. Humphrey Gocart perambulates stoically thru the writer's wheeze-whimsickly dialogue but the ivory-crapper aura of the plot funks up the fowl foully. D.H. should get his own bird.
Coming: THIN MAN RETURNS, ANOTHER THIN MAN, THINNER MAN, THINNEST MAN -four feature exhibit of Hasheesh Dammit features proving that merdre will out, sometimes as dysentery.

VILLAGE
Today:THE GLASS KEY;Don't be guided by Gide for Hammett's obviously using a ghost-writer, Colodny or Sol Chain, and its an improvement.
Tomorrow:RED HARVEST;Dachshund Hamcroquett's preference for red runs pink. We'll take Random, anyway. HS

Bernard Anastasia   *Bernie Kalb*   *Alva Morris*
Bill Glackin   *Al Loeffler*   *Oliver Pedigo*
Dick Jack   *Don L Miller*   *Hal Sykes*

2

soon became principally the buffer between the brass and the enlisted men on the staff. Once the paper happened to use "God damn" in an article. The chaplain telephoned to complain. Hammett talked to him and told him, "With the paper shortage the way it is, it's lucky God gets his name in the paper in any manner."

The paper was published at night, and Hammett usually got out of the sack around 9 p.m. He went to bed around 5 or 6 a.m. When the weather was fairly good, he would wake up early and take a walk, and his tall, spare frame, topped by a bushy white mane, could be seen plodding up and down the mountains that ring the island. Though he had been a crack screen writer during civilian days he went to only one movie in the Army– *Watch on the Rhine*, which he had adapted for the screen.

No GI's with whom he worked and lived regarded him as a man of prominence. He was known as "Sam," not "Dashiell" or "Dash," as he is referred to by civilian friends. While dining with friends in a New York restaurant shortly after his discharge Hammett was approached by a couple of men who knew him as an enlisted man. He asked them to join his party for a drink, and they kept referring to him as "Sam." One of Hammett's civilian friends, tiring of the name, at last appealed to the visitors to "please call him 'Dash'; I can't get used to 'Sam' at all."

The fact that he preferred "Sam" to "Dash," the fact that he "played it straight"–to quote him– as an enlisted man and that he didn't seek or accept any special privileges because of his age or prominence, the fact that he used the GI belt and razor, and the fact that he shared the GI suspicion of brass made him extremely popular.

Hammett's scorn of brass was legendary. A major at Dutch Harbor approached Hammett and said, "I've been doing a little bit of mystery writing, and I wonder if you would come to my quarters this evening and share a steak with me. I'd like to show you my stuff." Hammett replied, "Certainly, if you've got enough for all of us," pointing to the four enlisted men accompanying him. "Well, I don't know," stuttered the major.

"Oh, well, some other time, sir," said Hammett. He saluted and walked off.

The matter of a commission for himself was always a source of amusement to Hammett.

"Every time I was interviewed by some visiting newspaperman I was always asked why I turned down a commission," he used to say. "I always had to explain that no one ever offered me one, and I was damned if I was going to stand on my head to get one."

Hammett, like every other GI sweated out Information and Education problems, and while the dough never interested him–he once went seven months without hitting the pay line–he desired ratings as much as anyone else. He was a sergeant in the Medics in the last war and came up to the Aleutians as a corporal, and for a time it appeared he was doomed to remain one. "That would have left only PFC in Ordnance for me in the next war," he complained. However, he made T-4 after a year on Adak and subsequently, when he was transferred to Anchorage, in the Information and Education section of Headquarters, Alaskan Department, he made T-3.

"Now I can buck the line in case I ever want to go to a movie," he said.

Hammett spent the last six months of his overseas duty editing a monthly publication for the Alaskan Department's I&E section, but his superiors made one error with regard to the author last August. They sent him to Edmonton, Alberta, on temporary duty.

The writer checked into a downtown hotel in Edmonton, glanced out of the window and saw his first streetcar in two years, telephoned room service for food and headed for the bathroom and his first tub since he left Alaska.

Newspapers frontpaged his visit. He signed more autographs in one day than he had in three years. He was Dashiell Hammett, noted mystery writer, again.

Ten days later he returned to Anchorage, Alaska, and surprised everyone by putting in for his discharge on the age ruling.

"That atomic bomb frightens me, even though it's on our side," he told one friend. Later he said he thought it was the streetcars.

But, in a more serious mood, he confessed that he had gone stale on his Army job. "And the Army was the steadiest job I ever had since the last war," he solemnly remarked.

The one mystery Hammett never quite cleared up to the satisfaction of a great many of his friends was the reason why he joined the Army and volunteered for overseas duty. Many GI's were convinced Hammett wanted to get material for a book.

Leonard Lyons, New York columnist, said recently that Hammett is preparing a book and quoted the author as saying, "It will *not* be about Alaska or the Aleutians. It's about a guy who comes home and doesn't like his family."

Actually, the reason Hammett joined up was his personal campaign to fight fascism, a fight that he has been engaged in since 1936 and to which he has been devoting most of his time and money. As for the overseas duty, Hammett explains he didn't want to suffer the fate he had in the last war, when he never got farther than 20 miles from his home in Baltimore.

Maintaining his unpredictable manner to the last, Hammett left his barracks bags full of GI clothing on the air-freight dock at Anchorage when he took off for the States and showed up with just his toilet kit and sense of humor. Hammett was fully prepared for civilian life.

ARTICLE:

E. E. Spitzer, "With Corporal Hammett on Adak," *Nation* (5 January 1974): 6-9.

I feel I'm mainly responsible for Dashiell Hammett's going to jail and the only way I can try to ease my mind is by telling how it happened. I knew him for about two and a half years and two of those were on the island of Adak in the Aleutians during World War II, when we both were corporals in the Army. His rank, the weather and the war were factors in the Hammett I knew.

First, the weather. The Aleutians, stretching from Alaska almost to the tip of the Soviet Union, have the worst weather possible, since it combines constant dampness with constant wind and a constant cloud cover. On an average day the wind is 40 miles an hour, which means that what would call for gale warnings elsewhere is just another day in the Aleutians. On an unaverage day in the winter, the wind can rise to 140 miles an hour. Add to this a cold dampness and the continual overcast of low gray clouds for about 360 days a year,

and you have one of the most depressing places in the world, even without the occasional earthquakes.

It was the weather, even more than the lack of women, that produced in soldiers what was called the Aleutian Stare. In the early days our company took its meals in the mess of a National Guard Company that had been there a year, having arrived with the American invasion on the heels of the Japanese pull-out. On my first morning in the mess hall, I thought I had run into a collection of zombies. The guardsmen stared into their plates unseeingly and pushed food into their mouths mechanically. Then, like robots, they stood in line, scraped their plates, handed them in, and marched out dully into the howling snow. Later, I heard the story of a staff sergeant who had entered a mess hall of his own company and machine-gunned his own men.

I had been in the Aleutians for two years when one spring day, walking across the tundra, I found myself yelling, "All right, you sonofabitch wind, I've had enough of you! Now quit it! Stop it! Or I'll kill you!"

About a month before this, I was in front of Hammett in a chow line. (He claimed I always beat him to it and he was right.) We were standing in the cold muck of which the islands are made. Above us the lowering clouds raced along, while the wind pulled at us. In the distance was the snow-sprinkled peak of Mount Moffit, a mainly extinct volcano.

"Ugly, stinking place," I said, kicking the muck. "I've got to get out of here." Hammett said mildly, "You're looking in the wrong direction." He gestured with his spoon at the clouds and Mount Moffit.

I suddenly saw everything through his eyes and realized it could be considered beautiful, but I wouldn't give him the satisfaction or, more important, give up my right to bitch. I said elegantly, "Sam, you're full of shit," although I knew he was at least as right as I was.

That brings up a small but significant point. To those who knew Hammett in civilian life, he was called "Dash"; to those who knew him in the Army, he was "Sam," his full name being Samuel Dashiell Hammett. Sam himself never indicated

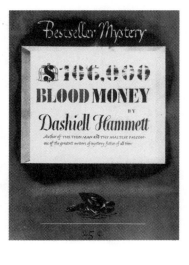

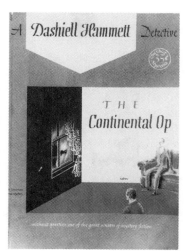

Between 1943 and 1951, Lawrence Spivak, with the editorial assistance of Ellery Queen, published nine collections of Hammett's pulp magazine stories. These volumes appeared under the imprints Mercury Mystery, Bestseller Mystery, and Jonathan Press. In 1961, the year Hammett died, the last Mercury Mystery volume, A Man Named Thin, *was published by Joseph W. Ferman.*

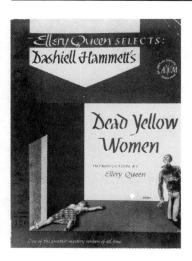

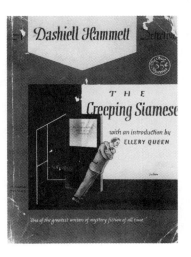

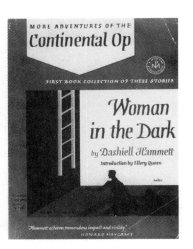

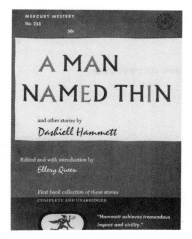

any feelings on the subject, responding or not responding equally to both.

Which brings up the matter of rank. Sam was a great unrespecter of rank, and since he was only an enlisted man, enlisted men did not respect him; only the brass did. Sam was pretty much at the height of his fame then. He was known as the author of *The Thin Man* and *The Maltese Falcon*. He was still play-doctoring for Lillian Hellman, but by cable, and it was said he got more cables than the commanding general. Also, there was the fact that he was over-age for an enlisted man and it was known he had volunteered.

What was not generally known was that, having taken him in as a volunteer, the Army decided he was a radical and not to be trusted. By the time it decided that, Sam was working in cryptanalysis on the island of Umnak in the Aleutians.

What to do with him? The Army transferred him to the island of Adak, attached him to Headquarters Company and gave him nothing to do. Sam, looking for something to do, asked the commanding officer of Adak, Brig. Gen. Harry Thompson, for permission to establish a newspaper.

Thompson, a bright, no-nonsense man, thought it would be good for morale and told Corporal Hammett that if any of the brass ever gave the corporal any flak, the corporal should tell the brass to complain to the general about their problem.

I saw a notable result of that instruction more than a year later in the newspaper quonset hut. Sam was in his usual position, lying in his sleeping bag on the wooden counter that served as the staff's desks. His head was on the mimeograph machine and he was reading a book on materialist philosophy when there was a brisk knocking on the door.

No one even looked up. The staff, which at that point included me, was busy typing and writing the next day's issue, and who the hell ever knocked on a door anyway? Presently, the door snapped open and in strode a major, all gleaming brass and still-shined shoes. He glanced about sharply, looking as though he expected someone would call attention, although regulations make that unnecessary when you're working.

It was as if he had not entered. Finally, after what to him must have been a pregnant pause, he walked briskly to where editor Bill Glackin was typing.

"Sergeant, where can I find Corporal Hammett?"

Without losing the rhythm of his typing, Bill nodded toward the rear where Sam lay contemplating the intricacies of Marxian dialectics, while his busy and well-trained slaves turned out the 4-page newspaper that had become famous throughout the chain.

The major marched up to Sam.

"Corporal Hammett?"

A rhetorical question, because no one else in the hut had snow-white hair, the face of a philosophical hawk and a corporal's stripes. Sam's eyes slowly came off the page, went up to the major's face and uniform, and came down to the page again.

"Corporal! I'm speaking to you!"

Intent on the page, Sam said nothing.

"Corporal, I've come to inspect your newspaper!"

Obviously a lie, but also obviously, one delivered by a field-grade officer and one whose dignity and position were being ignored in front of a group of enlisted men, including one Pfc.

Sam shifted his book to make it more comfortable.

"If you have a complaint, Major, make it to the general."

The major fell over his feet getting out of the hut.

Pfc. Dick Jack who didn't really believe that Sam was famous, said, "Boy, now you're going to get it, you stupid bastard."

Bernie Anastasia, one of our artists said, "All he wanted was your autograph, Sam. Why didn't you give it to him?" Bernie Kalb who was trying to learn to be a newspaperman said, "I guess that'll stop those klebes from bothering us." (Klebe was Bernie's current word for things he especially disliked or liked.)

It didn't stop the klebes entirely, but it did cut their visits to almost nothing.

Sam had staffed his newspaper entirely from our company. Ours was a Special Service outfit and contained not only an entertainment unit but a newspaper unit. The difference between the two units was that the entertainers had all been professionals, but the men in the newspaper unit had had almost no experience with a newspaper except reading one, and the short Army courses in journalism given them, along with calisthenics, close-order drill and bayonet practice during six weeks of basic training.

However, the group had been taught that a newspaper story is Who, What, When, Where and Why, and they all knew how to type and they had learned how to run a mimeo, so they were the best candidates Sam could find. (What Sam's influence on them was you can judge by the fact that at least two of the staff are still in the news business. Bill Glackin is on the Sacramento *Bee* and Bernie Kalb gives you the news on CBS-TV.)

Sam had some special theories about newspapers. He didn't think it was enough just to give the news. He believed that most people do not remember the background of most news stories—that they could not usually recall who had previously said what or done what to whom. Therefore, shortly after the beginning of each news story, his paper, *The Adakian*, gave the background of the story. This was done in brackets so you could easily distinguish it from the latest news and you could ignore it if it was already familiar.

Also, Sam did not believe in relying on any one news service to deliver the truth, particularly in wartime. The Armed Service network was furnishing a radio feed that combined AP, UP and INS, but that wasn't enough for Sam. He found a corporal with a formidable I.Q., who had taught history, and knew many languages, including Russian and German and Japanese. He set up a special shortwave receiving room at the post radio station for Robert Colodny.

Radio reception there where the Pacific meets the Bering Sea is phenomenal. Bob monitored Germany, Russia and Japan, among other countries. The result was a column in *The Adakian* of news and interpretation based on news reports from the major powers. The predictions were so accurate that soon General Thompson asked Corporal Colodny to prepare a weekly summary of the war for his personal use. This, despite the weekly summary he received from the Chiefs of Staff.

Movies were among the most important diversions on that bleak (beautiful?) island, so Sam trained our Hal Sykes to write movie reviews that encouraged you or discouraged you in one or two sentences. Sam felt that was all a review should do. After that, you ought to make your own judgments.

What was even scarcer than movies was humor, the humor you needed for your own equilibrium. Sam studded *The Adakian* with cartoons by three artists from our company. The humor was indigenous to the Aleutians and soon G.I.s all along the chain were mailing them home to explain what it was like. Eventually, the best cartoons were issued in a booklet, with a foreword by Sam. Probably the most important function of the cartoons was that they helped explain the G.I.s to themselves.

None of us knew that Sam had ever had a drinking problem. Even when beer finally became available, he never touched it. It was only when Sam visited civilization again that it emerged. Civilization in this case came to Sam via Joe Louis.

Louis arrived on Adak to give an exhibition, and to inaugurate an Army Boxing Tournament. The winners on each of the Aleutian Islands would compete with one another and the finalists would be flown to heaven, namely Anchorage, Alaska, where they would box the mainland winners.

The coverage by *The Adakian* was so complete and knowledgeable that the hand of a master was obvious. Naturally, the idea emerged to send Sam along with the boxing team, so that the whole Alaskan Department would have the advantage of his expert reporting.

Did he want to go? Maybe; otherwise why didn't he appeal to the general to let him stay behind? Did General Thompson insist he go to bring credit to Adak? Anyway, he went and his fall from the wagon was spectacular.

Main Street in Anchorage was a procession of bars and liquor stores. Sam didn't bother much with the liquor stores. Off the wagon, he was as effusive as he was withdrawn when sober. He wanted company for his drinking, anybody's company. And with his natural Toid Avenue and Toity-Toid Street tough-guy accent, he could talk to anybody. And did.

Smashed, crocked, jugged; loud, boisterous, talking nonsense, then eloquence, then just four-letter words. The gamut, including weeping.

EISLER CASE

CIVIL RIGHTS CONGRESS *of New York*

ROOM 402 • 112 EAST 19th STREET • NEW YORK 3, N. Y. • ORCHARD 4-5260

URGENT NOTICE!

Honorary National Chairmen
DR. BENJAMIN E. MAYS
DR. HARRY F. WARD
New York
President
DASHIELL HAMMETT
Vice-Presidents
JAMES EGERT ALLEN
PROF. LYMAN R. BRADLEY
REV. WILLIAM HOWARD MELISH
SAMUEL A. NEUBURGER
HOWARD DA SILVA
Chairman of Executive Council
MEYER E. STERN
Executive Secretary
LOUIS COLMAN

June 12, 1947

Dear Friend:-

You have probably read in the newspapers that Gerhart Eisler was convicted of contempt of Congress in U.S. District Court in Washington.

You have probably not heard that Eisler's defense counsel charged that Judge Alexander Holtzoff deprived the jury of the right to decide Eisler's guilt or innocence.

You have probably read in today's paper that Judge Holtzoff was disqualified from sitting in the contempt case of the officers and Board members of the Joint Anti-Fascist Refugee Committee. He refused to disqualify himself from the Eisler case, and, according to Carol King, Abraham J. Isserman and David Rein, who handled the defense, "...made many erroneous rulings, all of them of a serious nature, from the beginning to the end of the proceedings. They so prejudiced the case that the defendant's rights were taken from him without due process of law."

"When I was released from federal jail in April and the spurious charge dropped that I was a dangerous enemy alien, I said then that I did not expect a fair trial," Eisler declared upon his conviction. "I find now sorrowfully that I was right. The dice were loaded against me because of my political beliefs and not because I was in contempt of the Un-American Activities Committee. During the trial it was hard for me to tell the difference between the judge and the prosecutor for the government."

Gerhart Eisler will speak at a PUBLIC MEETING under the auspices of CRCNY at WEBSTER HALL, 119 East 11th Street, NYC, on MONDAY, JUNE 16 at 8 P.M. He will tell the real story of his trial in Washington. He will be assisted by his attorneys, Carol King and Abraham J. Isserman, who will tell the legal story and will outline the plans for the legal battles ahead. Of course, Civil Rights Congress will appeal, but the initial verdict in the case shows us that we cannot depend upon the courts to defend civil rights--the people MUST be the guardian of their own liberties. That's why ATTENDANCE AT THIS MEETING IS A MUST FOR EVERY ONE OF US. Admission is .35¢--and I hope to see you on Monday evening at Webster Hall.

Sincerely yours,

Dashiell Hammett
Dashiell Hammett

DH:el
uopwa 16-83

Beginning in 1946 Hammett was New York state chairman and national vice-chairman of the Civil Rights Congress, an organization that supported left-wing causes related to civil liberties. Gerhardt Eisler was convicted under the Smith Act, which made it unlawful to advocate the overthrow or destruction of the U.S. government. The Smith-Rankin committee was the U.S. House of Representatives Committee on Un-American Activities.

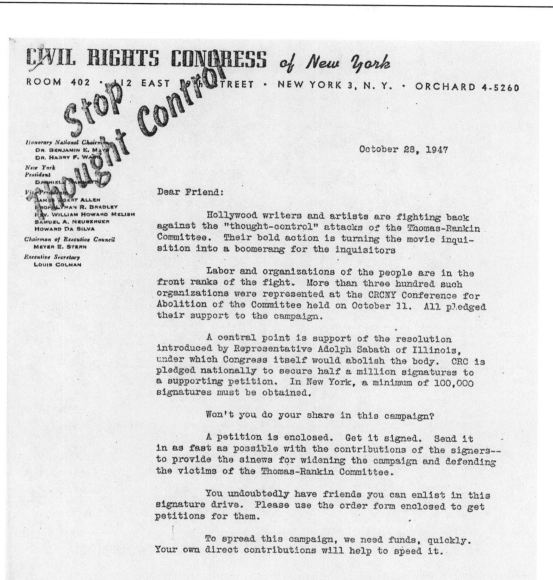

CIVIL RIGHTS CONGRESS *of New York*

ROOM 402 · 112 EAST 19th STREET · NEW YORK 3, N. Y. · ORCHARD 4-5260

Honorary National Chairmen
DR. BENJAMIN E. MAYS
DR. HARRY F. WARD

New York
President
DASHIELL HAMMETT

Vice-Presidents
JAMES EGERT ALLEN
PROF. LYMAN R. BRADLEY
REV. WILLIAM HOWARD MELISH
SAMUEL A. NEUBERGER
HOWARD DA SILVA

Chairman of Executive Council
MEYER E. STERN

Executive Secretary
LOUIS COLMAN

October 28, 1947

Dear Friend:

Hollywood writers and artists are fighting back against the "thought-control" attacks of the Thomas-Rankin Committee. Their bold action is turning the movie inquisition into a boomerang for the inquisitors

Labor and organizations of the people are in the front ranks of the fight. More than three hundred such organizations were represented at the CRCNY Conference for Abolition of the Committee held on October 11. All pledged their support to the campaign.

A central point is support of the resolution introduced by Representative Adolph Sabath of Illinois, under which Congress itself would abolish the body. CRC is pledged nationally to secure half a million signatures to a supporting petition. In New York, a minimum of 100,000 signatures must be obtained.

Won't you do your share in this campaign?

A petition is enclosed. Get it signed. Send it in as fast as possible with the contributions of the signers—to provide the sinews for widening the campaign and defending the victims of the Thomas-Rankin Committee.

You undoubtedly have friends you can enlist in this signature drive. Please use the order form enclosed to get petitions for them.

To spread this campaign, we need funds, quickly. Your own direct contributions will help to speed it.

Sincerely,

Dashiell Hammett

Dashiell Hammett

DH:el
uopwa 16-83

Abolish the Un-American Activities Committee

Stop AMERICA'S "THOUGHT POLICE"

ABOLISH THE UN-AMERICAN ACTIVITIES COMMITTEE

You know these thought policemen: John Rankin, J. Parnell Thomas and the rest.

They've shut up liberal radio voices. They're trying to force Hollywood to picture life their way. They're threatening government workers, smearing unions, trying to jail leaders of progressive organizations and minority parties.

They fight everyone but fascists to get at YOU.

That's why Civil Rights Congress is combatting the committee.

CRC is exposing its evil purpose.

CRC is testing its constitutionality by defending its victims.

Join in the campaign to abolish America's thought police—the Thomas-Rankin committee.

SIGN THIS PETITION. CONTRIBUTE

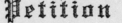

Petition

TO THE HOUSE OF REPRESENTATIVES:

WE UNDERSIGNED CITIZENS respectfully petition our Representatives to support and adopt House Resolution 46 (by Rep. Adolph J. Sabath) which would abolish the *Committee on Un-American Activities.*

In complete violation of the Bill of Rights, this truly un-American committee—

- Constitutes a thought police agency for the intimidation, persecution and suppression of American citizens, organizations and movements.
- Menaces America's great tradition of freedom.

Name	Address	City & State	Contribution

Not that I was there to see. I was back on Adak having been asked by Sam to fill in on the paper for Bill Glackin who went to Anchorage with him. But I had an accurate account of Sam's journey through Anchorage bars because there was no lack of witnesses.

I had another account of how Sam later sobered up in Anchorage and stayed sober. The reason? Part of it certainly was a change of assignment. Once the boxing matches were over, it was decided a more serious assignment would be fitting, so an orientation team was set up by Major Hurford, head of the Alaskan Department Special Service. This team had the mission of touring the chain and telling the men Why We Fight. The team consisted of four men, led by Corporal Hammett. That was a subject Sam took seriously; it was why he had enlisted. He went on the wagon again.

When Sam returned to Adak, he resumed the horizontal reading position, once again the teetotaler.

After the war, I saw Sam only three times. The first time was when he took my wife and me to the Stork Club. Sam had met my wife in Anchorage when she was with the USO, and when he had sobered up in preparation for travel with the orientation team.

At the Stork Club, he had his table up front, center. We were led there by the captain, who "Mr. Hammetted" continually, so that other patrons would know and they did, judging by their sidelong glances. Leonard Lyons came over, said a few words.

We reminisced, we drank. I got a little smashed; Sam got a lot smashed. After a while, he didn't make much sense. It seemed to me he felt a lack of interest in his life.

The second time I saw Sam was when he was teaching a course in mystery writing in a radical school otherwise devoted to social studies. You may or may not remember, but during and after World War II there was a brouhaha about building a new world with liberty and justice for all.

At this time, someone, and the temper of the times, convinced me that the downtrodden of the world needed a more ballsy version of the American Civil Liberties Union. It was called the Civil Rights Congress and all that it lacked was a name

that could attract public support, such as Dashiell Hammett. I was assured that he would be purely the honorary head, that he need do literally nothing. And all they wanted from me was to ask him to be on the letterhead.

Sam was the original nonorganization man, the ultra Private Private Eye, but evidently someone, and the temper of the times, had persuaded him he should lend his name and the teaching of a course in mystery-story writing to a left-wing school that was convinced the butler didn't do it—his employer did.

The building where Sam taught was crummy. Up one flight to a beat-up classroom with the kind of chairs they used to have in one-arm lunchrooms. I had timed it so that class was just breaking up. A few students clustered around Sam; I waited in the hall. When he came out, still surrounded, he looked at me a little surprised, but pleasantly.

I asked if I could see him privately for a moment. Of course. We stepped back into the classroom. I told him what was wanted of him. He said, sure. I said, thanks, and left.

You may remember that soon after World War II, the Red witch hunt began. They got hold of Sam and asked him to surrender the names of the members of his organization. Knowing Sam, I was sure he didn't know their names and didn't care to know them, but that's not what he told them. He told them he would not surrender the names. And they put him in jail.

I don't remember for how long. All I remember is that it seemed to be a helluva long time. And while he was in, I kept saying to myself that I should really go and see him. But I was so ashamed of what I had done that I didn't go.

Finally, they let Sam out of jail and by then he was real sick and I heard he went back to drinking.

The third time I met Sam was in a theatre lobby. All I could say was hello. He helloed back matter of factly.

My wife said to Sam. "I guess I should have written you."

Sam said, "Yes."

It wasn't too long after that, he died. My wife went to the funeral. I could not bring myself to go. Since then, I've argued the case with myself many times.

You can't really get people to do what they don't want to do, can you?

INTRODUCTION:

Introduction to *Wind Blown and Dripping* (Privately printed, 1945).

After the war, Hammett attempted to arrange publication of a collection of cartoons drawn by the Adakian *staff artists. When he failed, he arranged private publication of a pamphlet of their work and wrote an introduction.*

These cartoons originally were scratched into waxed paper stencils for our mimeographed daily newspaper at APO 980 in the Aleutians. This is a medium to make an artist long for the good old days when a craftsman had nice cave walls and handfuls of red and yellow ocher to work with. The hundred and fifty representative cartoons reproduced here have been dressed up a little with ink-line and wash; otherwise they haven't been tampered with.

Since our newspaper first appeared, fourteen months ago, we've run from two to four cartoons a day, depending on how much space we needed for maps, and our daily average through this period must have been at least three. That multiplies up to some twelve hundred and seventy cartoons in all. So far as I can figure out, no particular plan was followed in picking out the favored hundred and fifty for this book. Each of the three artists seems simply to have picked out the ones he happened–for one reason or another–to like. Some of my favorites are absent, but I'm too old and cagey to argue with artists unless I have to. And this lot is doubtless as truly representative as any I would select.

Military life in the Aleutians is not a whole lot like any kind of life anywhere else in the world, and life on one Aleutian island often differs a good deal from life on its neighbors. But we on the wet rock that's listed as APO 980 like to think our island is the norm, the others merely slight variants on our pattern. This, of course, is healthy provincialism which shouldn't bother anybody. In any case it's a cinch we are more like the rest of the Aleutians than we are like any other place and, if this book shows what we're like here, then it can safely be said to more or less show what we're all like up and down the Chain.

This business of showing what we're like is the heart of the whole thing. It's not so much a matter of showing outsiders what we're like–though we're not modest enough to have anything against that–what's important is showing ourselves. With the first-comers to the Aleutians it may have been different. Stepping off a landing boat in icy water and wading ashore on a new island–whether occupied by the enemy or not–was a clear-cut military operation that spoke for itself. But most of us weren't in that first wave–although millions and millions must have been in one first wave or another if you're a good listener–and our life here doesn't fit into any of the familiar martial patterns. Most war art, serious or comic, misses us.

There is in man a need to see himself, to have himself and his pursuits and environment expressed. This is the necessity that set early man to daubing his cave wall with ochered representations of the hunt, that set Anastasia, Pedigo and Miller to scratching mimeograph stencils with a stylus. No art can have an older, a more honorable, a more truly authentic basis.

This, then is our art and its people are us.

DASHIELL HAMMETT
Aleutian Islands
2 April 1945

STATEMENT:

"Dashiell Hammett," *Daily Worker*, 12 March 1947, p. 3.

This statement by Hammett was in response to a proposal by U.S. Labor Secretary Schwellenbach to the House Committee on Labor to outlaw the Communist Party in the United States.

"The proposal outlawing the Communist Party is a direct assault on American democracy, on American tradition of civil rights and liberties and of electoral freedom.

"It must be assumed that the Secretary of Labor acted as spokesman for the Truman adminis-

The radio serial Adventures of Sam Spade *(1946-1951) was sponsored by the Wildroot Company, who advertised the show in a long-running series of ads, such as the one above, in the Sunday comic sections of newspapers all over the country*

tration, of which he is a member, in making his statement before the House Labor Committee.

"President Truman and the Republican leadership to whom the proposal was directed need not be reminded that outlawing of the Communist Party was the first step taken by the Hitler administration to establish itself in power.

"We urge that every American now make his voice heard in defense of his country against the attack which is being leveled against it on the Hitler pattern from Washington itself. The chorus of American voices demanding that President Truman repudiate this proposal can stop the attack in its tracks."

AFFIDAVIT:

Affidavit of Dashiell Hammett, United States District Court, Southern District of New York, 20 September 1948.

In 1948 Warner Brothers, who had produced two movies based on The Maltese Falcon *(one in 1931 and one in 1941), sued various people associated with the CBS radio series "Adventures of Sam Spade" for copyright infringement and unfair competition. Warner Brothers had bought all broadcast rights to* The Maltese Falcon, *including the rights to the characters. Hammett's affidavit filed in connection with the suit provides a wealth of*

information about his professional dealings. The precedent-setting decision held that the characters: a literary work are not subject to copyright unless they are integral to the plot. The radio series continued on NBC until 1951, when it was cancelled because of Hammett's notoriety.

DASHIELL HAMMETT, being duly sworn, deposes and says:

I am the plaintiff above named and submit this affidavit in support of the plaintiff's motion for summary judgment.

I was born in St. Mary County, Maryland on May 27, 1894 and am and have been a resident and citizen of the State of New York for well over the past ten years excepting only the period from September 13, 1942 to September 6, 1945 when I was in Military service with the U.S. Army. Following my honorable discharge on the latter date, I resided at 15 East 66th Street, New York City until about December, 1947 when I moved to my present address of 28 West 10th Street, New York City, where I have since resided. I have at no time resided in or been a citizen of the State of Delaware.

Professionally, I am and have been an author for about the past 25 years. My writings have consisted mainly of fiction in the mystery or detective story field. I have lectured on and have also been a critic and reviewer of literature in those fields. During the year 1926 as well as during the years of 1930 and 1931 I was engaged and served in the latter capacities for the *Saturday Review of Literature* and the New York *Evening Post* respectively. Prior to 1929 when I wrote the mystery detective story entitled "The Maltese Falcon" I had written a number of detective stories and two novels entitled "Red Harvest" and "The Dain Curse." These writings were published and well received.

"The Maltese Falcon" was first published serially under that title about the latter part of 1929 in the periodical known as the *Black Mask* magazine. This work brought favorable response and as a consequence was published in book or novel form in early 1930 by the publisher, Alfred A. Knopf, Inc. The latter had received copyright assignments covering the work from the periodical publisher and had registered its own copyright on the book at about the time of its publication. The book successfully impressed critics and public alike.

This volume was translated and published in Denmark, Spain, France, England, Germany, Hungary, Sweden, and Portugal, as well as in English on the Continent. Other American editions besides Knopf's were put out by Grosset and Dunlop, McClure, the Modern Library, and Pocket Books. It was included in "The Hammett Omnibus" which has been published by Grosset and Dunlop, the World Publishing Company, and Pocket Books. Serializations have appeared in foreign newspapers and American magazines.

The following comments have been made about "The Maltese Falcon":

"The story has plenty of action, a good plot, excellent characterization, and a startling denouement * * *. This is not only probably the best detective story we have ever read, it is an exceedingly well written novel."

W. R. BROOKS
The Outlook, 2/26/30

"Mr. Hammett has written a fascinating story, thrilling from cover to cover, and amazing in its developments * * * Grand literature it is, a racy American sort of writing * * *."

Detroit News, 2/23/30

* * * combine the traditional elements of detective fiction with quick humor, hard, real characters and effective writing."

New York Post, 3/27/30

"Dashiell Hammett's 'The Maltese Falcon' is an excellent and thrilling mystery story."

STANLEY WALKER
New York Herald-Tribune
7/27/30

About this time, too, Warner Brothers Pictures, Inc., one of the major motion picture companies, became interested in making a motion picture of or based upon "The Maltese Falcon." Negotiations with said defendant company (hereinafter also referred to as "Warner's") took place in New York City, where I resided. After a price of $8,500. was fixed, Warner's sent over to the publisher Alfred A. Knopf, Inc. in New York City its proposed agreement (Exhibit "A" to Complaint) for execution by the publisher and myself. It was signed by the publisher and myself at the former's offices in New York City on June 30, 1930 and countersigned by Warner's also in New York City the day following.

In this work I for the first time employed the fictional private detective whom I named "Sam Spade." He is a leading character in the book. He was a figure originated and created from my imagination as well as my personal experience with private detectives garnered during the period from 1915 to 1922, when I was myself a Pinkerton (private) detective. In making his debut, "Sam Spade" too was well received in the select circle of fictional detectives. Ellery Queen, one of my colleagues in this field of literature refers to him as "the great Sam Spade" (introduction to "The Return of the Continental Op" published by Jonathan Press Inc., 1945) and comments at length about this character in his Introduction to the collection entitled "The Adventures of Sam Spade" hereinafter referred to. I subsequently employed Sam Spade as the central character in three later stories written by me from about 1932 to 1934 and first published in *Collier's* and the *American Magazine*. These stories were thereafter published in a collection of stories entitled "The Adventures of Sam Spade and other stories by Dashiell Hammett," two of these editions being published under the

1944 copyright of The American Mercury, Inc. Copies of these two editions will be handed up to the Court as Plaintiff's Exhibits "1" and "1a" hereto.

In utilizing Sam Spade as the central and leading character in these later stories after his successful debut in "The Maltese Falcon" I have been following a custom in detective story writing which is virtually as old as this form of literature itself. This branch of literature is generally regarded as dating from the emergence of the classic Sherlock Holmes stories over a half century ago. "A Study in Scarlet," the first of these stories by the late British author, Sir Arthur Conan Doyle, which recounted the exploits of the fictional detective, Sherlock Holmes, was published in England in 1887.

Some of the better known fictional sleuths who have followed Sherlock Holmes in a career of solving crime as recounted in different stories featuring new adventures of the same sleuth are:

Philo Vance ....by S. S. Van Dine
Perry Mason ....by Erle Stanley Gardner
Nero Wolfe.....................................by Rex Stout
Father Brown ....by G. K. Chesterton
Hercule Poirot ....by Agatha Christie
Hanaud...............................by A. E. W. Mason
Ellery Queen..........................by "Ellery Queen"
The Saint..............................by Leslie Charteris
Philip Trent...............................by E. C. Dentley
Max Carrados.........................by Ernest Bramah
Craig Kennedy ....by Arthur B. Reeve
Charlie Chan.........................by Earl Der Biggers

Indeed, I have followed this custom of using the same sleuth or sleuths as the central figure of successive different adventures in other instances besides Sam Spade. The Thin Man characters of "Nora and Nicky Charles" and the "Continental Op" are some of my well known characters who are such examples. They each appear in a number of different adventure stories which have been widely exploited through publications or motion pictures.

My four "Sam Spade" stories have been successful. Apart from republication, readers have inquired and have asked for more. Warner's has already produced three different motion pictures of or based on "The Maltese Falcon," the first and third under that title in about 1931 and 1941 and the second under the title of "Satan Met a Lady" in about 1936. Also, according to Warner's admis-

sion (Freston & Files letter to Regis Radio Corporation, May 13, 1948, Exhibit "2" hereto), a number of broadcasts have been made of dramatizations of "The Maltese Falcon" under the guise of a Warner's license. In fact, as late as December of 1947 the Columbia Broadcasting System, Inc. requested of Warner's a license for broadcasting "The Maltese Falcon," which proposed license Warner's refused to grant.

On May 15, 1946, there being an apparent demand for a radio series featuring further adventures of "Sam Spade," I granted the authorization to E. J. Rosenberg and Larry White for the use in radio and other media of the character "Sam Spade" and of the title "The Adventures of Sam Spade," as per copy of agreement with said parties hereto annexed as Exhibit "3." I have known said E. J. Rosenberg and Larry White for a number of years and know them to be residents of New York City, New York and Huntington, Long Island, New York respectively.

As will be noted the authorization and rights granted under said agreement relate solely and merely to the character "Sam Spade" and to the title containing such name. There is no grant or obligation with respect to any script or story content in which the character "Sam Spade" may be used or to which such title may be applied. In fact my warranties therein are expressly made inapplicable to the "scripts or substance" of any Sam Spade productions (Par. 6). I have never written, collaborated in the writing of, made suggestions for, approved or disapproved of, nor have I been consulted nor have I requested consultation concerning, the scripts or substance which have been the subject of weekly broadcasts for over two years under the title of "The Adventures of Sam Spade." These scripts and material have been prepared and written by others. Nor have I had any connection with any other phase of the presentation and production of this program other than that I have been referred to by name on each week's program at least twice as the creator of the character "Sam Spade."

Save for one or two possible interruptions, the aforementioned "Adventures of Sam Spade" radio series has been broadcast weekly on Sunday, 8:00 p.m., New York time, since July 12, 1946 over transcontinental radio networks embracing approximately 160 radio stations in various localities including every important city in the nation. It has been regularly originated and broadcast from a radio station in Hollywood, California. Throughout it has been commercially sponsored by Wildroot Company, Inc., a major national advertiser. Since about September 29, 1946 such weekly broadcasts have been over the Columbia Broadcasting System, Inc. network. Such weekly programs have been produced for such radio presentation by the Regis Radio Corporation.

The latter corporation organized and controlled by the aforementioned E. J. Rosenberg and Larry White, uses the Spade character and title for the above radio series pursuant to the aforementioned agreement for such use. That corporation has regularly paid me the stipulated royalty of $400.00 per broadcast (weekly) pursuant to that agreement.

Each of the weekly broadcasts in the "Adventures of Sam Spade" series is of a half-hour duration and involves with but a few exceptions a dramatization of a new, different and complete adventure or case of Sam Spade. The few exceptions are those programs which have presented a repeat of the same adventure which appeared in a prior week of the series or which have presented the same adventure spread over two successive weekly half-hour installments.

As shown in the accompanying affidavit of E. J. Rosenberg, President of Regis Radio Corporation, the program has been extensively and regularly advertised and promoted since its inception over two years ago. It is one of the most popular mystery programs on the air. In slightly over two years of regular broadcasting it has reached a total audience aggregating tens, if not hundreds of millions of listeners. Obviously such wide exploitation has made the name and character Sam Spade even better known to many millions of people. It can safely be said that there is scarcely a man, woman or child regularly listening to radio who has not thereby become familiar or better acquainted with the name and character Sam Spade. Indeed (as further shown in the above affidavit), when Howard Duff recently made his appearance as an actor in motion pictures, the press and even the defendant's own theatre ads referred to him typically as "radio's Sam Spade" or "Sam Spade of

radio."

Until this year the defendant had made no complaint concerning the Sam Spade program. It was not until after the refusal of the defendant late in December of last year to grant a radio license to Columbia Broadcasting System, Inc. for "The Maltese Falcon" and the use instead by Columbia Broadcasting System, Inc. on a "Suspense" program of January 10, 1948 of "The Kandy Tooth," another Sam Spade adventure story previously broadcast in the above Sam Spade series, that the defendant first began to make claims. Defendant's first claim letter to Columbia Broadcasting System, Inc. of January 29, 1948 (Exhibit "4" hereto) shows the defendant's particular pique over the use of the "Kandy Tooth," claiming that to be a *plagiarism* of "The Maltese Falcon" and its film version, and then further expands its claims to include all past Spade character and title uses.

In the later initial letter of May 13, 1948 to Regis Radio Corporation (Exhibit "2" hereto) defendant's attorneys set forth demands solely with reference to the name and character of Sam Spade. On June 1, 1948 I was notified by Regis Radio Corporation of Warner's claims for the use of the character "Sam Spade" and the title "The Adventures of Sam Spade" and advised that pursuant to the warranties in our agreement of May 15, 1946 (Exhibit "3" hereto), Regis would look to me for their prompt elimination.

It is evident from the above facts that the present or continuing assertion of defendant's claims to the character Sam Spade and any title featuring that name is and will be highly damaging to me.

Unless this Court declares that I as author am privileged to use such name and character free from let or hindrance on the defendant's part, I will be prevented from engaging in or authorizing similar independent dealings for new Sam Spade stories in the radio, television and motion picture fields. How costly this controversy can be to me and how valuable name and character rights such as those in question are is illustrated by the following typical facts: On January 15, 1934 I executed a contract with Metro-Goldwyn-Mayer Corporation for my story "The Thin Man" (Exhibit "8" hereto). This contract is similar to my instant Warner's contract of June 23, 1930 (Exhibit "A" to Complaint) except that it contains grants even possibly broader in favor of the motion picture purchaser. I received a consideration of $21,000 therefor. Subsequently, on October 23, 1934, I executed another motion picture agreement with the same producer for a sequel to the "Thin Man" story featuring the same central characters (Exhibit "9" hereto). For the latter story I received a consideration of $20,000. Notwithstanding, I later entered into the agreement of February 11, 1937 (Exhibit "10" hereto) with Metro-Goldwyn-Mayer wherein I expressly and specifically sold the right to the use of the "Thin Man" characters and name or title in connection with motion pictures for a consideration of $40,000.

Thus, aside from the loss of royalties and revenue with which I am threatened by the defendant's claims, I will be subjected to the further annoyance and expense of defending against such claims pursuant to the warranties that I would be obliged to give in connection with any of my such dealings for the name or character Sam Spade.

Although aware of the broadcast, the claims, and the litigation between Warner's and myself, the publisher of "The Maltese Falcon," Alfred A. Knopf, Inc., has made no claim with respect to the character Sam Spade or any title containing that name. As shown by the pleadings, the publisher has been named by Warner's as a former party plaintiff in Warner's California action by reason of Warner's having invoked a clause in our 1930 agreement (Exhibit "A" to Complaint). Thus, insofar as the controversy concerns the rights to the character Sam Spade or any title containing that name, it relates solely to my rights therein *vis-a-vis* Warner's.

I have fully and fairly stated the above facts herein to Leonard Zissu, Esq., my attorney, and as I am informed and verily believe: there is no genuine issue as to any material fact; I as plaintiff am entitled to judgment as a matter of law; there is no merit in the answer of the defendant but on the contrary such answer was interposed merely for the purpose of delaying this action to which there is no defense.

I hereby certify that all papers or parts thereof referred to in my affidavit or attached as exhibits thereto are true copies of such original papers or parts thereof.

Wherefore I respectfully pray that an order be made striking out defendant's answer and granting judgment in my favor for the relief sought in the complaint.

Dashiell Hammett.

(Sworn to by Dashiell Hammett, September 20th, 1948.)

BOOK REVIEW:

"A Man Called Hammett," *Times Literary Supplement* (London), 17 November 1950, p. 728.

The publication in London of The Dashiell Hammett Omnibus, *which included all five of his novels and four short stories, provided the occasion for a reassessment of his work.*

Mr. Dashiell Hammett must be considered unique among writers of detective fiction, not only by reason of the quality of his work, which may be held to place him in an altogether different category, but because, having actually worked for the Pinkerton Detective Agency, he has had personal experience of the type of work he describes. Doubtless the cases on which he himself worked were more prosaic and less exciting than *The Maltese Falcon* and *The Dain Curse*, and certainly less bloodthirsty than *Red Harvest* or other adventures of his own character, the Continental Op, who is given no name by his creator other than the aliases which he assumes in the line of duty; but one cannot avoid the assumption that Mr. Hammett's acquaintance with the routine of criminal investigation helped to create the illusion of reality which is so striking a feature of his stories and which distinguishes him so sharply from his countless imitators. He left the detective agency because, it is stated, "he was sick of poking his nose into other people's business"; and his early work appeared in American pulp magazines such as *Black Mask*, which, under the editorship of Joseph Thompson Shaw, printed many examples of "tough" writing. Mr. Hammett, and others of the "hard-boiled" school of which he was the founder were determined to bring mystery fiction down to earth, and to substitute flesh-and-blood characters for the cardboard abstractions—labelled "detective," "victim," "suspect" and "murderer"—which figured so prominently as protagonists in the armchair problems of that day.

Owing, however, to the requirements of the readers of these magazines, Mr. Hammett was often able to fulfil his ambition only at the expense of probability in the choice of subject-matter, and the plot-framework of his first Continental Op stories conformed to the pattern in vogue. But while the motives for the crimes unravelled were standardized (revenge for some past wrong, far-fetched manifestations of greed, robberies planned on a scale undreamed of by Professor Moriarty, &c.), the backgrounds and characters were presented with scrupulous realism, and the curt brutality of the style must have come as a salutary shock to those accustomed to the devitalized writing then current among practitioners in the thriller medium.

Mr. Hammett's prose was not only a stylistic innovation–for his stories appeared at a time when Mr. Hemingway himself was comparatively unknown–but it was an expression of the personality of the dour, forthright, ruthless detective who was his own chronicler. Deeds of incredible callousness–such as the holocaust on Couffignal Island, or the wholesale annihilation of the gangsters in *Blood Money*–were described with a terse matter-of-factness and a mastery of understatement rare even to-day, when Mr. Hammett's method is so often abused by second-rate writers ignorant perhaps of its origin.

Black Mask specialized in complete stories of approximately 15,000 words, a length peculiarly suited to the detective genre, imposing, as it must, a rigid economy of phrase and a concentration upon essential incident; and such pieces as *Dead Yellow Women* and *Golden Horseshoe*, in spite of the aforementioned crudities of plot, are models of their kind. Mr. Hammett also developed, during this formative period, a talent for directly engaging the reader's attention which should be an integral part of every writer's technical equipment; the opening sentences of *The Farewell Murder* will serve as a typical example:

> I was the only one who left the train at Farewell. A man came through the rain from the passenger shed. He was a small man. His face was dark and flat. He wore a grey waterproof cap and a grey coat in military style.

A sinister atmosphere is at once created by the darkness and flatness of the stranger's face, by the "short choppy steps" with which he walks through the rain; though he is in fact an unimportant minor character who plays no part in the drama of vengeance, avarice and murder in which the reader, like the anonymous narrator, is shortly to be embroiled.

The Continental Op, invariable hero of these early essays, was conceived in deliberately unromantic terms: short, stout, and 40 years old. His physical dissimilarity from the keen-eyed, hawk-faced detectives of the time, his sturdy common sense, disenchanted outlook, and unscrupulous attitude towards major criminals, were refreshing and unfamiliar in the field. He was, to quote Mr. Ellery Queen, the first truly American detective, and his first full-length adventure, *Red Harvest*, was the first truly American detective story. English readers, encountering it for the first time–for it has never before been published in this country–might dismiss this medley of civic corruption, gangsterism, and multiple murder as yet another shocker in the manner of *No Orchids for Miss Blandish*, but they should remember that it antedated the publication of that work by several years, and that it was printed at a date when the St. Valentine's Day massacre had become part of contemporary history, and when such events as are described in the book were by no means uncommon in the United States. The construction of the novel itself is also worthy of note, as is that of its successor, *The Dain Curse*. The latter is particularly interesting, being divided into three parts, each ending with a surprise revelation and a feasible explanation of the mystery, but keeping the real secret until the very last with an ingenuity unequalled even by Edgar Wallace at the height of his form. There are times during the perusal of these two books when even the most slavish devotee will suspect Mr. Hammett of wallowing in a mere blood bath, and certainly the *Black Mask* formula has not yet been entirely discarded; but it should be taken into consideration that the author was then engaged in combating the influence of the English crossword-puzzle school, and that his accounts of violence, perversion, and cruelty were deliberately selected to shock–like those of D. H. Lawrence or

Henry Miller in another sphere–and did not reflect a subconscious sadism of any sort.

Another convention which Mr. Hammett set himself to break down was the love-interest forced upon reluctant readers in the mistaken belief that it made for larger sales, and the lifelessness of the heroines involved, who existed only to be drugged, kidnapped, held to ransom, and to marry the detective in the last chapter, when their major function had been fulfilled. Mr. Hammett's feminine characters–Dinah Brand, with her smudged lipstick and the run in her stocking; the beautiful psychopathic liar Brigid O'Shaugnessy; Big Flora and the egregious Mimi–belonged to a very different species; of them all, Gabrielle in *The Dain Curse* perhaps approaches nearest to the conventional type. Apart from Gabrielle and Nancy Regan in *Blood Money*–and she is not entirely blameless in her conduct–Mr. Hammett's other women are all either mad or bad: Princess Zhukovski and the girl with silver eyes (the two forerunners of Brigid O'Shaugnessy); the knife-throwing Kewpie, the exotic Inés and the intriguing Janet Henry. The charming, sophisticated wife of Nick Charles might be cited as an exception, but she belongs to a later period, and like *The Thin Man* itself (the film of which is perhaps better known to many than the novel from which it was adapted) is conceived on a very different plane.

The Continental Op, however, remained true to the accepted moral code in resisting the blandishments of this bevy of tiger-women whenever their dangerous professional charm was turned upon him; unlike Sam Spade, his successor, who in *The Maltese Falcon* not only seduced his partner's wife but accepted the advances of a cold-blooded murderess in order to extract information from her, and later to hand her over to justice. Spade, the blond Satan with the V-shaped face, who was to become the prototype of countless "private eyes" in American fiction, had previously made his bow in a *Black Mask* novelette, *A Man Called Spade*, where his salient characteristics, rumoured dishonesty and disinclination to be pushed around by the official police were lightly sketched in, before the full-length portrait in *The Maltese Falcon* established him as an almost national figure in the United States. There can be little doubt that the story of the quest for that fabulous, golden, gem-studded

bird will live long in the history of romantic literature; for, as Mr. Ellery Queen has pointed out, its theme is basically as romantic as *The Moonstone* or *The Rajah's Diamond*, and the realistic label attached to the book by many critics is due to a confusion between the subject and the hard shell of style encasing it, even as the outer coating of lead concealed the presence of the jewelled Falcon beneath. In style *The Maltese Falcon* marks a considerable advance on the Continental Op stories and novels, technically excellent though these undoubtedly were: Mr. Hammett's prose had acquired a high polish, and the construction of his sentences revealed an almost fanatical care in selecting the *mot juste*, as his description of Caspar Gutman, Spade's antagonist, will show:

> A fat man came to meet him. The fat man was flabbily fat with bulbous pink cheeks and lips and neck, with a great soft egg of a belly that was all his torso, and pendant cones for arms and legs. As he advanced to meet Spade all his bulbs rose and shook and fell separately with each step, in the manner of clustered soap bubbles not yet released from the pipe through which they had been blown.

The graphic, visual quality of such writing cannot be denied, and the character of Gutman himself, compounded perhaps of Count Fosco and the president of the Suicide Club, with a touch of Long John Silver's genial capacity for treachery, belongs to the great rogues' gallery of fiction; for, like Stevenson–a writer with whom, in spite of their disparity of style and aims, he had more than a little in common–Mr. Hammett has a talent for creating villains on the grand scale. The elegant Chinese with the Oxford accent who dominates *The House in Turk Street*; the cringing Papadopoulos; the effeminate Joel Cairo; and the snivelling, brutal bully of *The Glass Key* may take up, with future generations, a place alongside Blind Pew, Israel Hands and the diabolical Case.

At the time of writing *The Maltese Falcon* Mr. Hammett was also much preoccupied, like Mr. Hemingway, with the mechanics of violence and the difficulty of conveying their effect on to paper; this preoccupation is revealed by his slow-motion account of Spade disarming Cairo, from which the following extract is taken:–

Then Spade smiled. His smile was gentle, even dreamy. His right shoulder raised a few inches. His bent right arm was driven up by the shoulder's lift. Fist, wrist, forearm, crooked elbow, and upper arm seemed all one rigid piece, with only the limber shoulder giving them motion. The fist struck Cairo's face, covering for a moment one side of his chin, a corner of his mouth, and most of his cheek between cheek-bone and jaw-bone. Cairo shut his eyes and was unconscious.

This method is repeated in his most important novel, *The Glass Key*, in which the detective *motif*, in this case the search for the murderer of dissolute young Taylor Henry, is subordinate to the psychological relationship between Ned Beaumont, the gambler, and his friend Paul Madvig, the politician–a relationship which is complicated by their rivalry for the dead playboy's sister. It is a book typical of its period–of the days of Cole Porter and Ted Lewis, when dance-music had a nostalgic dying fall and love affairs ended in "desolation, spoliation and uprooting." The symbolic dream which gives a title to the novel ensures, prophetically, the future unhappiness of the lovers, after Beaumont has prepared to elope with Janet and his friendship with Paul is finally broken up; suffering and futility were the order of the day: a pattern repeated, after a second world war, by contemporary existentialists in France at the moment of writing. The nihilistic intransigeance of Mr. Hammett's heroes is, however, unbacked by any philosophy, and perhaps the more terrible for that; Beaumont's dead-pan progress through the welter of beatings-up and brutality has at times the hallucinatory quality of a nightmare; and Mr. Hammett's harsh uncompromising method of presenting his story, in which no introspection is permitted to the characters, has more in common with the tenets of Mr. Wyndham Lewis than with the influence of the cinema, generally held to be responsible.

Mr. Hammett has not published a novel for more than 16 years, and it is to be hoped that he will soon complete the major work on which he is rumoured to be engaged; for at his worst he has provided us always with entertainment, while at his best he is an artist intent on presenting his intensely personal vision, in terms of action rather than psychology, of the violent, cruel and treacherous world we live in to-day.

TESTIMONY:

Transcript of Hammett's Testimony on 9 July 1951 before the U.S. Second District Court for the Southern District of New York, Sylvester J. Ryan Presiding. [from Shadow Man]

On 4 November 1949, The Civil Rights Congress bail fund, of which Hammett was a trustee, posted $260,000 bail for eleven men appealing their conviction under the Smith Act. Four of the eleven skipped bond, and in the first week of July the trustees of the CRC bail fund were subpoenaed to testify as to the whereabouts of the fugitives. As a result of his refusal to cooperate, Hammett was sentenced to six months in jail for contempt of court. He was taken into custody immediately as he left the witness stand.

AFTERNOON SESSION
2.30 o'clock P.M.

THE COURT: All right, now, Mr. Hammett, will you take the stand.

SAMUEL DASHIELL HAMMETT, called as a witness, being duly sworn, testified as follows:

THE COURT: Did you want to say something, Mr. Rabinowitz?

MR. RABINOWITZ: Your Honor, I wanted to note first that Mrs. Kaufman and I will both appear for Mr. Hammett.

And then I wanted to make a preliminary motion to quash the subpoena here on the ground that the subpoena bears the caption "United States v. Hall." There is no index number on the subpoena. I am unable to trace the action, and so far as I know there is no action pending in this court entitled U.S. v. Hall.

THE COURT: The witness is present in court. The Court will now proceed to examine him irrespective of the validity of any subpoena served upon him.

The motion is denied.

Mr. Saypol, you may proceed.

By Mr. Saypol.

Q. Mr. Hammett–

THE COURT: Before you begin, Mr. Hammett, so that you might understand your position here, you are called here as a witness by the Court. If, during the course of your examination you feel that it is necessary to consult with counsel before answering any question, simply ask the Court for

[196]

an opportunity to do so and the opportunity will be granted to you.

Do you understand?

THE WITNESS: Yes.

Q. Mr. Hammett, are you one of the five trustees of the bail fund of the Congress of Civil Rights? A. I decline to answer that question on the ground that the answer might tend to incriminate me. I am exercising my rights under the Fifth Amendment of the Constitution.

THE COURT: Mr. Saypol, I think the name of the fund was not correctly given by you in your question. I therefore suggest that you ask the question again.

MR. SAYPOL: All right.

Q. Mr. Hammett, I show you this–

THE COURT: No. Ask the question again so that we may get an answer to it.

Q. Are you one of the five trustees–

THE COURT: No. One of the trustees. Are you one of the trustees of the–

Q. –bail fund of the Civil Rights Congress of New York? A. I decline to answer. Do I have to repeat my reasons for declining to answer?

THE COURT: Yes.

A. (continuing) I decline to answer on the ground that the answer may tend to incriminate me, and I am relying on my rights under the Fifth Amendment to the Constitution of the United States.

THE COURT: I direct you to answer the question.

THE WITNESS: I decline to answer the question, your Honor, for the same reasons.

THE COURT: For the same reasons that you have given?

THE WITNESS: Yes.

Q. I show you Exhibit 6 in evidence, the minute book of the bail fund of the Civil Rights Congress of New York, and I direct your attention particularly to a minute dated November 14, 1949, which reads as follows:

"The trustees agreed to post bail up to $1,000 each for a 30-day period for the 16 members of the Federation of Greek Maritime Unions now held on Ellis Island.

"It was reported that on November 3, 1949 bail in the aggregate amount of $260,000 had been posted in the case of the 11 Communist leaders con-

victed under the Smith Act. This action was taken in pursuance of the authorization given by the trustees at their meeting on July 22, 1948."

Signed "Frederick V. Field."

I ask you, have you seen this minute book before? A. I decline to answer–

THE COURT: Showing the witness Exhibit No. 6; is that right?

MR. SAYPOL: Yes, your Honor.

A. (continuing) I decline to answer the question on ground that the answer may tend to incriminate me.

Q. Have you examined this–

THE COURT: Excuse me, Mr. Saypol.

Q. Have you examined this–

THE COURT: Excuse me, Mr. Saypol.

(To witness) I direct you to answer the question.

A. I decline to answer the question on the same grounds.

THE COURT: All right.

Q. Before you declined, did you examine this document that I handed you? A. May I consult counsel?

THE COURT: Yes, surely.

(Witness consults with counsel.)

MR. RABINOWITZ: May I ask to have the question read?

THE COURT: Yes.

(Question read.)

(Witness consulted with counsel.)

MR. SAYPOL: May the record show that the witness consulted with his counsel and returns to the witness stand now?

THE WITNESS: May I hear that question?

(Last question read as follows: "Before you declined did you examine this document that I handed you?")

Q. Government's Exhibit 6? A. Yes, now.

Q. Did you examine now the minutes that I referred to dated November 14, 1949? A. Yes.

Q. And after examining it do you decline to answer the question directed to you by the Court that you answer? A. I do.

Q. Referring to this minute dated November 14, 1949, which I have read, do you see in the left hand margin a group of initials, four to be exact? A. I do.

Q. Do you recognize those? A. I decline to answer that—now I would like before I decline to ask, do I recognize them as initials? I would say Yes.

By the Court.

Q. Do you recognize the handwriting of the individual? A. I decline to answer that on the ground that the answer may tend to incriminate me.

Q. I direct you to answer that. A. I decline, your Honor, for the reasons given.

By Mr. Saypol.

Q. Without telling me whether the first initials are those of yourself or somebody else, do they appear to you to be the initials D. H.? A. They do appear.

Q. Are they your initials? A. I decline to answer that question.

By the Court.

Q. Are they your handwriting? A. I decline to answer that question for the reasons given.

Q. That is, you feel that the answer may tend to incriminate you? A. Yes.

Q. I direct you to answer the question. A. I respectfully decline, for the reasons given.

Q. Let me ask you one question, Mr. Hammett—is that the name? A. It is.

Q. Have you any way conspired, aided or abetted or arranged or assisted in the arrangements for the nonappearance of Robert G. Thompson, Gilert Green, Gus Hall and Henry Winston, or any of them in this cause since the issuance of process against them? A. I decline to answer on the ground that the answer may tend to incriminate me.

Q. I direct you to answer. A. I decline to answer for the reasons already given.

Q. Do you know Robert G. Thompson? A. I decline to answer on the ground the answer may tend to incriminate me.

Q. I direct you to answer. A. I decline to answer for the reasons given.

Q. Have you seen Robert G. Thompson since Thursday, July 5th? A. I decline to answer on the ground the answer may tend to incriminate me.

Q. I direct you to answer. A. I decline to answer for the same reason.

Q. Do you know Gilbert Green? A. I decline to answer on the ground that the answer might tend to incriminate me.

Q. I direct you to answer. A. I decline to answer for the reasons given.

Q. Have you seen Gilbert Green since Thursday, July 5th? A. I decline to answer on the ground the answer may tend to incriminate me.

Q. Do you know Gus Hall? A. I decline to answer on the ground that the answer may tend to incriminate me.

Q. I direct you to answer. A. I decline to answer for the reasons given.

Q. Have you seen Gus Hall since Thursday, July 5th? A. I decline to answer for the reason that the answer may tend to incriminate me.

Q. I direct you to answer. A. I decline to answer for the reasons given.

Q. Do you known Henry Winston? A. I decline to answer for the reasons, on the ground—

Q. Take your time. A. (continuing)—that an answer may tend to incriminate me.

Q. I direct you to answer. A. I decline to answer for the reasons given.

Q. Have you seen Henry Winston since Thursday, July 5th? A. I decline to answer on the ground the answer may tend to incriminate me.

Q. I direct you to answer. A. I decline to answer.

THE COURT: Go ahead, Mr. Saypol.

By Mr. Saypol.

Q. When since last Monday, July 2nd, were you in New York last? New York City, I mean? A. The question was when since—

Q. When since Monday, July 2nd, have you been in New York City last.

(Witness left the stand to consult with counsel and thereafter returned to the stand.)

MR. SAYPOL: May the record show that the witness has returned to the witness box after consulting with both his counsel.

Q. Now then will you respond?

(Last question read by the reporter.)

A. I was in New York City from about 11 o'clock Thursday morning until around 4 o'clock Friday afternoon and from, oh, about 1 o'clock yesterday to the present time.

Q. You mean from Thursday, July 5th, until, when you say yesterday, you mean Sunday, July 8th? A. Yes.

Q. When before Thursday, July 5th, were you in New York City last? A. My best memory would be–oh, I had not been in New York City for, I think, one day short of two weeks. Two weeks. Friday, two weeks previous. One day. About 13 days.

Q. I direct your attention once again to this Exhibit 6. Will you please examine this minute, the minutes of the bail fund of the Civil Rights Congress of New York, dated May 18, 1949, reading as follows:

"The trustees surveyed the various acts of the bail fund from its first meeting to date. The auditor's report of the bail fund of the Civil Rights Congress of New York as of December 31, 1948, prepared by Bernard Ades, certified public accountant, was noted and filed. The trustees approved the payment of $340 to Mr. Ades for the preparation of this report on January 27, 1948, and for all other accounting services previously rendered to the bail fund. The trustees also approved the payment of $50 as rent for its safe deposit box at the Amalgamated Bank."

Signed "George Marshall, Secretary,
Bail Fund of the Civil Rights
Congress of New York."

Mr. Marshall was Mr. Field's predecessor, was he not? A. I decline to answer on the grounds that the answer might tend to incriminate me.

THE COURT: I direct you to answer.

THE WITNESS: I decline to answer for the reason stated.

Q. That answer was given after you followed the reading of this paper with me; is that so? A. It is.

Q. I direct your attention to the lefthand margin, the left side margin of this resolution of this minute of May 18, 1949, and you see there, do you not, the pen written initials, the first of which appear to be "D. H."? A. I do.

Q. Are those your initials? A. I decline to answer the question on the ground that the answer might tend to incriminate me.

THE COURT: I direct you to answer.

THE WITNESS: I decline to answer the question for the reasons given.

Q. Did you affix those initials? A. I decline to answer.

Q. Did you affix the initials "D. H."? A. I decline to answer the question for the reasons given.

THE COURT: I direct you to answer.

THE WITNESS: I decline to answer.

By the Court.

Q. Do you know the present whereabouts of Robert G. Thompson, Gilbert Green, Gus Hall and Henry Winston, or either of them? A. I decline to answer on the ground that the answer might tend to incriminate me.

Q. I direct you to answer. A. I decline to answer for the reasons given.

Q. Mr. Hammett, a bond was given in this court, four bonds were given in this court by the bail fund of the Civil Rights Congress of New York, to secure the appearance or to assure the appearance of these four individuals whose names I have just given you. The testimony before the Court is that you functioned as one of the trustees of that fund, for some time past. When these men were released on bail, they were released in the custody of the bondsmen, and since the bondsmen are members of an unincorporated association, in effect it means that they were released in the custody of those who operated and managed the affairs of this bail fund, and that they were released in the custody of the trustees, and the testimony before the Court indicates that you were one of the trustees, and by your refusal to answer you are not only violating the trust imposed in you, that you voluntarily assumed when you acted as a trustee for this fund, but you are thwarting the processes of this court. I feel that your claim of immunity has neither legal basis nor factual foundation. It is the intention of the Court, if you persist in your refusal to answer these questions which have been put to you, particularly those questions concerning the present whereabouts of these four men who were released under bail given by the bail fund of the Civil Rights Congress of New York, to deal with you just as dramatically as the law permits. I trust that you will not make that necessary. A. (No response.)

THE COURT: Next question.

By Mr. Saypol.

Q. Mr. Hammett, I direct your attention to this paper in Exhibit 6 which reads as follows:

"Minutes bail fund Civil Rights Congress of New York September 26, 1949.

"The trustees decided that it would be desirable to have two additional trustees, making a total of five.

"The trustees thereupon elected W. Alpheus Hunton and Abner Green as additional trustees of the bail fund of the Civil Rights Congress of New York."

Signed "Frederick V. Field, Secretary."

I direct your attention to the lefthand side of that paper where appear some written initials. I ask you if it appears to you that the first of those initials are "D. H."? A. It does.

Q. Did you write those initials? A. I decline to answer that question on the ground that the answer might tend to incriminate me.

THE COURT: I direct you to answer.

THE WITNESS: I decline to answer for the reasons given.

By the Court.

Q. Do you know whether the bail fund of the Civil Rights Congress of New York had a bank account? A. I decline to answer the question on the ground that the answer might tend to incriminate me.

Q. I direct you to answer. A. I decline to answer for the reasons given.

Q. Do you know whether the bail fund of the Civil Rights Congress of New York had a safe deposit box? A. I decline to answer the question on the ground that the answer might tend to incriminate me.

Q. I direct you to answer. A. I decline to answer for the reasons given.

Q. Do you know whether the bail fund of the Civil Rights Congress of New York had a checkbook? A. I decline to answer the question on the ground that the answer might tend to incriminate me.

Q. Do you know where such a checkbook of the bail fund of the Civil Rights Congress of New York is now located? A. I decline to answer because the answer might tend to incriminate me.

Q. I direct you to answer both of those questions. A. I decline to answer for the reasons given.

Q. Do you know whether the bail fund of the Civil Rights Congress of New York had a receipt book or a book which kept a record of the receipts? A. I decline to answer the question on the ground that the answer might tend to incriminate me.

Q. I direct you to answer. A. I decline to answer for the reasons given.

Q. Do you know where the receipt book or the book showing the receipts of the bail fund of the Civil Rights Congress of New York is now located, or who has its possession? A. I decline to answer on the ground that the answer might tend to incriminate me.

Q. I direct you to answer. A. I decline to answer for the reasons given.

MR. SAYPOL: Shall I go ahead, your Honor?

THE COURT: Yes, you may.

By Mr. Saypol.

Q. I show you Exhibit 6, Mr. Hammett, a paper which reads as follows, and will you read it along with me:

"Minutes of the bail fund of the Civil Rights Congress of New York, October 3, 1949.

"It was reported that W. Alpheus Hunton and Abner Green have accepted their election as trustees of the bail fund of the Civil Rights Congress of New York.

"It is further reported that they, together with the previous trustees, Dashiell Hammett, Robert W. Dunn and Frederick V. Field, signed the deed of trust the 26th day of September, 1949.

"A copy of the new deed of trust is attached.

"In view of the enlargement of the board of trustees it was decided to authorize either the trustees or the secretary and any other trustee to make decisions regarding the posting of bail in emergency situations."

Signed "Frederick V. Field, Secretary."

I direct your attention now to the group of initials on the lefthand side of the page, and ask you if it appears that the initials "D. H." appear at the point I have indicated? A. It does, sir.

Q. Those are handwritten initials? A. Yes.

Q. Are they your initials, Dashiell Hammett? A. I decline to answer the question on the ground that the answer might tend to incriminate me.

THE COURT: I direct you to answer.

THE WITNESS: I decline to answer for the reasons given.

Q. Now, Mr. Hammett, I direct your attention, finally, in this minute book, Exhibit 6, to the Minutes of the bail fund of the Civil Rights Congress of New York, October 28, 1949. You are following along with me? A. Yes.

Q. "The board of trustees instructed the treasurer at the earliest possible day to arrange for an audit of the bail fund books at the earliest possible date."

Signed "Frederick V. Field, Secretary," and I again direct your attention to the group of initials in the lefthand margin; do you see there what purports to be initials "D. H."? A. I do.

Q. You recognize them as such? A. As D. H.

Q. You say you recognize them as D. H.; do you recognize them as your handwritten initials? A. I decline to answer the question on the ground that the answer may tend to incriminate me.

THE COURT: I direct you to answer.

THE WITNESS: I decline to answer for the reasons given.

Q. Now, Mr. Hammett, I show you a group of four recognizances in the cases of Henry Winston, Robert Thompson, Gilbert Green and Gus Hall, and I state to you that these are Exhibit 1 in evidence; will you please examine them and tell me, tell the Court whether or not any of those documents bear your signature (showing)? A. Do you want all of this first?

Q. You can examine them one at a time.

THE COURT: You are showing the witness what paper?

MR. SAYPOL: I am showing him now the recognizance in the case of Henry Winston and am directing his attention particularly to the attached so-called trust agreement.

THE COURT: That is the recognizance which has been forfeited by the Court?

MR. SAYPOL: Yes, if the Court please—

THE COURT: And the question is?

Q. Will you see whether any of those documents bear your signature? A. (No response.)

Q. I likewise show you—one paper at a time. A. When he said "these documents," I took it for granted that—

THE COURT: Well, I don't want any confusion about it. Look first at the bail bond pertaining to the bail bond of this man Henry Winston. Those are the papers you now have in your hand.

Q. Do you recognize them as such? A. I decline to answer on the ground that—

Q. First, do you recognize those as the bail bond papers relating to Henry Winston, or the bail papers? A. Yes.

Q. Now, will you see whether any of those documents, particularly the trust agreement at-

tached to that group of documents, contains your signature? A. I decline to answer on the ground that the answer may tend to incriminate me.

THE COURT: I direct you to answer.

THE WITNESS: I decline to answer for the reasons given.

THE COURT: Now, pay particular attention to what appears to be a handwriting there on page–

(To Mr. Saypol) What page is that?

MR. SAYPOL: It is page 2 of the attached paper labeled "Agreement and Deed of Trust."

THE COURT: Pay particular attention to the signature which appears to be or purports to be the writing of one Dashiell Hammett. Will you look at that?

(Witness examines document.)

A. I decline to answer on the ground that–

THE COURT: Well, will you look at it?

(Witness examines paper.)

THE COURT: You don't decline to look at it, do you, Mr. Hammett?

THE WITNESS: No, your Honor.

THE COURT: Have you looked at it?

THE WITNESS: Yes, your Honor.

THE COURT: Have you seen a certain writing which purports to be a signature of Dashiell Hammett?

THE WITNESS: Yes.

Q. Is that your signature? A. I decline to answer on the ground that the answer might tend to incriminate me.

THE COURT: I direct you to answer.

THE WITNESS: I decline to answer for the reasons given.

THE COURT: Now will you take up the next bond?

MR. SAYPOL: Just one moment, if I may, your Honor.

Q. Mr. Hammett, I refer again to this minute dated October 3, 1949, and I direct your attention to the sentence which reads as follows:

"A copy of the new deed of trust is attached."

Is the deed of trust attached to the recognizance of Henry Winston the deed of trust which was referred to in that minute? A. I decline to answer on the grounds that the answer might tend to incriminate me.

MR. SAYPOL: Will your Honor make a direction?

THE COURT: No, not on that. It is a conclusion.

Q. I show you a group of papers, a part of Exhibit 1, comprising the recognizance in the case of the fugitive Robert Thompson, and I direct your attention particularly to the paper labeled "Agreement and Deed of Trust," the second page thereof, and I ask you to examine it, and having examined it, tell us whether or not it bears your signature, Dashiell Hammett?

THE COURT: Or whether or not it is a photostat of your signature?

A. I decline to answer the question on the ground that the answer might tend to incriminate me.

THE COURT: I direct you to answer.

THE WITNESS: I decline to answer for the reasons given.

Q. You still decline? A. Yes.

Q. I show you a group of papers constituting the recognizance in the case of the fugitive Gilbert Green, and I direct your attention particularly to the paper labeled Agreement and Deed of Trust, the second page thereof, and ask you to examine it and having examined it tell me whether on that photostat appears a replica of your signature Dashiell Hammett? A. I decline to answer on the ground the answer may tend to incriminate me.

THE COURT: I direct you to answer.

THE WITNESS: I decline to answer.

Q. Similarly I show you a group of papers in the case of the fugitive Gus Hall, which are part of Exhibit 1, and direct your attention to those papers described as Agreement and Deed of Trust, the second page thereof, and ask you whether there appears a replica on the photostat of your signature Dashiell Hammett? A. I decline to answer on the ground the answer may tend to incriminate me.

THE COURT: I direct you to answer.

THE WITNESS: I decline to answer for the reason given.

Q. In each of the group of four sets of papers I have shown you, I show you in the group relating to the fugitive Gus Hall a replica of what appears in the other sets and which is described as a certificate of deposit of the bail fund of the Civil Rights Congress of New York, and I direct your attention particularly to the lower lefthand margin where the following appears, trustees, and then there are a group of six names, the first of which is Dashiell Hammett, Chairman. Will you examine that and tell me whether or not you are the Dashiell Hammett who was chairman of that fund? A. I decline to answer on the ground that my answer may tend to incriminate me.

THE COURT: I direct you to answer.

THE WITNESS: I decline to answer.

MR. SAYPOL: It seems to me that this stage, if the Court please, between the minutebook and these documents on the strength of which the Court entered into an agreement of bail with these trustees of whom Mr. Hammett is one–

THE COURT: Does it appear that Mr. Hammett is the chairman of this fund?

MR. SAYPOL: So it indicates on this certificate of deposit, and on the basis of the indication so far from Exhibit 6, the minutebook indicating the participation of Dashiell Hammett in the activities of this Fund, Mr. Hammett is a representative so that his answers are not tolerable under the White case, and I ask Mr. Hammett now whether he is familiar with the record keeping practices of this fund particularly the record of receipts in the form of stubs which are attached originally to each certificate of deposit and retained by the fund evidently as a record of receipts which have been issued.

Are you so familiar, Mr. Hammett?

THE WITNESS: I decline to answer that question on the ground that my answer might tend to incriminate me.

THE COURT: I direct you to answer.

THE WITNESS: I decline to answer.

By Mr. Saypol.

Q. Mr. Hammett, the Court is desirous here of obtaining for its examination records of the bail fund of the Civil Rights Congress of New York of which you are one of the trustees and the chairman of the fund, and those records which indicate the deposit of money and the sources of those deposits, and I ask you whether you are willing to produce those? A. I decline to answer the question on the ground the answer may tend to incriminate me.

Q. I take it then that you are unwilling to do so. A. Is that a question?

Q. Well, I ask you are you willing or unwilling? A. I decline to answer the question on the ground that the answer may tend to incriminate me.

THE COURT: I direct you to answer.

THE WITNESS: I decline to answer for the reasons given.

Q. Well is it the question you decline to answer or the production that you refuse to make on the premise that it would be incriminating you?

MR. SAYPOL: I am trying to be clear. I don't know whether the witness refuses to answer the question or refuses to produce the records.

THE COURT: The witness gives every indication of understanding the question. However, he may answer the question.

(Last question read.)

THE COURT: Suppose you ask him again.

Q. Mr. Hammett, I ask you whether or not you were willing to produce the records including the record of deposits in the form of receipts, receipt books of this bail fund of the Civil Rights Congress of New York? A. I decline to answer the question on the ground that the answer may tend to incriminate me.

THE COURT: I direct you to answer.

THE WITNESS: I decline to answer for the reason given.

THE COURT: Mr. Hammett, I direct you to produce as chairman and trustee of the bail fund of the Civil Rights Congress of New York all books, records, papers and documents pertaining to that fund which are in your possession or under your control. Will you comply with such a direction?

THE WITNESS: May I consult with counsel?

THE COURT: Yes.

(Witness left the stand and conferred with counsel and thereafter returned to the stand.)

THE WITNESS: Without conceding that I have the ability to or can produce such documents I must decline to produce them.

THE COURT: I direct you to produce them.

THE WITNESS: I must decline for the same reason.

THE COURT: For the reason that the production will tend to incriminate you?

THE WITNESS: Yes and without conceding that I have any ability or can.

By the Court.

Q. I will ask you this specific question: Have you now in your possession or under your control any books, records and documents of the bail fund of the Civil Rights Congress of New York? A. I must decline to answer that question on the ground that the answer may tend to incriminate me.

Q. I direct you to answer. A. I decline to answer.

MR. SAYPOL: I think I need not ask any more, and I ask the Court adjudge this witness in contempt.

THE COURT: Mr. Rabinowitz and Mrs. Kaufman, I will give you an opportunity, if you desire to avail yourselves of it, of asking this witness any question that you feel may assist the Court in determining the merits of this claim which he has asserted to the various questions and directions which have been asked of him and made to him. Do you desire to ask this witness any question, Mr. Rabinowitz?

Mrs. Kaufman: May we confer a moment?

THE COURT: Yes. Is the marshal present in court?

A Deputy Marshal: Yes.

MR. RABINOWITZ: I have nothing.

THE COURT: Mrs. Kaufman, do you desire to?

Mrs. Kaufman: I have no questions, your Honor.

THE COURT: Step down, Mr. Hammett, before the bar of the Court.

(The witness stepped down from the witness stand.)

THE COURT: Mr. Hammett, I find you guilty of contempt of court for your failure and refusal to comply with the directions of the Court and to make answer to questions asked of you, and to directions of the Court made to you to produce books, documents and records the bail fund of the Civil Rights Congress of New York.

The minutes of this proceeding in which you committed contempt and in which your contumacious conduct has occurred have not as yet been transcribed. The hearing has not yet been concluded. I direct the stenographer forthwith and without undue delay to transcribe these minutes, and I commit you now to the custody of the marshal, to be incarcerated by him until 8 o'clock this evening, at which time you will be arraigned before me, and I will impose sentence and make such certificate as is required by Rule 42-A of the Federal Rules of Criminal Procedure, Title 18, of the United States Code. The marshal will have custody of this man.

MR. RABINOWITZ: May I make a motion for reconsideration and argue it, or would you prefer that that be done tonight?

THE COURT: It may be heard now, if you desire, or I will hear you later on at half past seven, if you want to be heard then, or at 8 o'clock.

MR. RABINOWITZ: I prefer to be heard then.

THE COURT: Whatever suits your convenience, counsel.

MR. RABINOWITZ: All right.

THE COURT: That will be in this room. At that time the marshal will then bring this man Dashiell Hammett before the Court. That will be at 7:30 instead of 8 o'clock.

Mr. Hunton–

MR. RABINOWITZ: Your Honor, may I suggest that the witness be paroled in my custody until 7:30 tonight? There doesn't seem to be any advantage in taking him into custody now. No gain can be served by it.

THE COURT: The advantage is that perhaps there will be some respect for the dignity and authority of this Court.

MR. RABINOWITZ: Well, I doubt whether–

THE COURT: I have endeavored to be most patient, counsel, with these various witnesses who have appeared before me, and they have consistently and repeatedly flaunted the jurisdiction and defied this Court. I think the dignity of the Court and the majesty of its process requires immediate commitment.

The application to parole the man further is denied.

At the 7:30 session:

THE COURT: Samuel Dashiell Hammett, will you stand, please?

(Defendant Hammett arises.)

THE COURT: Samuel Dashiell Hammett, I have found you guilty of contempt of this court by reason of your refusal to answer questions, and by reason of your refusal to produce or give evidence of the location of certain books, records and documents in your possession, or under your control, relating to the bail fund of the Civil Rights Congress

of New York, and more specifically as is set forth in the certificate which I have made, and which I am about to sign under Rule 42(a) of the Rules of Criminal Procedure, and I will sign the certificate.

Counsel, you have seen a copy of it.

MR. RABINOWITZ: Yes, your Honor.

THE COURT: Do you waive, on behalf of this man, the reading of this paper?

MR. RABINOWITZ: Yes, your Honor.

THE COURT: I have signed the certificate as was required by Rule 42(a) of the Federal Rules of Criminal Procedure. I give it to the clerk to file and make part of the records of this case (handing to clerk).

Samuel Dashiell Hammett, have you anything to say as to why judgment should not be pronounced upon you by this Court?

Defendant Hammett: Not a thing.

THE COURT: I adjudge and order that you, Samuel Dashiell Hammett, be committed to the custody of the Attorney General or his authorized representative for imprisonment for a period of six months or until such time as you may purge yourself of the contempt of this Court. I certify the certificate on file.

MR. RABINOWITZ: Now, your Honor, I would like to make a motion.

THE COURT: Very well. You may.

MR. RABINOWITZ: Your Honor, I would like, at this time, to make a motion that the execution of the sentence be stayed and that the contemnor be released in reasonable bail to be set by your Honor.

Now, I know that similar motions were made in the other two cases, and that your Honor denied them, and the ground for denying them was that a granting of such an application would be an admission on your Honor's part.

THE COURT: It might be construed as such.

MR. RABINOWITZ: It might be construed as an admission on your Honor's part.

THE COURT: I don't like the word "admission." Acknowledgment, if you will.

MR. RABINOWITZ: Very well, your Honor. That there were substantial questions of law involved. I submit, your Honor, that there are in this case, more perhaps than in the others, very substantial questions of law involved, and that it would be grossly unfair to have this contemnor placed in custody pending an appeal which, in the nature of things, cannot be heard until the fall, when there are certainly substantial questions of law. If it were not for your Honor's ruling, I think that the questions were not even substantial, that they were all on the side of the defendant here, but evidently I am wrong in that respect.

THE COURT: I think your advocacy blinds your judgment.

MR. RABINOWITZ: Well, I don't think it does always; sometimes I turn out to be right.

THE COURT: Not always, but that frequently happens to counsel.

MR. RABINOWITZ: Well, perhaps it does and perhaps it does not. Only time will tell.

In any event, in this case, your Honor, I request, and I submit that there is a very substantial question involved, and that therefore it would be appropriate for your Honor to set that aside and–

THE COURT: Your application is denied. I see no reason why this man's case should be treated any differently from the others. In fact, I was inclined, counselor, at first, to impose a longer sentence upon him because he had seen an example of what happened to Field, and he knew what was going to happen or had reason to believe that some punishment would be visited upon his co-trustee, Hunton, and he occupies the important position, not only of trustee, but he occupies the important position of chairman of this fund, and in addition I felt that his claim of privilege was especially unwarranted and unjustified, either in law or in fact, because he had executed a paper to be submitted to this Court at the time bail was accepted, in which he represented himself to be a trustee of this fund.

On the stand he refused, on his claim of privilege, to admit or state that he was a trustee of this fund. I feel that I have dealt with him extremely leniently.

MR. RABINOWITZ: Well, your Honor, I think that while recognizing the way your Honor feels–

THE COURT: Well, I am glad that you appreciate my position, counselor.

MR. RABINOWITZ: The moral feelings of your Honor on this subject have nothing to do, or have very little to do with the legal question that is involved, and–

THE COURT: Well, except by way of punishment, I wanted you to know just how I felt about it, and I am glad that you appreciate my position.

INTERVIEW:

"Dashiell Hammett Has Hard Words for Tough Stuff He Used to Write," *Los Angeles Times*, 7 June 1950.

"This hard-boiled stuff–it is a menace." Dashiell Hammett made that remark–or confession–yesterday at the Beverly Wilshire Hotel.

Hammett is a first-class writing man from Manhattan. He has written five mysteries and innumerable short stories of various plots. He is now working on a sixth novel to be titled "December 1."

In a period when most writers reside in remodeled barns in Connecticut and Vermont, Hammett lives on Lower Manhattan and plays the table d'hotes. He seldom gets farther west than Philadelphia.

He came out to see his daughter, Mrs. Josephine Marshall of Westchester, who is wife of a Douglas Aircraft mechanical engineer.

"Are you up to something in Hollywood?" he was asked.

"Positively not," he replied, and that was that.

The reason Hammett denounces the hard-boiled stuff he used to write with such relish and profit is that it has become old hat.

"It went all right in the Terrible 20s," he explained. "The bootlegger days. The racketeering days. There are racketeers now, to be sure, but they are nice, refined people. They belong to country clubs."

Hammett paused and looked as if he were going to say something unexpected. He did.

Tribute to Belgian

"Do you know," he went on, "the best mystery writer today is a Belgian who writes in French? His name is Georges Simenon. His latest book, which has been translated into English, is titled 'The Snow Was Black.' "

"What makes him the best?"

"Well, he is more intelligent. There is something of the Edgar Allan Poe about him."

Alpheus Hunton, Hammett, Frederick Vanderbilt Field, and Abner Green, the trustees of the Civil Rights Congress bail fund

After that tribute to a rival, Hammett toddled off to meet his daughter to go on a trip to the beach. Papas are about the same, whatever they do for a living.

ARTICLE:
Oliver Pilat, "The Strange Case of Dashiell Hammett," *New York Post*, 23 July 1951, pp. 2, 24; 24 July 1951, pp. 2, 23; 25 July 1951, pp. 4, 46; 26 July 1951, p. 14; 27 July 1951, p. 28.

The sensationalistic Post *attacked Hammett in this five-part series published two weeks after he was sentenced to prison. While this article is factually unreliable, it is an accurate representation of the anti-Communist sentiment of the press.*

Samuel Dashiell Hammett, whose literary split personality has long intrigued students of the modern detective story, now finds himself in a jam as startling as any ever encountered by his fictional heroes, those hard-boiled yet perceptive private eyes known as Ned Beaumont, Sam Spade, and Nick Charles (The Thin Man).

The 57-year-old ex-writer, a tall, grey-haired man no fatter than a razor blade, was sentenced on July 10 to six months in Federal Prison by Judge Sylvester Ryan for criminal contempt of court, after refusing to answer 33 questions concerning the flight from justice of four U.S. Politburo members convicted of Communist conspiracy.

So far Hammett has failed to get out on bail, pending appeal of his sentence. On one occasion, Murial Alexander, his secretary, brought $10,000 in cash before U.S. Commissioner McDonald as bail, only to withdraw it when questions were asked as to its source.

The prevailing judicial attitude toward Hammett, and his own concern over possible self-incrimination in case he did–as his Continental Op would say–come clean on the underground dive of the convicted Politburo members, show a mutual understanding of the realities embodied in the Subversive Activities Control Act of 1950.

Yet Dashiell Hammett has served as chairman of the national bail fund of the Civil Rights Congress, which sprang such arch conspirators as Gerhart Eisler, who escaped to Eastern Germany to assume direction of Communist propaganda there.

In 1946, Dashiell Hammett emerged as head of the New York chapter of the CRC. In 1947 the CRC was branded Communist and subversive by Attorney General Clark. As of today, according to Morris Dweck, public relations director of CRC, Hammett is still head of the New York chapter.

Now Hammett is no pinhead. If he is up to his thin neck in Communist intrigue, he must have given some thought to it, stumbled into it or been driven by personal frustration and despair. The obvious question is, how did he get where he is today?

As a resident of the Federal House of Detention on the West Side, Hammett is presently not in a position to speak for himself. Permission to visit him was denied by A. H. Conner, acting director of the Bureau of Prisons.

Even if permission had been granted, there was no assurance Hammett would talk. Mrs. Mary Kaufman, his lawyer, agreed to ask him about an interview, but she had doubts that he would be interested. Friends said he was "not neurotic about publicity," and didn't care much whether his motives were understood or not.

In recent years, Hammett has turned seclusive. He has lived alone in an apartment in Greenwich Village, coming alive chiefly at night, to walk and talk, and roam the night spots, and drink and read. He has maintained close relationships with fewer and fewer persons, and to them he has seemed an increasingly tragic figure.

The basic, startling, almost shocking fact about Dashiell Hammett, mentioned by some of his old friends, is that this discoverer and prophet of a new kind of hero for detective stories, which probably reach more people in America than any form of writing outside of the newspapers, has done no fictional writing in his own field for 17 years.

The rough and tough detective, all elephant hide outside and pulp within, who is so strongly sexed and yet semi-impervious to feminine wiles, who cares less about right or wrong than getting a job done; this fictional prototype which Hammett invented and made part of our literary tradition, continues to intrigue millions of radio listeners and readers. But Hammett himself has faded out of the picture.

The last Hammett thriller was "The Thin Man," published by Knopf in 1934, and dedicated to Lillian Hellman, the famous playwright, who classes as a personal rather than a political friend.

That was the year Hollywood called.

Hammett was rooming with another man in a Greenwich Village apartment when he got an offer to shape up a movie version of "The Thin Man."

"It's all yours," he told his room-mate, waving his hand around his possessions. "I've got what I wanted!"

It didn't turn out quite that way.

From the early '30s until 1949, Hammett worked at intervals in Hollywood for Warner Brothers and other studios, at salaries ranging up to $1,500 a week, but not really as a writer. What the movie moguls used him for was as a technical expert, and a trouble-shooter. He had to patch up scripts, and keep the story moving after the cameras had started shooting.

This sort of thing was devastating to a man with a finicky, perfectionist approach to writing. There were signs of its impact in an increasing disorderliness of living. One year an actress named Elise de Viane collected $2,500 from him in damages, on the ground that he had beaten and attempted to attack her during a dinner party in his apartment. Another year, Hammett was sued for making a shambles out of a home in Princeton, N.J., which he had rented in hope of getting some work done.

When a play he had written failed to materialize, Hammett took a gruff, cynical attitude toward a producer who was interested in him.

"Playwriting is a jerk way of writing," he declared. "You write centuries. Today there is another play and somebody tells you to fix it up. You fix it up and then some actor won't play it that way, and you fix it up again. Then something else happens, and you fix it up again. What's the use, when you can write a full-length book and they don't change a word."

Dashiell Hammett's friends agree on his "pure attitude" toward writing. He was a tremendously careful and painstaking workman in the days between 1928 and 1934 when he was grinding out the stories for which he is famous.

Hammett never let anything go to a magazine or a publisher until it was the very best he felt he could do. He was content to work at first for pulp magazines because of the leeway they gave him in working out his style. He had a rare quality of being able to evaluate his own work critically, logically and impartially. Money interested him in those early days less than the development of his skill.

Toward fiction editors who thought they knew what he was doing better than himself, Hammett frequently exhibited a pixyish sense of humor.

One large magazine bought a story, then required revision. Hammett agreed to fix it up, but kept putting off the work. Finally the editor sent out a man to locate the writer. When that failed the editor decided to track down Hammett himself.

Making the rounds in the nightclub belt, the editor went from one to another of Hammett's favorite haunts. In each he was told, "Why, yes, Dash was here just a few minutes ago. I think he went on to such and such a place."

The chase continued until dawn, with the editor still a few minutes behind Hammett. Finally the editor went home for a few hours sleep. When he reached his office at 11 a.m., the revised work, complete and beautifully typed, lay on his desk, apparently having been completed before the chase began.

Perhaps the only thing in Hollywood which came out right for Hammett was his motion picture treatment in 1945 of Lillian Hellman's "Watch on the Rhine," for Warner.

In 1949, he was hired by Paramount to write the movie version of Sidney Kingsley's "Detective Story," but he couldn't finish the job.

More than one writer has been upset by Hollywood. The obvious remedy is to get away. Hammett got away periodically; in fact he spent most of his time in the East. Friends said he was planning a philosophical novel, but it didn't appear.

In 1939, Lillian Hellman was quoted in a New Yorker profile as being excited by a new Hammett detective novel which was in the works, but Hammett didn't finish the novel. In 1940, Hammett told a night club columnist all about a new book, entitled "There was a Young Man," concerning a man with 17 children.

Though there were several murders in the story, "There Was a Young Man" would not be mystery because the murders would be solved in the middle of the book, Hammett said, thus allowing him to escape from Knopf, which had a contract for all his mysteries, and give Vanguard a chance at some profit.

The Thin Man may have been spoofing the nightclub columnist, Vanguard or himself, but in any event, the novel about the man with 17 children never appeared.

Hammett always made a fetish of appearing lazy. "I'm a two-fisted loafer," he told one interviewer at the height of his productive period, in 1934.

"I can loaf longer and better than anybody I know," he continued. "I did not acquire this genius. I was born with it. I quit school when I was 13 because I wanted to loaf. I sold newspapers for a while, loafed, became a stevedore, loafed, worked in a machine shop, loafed, became a stock broker, loafed, went into the advertising business, loafed, tried hoboing in earnest, loafed, became a Pinkerton detective, and loafed."

Increasingly, between 1934 and 1951, Hammett made the point to friends that there was no reason to struggle with serious writing when he was assured of a comfortable income while loafing. Men producing packaged radio shows in New York were willing to pay $400, $500 or $600 a week just for the use of The Thin Man, Sam Spade or the Fat Man.

With anywhere from $1,000 to $1,500 a week pouring in from radio alone, without the necessity of hitting a typewriter key, why should he strain to produce enduring literature, Hammett demanded.

The point was a reasonable one, provided it was made sincerely. In fact, Hammett did strain, now toward a play; now toward a philosophical novel; now toward a murder story which would not be a mystery. Out of all his straining came nothing. That's what made his pretended delight in loafing only a screen for professional frustration.

Dashiell Hammett was married in 1920, to a woman who had nursed him to health from tuberculosis. They had two daughters. Somewhere along the line the family broke up, and friends of Hammett in the East knew only that his wife and daughters lived somewhere in California, the couple having secured a quiet divorce.

For several summers, Hammett rented places in the suburbs of New York, once in Port Washington, once in Pleasantville.

He had a dog, but the dog died, and he purchased no successor. He fumbled with fishing and hunting for a while, with his technician's concentration on just the right kind of tackle and gun, and the right approach to the game, but that dulled, too, and nothing similar succeeded it.

During the last two or three years, friends say Hammett's chief remaining relaxation, nightlong reading, when the light was somehow surer and the silence permitted complete concentration, began to lose its savor. Poker no longer interested him. Of all his night-living diversions, only drinking remained, and in drinking, what counted with Hammett, was the effect, not the means.

Lillian Hellman's latest play, "Autumn Garden," which she wrote "for Dash," has a central character, a man who has frittered away his talents until virtually nothing is left of them, or him. In almost the last lines of that play, produced last Spring, this character says:

> I live in a room and I go to work and I play a game called getting through the day while you wait for night. The night's for me–just me–and I can do anything with it I want. There used to be a lot of things, but now there's a bar and another bar, and the same people in each bar.
>
> When I've had enough I go back to my room–or somebody else's room–and that never means much one way or the other. A few years ago I'd have weeks of reading–night after night–just me. But I don't do that much any more. And a few years ago, I'd go on the wagon twice a year. Now I don't do that anymore. And I don't care.

Old friends of Dashiell Hammett don't say, nor does Lillian Hellman say, that her character was drawn from him, but others have noted the resemblance.

The magnificent detective stories of Dashiell Hammett are not, strictly speaking, mysteries. What intrigues the reader is not just the who-dun-it angle but how Hammett's private eye operates in a maze of cross purposes, some sexual titillation, considerable violence and repeated death.

Though most of the characters in a Hammett detective story are recognizable as people, the subject matter is unreal and sensational in the extreme. The resulting contrast is Hammett's own plight.

Hammett likes to joke that he takes no exercise more vigorous than rolling his own cigarets. For decades he has led an owl-like existence, mostly at night, oiling his internal combustion machine as much with alcohol as with food.

It seems odd for a former TB case, 57 and frail, to stick his chin out in front of a six-months Federal prison sentence by refusing to disclose how the Civil Rights Congress dug a hole in the ground for a quartet of convicted Communist arch-conspirators.

But it is not surprising to his friends. Outside of his specialized form of literary genius (now withered by long disuse), they say Hammett's chief qualities, as revealed by his career, have been cynicism, an impulse toward martyrdom and an amazing physical endurance.

Samuel Dashiell Hammett was born May 27, 1894, in St. Mary's County on the Western Shore of Maryland. His parents moved to Philadelphia, then back to Baltimore, and there, at the age of 14, in the middle of his freshman year at the Polytechnic Institute, the boy repudiated the formal education process.

The point to remember, according to his friends, it that young Hammett left school, not because of failure in exams or financial difficulties, but because he decided classroom work was the bunk. He wanted to get down to bedrock realities of life. He got down, by taking a variety of jobs, including manual work like stevedoring, for which he was physically unfitted.

Ever since his creative well began to run dry in the middle 30s, "Dash" Hammett interviews with the press have been compounded of such bitterness and whimsy that they cannot be relied upon as guides to the details of his life. But in 1929, when his first two novel-length detective stories–"The Dain Curse" and "The Red Harvest"–appeared in book form, thrusting him, blinking, into the limelight, he gave a frank statement to one interviewer.

"My first dive into bread-winning," he said, "was as a messenger boy for the Baltimore & Ohio Railroad, though I had dipped my toes in before that by selling newspapers after school. Later I drew wages as a junior clerk, very junior, in an advertising office.

"Then I went into a stock broker's office. There was a place! I could seldom get the same approximate total twice in succession out of any column of figures, but still more seldom managed to get down early enough in the day to make any of my mistakes before noon. They had a weird notion that one should be there all day.

"Well, of course, when such a situation arises something is bound to happen. It did. Maybe I should have gone in for journalism. . .''

Maybe he should have, at that. The hours are frequently irregular, and a newspaperman, almost by definition, is a verbal-minded person, not necessarily intelligent, with a tough hide and a sensitive set of inner relations. Hammett heroes frequently play poker with reporters and recognize them as kindred souls.

As a matter of fact, Hammett did become a reasonable facsimile of a newspaper man for a brief period. In the early 20s, he contributed literary reviews of thrillers to the old New York Evening Post. As a former detective with a feeling for words, he discovered quickly that most of the practitioners in the fictional field had no conception of the mechanics of the trade. If they could get away with phoney stuff, he thought, maybe he could put his own knowledge of detective work to good advantage. That was the way he became a writer.

It wasn't a simple process, of course. Looking back now, you can see how Dashiell Hammett, like Somerset Maugham and many another writer, stumbled from failure in other fields while sharpening his hidden talent for writing. He was a timekeeper in a cannery, and in a machine shop; regular hours and reliability were the only requirements, but he couldn't or wouldn't meet even them, for long.

For a while, the lean giant tried swinging a hook as a longshoreman. The job had one advantage; it went by the hour, and a man didn't need to work every day, or even all day, if he chose. Sometimes when he elected to work by appearing for a shape-up at the end of a pier, the hiring boss' jabbing index finger would pass over him in the crowd, and provide temporary leisure anyway.

But the work was basically too strenuous. Hammett had to quit finally, and after a rest he became a detective agency operative for Pinkerton.

In describing his career as a detective, Hammett usually says it lasted seven or eight years. But the Pinkerton records show that he came to work for them in Baltimore on April 5, 1917, and left–after several prolonged absences for reasons of military service and illness–on Feb. 10, 1922.

He quit professional snooping because he couldn't stand the gaff physically. He wasn't particularly successful as a private eye, either. On several occasions he would probably have been fired, he confesses, except for the literary quality of his reports.

The ashy taste associated with all his activities extended to military service. Hammett liked to remind friends cynically that Dashiell was an old family name coming from the De Chiels, French ancestors whose boast was that they fought in every war, and never won.

Dashiell Hammett got into two wars, but says no fighting. He joined the Motor Ambulance Corps as a sergeant in World War I, but came down with tuberculosis. It took him 10 years to lick the Bug and by the time he finally satisfied the doctors, in 1927, he was pretty well launched as a writer of trail-breaking shorts in the pulps.

It was suggestive of self-contempt, or, at the very least, a cynical under-appraisal of his own worth–that Dashiell Hammett used Peter Collinson as a pen name for his first excursions in the who-dun-it field. According to his own explanation, Peter Collins was an 18th century gang phrase for "nobody." He added "son" to describe himself as "Nobody's Son."

By the time World War II rolled around, Hammett was sitting pretty. He had an assured income from radio and movie adaptations of his works, without any need for disturbing a typewriter key on his own account.

Why work, when it wasn't necessary, he asked acquaintances cynically. Some friends, however, sensed a growing frustration over being unable to expand a literary approach which had aroused more imitation than that of Ernest Hemingway.

Whatever the reason, Hammett decided to ignore his age, which was 47, and enlist again. Rejected promptly as too thin, he cleared the hurdle of weight by eating bananas until he was sick. Again he was rejected as a poor military risk, this time because of his tubercular past. Hammett tried another doctor; after an incredulous glimpse at the writer's chest scars, this doctor opined that a man who fought to get into battle despite such scars would undoubtedly summon enough resolution to finish the job.

So Dashiell Hammett, a corporal this time, was sent up to Alaska, and then to Adak, in the Aleutians, where he sat out two years of war under conditions of extreme hardship. He edited a local newspaper and conducted some radio shows. One winter he lived in a hut from which men had been known to depart on a visit to a nearby outhouse, only to be blown by wind and snow off the path and never seen again.

Writing home to friends in a tone unusually buoyant for him, Hammett wondered which was worse, snow up to the waist in winter, or mud up to the waist in summer. He claimed to be the only military man who realized the full beauty of the Aleutians. Everybody up there tended to walk with heads down, he said, thereby missing the magnificent mountains and lakes which he surprised by raising his head. Some day, in time of peace, he would return to the Aleutians for a visit, perhaps even to live, he said.

Whatever his private doubts as to his wartime achievements, Hammett showed an endurance far beyond anything suggested by his appearance. He not only survived the second war, but managed to produce with Cpl. Robert Colodny as co-author and Major Henry W. Hall as supervisor, a workmanlike 15,000-word pamphlet entitled:

The Battle of the Aleutians, a graphic history, 1942-43, in honor and memory of the men of the North Pacific theater who died so that a continent might be free.

Yet this same Hammett, six years later, gets tossed in the clink for involving himself in a Communist conspiracy which, according to the Government, is designed to end freedom on the American continent.

You need a Sam Spade, or the Thin Man himself, to unravel a mystery like that!

Dashiell Hammett's fictional operatives provide some clues to the type of thought and behavior which led their creator down a long road of personal and professional frustration to a Federal prison cell.

For one thing, the chief concern of Ned Beaumont, Sam Spade, Nick Charles (The Thin Man) and the other Hammett private eyes is always to finish a job, regardless of its messiness, or its economic, political or moral overtones. The job in turn is defined by a client, who may be a law-abiding citizen in trouble, a ruthless employer trying to break a strike or a promiscuous wife trying to frame her husband for a divorce.

To these heroes, whose appeal lies in professional competence and a total lack of illusion, the quality of the client is always less important than the size of the fee. Once involved in a client relationship, the Hammett-type of private eye is prepared for anything from fornication to theft, and from mayhem to murder.

If out of boredom, guilt, hatred of society, sheer incapacity or some combination of these qualities, Dashiell Hammett came to consider the Communist Party his client, that could explain his willingness to bury his frail carcass in jail for half a year rather than tell what he knows about the underground flight of a quartet of U.S. Politburo officials.

An alternative explanation is that he keeps mum to protect more or less innocent friends induced by him or others to contribute to the bail fund of the party-line Civil Rights Congress. Even there the client analogy persists: Hammett heroes are forever being browbeaten and slugged, without success, by the police in an effort to obtain information which they consider confidential or damaging to a client.

It doesn't matter very much to these detectives whether the information is required in the public interest; a client is a client, and that's enough.

Dashiell Hammett did more than probe deeply into the business of private sleuthing. He identified himself with its code of conduct. His fictional heroes are composites of detectives he met and admired during his own periodic tricks of duty as a Pinkerton man, but they are bound together by the solvent of his own personality and experience. One hero is tubercular (Hammett was a TB patient for a decade), another is a dipsomaniac (Hammett was always a heavy drinker) but they, like the healthier heroes, are all detectives.

It is even possible to suggest, by tracing the line of descent from one Hammett hero to another, why the author ceased to write and became an easy mark for formularized political philosophy with a paranoiac base.

"The 'op' I use," said Hammett in 1929, when he was getting his first glimpse of fame, "is the typical sort of private detective that exists in our country today. I've worked with half a dozen men who might be he with few changes. Though he may be 'different' in fiction, he is almost pure type in life.

"I've always tried to hold him close to the type as possible because what I see in him is a little man going forward day after day through mud and blood and death and deceit–as callous and brutal and cynical as is necessary–towards a dim goal, with nothing to push or pull him towards it except that he's been hired to reach it–a sort of Manuel whose saying is: 'The job's got to be done.' "

The agencies for which the fictional operatives of Hammett work recall inevitably the one for which the author worked, and the locales of the stories, places like Baltimore, Spokane, Seattle and 'Frisco, are places where Hammett did much of his detective work. Quite a few of the thugs described in Hammett fiction are lifted bodily from life.

"Girl Hunt," for example, describes a big gangster named McCloor. His prototype in real life, Babe McCloor, was a member of Jimmie the Riveter's mob of stickup artists who were rounded up on the West Coast by the Pinkertons in the winter of 1921-22. Babe McCloor was nabbed in the Seattle Post Office. On the way to the railroad station, despite handcuffs, the Babe made a dive for a deputy's gun and shot it out, right there in the street, until he was full of lead.

Dashiell Hammett's basis for appraisal of a lawbreaker, as evidenced by his own fiction, is not so much whether he is a menace to society as whether he is competent and lives by his code. He liked to tell friends about Jimmie, a Detroit mobster with whom he got on social relations during the course of his Pinkerton work.

"Once I was sitting with Jimmie when a fight started across the room," he recalled. "Jimmie tossed a .45 colt into my lap. 'Will you hold that gun for me,' he asked, 'I wanna get into this fight.' "

To one fellow mystery writer, Hammett confessed whimsically that if, in re-reading his own preliminary draft of a story, he came to the conclusion that an underworld character had acted improperly (contrary to code), he would revise the yarn to "kill him off." He explained: "Why not? If somebody works for you and you don't like him, you fire him, don't you?"

The implication is that the crooks in a Hammett novel surviving this verbal assassination by their own author must have been attractive to him, one way or another.

Hammett handled some big cases as a Pinkerton man, including those involving Nicky Arnstein and Fatty Arbuckle, but the plots of his stories are hopped up and almost incredible. What saves them from silliness is that the sensational events center around a hero who represents an enlarged composite picture of a relatively realistic private eye.

In a sense, Sam Spade or The Thin Man is the super-sleuth Dashiell Hammett would have liked to have been. "Being a professional busybody requires more energy, more dogged patience than you'd suppose," he confessed on one occasion. "I got so tired, I just had to give it up. . ."

Estimating an author's relation to his own characters is ticklish business, at best. Dashiell Hammett's case presents special difficulties. Asked by a reporter to cite a big case on which he worked as a Pinkerton man, he was likely to say, deadpan:

"My biggest case involved the theft of a Ferris wheel. I solved that case by the process of elimination. I eliminated everything but carnivals. I went from carnival to carnival until I found one which had a Ferris wheel without a receipted bill for sale. Not bad, eh?"

In talks with friends, the detective story writer revealed a tremendous capacity for isolating

In October 1934, Hammett signed a contract with MGM. Though he did little work and often refused to cooperate with his bosses, the contract brought Hammett about $100,000 per year during the middle 1930s. Hammett's first complete screen story for MGM, After the Thin Man, *was first published in 1987.*

colorful and contrasting detail, out of his own experiences. He liked to tell about the chief of police down South who gave him a careful description of a wanted criminal, complete to a mole on his neck, but neglected to mention that he had only one arm . . . or the forger who left his wife because she learned to smoke cigarets while he was in jail.

Conventional morality never comes out very well in the Hammett detective stories, or in the nuggets of experience which he would pull out of his conversational pockets from time to time for the amusement of friends. He liked to remark that burglary was the poorest trade in the world, that picking pockets was the easiest, and that the embezzlers he had known were almost invariably non-smokers and non-drinkers.

If you read the Hammett mysteries carefully, you are amazed at the miasma of paranoiac suspicion in them. Nobody trusts anybody. Lying is the chief method of communication among characters concealing varying degrees of perversity. The fact that in several mysteries—and particularly in the bloodiest of them all, "The Dain Curse"—the murderer, or chief murderer, turns out to be the closest friend of the private eye, is perhaps significant.

You may remember Javert, Victor Hugo's detective who either had to be a detective or a first-class crook. The distinction between the two categories becomes rather blurred in a Hammett detective story.

"Red Harvest" suggests most clearly, of all the Hammett novels, the suppressed feeling of guilt which rides along on each lawless adventure of a private eye. The story is located in the town of Personville (pronounced Poisonville) and the problem is how to rid a State of gangster control without embarrassing the industrialist who brought in the gangsters originally to break a strike.

The industrialist, is, shall we say, a crook on his own hook, but he is also a client, and clients are above the law. This particular client decides periodically to reverse the field and make a new deal with the gangsters. Such behavior presents special difficulties for the private eye, since the police are in the industrialist's control, and some of the gangsters are already displeased by the intrusion.

The solution is simple: by breaking a few laws on his own crooked hook, by lying, boldness and durability, the detective gets all the gangsters mad at each other, so mad that they shoot and stab and kill until not one of them is left. The only survivors are the detective and his now virtuous client, the industrialist. At one point it occurs to the private eye that an orgy of death, as a method of doing a job, is somewhat messy and roundabout, but the question is never pursued.

After meeting problems like this, or even lesser problems of the same sort, you can understand that an operative with any spark of decency would become, in Hammett's words, a little "tired." This happens. As you shift from detective to detective, chronologically, in the Hammett series of fictional heroes, you come at last to Nick Charles (The Thin Man), who spends more time drinking than he does in solving crimes. The only reason he does any work at all is because he is nagged to it by a wife from whom he is drifting apart.

The Thin Man wants to stop work, and drift, and drink. Dashiell Hammett, after creating the Thin Man in 1934, did stop work, and drift, and drink, for 17 years. The analogy between the two is almost too close for comfort.

Women in Dashiell Hammett detective stories seem to be forever flashing their charms at the hero, a hard-boiled but conscientious detective agency operative, in a vain effort to divert him from duty.

The operative takes them in stride, so to speak. He loves them and is extremely suspicious at the same time, a curious pattern of masculinity which has been widely copied. The charmers don't seem to mind being pushed around and in-

The house on Cleveland Avenue in Princeton, New Jersey, that Hammett rented in 1936

sulted so long as the operative operates with appropriate gestures of affection.

On paper the Hammett formula for influencing the fair sex seems irresistible, but in practice it develops certain flaws which will be alluded to later.

It should be noted that Hammett heroes, though consistently amative as well as combative, vary considerably in restraint.

The early Continental Op seems almost a Puritan compared to the later Sam Spade. Ned Beaumont acquires a certain distinction among the private eyes by willingness to consider marriage as a sequel to romance. Nick Charles (The Thin Man) is actually married, though hardly house-broken.

Whether they yield quickly or slowly to temptation, or not at all, the Hammett heroes share an inscrutable, unshakable determination not to permit dalliance to get in the way of the job.

The most memorable scene in Hammett fiction occurs in "The Maltese Falcon" when Brigid

O'Shaughnessy, a seductive criminal if there ever were one, cannot believe that Sam Spade will "send her over," that is, put her in the hoosegow.

"You've been playing with me?" she moans at one point. "Only pretending you care . . . You didn't–don't–I-love me?"

Spade replied: "I think I do. What of it . . . I won't play the sap for you."

When she deplores this attitude, Spade notes that she came into his bed to stop him from asking questions. Though he enjoyed her company, he cannot ignore the fact that she murdered his partner "like swatting a fly" and might get around to murdering him some quiet evening. Even as Spade makes his difficult decision, the author notes that he looks hungrily from the girl's feet to her hair, and vice versa.

In an earlier opus, called "The Dain Curse," the Continental Op is described by a girl as a "nice monster without any human foolishness like love in him." He is fat and 40, but the spark is still smoldering, as becomes evident after he has cured a somewhat battered young lady named Gabrielle of the drug habit. She is delighted when he remarks that the task has not been revolting and that he would do it over again if he had the chance.

"You mean–" she says.

"I don't mean anything that I'll admit," returns the detective. He adds:

"If you're going to parade around with that robe hanging open you're going to get yourself some bronchitis. You ex-hopheads have to be careful about catching cold."

Can you blame the poor girl for weeping a little?

In "Red Harvest," the Hammett hero goes to sleep in the apartment of a soiled dove named Dinah Brand, after absorbing laudanum in gin to forget his troubles. Imagine his embarrassment when he wakes up to find the girl without any clothes, an icepick in her breast, and his hand on the handle of the icepick! The murder adds to the hero's troubles, since he cannot be certain for a while whether he got impulsive during his coked-up sleep, but in the end the tragedy serves to assist him in completing his job, which is, after all, the important thing to a Hammett hero.

By ordinary fictional standards, "The Glass Key" is probably Hammett's best job. Here the hero has less boilerplate in him. He seems to be tubercular, he gambles, he hesitates and he makes mistakes, yet he gets his girl in the end, which is not unknown in real life. It would seem reasonable to believe that Ned Beaumont is closer to the character of the author than some of Hammett's brassier detectives.

Dashiell Hammett married Josephine Anna Dolan, of Anaconda, Mont., in 1920, when she was nursing him through one of a series of TB attacks which did not subside until 1927. The couple had two daughters, and were subsequently quietly divorced. Mrs. Hammett took the girls to live with her in California, Hammett established a home in Greenwich Village, and there the episode ended. Hammett never discusses it with friends.

In the years since the divorce, those who know Hammett fairly well declared there has been no romantic attachment in his life of sufficient intensity to upset his determination to do his duty, if he had one to do.

An obvious caution at this point: despite similarities between Hammett and some of his heroes, such as their mutual lack of illusion and their habit of working and playing at night, the author is clearly more complex than any of his creations. Hammett reads Dickens, Thackeray and Tolstoy as well as such hard-boiled moderns as Ben Hecht and William Faulkner. He esteems the poetry of Robinson Jeffers, and is supposed to have written some verse of his own, many years ago.

Since he ceased writing detective novels in 1934, Hammett has developed one minor interest after another, absorbing details with a technician's thoroughness, then getting bored and trying something else. One continuing interest has been professional baseball records, batting averages, scores, things like that. He is also said to have studied boxing records fairly thoroughly.

Heroes in the Hammett tradition never trust their friends, and with good reason, since their friends frequently turn out bad.

Hammett differs from them in this respect. He has maintained a number of close literary friendships. It has pleased him from time to time to help financially young writers who have attracted him by some clear gift. He has also helped relatively established writers by the unflinching candor of his criticism of their literary first-drafts, regardless of the sex or sensitiveness of the author.

As an example of thoughtfulness, it is mentioned that Hammett has sent a lively, informative letter once a week for many years to the bedridden wife of an old friend.

In pursuit of further information as to the social life and attitudes of Dashiell Hammett, a Post operative went around the other day to Hammett's apartment on the second floor of a four-story brownstone at 28 W. 10th St.

There was no hope of catching Hammett at home, since the 57-year-old author is in the Federal House of Detention, serving out a six months contempt sentence for refusing to discuss the bail fund of the Civil Rights Congress which had helped four U.S. Politburo leaders to go underground.

Closed windows and drawn white curtains on the second floor front added to the impression that nobody was home. Just for the fun of it, the Post operative pushed the Hammett bell. To his great astonishment, a buzzer sounded, and the door opened at his push. In an apartment doorway on the first floor stood a somewhat buxom young lady, with wise eyes and a red mouth, who looked vaguely familiar. She smiled at the Post operative, or was it at the middle-sized, smiling gentleman who had come in just after him?

"I'm looking for some information on Dash Hammett," the Post operative announced in a loud tone. "Why don't you go to his office?" suggested the middle-sized smiling gentleman. Before the Post operative could ask where the office was, the girl with the red mouth opened up. Tossing her head, she said several icy things which he failed to take down in his notes, but the basic idea was that Mr. Hammett was in trouble enough, without people talking about him. Then she and the other man went inside.

A pasted sign near Hammett's bell said packages would be taken by the superintendent at 32 W. 10th St. As the Post operative pushed the doorbell there, he suddenly remembered who the girl with the red mouth was. She was Miriam Alexander, Hammett's secretary, the one who had tried to put up $10,000 bail in court, only to withdraw it

when questions were asked in court as to its source.

The superintendent, or perhaps it was her daughter, seemed rattled, perhaps impressed, by the Post operative. She said she kept packages for Hammett until Miss Alexander called for them. That was funny, the Post operative said, since Miss Alexander lived in the same house. Why didn't she take the packages directly?

A young man now appeared. He said Miss Alexander was not always home, and anyway there had been no packages, recently.

The Post operative went next to the Civil Rights Congress office, 23 W. 26 St., to look at Dashiell's desk, but everybody there from National Executive Secretary Patterson to Public Relations Director Dweck denied that he worked there, and refused to hazard any guess as to where his office might be. The operative went around again to 28 W. 10th St., where he noticed for the first time there was no name on the bell for the ground floor, though there were names on the bells for all the other apartments. He pushed the bell, but there was no answer.

No Continental Op ever gives up easily, so the Post Op came opping around the next day. This time the ground-floor bell was answered by a maid who said she would give the Op's telephone number to Miss Alexander. That was the end of it. Miss Alexander never called.

Thinking it over, the Post operative concluded his technique had slipped somewhere. Perhaps if he had come up to the girl with the red mouth and growled gutterally: "You're so beautiful you make me sick!" in the tradition of all Hammett heroes, she would have melted and told him what he wanted to know.

During his pre-fiction days as a Pinkerton operative, Dashiell Hammett says he particularly admired two techniques of wringing a confession from a suspect. One was called "talking to the mug about his mother." An associate of Hammett was famous for this. He would stir the criminal to tears, he would even flop down on his knees to pray for him, before turning him over to the cops.

Hammett personally had greater success with a more subtle method, called "seeing the side of the other fellow." He would explain to a thug he realized he (the thug) meant nothing by shooting his girl, but if the matter were not properly explained, it would look bad. Variations of this technique worked frequently, Hammett noted, because lawbreakers were often anxious, deep down inside, to confess.

At the present time, Hammett is residing, under a six months lease, at the Federal House of Detention, 427 West St., instead of at his Greenwich Village apartment, 28 W. 10th St., because he refuses to come clean about his own role, and that of the Civil Rights Congress bail fund under his control, in the underground disappearance of four convicted U.S. Politburo leaders.

It is doubtful whether talking to Hammett about his mother, or even "seeing his side," would make him very loquacious at this time. Techniques like these work only when applied unemotionally against emotional subjects. An operative on an operative simply means a standoff.

David T. Bazelon, who did a nice (in the sense of delicate) analysis of Dashiell Hammett in Commentary Magazine a couple of years ago, classed the detective story pioneer as a debunker, in the cultural tradition of the late '20s and early '30s, along with the fiction of Hemingway, Faulkner, Dos Passos and Farrell, the criticism of Edmund Wilson "and the whole complex of expression connected with the diffusion of Marxist ideas and the growth of political consciousness."

Something more must be said about Dashiell Hammett, personally and psychologically, which points directly toward a Communist affiliation he has never avowed. He classes as a technician rather than as an artist. He wants eternally to know how; not why. Call him a persistent professional, if you will, rather than an amateur, which in its original meaning had something to do with love.

Hammett heroes know the technique of love, nothing about the tender emotion itself. Hammett himself seems to have no love for things, or people. One of his oldest friends always thought of him as eccentric, possibly because he never observed routine precautions against hurting other people's feelings. If a playwright, on the verge of suicide because of unfavorable criticism of his new play, asked Hammett as a friend to give his view, Hammett would feel obliged to say the thing

stunk, if that was his actual reaction.

"Dash never does anything in a superficial manner," says one acquaintance. He does not draw the conclusion, but it is inevitable; once having been involved in Communist intrigue as far as it appears on the surface, a man constituted like Hammett, with insufficient breadth of social and political vision, and with frustration gnawing at him, must inevitably as a technician have gone further.

Persons on the fringe of Hammett's life are understandably reluctant to consider him an active factor in a totalitarian foreign conspiracy. They say he doesn't put CP propaganda in his creative writing. Inasmuch as no detective story novel from his typewriter has appeared since 1934, and the non-mystery novel scheduled by one publisher for 1940 was postponed and postponed and never did appear, that can be conceded for the last 17 years.

Take "The Thin Man," Hammett's last and possibly best-known work, which William Powell and Myrna Loy made into such a successful movie. It contains a character named Alice Wynant, who is so silly, about names and everything else, that when her brother goes to a hospital for removal of his tonsils, and she notices a hearse moving in the street, she pales and exclaims: "I wonder if that could be whats-his name?"

Now Nitwit Alice has a phobia about Communism. It develops that she has not spoken to her brother, a really intelligent scientist for five years, because he "gave an interview to one of the papers saying he didn't think the Russian Five Year Plan was necessarily doomed to failure. Actually he didn't make it much stronger than that."

Alice's brother gets killed eventually by a crooked lawyer, for a capitalistic motive known as money, but Alice pushes her own theory, that "he's become a Communist," and "The Communists will kill him in the end . . . over some secret they betrayed." When Hammett's private eye hears this theory, he groans: "Oh my God."

Hammett detective stories are extremely lean as a rule. The pro-Communist padding doesn't add a thing, but it gets in there, just the same.

In 1934, when Hammett was going out of his way to ridicule the notion that Communists stole secrets, Harry Gold, who eventually acquired the atomic bomb secret for his Soviet superiors, was agreeing to start industrial espionage in Philadelphia, and Whittaker Chambers was already acting as a faceless courier in Washington and New York, for an extremely well organized espionage ring.

Many a 1934 pro-Communist lived to outgrow his idealistic foolishness. There is no indication that Dashiell Hammett did. There is nothing to show he was ever idealistic either. He traveled socially in the best Hollywood and New York fellow-traveling circles. If you didn't know The Thin Man and Sam Spade, you might think he was one of the dupes, but can you imagine either one of them being fooled by a false face of any kind?

Dashiell Hammett was not by nature a joiner. For example, he never joined the Mystery Writers of America. He was about the only successful practitioner in his field who refused to join. Yet he kept popping up, and popping up, on the Stalinist letterheads. One theory, incidentally, about Hammett is that he became a Communist out of the personal and professional frustration involved in being unable to progress as a writer. An alternative possibility, unexplorable without more facts, might be that he failed to write for the last 17 years because he was too absorbed in secret Communism.

In 1938, Hammett signed a statement appearing in the Daily Worker in support of the Moscow trials. This could hardly be classed as a politically unsophisticated gesture.

Late in the Fall of 1939, after the Hitler-Stalin pact had switched the Communist Party, U.S.A., from a policy of conciliation to one of extremism, Hammett made public the names of 62 Americans, including some fairly well known scientists, educators, writers and artists, whose signatures had been secured on a statement deploring attempts to suppress the Communist Party.

This was the beginning of Hammett's career as a Communist operator; he was not only a spokesman for the signers, he revealed, but he was one of a group of four persons who has collected signatures.

In June, 1941, Hammett was elected, unanimously, as president of the League of American Writers, chief literary Communist front, at a New York convention where 450 delegates unanimously approved eight party-line resolutions. Support was voiced for the CIO-repudiated strike at the North American Aviation Co., in Los Angeles, one of a series of political strikes designed by the party to cripple U. S. aviation production. Harry Bridges got a pat on the back as a patriotic labor leader, and the American Peace Mobilization won approval from Hammett and his followers.

Hitler double-crossed Stalin before Stalin could double-cross Hitler, and the American Communist Party doubled resourcefully in its tracks, like Sam Spade. Hammett kept on a trail which would have thrown a Continental "Op." He became a violent supporter of war preparations; when the U.S. got into the conflict, he donned uniform at an age when he might better have stayed home.

Assigned intelligence desk duty in Alaska, Hammett was known fairly widely as a Communist to rank-and-file associates. He was patriotic, in a Russian sense, and became involved in at least one hastily suppressed fracas, according to a man who served with him.

After the war, the detective story writer emerged as head of the New York State branch of the newly-formed Civil Rights Congress, which did yeoman work for the Communist Party under an idealistic pose.

By this time Hammett was receiving $1,000 a week or more out of packaged radio shows using the name of his detective heroes but requiring no work at all on his part. He was able to toss large bills into the pot at Communist fund-raising meetings without feeling any pain. He went along with every wrinkle in the party movement, from the Henry Wallace campaign for President to the phony world peace drives. He lectured at and became a trustee of the Communist Jefferson School of Social Science.

The strange thing is this: despite activity in behalf of two-score or more Communist fronts, including press conferences, letter-writing and occasional speech-making, there is no evidence that Dashiell Hammett, who provided such an original approach to detective story fiction, ever came up with a single fresh or surprising idea in the social or political field.

So far as the record shows, Hammett possesses no more of a social or political philosophy now than he did in his Pinkerton days. He is still concerned entirely with doing a job, no longer as

Hammett testifying before the McCarthy Committee

an operative for a detective agency, but as an operative for the Communist Party.

TESTIMONY:

Hammett's testimony before the Permanent Subcommittee Investigation of the Senate Committee on Government Operations, 26 March 1953.

When Hammett was called to testify before the McCarthy committee, which was invesitgating the purchase by the State Department of books written by Communists, he was wracked with financial problems and ill health. Roy Cohn, chief counsel to the committee, assisted in the questioning. After his testimony Hammett's books were removed briefly from State Department libraries until President Eisenhower had them replaced.

MR. COHN: The next witness is Mr. Dashiell Hammett.

THE CHAIRMAN: Mr. Hammett, will you raise your right hand? In this matter now in hearing be-

fore the committee, do you solemnly swear to tell the truth, the whole truth, and nothing but the truth, so help you God?

MR. HAMMETT: I do.

MR. COHN: Could we have your full name, please, sir?

MR. HAMMETT: Samuel Dashiell Hammett.

MR. COHN: Samuel Dashiell Hammett. Is that right?

MR. HAMMETT: That is right.

MR. COHN: And what is your occupation?

MR. HAMMETT: Writer.

MR. COHN: You are a writer. Is that correct?

MR. HAMMETT: That is right.

MR. COHN: And you are the author of a number of rather well-known detective stories. Is that correct?

MR. HAMMETT: That is right.

MR. COHN: In addition to that, you have written, I think, in your earlier period, on some social issues. Is that correct?

MR. HAMMETT: Well, I have written short stories that may have–you know, it is impossible to write anything without taking some sort of stand on social issues.

MR. COHN: You say it is impossible to write anything without taking some sort of stand on a social issue. Now, are you the author of a short story known as Nightshade?

MR. HAMMETT: I am.

MR. COHN: I might state, Mr. Chairman, that some 300 of Mr. Hammett's books are in use in the Information Service today located in, I believe, some 73 information centers; I am sorry, 300 copies, 18 books.

You haven't written 300 books; is that right?

MR. HAMMETT: That is a lot of books.

MR. COHN: There are 18 books in use, including some collections of short stories and other things, and there are some 300 copies of those located in some 73 information centers.

Now Mr. Hammett, when did you write your first published book?

MR. HAMMETT: The first book was Red Harvest. It was published in 1929. I think I wrote it in 1927, either 1927 or 1928.

MR. COHN: At the time you wrote that book, were you a member of the Communist Party?

MR. HAMMETT: I decline to answer, on the grounds that an answer might tend to incriminate me, relying on my rights under the fifth amendment to the Constitution of the United States.

MR. COHN: When did you write your last published book?

MR. HAMMETT: Well, I can't really answer that. Because some collections of short stories have been published. I imagine it was some time in the thirties, or perhaps the forties.

MR. COHN: In the thirties or forties. At the time you wrote your last published book were you a member of the Communist Party?

MR. HAMMETT: I decline to answer on the grounds that an answer might tend to incriminate me.

MR. COHN: If I were to ask you, with reference to these books, whether you were a member of the Communist Party at the time you wrote the books, what would your answer be?

MR. HAMMETT: Same answer. I would decline to answer on the grounds that an answer might tend to incriminate me.

MR. COHN: Mr. Hammett, are you a member of the Communist Party today?

MR. HAMMETT: I decline to answer on the grounds that an answer might tend to incriminate me.

THE CHAIRMAN: Mr. Hammett, let me ask you this. Forgetting about yourself for the time being, it is a safe assumption that any member of the Communist Party, under Communist discipline, would propagandize the Communist cause, normally, regardless of whether he was writing fiction books or books on politics?

MR. HAMMETT: I can't answer that, because I honestly don't know.

THE CHAIRMAN: Well, now, you have told us that you will not tell us whether you are a member of the Communist Party today or not, on the ground that if you told us the answer might incriminate you. That is normally taken by this committee and the country as a whole to mean that you are a member of the party, because if you were not you would simply say, "No," and it would not incriminate you. You see, the only reason that you have the right to refuse to answer is if you feel a truthful answer would incriminate you. An answer that you were not a Communist, if you were not a Communist, could not incriminate you. Therefore, you should know considerable about the Communist movement, I assume.

MR. HAMMETT: Was that a question, sir?

THE CHAIRMAN: That is just a comment upon your statement.

Mr. Counsel, do you have anything further?

MR. COHN: Oh, yes.

Now, Mr. Hammett, from these various books you have written, have you received royalty payments?

MR. HAMMETT: I have.

MR. COHN: And I would assume that if the State Department purchased 300 books, or whatever it was, you would receive some royalties?

MR. HAMMETT: I should imagine so.

MR. COHN: Could you tell us, without violating some secret of the trade, just what your royalties are, by percentage?

MR. HAMMETT: Well, it is not a case of violating a secret of the trade. I would have to look up contracts. And they vary, as a matter fact. On the books published by Alfred Knopf, $2 or $2.50 books, or whatever they were, I think it starts at 15 percent. On the short-story collections, most of which were reprints, the royalties are lower than that.

THE CHAIRMAN: Did any of the money which you received from the State Department find its way into the coffers of the Communist Party?

MR. HAMMETT: I decline to answer, on the grounds that an answer might tend to incriminate me.

THE CHAIRMAN: Let me put the question another way. Did you contribute any royalties received as a result of the purchase of these books by the State Department to the Communist Party?

MR. HAMMETT: I decline to answer, on the grounds that an answer might tend to incriminate me.

THE CHAIRMAN: You have the right to decline.

MR. COHN: Now, is it a fair statement to make that you have received substantial sums of money from the royalties on all of the books you have written?

MR. HAMMETT: Yes; that is a fair statement.

MR. COHN: And you decline to tell us whether any of those moneys went to the Communist Party?

MR. HAMMETT: That is right.

MR. COHN: Now, Mr. Hammett, is it a fact that you have frequently allowed the use of your name as sponsor and member of governing bodies of Communist-front organizations?

MR. HAMMETT: I decline to answer, on the ground that an answer might tend to incriminate me.

MR. COHN: Mr. Hammett, is it a fact that you recently served a term in prison for contempt of court?

MR. HAMMETT: Yes.

MR. COHN: And from what did that arise?

MR. HAMMETT: From declining to answer whether or not I was a trustee of the bail bond fund of the Civil Rights Congress.

THE CHAIRMAN: May I ask the photographers not to use any flash pictures while the witness is testifying?

MR. COHN: Now, you said it was for refusal to answer. The fact is: You were a trustee of the bail fund of the Civil Rights Congress. Is that right?

MR. HAMMETT: That was the question that I went to jail for not answering; yes.

MR. COHN: Well, let me ask you: Were you a trustee of the bail bond fund of the Civil Rights Congress?

MR. HAMMETT: I decline to answer on the grounds that an answer might tend to incriminate me.

MR. COHN: And is it a fact that the Government's allegation was that you were one of the sureties on the bond of four fugitive Communist leaders, that when they disappeared and ran away you were called in to see if you could aid the court in discovering where they were, and that a number of questions were put to you concerning their whereabouts, your activities as a surety, as a trustee of the group that had put up the money for the bail bond, and that you refused to answer?

MR. HAMMETT: I don't remember. I don't know whether I was asked anything about their whereabouts.

MR. COHN: Well, I will ask you: Do you know the whereabouts of any of the fugitive Communist leaders?

MR. HAMMETT: No; Gus Hall, I read, is in jail.

MR. COHN: You know Gus Hall has been captured. How about the other three?

MR. HAMMETT: I don't know.

MR. COHN: You say you don't know?

MR. HAMMETT: I don't know.

THE CHAIRMAN: You say you do not know where they are at this moment. Did you know where they were at any time while the Government was searching for them?

MR. HAMMETT: No.

THE CHAIRMAN: You did not. Do I understand that you arranged the bail bond for the fugitives?

MR. HAMMETT: I decline to answer, on the grounds that an answer might tend to incriminate me.

MR. COHN: Did you contribute any of the money that went toward the bail, which made it possible for these Communist leaders to go free on bail, and later to abscond?

MR. HAMMETT: I decline to answer, on the grounds that an answer might tend to incriminate me.

THE CHAIRMAN: Have you ever engaged in espionage against the United States?

MR. HAMMETT: No.

THE CHAIRMAN: Have you ever engaged in sabotage?

MR. HAMMETT: No, sir.

THE CHAIRMAN: Do you believe that the Communist system is better than the system in use in this country?

MR. HAMMETT: I can't answer that question, because I really don't know what it means: is the Communist system better than the system used in this country?

THE CHAIRMAN: Do you believe that communism as practiced in Russia today is superior to our form of government?

MR. HAMMETT: Well, regardless of what I thought of communism in Russia today, it is doubtful if, you know, any one sort of thing—one is better for one country, and one is better for the other country. I don't think Russian communism is better for the United States, any more than I would think that some kind of imperialism were better for the United States.

THE CHAIRMAN: You seem to distinguish between Russian communism and American communism. While I cannot see any distinction, I will assume there is for the purpose of the questioning. Would you think that American communism would be a good system to adopt in this country?

MR. HAMMETT: I will have to decline to answer that, on the grounds that an answer might tend to incriminate me. Because, I mean, that can't be answered "yes" or "no."

THE CHAIRMAN: You could not answer that "yes" or "no," whether you think communism is superior to our form of government?

MR. HAMMETT: You see, I don't understand. Theoretical communism is no form of government. You know, there is no government. And I actually don't know, and I couldn't, without—even in the end, I doubt if I could give a definite answer.

THE CHAIRMAN: Would you favor the adoption of communism in this country?

MR. HAMMETT: You mean now?

THE CHAIRMAN: Yes.

MR. HAMMETT: No.

THE CHAIRMAN: You would not?

MR. HAMMETT: For one thing, it would seem to me impractical, if most people didn't want it.

THE CHAIRMAN: Did you favor the Communist system when you were writing these books?

MR. HAMMETT: I decline to answer, on the grounds that an answer might tend to incriminate me.

THE CHAIRMAN: Senator McClellan, did you have a question?

SENATOR MCCLELLAN: You are declining to answer many questions, taking refuge in the privileges of the fifth amendment of the Constitution, because you are afraid you might incriminate yourself if you answer the questions. Are you sincere and honest in making that statement under oath?

MR. HAMMETT: Very sincere, sir. I really am quite afraid that answers will incriminate me, or will tend to incriminate me.

SENATOR MCCLELLAN: Since you say you are afraid: Do you not feel that your refusal to answer is a voluntary act of self-incrimination before the bar of public opinion? Are you not voluntarily, now, by taking refuge in the fifth amendment to the Constitution, committing an act of voluntary self-incrimination before the bar of public opinion, and do you not know that?

MR. HAMMETT: I do not think that is so, sir, and if it is so, unfortunately, or fortunately for me in those circumstances, the bar of public opinion did not send me to jail for 6 months.

SENATOR MCCLELLAN: Violation of a law sent you to jail; being caught; is that what you mean? Public opinion, as against being caught? Is that what you are trying to tell us?

MR. HAMMETT: No, sir.

SENATOR MCCLELLAN: I did not want to misunderstand you. I thought maybe public opinion or at least judicial opinion had something to do with your going to jail. That was not a voluntary act, was it?

MR. HAMMETT: Going to jail?

SENATOR MCCLELLAN: Yes.

MR. HAMMETT: No, sir.

SENATOR MCCLELLAN: Well, public opinion must have had something to do with it, or judicial opinion at least.

Hammett, near the end of his life, with Mrs. Richard Wilbur. In 1956 Hammett suffered a heart attack at Lillian Hellman's house on Martha's Vineyard, where he was visiting. From 1952 until just before his death, he lived rent-free in a four-room gatekeeper's cottage on the estate of a friend in Katonah, New York.

I do not want to misjudge anyone. I do not think the public wants to. We want to give you every opportunity to be fair to the committee, to be fair to yourself, to be true to your country, if you care anything for this country. And I would like to ask you this question: Would this committee and the public in general be in error if they judged from your answers, or rather your lack of answers, to important questions, and from your demeanor on the witness stand here, that you are now a Communist, that you have been a Communist, and that you still follow and subscribe to the Communist philosophy? Would we be in error if we judged you that way from your actions?

MR. HAMMETT: I decline to answer that question, because the answer might tend to incriminate me.

SENATOR MCCLELLAN: Then we are free to judge according to our observations and conclusions based on your refusal to answer and your demeanor on the stand.

MR. HAMMETT: Is that a question, sir?

SENATOR MCCLELLAN: Well, if you want to answer it, it is a question. Do you want to take refuge under the Constitution again?

MR. HAMMETT: Yes, sir.

SENATOR MCCLELLAN: All right. That is all.

THE CHAIRMAN: For your information, in case you do know it, Mr. Budenz, the former editor of the Communist Daily Worker, gave you as one of those used by the Communist Party to further the Communist cause, and gave your name as a Communist under Communist Party discipline, recognized by him as such. If you care to comment on that, you may.

MR. HAMMETT: No, sir. I have no comment to make.

THE CHAIRMAN: I have no further questions.

MR. COHN: I would like to ask: Is Mr. Budenz being truthful when he told us that you were a Communist?

MR. HAMMETT: I decline to answer, on the grounds that an answer might tend to incriminate me.

[223]

MR. COHN: When he told us that you were under Communist discipline?

MR. HAMMETT: I decline to answer, on the same grounds.

THE CHAIRMAN: May I ask one further question: Mr. Hammett, if you were spending, as we are, over a hundred million dollars a year on an information program allegedly for the purpose of fighting communism, and if you were in charge of that program to fight communism, would you purchase the works of some 75 Communist authors and distribute their works throughout the world, placing our official stamp of approval upon those works?

Or would you rather not answer that question?

MR. HAMMETT: Well, I think—of course, I don't know—if I were fighting communism, I don't think I would do it by giving people any books at all.

THE CHAIRMAN: From an author, that sounds unusual.

Thank you very much. You are excused.

INTERVIEW:

James Cooper, "Lean Years for the Thin Man," *Washington Daily News*, 11 March 1957.

This was Hammett's last public interview.

Three typewriters stand mute as tombstones in a wooden caretaker's cottage outside New York.

Still in pajamas at noon a lean, 6-ft. man with bushy hair, startlingly white in contrast to his black scars of eyebrows and moustache, paces the floor without a glance at the keyboards, dusty in the bright sunshine, intensified by the blue-white snow outside.

Once all three typewriters were needed to keep pace with the output of the haggard-looking man, and brought him as much as $100,000 a year.

For this is Dashiell Hammett, the creator of "The Thin Man" stories and regarded as the father of the tough detective vogue in mystery thrillers.

But at 62, and looking older, the man who could pass for his own hero is father of no more brain children.

It is more than seven years since the typewriters clacked, and in keeping with his own description now of being "a two-fisted loafer" Mr. Hammett shows no signs of the old spark that ignited his fame.

If you draw his attention to the silent machines he says:

"I keep them chiefly to remind myself I was once a writer."

The fact that he is being sued for $110,000 for back income tax, offers no spur. He says:

"All my royalties are blocked. I am living on money borrowed from friends."

Yet as he gazes listlessly over the lonely countryside from his isolated cottage there must be times when he reviews a life as bizarre as any of his whodunits.

At 14 he decided "formal education is bunk." He left school to work at jobs unfitted to a frail frame that was later racked by tuberculosis.

Authentic

He was a messenger, a laborer, stevedore and then stumbled into the job that laid the foundation of his fortunes—a detective for the Pinkerton Private Agency.

His one big case involved film star Roscoe (Fatty) Arbuckle.

The work was too hard and in 1922 after five years he had to quit.

"I would have been fired anyway," he says, "except for a literary quality about my reports."

For a while he wrote literary reviews. It was not until 1929 that he jumped to fame with his detective stories "The Dain Curse" and "Red Harvest," a title that proved prophetic.

Mr. Hammett explains his success: "I found I could sell the stories easily when it became known I had been a Pinkerton man. People thought my stuff was authentic."

Success

Then in 1934 came his greatest success. "The Thin Man," made famous thruout the world by Hollywood films with William Powell and Myrna Loy and Asta the dog. Royalties poured in from the films, from the books and from radio serials.

"But I was never too enthusiastic about the detective stories. The Thin Man always bored me."

Yet The Thin Man took him to Hollywood at $1200 a week and later brought him as much as four times that a week for radio serials.

He became soured and complained: "Play writing is a jerk's way of making a living. You do a play and someone tells you to do it over. Then some actor won't do it that way and you fix it for him again. What is the good?

Going Down

He quit Hollywood. His marriage to the girl who nursed him thru tuberculosis ended in divorce. The real-life Thin Man began to be seen in Left-wing circles around Greenwich Village, the Chelsea of New York. Finally in 1951 he went to jail for contempt of court for refusing to say who put up bail for convicted communists.

He served only five months but emerged an even lonelier man, content now to do little more than cook for himself and bring in wood for his log fire.

"I am concentrating on my health. I am learning to be a hypochondriac. I stopped writing because I found I was repeating myself. It is the beginning of the end when you discover you have style.

"But the thing that ruined me was the writing of the last third of 'The Glass Key' in one sitting of 30 hours."

He looked towards the three dusty typewriters and said: "Ever since then I have told myself: 'I could do it again if I had to.'"

Like Home

If working as a real live detective could produce "The Thin Man," could not his experiences in jail create another best seller?

Why did he not write in jail?

"I was never bored enough. I found the crooks had not changed since I was a Pinkerton man. Going to prison was like going home."

"The best detectives are the ones who do not get into trouble."

OBITUARY:

"Dashiell Hammett, Author, Dies; Created Hard-Boiled Detectives," *New York Times*, 11 January 1961, p. 47.

Dashiell Hammett, the dean of the so-called "hard-boiled" school of detective fiction and author of "The Maltese Falcon," died yesterday morning at the Lenox Hill Hospital. He was 66 years old.

Mr. Hammett had been ill several times in the last four years with a lung ailment. He contracted tuberculosis while serving overseas in World War I but recovered after a long convalescence.

Mr. Hammett won his fame as an author in the late Nineteen Twenties and early Thirties. He put his name to a series of detective novels whose characters were, by modest estimate, at one remove from the stuffy, formal sleuths who moved through the mystery fiction of the day, disdaining evil. Before him paragons had trapped scoundrels in the dark lair of their own duplicity.

Mr. Hammett brought the form a step closer to reality. His detectives were tough or urbane or both, but they were by no means inaccessible to the common temptations of man. They were drawn in part from the writer's eight years of experience as a Pinkerton agent.

Created Sam Spade

Probably his most famous creation was the detective, Sam Spade, from "The Maltese Falcon," a man whose name was eloquent of his rough-cut, get-to-the-core-of-things style.

His novels included "The Glass Key," "The Dain Curse," "Red Harvest" and the famous "The Thin Man."

After 1935 he produced little to match his first works, though he long continued to enjoy the accessory benefits of having his writing adapted to virtually every form of entertainment–radio, motion pictures, television, magazine serialization, even cartoon strips.

Mr. Hammett's association with various left-wing causes from about the time of World War II led finally to a conviction for contempt of court in 1951.

He had been a trustee of the bail fund of the Civil Rights Congress, an organization that was designated by the Attorney General as a Communist front. The fund had posted bond for four top Communist leaders who jumped bail. Mr. Hammett and three other trustees were sentenced for refusing to name persons who contributed to the fund. The author served six months at the Federal Correctional Institute near Ashland, Ky.

Les Tremayne and Claudia Morgan, the voices of Nick and Nora Charles from 1946 to 1948 when The Adventures of the Thin Man *was broadcast on CBS Radio. Though Hammett refused to write the scripts, to meet with the scriptwriters, or even to take calls from the production department, he was paid $500 per week for the use of his name in connection with this popular weekly radio show, which ran from July 1941 to September 1950, with an interruption during the war. It was, at various times, broadcast by NBC, CBS, and ABC.*

Invoked Fifth Amendment

Called before the Senate Permanent Subcommittee on Investigations headed by the late Senator Joseph R. McCarthy of Wisconsin, Mr. Hammett invoked the Fifth Amendment when asked if he was then or had been at any time a member of the Communist party. He told the committee that he was "sincerely afraid" he might incriminate himself.

Mr. Hammett's prose style invited such descriptive words as "lean, driving, hard." His work was several times likened to that of Ernest Hemingway by qualified critics and, in one case at least, it was Hemingway, not Hammett, who was the beneficiary of the comparison. Another writer said that Mr. Hammett's work was not fiction but "life magnified."

In 1953, Mr. Hammett's novels were plucked from the shelves of seventy-three of 189 American libraries overseas as a result of a volley of State Department confidential directives, based largely on testimony before the McCarthy committee.

Ten memorandums went out to the libraries, listing Mr. Hammett and fifteen others as undesirable authors. While the eleventh memorandum was being prepared, President Eisenhower told a

news conference that he thought "someone got frightened." He said that he would not himself have removed Mr. Hammett's books. Soon thereafter a new directive went out, authorizing the return of Mr. Hammett's books from storage to circulation.

Mr. Hammett was always placing distraction in the way of his heroes, usually in the persons of young women. It was typical enough of his detectives to spend a lavish evening in the company of one, neglecting no favor, and then to ransack her purse for the ultimate clue.

In a newspaper interview Mr. Hammett once described his view of a character this way:

"I see in him a little man going forward day after day through mud and blood and death and deceit–as callous and brutal and cynical as necessary–towards a dim goal, with nothing to push or pull him towards it except he's been hired to reach it."

Native of Maryland

This indifference to ordinary morality joined to devoted pursuit of a private code was a frequent trait of Hammett characters. It was written of Nick Charles, "The Thin Man" hero, that he "devoted himself to an intensive study of the liquor problem from the consumer's standpoint."

Mr. Hammett was born on Maryland's Eastern Shore and put in three years at the Baltimore Polytechnic Institute, which he left at the age of 13. He worked as a newsboy, freight clerk, railroad laborer, advertising man as well as Pinkerton detective. He once caught a man who had stolen a Ferris wheel.

Mr. Hammett, a slender 6-foot-tall man with a crest of gray hair, was a painstaking craftsman who worked and reworked his stories until he was satisfied he could do no better. He was a night worker, and sometimes, if pressed, worked on a book or motion picture thirty-six hours at a stretch.

In keeping with his request, arrangements have been made for Mr. Hammett to be buried Friday in the Arlington National Cemetery. Mr. Hammett served as a sergeant with the Motor Ambulance Corps in the First World War. In World War II, at the age of 48, he enlisted in the Army and served for two years in the Aleutian Islands.

Mr. Hammett's latest residence was at 63 East Eighty-second Street as the house guest of Lillian Hellman, the playwright. Miss Hellman will speak at the funeral service at 4 P.M. Thursday at the Frank E. Campbell Funeral Church, Madison Avenue at Eighty-first Street.

Mr. Hammett's marriage in 1920 to Josephine Annas Dolan of Anaconda, Mont., ended in divorce. Surviving are two daughters, Mrs. Mary Miller and Mrs. Josephine Marshall, and four grandchildren.

OBITUARY:
M. N., "A Gentle Man Who Wrote about the Underworld," *Daily Worker*, 29 January 1961, p. 4.

He was a gentle man who wrote about underworld toughs.

He was best known for his "The Thin Man," "Maltese Falcon," "Red Harvest" and his indomitable, dodo-voiced, dourly sentimental detective of detectives Sam Spade. Yet Dashiell Hammett was least known by the public for the man of principled belief, who believed in enacting his principles, as his friends best knew him.

He went to prison for his principles.

He underwent his trial by fire in the midst of the McCarthy hysteria when he was serving as a trustee of the Civil Rights Congress bail fund and refused to reveal the names of contributors to the bail fund.

He stood up to McCarthyism in the best tradition of his own tough-minded heroes.

He was a heretic who could never stomach hypocrisy and sham, sanctimonious or callous, in high places or low.

He was the chronicler of brutality in our national life, but he hated brutality.

He was the portrayer of the modern cynic to perfection, but he was as romantic as a schoolboy.

He was a master of lean dialogue, quick action, and the hard plotted story. He was an old pro.

He said of his writing: "The contemporary novelist's job is to take the pieces of life and arrange them on paper, and the more direct their passage from street to paper the more lifelike they should turn out." Writers, he said, should "make what is set down seem truly contemporary, to give the impression of things really happening here and now, to force upon the reader a feeling of immediacy."

He was often ignored by the smug literati and academic critics of his own land, but in Europe he was thought of as a writer of stature. He was hailed in France by the side of Ernest Hemingway as true creator of the American spirit in literature.

He was a realistic lover of America.

He believed in equality, in civil rights, in peace, but he more than believed in them. He acted.

He believed in socialism.

He did not preach, he practiced.

He was a member of the League of American Writers, the Civil Rights Congress, and many groups dedicated to the fight for a good life.

He was once asked if he opposed fascism and Franco. He replied: "It is very difficult for me to believe that anybody can still (this was in 1938) have any honest doubts about Franco and fascism, either separately or as a team . . . I am against Franco and fascism."

Reba Hammett, Dashiell's sister

He was made ill by the corruption he saw, by the "death and deceit" he experienced. He died of this illness.

Last week, when Dashiell Hammett was laid to rest, his funeral was attended by the great of literature and the bold of politics. One of the mourners was Louis Weinstock, The Worker's general manager, who had met the novelist in prison, an old meeting place for fighters.

"He was a good man", Louis Weinstock said of him, simply. "He was a good man."

ARTICLE:
Philip Durham, "Hammett: Profiler of Hard-Boiled Yeggs," review of *The Novels of Dashiell Hammett, Los Angeles Times*, 21 November 1965, Calendar Section, p. 1.

By the mid 1960s, the suppression of Hammett's works that had occurred after his imprisonment ended, and his reputation was restored.

What can one say about the novels of Dashiell Hammett except that they are as superbly written as one remembers them from more than 30 years ago? Here are five novels, all familiar to my generation: "Red Harvet," "The Dain Curse," "The Maltese Falcon," "The Glass Key" and "The Thin Man." But for the present generation–whose only contact with Hammett may be through a television rerun of "The Maltese Falcon"–Knopf could have provided a preface. A short one might have gone like this:

What is now known in America and England as the Black Mask school of writing began in the early spring of 1920 in a pulp magazine called Black Mask, founded by Henry L. Mencken and George Jean Nathan. After six months Mencken and Nathan sold their pulp magazine for a nice profit. Under the subsequent editorship of such capable men as Phil Cody and Harry North, Black Mask took on a specific character. Within two or three years the heroic man of violence emerged. The private investigator was poised and indestructibly ready to take over as the protector of American ideals.

Editor Had Vision

The "golden decade" of Black Mask began in November, 1926, under the editorship of Capt. Joseph T. Shaw. The new editor had a vision–that through Black Mask he could make a unique contribution to American literature. In the pages of his magazine Shaw singled out the stories of Dashiell Hammett as approximating what he had in mind: "simplicity for the sake of clarity, plausibility and belief." Shaw wanted action, but he held that "action is meaningless unless it involves recognizable human character in three-dimensional form."

With Shaw as the editor and Hammett as the leader, the Black Mask school flourished for 10 years. The editor insisted that his writers observe a cardinal principle. They were to create the illusion of reality by allowing their characters to act and talk tough rather than by making them do it. Instead of telling the reader how infallible the actors were, the authors permitted their heroes to demonstrate their abilities.

Perhaps the best known hero of the Black Mask school was the Continental Op (the private operator from the San Francisco office of the Continental Detective Agency). Dashiell Hammett, the creator of the Op, had had a varied career, including service in World War I and several years as a Pinkerton detective. Hammett–who knew a man who once stole a Ferris-wheel–began to turn his experiences into stories.

Dashiell Hammett, as the leader of the hard-boiled school of detective fiction, began to experiment with writing techniques. In his Black Mask stories he worked with plot, trying to keep it from becoming too obviously stereotyped. He created a protagonist in his short stories who would later stand up in longer works of fiction. He used the theme of the rugged individualist righting social wrongs. He concentrated on the objective, hard-boiled style, trying to make it as action-packed as possible.

In his Black Mask short stories from 1923 to 1927, Hammett developed his style. According to Raymond Chandler, Hammett "was spare, frugal, hard-boiled, but he did over and over again what only the best writers can ever do at all. He wrote scenes that seemed never to have been written before."

The clipped prose, the Hammett trade-mark, appeared in the early stories. Action abounded, but the economy of expression implied even more action than was visible. "The Golden Horseshoe" provided an example of violence in tempo.

A character named Gooseneck fired at one called Kewpie at the moment she threw a knife at him. Kewpie was "spun back across the room–hammered back by bullets that tore through her chest. Her back hit the wall. She pitched forward to the floor." The knife caught Gooseneck in the throat, and he "couldn't get his words past the blade."

In "Women, Politics and Murder" the style rattled like machine-gun fire: "My bullet cut the gullet out of him."

The hero of the short stories developed with the style. Although he played the traditional knightly role, he did not look the part. He was nameless, fat and 40.

In "Zigzags of Treachery" he did not like eloquence because "if it isn't effective enough to pierce your hide, it's tiresome; and if it's effective enough then it muddles your thoughts." He was not "a brilliant thinker," yet he had "flashes of intelligence." He was a man of action who liked his jobs to be "simply jobs–emotions are nuisances during business hours."

By 1927 Hammett was ready for more sustained fiction. His hero, style and setting had developed beyond the limits of the short story. In February and May of 1927 Black Mask carried two of Hammett's long stories–"The Big Knock-Over" and $106,000 Blood Money"–which were published together as his first novel. One hundred and fifty of the country's finest crooks gathered in San Francisco where they simultaneously knocked over the Seaman's National and the Golden State Trust. During the noisy affair 16 cops were killed and three times that many were wounded; 12 bystanders and bank clerks were killed; and the bandits lost seven dead and had 31 of their number taken as bleeding prisoners. After the shooting died down, the Op and two assistants took over the job. They took care of the crooks who were left and then tidied up the town.

If there is such a thing as the poetry of violence, Hammett clearly achieved it in his first novel, "$106,000 Blood Money." The Continental Op got with the rhythmical spirit of the occasion: "It was a swell bag of nails. Swing right, swing left, kick, swing right, swing left, kick. Don't hesitate, don't look for targets. God will see that there's always a mug there for your gun or blackjack to sock, a belly for your foot."

During the 32 months from November 1927 to June 1930, Dashiell Hammett's four important novels were published serially in Black Mask–"Red Harvest," "The Dain Curse," "The Maltese Falcon" and "The Glass Key." They were clearly his best fiction, but they were successful only because he had previously worked out everything in them in his short stories. The first two continued the Op as the first person narrator, although he changed character somewhat in the second. The

NY 93-1210

DETAILS:

This investigation was predicated upon a letter received from Assistant United States Attorney DANIEL F. McMAHON, Chief, Civil Division, Southern District of New York, under date of March 26, 1957, requesting that an agent be assigned to conduct a financial investigation of the debtor. He explained that a default judgment in the amount of $140,795.96 for tax deficiencies had been filed on February 28, 1957, against HAMMETT.

On April 5, 1957, Assistant United States Attorney McMAHON was contacted in this regard by ███████████ McMAHON made available the files of his office relating to this matter ██████

The following pertinent information was contained in a report of an Examination in Supplementary Proceedings which was conducted on March 26, 1957, at the United States Court House, Foley Square, New York. HAMMETT lives in the gate cottage located on the estate of ████████████ located at Orchard Hill Road, Katonah, New York. He has lived there for about 4½ years rent free. He is single, having been divorced in 1936, and has no bank accounts or safe deposit vaults or boxes whatsoever. He has no boarders or subtenants living with him and lives alone.

HAMMETT stated he has two children and three grandchildren. His children are MARY JANE HAMMETT and JOSEPHINE MARSHALL, both of whom reside in California. HAMMETT is not presently employed as the result of a heart attack which he suffered about 1½ years ago resulting in a shortness of breath and complications with his lungs and diaphragm.

He is not presently receiving royalties from any books or literary productions, and has not done so for several years because of tax liens imposed by federal and sta

After Hammett was released from prison, federal and New York State tax examiners determined that he owed a total of $140,795.96 in back taxes. When Hammett failed to respond to a court subpoena regarding this matter, a default judgment was entered against him, and the FBI was asked to interview him to determine his ability to pay. He was without income or financial resources from 1951 until his death in 1961. The tax liability grew, with interest and penalties, to over $180,000.

NY 93-1210

1957

income tax agencies. He stated that his income for the past year had been somewhere around $30, from an investment in the play "Death of a Salesman." He stated that he has been living on loans from friends since December, 1951, when he got out of jail.

He stated that he owns no stocks, bonds or other securities, and receives no pensions of any kind. According to HAMMETT, he holds no mortgages, has no insurance policies of any type, and is not presently engaged in any business venture either actively or passively. He explained that he had a book which he had started some years ago, but he had done nothing for the past couple of years. This book is entitled "Tulip," and is the only book on which he is presently working.

He explained that some years ago he had had a couple of radio shows, and had had three at one time, but the last of them, "The Fat Man," went off the air sometime between July and December, 1951, while he was in jail.

HAMMETT noted that the royalties to which he was entitled would normally come to him through his agent, The Music Corporation of America, or through Regis Radio. Also from ALFRED A. KNOPF, a publisher. The Music Corporation of America is still his agent, and he has had no other agent in the past ten years. The last time he received any remuneration from any of the above sources was approximately in 1951 or 1952.

HAMMETT stated that he owned no car, and that his personal property consisted only of the majority of the furniture contained in the four room gate cottage in which he presently resides. He stated that he is not aware of being the beneficiary under any will.

He stated that the present obligations which he can recall are one for about $300 to the Burrell Clipping Bureau, White Plains, New York; to Bernard Rice, Associates, his accountant, for about $1,000; to the federal government; and New York State in the amount of $15,000 or $16,000.

NY 93-1210

HAMMETT stated he has never been in bankruptcy, and does not know of any garnishee proceedings against him. His last bank account was at the Amalgamated Bank, Union Square, New York. He has not transferred any monies or properties to anyone in the past five years, and is not making payments to any of his present creditors. He has no obligations to his former wife as a result of their divorce.

According to the report of the Examination, the government made an application to direct HAMMETT to fully disclose the identity of all persons to whom he is obligated, including those making loans to him for his present subsistence. This application was denied by United States District Judge NOONAN.

HAMMETT knew of no monies owed to him. He explained that he had no reason to anticipate any change in his financial position. HAMMETT stated that he has had no other occupation than that of a writer since 1928. He gave his date of birth as May 27, 1894.

The records of the Credit Bureau of Greater New York, as furnished by ~~redacted~~ to ~~redacted~~ on May 21, 1957, contained the following pertinent information:

DASHIELL HAMMETT has resided at 28 West 10th Street, New York City, Hardscrabble Farm, Pleasantville, New York ~~redacted~~ 15 East 66th Street, New York City, the Hotels Plaza and Lombardy, New York City, on Cove Road, Huntington, Long Island, and in Santa Monica, California. His occupation is listed as an author and his bank is the Amalgamated Bank. He has charge accounts with the following:

. Brooks Brothers
346 Madison Avenue, New York City

NY 93-1210

A. Sulka and Company
661 5th Avenue, New York City

Tripler and Company
366 Madison Avenue, New York City

Bloomingdale's
59th Street, New York City

Abercrombie and Fitch
360 Madison Avenue, New York City

Finchley, Incorporated
564 5th Avenue, New York City

Holliday Book Shop
49 East 49th Street, New York City

Hotel Pierre
2 East 51st Street, New York City

Brentano's Book Stores
1 West 47th Street, New York City

McCutcheons
609 5th Avenue, New York City

The files contain the following record of litigations:

June 5, 1939	a judgment by Walter G. McCarty Corporation for $5,286. This was satisfied of record on May 18, 1942 and has been disputed.
January 13, 1956	Federal tax lien filed in Manhattan on HAMMETT, care of Bernard Reis and Company, 10 East 40th Street, for $7,340.

NY 93-1210

March 7, 1955	Judgment filed New York County in favor of State Tax Commission for $496.83.
August 1, 1956	Federal tax lien filed in Manhattan for $3,039.57 under #F4218.
April 2, 1957	Judgment filed in Westchester County in favor of the United States Government for $140,747.96.
May 7, 1956	Judgment filed in Westchester County in favor of CARMELA MONEA for $316.95, Attorney J. M. PARISH

On May 21, 1957, ██████████████, Yorktown Office, County Trust Company, Yorktown Heights, New York, advised after a check of the Central Files of the Bank located at White Plains, New York, that there is no record either past or present of any transactions by the bank with HAMMETT or ███████████████ stated that both individuals are unknown to him.

███████████████ Assistant Cashier and Branch Manager, Bedford Hills Office of the National Bank of Westchester, Bedford Hills, New York, advised on May 21, 1957, that SAMUEL DASHIELL HAMMETT and ████████████████ do not have accounts at his bank and are not known to him.

- P -

- 6 -

third developed the swaggering Sam Spade. And the fourth created a variation on the character in Ned Beaumont and also used the third person viewpoint.

"Red Harvest" (dedicated to Joseph Shaw) was originally a group of separate stories referred to under the general title "The Cleansing of Poisonville." They revolved around the Op at his hard-boiled best. The Op set out to clean up a crime-ridden city by playing everyone off against the middle. By his own count one and a half dozen criminals were murdered. He admitted that he could "swing the play legally," but he decided that it was "easier to have them killed off, easier and surer."

The Op did not allow himself any sexual diversion, but he did go in for some very heavy drinking.

Hollywood Influence

Dashiell Hammett's last major effort, "The Thin Man," was obviously written under excessive Hollywood influence. The original version of the novel had been planned and begun in 1930, in the style of that period. Only 65 pages were completed. The setting was San Francisco and its environs, the viewpoint the third person, the detective a kind of modified Op.

The most interesting aspect of the fragment was the unreal quality that Hammett insisted on attaching to the hero. He was referred to as untouchable, as not even a corpse but a ghost, as one with whom it was impossible to come into contact–like trying to hold a handful of smoke.

It was three years, one of which was spent in Hollywood, before Hammett returned to his fragment. Unable or unwilling to continue it, he wrote a different novel by the same name.

"The Thin Man," dedicated to Lillian Hellman, was not published in Black Mask. It is a good novel in the older tradition of detective fiction but it does not belong in the Black Mask school.

For some, Dashiell Hammett wrote beyond the tradition of detective fiction by specifically expressing the giddiness of the 1920s–the period when violence and brutality were accepted as simply a part of the times. For many, Hammett's hero spoke for men who had lost faith in the values of their society.

ESSAY:
Ross Macdonald, "Homage to Dashiell Hammett," *Mystery Writers' Annual* (April 1964): 8, 24.

I have been given some space to speak for the hardboiled school of mystery writing. Let me use it to dwell for a bit on the work of Dashiell Hammett. He was the great innovator who invented the hardboiled detective novel and used it to express and master the undercurrent of inchoate violence that runs through so much of American life.

In certain ways, it must be admitted, Hammett's heroes are reminiscent of unreconstructed Darwinian man; *McTeague* and *The Sea Wolf* stand directly behind them. But no matter how rough and appetent they may be, true representatives of a rough and appetent society, they are never allowed to run unbridled. Hammett's irony controls them. In fact he criticized them far more astringently and basically than similar men were criticized by Hemingway. In his later and less romantic moments Hammett was a close and disillusioned critic of the two-fisted hard-drinking woman-chasing American male that he derived partly from tradition and partly from observation, including self-observation.

Even in one of his very early stories, first published by Mencken in *Smart Set*, Hammett presents a character who might have been a parody of the Hemingway hero, except that he was pre-Hemingway. This huge brute is much attached to his beard. To make a short story shorter, the loss of his beard reveals that he used it to hide a receding chin and make him a public laughingstock. This isn't much more than an anecdote, but it suggests Hammett's attitude towards the half-evolved frontier male of our not too distant past. Shorn and urbanized, he became in Hammett's best novels a near-tragic figure, a lonely and suspicious alien who pits a hopeless but obstinate animal courage against the metropolitan jungle, a not very moral man who clings with a skeptic's desperation to a code of behavior empirically arrived at in a twilight world between chivalry and gangsterism.

Like the relationship of Charles Dickens and Wilkie Collins, the Hemingway-Hammett influence ran two ways. Hammett achieved some things that Hemingway never attempted. He placed his characters in situations as complex as those of life, in great cities like San Francisco and New York and Baltimore, and let them work out their dubious salvations under social and economic and political pressures. The subject of his novels, you might say, was the frontier male thrust suddenly, as the frontier disappeared, into the modern megalopolis; as Hemingway's was a similar man meeting war and women, and listening to the silence of his own soul.

Hammett's prose is not quite a prose that can say anything, as Chandler overenthusiastically claimed it could. But it is a clean useful prose, with remarkable range and force. It has pace and point, strong tactile values, the rhythms and colors of speech, all in the colloquial tradition that stretches from Mark Twain through Stephen Crane to Lardner and Mencken, the Dr. Johnson of our vernacular. Still it is a deadpan and rather external prose, artificial-seeming compared with Huck Finn's earthy rhetoric, flat in comparison with Fitzgerald's more subtly colloquial instrument. Hammett's ear for the current and the colloquial was a little too sardonically literal, and this is already tending to date his writing, though not seriously.

Analysis of any kind is alien to this prose. Moulding the surface of things, it lends itself to the vivid narration of rapid, startling action. Perhaps it tends to set too great a premium on action, as if the mind behind it were hurrying away from its own questions and deliberately restricting itself to the manipulation of appearances. It is in part the expression of that universally-met-with American type who avoids sensibility and introspection because they make you vulnerable in the world. At its worst such prose can be an unnecessary writing-down to the lowest common denominator of the democracy. But at its best it has great litotic power, as in some of Hemingway's earlier stories, or in the haunting chapter where Sam Spade makes devious love to Brigid by telling her the story of Flitcraft:

"A man named Flitcraft had left his real-estate office, in Tacoma, to go to luncheon one day and had never returned. He did not keep an engagement to play golf after four that afternoon, though he had taken the initiative in making the engagement less than half an hour before he went out to luncheon. His wife and children never saw him again. His wife and he were supposed to be on the best of terms. He had two children, boys, one five and the other three. He owned his house in a Tacoma suburb, a new Packard, and the rest of the appurtenances of successful American living."

Sam Spade is Flitcraft's spiritual twin, the lonely male who is not at ease in Zion or in Zenith. He is inarticulate about himself, like Babbitt is aware only of a deep malaise that spurs him on to action and acquisition. *The Maltese Falcon* is a fable of modern man in quest of love and money, despairing of everything else. Its murders are more or less incidental, though they help to give it its quality of a crisis novel. Its characters act out of the extreme emotions of fear and guilt and concupiscence, anger and revenge; and with such fidelity to these passions that their natures almost seem co-terminous with them.

Driven by each and all of them, Sam Spade strips away one by one the appearances which stand between him and the truth, and between him and the complete satisfaction of his desires. His story ends in drastic peripeteia with the all but complete frustration of his desires. His lover is guilty of murder; the code without which his life is meaningless forces him to turn her over to the police. The black bird is hollow. The reality behind appearances is a treacherous vacuum. Spade turns for sardonic consolation to the wife of his murdered partner (whose name was Archer). It is his final reluctant act of animal pragmatism.

Probably Hammett intended the ultimate worthlessness of the Maltese Falcon to be more than a bad joke on his protagonist. I see it as the symbol of a lost tradition, representing the great cultures of the past which have become inaccessible to Spade and the men of his time. It represents explicitly the religious and ethical developments of the Mediterranean basin, Christianity and knight-errantry. Perhaps it stands for the Holy Ghost itself, or rather for its absence.

In any case the bird's lack of value implies Hammett's final comment on the inadequacy and superficiality of Sam Spade's life and ours. If only his bitterly inarticulate struggle for self-realization were itself more fully realized, the stakes for which he plays not so arbitrarily lost from the beginning (a basic limitation of the detective story is that its action is pre-ordained, in a sense, by what has already happened), Sam Spade could have been a great indigenous tragic figure. Maybe he is. I think *The Maltese Falcon*, with its astonishing imaginative energy persisting undiminished after a third of a century, is tragedy of a new kind, deadpan tragedy.

ARTICLE:

Richard T. Hammett, "Mystery Writer Was Enigmatic Throughout Life," *Baltimore News-American*, 19 August 1973.

This article by Hammett's nephew provides the only statement made by Hammett's brother, Richard. After Hammett left Maryland in 1920, they rarely saw one another. During the 1940s when Richard Hammett, was a successful oil company executive in New York City, he and Dashiell visited occasionally, though they never developed a close relationship.

It is not an easy job to write an objective story about a controversial figure, especially when that person is your uncle.

The controversial person was a St. Marys County native called Samuel D. Hammett, best known as Dashiell Hammett. In literary circles he is considered to be the father of the modern hardnosed detective story. But as a writer, he was a master of the short story almost unsurpassed in American literature.

He came by it honestly. After holding down a variety of jobs he followed up a blind newspaper ad and became a Pinkerton detective, a background he said he used in many of his novels.

He probably was best known for "The Thin Man" which was an instant success when printed during the 1930s and became the basis for a series of movies starring William Powell and Myrna Loy.

Often glossed over is the fact that he created the great "private eye" Sam Spade, the Continental Op, and also authored a plethora of short stories, many of which did not deal with crime.

Dashiell Hammett was born in 1894, the son of a Southern Maryland farmer-politician.

He might still be there had his father not been run out of the county more or less on a rail. A popular but impecunious Democrat, he was persuaded to run for Congress as a Republican in return for Republican financial support. He lost; and

eventually was forced to sell his farm and move to Philadelphia and then Baltimore, where Dashiell grew up in the family home at 212 North Stricker Street.

Few remember much of his childhood. My father said he was not a particularly remarkable child except for being quite stubborn at times, a trait U.S. Senate investigators were to discover some years later.

He was a Baltimore Polytechnic dropout prior to World War I in order to go to work to help the family. During that war he enlisted and managed to get as far as Camp Meade as a medical sergeant before being discharged for physical disability (tuberculosis).

While a Pinkerton agent for eight years he investigated the Fatty Arbuckle and Nicky Arnstein cases. He often said his first promotion as a detective came when he captured a man who stole a Ferris wheel. Also while with Pinkerton he was involved in a number of strikebreaking incidents, which may explain his later involvement in labor and leftist causes.

During the thirties and forties he became involved in a number of organizations, some of which were labeled "Communist Fronts." My father feels that the Pinkerton methods of strikebreaking influenced his turn to leftist groups.

During the same period–according to Lillian Hellman–his friend and bed partner for 31 years, he also was the "hottest piece of property" in Hollywood. He wrote the screen play for "The Watch on the Rhine," which was adapted from Miss Hellman's stage production of the same name, as well as many others.

He was being considered to do the screen play for "The Detective Story" which starred Kirk Douglas, when the Joe McCarthy witchhunt of the 1950s hit. He was among the many writers who suddenly became persona non grata in the studios; a name on the "blacklist."

Among his activities allegedly–had been raising bail money for Gerhard Eisler, an American Communist. Eisler promptly jumped bail or fled on a Polish ship to ultimately end up in Moscow.

Hammett was summoned before the McCarthy committee, but stubbornly refused to say where the $80,000 bail money came from. For this he was sentenced to six months in jail for contempt of Congress.

Miss Hellman insists that he was only a trustee of the American Civil Rights Congress and never knew the names of the contributors. Another theory advanced is that he refused to talk to protect a number of "little people" who gave a dollar or two to a cause that rightly or wrongly they believed in at that time.

In any event he spent his six months in jail, and upon release was hauled up before the committee again and again refused to talk.

Sen. John McClellan, D-Ark., said testily, "Mr. Hammett, you certainly don't think much of the power of American public opinion, do you?" The reply was, "Senator, it wasn't American public opinion that put me away for six months, it was your committee and a judge."

The committee gave up.

At the time all this was going on I was in the Navy and much of what I have said was gleaned from conversations with my father and old newspaper files. They jibe.

After his period as the "hottest property in Hollywood" he fell on bad times. He was not only on the then lethal studio blacklist, but either couldn't or wouldn't write. He also had spent large sums in legal fees during his long ordeal. The Internal Revenue Service attached nearly everything he owned for tax claims.

Despite being invalided out of World War I, he managed to get into the Army in World War II. The Army in its wisdom processed him, decided they had a good mind on their hands and sent him to school to be a cryptographer.

Family story has it that after he had learned all about codes the Army finally learned all about him. The story is that someone said, "My God, we may have a Communist on our hands. Send him someplace where he'll never see a code."

Whatever the reason, Hammett wound up in the Aleutians. Miss Hellman described him as saying his greatest contribution to the war effort was assuring young men they would not lose their virility by staying in the womanless Arctic for several years; at the time he was 50.

After the war his health began to fail. He drank heavily for a number of years, then suddenly quit. Miss Hellman thinks he quit because a doctor told him he couldn't, and he was contrary enough to show him.

Unfortunately no one in his immediate family really knew him well after World War I. A very private person, he left Baltimore, seldom to return. However, what he considered his best book, "The Glass Key," had clearly a Baltimore setting.

He had married his Army nurse at Camp Meade and had two daughters.

What little the family knows of him came from letters he sent to his sister, the only person in his family with whom he maintained any contact.

The man was an enigma, even to those who knew him best. In her autobiography, "An Unfinished Woman," Miss Hellman devotes several chapters to him and in effect admits she did not entirely understand him after a 31-year-relationship.

On Jan. 10, 1961, Dashiell Hammett died at the age of 67 in New York's Lenox Hill Hospital.

He had lived his life the way he wanted to live it, for his own reasons.

ARTICLE:

James H. Bready, "Books and Authors," *Baltimore Sun*, 8 May 1966.

For this article the author interviewed Hammett's sister Rebecca. This is the only printed statement she made about her brother.

I came across Lillian Hellman's memoir in the *New York Review* of Books, and reading it gave me the fanciest tingle in a long time. Imagine, a man and a woman calling each other best friend for 30 years, loving, fighting, collaborating, above all understanding and abetting each other. Still, I thought afterward, all this is New York and California. Nobody's ever really done the story of his formative period, as Marylander and particularly as Baltimorean. Even when he came back in 1939 to give a political-cause speech, the papers didn't interview him. It's five years now since his death, and nearly 50 years since he left here–but what the heck, I said, let's switch it around and put a tail on the celebrated private op; let us, all quiet-like trail Dashiell Hammett.

I poured myself a Sam Spade-size drink, I lit a thin, green-dappled cigar (Ned Beaumont–"The Glass Key"). I wrote to Miss Hellman (to whom "The Thin Man" is dedicated). She was nice about it–having met him in 1930, when he was 36 and she was 25, she is no authority on the life he left behind in 1918 when he was originally sent west, to an army hospital. He had survived World War I's flu epidemic only, in a dank barracks at old Camp Meade, to come down with t.b. Had I, she wrote back, tried his sister, in Charlotte, N.C.?

Putting a little Bogart into the voice, I called Information, and Mary Astor straightway came back at me with the number, and there I was dialing Miss Rebecca Hammett. She was home–she was still up–she was glad to hear about the anthology of her brother's short stories that Random House will publish next month, with Miss Hellman's glowing memoir as its preface. And, Miss Hammett had memories. There were three of them, girl, boy, boy: Rebecca (Aaronia Rebecca, actually–remember, in "The Dain Curse," Joseph Haldorn's wife Aaronia?), and Samuel Dashiell (called by his middle name, too, with stress on second syllable–their mother's family, from Baltimore, once spelled it de Chiel) and Richard Thomas 3d. Their grandfather worked 200 or more acres of tobaccoland at Jarboesville, in St. Marys county (where interrelated Hammetts still abound). Dashiell Hammett was born there. But his father disliked farming and in 1898 moved his family to Baltimore, going to work for the Safe Deposit and Trust Company and living on North Stricker street–she paused, hardly a second–at No. 212, opposite the old orphan asylum.

My neat script was filling page after notebook page. Dashiell ("Dash" is from later years) did his first book reading at Branch 2, like his neighbor Mencken before him. A year at Poly and he had had enough of all schools. He got a job, the first of many, as messenger boy at the B.&O.

A Wild One

Year after year, on into the war, city directories listed Hammett, S. Dashiell, as "clk"; but at some point he became a Pinkerton's Inc. operative, regardless of his build. Nervously, I flicked my mustache with my thumb. How tall was your brother, I asked; how thin? He was six-two and he never weighed more than 145, she said. I stayed with my streak. Are you tall too? I asked. Five-five and I'm 84 pounds, she said. I'm 73 years old and still entirely making my own way, in business. My

trouble, I said to myself, is I set out to impress a woman and every time she impresses me instead and what would *Nick Charles* say to *Nora* now? Her other kid brother, after many years with Esso, is retired and living in Charlotte.

Dashiell was a wild one, she said. Father didn't like it–he never touched a drop and only died in 1948 when he was 85. Dashiell would tell me stories about his adventures, but I've forgotten them–never knowing how much to believe. In the hospital he married his nurse, a good-looking girl from Montana; they were divorced and she may be alive, out West, which is where their two married daughters are. The doctors told him he had only one more year, so he left the hospital, saying he didn't mind dying but he did mind doing it there. But then the t.b. stopped–an arrested case, they told him. He said what stopped it was whiskey.

He couldn't be an op any more so he started writing for the pulps. He'd start around midnight and type until it was light–slowly, with butts but no booze, a few hundred words a night, never rewriting. That was the way he did his five novels in five years, including the four they made into movies. Once in the 1930s he invited Rebecca to come to New York and they shared an apartment some months. Then he grew less interested in writing and more interested in causes. Then, still getting disability pay from his first World War he went into his second at 48–again, as an EM.

Alcoholism didn't get him–he finally swore off altogether–but emphysema and lung cancer did. Robert Graves and Andre Gide and Sinclair Lewis had hailed his work, maybe relishing the hard-boiled atmosphere, maybe liking the plausible people. He would rather have impressed them with the serious, nondetective novel he started but never finished. In North Carolina, a sister who passes up night-time television's movie reruns to reread English literature classics, and other people in Baltimore and elsewhere, wonder whether anybody from the early days still has firsthand Hammett stories worth writing down; and especially, whether an old-file drawer somewhere still contains any of his detective-agency case reports, written in language that ensured his job even if somebody did make off with the object to be guarded, that falcon supposed to have been fashioned out of gold and jewels by the Knights of Malta.

ARTICLE:

Bernard Kalb, "Remembering the Dashiell Hammett of 'Julia'," *New York Times*, 25 September 1977, pp. D 15-16.

Bernard Kalb was on the staff of The Adakian.

Suddenly–tumbling from the attic of my memory–bits, pieces and people from an island in the Aleutians during World War II; icy williwaws that numbed my life for a couple of years in the early 1940's, a mimeographed Army newspaper called The Adakian and a corporal we all knew as Sam.

All this bric-a-brac has just been dusted off, and the reason is that Sam, who died in 1961, is alive again–on the screen. To the outside world, he was known as Dashiell Hammett–his full name had a Samuel before his best-selling name–and Hammett figures prominently in a new movie called "Julia," based on a chapter in Lillian Hellman's autobiographical "Pentimento." Hammett is portrayed by Jason Robards in a way that captures the essence of the man: Sam was more of a listener than a talker, and when he did talk he often talked the way his characters did–economically, to the point. More than three decades later, I can still hear the echo of Hammett.

It took a World War to introduce us. Sam was famous, rich and almost 50–achievements beyond our wildest dreams. We were a bunch of enthusiastic semi-literates, mostly in our early 20's, white and black, who had been trained to serve interchangeably as infantrymen or journalists. We landed on Adak in December, 1943. Hammett had already been there several months, and we were thrown together in a quonset hut that would serve as a city room. Our assignment, with Sam as editor, was to turn out a newspaper for the thousands of G.I.'s on that desolate dot in the North Pacific.

The Hammett I remember was a bayonet of a man–tall, thin, with a constant glint of a smile. I was too unsophisticated to interpret that crinkled look, topped by a tassel of white silky hair, but in retrospect, I guess the word is *bemused*. Sam's

being bemused was inevitable. Here he was–author of "The Maltese Falcon" and "The Thin Man," among other detective classics; play doctor; screen writer of, among other things, Hellman's "Watch on the Rhine"–and here he was now, in the midst of an assemblange of callow recruits, on a barren island, back in uniform for his second World War.

What do I recall of the Sam Hammett of the Aleutians? Over coffee in the mess hall or during the long nights of putting out our four-page newspaper, we'd all exchange life stories; clearly, Sam's was the most interesting–and not only because his was the longest. The way I remember it, he had served in World War I and had contracted tuberculosis somewhere along the line. That led to treatment in veterans' hospitals, and it was while he was on his back, perhaps reliving his earlier experiences as a Pinkerton operative, that he began testing himself as a writer–first for the pulps, later in the novels that were to introduce a new genre of detective fiction. Sam once told us that, when he volunteered to join World War II, he was able to pass the physical only when he agreed to have all his remaining teeth pulled.

Occasionally, under questioning–and we were immensely curious about all the famous people he knew–Sam would share a bit of his civilian life with us. Once I remember his reading an excerpt from a letter Lillian Hellman had sent during a visit to the Soviet Union. I did not then know the depths of the Hammett-Hellman relationship, but I recall Sam's sense of excitement as he quoted a few of the lines she had written about her visit to the Russian troops. Her eyewitness account lifted us out of our Aleutian stagnancy and placed us at the front lines.

It may have been his connection with Hellman–or his intellectual need to explore whatever resources were lying around in the quonset hut–that prompted him to enlist the aid of a few of us in brushing up on his Yiddishisms. He was particularly fond of the word "punim"–face–which he pronounced "poonim"–with a slight Southern drawl. (Hammett was born a Catholic, in Maryland.) He once, in fact, jokingly confided that he would have liked to call our newspaper The Adakian, "The Adaknik"–but he thought not enough people would appreciate it.

Hammett emerges from memory partly blur, partly vivid. If he had been, pre-induction, a man-about-town, I don't recall his being particularly gregarious in khaki. Not that he wasn't friendly; he was—but he was not an intimate part of the mix. This may have been a result of the unworldly company the Army forced him to keep or the sheer generation gap.

I must confess that on one occasion I inadvertently added to the gap. It had to do with working through the night. Ours was a morning newspaper; Sam wanted it that way. That meant that we were on the job from before midnight to breakfast, reading the incoming news file, monitoring shortwave broadcasts, preparing our copy. "This is your newspaper," Sam wrote in an editorial initialed D. H. in the first edition of The Adakian, Jan. 29th, 1944. "If we ever forget it—lower the boom on us." Well, without intending to lower the boom on him, I found myself suggesting early one morning that the all-night shift might not be the ideal spot for anyone over, say, 25.

Thirty-three years later, I still remember—with considerably greater vividness—the way he looked at me, first with surprise, then with tolerance, then with an amused smile. Sam stayed on that night, of course, and hundreds of other nights. As a birthday present we ran a special private edition of The Adakian in May 1944, with a headline "Hammett Hits Half-Century." He was delighted.

Yet Hammett was more of a hermit than a handshaker. He preferred silence to small talk, and I think that his retiring style, weighted by his fame and his age, had an occasionally inhibiting impact on our noisy spontaneity. One indelible impression—a kind of snapshot in my mind—that I still retain is of Hammett in the horizontal position, full-length on a rectangular work table, either reading a book on political philosophy or composing a caption for a cartoon that would convey the bleakness of the Aleutians. Indeed, he spent a lot of time in that position, and if it weren't for that surprising prematurely white thatch, you'd swear that wasn't a man stretched out but a discarded uniform.

Our newspaper had three cartoonists, and their drawings and their captions were meant to be a wry comment on G.I. life on a frozen archipelago between Alaska and the Soviet Union. But Sam's captions were the most incisive, the most humorously illuminating. I riffle—now—through a 1945 paperback of those drawings, and I can still pick out the Hammett lines. One cartoon shows a G.I. in a parka staring at the wet Aleutian weather and saying defiantly: "Go ahead—rain!" Another shows a G.I. pointing out the sights to a newcomer: "There's nothing over there, too." A third shows a couple of soldiers gazing at the snow-covered mountains. "Awright," says the caption, "but there's a limit to what beauty can do for ya."

This anthology was, in a way, a diary of our stay in the Aleutians. "There is in man a need to see himself," Sam wrote in a preface dated April 2, 1945, "to have himself and his pursuits and environment expressed. This is the necessity that sent early man to daubing his cave wall with ochered representations of the hunt, that set Anastasia, Pedigo and Miller [our three artists] to scratching mimeographed stencils with a stylus. No art can have an older, a more honorable, a more truly authentic basis. This, then, is our art and its people are us."

Though we spent a couple of years together, we knew very little about Sam's private life. Hammett's fame as a drinker, for example. All the time he was with us on Adak, Sam and alcohol went their separate ways, but we did manage—once—to get a glimpse of him in high spirits. He was just back from an assignment that had taken him to the temptations of mainland Alaska, and he returned to our quonset in a party mood. He ran over with stories, jokes, gossip; we were exhilarated by this burst of liveliness into our sodden, repetitious world. But I remember that Sam was so overwhelmed by his imbibing that his false teeth had somehow slipped loose of their moorings. The upshot was that his lips and his choppers were not in synch; his mouth would form one set of words while his teeth clicked out a contrasting set of rhythms.

As for his politics, I would later read in one of Hellman's books that she was fairly sure that Hammett joined the Communist Party in 1937 or 1938, but that she didn't know because she never asked him. If he had, he did not, to the best of my memory, ever talk about that to us; in fact, I don't remember his talking much about politics.

But there was a morning–after V. E. Day and after V. J. Day–that Sam provided us with a clue to his political reputation. He had just been invited to see the commanding general of the island. The way Sam told it, the general said he'd been told that Sgt. Hammett (by then, Hammett had been promoted) was some kind of radical. But the general was quoted as saying he still wanted Sgt. Hammett to keep it as good a newspaper as ever. Sam seemed bemused. There was always some speculation that Sam's political leanings had won

him a ticket–not to the main battlegrounds of the war–but to the out-of-the-way Aleutians.

After the war, I pretty much lost touch with Sam. Once, I read that he was teaching mystery writing at a Marxist-oriented school in New York. I dropped by on the chance of saying hello, but it turned out that the class was filled. I couldn't get past the front door. Another time I ran into him on a street in the Village. We self-consciously exchanged a word or two. The war was over. We were back in our separate worlds.

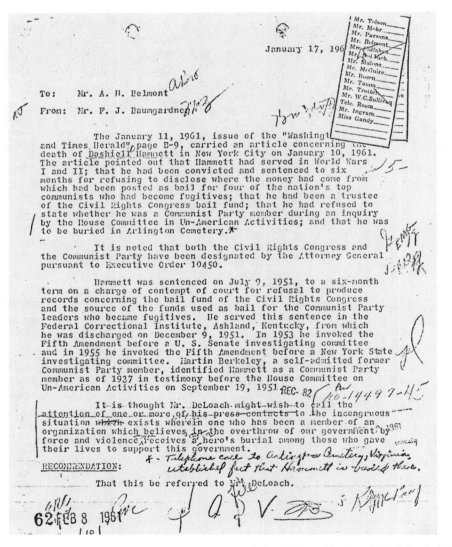

No action was taken on this recommendation that Hammett's burial be publically criticized by the FBI.

ROSS MACDONALD
[Kenneth Millar]
(13 December 1915-11 July 1983)

See the Kenneth Millar entries in the Dictionary of Literary Biography, *volume 2,* American Novelists Since World War II *and* Yearbook 1983.

BOOKS:

The Dark Tunnel, as Kenneth Millar (New York: Dodd, Mead, 1944);

Trouble Follows Me, as Kenneth Millar (New York: Dodd, Mead, 1946);

Blue City, as Kenneth Millar (New York: Knopf, 1947; London: Cassell, 1949);

The Three Roads, as Kenneth Millar (New York: Knopf, 1948; London: Cassell, 1950);

The Moving Target, as John Macdonald (New York: Knopf, 1949; London: Cassell, 1951);

The Drowning Pool, as John Ross Macdonald (New York: Knopf, 1950; London: Cassell, 1952);

The Way Some People Die, as John Ross Macdonald (New York: Knopf, 1951; London: Cassell, 1953);

The Ivory Grin, as John Ross Macdonald (New York: Knopf, 1952; London: Cassell, 1953);

Meet Me at the Morgue, as John Ross Macdonald (New York: Knopf, 1953; London: Cassell, 1954);

Find a Victim, as John Ross Macdonald (New York: Knopf, 1954; London: Cassell, 1955);

The Name Is Archer, as John Ross Macdonald (New York: Bantam, 1955; London: Fontana, 1976);

The Barbarous Coast, as Ross Macdonald hereafter (New York: Knopf, 1956; London: Cassell, 1957);

The Doomsters (New York: Knopf, 1958; London: Cassell, 1958);

The Galton Case (New York: Knopf, 1959; London: Cassell, 1960);

The Ferguson Affair (New York: Knopf, 1960; London: Collins, 1960);

The Wycherly Woman (New York: Knopf, 1961; London: Collins, 1961);

The Zebra-Striped Hearse (New York: Knopf, 1962; London: Collins, 1963);

The Chill (New York: Knopf, 1964; London: Collins, 1964);

The Far Side of the Dollar (New York: Knopf, 1965; London: Collins, 1965);

Black Money (New York: Knopf, 1966; London: Collins, 1966);

The Instant Enemy (New York: Knopf, 1968; London: Collins, 1968);

The Goodbye Look (New York: Knopf, 1969; London: Collins, 1969);

The Underground Man (New York: Knopf, 1971; London: Collins, 1971);

Sleeping Beauty (New York: Knopf, 1973; London: Collins, 1973);

On Crime Writing (Santa Barbara, Cal.: Capra, 1973);

The Blue Hammer (New York: Knopf, 1976; London: Collins, 1976);

Lew Archer Private Investigator (New York: Mysterious Press, 1977);

A Collection of Reviews (Northridge, Cal.: Lord John Press, 1979);

Self-Portrait: Ceaselessly into the Past, edited by Ralph B. Sipper (Santa Barbara, Cal.: Capra, 1981);

Early Millar: The First Stories of Ross Macdonald & Margaret Millar (Santa Barbara, Cal.: Cordelia Editions, 1982);

Strangers in Town, edited by Tom Nolan (Norfolk, Va.: Crippen & Landry, 2001).

BIOGRAPHIES:

Matthew J. Bruccoli, *Ross Macdonald* (New York & San Diego: Harcourt Brace Jovanovich, 1984);

Tom Nolan, *Ross Macdonald* (New York: Scribner, 1999).

BIBLIOGRAPHY:

Matthew J. Bruccoli, *Ross Macdonald/Kenneth Millar: A Descriptive Bibliography* (Pittsburgh: University of Pittsburgh Press, 1983).

ARCHIVES:

Kenneth Millar's papers and manuscripts are at the University of California-Irvine Library.

ESSAY:

Introduction to *Kenneth Millar/Ross Macdonald: A Checklist,* by Matthew J. Bruccoli (Detroit: Bruccoli Clark/Gale Research, 1971), pp. xi-xvii.

Millar's introduction to the first separately published bibliography of his work traces his career and acknowledges literary debts. He and his mother were deserted by his father when Kenneth was four, and he had to overcome the obstacles of poverty to obtain an education. Abandoned children and the quest for parents are recurring themes in his work. Millar's tribute to Raymond Chandler ("He wrote like a slumming angel. . . .") has been widely quoted.

Having a bibliography put together is in some ways like being psychoanalyzed. Forgotten days of your life are rediscovered. But where the effect of a successful analysis is to revalue and in a sense revoke the past, a successful bibliography puts it permanently into the record. . . .

To be confronted all at once with the record of nearly everything that one has ever written can be a sobering experience. A bibliography is to an old writer what a rap sheet is to a three-time loser.

Is it possible that this man can be rehabilitated? the internal prosecutor says to the imaginary judge. Just look at his record, your honor. He committed his first public crime when he was fifteen, and he has been helplessly repeating it for nearly forty years. The only way to protect society from this incorrigible malefactor is to lock him up and throw away the key.

One is moved to explanation and apology. I was born with a fatal predisposition to words. Both my father and my grandfather were journalists, and there were writers on my mother's side of the family. My Uncle Rob, with whom I lived for a while after my parents were separated, used to tell me animal stories every weekday, and on Saturdays he took me to the movies to see such serials as Pearl White's "Plunder." The terrors with which the episodes ended, the satisfactions with which they began, left a permanent impression on my nerves. My own life, as I moved from home to home and relative to relative, seemed as episodic and unpredictable as a movie serial, or the *Black Mask* fiction I read in my teens.

I began to write verse and fiction before I reached my teens. When I was twelve, resident in a boys' school in Winnipeg, I filled the empty hours when the gym was closed writing a sheaf of western stories and a long narrative poem about Bonnie Prince Charlie. I think I was searching for a tradition that would relate to my life and the place. My grandfather came from Scotland; Prince Charlie and the Stuarts were its lost kings. The Canadian west, a remote province of Great Britain which is only now being staked out by native imaginations, seemed infinitely cold and empty in those winters.

The crash of 1929 propelled me out of the school in Winnipeg, where my father's sister had

Introduction

The process of having a bibliography put together is in some ways like being psychoanalyzed. Forgotten facts of your life are retrieved. But where the effect of a successful analysis is to revolve and in a sense revoke the past, a successful bibliography puts it permanently into the record. A psychoanalyst may hazard an educated guess that once upon a time his subject entertained a certain fantasy; Dr. Bruccoli is in a position to prove it.

To be confronted all at once with the record of nearly everything that one has ever written can be a sobering experience. A bibliography is to an old being writer what a rap sheet is to a three-time loser.

Is it possible that this man can be rehabilitated? the virtuous prosecutor says to the imaginary judge. Just look at his record, your honor. He committed his first public crime when he was fifteen, and he has been helplessly repeating it for nearly forty years. The only way to protect society from this incorrigible malefactor is to lock him up and throw away the key.

One is moved to explanation and apology. I was born with a fatal predisposition to words. Both my father and my grandfather were journalists, as were some others on my mother's side of the family. My Uncle Rob, with whom I lived for a while after my parents separated, used to tell me serial stories every weekday, and on Saturdays he took me to the movies to see Pearl White's "Plunder." The terror with which the episodes ended, the satisfaction with which they began, left a permanent impression on my nerves. My own life, as I moved from home to home and relative to relative, seemed as episodic and unpredictable as a movie serial, or the Black Mask fiction I read in my teens.

I began to write mass and fiction before I reached my teens. When I was twelve, a resident in a boys' school in Winnipeg, I filled the

been paying my tuition. After a year with my mother's sister, Laura, in Medicine Hat, Alberta, I went back to the family's original home in Ontario, and lived with my mother in her mother's house until I finished high school. The year I graduated, 1932, I counted the rooms I had lived in during my first sixteen years, and got a total of fifty. Novelists are made, if they are made at all, out of uncertain beginnings and long delayed completions, like their books.

Canada was alive with lyric poets at that time, but had few novelists. Its dominant prose writer was Stephen Leacock, acknowledged as the founder of modern North American humor by Robert Benchley and Scott Fitzgerald. I was reading Dashiell Hammett and Dostoevsky, but my first published story was a parody of Conan Doyle written under the obvious influence of Leacock.

My wife Margaret Millar keeps in a special box a copy of the Kitchener Collegiate Institute *Grumbler* in which this first story appeared. Her own first story, about a dying pianist in Spain, is in it, too. Elsewhere in that old school magazine, dog-eared after nearly forty years, we can find more direct images of our adolescent lives. Margaret and I are there with the other members of the high school debating team, gazing confidently out of the picture on the page into eight more years of depression and six of war.

About six years later, in another city, I walked into the public library and found Margaret reading Thucydides in Greek. From then on, we saw each other nearly every day. I was just back from Europe, determined to become a writer. Margaret confessed she had the same ambition. We were married in June, 1938, the day after I graduated from college, and honeymooned at summer school in Ann Arbor. In the fall we went on to the University of Toronto, where I prepared to become a high school teacher.

The following spring I became at the same time the father of a daughter and a professional writing for money. My main market was the Toronto political and literary weekly, *Saturday Night*. I lightly bombarded the editor, B. K. Sandwell, with verses and humorous sketches, and my first few realistic stories. *Saturday Night* came out on Saturday morning, and we used to walk up Bloor Street to see if anything of mine had been printed

that week. Payment was just a cent a word, but the early joys of authorship were almost as sweet as sex. I felt as if Toronto, that unknown city of stone, had opened an eye and looked at me, then relapsed into her dream of commerce.

We had a very Canadian eagerness to make something of ourselves. While I taught in our old high school in the winter, and studied at Ann Arbor in the summer, Margaret began to write mystery novels. Her books were humorous at first, then veered through the Gothic mode toward tragedy. Their success enabled me to leave high school teaching after two years and accept a full-time fellowship at the University of Michigan. Margaret's work was enabling to me in another way. By going on ahead and breaking trail, she helped to make it possible for me to become a novelist, as perhaps her life with me had helped to make it possible for her.

My first novel was written in Ann Arbor in the fall of 1943. I worked on it at night in one of the offices of the main classroom building, and the book preserves some of the atmosphere of that empty echoing pile. Part of the terror that permeates the book was my own terror, I think, at the act of committing myself to a long piece of writing. It also reflects less immediate experiences. In the winter of 1936-37 I had dropped out of school and gone to Europe, where I spent two months in Nazi Germany. More recently, I had been turned down on physical grounds for a commission in the United States Naval Reserve. Later the Navy relaxed its standards and by the time *The Dark Tunnel* was published, I was in Officers Candidate School at Princeton. My second book was written a year or so later aboard an escort carrier in the Pacific. Then I came home to California, where Margaret and our daughter now lived, and between March 1946 and the end of that year, in a kind of angry rapture, wrote *Blue City* and *The Three Roads*.

The first was about the underlife of an imaginary American city, abstracted from the several cities the war had taken me to. *The Three Roads* was my first California novel, written when I had spent no more than a few days on leave in Los Angeles. But I had met writers there–Joe Pagano, Elliot Paul, John Collier–and they gave me the feel of that extraordinary city. It seemed like the capital of an unknown civilization, barely remembered, or dimly foreseen.

One of the two main characters in *The Three Roads*, Paula West, begins a railroad journey from San Diego to Los Angeles as follows:

> The shining metal streamliner standing beside the station added the final touch to her allegory. It was the impossible future superimposed upon the ugly present in the presence of the regretted past. There was no continuity between the tenses, she thought. You passed from one to the other as a ghost passed through a wall, at the risk of your own reality. The spotless interior of this streamlined future was crowded with unreal passengers waiting to be transported, appropriately enough, to Los Angeles.

Such a moderately ambitious passage as this brings up the question of why I chose to write crime fiction instead of straight fiction. I had less choice than the reader may suppose. My one attempt to write a regular autobiographical novel about my unhappy childhood turned out so badly that I never showed it to my publisher. I left the manuscript, I think, in an abandoned blacking factory. The deadly game of social Snakes and Ladders which occupied much of my youth had to be dealt with in another form, more impersonal and objective.

* * * * *

In my opinion, the distinctive qualities of The Ivory Grin, *and the valuable elements in the convention from which it derives, are vividness and honesty of characterization, the close technical interaction of "narrative" or "drama," and plot; the amount of life packed into it; the chance at tragic passion. The physical violence which has become the hallmark of the "hardboiled school" has tended to kill it off with literate readers, and* Grin *was written in rather explicit reaction to this excess, the idea being to increase the psychological, social, moral range of the form while retaining the virtues noted above.*

From a letter to David Herrmann, 20 September 1951.

* * * * *

I had other reasons for writing detective stories. The work of Hammett and Chandler and their fellow-writers seemed to constitute a popular and democratic literature such as Frank Norris had called for in "The Responsibilities of the Novelist." Their heroes seemed to continue in highly complicated urban environments the masculine and egalitarian frontier traditions of Natty Bumppo and his nineteenth-century descendants. Their abrupt and striking scenes seemed to reflect the disjunctions of an atomized society. Their style, terse and highly figured, seemed not quite to have reached the end of its development.

Certainly the world they wrote about had not. The rush of change which the war had started continued and accelerated afterwards, particularly in the empty spaces of California. It seemed that a brave new world was being born here, on the last frontier, and people migrated to it as we had from all over the continent. I wrote about the far side of the brave new world, in a series of hardboiled detective stories which began in 1949 with *The Moving Target*.

"Hardboiled" is rather a misnomer for this kind of story. Its distinctive ingredient is a style which tries to catch the rhythms and some of the words of the spoken language. While the essential features of its plot are a crime and a solution, there is room in the form for complexities of meaning which can match those of the traditional novel. It is a form which lends itself to the depiction, at the same time energetic and disenchanted, of the open society which California in the years just after the war was struggling to become.

I needed time, and deeper personal knowledge of that society, before I could make it entirely my own in fiction, or make the California detective novel my own. Raymond Chandler was and remains a hard man to follow. He wrote like a slumming angel, and invested the sun-blinded streets of Los Angeles with a romantic presence. While trying to preserve the fantastic lights and shadows of the actual Los Angeles, I gradually siphoned off the aura of romance and made room for a completer social realism. My detective Archer is not so much a knight of romance as an observer, a socially mobile man who knows all the levels of Southern California life and takes a peculiar wry pleasure in exploring its secret passages. Archer tends to live through other people, as a novelist lives through his characters.

In the course of the first three Archer novels, I tried to work out my own version of the "hardboiled" style, to develop both imagery and structure in the direction of psychological and symbolic meaning. In the fourth, *The Ivory Grin* (1952), I extended the range of the form beyond California, touching on Boston and Montreal, Chicago and Detroit; and doing a portrait of a gangster family which was unblurred by any romantic admiration. But it took me five more novels, and seven more years, to work out within the limits of this rather difficult craft the kind of story that I was aiming at: a story roughly shaped on my own early life, transformed and simplified into a kind of legend, in *The Galton Case*.

Even here I approached my life from a distance, and crept up on it in disguise as one might track an alien enemy; the details of the book were all invented. But there was personal truth in its broad shape, as I have explained elsewhere. In crossing the border from Canada and making my way in stages to my birthplace in California, I had learned the significance of borders. They make the difference between legitimacy and fraudulence, and we cross them "as a ghost passes through a wall, at the risk of our own reality."

Perhaps *The Galton Case* validated my journey, and made it possible for my mind to look both north to Canada and south to Mexico and Panama, in later books like *The Zebra-Striped Hearse* and *Black Money*. At any rate it thawed my autobiographical embarrassment and started a run of somewhat more personal fiction which has, for better or worse, gone on unabated ever since. Of my twenty-three books, the three I have just named are among my favorites. They have a certain intensity and range.

But one writes on a curve, on the backs of torn-off calendar sheets. A writer in his fifties will not recapture the blaze of youth, or the steadier passion that comes like a second and saner youth in his forties, if he's lucky. But he can lie in wait in his room—it must be at least the hundredth room by now—and keep open his imagination and the bowels of his compassion against the day when another book will haunt him like a ghost rising out of both the past and the future.

* * * * *

BOOK EXCERPT:
Matthew J. Bruccoli, *Ross Macdonald*, pp. 18-19, 22. *This discussion of the loosely applied term* hard-boiled *attempts to identify it as a literary technique that depends more on style than on material.*

Millar properly insisted that the hard-boiled technique is more the result of style or language than of material or action. "The mystery writer pretends, you know, to be writing hard-boiled, realistic material, almost something that has been written down verbatim out of somebody's mouth, and yet if you take a close look at it, you'll find that much of it is lyrical material; the characters talk a highly charged poetic prose. I think this is true of Hammett, and of Chandler, and of me too. You might call it romanticism of the proletariat."[1] In the hard-boiled novel there is brutality as the hero absorbs or delivers considerable punishment. But the distinctive element is provided by the stylistic response to the material: a matter of tone and point of view.

The earliest *Oxford English Dictionary* citation for *hard-boiled* with the meanings "hardened," "callous," "hard-headed," "shrewd," "of measures, practical" is an 1886 usage by Mark Twain; but the *OED* provides no example of the word as a critical term. A working definition of *hard-boiled literature* is: realistic fiction with some or all of the following characteristics—objective viewpoint, impersonal tone, violent action, colloquial speech, tough characters, and understated style; usually, but not limited to, detective or crime fiction.

The hard-boiled style—more accurately, a combination of styles—was not the innovation of any writer. It was developed by many writers using the American language and the American experience in ways that fused in the late twenties and seemed to provide a voice for the bitter thirties. (Two of the masters of this American style—Chandler and Millar—were raised outside the United States; and Millar claims that his Canadian education sharpened his sense of American speech.) The evolution of the hard-boiled style owes much to Ernest Hemingway, but Hammett was publishing stories in *Black Mask* before Hemingway's work was known in America. Millar has acknowledged that "Hammett and Crane

Millar as a teacher at the Kitchener-Waterloo Collegiate Institute, circa 1940, the school he had attended (Inward Journey, edited by Ralph B. Sipper)

taught me the modern American style based on the speaking voice."[2] When Millar was asked to provide a statement on Hammett in 1972, he wrote: "Hammett was the first American writer to use the detective story for the purposes of a major novelist, to present a vision, blazing if disenchanted, of our lives. As a stylist he ranked among the best of his time, directly behind Hemingway and Fitzgerald. As a novelist of realistic intrigue with deep understated poetic and symbolic overtones, he was unsurpassed in his own or any time."[3] The hard-boiled technique is not limited to the detective genre, but it has received most of its development in crime fiction because the material lends itself to objective and understated treatment. Since the manner is easily imitated, serious writers of hard-boiled detective fiction have had to struggle for proper assessment against a host of hacks.

NOTES: 1. Clifford A. Ridley, "Yes, Most of My Chronicles Are Chronicles of Misfortune," *National Observer*, 31 July 1976, p. 17.

2. Macdonald, "In the First Person," *Self-Portrait*, edited by Ralph B. Sipper (Santa Barbara: Capra, 1981), p. 41.
3. Millar to Ashbel Green, 29 May 1972.

PARODY:

Ken Miller [sic], "The South Sea Soup Co.," *The Grumbler* (1931), pp. 23-25.

Millar's first appearance in print was a burlesque of Sherlock Holmes in the annual of the Kitchener-Waterloo Collegiate and Vocational School when he was fifteen.

The ambitious young investigator, Herlock Sholmes, yawned behind his false moustache and poured for himself a cocaine-and-soda. He then lightly tapped with his knuckles a Burmese wacky-wara, which he had secured from an Oddfellows' Temple in French Indo-China. For it was thus he summoned his obtuse assistant, Sotwun. Sotwun crawled into the room, an idiotic expression on his face.

"I say, Sotwun, I'm sorry to disturb your reading of the 'Ju-Ju Journal' for March 1, 1927."

Sotwun stood awed by Herlock's amazing perspicuity and perspicacity. "How did you know that I was reading that, huh?"

Sholmes smiled and explained:

"Well, there's a minute speck of fresh plaster-of-paris on your nose. The only place there is fresh plaster-of-paris in these rooms is the nose on the bust of Julius Caesar in the next room, which I repaired this morning. Therefore your nose must have touched the nose of the bust. As I have often noticed your resemblance to a monkey, physically and mentally, Sotwun, I thought you must have imitated some picture you saw. The only picture in this house of people touching noses is in the Ju-Ju Journal for March 1, 1927, which I scanned several years ago."

When Sotwun had overcome his astonishment, Sholmes explained the reason for his summons.

"Sotwun, has the South Sea Soup Company yet accepted my application for the position as head of their detective force, whose business is to discover oysters in their oyster soup? No? How strange!

Just then Herlock sneezed,

"Aha!" said he, "the 'phone!"

Dust jacket for Millar's first book, a 1944 spy novel written while he was a graduate student at the University of Michigan

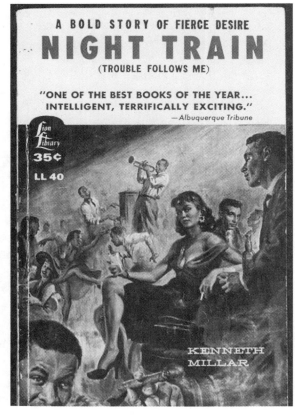

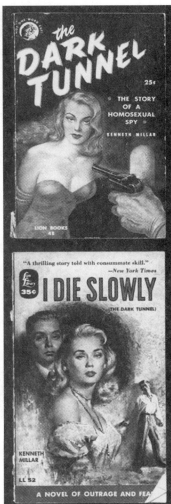

The paperback editions for the early Millar novels attempted to make his work more commercial by changing the titles and providing lurid art.

Instead of ringing, his telephone had been made to loose a quantity of gas when-ever there was a call. This gas had the peculiar property of causing one to sneeze. Thus Sholmes could be informed of the call without any undesirable noise.

He lifted the receiver. Immediately he recognized the voice of a man sixty-three years of age, wearing a brown suit and other clothes, who had been married eighteen times.

The strained voice said, "Mr. Sholmes? Oh! Come quickly to the office of the South Sea Soup Company. Mr. Ox-Tailby has been murdered!"

Nonchalantly flicking an imaginary speck of dust from his eyebrow, Sholmes quickly undressed himself and donned his clothes again, thus changing his appearance from that of a handsome, thoughtful, young man to that of a good-looking, pensive youth. He then bounded out of the room and down the stairs, eight at a time, tying his shoelace and lighting his opium-pipe on the way.

He then hailed a passing cab and rode his bicycle, with Sotwun running behind, to the office of the South Sea Soup Company.

With a burst of speed he burst into the room, bursting his vest-buttons.

There on the floor lay the corpse of Oswald Ox-Tailby, the gravel commissioner in the company's barley department, a bullet-wound in its chest. The body, to the experienced eye of Herlock Sholmes, was evidently quite dead.

Sholmes thought steadily for a full second. Then,—"Aha! Sotwun, go and ask Raring Riley, my Limehouse man, to look up Jamaica Jo."

For seventeen minutes and forty-five seconds the occupants of the room, friends and colleagues of the murdered man, stared at Herlock's thoughtful brow. Then Sotwun came into the room with somebody behind him.

Nonchalantly flicking an imaginary speck of dust from his necklace, Sholmes said, "Allow me, gentlemen, to introduce to you Miss Josephine Bartley, commonly appellated Jamaica Jo."

It was a woman!

"Miss Bartley," said Sholmes, "has anyone ever said you were beautiful?"

The woman blushed. "Why, yes, sir. My sweetheart has often said so."

With a cry of triumph, our hero grasped her by the arm. "Tell me where he lives," he thundered.

The woman gave him the street and number and he drove his bicycle madly to the designated dwelling. He ran to the door, struck it violently, and deftly handcuffed the man that answered.

Before giving him time to speak Sholmes flung him across the handle bars of his bicycle and, drawing on his vast resources of Herculean strength, pedalled back to the office.

"Here is your man!" he said, nonchalantly flicking an imaginary speck of dust from his moccasins, which he had secured while hunting colleoptera in the Antarctic.

Everyone shouted, "Huh?"

"I suppose you wish me to explain," said the detective, as he took out his grammar-book to continue his study of the Lithuanian tongue.

Assent was evidenced.

Sholmes began: "The first thing that struck me when I entered this room (besides that dictionary yonder) was that the corpse had a bullet-wound in it. This reminded me of the famous Ugga-Wulla case which you all must remember. In that case the murdered man also had a bullet-wound in him. The similarity of the two crimes is astonishing, as I have just shown you, and consequently I deducted that the same criminal committed them both. I had already solved this Ugga-Wulla mystery, though I forgot to denounce the murderer to the police. The murderer was Black Bleerstone.

"My Limehouse man, Raring Riley, had told me a month before that Black Bleerstone was the lover of this woman, Jamaica Jo. Black Bleerstone, having once used a pair of spectacles from Woolworth's, has very poor eyesight. To confirm the message that Bleerstone was her lover, I asked Jo if anyone had ever called her beautiful. She said that her lover had, and, as only a man with poor eyesight would call her beautiful, her lover is a man with poor eyesight. That man there is her lover, and he has, as you perceive by his powerful spectacles, poor eyesight. And Bleerstone has poor eyesight! The coincidence is too great, and the man that killed Oswald Ox-Tailby stands before you in the person of Black Bleerstone, Jamaica Jo's lover."

Then forth from the circle of onlookers strode Peter P. Soup, the superintendent of horse-flesh cutting in the chicken-soup department, and said, "Herlock Sholmes, I cannot let an innocent man go to the scaffold. I am the man who killed Oswald Ox-Tailby, for he made the vile insinuation that I did not put any veal in our last week's output of chicken-soup. But I did! Lots of it! Didn't I, my friends?" and he turned a pleading face to his former co-workers.

"No, you didn't. Only horse-flesh," said they. On these fateful words Sholmes, nonchalantly flicking an imaginary speck of dust from his boxing gloves, which he had secured in Hindustan during the Boxer Rebellion, threw himself at Peter P. Soup, self-confessed murderer.

But Soup, with one blow of his mighty fist, strengthened by years of pounding horse meat to make it as tough as ordinary spring chicken, knocked Herlock through the open window.

Sholmes alighted unhurt on the grass below.

Nonchalantly flicking several thousand real specks of dust from his face, Sholmes ran back into the office just in time to see Peter P. Soup place a little white pellet in his mouth. Sholmes tried to take it from him, but he was too late, for the mint from a slot-machine had been swallowed. In a few seconds it began to do its deadly work. Soup fell to the floor, his limbs slowly stiffening. With his last breath he sang that fine old song so reminiscent of slot-machine mints in general, "Rock of Ages."

After these evidences of his detective abilities, Sholmes was accepted as the head detective of the South Sea Soup Company's detective force.

But he never succeeded in finding an oyster in the oyster-soup, although he found several oyster-shell buttons.

* * * * *

Both Margaret and I were writing mysteries at this time. [W. H. Auden] was most encouraging to us. That kind of push is unbelievably important to a young writer. Auden was the greatest poet in the English speaking world at that time. It gave us a shove in the direction in which we were going anyway. It just couldn't have been equaled in any other way. It marked a point in my life where I chose to become a fiction writer rather than a man who writes about other people's writings as a scholar; that's where I was headed. I would have done both, actually, but this straightened me out and put me on the creative path.

"Ross Macdonald Interview" [excerpt], *Mystery* (November/December 1979)

* * * * *

BOOK EXCERPT:
Matthew J. Bruccoli, *Ross Macdonald*, pp. 30-32.

Millar's series hero Lew Archer was introduced in The Moving Target *(1949), his fifth novel and the first to appear under the John Macdonald by-line. As Archer's character developed in subsequent novels, the connections between author and hero became more personal.*

In *The Moving Target*, Lew Archer is a Los Angeles private detective who operates a one-man agency. He is thirty-five years old and separated from his wife, who dislikes his work. Formerly a member of the Long Beach Police Force, he had been fired for his opposition to municipal corruption. Archer is intelligent, courageous, and good with his fists. He absorbs beatings and administers them; Archer vows to get one of his assailants and drowns him. If Millar had a model for Archer, it was Chandler's Philip Marlowe rather than Hammett's Sam Spade (who appears in one novel, *The Maltese Falcon*). Like Marlowe, Archer is a knight-errant, a free lance with a highly developed system of morality; but he is less romantic than Marlowe and, at the same time, more introspective in this first appearance.

> I used to think the world was divided into good people and bad people, that you could pin responsibility for evil on certain definite people and punish the guilty. I'm still going through the motions. . . . When I went into police work in 1935, I believed that evil was a quality some were born with, like a harelip. A cop's job was to find those people and put them away. But evil isn't so simple. Everybody has it in him, and whether it comes out in his actions depends on a number of things. Environment, opportunity, economic pressure, a piece of bad luck, a wrong friend. The trouble is a cop has to go on judging people by rule of thumb, and acting on that judgment.[1]

Marlowe doesn't find it necessary to explain his code of conduct. He does what he does for himself. But if the early Archer is righteous, he isn't self-righteous.

An unusually well-read man, Millar has acknowledged the influence of the Icelandic saga of Grettir the Strong, a tenth-century outlaw-hero, on his detective: "The hard-boiled detective story is, literally, epic in intention. These are sagas in which the idealized figure of the hero–Spade, Marlowe, Archer if you will–proceeds along a chain of events, a sequence of narratives, that ranges through a whole society and, hopefully, expresses it."[2] The name Archer is also borne by Spade's partner, Miles Archer, but Millar has said that the tribute was unconscious. (Millar was a Sagittarius.) Lew came from Lew Wallace, the author of *Ben-Hur*, because Millar liked the sound of it. The aspirational connotations of the name Archer are appropriate for Millar's detective, who is introduced in a novel titled *The Moving Target*.

Lew Archer provides what Millar has described as a welder's mask or a protective shield between author and material that is too hot to handle. Archer not only tells the story; his investigations cause things to happen and extend the web of causality. But he is not the hero; the novels are not about Archer. "He is less a doer than a questioner, a consciousness in which the meanings of other lives emerge. This gradually developed conception of the detective hero as the mind of the novel is not wholly new, but it is probably my main contribution to this special branch of fiction."[3] Millar had been impressed by "the talking voice" in Cain's *The Postman Always Rings Twice* (1934): "You can say almost anything about almost anything with a tone like that, I realized."[4]

Millar has remarked that "I wasn't Archer, exactly, but Archer was me."[5] His treatment of Archer's point of view allows both identification and separation: "I can think of few more complex critical enterprises than disentangling the mind and life of a first-person detective story writer from the mask of his detective narrator."[6] Archer is the voice of the author, but he is also the distancing character Millar has created. Millar might well have said that he wasn't Macdonald, exactly, but Macdonald was Millar. The pseudonym provided another layer of insulation between writer and material. If Macdonald is a persona for Millar, then there is a double-play combination: Millar to Macdonald to

Lieutenant (j.g.) Kenneth Millar. During World War II he served as a communications officer on the escort carrier Shipley Bay (Inward Journey, *edited by Ralph B. Sipper)*

Archer. This idea is intriguing, but it is necessary to remember that *The Moving Target* was originally intended for publication under Kenneth Millar's name. Nonetheless, the Macdonald mask became an increasingly comfortable fit: "Archer, over the years, has become more myself, as I have become more myself. It took a good many years for me to get into my own background and see it and reflect it."[7]

Notes:

1. John Macdonald, *The Morning Target* (New York: Knopf, 1949), p. 109.
2. Raymond F. Jones, "A New Raymond Chandler?," *Los Angeles Magazine*, March 1963, p. 58.
3. Ross Macdonald, "The Writer as Detective Hero," *Show*, January 1965, pp. 34-36. Also in Macdonald, *Self-Portrait*, p. 121.
4. Robert Easton to MJB, 22 September 1982.

5. Macdonald, "The Writer as Detective Hero," in *Self-Portrait*, p. 113.
6. Macdonald, "Down These Streets a Mean Man Must Go," in *Self-Portrait*, p. 7.
7. Ed Wilcox, "The Secret Success of Kenneth Millar," *New York Sunday News*, 21 November 1971, p. 159.

LETTER:

Raymond Chandler to James Sandoe, 14 April 1949, *Selected Letters of Raymond Chandler*, edited by Frank MacShane, pp. 163-164.

Chandler's reaction to the first Lew Archer novel, expressed in a letter to mystery-fiction critic Sandoe, was unfavorable. Although Chandler recognized its skill, he objected to Macdonald's stylistic self-consciousness.

6005 Camino de la Costa
La Jolla, California
April 14th. 1949

Dear Sandoe:

Have read *The Moving Target* by John Macdonald and am a good deal impressed by it, in a peculiar way. In fact I could use it as a springboard for a sermon on How Not to be a Sophisticated Writer. What you say about pastiche is of course quite true, and the materials of the plot situations are borrowed here and there. E.g. the opening set up is lifted more or less from *The Big Sleep*, mother paralyzed instead of father, money from oil, atmosphere of corrupted wealth, and the lawyer-friend villain is lifted straight out of *The Thin Man*; but I personally am a bit Elizabethan about such things, do not think they greatly matter, since all writers must imitate to begin with, and if you attempt to cast yourself in some accepted mould, it is natural to go to the examples that have attained some notice or success.

What strikes me about the book (and I guess I should not be writing about it if I didn't feel that the author had something) is first an effect that is rather repellent. There is nothing to hitch to; here is a man who wants the public for the mystery story in its primitive violence and also wants it to be clear that he, individually, is a highly literate and sophisticated character. A car is "acned with rust" not spotted. Scribblings on toilet walls are "graffiti" (we know Italian yet, it says); one refers to "podex osculation" (medical Latin too, ain't we hell?). "The seconds piled up precariously like a

tower of poker chips," etc. The simile that does not quite come off because it doesn't understand what the purpose of the simile is.

The scenes are well handled, there is a lot of experience of some kind behind this writing, and I should not be surprised to find the name was a pseudonym for a novelist of some performance in another field. The thing that interests me is whether this pretentiousness in the phrasing and choice of words makes for better writing. It does not. You could only justify it if the story itself were devised on the same level of sophistication, and you wouldn't sell a thousand copies, if it was. When you say, "spotted with rust," (or pitted, and I'd almost but not quite go for "pimpled") you convey at once a simple visual image. But when you say, "acned with rust" the attention of the reader is instantly jerked away from the thing described to the pose of the writer. This is of course a very simple example of the stylistic misuse of language, and I think that certain writers are under a compulsion to write in recherché phrases as a compensation for a lack of some kind of natural animal emotion. They feel nothing, they are literary eunuchs, and therefore they fall back on an oblique terminology to prove their distinction. It is the sort of mind that keeps avant garde magazines alive, and it is quite interesting to see an attempt to apply it to the purposes of this kind of story.

R. C.

* * * * *

Every time Chandler would have a new book published, I'd dash down to the lending library–I couldn't afford to buy books at that time–and read right through it the first night. I just can't overestimate the extent he influenced me at the time, turning me in the direction I took at that time as a writer.

"Ross Macdonald Interview" [excerpt], *Mystery* (November/December 1979)

* * * * *

LETTER:

To Alfred A. Knopf, 1952, *Inward Journey*, edited by Ralph B. Sipper, pp. 37-42.

This letter to his publisher was written when Millar's career seemed to be stalled. At that time the paperback

Dust jacket for the first Lew Archer novel and the first John Macdonald novel, published in 1949

rights to his novels were an important consideration for Knopf, and Pocket Books complained that the Lew Archer novels weren't close imitations of Raymond Chandler.

Your letter is a hard one to answer. I'll do my best to answer it as well and candidly as I can, even though that will probably require me to discuss myself and my work in what may seem to be an immodest fashion. First of all, I agree with everything that Pocket Books says, except that I seriously doubt the competence of any expert to revise the book for the better. I don't mean that it can't be improved, or that I'm not open to editorial suggestions for rewriting. I am. But I question the point of view from which Pocket Books would like to see the book revised, and I question it on a number of grounds. Their assumption seems to be that my work in general, and this book in particular, is an imitation of Chandler which fails for some reason to come off. Granting that I owe a lot to Chandler, and to Hammett, I have never been a slavish disciple of either. Though I lack Hammett's genius and the intensity which Chandler sustained in his first four novels, I am not wasting my time trying to be one or the other. I am interested in doing things which neither of them was able or willing to do. Let us say that Hammett's subject was the conflict of powerful amoral forces in a money society. (You see, I take Hammett seriously. I think he is a better and more original writer than Steinbeck, for example, and will last

longer.) Let us say that Chandler's subject is the evilness of evil, and his highest achievement, the vivid scene of conflict between (conventional) evil and (what he takes to be) good. His unit is the scene, and his overall plots are generally helter-skelter and based on the tired device of blackmail. For that and other reasons, I can't possibly accept Pocket Books' notion that Chandler is the last word in the mystery or that I differ from him only to err. With all due respect for his power, which I am willing to admit I do not match, but which I also insist I do not try to duplicate, I can't accept Chandler's vision of good and evil. It seems to me that it is conventional to the point of old-maidishness, that it is anti-human to the point of sadism (Chandler hates all women, and really likes only old men, boys, and his Marlowe *persona*), and that the mind behind it, for all its tremendous imaginative force, is both uncultivated and second-rate. Since my own mind is neither, it would be simple self-stultification for me to take Chandler as my model and arbiter. His fifth novel is his own self-parody and criticism, clearly displaying the inherent corruption of his view.

My subject is human error. My interest is the exploration of lives. As Pocket Books points out, my stories lack a powerful contrast between good and evil, because I don't see things that way. I did, partly, when I wrote *Blue City;* it was about a town where I had suffered, and several of the characters were based on people I hated. But even the murderers in the last five books have seemed

Paul Newman starred in the 1966 movie version of The Moving Target. *The title was presumably changed to* Harper *because of the actor's lucky-H superstition.*

more human than "bad" to me. I would rather understand them than condemn them. I would rather display them in characteristic postures and sum up their lives and the reasons for their lives than cause a self-righteous hero to denounce them or push them around for the sake of action. Because my theme is exploitation rather than conflict, my fables lack punch. But it would spoil them in my eyes to superadd punch. My whole structure is set up to throw insight into lives, not undramatically I hope; its background is psychological and sociological rather than theological. I suppose you could ask whether I should be writing mysteries at all. The answer is that I have been writing mysteries which are good in the opinion of the critics and my colleagues, not so good as Chandler's perhaps and certainly not so popular, but my own. I have been using the form for my own purposes, as any good writer has to use his form. My hope has been to write "popular" novels which would not be inferior to "serious" novels. As I said, I have barely started.

I chose the "hardboiled" form in the first

place because it offered both a market and a convention or structure with which almost anything could be done, a technique both difficult and free, and adapted to the subject matter I am interested in. But I have been doing my best to improve the form, and to write real novels in it. I'm not exactly a money writer, and think I discern in myself the potentiality of first-rate work, and because I take the mystery seriously as a form of the novel, I couldn't very well let Pocket Books tell me what to write or how to write it. Though I admire their incomes, I have no respect for most of the mystery writers they reprint. Furthermore I have a notion that in spite of the Spillane phenomenon which hasn't much to do with the mystery as such but which probably has a lot to do with paperback publishers' notions of what a good mystery should be– the future of the mystery is in the hands of a few good writers. The old-line hardboiled mystery, with many guns and fists and fornications, has been ruined by its own practitioners, including Chandler. Spillane pulled the plug. I refuse to fol-

Publisher Alfred A. Knopf with the Millars in Santa Barbara (photo by Hal Boucher)

low it down the drain, because I'm thoroughly convinced that I'm writing something better. That is what my taste and judgment tell me. I can't afford to abdicate them. If I did, I would have to give up my serious literary and novelistic intentions and write for the slick magazines. I've only tried to write one slick story. It sold. I used the $3500 to finance my doctorate.

If I puzzle Pocket Books, Pocket Books also puzzles me when they seem to take it for granted that the new book is a hardboiled mystery, or my idea of a hardboiled mystery. It isn't. Of course it is a variation or offspring of the hardboiled form, but what distinguishes it from the run-of-the-mill hardboiled mystery is the very tone (which I've tried to make literate, humane and, let us face it, adult) to which they object. I can write an ordinary hardboiled mystery with all sorts of shenanigans and gunplay with my eyes closed. I've spent several years developing a form of my own. To

jazz it up would be unfortunate, according to my lights, and I seriously doubt if that would make it more saleable. If I can trust my own ear as representative–and I always have trusted my own ear–the public ear may be getting tired of jazzy effects. I expect an audience for my attempt to combine the "popular" and the "sensitive" hero, and to forge a style which combines literacy and flexibility with the virtues of the American–colorful–colloquial. Am I optimistic in thinking that the popular audience is growing up?

Now this may seem an exaggerated and swell-headed response to a perfectly just criticism. Compared with Chandler, my book is lacking in some of the more obvious forms of excitement. My murders are few and offstage. There are no gangsters. My main villains are a pathetic old psychoneurotic and a trapped housewife. My heroine gets upset and makes mistakes. My hero is sexually diffident, ill-paid, and not very sure of himself. Compared

The identity of John Ross Macdonald was revealed on the dust jacket for Find a Victim *(1954). The X-ray had been used on the* Meet Me at the Morgue *(1953) jacket.*

with Chandler's brilliant phantasmagoria this world is pale, I agree. But what is the point of comparison? This is not a Chandler book. The characters are less remarkable but more lifelike, for example, and the reader gets to know them better. None of my scenes have ever been written before, and some of them have real depth and moral excitement. I venture to say that none of my characters are familiar; they are freshly conceived from a point of view that rejects black and white classification. There is none, or a good deal less, of the Chandler phoniness. The plot makes sense, and could actually have happened. I could go on for pages. I already have.

I repeat, though, that I know the book is improvable. Any book is, at least any book of mine. If anyone has any ideas about how to give it more speed or power or vividness, without sacrificing the values it already has for me, I'll be glad to go to work on them. My sole objection is to the idea that it is a hardboiled story which misses fire. I'll see if I can write a jacket description as you suggest. And of course I'll have all these things in mind as I write the new book coming up. My main intention in this letter has been to assure you that I know what I'm doing and fully expect to be going strong twenty books from now. I couldn't possibly feel that way if I placed my standards outside my own judgment. But on the other hand I'm eager to make a living. Between Spillane and Charybdis is where I am.

What is Pocket Books so worried about? Lee Wright herself (along with various other connoisseurs) named *Moving Target* as the best American non-Simon and Schuster mystery of its year. With the exception of *Drowning Pool*, my books since *Target* have been getting better. Any mystery writer can be made to look bad by comparing him with Chandler, *from Chandler's point of view.* After all Chandler is universally recognized as the American master of the mystery story, along with Hammett (though I think the latter is far and away the more important writer). I'd prefer to be compared with the current crop. And please give me a little more time. Chandler had been writing for at least fifteen years before I ever thought of writing a mystery, and I turned professional just six years ago. My peak is still coming, and I've yet to find the form that suits my talent. I only know it isn't behind me.

Still, I'm willing to bet that Pocket Books will have to order a second printing of *The Way Some People Die*. In spite of its dismal record in hard cover, I'm convinced that it can be sold in paper. If it fails, I'll be in a mood to write you a *Dark Blue City. Blue City*, by the way, took exactly two months and I wrote two other books the same year.

I have no objections to *The Convenient Corpse* as a title, though it doesn't exactly jar me all the way down to my heels. It's a nice neat ordinary title. By all means use it, though I don't quite catch its relevance to the book; that doesn't matter. What do you think of *The Sinister Habit*? It's a phrase from Cocteau, the reference being to "the sinister habit of asking questions."

Well, I've written more than I intended to, let my hair down in fact. I hope I haven't labored *my* point of view. If I turn out to be Athanasius against the world, I'll rewrite places where the story drags or characters fade out. Show me the places. I certainly don't think the whole book needs rewriting. It's already had a lot of it. Don't you think it's a good well-paced story as it stands, and that perhaps a main difficulty comes from pigeon-holing it as a hardboiled item? While no one would mistake it for a *major opus*, I must confess I was pleased with the characterization–the characters seemed more human than in anything I've done, closer to life–and more than pleased with the plot. The trouble with a highly organized plot, such as I have a predilection for, is that it determines and controls the movement of the story. I know I have a tendency to underplay the individual scenes, to make the book the unit of effect. Chandler practices, and has stated, the opposite theory: that a good plot is one that makes good scenes. I don't wish to give the impression that he's my *bête noire*. Hell, he's one of my masters. But I can see around him, and am in growing disagreement with much of his theory and practice. That is why the present book, which is more different from Chandler and more like myself than any of the other Macdonald books, is important to me, and why I have set out my ideas about Chandler at such length. As I see it, my hope of real success as a writer, both artistic and commercial, resides in developing my own point of view and craft and technique to the limit. Chandler had something to say or tell, and said it powerfully. I have something different to say, about similar subjects and the same society. The satisfaction of saying it and the hope of saying it better are more important to me than my status as a commercial artist would seem to warrant. But if I overvalue my work, that is the defect of the virtue of believing in what I am doing. My peculiar ability to take the mystery as a serious form is half my strength as a mystery writer. I only wish *The Convenient Corpse* were a better example of what I am talking about. Now it's up to me to write one.

I'd rather do that than rewrite the book that I have just finished writing and rewriting. My standards are high even though they may be mistaken, and I never let a book out of my hands until I've given it everything that I happen at the moment to have. One of my obvious problems, though, is doing a first-rate job on a book which will ultimately bring me about three thousand dollars, which is scarcely enough to live on for six

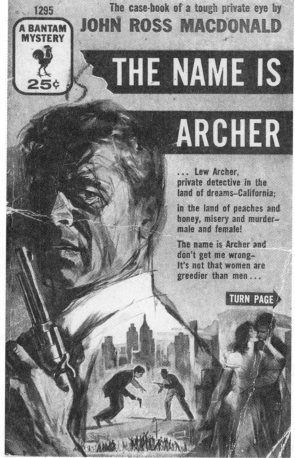

Front cover for the first collection of Macdonald's short stories, a paperback original published in 1955

months. *If* Pocket Books decides to take it–is that the question at stake? I realize, of course, that your and Pocket Books' intention is to find ways and means of improving sales and incidentally my income. In the light of that, I hope my counter assertion doesn't sound churlish. I suppose I was a little startled by the suggestion that experts might sharpen my book up for me. If any rewriting has to be done, I feel I must do it myself. Revision by persons other than the writer might possibly work for a book, but it cannot work for a writer. That is why Hollywood writers lose their morals so quickly and their writing ability eventually, and why movies in general are so bad. A writer has to defend his feeling of free and joyful creation, illusory as it may be, and his sense that what he is writing is his own work.

COMMENTS ON WRITING:

Herbert Harker's notes on conversations with Millar, Harker to Matthew J. Bruccoli, 24 October 1982.

Millar taught writing courses in the Adult Education Division of Santa Barbara City College during the 1950s. He encouraged Harker, one of his students, to write a first novel, Goldenrod *(published in 1972). Harker made a record of Millar's obiter dicta.*

A story should be a circle.

Causality. Everything is connected.

Keep it a secret, like a gestation.

Writing is essentially a private task, and for it to flourish, it must remain that way.

The story is not the string, and it is not the knot. It is the undoing of the knot.

When I find myself with an unsolvable problem, I sit and gloat for two days. It is in the working out of these problems, the building up to their solution, that the story comes into being.

The control of ideas is only possible through language. And by practice we learn to use the subconscious so that it feeds into the conscious mind at the proper level. This is true of life as well as literature. Our symbols grow spontaneously, not by taking thought.

We are all caught in the web of language. We cannot change it. All we can do is learn to understand and use it. It is a marvelous trap, of course. But we cannot escape it.

The poet, when he uses a word, is conscious of its complete history—all the places where it has been used before—and uses it with all this in mind, then puts his own spin on it. The prose writer must also be aware of the tradition of his language. The principal word in a paragraph explains that paragraph and provides its context, just as the paragraph provides the context for the word.

I think sometimes writers do better under pressure–stress. Not in the early stages of work. One can't stay in the air that long. But as we work to bring it all together, we need great effort, great concentration, as if we were preparing to pilot a suicide plane. . . . That's quite literally true. We want to consume everything that's *in us* at the time, in one great flash.

[On psychiatric problems] These can be overcome, won back, made productive. That is one of the great things we are engaged in–or should be engaged in–in our lives, the reclaiming of these swamps and deserts which are the result of our earlier experiences.

PREFACE:

Kenneth Millar, "A Preface to *The Galton Case*," *Afterwords*, edited by Thomas McCormack (New York: Harper & Row, 1968), pp. 146-159.

Millar wrote The Galton Case *after a year of psychiatric treatment: "There's no question that my work has deepened since then. Freud was one of the two or three greatest influences on me. He made myth into psychiatry, and I've been trying to turn it back into myth again in my own small way."*

Detective story writers are often asked why we devote our talents to working in a mere popular convention. One answer is that there may be more to our use of the convention than meets the eye. I tried to show in an earlier piece how the literary detective has provided writers since Poe with a disguise, a kind of welder's mask enabling us to handle dangerously hot material.

One night in his fifth year when we were alone in my house, my grandson Jimmie staged a performance which demonstrated the uses of disguise. His main idea seemed to be to express and discharge his guilts and fears, particularly his overriding fear that his absent parents might punish his (imperceptible) moral imperfections by never coming back to him. Perhaps he had overheard and been alarmed by the name of the movie they were attending, *Divorce American Style*.

Jimmie's stage was the raised hearth in the kitchen, his only prop a towel. He climbed up on the hearth and hid himself behind the back of an armchair. "Grandpa, what do you see?"

"Nothing."

He put the towel in view. "What do you see now?"

"Your towel."

The Barbarous Coast (1956) was the first Ross Macdonald novel. The dust-jacket flap explains that the byline has been changed to avoid confusion with John D. MacDonald.

He withdrew the towel. There was a silence. "What am I doing with my towel?"

I guessed that he was doing something "wrong," and that he wanted me to suspend judgment. "You're chewing it," I said boldly.

"No. But I have it in my mouth."

My easy acceptance of his wickedness encouraged him to enact it before my eyes. His head popped up. He was completely hooded with the towel, like a miniature inductee into the Ku Klux Klan.

"I'm a monster," he announced.

Then he threw off the towel, laughing. I sat and watched him for a time while the hooded monster and the laughing boy took alternate possession of the stage. Finally, soothed and purged by his simple but powerful art, Jimmie lay down on the cushioned hearth and went to sleep.

His little show speaks for itself, and needs no Aristotle. But let me point out some connections between his monodrama and my detective fiction. Both draw directly on life and feed back into it. Both are something the artist does for his own sake. But they need an audience to fulfill even their private function, let alone their public ones. Disguise is the imaginative device which permits the work to be both private and public, to half-divulge the writer's crucial secrets while deepening the whole community's sense of its own mysterious life.

I was forty-two when I wrote The Galton Case. It had taken me a dozen years and as many books to learn to tell highly personal stories in terms of the convention I had chosen. In the winter of 1957-1958 I was as ready as I would ever be to cope in fiction with some of the more complicated facts of my experience.

Central among these was the fact that I was born in California, in 1915, and was thus an American citizen; but I was raised in Canada by Canadian relatives. After attending university in Canada, I taught high school there for two years. In 1941, in one of the decisive moves of my life, I came back to the United States with my wife and young daughter, and started work on a doctorate in English at the University of Michigan.

It was a legitimate move, but the crossing of the border failed to dispel my dual citizen's sense of illegitimacy, and probably deepened it. This feeling was somewhat relieved by a couple of years in the American Navy. After the war I closed a physical circle, if not an emotional one, by settling in California, in Santa Barbara. At the same time I took up my lifelong tenancy in the bare muffled room of the professional writer where I am sitting now, with my back to the window, writing longhand in a Spiral notebook.

After ten years this writing routine was broken by circumstances which my later books more than adequately suggest. My wife and I lived in the San Francisco area for a year, and then came

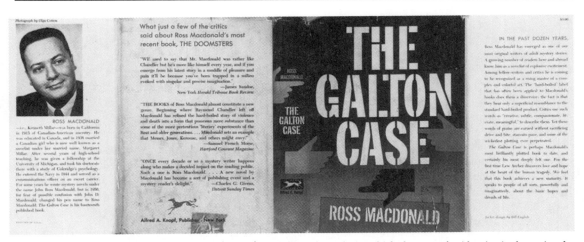

Dust jacket for the 1959 novel regarded as Millar's breakthrough work, in which the quest for identity is the major theme

back to Santa Barbara. We rented a house on a cliff overlooking the sea and lived in it for a winter and a summer.

The Pacific had always lapped like blue eternity at the far edge of my life. The tides of that winter brought in old memories, some of which had drifted for forty years. In 1919, I remembered, my sea-captain father took me on a brief voyage and showed me a shining oceanic world from which I had felt exiled ever since, even during my sea duty in the Navy.

Exile and half-recovery and partial return had been the themes of at least two earlier books, *Blue City* and *The Three Roads* (which got its title from *Oedipus Tryannos*). I wrote them in 1946, the year I left the Navy and came back to California after my long absence. These novels borrowed some strength from my return to my native state but they missed the uniquely personal heart of the matter—matter which I will call Oedipal, in memory of that Theban who was exiled more than once.

In the red Spiral notebook where I set down my first notes for *The Galton Case*, Oedipus made an appropriately early appearance. His ancient name was surrounded by a profusion of ideas and images which I can see in retrospect were sketching out the groundwork for the novel. A crude early description of its protagonist turns up in two lines of verse about a tragicomic track meet:

A burst of speed! Half angel and half ape,
The youthful winner strangles on the tape.

Two lines from another abortive poem—

Birds in the morning, scattered atomies:
The voice is one, the voice is not my own.–

were to supply an important detail to the closing page of the completed novel. The morning birds appear there as reminders of a world which encloses and outlasts the merely human.

A third and final example of these multitudinous early notes is one for an unwritten story– " 'The Fortieth Year' (downgrade reversed by an act of will)"–which recalls my then recent age and condition and suggests another character in the novel, the poet Chad Bolling. This middle-aged San Francisco poet is at the same time an object of parody and my spokesman for the possibilities of California life. Bolling's involvement in the Galton case takes him back to a sea cliff which he had visited as a young man, and he recovers some of a young man's high spirits:

He flapped his arms some more. "I can fly! I breast the windy currents of the sky. I soar like Icarus toward the sun. The wax melts. I fall from a great height into the sea. Mother Thalassa."

"Mother who?"

"Thalassa, the sea, the Homeric sea. We could build another Athens. I used to think we could do it in San Francisco, build a new city of man on the great hills. A city measured with forgiveness. Oh, well."

Not long after this outburst, Bolling sits down to write his best poem in years, as he says.

While I am not a true poet, I am content to have Bolling represent me here. He shows the kite-flying exuberance of a man beginning a lucky piece of work, and speaks unashamedly for the epic impulse which almost all writers of fiction try to service in some degree.

It was a complex business, getting ready to write even this moderately ambitious novel. Dozens of ideas were going through my mind in search of an organizing principle. The central idea which was to magnetize the others and set them in narrative order was a variation on the Oedipus story. It appears in the red notebook briefly and abruptly, without preparation: "Oedipus angry vs. parents for sending him away into a foreign country."

This simplification of the traditional Oedipus stories, Sophoclean or Freudian, provides Oedipus with a conscious reason for turning against his father and suggests that the latter's death was probably not unintended. It rereads the myth through the lens of my own experience, and in this it is characteristic of my plots. Many of them are founded on ideas which question or invert or criticize received ideas and which could, if brevity were my forte, be expressed in aphorisms.

Neither plots nor characters can be borrowed, even from Freud or Sophocles. Like the moving chart of an encephalograph, the plot of a novel follows the curve of the mind's intention. The central character, and many of the other characters, are in varying degrees versions of the author. Flaubert said that he was Madam Bovary, William Styron that he became Nat Turner. The character holding the pen has to wrestle and conspire with the one taking shape on paper, extracting a vision of the self from internal darkness—a self dying into fiction as it comes to birth.

My mind had been haunted for years by an imaginary boy whom I recognized as the darker side of my own remembered boyhood. By his sixteenth year he had lived in fifty houses and committed the sin of poverty in each of them. I couldn't think of him without anger and guilt.

This boy became the central figure of *The Galton Case*. His nature and the nature of his story are suggested by some early titles set down in the red notebook: "A Matter of Identity," "The Castle and the Poorhouse," "The Impostor." He is, to put it briefly and rather inexactly, a false claimant, a poorhouse graduate trying to lie his way into the castle.

"The Castle and the Poorhouse," old-fashioned and melodramatic as the phrase is, accurately reflects the vision of the world which my adult imagination inherited from my childhood. It was a world profoundly divided, between the rich and the poor, the upright and the downcast, the sheep and the goats. We goats knew the moral pain inflicted not so much by poverty as by the doctrine, still current, that poverty is always deserved.

In the first winters of the Depression in Ontario, skilled factory workers were willing to put in a full week on piecework for as little as five dollars. The year I left high school, 1932, I was glad to work on a farm for my board alone. Healthy as that year of farm life was, it was a year of waiting without much hope. I shared with many others the dilemma of finding myself to be at the same time two radically different kinds of people, a pauper and a member of the middle class. The dilemma was deepened by my fear that I'd never make it to college, and by my feeling of exile, which my mother had cultivated by teaching me from early childhood that California was my birthplace and natural home.

Such personal dilemmas tend to solidify along traditional philosophic lines. In a puritanical society the poor and fatherless, suffering the quiet punishments of despair, may see themselves as permanently and justifiably damned for crimes they can't remember having committed.

The Platonic split between more worthy and less worthy substances, idea and matter, spirit and flesh, widens under pressure. The crude pseudo-Darwinian dualism of my own phrase, "half angel and half ape," suggests an image of man not only divided but at war.

The Galton Case was an attempt to mend such gross divisions on the imaginative level. It tried to bring the Monster and the Laughing Boy into unity or congruence at least, and build a bridge, or a tunnel, between the poorhouse and the castle.

. . . to take the psychic event which has occurred in all of us, the guilty loss of togetherness and innocence, and put it back into the external world where it has its repercussions.

From a BBC interview.

The castle is represented by the Galton family's Southern California estate, described as if it was literally a medieval demesne: "The majestic iron gates gave a portcullis effect. A serf who was cutting the lawn with a power-mower paused to tug at his forelock as we went by." The old widow who presides over this estate had quarreled with her son Anthony some twenty years ago, and Anthony had walked out and disappeared. Now Mrs. Galton has begun to dream of a reconciliation with her son. Through her attorney she hires the detective Lew Archer to look for him.

My earliest note on Anthony Galton will give an idea of his place in the story. A very young man and a poet, Anthony deliberately declassed himself in an effort, the note says, "to put together 'the castle and the poorhouse.' He changed his name (to John Brown) and became a workingman . . . Married under his pseudonym, to the common law wife of a man in jail," he was murdered when the other man got out.

About one-third of the way through the novel, the detective Archer is shown an incomplete set of human bones which prove to be Anthony Galton's. At the same time and the same place–not many miles up the coast from the Northern California town where I was born–Archer finds or is found by a boy who represents himself as Anthony's son and calls himself John Brown. The rest of the novel is concerned with this boy and his identity.

Perhaps I have encouraged the reader to identify this boy with me. If so, I must qualify that notion. The connections between a writer and his fiction, which are turning out to be my present subject, are everything but simple. My nature is probably better represented by the whole book than by any one of its characters. At the same time John Brown, Jr.'s life is a version of my early life: the former could not have existed without the latter.

The extent of this symbiosis can be seen in the two false starts I made on the novel, more clearly than in the finished product, where personal concerns were continually reshaped by overriding artistic needs. The most striking fact about these early versions is that they begin the story approximately where the completed novel ends it. Both Version One and Version Two, as I'll call them, are narrated by a boy who recalls aspects of my Canadian boyhood. The other characters including the father and mother are imaginary, as they are in the published novel.

In Version One the narrator's name is Tom. He lives on the poorer side of London, Ontario (where I attended university and in a sense graduated from the "poorhouse" of my childhood). Tom has finished high school but has no prospects. At the moment he is playing semi-pro pool.

He is challenged to a game by an American named Dawson who wears an expensive suit with a red pin-stripe in it. Tom wins easily and sees, when Dawson pays, that his wallet is "thick with money–American money, which always seems a little bit like stage money to me." From the standpoint of a poor Canadian boy, the United States and its riches seem unreal.

Tom has a taste for unreality. He had done some acting in high school, he tells Dawson.

"Did you enjoy acting?"
Did I? It was the only time I ever felt alive, when I could forget myself and the hole I lived in, and turn into an imaginary character. "I liked it, yeah."

Tom is not speaking for me here. I don't like acting. But it is probably not a coincidence that the American, Dawson, is a Ph.D. trained, as I was trained at the University of Toronto, "in the evaluation of intelligence."

Dawson is testing the boy's memory and acting ability and talking vaguely about hiring him, as Version One died in mid-sentence on its thirteenth page. This version suffered from lack of adequate planning, and from the associated difficulty of telling the boy's complicated story in his own simple person. Neither structure nor style was complex enough to let me discover my largely undiscovered purposes.

But immediately I made a second stab at having the boy narrate his own story. His name is

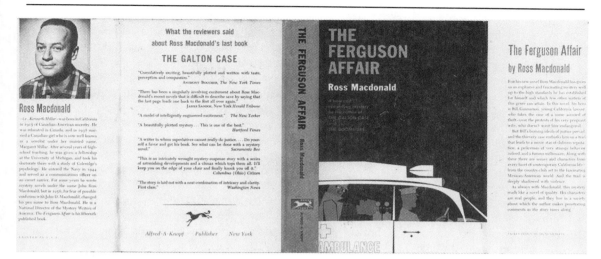

Dust jacket for the 1960 novel in which Lew Archer did not appear

Willie now, and he lives in Toronto, almost as if he was following in my footsteps. He has an appointment with an American, now named Mr. Sablacan, who is waiting for him at the Royal York Hotel.

Willie never gets there. All of Version Two takes place in his home, in the early morning. This rather roughly written six-page scene breaks the ground for my book and introduces some of its underlying themes: the hostility between father and son, for instance, here brought to an extreme pitch:

> *The old man was sitting at the kitchen table when I went down. He looked like a ghost with a two-day beard. The whole room stank of wine, and he was holding a partly empty bottle propped up between his crotch.*
> *. . . I kept one eye on him while I made breakfast.*
> *. . . He wouldn't throw the bottle as long as it had wine in it. After that, you never knew.*

The shades of Huck Finn and his father are pretty well dispelled, I think, when the boy's mother comes down. She approaches her drunken husband "with that silly adoring look on her face, as if he was God Almighty giving her a break just by letting her live. 'You've been working and thinking all night,' she said. 'Your poor head needs a rest. I'll fix you a nice cup of tea . . . ' "

Later, she stops an argument between the father and the boy by silencing the father.

> *He sat in his chair and looked down into his bottle. You'd think from the expression on his face that it was a telescope which let him see all the way down to hell. All of a sudden his face went slack. He went to sleep in his chair. The old lady took the bottle away from him as if he was a baby . . .*
> *. . . I sat and ate my breakfast in silence. With the old man propped up opposite me, eyes closed and mouth open, it was a little like eating with a dead man at the table.*

My story had begun to feed on its Oedipal roots, both mythical and psychological. Relieved by the mother of his crotch-held bottle, the father has undergone symbolic death. The short scene ends with the boy's determination to get away not only from his father but from his mother:

> *She'd go on feeding me until I choked. She'd be pouring me cups of tea until I drowned in the stuff. She'd give me loving encouragement until I suffocated.*

Version Two was a good deal more than a false start. Swarming with spontaneous symbolism, it laid out one whole side, the sinister side, of the binocular vision of my book. In fact it laid it out so completely that it left me, like Willie, nowhere to go but away. I couldn't begin the novel with the infernal vision on which part of its weight would finally rest; the novel must converge on that gradually. But by writing my last scene first, in effect, and facing its Medusa images—poverty and family failure and hostility—my imagi-

[265]

nation freed itself to plan the novel without succumbing to the more obvious evasions.

Even so, as I was trying to finish the first draft, I got morally tired and lost my grip on my subject, ending the book with a dying fall in Nevada. My friend John Mersereau read this draft—entitled, appropriately, "The Enormous Detour"—and reminded me that a book like mine could not succeed as a novel unless it succeeded in its own terms as a detective novel. For my ending I went back to Version Two, which contains the dramatic essence of the final confrontations. Willie's scene with his parents served me well, leading me into the heart of my subject not just once but again.

A second break-through at the beginning, more technical and less obviously important, came with my decision to use the detective Archer as the narrator. This may seem a small matter, but it was not. The decision on narrative point-of-view is a key one for any novelist. It determines shape and tone, and even the class of detail that can be used. With this decision I made up my mind that the convention of the detective novel, in which I had been working for fifteen years, would be able to contain the materials of my most ambitious and personal work so far. I doubt that my book could have been written in any other form.

Miss Brigid Brophy has alleged against the detective story that it cannot be taken seriously because it fails to risk the author's ego and is therefore mere fantasy. It is true as I have noted that writers since Poe have used detectives like Dupin as a sort of rational strong point from which they can observe and report on a violent no-man's-land. Unfortunately this violent world is not always fantastic, although it may reflect psychological elements. Miss Brophy's argument disregards the fact that the detective and his story can become means of knowing oneself and saying the unsayable. You can never hit a distant target by aiming at it directly.

In any case I have to plead not guilty to unearned security of the ego. As I write a book, as I wrote *The Galton Case*, my ego is dispersed through several characters, including usually some of the undesirable ones, and I am involved with them to the limit of my imaginative strength. In modern fiction the narrator is not always the protagonist or hero, nor is the protagonist always single.

Certainly my narrator Archer is not the main object of my interest, nor the character with whose fate I am most concerned. He is a deliberately narrowed version of the writing self, so narrow that when he turns sideways he almost disappears. Yet his semi-transparent presence places the story at one remove from the author and lets it, as we say (through sweat and tears), write itself.

I remember the rush of invention that occurred when the emotional and imaginative urges, the things *The Galton Case* was to be about, were released by Willie's scene with his parents, and channeled by my decision to write the book from Archer's point of view. The details came unbidden in a benign avalanche which in two or three days filled the rest of the red notebook. The people and the places weren't all final, but they were definite enough to let me begin the wild masonry of laying detail on detail to make a structure. (Naturally many of the details came in already organized gestalts: people in relationship, events in narrative order.)

Detective novels differ from some other kinds of novel, in having to have a rather hard structure built in logical coherence. But the structure will fail to satisfy the mind, writer's or reader's, unless the logic of imagination, tempered by feelings and rooted in the unconscious, is tied to it, often subverting it. The plans for a detective novel in the making are less like blueprints than like travel notes set down as you once revisited a city. The city had changed since you saw it last. It keeps changing around you. Some of the people you knew there have changed their names. Some of them wear disguises.

* * * * *

The underlying theme of many of my novels, as I read them now, is the migration of a mind from one place and culture to another. Its purpose, like the dominant purpose of my young life, was to repossess my American birthplace by imaginative means and heal the schizophrenic pain.

From "Foreword," *Archer in Jeopardy* (1979).

* * * * *

Take for example Dr. Dawson who lost a game of pool to Tom in Version One and became, in Version Two, a Mr. Sablacan waiting for Willie at the Royal York. In my final notes and in the novel itself he has become Gordon Sable, identifiable with his earlier personae by his name and by the fact that, like Dr. Dawson, he wears a suit with a wicked red pin-stripe in it. His occupation has changed, and his function in the novel has expanded. Gordon Sable is the attorney who hires Lew Archer on Mrs. Galton's behalf to look for her lost son Anthony.

Archer and Gordon Sable know each other. The nature of their relationship is hinted at by a small incident on the first page of the novel. A line of it will illustrate some of the implications of style, which could be described as structure on a small scale. Archer sits down on a Harvard chair in Gordon Sable's office, and then gets up. "It was like being expelled."

In a world of rich and poor, educated and disadvantaged, Archer's dry little joke places him on the side of the underdog. It suggests that he is the kind of man who would sympathize with the boy impostor waiting in the wings. And of course it speaks for the author–my own application for a graduate fellowship at Harvard was turned down thirty years ago–so that like nearly everything in fiction the joke has a private side which partly accounts for its having been made. The University of Michigan gave me a graduate fellowship in 1941, by the way, and my debt to Ann Arbor is duly if strangely acknowledged in the course of John Brown, Jr.'s story.

Detective stories are told backward, as well as forward, and full revelation of the characters and their lives' meanings is deferred until the end, or near the end. But even deeper structural considerations require the main dynamic elements of a story to be laid in early. For this and other reasons, such as the further weight and dimension imparted by repetition, it is sometimes a good idea to let a character and his story divide. One part or aspect of him can perform an early function in the story which foreshadows the function of his later persona, without revealing too much of it.

John Brown, Jr., as I've already said, doesn't enter the story until it is one-third told. I decided, though hardly on the fully conscious level, to provide John with a stand-in or alter ego to pull his weight in the early part of the narrative. When I invented this other boy, and named him Tom Lem-

berg, I had totally forgotten that Tom was the name of the boy in Version One who beat Dr. Dawson at pool. But here he is in the novel: an earlier stage in the development of my boy impostor. A specimen of fiction, like a biological specimen, seems to recapitulate the lower stages of its evolution. I suspect Tom had to be brought in to validate my novel, proving that I had touched in order all the bases between life and fiction. At any rate the book comes alive when Archer and Tom Lemberg, two widely distinct versions of the author, confront each other in Chapter Five.

This confrontation with Tom of course prefigures Archer's confrontation with the boy impostor John. Tom serves an even more important purpose at the beginning of the book, when he is held responsible for the murder of Peter Culligan. The structure of the story sufficiently identifies Culligan with the wino father, so that Culligan's death parallels and anticipates the final catastrophe. Like the repeated exile of Oedipus, the crucial events of my novel seem to happen at least twice. And like a young Oedipus, Tom is a "son" who appears to kill a "father," thus setting the whole story in circular motion.

I have told a little too much of that story for comfort, and a little too much of my own story. One final connection between the private story and the public one should suffice. When Archer opens the dead Culligan's suitcase, "Its contents emitted a whiff of tobacco, sea water, sweat, and the subtler indescribable odor of masculine loneliness." These were the smells, as I remembered and imagined them, of the pipe-smoking sea-captain who left my mother and me when I was about the age that grandson Jimmie was when he became a monster in my poor castle, and then a laughing boy, and fell asleep.

BOOK REVIEW:

Ross Macdonald, "Research into the History of Detective Fiction," *San Francisco Chronicle*, 15 February 1959, p. 29.

*In this review of A. E. Murch's The Development of the Detective Novel *Millar reiterates his position that mystery fiction merits serious consideration as literature– in opposition to the critics who regard it as providing puzzles and escapism.*

Kenneth Millar, 1961 (photo by Ray Borges)

Readers, and critics, of mystery fiction seem to be divided into at least two main camps. There are those who feel that the English story of scientific detection à la Sherlock Holmes represents the mystery at its peak, and that everything since has been a falling-away. Dr. Jacques Barzun is the most vocal current laudator of crimes past. Then there are others who consider that the mystery novel is a form of the novel proper, subject like its other forms to the endless new developments which the word "novel" suggests. According to this second view, the contemporary movement of mystery fiction in a variety of directions—social, psychological, poetic, symbolic, philosophic—means that it is rejoining the literary mainstream where it belongs.

To say that the first is the English view would be to distort the opinions of many English writers from G. K. Chesterton to Dorothy L. Sayers and Josephine Tey. In the introductory chapter to her history, Mrs. Murch quotes Chesterton to the effect that "the detective story . . . is the earli-est and only form of popular literature in which is expressed some sense of the poetry of modern life." But Mrs. Murch does nothing with this promising approach. She regards the detective story as "a game of skill," presumably something like croquet. But the standards of the game are degenerating. The mallets turn into flamingoes in your hands. Enemy agents have planted land-mines under the lawn.

As a member of the enemy who also happens to be an Anglophile, I am glad to report that Mrs. Murch is a sound scholar whose researches into the history of detective fiction give us aid and comfort. Following the lead which Dorothy Sayers provided in the introduction to her famous anthologies, she goes far back behind Poe, who has been the point of departure for most scholars. She glances at the picaresque novel culminating in Defoe (but Nash is omitted), and gives more than passing attention to the Gothic novel from Horace Walpole to Charles Brockden Brown. The influence of Vidocq on Balzac, and then of Balzac on Wilkie Collins, is clearly established. Collins in turn helped Dickens to overcome the centrifugal forces in his plot structures. Those narrative techniques, those complications and completions, which are the essence of the mystery form are shown to be a rather central feature of nineteenth-century fiction.

The second half of the book includes a sound comparison of the modern English, French, and American schools which could have been used as a structural device to control the mass of twentieth-century material. But under the pressure of this mass, Mrs. Murch allows her history to deteriorate towards mere bibliography, without the virtue of completeness. Brockden Brown's inheritor William Faulkner, for instance, does not appear in the index. Yet that great novelist has written detective fiction in its narrowest, as well as its broadest, sense.

It is dangerous for a scholar, however diligent, to tackle an immense subject with hand-me-down critical tools. Mrs. Murch's limitations may be indicated by her opinion that "criminal psychology" bears "little relation to detection." Her overall implication is, I fear, that crime fiction should stay away from the realities of modern life. Like that of her fellow-nostalgic Dr. Barzun, Mrs. Murch's sensibility seems attuned to the spirit of a simpler time. As one of the key literary expressions of contemporary sensibility, the mystery novel awaits a more searching examination from a less escapist point of view.

It grieves me to say this, because mystery writers are traditionally grateful for small scholarly mercies, and Mrs. Murch's book contains many good things, including a youthful likeness of the lady I love.

REVIEW:

Anthony Boucher, Review of *The Far Side of the Dollar, New York Times Book Review*, 24 January 1965, p. 42.

Boucher, a novelist and critic, was a friend and admirer of Millar. Many readers ranked The Far Side of the Dollar *as Millar's best novel up to then.*

Without in the least abating my admiration for Dashiell Hammett and Raymond Chandler, I should like to venture the heretical suggestion that Ross Macdonald is a better novelist than either of them. He owes an immeasurable debt to both in the matter of technique and style; but he has gone beyond their tutelage to develop the "hard-boiled," private-eye novel into a far more supple medium, in which he can study the common and the uncommon man (and woman) as well as the criminal, in which he can write (often brilliantly and even profoundly) not only about violence and retribution but simply about "people with enough feeling to be hurt, and enough complexity to do wrong"–to quote from his latest, *The Far Side of the Dollar* (Knopf, $3.95).

A 17-year-old boy has run away from a curious sort of psychotherapic prep school, and private detective Lew Archer is called in to find him. It is a quest which illumines the war of the generations, odd corners of Hollywood, a 20-year-old sin and even a part of Archer's own past. It involves violence and murder, strong action and skillful deciphering–and above all a compassionate understanding of people, old and young, caught up in this moment of time.

* * * * *

SPEECH:

"Murder in the Library," *Mystery Writers' Annual* (1965), p. 2.

In 1965 Millar was elected president of the Mystery Writers of America, a position his wife had held earlier.

I thank you for the very special honor, which I won't deny I've aspired to, the more intensely in the years since Margaret Millar was elected President of MWA.

My memory wanders much further back, to the high school days when my distinguished predecessor and I were always bumping into each other in the stacks of the Kitchener (Ontario) Public Library. We were preparing ourselves for a life of crime by reading our way through the mystery section, a category which the librarian (Miss Mabel Dunham, a novelist in her own right) interpreted loosely. I had read all of *Crime and Punishment* before I realized that I had been conned by an expert.

There may be a point, after all, in this not very pointed reminiscence. As custodians of the mystery tradition in America, I think we should interpret its limits loosely and with a certain pride and hopefulness. While there may not be a Dostoevsky among us, our craft has provided the matrix for some of the classics of our literature.

Under the pressure of publishers' deadlines and bills that have to be paid, it isn't easy to try and write for some word-happy kid haunting a provincial library who might just possibly find in our work a viable tradition, native as jazz, complex in potential as Elizabethan drama. But if we write with an eye to that possibility, we may stumble into some new excellence.

REVIEW:

Macdonald, Review of *Cain x 3, New York Times Book Review*, 2 March 1969, pp. 1, 49-51.

Millar's review of the James M. Cain omnibus volume (The Postman Always Rings Twice, Mildred Pierce, Double Indemnity) *paid tribute to Cain as an influence on American written speech and as a literary artist. Millar acknowledged his debts to Cain's style elsewhere.*

Over the past 40 years the West Coast crime novel has given us perhaps our most persistent literary impression of California. James M. Cain was one of the great inventors of this form and the im-

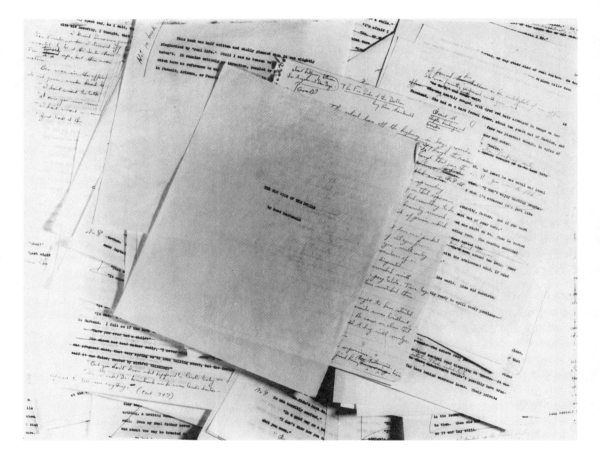

Working draft for The Far Side of the Dollar, *1965 (University of California–Irvine)*

James M. Cain

ages it projects. Not even Raymond Chandler, with his lyrical sweet-and-sour sense of place, ever put together more haunting landscapes and cityscapes. Now Alfred A. Knopf has collected three of the earliest and best Cain novels—"The Postman Always Rings Twice," "Mildred Pierce," and "Double Indemnity"—and reissued them in a single volume.

The human figures in Cain's landscapes are in terribly rapid motion, most of it downhill, as in a vision of judgment. In the first two pages of "The Postman Always Rings Twice" (1934) Frank Chambers is thrown off a truck near a roadside restaurant where he scrounges lunch and takes a job from the owner, Nick the Greek, having seen Nick's wife, Cora:

"Except for the shape, she really wasn't any raving beauty, but she had a sulky look to her, and her lips stuck out in a way that made me want to mash them in for her."

A few pages further on we are shown with even more shocking immediacy the physical aggressiveness of a passion which is going to lead to murder: "I bit her. I sunk my teeth into her lips so deep I could feel the blood spurt into my mouth. It was running down her neck when I carried her upstairs." The intensity of this passage, even if it is slightly overdone, transmutes the blood into sym-

bol, the stuff of art. It is a far cry from "Tristan and Isolde," but not so far from "Cavalleria Rusticana." The violence and desolation and the freeze-dried pity of Cain's California are reminiscent of Verga's Sicily.

Mr. Cain is a conscious and deliberate artist, and the structure of "The Postman Always Rings Twice" has the moral and symbolic overtones hinted at in the title. In the course of their first attempt to kill the Greek, Frank and Cora discover that they are not after all alone in the universe. A cat short-circuits the lights and interrupts the murder. Cats, which recur throughout Cain's work, represent certain kinds of power and grace that are fascinating but alien to men. Cora is called a "hell cat." The power or fate that runs through the universe—Cain's Postman?—is catlike in its toying with human beings.

Everything that happens in this novel happens twice, the first time with a twist (the cat dies instead of the Greek), the second time with a reverse twist. Even details are used in this way, notably in the second, successful, murder attempt. Nick has a fine tenor voice, and just before Frank kills him, he is trying out the echo in Malibu Canyon. Just after Frank kills him:

"Then Cora, she gave a funny kind of gulp that ended in a moan. Because here came the echo of his voice. It took the high note, like he did, and swelled, and stopped, and waited." Taken by itself, the posthumous high note would be no more than a fine operatic flourish ending a chapter. But when such recurrences continue to recur, they must be allowed their meaning. The echo of the dead man's voice hints at something out there in the void, like an echo of the voice of the ghost of God.

There is a new generation of readers for Cain's stories—"Cain x 3" should make its way into the universities—and I won't spoil this one for them by poking any further into its coiled surprises. Some unprepared readers may wonder, though, why a serious writer like Cain, setting two passionate fools at odds with an ironic universe, and hoping, as he said, to "graze tragedy," should put his story in the mouth of an illiterate hobo. The answer is simply that the vernacular, and the people who speak it, are the main source of his imaginative strength. Cain once confessed that the art of fiction eluded him until he heard a Western roughneck talk.

Mark Twain and Melville and Whitman, more recently Norris and Crane, had shown what writers could do with our vulgar language. In the decade before Cain emerged as a novelist, Dashiell Hammett had developed the spoken word into a polished vehicle for his hard-boiled detective stories. Cain has denied that Hammett influenced him, and I can see no evidence of direct influence. It is more than likely, though, that H. L. Mencken, the Sage of Baltimore, provided the connection between these two natives of Maryland by influencing them both. Cain knew him at a time when Mencken had just come up dripping with information from his first deep immersion in the American language. And when the Western roughneck spoke within his hearing, Cain must have experienced that coming together of the already known and the freshly heard which opens the imagination to new life.

In "Mildred Pierce" (1941), the longest and last written of these three books, Cain's language has changed, losing some of its poetic power and pace. While it is, like "Postman," a Depression novel, its people are predominantly middle class. Their language, partly canned and partly perishable, is less reliable and less inspiring than the low vernacular. For this and other reasons, the two languages spoken and written, which a novelist must listen to binaurally as he writes, fail sometimes to fuse at the level of sensibility.

A first novel can be a kind of index to an author's ensuing work, and in some respects "Mildred Pierce" was an offshoot of "Postman." After they killed the Greek, and "beer came back," Cora wanted to expand the restaurant, but Frank wasn't interested. Mildred Pierce lives out Cora's middle-class dream. This time the husband doesn't have to be killed. He walks out, and tragedy modulates into black, or dark brown, comedy.

Cain's primal vision of woman as the passionate hellcat divided into Mildred on the one hand and her daughter Veda on the other. Mildred is good in bed–"voluptuous" is Cain's favorite adjective for her–but not profoundly interested in sex. Even her passion for the dollar is rather absent-minded. The entrepreneurial gift which converts her from a waitress into the head of a small restaurant chain is largely a matter of luck which eventually runs out. She's a gutty pleasant mindless woman who makes good pies and bad decisions.

Her daughter Veda is a handsome prodigy who talks like a book and hates her mother for her lack of class. But she is willing to use Mildred's earnings in her own drive to become a coloratura soprano. The grotesque ending of her story, which has to do with her voice changing, hints at the sexual disturbances which underly Veda's pathological coldness and recalls Cain's novel "Serenade" (1937), another story of vocal and psychic problems.

Veda's story provides Mildred with her central motive: her unrequited passion for her daughter is her only real hint of a spiritual life. But the tricky handling of the Veda plot-line cuts across the true grain of the book. Its main development is large and simple, almost Dreiserian: it is the story of a fairly ordinary woman who loses her husband and her place in life, by sheer hard work makes a new false place for herself, then loses that. Some of the most brilliant passages are detailed accounts of how things happen in the world of business: how to open a restaurant, how to lose one. Cain's wonderful eye for everyday detail recalls the fact that he started as a journalist; and after more than a dozen novels he persists in styling himself, in his "Who's Who" entry, a "newspaperman."

Though her crucial adventures are more financial than sexual, Mildred does have a part-time lover, a Pasadena gentleman of leisure named Monty Beragon. Even this romantic figure is gradually converted, in the central movement of the book, into a mere economic man, and is dragged at the wheels of Mildred's tin-Lizzie ambition. As the novel proceeds on its rather circular course, the lives and fates of the characters seem to be walled in, fixed in a vision of usury both economic and personal. The conception is broad-gauged, and prophetic of our anomie, but it falls a bit short in the execution, particularly in the eccentric structure.

When, at the height of his powers, in 1936, Cain wrote "Double Indemnity," he had learned, as few writers ever do, how to dispense with everything inessential. Yet his telegraphic art made room for a remarkable variety of characters and

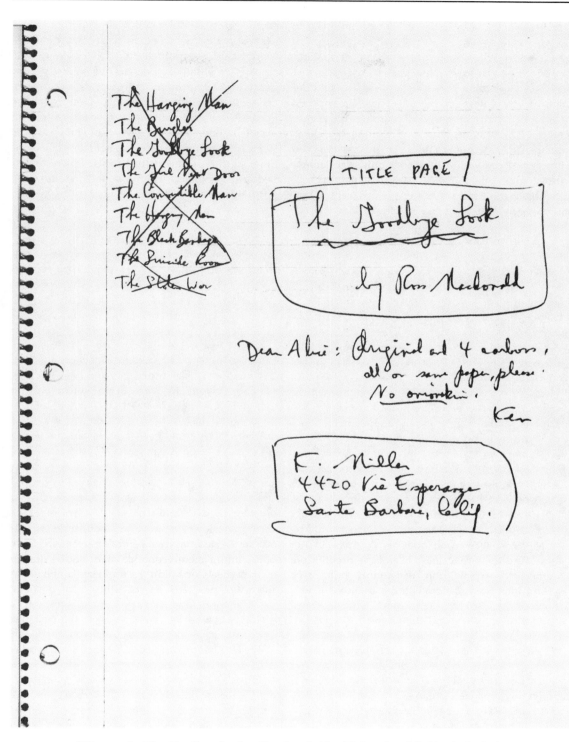

Title page for The Goodbye Look *with rejected titles (University of California–Irvine)*

scenes. This short novel of fewer than 40,000 words has, like "The Great Gatsby," the effect of a rather large action boiled down to a concentration approaching that of dramatic poetry.

Cain's account of a wasting, utterly damnable love affair never even stops for a love scene, let alone a bedroom scene. But it isn't an action story. Its critical actions are psychological and moral. The hero, Walter Huff, is an insurance salesman who decides, with the help of a woman named Phyllis Nirdinger, to murder her husband and cheat his own company out of $50,000: "What I was doing was peeping over that edge, and all the time I was trying to pull away from it, there was something in me that kept edging a little closer, trying to get a better look."

Walter Huff's moral condition recalls Kierkegaard, who wrote, in "The Sickness Unto Death," that innocence is like standing on the edge of a chasm; you can't look down without becoming guilty. In his Kierkegaardian despair, the smiling desolation of his life, Walter is driven to gamble for money he doesn't need and a woman he comes to abhor. Beyond that he is playing for the highest stakes of all, to see if he has a soul which he can lose. It seems he has. After the murder he mumbles the Lord's prayer, and then "couldn't remember how it went."

Cain, whose novels instructed Camus (as Tom Wolfe points out in his introduction), was an important precursor of the existentialist school of fiction both in his portraits of alienation and despair, and his ultimate concern with good and evil. Like most 20th-century writers, he tends to define virtue in terms of its absence. Occasionally he slips toward diabolism, and if "Double Indemnity" has any weakness at all, it is connected with Phyllis Nirdinger's complete lack of humanity. In the course of their bloody transactions, Walter gradually recognizes that he is paired with a monster. At the very end Phyllis takes on an almost supernatural aura, for which Cain has carefully prepared in the course of the book: "She's made her face chalk white, with black circles under her eyes and red on her lips and cheeks. . . . She looks like what came aboard the ship to shoot dice for souls in the 'Rime of the Ancient Mariner.' "

In this reference to Coleridge's figure of essential evil, the "Nightmare Life-in-Death," Cain delib-

erately grounds his moral vision in that of the great Romantic who experienced before Kierkegaard the sickness unto death. I think Cain was telling us as well that like Walter Huff he was playing for the highest available stakes.

It seems clear by now that Cain has taken them. He has won the unfading laurels with a pair of native American masterpieces, "Postman" and "Double Indemnity," back to back.

REVIEW:

William Goldman, Review of *The Goodbye Look*, *New York Times Book Review*, 1 June 1969, pp. 1, 2.

This review by novelist and screenwriter Goldman (who wrote the screenplay for The Moving Target, *produced as* Harper) *was headlined "The finest detective novels ever written by an American." It helped to make Macdonald's twenty-first novel a best-seller.*

A decent, disturbed young man, who may be a murderer, takes an overdose of sleeping pills. Lew Archer, a California private detective who has been looking for him, finds him and drives him to the nearest hospital. But when he gets there, Archer discovers that no one at the hospital can help: "There had been a recent auto accident, and everybody on the emergency ward was busy. Looking for a stretcher, I opened a door and saw a dead man and closed the door again."

Only the doors don't stay closed. They never do in Ross Macdonald's novels. The corpses keep coming and long before "The Goodbye Look" has reached its terminal sum, it is evident that this is another stunning addition to the Archer books, the finest series of detective novels ever written by an American.

There are 15 of them now, turned out slowly over a period of 20 years. Though the first half dozen or so were enormously influenced by Dashiell Hammett and Raymond Chandler (Archer, in fact, was named after Miles Archer, Sam Spade's murdered partner in "The Maltese Falcon"), Macdonald's novels of the last decade have been of a texture never done by anyone before.

Telling the plot of any novel is unfair. Telling the plot of an Archer is impossible. The books are so ramified, Delphic and dark that you can either give a one sentence synopsis, or just hand over the novel and say "Read!": nothing in between.

"The Goodbye Look" is about a not particularly valuable Florentine gold box that has been stolen and that Archer is hired to find. Inside of 30 pages, he has not only located the thing, he knows pretty well who stole it. But then the first dead corpse appears, and the real stuff of the book begins.

The phrase "dead corpse" is not a redundancy, for in Macdonald's books, it's not just the deceased who qualify; everyone around is dead or dying. And has been for years. For if there is no way of detailing a specific Archer plot, there is a kind of over-all structure that tends to fit the late novels: in general, perhaps a full generation before the present time of the novel, two people come together, neither of them lethal alone, but united, deadly. And they do something terrible. They murder or steal or assume different identities. Or all three. It is a wild compulsive drive that operates on them. Sometimes what they do they do for money or lust or power. But mostly they do it for love. And they get away with it. And everything is quiet.

Until Archer comes. Usually he is hired for something standard: my wife has left me–find her; my husband has a mistress–tell me who; my Florentine box is gone–get it. So he begins, and gradually, obliquely, the generation-old crime is scratched alive. He goes on. People lie to him; people always lie to him. He expects it, he goes on. People sometimes try to stop him. He expects that too. That's their job; his is to go on. And so he does, till all the truths are told.

Macdonald has written that Archer "is not the main object of my interest, nor the character with whose fate I am most concerned." He also has said, "when he turns sideways, he almost disappears."

We should all be so thin. Archer is aging and vulnerable and full of the sadness of the world. In "The Goodbye Look," while a woman, once rich, screams at him in anger, he thinks that "it was probably sorrow she was feeling. She'd stepped on a rotten place and fallen through the floor and knew she was trapped in poverty forever." Earlier, he has been listening as a man tries to force a reconciliation with his wife, both verbally and physically,

and Archer thinks: "He was saying and doing all the wrong things. I knew, because I'd said and done them all in my time."

That's the great thing about Archer–he's done it all and he knows that we've all fallen into a rotten place. Still, he plods along, a modern miserable Diogenes who makes his money from other people's suffering, a nosy guy with a passion for mercy who likes to move into other people's lives and then move quickly out again so he won't get bored. Nothing surprises him. Nothing shocks him. And he is continually horrified at the things we do to each other.

It is Archer's desperate and growing compulsion to get in and out of the lives he is visiting that gives these novels their strange irresistible narrative pull. I say "strange" because there is a tendency to think of Macdonald as a writer of hardboiled books, the sort of work that draws its readability from the author's skill at piling on portions of sex, wisecracks, violence and death.

Well, there are wisecracks in "The Goodbye Look"; maybe half a dozen in 243 pages. And sex–readers of Macdonald will be shocked to learn that there is a sex scene in this newest novel. Archer actually makes it with somebody in two paragraphs, three sentences, six lines. As follows: "She was willing to be taken. We shed our clothes, more or less, and lay down like wrestlers going to the mat under special rules, where pinning and being pinned were equally lucky and meritorious.

"She said at one point, between falls, that I was a gentle lover."

Now that's the kind of stuff that'll have them lining up at the 42nd Street bookstores.

As for violence and death, the most vicious word in the longest fight is "jabbed" and the whole thing is really a lovely image of a man growing old, as in stop-time pictures. And here, finally, is a verbatim description of the first death, as gory as any in the book: "I looked in through the rear window and saw the dead man huddled on the back seat with dark blood masking his face."

The point to all this is that Macdonald's work in the last decade has nothing remotely to do with hard-boiled detective novels. He is writing novels of character about people with ghosts.

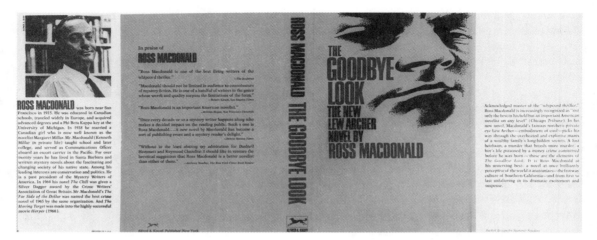

Dust jacket for The Goodbye Look *(1969), Macdonald's first best-seller*

Ghosts is his theme. All his characters have them and so do all of us. We have each experienced those crazy moon-moments when we considered pitching everything and taking off with the rich divorcee down the hall. Macdonald's people do it, that's the only difference.

Like any first-rate writer, he has created and peopled his own world. Nobody writes southern California like Macdonald writes it. All those new rich people, the perfect front lawns where no one but the gardener ever treads, the dustless houses with their huge picture windows facing other picture windows—there's something unalive about it all. And since Macdonald's characters are all dying anyway, that's what makes him their perfect chronicler. At any rate, his world is every bit as tactile as O'Hara's Pennsylvania.

I moved into Macdonald's world last night. I was going across the East 50's and in the darkness, alongside a famous French restaurant, a couple was kissing wildly. The kiss held and held and I'm nosy too and finally as they broke, I saw them: the man was dressed very expensively, very mod: he was suntanned and handsome and well into his fifties. The girl was young. But there were two things terribly wrong, for as they held each other close, their faces were hidden from one another, and neither of them showed the remotest sign of passion. And besides that, the girl wasn't pretty. She was tacky and stout and why had they been kissing like that, feigning desire in the darkness? What were their lies and when would they surface and who was going to suffer when they did?

There are some artists whom we tend to think of only as entertainers. Alfred Hitchcock for example. But it's my guess that of all the American movies of the sixties, "Psycho" is going to last as long as any. It scared the be-Jesus out of us, and everyone said it was "skillful" but almost nobody said it was "good," at least not in any esthetic way. Well, it was good. It hit, unpretentiously, at something terrifying and perennial in us all, something back beyond memory and below the level of speech.

I think Macdonald is that kind of unpretentious artist. This year, everybody's plotzing over "Portnoy." It is "important" and "significant" and "brilliant" and "a bulls-eye," and I thought it was a repetitious bore. And after the 50th masturbation novel floods our friendly neighborhood bookstore, I think the critics are going to scramble a bit to explain their adjectives, just as they had to scramble a decade back after James Gould Cozzens made the cover of Time

I'm not saying "The Goodbye Look" is going to outlast the Roth. But James M. Cain was the lead review in this journal a few months ago—a week after a new book by Pearl S. Buck, who won the Nobel Prize back in the 1930's, when those Cain novels were first appearing, was buried on page 35. It's too soon to assess Ross Macdonald.

All I know is I've been reading him for 20 years and he has yet to disappoint. Classify him how you will, he is one of the best American novelists now operating, and all he does is keep on getting better.

REVIEW:

Eudora Welty, Review of *The Underground Man, New York Times Book Review,* 14 February 1971, pp. 1, 28-30.

This review by a distinguished writer consolidated the acclaim received by Millar's previous novel, The Goodbye Look. The Underground Man *was his most successful book. Millar and Welty had not met when she wrote this review, but they subsequently became warm friends and dedicated books to each other.*

Curled up, with an insulted look on his upturned face, and wearing a peppermint-striped shirt, the fresh corpse of a man is disclosed in a hole in the ground. From the scene of the crime the victim's little boy is carried off, nobody knows why, by a pair of troubled teen-agers. And at the same time, a deadly forest fire gets its start in these hills above Santa Teresa: whoever murdered Stanley Broadhurst must have caused him to drop his cigarillo into the dry grass. So opens the new novel by Ross Macdonald, "The Underground Man." It comes to stunning achievement.

A Forest Service man looks into the killing to find out who was responsible for the fire; but Lew Archer goes faster and farther into his own investigation, for a personal reason. That morning, he had met that little boy; they fed blue jays together. He promises the young widow, the child's mother, to find her son and bring him back.

The double mystery of Santa Teresa cries urgency but is never going to explain itself in an ordinary way. For instance, it looks as if the victim himself might have dug the hole in which he lies. ("Why would a man dig his own grave"?–"He may not have known it was going to be his.") With the fire coming, Archer has to work fast. The corpse must be quickly buried again, or be consumed with his murder unsolved. This, the underground man of the title, waits the book out, the buried connection between present threat and something out of the past.

"I don't believe in coincidences," Archer says, as the investigation leads him into a backward direction, and he sees the case take on a premonitory symmetry. And it is not coincidence indeed, or anything so simple, but a sort of spiral of time that he goes hurtling into, with an answer lying 15 years deep.

He is to meet many strange and lonely souls drawing their inspiration from private sources. On the periphery are those all but anonymous characters, part of the floating population of the city, evocative of all the sadness that fills a lonely world, like some California versions of those Saltimbanques of Picasso's ("even a little more fleeting than ourselves") drifting across the smoke-obscured outskirts. They are the sentinels of a case in which everybody has something to lose, and most of the characters in this time-haunted, fire-threatened novel lose it in the course of what happens–a son, or a husband, or a mountain retreat; a sailing boat, a memory; the secret of 15 years or the dream of a lifetime; or a life.

Brooding over the case is the dark fact that for some certain souls the past does not let go. They nourish the conviction that its ties may be outlived but, for hidden reasons, can be impossible to outgrow or leave behind.

Stanley Broadhurst died searching for his long-lost father. The Oedipus story, which figured in Mr. Macdonald's "The Galton Case" and "The Chill," has echoes here too. But another sort of legend takes a central place in "The Underground Man." This is the medieval tale of romance and the faerie.

It is exactly what Archer plunges into when he enters this case. Finding his way, through their lies and fears, into other people's obsessions and dreams, he might as well be in a fairy tale with them. The mystery has handed him what amounts to a set of impossible tasks: Find the door that opens the past. Unravel the ever-tangling threads of time. Rescue the stolen child from fleeing creatures who appear to be under a spell and who forbid him to speak to them. Meet danger from the aroused elements of fire and water. And beware the tower.

But Archer's own role in their fairy tale is clear to him: from the time he fed the blue jays with the little boy, he never had a choice. There is

The Underground Man was on the New York Times best-seller list for seventeen weeks in 1971

the maze of the past to be entered and come out of alive, bringing the innocent to safety. And in the maze there lives a monster; his name is Murder.

* * * * *

The movement of the story could be described as the central character's gradual discovery that he is an underground man, to put it mildly.

What do I mean by an underground man? A character who represents the author, perhaps, but is given no special indulgence; who reflects a lack of interest in, even an impatience with special privilege–a sense of interdependence among men–a certain modesty. The central vice of the traditional hero, who easily accepts his own superiority, is hubris, an overweaning pride and expectation. The central vice of the underground accidie, moral and social sloth, a willingness to live with whatever is, a molelike inclination to accept the darkness. Perhaps these are the respective vices of aristocracy and democracy.

Among the classless men of our democracy the private detective has become a representative figure.

From *Self-Portrait*, edited by Ralph B. Sipper (Santa Barbara: Capra Editions, 1981).

* * * * *

All along the way, the people he questions shift their stands, lie as fast as they can, slip only too swiftly out of human reach. Their ages are deceiving, they put on trappings of disguise or even what might be called transformations. As Archer, by stages, all the while moving at speed, connects one character with the next, he discovers what makes the sinister affinity between them.

"Robert Driscoll Falconer, Jr., was a god come down to earth in human guise," the older Mrs. Broadhurst, mother of the murder victim, has written in a memoir of her father, and here her Spencerian handwriting went to pieces: "It straggled across the lined yellow page like a defeated army." Mrs. Crandall, the mother of the runaway girl, is "one of those waiting mothers who would sit forever beside the phone but didn't know what to say when it finally rang." Another character being questioned plays "a game that guilty people play, questioning the questioner, trying to convert the truth into a shuttlecock that could be batted back and forth and eventually lost." And the violence and malice of another character "appeared to her as emanations from the external world."

These people live in prisons of the spirit, and suffer there. The winding, prisonlike stairs that appear and reappear under Archer's hurrying feet in the course of the chase are like the repeated questionings that lead most often into some private hell.

And of course unreality–the big underlying trouble of all these people–was back of the crime itself: the victim was obsessed with the lifelong search for his father; oblivious of everything and everybody else, he invited his own oblivion. In a different way unreality was back of the child-stealing. "As you can see, we gave her everything," says the mother standing in her runaway daughter's lovely white room. "But it wasn't what she wanted." The home environment of the girl and others like her, Archer is brought to observe, was "an unreality so bland and smothering that the children tore loose and impaled themselves on the spikes of any reality that offered. Or made their own unreality with drugs."

The plot is intricate, involuted, and complicated to the hilt; and this, as I see it, is the novel's point. The danger derives from the fairy tales into which people make their lives. In lonely, fearful, or confused minds, real-life facts can become rarefied into private fantasies. And when intensity is accepted–welcomed–as the measure of truth, how can the real and the fabricated be told apart?

We come to a scene where the parallel with the fairy tale is explicit–and something more. It is the best in the book–I can give but a part.

"I made my way up the washed-out gravel drive. The twin conical towers standing up against the night sky made the house look like something out of a medieval romance. The illusion faded as I got nearer. There was a multi-colored fanlight over the front door, with segments of glass fallen out, like missing teeth in an old smile. . . . The door creaked open when I knocked."

Here lives a lady "far gone in solitude," whose secret lies hidden at the heart of the mystery. She stands there in "a long full skirt on which there were paint stains in all three primary colors." She is a painter–of spiritual conditions, she says; to Archer her pictures resemble "serious contusions and open wounds" or "imperfectly remembered hallucinations."

" 'I was born in this house,' she said, as if she'd been waiting fifteen years for a listener." (And these are the 15 years that have done their worst to everybody in the novel.) " 'It's interesting to come back to your childhood home, . . . like becoming very young and very old both at the same time.' That was how she looked, I thought, in her archaic long skirt–very young and very old, the granddaughter and the grandmother in one person, slightly schizo."

"There were romantic tears in her eyes" when her story is out. "My own eyes remained quite dry."

Millar with Eudora Welty

Fairy tale and living reality alternate on one current to pulse together in this remarkable scene. The woman is a pivotal character and Archer has caught up with her; they are face to face and there comes a moment's embrace. Of the many brilliant ways Mr. Macdonald has put his motif to use, I believe this is the touch that delighted me most. For of course Archer, this middle-aging Californian who has seen everything in a career of going into impossible trouble with his eyes open, who has always been the protector of the weak and the rescuer of the helpless, is a born romantic. Here he meets his introverted and ailing counterpart–this lady is the chatelaine of the romantic-gone-wrong. He is not by nature immune, especially to what is lovely or was lovely once. At a given moment, they may brush close. As Archer, the only one with insight into himself, is aware.

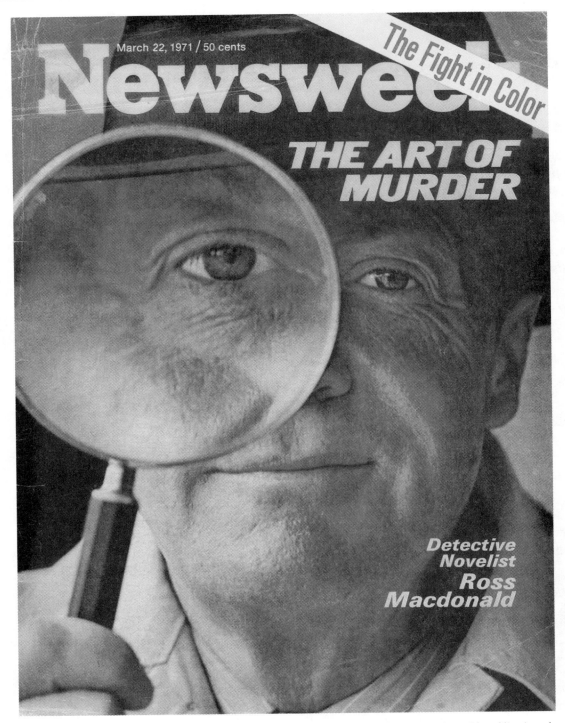

Cover for Newsweek issue with profile of Ross Macdonald, which appeared in connection with publication of The Underground Man.

Time pressing, time lapsing, time repeating itself in dark acts, splitting into two in some agonized or imperfect mind–time is the wicked fairy to troubled people, granting them inevitably the thing they dread. While Archer's investigation is drawing him into the past, we are never allowed to forget that present time has been steadily increasing its menace. Mr. Macdonald has brought the fire toward us at closer and closer stages. By the time it gets as close as the top of the hill (this was the murder area), it appears "like a brilliant omniform growth which continued to grow until it bloomed very large against the sky. A sentinel quail on the hillside below it was ticking an alarm." Then, reaching the Broadhurst house, "the fire bent around it like the fingers of a hand, squeezing smoke out of the windows and then flame."

Indeed the fire is a multiple and accumulating identity, with a career of its own, a supercharacter that has earned itself a character's name–Rattlesnake. Significantly, Archer says, "There was only one good thing about the fire. It made people talk about the things that really concerned them."

What really concerns Archer, and the real kernel of the book, its heart and soul, is the little boy of six, good and brave and smart. He constitutes the book's emergency; he is also entirely believable, a full-rounded and endearing character. Ronny is the tender embodiment of everything Archer is by nature bound to protect, infinitely worthy of rescue.

When Archer plunges into a case his reasons are always personal reasons (this is one of the things that make us so much for Archer). The little boy for as long as he's missing will be Archer's own loss. And without relinquishing for a moment his clear and lively identity, the child takes on another importance as well: "The world was changing," says Archer, "as if with one piece missing the whole thing had come loose and was running wild."

If it is the character of the little boy that makes the case matter to Archer, so it is the character of Archer, whose first-person narrative forms all Mr. Macdonald's novels, that makes it matter to us. Archer from the start has been a distinguished creation; he was always an attractive figure and in the course of the last several books has matured and deepened in substance to our still greater pleasure. Possessed even when young of an endless backlog of stored information, most of it sad, on human nature, he tended once, unless I'm mistaken, to be a bit cynical. Now he is something much more, he is vulnerable. As a detective and as a man he takes the human situation with full seriousness. He cares. And good and evil both are real to him.

Archer knows himself to be a romantic, would call it a weakness–as he calls himself a "not unwilling catalyst" for trouble; he carries the knowledge around with him–that's how he got here. But he is in no way archaic. He is at heart a champion, but a self-questioning, often a self-deriding champion. He is of today, one of ours. "The Underground Man" is written so close to the nerve of today as to expose most of the apprehensions we live with.

In our day it is for such a novel as "The Underground Man" that the detective form exists. I think it also matters that it is the detective form, with all its difficult demands and its corresponding charms, that makes such a novel possible. What gives me special satisfaction about this novel is that no one but a good writer–*this* good writer–could have possibly brought it off. "The Underground Man" is Mr. Macdonald's best book yet, I think. It is not only exhilaratingly well done; it is also very moving.

Ross Macdonald's style, to which in large part this is due, is one of delicacy and tension, very tightly made, with a spring in it. It doesn't allow a static sentence or one without pertinence. And the spare, controlled narrative, built for action and speed, conveys as well the world through which the action moves and gives it meaning, brings scene and character, however swiftly, before the eyes without a blur. It is an almost unbroken series of sparkling pictures.

The style that works so well to produce fluidity and grace also suggests a mind much given to contemplation and reflection on our world. Mr. Macdonald's writing is something like a stand of clean, cool, well-branched, well tended trees in which bright birds can flash and perch. And not for show, but to sing.

A great deal of what this writer has to tell us comes by way of beautiful and audacious similes. "His hairy head seemed enormous and grotesque on his boy's body, like a papier-mâché saint's head on a stick": the troubled teen-ager's self-absorption, his sense of destiny–theatrical but maybe in a good cause–along with the precise way he looks and carries himself, are given us all in one. At the scene of evacuation from the forest fire, at the bottom of a rich householder's swimming pool "lay a blue mink coat, like the headless pelt of a woman." A sloop lying on her side, dismantled offshore, "flopped in the surge like a bird made helpless by oil." The Snows, little old lady and grown son: "The door of Fritz's room was ajar. One of his moist eyes appeared at the crack like the eye of a fish in an underwater crevice. His mother, at the other door, was watching him like a shark."

Descriptions so interpretive are of course here as part and parcel of the character of Archer who says them to us. Mr. Macdonald's accuracy of observation becomes Archer's detection–running evidence. Mr. Macdonald brings characters into sudden sharp focus too by arresting them in an occasional archetypical pose. The obsessed Stanley is here in the words of his wife: "Sometimes he'd be just sitting there shuffling through his pictures and his letters. He looked like a man counting his money." And Fritz in the lath house, where Archer is leaving him, complaining among his plants: "The striped shadow fell from the roof, jailbirding him."

INTERVIEW:

"An Interview with Ross Macdonald," *Concept, 12* (1971): 33-45.

This interview was conducted by three students from Santa Barbara City College and appeared in the college literary magazine. Millar had taught writing classes at SBCC and encouraged local writers.

INTERVIEWER: Mr. Millar, to what extent do you construct the preliminary foundations for your novel before you begin the actual writing?

MILLAR: Before I actually start writing I sometimes fill three or four notebooks; as much as 200 pages. I make sometimes notes almost as big as the novel and I spend more time on the e preparation than I do on the writing. I'll spend perhaps six months getting ready with my notes and five months writing the book.

INTERVIEWER: Do your notes incorporate scenes which you will use in the novel?

MILLAR: Very occasionally I will write a scene or an idea for a scene, but generally it's just structure and relationships between people and events.

INTERVIEWER: How much depth do you give your characters in your notes?

MILLAR: I don't try to write in depth about them, but I write a great deal about them. The truth is that the characters only come complete when I write the actual book. Everything comes together at once. Characters are subject to change until I actually start writing my final draft.

INTERVIEWER: Then you don't have a set personality in mind when you introduce a character?

MILLAR: I have some idea, but it's subject to change. It really gels when I start to write the book but that is subject to change too. Sometimes I change midway through. Everything is subject to change right up to the end.

INTERVIEWER: Including the plot?

MILLAR: Yes, I wasn't sure how the present book, *The Underground Man*, was going to end until I got about fifty pages from the end.

INTERVIEWER: Neither was I when I was reading it.

MILLAR: If I wasn't sure how could you be–that is desirable in fiction; everything should be up in the air.

INTERVIEWER: You've been using Lew Archer as your detective for many years. Would you say that the Archer in *The Underground Man* is more real than the Archer in–let's say *The Galton Case* which you wrote in the mid 50s?

MILLAR: What do you mean real?

INTERVIEWER: Well, for instance, in *The Galton Case* there were a few scenes in which the dialogue didn't seem consistent with Archer's character, and there was one scene where he was surrounded by men who had just given him a brutal beating and he made the foolish move of attacking them and receiving another beating. This seemed like a silly thing for an experienced man like Archer to do.

MILLAR: Well, this can happen in life though, but I would say that *The Galton Case* marks the end of a transition. I started off writing hard-boiled novels in a tradition in which the sort of event you mentioned was very common. This type of event isn't so likely to happen in the later books simply because I have a more mature idea of what Archer is. Let's say I put my own stamp on the tradition instead of just following the tradition.

INTERVIEWER: You mean you have matured Lew Archer as you have matured yourself? Rather than write a Lew Archer who would be more acceptable to your readers?

MILLAR: Well, of course, my readers are probably changing, too. We are all changing, but it isn't a deliberate attempt to make Lew Archer more acceptable, it is a changing conception. It has to do with my growing older I am sure. But it also has to do with the maturing form; you are more or less at its mercy until you master it and are able to change it yourself.

INTERVIEWER: Was *The Galton Case* the turning point, then?

MILLAR: Yes. I have always regarded that as a turning point. There are things in it that are from the tradition, and other things that mark a new departure. Not just for me, but for the hard-boiled mystery novel.

INTERVIEWER: How did you get into that form in the first place?

MILLAR: Well, it always interested me. You get into what you are really fascinated by. The detective story was about my favorite reading when I was in high school. I started reading Hammett when I was 13-14–when he was just coming out in the original editions. I also read a great many of the British mystery novelists. As a North American, I couldn't very well follow in the footsteps of the British mystery novelists; it is an entirely different tradition, and it doesn't really apply too well to North American experience. How did I originally get involved with this though? I think Poe was the writer who got me involved in tales of mystery and imagination, as he called them. I started reading Poe very early.

INTERVIEWER: About how early?

MILLAR: Oh, 12, I'd say. I was reading Dickens before that. Dickens was another writer who wrote a great deal about crime. Those are some of the literary influences that got me involved in it very early.

INTERVIEWER: Do you know any private detectives?

MILLAR: Yes, I do.

INTERVIEWER: Was that an interest that came before you started writing detective novels, or after?

MILLAR: Well, I have been writing detective novels for a long time. I have been writing crime novels for twenty-eight years; since before I came to California; so nearly everybody I know now I have come to know since I started writing crime novels. My most recent acquaintance among private detectives came here on account of my books. He was interested in setting up ethical standards for the behavior of private detectives, and he thought Archer would make a good model. He actually was interested in improving the ethics of private detectives.

INTERVIEWER: That was something I noticed about Archer too; he seemed much more compassionate than–what do I have to compare to–private detectives I have read about and seen on TV, but still he seemed more like a more compassionate character.

MILLAR: Like other people in real life, private detectives are better than the breed of them you see on TV. I've known a couple of other private detectives, both of whom are compassionate men, and understanding men, and imaginative men.

INTERVIEWER: That was what made me wonder if maybe you had been one, or probably had good friends who were.

MILLAR: No, I never was. Nearly everything I have Archer do I just make up. But it is true I have known all together four good private detectives.

INTERVIEWER: Let's discuss the literary relation of the detective novel, the mystery novel, and the spy novel, and how they are generally placed in one camp or another: fine tradition but just not great literature; the technique and the skill of the writer determining whether it is good or bad. Do you have any feelings about why it is only people like Poe, or Conan Doyle who are regarded as great literary people?

MILLAR: Poe is regarded as a great literary figure because he is. He is one of the seminal writers in North American literature. Now Conan Doyle is not really a great literary figure. Nobody would regard him really as a great writer. He was important for a great creation, which incidentally was to a large extent lifted from Poe. If you study Poe's short detective stories, of which there are several, "Murders in the Rue Morgue," "The Purloined Letter," and then compare them with a story by Conan Doyle, you'll find the whole Holmes-Watson set up was imitated from Poe. The reason why Conan Doyle was so successful was because he was a heck of a good plotter, but mainly he got in there first. He saw the possibilities of the form and used it. He really wasn't a great writer, though; let's face it. But Poe was. Because he was profoundly original. He almost invented not only the detective story, but also what you call tales of mystery and imagination. You know what I mean–the weird tales–those are the two you mentioned. I think what happens to the mystery form depends entirely on whose hands it falls into. It can be literature or not depending on who is writing it. I regard the works of Dashiell Hammett as literature, of course, and so do most other people whose judgment is valid.

INTERVIEWER: How do you regard your own novels?

MILLAR: In both the tradition of the mystery novel and also the tradition of literature, I think they're right in the main stream of the hard-boiled mystery novel. Just where I tried to put them. I have been working on that for twenty years.

INTERVIEWER: Do you think–that posterity will raise you to–where let's say Hammett is, or Raymond Chandler, or even Poe?

MILLAR: I don't know about posterity. We will be lucky if we have any. I mean that seriously. The whole future is so indeterminate that–I started out aiming at posterity. Now I'm just aiming at the present.

Interviewer: As a result of society or your own feelings about literature do you anticipate anything apocalyptic in this society, in California, or the country, or the world, or is that attitude just the result of your having written for twenty-eight years?

MILLAR: It has nothing to do with my writing. I'd feel the same if I weren't a writer. No, it is the possibility of nuclear disaster.

INTERVIEWER: Do you think it is a very real possibility right now?

MILLAR: It is a possibility all the time. As long as human beings have the power to do it, it can happen. Human beings are capable of anything.

INTERVIEWER: Is that where you would place the emphasis? On nuclear disaster?

MILLAR: To me that is the biggest danger still.

INTERVIEWER: A theme that comes through fairly strong in your novels is the crumbling of our family structure and its effect on society. Would you rate that as one of our biggest problems?

MILLAR: As somebody pointed out, in fact many people have pointed out, we are moving out from what they call the stem family to the nuclear family. The stem family being the family where several generations that are ruled over by the male head of the family, as on a farm, or among the working classes still in our cities to some extent–the white working class–to the nuclear family which consists of father, mother and children. I think we are in a period of transition to even more diluted family structure than that.

INTERVIEWER: A structure resulting from the broken home?

MILLAR: Eventually we'll just have to stop regarding it as a broken home and start regarding it as a new kind of home.

INTERVIEWER: Is that what you mean by diluted then, divorce and things?

MILLAR: Yes. If we keep regarding the one marriage, for example, as the only possible thing, and anything else is a broken home, you are going to have an awful lot more broken homes than not. So we are going to have to, I guess, start thinking, as we have already, in terms of making divorce easy, which we have done here in California in the last year. It has been a step in the direction of even less family structure.

INTERVIEWER: But does this solve the problem of a degenerating society?

MILLAR: It doesn't solve any problems. We still have to solve our problems whether we maintain one family-like structure or another; the problems have to be solved by individual human beings assuming responsibility for other people they are in relationship with whether it be their own children or not.

INTERVIEWER: Personally, how comfortable are you with the idea that the family structure seems to be getting thinner and thinner?

MILLAR: Well, you see, it's really a tragic situation if you look at it in terms of past values and past situations in which I was brought up, but things change, and you change tragedy into something else by understanding it. It's unfortunate, really, in a way, that this should be the example. I don't know. Many of my friends are divorced, and I know how many of their children suffer from it. The truth is one parent can do a pretty good job, and "parent" doesn't even have to be the child's blood parent. That is what I am saying. There are still relationships, important relationships with people who are not related to you. And many children do have such relationships and grow up successfully. You have to pick up your relationships where you can in a much more fluid society. You can't just depend on a rigid structure in which you remain in a fixed relationship to your father. Your father might be off married to somebody else, but there might be a substitute father available, or a father surrogate, your mother's next husband, perhaps, or perhaps not, perhaps somebody you just meet in another relationship with the family. Most meetings now don't occur within the family.

INTERVIEWER: You recently stated in a *Newsweek* article that the Oedipus myth was your favorite myth.

MILLAR: That is just the one I have used most. The one I think you should mention—just finishing up what I said to you. This question of the father substitute comes out very strong in *The Underground Man* where Archer becomes a kind of father substitute for the little boy. It's an illustration of what I'm talking about. Of course, that is what the book is about to a great extent.

INTERVEIWER: You have said that Archer's function is to be the imaginative catalyst–that he makes it possible for you to dredge up material which you wouldn't be able to dredge up writing in your own person. How much of your own life do you inject into the characters directly, and how far do you remove yourself by using Lew Archer instead of yourself?

MILLAR: Yes, I've said that, and the whole apparatus of the detective story, the whole apparatus and tradition is to provide what I once described as a welder's mask which enables you to handle dangerously hot material.

INTERVIEWER: You've also said that everybody has a bit of Oedipus in them, and I was wondering whether this could be brought up to a societal level, where people are alienated from each other by "technical apparatus"–people seeking a spiritual father to be a traitor to–to find that father so that he can die and be replaced by that person. And then the person can go on, and be free to be nobody's son, so to speak, as it is somewhat like, well, here in Southern California, where people are very free in a physical way from each other–actually so free from each other in a psychological way that, as you pointed out in your books, they walk around lonely and sad. In Southern California there is a mass of lonely alienated people.

MILLAR: I think actually this is true in all parts of the country. I just happen to be writing books in California. People in the other parts of the country read it and say, "Aha, that's the way it is in Southern California." They don't realize it's true of them, too. The products of what we are describing as this technological society have disrelated people under all the old forms, and I agree with what you said about the need to identify the father and become disengaged from him. I recognize that there are potential fathers everywhere for young people or for anybody else. I don't see any particular virtue or magical quality in blood relationship at all. In fact, I think it's been very much overrated.

INTERVIEWER: If anything, would you say it could be harmful in some cases?

MILLAR: Yes, I think so–I think so because people who are bound together by blood relationships also have the same heredity. It makes it tough on both of them.

INTERVIEWER: You did your doctoral dissertation on Coleridge, I believe.

MILLAR: Yes.

INTERVIEWER: I'd like to read something Coleridge wrote; I am quoting it as a secondary source from a book of Borges who quotes Coleridge as writing: " . . . in our dreams, images represent the sensations we think they cause. We do not feel horror because we are threatened by a sphinx. We dream of a sphinx in order to explain the horror we feel."

Could you react to this statement by Coleridge, as regarding your own books? Can you see any connection between some of the things that you write and the myth we hold within our minds, of people going to look for their fathers after fifteen years of disattachment and physical disassociation? Also, how about dreams? How much, if at all, do you rely on them and how do they affect you?

MILLAR: I can't relate it to Coleridge in the sense of using Coleridge to explain me, because what he said there is a very simple statement really; this is just that you lie down and you go to sleep and it starts to rain, and you might dream that you are in a flood. That is all he is saying there really; he is saying the dream is created by a physical sensation which you experience while you're sleeping. It really doesn't do much to explain dreams. Coleridge was a great psychologist, but not in the area of dreams–his own dreams were so God-awful that he couldn't really face up to them and do a Freudian analysis at all. In this case he is really reducing the importance of dreams; he is not trying to do anything big there.

INTERVIEWER: Do you really think he was saying that it is physical sensation? I think he used the example of horror and I thought he meant that during your daily life you feel some horror, and in your dreams you are making a thing that would react to it.

MILLAR: Yes, you're right. You are quite right. There was more to it than I said. He was talking about moral facts. Nevertheless, what he is saying is pretty simple, compared with what we have learned about dreams–but what is your question again?

INTERVIEWER: How to relate Coleridge's statement to your works. For instance, Lew Archer, his character, his life, his ideals, and your own.

MILLAR: I think my books are related to the unconscious life the same way that dreams come out. Sometimes, I get an authentication of what I am writing by dreaming. Sometimes I'll have a dream that'll suggest something I'm writing. I can't immediately give you an example, but the two things do go hand in hand. You might think of books as rationalized nightmares, but they are not really nightmares because they are related to what is going on in the world. And they make an attempt to describe what is going on in the world, not in factual terms, but in imaginative terms. They are half-way between a sociological report and a nightmare.

INTERVIEWER: Do you have any aspirations to write in any other literary genres: play-writing, or film scripts, or poetry, or *do* you write other things and just keep it secret?

MILLAR: I have written a lot of verse but not much recently, and I don't have the facility for it that I had when I was younger. I realized especially after I came to know some good poets that I wasn't a poet. I think I prefer to do what I am good at. Every now and then there is a poem in one of my books, and it is generally one that I wrote some years ago.

INTERVIEWER: Was "Luna" in *The Galton Case* one of them?

MILLAR: Yes. I wrote that when I was 19 and in college. That is probably as good a poem as I ever wrote. Poets who don't develop past the age of 19 ought to give up and I did. I don't have any ability, special ability, to write screen plays. I collaborated on one once, and it didn't come off to my satisfaction, or anybody else's. I would have liked to write plays; in fact, my original ambition in college was to write plays. For that reason I acted in a couple of plays to get some stage experience to write out of. But after that I wasn't in contact with the theater, and a play-wright without a theater is like a man without any legs trying to walk. I just gradually gave up the whole idea of becoming a playwright. Once you have become established in a form and have learned how to make the form express what you want to say, you don't feel much like going back and starting on a different form. I told Brooks Atkinson, whom I got involved with a few years ago (for about 35 years he was the *New York Times* drama critic), that I once wanted to be a playwright, but that I never made it. He said I was extremely lucky, given the condition of the American theater today. That is true. It is a very tough place for a man to try to make a living or make his way as an artist, and even some of the very good ones have fallen.

INTERVIEWER: How do you feel about something like state support or a national foundation set up by the government or the states to support the arts? Do you think it would work in any beneficial way for the artists of America?

MILLAR: It is working now, in a sense. We don't have government support for novelists, but we do have Guggenheim fellowships, which are essentially government supported. The Guggenheim foundation is tax free; the Guggenheim fellowships are paid for by the taxpayers, essentially.

INTERVIEWER: Aren't they given to the people who have something out already, something of substance, and who are just about on their way?

MILLAR: Yes, in order to get a Guggenheim fellowship you have to have done something already; nevertheless, they seem to work pretty well for a general class of writing. Generally high-brow writing. I don't know of any popular writers who have gotten Guggenheims. The trouble with government support of the arts, such as they have made in Russia, is that they also give government the power to withhold support to the extent of practically blanking a man out, as they tried to recently with Solzhenitsyn. Unless you can be sure of the purity of the intentions of your government, it might not be the best idea in the world for the arts to be taken over on a grand scale. One of the things that gives the current administration's attack on the TV networks the strength and the importance that it has is the fact that the government has the right to license television, and they can withhold licensing. They are in a position to shut down television stations if they really want to. If they can get away with it. So there are things to be said on both sides. I think it would be desirable, of course, for our government to do more for the arts, as the governments normally do in other countries, but I don't think the popular writing that we are talking about would necessarily benefit from it. Popular writing is not just written between the writer and the page; it is between the writer and his audience, and part of the enormous excitement of writing for popular audiences is that relationship with your audience. You have to catch it and you have to hold it; that is part of the writing. I am glad you brought that up. I am much happier than I would be working for the damn government. Under our free economic system, this seems like an awfully good way to make a living, if you can do it.

INTERVIEWER: Do you think even with the controls that we have in this democratic system that it would ever get to a point where the government could pressure a writer to write or not write a certain way?

MILLAR: I have seen what happens in universities and it is true that I don't know much about pressure being brought to bear on creative writers in universities; ordinarily they're allowed to follow their own paths. I do know this, though, that sometimes the people who do the choosing of the guy who is going to get the help are not competent. And this is generally true in bureaucracies, both academic and governmental. The guys who are making the choice may more resemble Boss Daley than Virginia Woolf.

INTERVIEWER: You were speaking before of your desire to write plays. You have been writing twenty-eight years, but when did you decide mystery was what you were going to pursue?

MILLAR: Twenty-eight years ago.

INTERVIEWER: After your first novel?

MILLAR: My first novel was a spy novel. I have only written one novel that was not in the general crime field, and it was terrible. It was so bad I never sent it in. It was the traditional boyhood and youth novel.

INTERVIEWER: *Catcher in the Rye* type?

MILLAR: I wish it had been!

INTERVIEWER: When, in the sequence of your novels, was this?

MILLAR: It was my fifth.

INTERVIEWER: Then you weren't quite sure that the mystery vein was the way you wanted to go?

MILLAR: Well, it wasn't that so much. I wanted to do this other. My life was complicated, or made easy, in another sense, by the fact that my wife was a mystery writer.

INTERVIEWER: Before you?

MILLAR: Yes, she started writing mysteries around 1940. There is no question that if it hadn't been for her breaking the ground–I worked with her on her books as a critic, and so on, thus learning how to do it–I might never have become a mystery writer in spite of all my interest in the form.

INTERVIEWER: Would you have gone on to some other form?

The paperback sales of Millar's books in England during the 1970s were probably stimulated by the covers.

MILLAR: I was already writing. I was writing for publications from 1939 on. I was writing other things, short stories, verse, humorous skits.

INTERVIEWER: Are you going to keep pursuing the mystery vein?

MILLAR: Yes, I'll pursue it to the point where it's no longer useful to me. You see, I'm still finding things to do with it.

INTERVIEWER: In this country there seems to be an idea that a writer has to suffer life and endure all torments before he can write and be accepted. Hemingway and Fitzgerald are good examples. Why do you think this is?

MILLAR: It is very difficult to learn how to be an American writer and how to survive, but it is not true that you have to suffer. Fitzgerald, for instance, only wrote one great novel, a very short novel, *The Great Gatsby*, that was considered great, and he wrote it before he went through his great problems. Yet on the basis of that book he is being acclaimed as the greatest of contemporary fiction writers. In the United States a writer enters into a fraternity of sickness partly because of our basically egalitarian society. English writers enter a higher class and are protected by it.

INTERVIEWER: How about writers and alcohol?

MILLAR: Why are writers alcoholics? A reaction to the wound peculiar to this country. You must be wounded to have the wherewithal to write, like the Greek who had to be wounded to pull the bow.

INTERVIEWER: What advice would you give to young writers today?

MILLAR: Young writers? Try to find out what you're good at. Young writers, I think, some of them, aim too low but most of them aim too high. To limit themselves to purely literary writing is a false limitation imposed by the universities. Of course, there is a lot of crap in popular writing too. As a young writer you have to write what you can write in order to develop into what you're capable of.

INTERVIEW:

Sam Grogg, Jr., "Ross Macdonald: At the Edge," *Journal of Popular Culture,* 7 (Summer 1973): 213-222.

Millar makes the point that he adapted the detective-novel form to the purpose of writing about contemporary American life.

This interview took place over two days in Santa Barbara, California. We sat in Millar's cabaña at his beach club on the edge of the Pacific Ocean. During our talk, Millar would occasionally glance at the offshore oil-rigs not too far away. But flights of migrating seabirds would bring back his attention and he would smile.

GROGG: What do you think of the critical attention which has been recently given to your work? Do you think you deserve it?

MILLAR: Yes. Although, I'm surprised by it. You don't always get what you deserve. A writer gets used to not having attention, inattention. I did.

GROGG: What's most important to you: critical attention or the fact that millions of people read your novels?

MILLAR: The second. But I like both. I'll tell you the truth, though, it's good for a writer to spend the greater part of his working life without getting too much attention. I think it's somewhat distracting. It's better just to do your work than to be a writer with a capital "W." And I'm still trying to do that. I haven't let this new attention change my way of life at all. I'm living very much the way I did twenty years ago. Except that I have more money.

GROGG: Can you ever see yourself writing for the critics first and those millions second?

MILLAR: I wouldn't know how to write for the critics. All I really know is how to tell my own kind of story. I really wouldn't know how to do anything different.

GROGG: Have you ever had any criticism that has really affected you adversely?

MILLAR: Well, my books were frequently dismissed by reviewers.

GROGG: Do you think that was because they were "detective" novels rather than "novel" novels?

MILLAR: Partly that and partly the fact that they're in the "hard-boiled" vein. That was regarded as "infra dig" for a long time–below the level of adult attention by some critics. And this was true, unfortunately, of some of the most powerful critics. By critics, I really mean "reviewers." The "critics" really have no part in this at all. And I was hurt by Raymond Chandler's dismissal of my work. But that's understandable, too. His work and mine are really quite different.

GROGG: You mentioned the "hard-boiled" tradition. How has that tradition influenced you, and how have you tried to influence it?

MILLAR: Well, I think all writers who have any serious interest in writing start out with something that's been done before, a tradition if that's what you want to call it, and gradually make an attempt to infuse that tradition with their own ideas and attitudes. That's what I've been doing. In other words, I've been trying to mold the tradition my own way.

GROGG: George Grella has pointed out that the "hard-boiled" detective novel is appropriate for reflecting American attitudes and values. Do you agree with this idea of appropriateness?

MILLAR: Yes. I think the American "hard-boiled" detective novel was invented to reflect American society, which was and is still becoming an equalitarian society. Everything is in process of change. Although it's true that things are changing in England and Europe too, they are changing very slowly and, so to speak, against the grain. And that grain is represented by the English detective story which is highly formalistic and socially stratified.

GROGG: But your novels, which deal with this "nouveau-riche" society of southern California, seem almost to represent a bridge between the "hard-boiled" and the "formal" detective novel traditions.

MILLAR: It's sort of inevitable that that should happen because I was brought up in Canada which is kind of a cultural bridge between England and the United States. I was raised not only on the American "hard-boiled" tradition, but also on the English tradition. There is, I think, in my work a melding of the two, to some extent. With emphasis on the American, though. Incidentally, in a new society when people are rich, they're inevitably "nouveau-riche," and to have a family that goes back three generations of known people or successful people almost constitutes being an aristocrat.

I have certain advantages from having been brought up in two cultures, Canadian and American. They're closely related but, nevertheless, they're different enough so it's like looking through binoculars as compared with looking through a telescope. You see things in more depth. Having not only studied literature and history, but taught them in Canada before I became an American writer, I can see American life in relation to another culture which I know equally well. I really know the Anglo-Canadian culture more deeply and thoroughly than I do the American culture. The things you know best are what you learn between the ages of five and twenty-five. Of course, we write out of our experience. So, I think

I can refer to myself as a North American novelist, although nearly all the action of my books takes place in the United States. There's an advantage in being different. You know that Canadian background is really an essential differentia of my books. It would be hard to point out how. For me to point it out. But I know that's the difference.

You can't understand one culture without having known another. This is true of all knowledge. There has to be a comparison possible. If you just know one culture, there's nothing to say about it, nothing to know about it. It's just there. You see, I am a scholar trained as a teacher in history, both ordinary history and intellectual history and, somehow or other, that background of historical knowledge and the full knowledge of another culture and of a native culture enables me to, I think, write more fully about the American culture. Which is mine by choice. You see, I'm really just in the same situation that Americans are in, only intensified. The American culture is still a development from the English culture, let's say European, though primarily from the English. Since I came from a place that was sort of a half-way point in the development from English to American, i.e. Canadian culture in America, my books are at the same time quite intimate in relation to American life, and also somewhat distanced.

GROGG: Space, this natural environment of Santa Barbara and southern California, seems quite important in your work. Why have you chosen this agrarian, natural setting for Archer to traverse?

MILLAR: It's the part that really interests me. Other people have done the city over and over again. You know, there's a certain advantage in getting out into the open, where there's a little more dilution of people by nature and that sort of thing. I think this is the ideal mix, myself, for civilization. And I'm not alone in thinking that. I talked to Constantinos Doxiadis when he was here in Santa Barbara. He called attention to the fact that Santa Barbara was approximately the size and general shape of what he considered the ideal city, Periclean Athens. Same population. The fact that everything, downtown anyway, is within walking distance. The city's small enough so that everybody, so to speak, can get to know everybody else if he wants to. No high-rise pressing you down into the

earth and cutting off the sky and the view. Doxiadis said it was his conception, or corresponded to his conception, of the ideal city.

GROGG: There seems to be a slow-down, or calmness out here.

MILLAR: That's true, there is a slow-down, and an opening out. I mean you're exposed to space out here. You're not surrounded by people and buildings.

GROGG: This area, Santa Barbara, is certainly almost an idyllic setting.

MILLAR: With a very high murder rate. We've got six or seven unsolved murders just along the beach in the last three years. Life in California does have a fairytale aspect. It seems unreal unless you get into the interior of it. Unless you really understand how people are living here, it looks like a dream. Everything seems to be a delightful movie-like fantasy on the surface.

GROGG: Nature and the landscape are a constant reference point in your Archer novels.

MILLAR: I just feel that man's connection with nature is indispensable to him. And a society or an individual literally goes insane if they lose touch entirely with natural rhythms and natural forces, both exterior and internal. And the two are in touch with each other. They speak back and forth to each other, the external Nature and the inner nature of man. As Wordsworth said: "One impulse from a vernal wood/may teach you more of man/of moral evil and of good/than all the sages can." Now that's an overstatement, but that's the sort of reference I'm going back to when I use Nature. And the destruction of Nature is a serious moral crime because it destroys man and his ability to live in the world.

GROGG: That's why the offshore oil rigs and the recent oil spills must have affected you very deeply.

MILLAR: Well, (pause). It's been the most important public event in my life during the last several years. And I've written three articles and a book about it.

GROGG: How do you write? What is the process behind a Macdonald novel?

MILLAR: I generally spend about six months preparing to write. I'll fill notebooks with ideas, plot developments, and so on. Generally, there will be several ideas for books going on simultaneously. Sooner or later I feel ready to start a book. I drop away the ideas that I'm not going to use, make a choice, and start writing. And I generally find that everything I've written in the notes gets absorbed into the one book.

I really just write them the way I like them in the hope that somebody else will like them too. But I think that people like a rapid story clearly told, but also with some depth. The mind isn't satisfied, even the young mind, by an account of life that doesn't give the depths of life.

GROGG: You mention that a "rapid story clearly told," is one of your goals as a detective novelist. But in your attempt to get at that goal you present some of the most complicated and finely wrought plots ever devised.

MILLAR: To me, the essence of the novel is its structure. It doesn't have to be as intricate as we're talking about. But you see, I get ideas that can only be worked out intricately. There is no way, for instance, that I would have written *The Chill* except in terms of that complex plot. It covers the whole lives of a number of people. There's just no other way to tell the story. And oddly enough, as I said, I get read by fifteen-year-old kids and, I don't know how they do it, but they seem able to understand my books.

GROGG: What do your novels turn on? Is it the story, the structure? Is it Archer? Chandler, for instance, placed a great deal of emphasis on his hero, Philip Marlowe. Do you feel that such focus is important in your novels?

MILLAR: Not nearly to the extent that Chandler's books do. That's one of the troubles of the Chandler books. He's too bound up with his hero, who is a self-projection, of course. And he doesn't move freely enough into other lives. He's constantly coming back to the subjective experience of Marlowe, whom I don't find all that interesting. I find the other characters in Chandler's books more interesting, although Marlowe is a fine creation. I'm just speaking in terms of how I'd do it. And I really have tried to play down, to a certain extent, the personality of the detective and to make him more a means of getting into the lives of other people. He represents the author, but not with the idea of blowing him up large. He's essentially a narrator. A man who gets around in order to narrate, looking at it from just the technical point of view.

And he's an eye. And an ear. He's a man too, but I'm not writing about him in that capacity so much. I leave out his private life. In fact, I become very impatient with detective stories that devote too much space to the private life of the author as represented by the detective. Many of the other characters are at least as interesting to me as Archer is. And some of them are just as representative of me as Archer is.

GROGG: In an early novel of yours, *Trouble Follows Me*, the hero, Sam Drake, spends much of the closing chapter pointing out the importance of the gun. In your latest novel, *Underground Man*, there is extremely little emphasis on the gun or gunplay. In fact, I don't believe Archer ever carries one. Why this change in attitude towards the gun?

MILLAR: When I took up writing the books we're talking about, the form was essentially a novel of violence. That's what *Trouble Follows Me* is. It's a social novel with its dealings with the racial theme expressed in terms of violence. But as one develops, one tries other ways, perhaps more subtle ways, of dealing with the subject matter. I have, myself, an objection to guns. I hate the idea of there being so many guns floating around in our society constantly being used to kill people. You know, when you write about a person like Archer—I won't call him a hero, but he is intended to be a kind of middle representative of American man—you want him to do the things that are representative in a good sense rather than a negative sense. In other words, I like him to be able to operate without violence, though he's sometimes subjected to it and he has to fight back. This is a concept that gradually grew over the years. It corresponds to real life, too. The detectives that I know don't carry guns ordinarily.

GROGG: Archer seems to be continually involved with broken marriages and, for the most part, finds himself in search of the missing pieces trying to put things back together again.

MILLAR: I'm profoundly concerned with broken marriages. I was the child of one. I'm sure that has a lot to do with it. Don't forget, though, that the Archer novels, and mystery novels in general, are about various kinds of brokenness. It's various kinds of social, psychological, and moral brokenness that lead to crime. In our society, which is virtually a society of broken marriage (we have almost a fifty percent divorce rate), a man who's really trying to write honestly about the problems of the society will focus on some of these things. In other words, they're not just a personal interest, though they are that; they also reflect, or try to reflect, the truth of what's happening to society. We seem to be moving away from the traditional concept of marriage. And you write about what's there. Writers don't have much control over their material. It's there. And it's not only outside, but it's in them too.

GROGG: Archer, too, is a product of a broken marriage.

MILLAR: I didn't realize how important it was going to be in the first book when I made him a divorced man, but it seems to have become a central part of his life, his loneliness.

GROGG: Archer seems to make little contact, other than official, with the opposite sex. Why the sexlessness of your detective fiction?

MILLAR: I'm deliberately, in my work, trying to get away from the idea that the private detective is a sex hero. I'm playing down that aspect because I'm interested in a different sort of image, model, and man. I'm trying to make him a man first. I'm also concerned with the fact that my books are read by people from age fourteen or fifteen up. I started my life as a high school teacher, and I'm concerned with the kind of character I present. I'm not offering Archer as a model man, but I set limits to the things he does because he's a moral man. He's not a model of morality, but like several good private detectives I know, he's a better man than most of the people he has to work with. That's what makes him effective. He's in control of himself. He's not a moral ideal, not a paragon, but a guy that is fairly trustworthy. And he's not in it just for the money and he has a vision of the way things ought to be. Of course, these things are just signs that he's a human being. All human beings hate to lie. And all human beings have a vision of something good that they'd like to see played out in life. The only people who don't are the very sick and the criminal, who are essentially the same, that is the same group, the mentally sick people and the criminal.

GROGG: In *The Moving Target*, the first Archer novel, Archer intimates that he is "a new kind of detective." What's new about him?

MILLAR: Well, I intended him to be both new and old. If there is any novelty in him in *The Moving Target*, I think it's in the fact that his explorations are essentially of people and their lives rather than of terrain and clues. He's a psychological and moral detective. I can't claim that that's a wholly new development, but in the context of the American "hard-boiled" tradition, there is something a bit new about it. And later, of course, I was able to develop him in that direction.

GROGG: What kind of guy is Archer?

MILLAR: Well, I've written eighteen books about him, and I've sort of covered the subject. But I consider him a man who's limited by his job and by his nature. He's not a great hero type in either the physical or the intellectual sense. He's a man who is in touch with the ordinary and content to be fairly ordinary. And at the same time he has moral interests and humane interests which are reflected not so much in what he does, but in how he does it. He takes his job seriously. I mean he's not just concerned with running down a criminal. He's concerned with the whole interrelationship of people that produces crime and is affected by crime. His primary interest is understanding other people's lives. And trying to make sense of them. Archer has two aspects. In one aspect he's an ordinary man, a private detective doing a not terribly well-paid job and working hard at it. And there's the other aspect of him where he's the representative of the novelist in the novel, and, in a sense, the mind of the novel. It's his observing mind in which things are put together and in which the whole novel exists, in a sense. So, he has, like all first-person narrator-characters, two aspects that have to be distinguished from one another. One is the man, the other is the voice of the novel, and readers don't seem to have any trouble making that distinction. They like a little literary sophistication. Even the fourteen or fifteen year olds. It's true, though, there hasn't been very imaginative understanding of the nature of first-person narration in criticism. I've never seen it explained clearly. It's basically simple enough. What I've said was simple enough.

Archer really isn't the hero of these books, in the old-fashioned sense. He's more of a narrator and observer than hero, although he's on the scene the whole time. But what happens, happens essentially to a lot of other people, twenty or more people in every book. It's their story that he tells, not his own. You never get to know very much about Archer's life apart from his working life.

GROGG: Archer refers to himself in a few places as a modern day Natty Bumppo. Does he function as a contemporary Bumppo?

MILLAR: Yes, of course. I think that the whole idea of the . . . let's call him the benevolent hunter, came to us through Natty Bumppo. Natty didn't originate in Cooper's book, though. He originated in the men who existed behind the books. And Archer is, to a certain extent, a descendant both socially and literarily of those men. It's the western tradition. The west was further east when Natty Bumppo existed. Our west has gradually moved from the Atlantic seaboard to the Pacific seaboard.

GROGG: Often in your books, the reader is treated to a glimpse of a revelation about himself and the society in which he lives. Archer, in fact, becomes as much a public eye as he is a private eye.

MILLAR: That's what a writer is supposed to be. I wouldn't describe myself as a seer, but I do have moments of what I would call penetration in my life. I think all writers do. That's what makes them want to write. And, of course, what you see isn't always negative, but often highly positive.

GROGG: Archer has better than average perception and penetrating abilities also.

MILLAR: Good detectives do. You have to remember, though, Archer is not just a detective, not just a fictional detective. He's also the narrator of a novel. So, he gets automatically endowed with all of the literary and imaginative qualities that the author has. Huckleberry Finn is a twelve or thirteen year-old boy. He's also a great poet. He's the vehicle of some of the greatest poetic prose ever written. Archer is more than himself. He's also the voice of the novel.

GROGG: Julian Symons in his recent study of the crime novel, *Mortal Consequences: A History from the Detective Story to the Crime Novel*, has mentioned your repeated use of the Oedipal-Electra themes as evidence of your unwillingness to experi-

ment with new themes and ideas. Do you think that this might be a valid criticism of your work?

MILLAR: Well, possibly it is, but it's a criticism that could be made of almost any serious writer. Every writer has his themes and follows them to the end. Of course, there's a compulsive return to certain themes, but that's not peculiar to me. There's a similar compulsive return to her themes in the work of Patricia Highsmith, who is Julian Symons' favorite author of crime fiction. Symons' own work, though there are some returning themes, does try to go on to new territory every time. But I find that my own territory continually changes and deepens under my eye. This kind of originality may be missed by an alien eye like Julian's.

The structure of my books has often been described as Freudian, meaning that what happens to you in early childhood is determinant. Though that's more than Freudian. People knew that long before Freud. But the peculiar tone and attitude in which these ideas are expressed, I guess, is Freudian. I'm certainly a disciple of Freud. Freud was a revelation to me, a major part of my education, and my wife's. But there have been other psychiatrists and analysts since that have been very influential on me and other writers. The existentialist school of psychoanalysis, for example. Still I think I can claim that in my later books I have made the ideas my own, given them my own leverage and meaning in the structures.

GROGG: Reading your novels, one is struck by the actionlessness of them. They are clearly from another mold than the typical ripsnorting mystery yarns.

MILLAR: That kind of fiction and the kind of fiction I write offer two kinds of satisfaction. One is essentially fantasy, and the other while it has its element of fantasy, is essentially realistic. That is, the satisfactions are the satisfactions you get from recognizing reality rather than from going off on some dream-adventure. I don't pretend that it's a lot of fun to be Archer. Still he does move around a great deal, and I wouldn't describe either him or the books as actionless.

GROGG: Archer's attempts to understand people's lives rather than to trace step-by-step the development of a case seem to come out of a nonlinear rather than linear sense of logic. He seems more interested in inter-relationships and patterns than with linear deduction. Is he the appropriate hero for the McLuhan age of non-linearity? Is there a connection between Marshall McLuhan's ideas and your fiction?

MILLAR: Yes. I think there's some connection between McLuhan's ideas and my narrative practice. Of course, I've been a great fan of McLuhan for twenty years, ever since *The Mechanical Bride*. I know him. I've audited one of his courses. We exchange all our books. I'm complimented by the idea because McLuhan is one of our great modern "understanders," I think. I don't pretend to be. And I'm not trying to write overtly intellectual material. I, of course, have been trying to use the detective novel, this is not accidental, to use it and change it into a form that could be used to express new perceptions and new meanings including the new "wholenesses" that you have to pick up. You have to look at a scene and pick it up quickly, nowadays, because it's changing. And that's essentially what Archer is doing. That's why I have to keep writing new books. The scene keeps changing. It's changed enormously in the twenty-five years that I've been working on this, and so have I changed. Therefore, the books have changed.

I'm really trying to write about contemporary life. I've found the detective form useful for this. In fact, that's why I write in this form. The old linear novel just comes to pieces under the new conditions of life. I found I couldn't write about them any other way. I'm trying to set up typical patterns that can be used for understanding contemporary life. I'm not really offering the novel as a substitute for science, psychology, sociology, etc. Nevertheless, the novel is one of our most important tools for learning how to understand life and to apprehend it later. Isn't that true? It's almost traditional over the last century that fiction has been a main tool of social understanding. If you wanted to stretch it a little, you could include drama and now, of course, the movies. We learn to see reality through the popular arts we create and patronize. That's what they're for. That's why we love them. Yearning for reality and the pleasure of it and the knowledge of it are the basis of art.

GROGG: But the reality of the detective novel is often an exaggerated one. For instance, almost all detective novels focus on the crime of murder. Why murder and not some other crime?

MILLAR: It's the ultimate crime. It's the ultimate crime in a secular society, and the mystery novel is essentially the expression of a secular society. But it's really symbolic. Murder stands for various kinds of crime. And, in fact, in my books it reflects other kinds of crime. It's the objective correlative, you might say, of spiritual death. That's why I write about extreme situations such as murder. They are a metaphor for our daily lives. We live in extreme situations in the United States. We're close to the edge in many ways. Which is quite thrilling too. It's an interesting way to live, if you can survive it.

GROGG: Taking your Archer novels together, one might point out that your work is of epic magnitude.

MILLAR: No, I wouldn't say epic in "magnitude," but perhaps epic in nature. You see, there are various kinds of epics. Some of the Icelandic and Norse sagas are not particularly big or particularly mythical. The *Saga of Grettir the Strong*, which is a very good one, and was very influential on me, is about a man who could have been an actual man and probably was. The essence of it, combined with his strength, was a kind of understated wit. One of the things you have in the back of your mind, hopefully, when you start a series is that it may turn out to be something that will take up and embody the characteristics of the society which you are writing about. That's what epic is for. That's what I have in mind. By epic, I don't mean something enormous or something terribly ambitious. A writer who can write a long novel or series of novels about a society and express it rather fully is doing a kind of epic work. Whether it's of great magnitude or not doesn't matter. Of course there are seventeen novels about Archer now. That's long.

GROGG: Why use the detective novel to work out your vision of society?

MILLAR: Well, people should work on what interests and fascinates them. It seems to be the form that suits me. I don't find myself thinking in terms of straight novels. Perhaps it's because I have a rather complex attitude towards society and towards life in general. And a somewhat "downbeat" attitude, at least superficially "downbeat." Though, I think, in general, the Archer books could be called hopeful. By definition, of course, the mystery novel is "downbeat." It has to do with crime, crime and punishment. But there are other things in my novels, too–other values. I haven't run out of things to do in the detective form yet.

GROGG: What have your novels done for you personally?

MILLAR: I think they've deepened my understanding of life. They've made me, in recent years at least, a good living. They've made me into a writer instead of something else. I used to be a teacher. And while writing is a much lonelier life, it has satisfactions that you don't get out of teaching. For one thing, it's a rarer form of life. Let's put it this way, my novels have made me into a novelist.

INTERVIEW:

Jerry Tutunjian, "A Conversation with Ross Macdonald," *Tamarack Review*, 62 (1974): 66-85.

This interview was conducted after publication of The Underground Man. *Although Millar did not relish his celebrity status, he was generous in granting interviews and took them seriously. The statement here that "What makes a novelist is the inability to forget his childhood" provides a key to his work.*

TUTUNJIAN: When you came to California in the early forties you said it seemed to you that this could be the brave new world. Talking about San Francisco, the poet Chad Bolling in *The Galton Case* says the city could be the New Athens. After thirty years in California, have your views changed? Do you still think this could be the brave new world?

MACDONALD: Chad Bolling wasn't speaking for me; he was speaking for himself about the New Athens. He was speaking as a poet with poetic license. However, the general idea was mine– that here was the possibility of making a new civilization–and the answer is yes, we are making a new civilization and it is one of the leading new places in the world. It seems to me to be perhaps the central place in the world, and the bellwether of the world at the present time. Technological civilization since the war was essentially a California in-

vention. One of the men who invented modern technology in the broadest sense lives just up the street from me, for example. Another thing that represents the brave new world or at least the hopeful new world is the development of environmentalism. It really grew out of California first and has spread first all over the country and now all over the world.

TUTUNJIAN: Yes, but there's the other side of the coin. Some call it the California dream and others call it the California nightmare.

MACDONALD: This is true of all high civilizations–they have two sides to their coin. You find if you look at any high civilization, historical or current, it has the underside too. That nightmare exists in all civilizations, but in a really high civilization it's realized in art. It becomes part of the consciousness of the people and it becomes possible for them to awaken from the nightmare, which is what civilization is for.

TUTUNJIAN: Would you consider Canada in the seventies as a brave new world? For the first time in many years, the number of Americans moving to Canada last year was more than the Canadians moving to the United States. These were not just draft-dodgers but professional people.

MACDONALD: I certainly would consider Canada as a brave new world. I'm afraid, though, unless it's more careful than it has been it could just follow the U. S. down the same route.

TUTUNJIAN: What's that route?

MACDONALD: Oh, economic overdevelopment–emphasis on money and things like that. But there are many respects, as you well know being a Canadian, in which Canada is superior to the U. S. Civil discipline, for example, is infinitely better in Canada than it is here, and it's a much more stable civilization but it's also somewhat subdued. It hasn't become itself yet. It's only beginning to produce its own novels and its own view of life over against the U. S. and Britain. You know, Canada was very much in two senses a provincial society from the beginning–I won't say when I left but in the beginning. It's by definition a provincial society, and it takes a long time for a provincial society to grow up; particularly when it's dominated from two sides as Canada has been– first by Britain and then at the same time by the

U.S.–culturally by one and economically by the other.

TUTUNJIAN: Would you have left Canada now if these were the forties rather than the seventies?

MACDONALD: I didn't leave Canada for any reason having to do with Canada. But certainly because opportunity was given to me in the U. S. which wasn't given to me in Canada. I was offered a fellowship at the University of Michigan. However, behind that is the fact that I was born in the U. S. I knew it; I'd been taught by my mother from childhood to regard myself as an American, and when I got a chance to come to the U. S. I seized it gladly because I regarded myself as an American. I really am of course both American and Canadian. You can't live as I did throughout your childhood and younger years in a country like Canada without becoming a Canadian in thought and feeling.

TUTUNJIAN: Have you forgiven Kitchener, Medicine Hat, St. John's School in Winnipeg, and your childhood in Canada? Have you forgiven Canada? Have you reconciled with your childhood?

MACDONALD: We never forgive our childhood. What makes a novelist is the inability to forget his childhood. I can document that. Not just from my books. *Oliver Twist* was the first important book I ever read–I was 11 years old when I read it and it probably had a lot to do with making a writer out of me. From then on I wanted to be a writer. I keep going back to my childhood in memory and also in fact. I have revisited Medicine Hat. I go back to Kitchener from time to time, and I think that the combination of fascination with one's own past and the desire to understand it really is the making of a novelist. I went back to Wiarton in 1971 for the first time in forty years.

TUTUNJIAN: How much do you remember from your days in St. John's School in Winnipeg?

MACDONALD: Well, it was on the whole an interesting and useful experience to me. I learned a lot, not only in terms of study where I did very well, but I became a gymnast. We had very good training in gym. Our gym teacher had been the British Empire champion, and I spent most of my spare time in the gym, which was open all the time including the evenings. It really laid the basis for my whole physical life. The library on the other hand was open only on Sunday afternoons,

which gives you some idea of how British-style Canadian prep schools regarded the relative importance of the gymnasium and the library.

TUTUNJIAN: What books were you reading then?

MACDONALD: Jimmy Valentine and Frank L. Packard are the first ones I think of.

TUTUNJIAN: It was at that school that you met wealthy kids and for the first time in your life you came in contact with the so-called upper class.

MACDONALD: It wasn't really the first time I had been in contact with wealthy people. It was the first time I got to know them intimately. My aunt who lived in Winnipeg and sent me to that school was wealthy too. My aunt Margaret–my father's sister.

TUTUNJIAN: What do you remember about your days at St. John's School and your rich classmates?

MACDONALD: That's so far back I hardly remember anything about them, but I think I learned something about the Canadian class structure and I'm sure I also evolved a desire to rise in it– not always be at the bottom. It stirs your ambition to be taken out of one place and put in contact with something higher or better in the economic sense and also in the social sense.

TUTUNJIAN: When did you begin writing?

MACDONALD: I started writing seriously from about the age of 12 and didn't show my work to anybody except one man, my cousin Sheldon Brubacher, who is also from Kitchener. He got his M.A. in English at the University of Toronto. He was a teacher all his life in the Toronto high schools and he was highly encouraging to me. He said that my early poems resembled the work of important writers that he knew of, the juvenile work.

TUTUNJIAN: Reading your pieces in *Saturday Night*, which you wrote in the late thirties and early forties, I couldn't help noticing the generous amount of humour and satire in practically every piece.

MACDONALD: The *Saturday Night* market wanted that. I wrote for that market, and you know Canadian literature was based on Leacock at that time. In fact, it still is. Robertson Davies is still writing under the influence of Leacock. You can make a direct connection, and I'm sure he would, between *Sunshine Sketches of a Little Town* and *Fifth Business*. That's in direct line from Leacock, at the beginning.

TUTUNJIAN: Let's talk about Kitchener in the thirties. You were there as a child, then as a high-school student, and later as a high-school teacher. What kind of place was it?

MACDONALD: Well, I think it was a place boiling with promise of all kinds, both economic and cultural. You know some years later Bob Ford, my friend who is now the Canadian ambassador to the Soviet Union, told me there are only two places in the world where young people are really working hard (he meant in school particularly)–that was the Soviet Union and Canada. This was true of Kitchener in the thirties. We really worked hard. I don't claim for myself so much that I worked hard. I hadn't reached the point of working hard yet. I was still very young. But there was a really ambitious attitude on the part of the people and it still continues in Kitchener. It's a powerful town and I think a very good town to be brought up in.

TUTUNJIAN: Did you enjoy your childhood in Kitchener?

MACDONALD: I can't say I enjoyed it because I had too many problems, economic and emotional and so on. You know my father was terribly ill, in dying condition, during those years, and he eventually did die.

TUTUNJIAN: When did he move from Vancouver to Kitchener?

MACDONALD: My father and mother separated in Vancouver when I was three years old and my mother and I went back to Kitchener where her mother and sister and brother were living. We lived a good deal of the time with my grandmother in Kitchener. Meanwhile my father stayed on in B.C. He was a harbour pilot in Vancouver harbour. He was in love with the sea. He wouldn't leave it. He had a series of strokes, though, the first of which occurred even before I was born. (He was forty-one when I was born.) They gradually did him in. He came back to Ontario, where he had originated too, in bad shape and had to be hospitalized. He spent years in the hospital, where he actually died. He died in the Ontario Government Hospital in Toronto. I guess it was about 1932.

TUTUNJIAN: He left some life insurance which enabled you to go to the University of Western Ontario.

MACDONALD: Yes, he left–I think it was $2,500 insurance. My mother took out an annuity in my name (she had no money of her own) which enabled me to go to college.

TUTUNJIAN: When did your mother die?

MACDONALD: It was in December of 1935.

TUTUNJIAN: Your mother has played a very important part in your life. Reminiscing about your childhood, you have said, referring to your mother: 'She had kept my spirit alive all those years.'

MACDONALD: It's what mothers generally do if they're good mothers. She was the one person that was continuous in my life and whom I could depend on and she was always on my side and encouraging me to become a human being. She was ambitious for me to some extent, too.

TUTUNJIAN: *The Galton Case*, which has a great deal of Canadian background, has been considered by many as a turning-point in the Archer books. Do you agree with that observation?

MACDONALD: It was the book in which I first seemed to be able to say some of the things that were unique and personal to me. Before that I was writing in the traditional form. I was writing my own books, but I wasn't writing about my own life. You don't write about your own life, but you derive the shapes of your fiction from your own life–sort of make a myth out of your own life.

TUTUNJIAN: Your first book was too autobiographical and subjective. It was never published. I understand you have never shown it to a publisher.

MACDONALD: That was an autobiographical book. It wasn't my first book, though. *The Dark Tunnel* is my first book. This book that we're talking about was written in the late forties. It was my fifth book. I still have it.

TUTUNJIAN: What do you remember from your *Saturday Night* days?

MACDONALD: Well, I was going to the University of Toronto, Ontario College of Education, preparing to be a high-school teacher. Margaret and I had married the previous summer and we were expecting a child. Along towards late spring I had obtained a job teaching for the following fall in Kitchener High School. We ran out of money so I started writing. I wrote a number of stories for Canadian Sunday-School papers for various age levels and also started sending things to *Saturday Night*–verse and prose, mostly short humorous things. It made me very happy when they took them. We were living in Toronto that summer. We used to rush home on Saturday morning when it came out and buy a copy to see if they had bought anything that week. They paid a cent a word. That was important money.

TUTUNJIAN: How often were you able to sell articles to *Saturday Night?*

MACDONALD: I sold them for several years. I was in the paper every week or two.

TUTUNJIAN: At the time *Saturday Night* had a regular crime-book reviewer. Were you interested in reviewing crime books then?

MACDONALD: I wasn't reviewing crime books in particular. They sent me a few. *Saturday Night* also had a column called *The Passing Show* and I was a regular contributor to that for several years. Even after I went to Michigan I was contributing every week. They had me on a regular basis, paying me so much a week. It was an anonymous column called *The Passing Show.*

TUTUNJIAN: You wrote a funny piece about typing rather than longhand, based on a quotation from Sir Charles G. D. Roberts.

MACDONALD: That was the first thing I ever sold. I never did write on a typewriter. My wife used to type my things for me. There's a story about that. When I decided to try my hand at writing to make some money, while I was waiting to begin work as a teacher, I didn't have a typewriter. At that time there was a radio program in Toronto–a question-and-answer show–where the contestants were given prizes. They announced one week that the prize of an Underwood portable typewriter would be given the following week. I told Margaret I was going to win that typewriter and I did. So we had a typewriter and that enabled me to start writing professionally.

TUTUNJIAN: You didn't like Toronto then. Describing Toronto in your first book, *The Dark Tunnel*, you wrote: 'Early twilight hung over the city like a thin, grey haze and made the lake a sheet of striated lead, stretching to a leaden horizon. . . . Down the long, drab streets the neons trembled in the gathering air, glowing blue and red and green with a quiet, inhuman lustre.'

MACDONALD: I never met anybody who was very crazy about Toronto. I like it now, but at that time it was pretty much a buttoned-up and closed-down city and it just didn't have the spirit of life in it that it has now. It was a vast provincial capital that hadn't realized itself, but I believe it's doing that now.

TUTUNJIAN: Did you mix with the Toronto literary circle in the late thirties?

MACDONALD: I never mix much in literary circles as such, although I have a lot of friends who are writers, particularly around here.

TUTUNJIAN: Have you kept in touch with Canadian literature? Would you like to comment on Margaret Laurence, Robertson Davies, Morley Callaghan, and Marshall McLuhan?

MACDONALD: I don't have any comment about Margaret Laurence, because I don't know her or her work to any extent. She's played no part in my life; maybe she will yet, though. I haven't gotten around to really reading her novels. Marshall McLuhan is a dear friend of ours and a delightful man and also a very great scholar. When he taught one summer out here at the University of California in Santa Barbara I went and audited his course, and I think I got more out of that than out of any course I ever sat in on or heard of. It was a brilliant historical survey of the technological aspects of civilization–the influence of technology in the development of culture. It is one of his great subjects. I've seen him since then, both here and in Toronto. We correspond and send each other our books.

TUTUNJIAN: I understand he also sends you jokes.

MACDONALD: Yes, and books. He sends me more books than I send him because he writes more.

TUTUNJIAN: What about Robertson Davies?

MACDONALD: I don't know Robertson Davies but I greatly enjoy his writing. I always have. We were, so to speak, together on *Saturday Night* in the old days. He joined *Saturday Night* a year or two after I did and I thought he was a great wit and I still do. Now of course, he's more than that– he's a very good novelist and a great literary critic too.

TUTUNJIAN: How about Morley Callaghan?

MACDONALD: He was the Canadian writer who had the most influence on me.

TUTUNJIAN: In addition to Stephen Leacock?

MACDONALD: I wouldn't say the influence of Stephen Leacock was so important to me except in terms of the humorous stuff I wrote when I was younger. Except in the sense of subject matter: Leacock did write about people known to him in *Sunshine Sketches*. You know, just to see another writer, an older writer, deal with life around him makes it possible for younger writers to do the same thing. So in a broad sense he was all-important. He was the one Canadian writer who was writing about the life around him. Although he didn't do it consistently: he wrote an awful lot of purely fantastic humour. Morley Callaghan was the one that we all most admired and wanted to emulate. He wasn't exactly a crime writer, or what you might call a member of the hard-boiled school, but his style belonged in that category. I think it had a great influence on me. I still have an enormous admiration for his work. I think he's underestimated because he just happened to fall under the shadow of world figures like Hemingway and Fitzgerald with whom he doesn't quite compete, but I think he's a first-rate writer. I think his short stories in the long run will turn out to be his most important work, as in the case of Chekhov. He's a Chekhovian writer.

TUTUNJIAN: Since leaving in the forties, how many times have you been back to Canada?

MACDONALD: Oh, altogether perhaps eight times.

TUTUNJIAN: What are the changes you have noticed on subsequent visits?

MACDONALD: Well, I am afraid that question is so broad it's difficult to answer. Canada has developed from a rather remote provincial area to a developing centre of civilization. I think it has only begun to become a centre of civilization in the deepest sense. That is, until now, it has been a secondary centre, so to speak–an offshoot of London and New York. It probably should develop in the next generation.

TUTUNJIAN: Going back to your Canadian childhood, you have said your mother instilled in you the feeling that you were an American. That you were born in California.

MACDONALD: That's right. It was true. It was important to her that I had been an American. I could think of various reasons why. Being an American in those days in Canada was regarded as superior. That's the nature of a province. But in this case it wasn't a matter of rich cousins, it was a matter of the fact that I was born near Stanford University, for example, and she wanted me to attend Stanford University.

TUTUNJIAN: As a child did you always feel you were an American rather than a Canadian?

MACDONALD: No, a young boy is not so certain of anything as that. It was something I held on to.

TUTUNJIAN: Marshall McLuhan and I talked about being from two different countries–the identity crisis (American or non-American) so prevalent in your books.

MACDONALD: He's from two different countries too, in a sense.

TUTUNJIAN: He disagrees with you in one sense. He says you can't be a stranger in North America whether you are Canadian or American, as long as you speak the English language you are North American. There is no border, no difference between Americans and Canadians, he told me.

MACDONALD: What he says is true in a very broad sense, but in the important detailed sense in which people feel and live, it's not true. There most definitely is a border and it was an important border at one time, now no longer so important. But don't forget McLuhan himself spent many years in the U.S. and he sees things partly as an American; but even more important is the fact that he went to Cambridge, and the result is that he is a cosmopolite–almost a professional cosmopolite or a citizen of the global village. What can be true for him with his peculiar special background and his special attitude isn't necessarily true of another citizen of the global village. For anybody who wants to live in the United States, to be an American by birth is a great advantage. My mother was right. It was important that I should be an American and in fact if I had stayed in Canada as a Canadian writer I would never have been able to write the books I have written. Canada just didn't provide the variety of material that I needed or the conflict between the two places.

TUTUNJIAN: While reading the short stories you wrote for your high-school yearbook, I couldn't help noticing that your style had already begun to take shape: the metaphors and similes.

MACDONALD: My basic style hasn't changed, it's just been purified.

TUTUNJIAN: Another facet of your early writings is your love of the sea.

MACDONALD: Yes, I've always been crazy about the sea. I started swimming in the Pacific when I was three years old in Vancouver and I'm still doing it. I also chose the Navy when I went into service. The fact that my father was a master mariner had a great deal to do with that. But going back to the previous question, I was a Canadian born in the U.S. and an American living in Canada, whichever you want to call it, but this was very typical. I read some years ago that one-seventh of all Canadians were living in the United States at that time. I imagine it's still true. There's part of the Western movement which occurred in Canada and the United States and that was that Canadians went west and then south. Very many Canadians did what my parents did. They went west and then south (Oregon and California) and then many of them went back again. It wasn't at all peculiar to my situation–the general movement, a western and southern movement.

TUTUNJIAN: In addition to Dashiell Hammett, Raymond Chandler, and James M. Cain, what other writers do you admire?

MACDONALD: Look around you. This is just part of my library–Hemingway, Vonnegut. Kafka is very important to me. Scott Fitzgerald is my dream writer.

TUTUNJIAN: Do you still read *The Great Gatsby* once a year?

MACDONALD: About once a year. Gatsby is in modern times the central artistic expression of the American experience. It's about American idealism destroyed by American greed. It's about the struggle for the soul of America by opposing forces–idealism on one hand and money power on the other–misplaced idealism.

TUTUNJIAN: How about more recent writers–say Norman Mailer and Philip Roth?

MACDONALD: I admire Philip Roth very much. It happens I have just been reading *Portnoy's Complaint* and I don't really think it's his best work. I don't think any of his novels have quite come up to his short stories yet. He's still a young writer, with a marvelous original mind. Mailer really stopped being a serious novelist a long time ago. He's a very interesting autobiographical essayist and a general journalist, but I have a particular penchant myself for the novel. I wish he had remained a novelist. He's become a superstar, and you know that doesn't agree too well with being a novelist, which is essentially a lonely silent job.

TUTUNJIAN: What other writer is doing what you are doing?

MACDONALD: I don't know–it's a hard question to answer. For one thing the writer never knows really what he's doing.

TUTUNJIAN: The prevailing subject matter in your books is the family.

MACDONALD: This has been the traditional subject matter of the novel almost from the beginning.

TUTUNJIAN: How about the sins of the fathers visited upon the sons, the Oedipus Complex which frequently appears in the Archer books?

MACDONALD: There's a continuity between the past and the present. That's what the novel is about. Practically all novelists are writing on that general subject. The idea that the parents influence their children, the children respond and react both positively and negatively, is the substance of most fiction traditionally, not quite so much right now. There haven't been so many family novels written lately as there were. What my books are about is essentially contemporary life interwoven with the realization that however contemporary and new everything appears to be the understanding of it reaches back into the past. I can't speak fully about contemporary novelists because I'm not a student of contemporary novelists.

TUTUNJIAN: A few weeks ago a friend and I were discussing the similarities between your life and style and that of Raymond Chandler.

MACDONALD: Yes, there is. He was an Anglo-Canadian-American.

TUTUNJIAN: His parents separated when he was quite young–as your parents did. He grew up in England with an aunt–you stayed with your Aunt Margaret in Winnipeg. He was in the service as you were.

MACDONALD: Right. He went to an English boys' school not unlike the boys' school that I went to in Winnipeg.

TUTUNJIAN: He was fascinated with the use of the language as you are, the correct usage of words.

MACDONALD: Yes, we have in large part the same cultural background. It's interesting, isn't it, that the cultural background produced books that in many ways are similar, and as you pointed out my style hasn't changed, essentially hasn't changed, since I was in my teens, which was long before Chandler was writing or available to me. Many people have assumed my imitation of Chandler, which of course is true to some extent, but I wouldn't have written very differently if Chandler hadn't existed. He did open up possibilities, though, for me in writing mystery novels of a particular kind–American vernacular mystery novels. He and Hammett. Hammett actually was a greater influence on me than Chandler was. I read him much earlier.

TUTUNJIAN: What do you think now of Hammett as a writer?

MACDONALD: I think Hammett is a first-rate writer and very nearly a great writer. Chandler is not quite in that same league. He's a very good writer but I don't think the energy in his books is going to last as long as that in Hammett–in fact it hasn't. Hammett is more alive now than Chandler is. Chandler's best books in my opinion are his first four. Some people like *The Long Goodbye* better, but I don't. It doesn't have the same speed and excitement or the same velocity of language.

TUTUNJIAN: You've said that Lew Archer's name comes from Miles Archer of *The Maltese Falcon*. There is a character in *The Maltese Falcon*, the brother-in-law of Miles Archer, and his name is Phil Archer. Maybe he's the character who gave his first name to Philip Marlowe.

MACDONALD: Very likely. I'd forgotten that Archer had a brother-in-law.

TUTUNJIAN: He had a brother-in-law who came from out of town and his name was Phil Archer.

MACDONALD: That's interesting. It's true, as I said long ago, we all came out from under Hammett's overcoat. That's what was said about Gogol, isn't it?

TUTUNJIAN: I don't agree with that. I think you have started something totally different.

MACDONALD: I am not talking about what I did after I came out from under the overcoat. I am talking about where I came out from. I certainly tried to start something different. I've tried to enlarge the boundaries of the mystery novel both in subject matter and in style, and in what you might call intellectual and linguistic content. In other words I've tried to write it as if I were writing straight novels, for keeps.

TUTUNJIAN: Don't you think it's sort of patronizing to say Ross Macdonald's books aren't just detective books, they are literature?

MACDONALD: Well, there is a difference between a detective novel and a straight novel. Any kind of popular literature has a hard time being accepted by taste makers, particularly in schools. It takes time. To take the most superb example of popular literature that has ever been written, Shakespeare wrote popular literature in the sense that it was intended to appeal to the whole civilization, not just to a group. He was writing for the groundlings as well as the aristocracy. Shakespeare wasn't really recognized as a very great poet until the nineteenth century. I mean fully accepted in the sense of the schools.

TUTUNJIAN: Do you think one day you, Hammett's and Chandler's books will be taught in high schools?

MACDONALD: My work is being taught in high schools and colleges right now.

TUTUNJIAN: Where?

MACDONALD: I hear from teachers in various parts of the country. My books are being taught at Harvard, Yale, University of New York at Buffalo, and the University of California.

TUTUNJIAN: Although you admire Chandler, in a letter to a friend Chandler called you a literary eunuch because you had described an old car as 'acned with rust'. Chandler has also said some nasty things about you in a letter to a critic.

MACDONALD: Many letters. He wrote many letters running me down. He was getting old and I was a competitor. Sometimes as you get older it's hard to enjoy your competitor. I'm sure his reactions were honest. He didn't have the same reaction to me that I have to my younger competitors. I try to help them.

TUTUNJIAN: Is it true that you edit the manuscripts of several young writers?

MACDONALD: No, I don't edit them. I just read them and make suggestions. I don't want to give the impression that I'm the man behind certain writers. There's one young Canadian writer who was actually a student of mine–I used to teach writing here and I first got to know him as a student about fifteen, sixteen years ago–Herb Harker (the book *Goldenrod* was his first novel). I gave Herb encouragement over the past fifteen years. I'm very pleased to see the success he had with that book.

TUTUNJIAN: Going back to mystery writers, what do you think of Stanley Ellin?

MACDONALD: He's always been one of my favorites. I think he's line for line just about the best writer in the business. I think many of his short stories are classics. I particularly like the one about White and Black–the chess story.

TUTUNJIAN: What about John D. MacDonald, the creator of Travis McGee?

MACDONALD: I think he's a strong talent, but he's not one of my favorite writers.

TUTUNJIAN: Are there any other mystery writers you admire?

MACDONALD: Eric Ambler has always been a particular favorite of mine. I like Julian Symons very much too.

TUTUNJIAN: Symons says he doesn't think Archer has helped your books. He thinks your books would have been better had you moved Archer out of California.

MACDONALD: Well, that would involve my moving, too. My dear friend Julian is not qualified to judge the possibilities of California. As far as I know he only spent about three days here. He spent most of them with me.

TUTUNJIAN: He said the same thing about Nicholas Freeling's Inspector Van der Valk. *In Bloody Murder*, Symons said the detective wasn't helping the books. That the books were hindered by the detective.

MACDONALD: There are different ways to write books. Julian has his way and I have mine. It's a different tradition. There's a great difference between the English and American tradition. Of course I have written several books, including some of the Archer books, going far beyond Califor-

nia. As you know, I was writing books before I came to California, but I chose to live in California because it was to me intensely interesting–the central place as far as America was concerned–and I don't think Julian understands that. He doesn't understand California as an important subject. He thinks it is a remote, strange, sunlicked province. What else would he know, spending only three days here? He wrote about Yugoslavia, for example, and he probably regards my writing about California in the same way as his writing about Yugoslavia. Whereas I am writing about my home, the thing that's essential to me. Everything that goes on here is of the highest interest to me. He actually suggested to me that I should come and write a book about England, which for an American writer, in my tradition at least, would be very difficult. But he's very much of a traditional John Bull and I don't think he regards anything that happens outside of England or Western Europe as of any great importance.

TUTUNJIAN: Referring to Chandler, you've been quoted as saying: 'While trying to preserve the fantastic lights and shadows of the actual Los Angeles, I gradually siphoned off the aura of romance and made room for more complete social realism.'

MACDONALD: I've deepened the use of imagery. I've changed it from the imagist to the symbolist, where it is intended to have deep psychological and social meanings. Much of the meaning in my books comes in the imagery. It's not just a decoration, it's the carrier of meaning, and I learned how to do it, to the extent that I can do it, from the poets. That's one respect. Another is that I've slightly purified the style. It's the vernacular, yes, but it's a purified vernacular. I don't think it's going to decay, as most vernacular stories do, for that reason. It's written with one ear to what people say and the other ear to the *Oxford English Dictionary* and the old English classics and American classics.

TUTUNJIAN: There is too much colloquialism in the Chandler books–

MACDONALD: Yes, that's what I'm talking about. It dates, and I'm trying to write so that it doesn't date; but naturally it's going to date some. Hammett is beginning to date a little bit, too. A writer should try to handle the language so it sounds exactly the way people talk or think, so it won't date. That means you have to have a very deep sense of what constitutes purity of diction. I think purity of diction is my main strength as a writer, using the vernacular style as possibly a pure style. It's pretty much the same style as Fitzgerald used. He was my master. He writes what appears to be a vernacular style which is actually very pure, and influenced by poetry.

TUTUNJIAN: I have always thought of you as a poet.

MACDONALD: My intention has always been to write dramatic poetry in a new form. Since there was no opportunity to write dramatic poetry for the theatre in Canada as I was growing up—you have to have a living theatre in order to be a playwright—I found another way to make my attempt to write dramatic poetry. Large sections of my early books are loose blank verse. I'm not saying this is desirable, but it's true.

TUTUNJIAN: This vernacular is, of course, important to you as a democratic means to cut down social barriers.

MACDONALD: Of course to me it's the only possible literature of a democracy—something that can be read by more than one class.

TUTUNJIAN: What would be your response to the French Academy whose job is to clarify the French language, take out all the colloquialisms and slang and keep the language in its pure classic form?

MACDONALD: They're turning their backs on possible enrichment of the language.

TUTUNJIAN: What about the slang or lingo used by the communications media, the bureaucracy, advertising, government, and the legal profession? What happens when people start picking them up? Would you be forced to use the slang?

MACDONALD: When a writer who aims at purity uses language that he considers impure he places it in the context in such a way that his knowledge of its impurity is telegraphed to the reader; in other words you can use language like that, but you put a little curve on it in the context so that the reader knows that you know that this isn't the correct word.

TUTUNJIAN: Discussing the differences between your and Chandler's work, you have said you took out the aura of romance from the California Chandler depicted in his books. Would you like to elaborate on that?

MACDONALD: Because of Chandler's rather ferocious attacks on me, some of which were deliberately intended to hurt my reputation, I can't discuss Chandler with a completely clear conscience. I'm not at ease with Chandler, as I am talking about these other writers, because he tried to damage me. I don't want to turn around and try to damage him. To answer your question as honestly as I know how, Chandler was essentially a pre-war writer. I don't mean pre World War II but pre World War I. His background was the whole great English nineteenth century, which was a romantic century, and he started writing in England around the turn of the century. His early work, which is only now becoming known about, was somewhat decadent and romantic work. Although he changed his subject matter and gathered an enormous volume of rich material here in California, that aspect of decadence and romanticism remained in his work. The pathos of female sensuality, that sort of thing. Actually it goes back to his English background, the century that stood behind him. I've tried to use some of the same materials but look at them more coolly, not romantically, not so emotionally, and make more intelligible structures out of these materials.

TUTUNJIAN: There is also a difference between Chandler's and your characters. His are more *outré*. His people are often involved in some criminal subculture while yours are more everyday, ordinary characters.

MACDONALD: This is what your crime novel is about to a great extent.

TUTUNJIAN: You once said detective fiction is a window on contemporary reality in the United States. It seems to me that only a very small group of detective-book writers are doing this seriously. Detective-book writing is dying—there are not many great detective-book writers in America.

MACDONALD: Well, we've named several—we've named Eric Ambler.

TUTUNJIAN: But he is a thirties and forties writer. He is not American; he is British.

MACDONALD: He has spent a lot of his time in this country, though. There are a lot of us, but we're sort of between generations. There are some of us who are trying to carry over from one genera-

Kenneth Millar in Burritt Alley, San Francisco, the scene of Miles Archer's murder in The Maltese Falcon
(University of California-Irvine)

tion to the next. There are a lot of good writers working the U.S. in this field that you don't know about because they haven't become known yet. I could think of a couple right away. Roger L. Simon of Los Angeles, Joe Gores and Colin Wilcox, both San Francisco writers, both more than promising, but neither one of them has been recognized as a good writer. I was writing for twelve to fifteen years before I had any recognition at all. This is particularly true of the mystery field. It takes a long time for a writer to make any impact. Half my books were written before anybody knew my name.

TUTUNJIAN: Literary critics in France have given up on the detective book presumably because the 'detective genre has used up all its possibilities.' They seem to be saying the detective-book genre is dead.

MACDONALD: I'm not concerned about that. It just never occurred to me. The answer to it is to find something new to say, perhaps writing something new and different and perhaps not calling it detective stories. We will continue to be writing about crime and human collisions. That's the very essence of dramatic literature, no matter what you want to call it. Of course a lot of writers are coming up with a new approach to crime stories. The idea of the detective who goes out and solves crimes may eventually lose interest for people, but it hasn't happened yet.

TUTUNJIAN: Considering your academic background, did you ever feel you had to justify your work?

MACDONALD: No, I thought that my crime fiction was a lot better than my doctoral dissertation. I've always been read by literate people. Some of my best friends are university professors. I never lost touch with that kind of life. Last November I went to the University of Michigan and was given a 'distinguished achievement award.' It's the university where I wrote my dissertation. There isn't really a split between me and the university. They invited me to come and teach there this year. I wouldn't leave California. I just mentioned that to prove there has not been a split. Who do you think my readers are?

TUTUNJIAN: I don't know. I've seen people read your books in buses, subways, colleges and universities. I was surprised to hear that you're not aware of your popularity in Canada.

MACDONALD: I don't get any figures on Canadian sales. I don't know anything about it. I just judge who my readers are from where I get my letters. I don't get many from Canada.

TUTUNJIAN: Talking about your popularity and Canadian fans, Marshall McLuhan told me that in your books the milieu was the main plot while the actual story line was the sub-plot. Do you agree with that statement?

MACDONALD: Well, not just place but society. What makes up the plot is the relationships between various members of a society and the various levels of a society. It's not just a flat place, it's a tiered society with relationships between the lower depths and the upper regions. It's tiered in terms of time, and my novels explore both social and temporal tiers.

TUTUNJIAN: Although you don't seem to socialize much with the people here, you know a lot about various levels of California society–the rich and the poor, Mexicans, middle classes, lower classes–where did you get all this information about the California class structure, while living in Santa Barbara?

MACDONALD: Hugh Kenner asked me that question once, back in the late forties. Where did I find out so much about Americans? In *Ontario*, I told him.

TUTUNJIAN: If you were a literary critic, say in the year 2001 looking back, evaluating the work of Ross Macdonald, what would you say or like to say?

MACDONALD: I would say that I feel unqualified to judge this writer as he is a close personal relative. I think I've succeeded in some of the later books in writing serious dramatic fiction on a detective framework. That's what I've been trying to do. That's what I'd like to be able to say in another generation.

ARTICLE:
George Grella, "Evil Plots," *New Republic*, 173 (26 July 1975): 24-26.

Professor Grella of the University of Rochester identified four recurring interlocked plots in the Lew Archer novels: "The Quest of the Archer, The Search for the Past, The Metamorphic Pattern and The Mythic Plot."

Any reader who can recognize the difference between an automatic and a revolver knows that Ross Macdonald is the most distinguished living practitioner of what has become known as "hard-boiled" detective fiction and a worthy successor to Dashiell Hammett and Raymond Chandler. In the 25 years that he has been chronicling the adventures of his private eye, Lew Archer, Macdonald has achieved, along with his great popularity, a certain respectability as well. This chiefly means that his works are no longer reviewed back among the literary equivalent of the truss ads but are now featured prominently on the front pages of the leading book reviews (there are a few). As a result some literary critics have discovered some of the most striking characteristics of the Archer books: the close attention to the Southern California subculture, the highly wrought metaphors, the saintly private eye hero, the intensely complicated plots. Among their many excellences, the plots of the Lew Archer novels distinguish them from all other detective fiction. The books seem, at times, to consist entirely of plot, to be about their plots, to be in fact all plot.

Virtually every reviewer remarks on the richly exfoliating complexity of Macdonald's plots: they are dizzying to follow, almost impossible to summarize. Picking up a Lew Archer novel after an interruption, the reader must try to untangle the snarled thread of events with an arduous effort of recollection; along with Archer and other characters, we find it very hard to know where we've been, where we are, and where we are going. Because the novels are usually informed by numerous overlapping and superimposed plots, their differentiation, as well as their ultimate congruence, becomes a subtle and delicate task.

There appear to be four important plots in the Archer books, which turn out to be four versions, or stages, of one complicated sequence of actions; they can be separated artificially, though of course they form a shapely and organic unity. At the risk of sounding both melodramatic and pretentious, I have invented a set of terms for these plots: The Quest of the Archer, The Search for the Past, The Metamorphic Pattern and The Mythic Plot.

The Quest of the Archer is the primary plot, the actual detecting job, a relatively simple and routine affair as Lew Archer describes it. He is hired to perform a specific, comprehensible task–to locate a missing spouse or a runaway child, to recover some stolen property, to investigate the heir to a fortune. He follows the usual procedures in the usual manner: he questions witnesses, makes phone calls, notes times and dates, and so forth, practicing his profession as it should be practiced, acting like a detective in a detective novel. He moves about in a more or less straightforward and logical fashion through a geographically limited space in a relatively short period of time. This is the simple detective plot, and the ease with which it is followed is merely the result of Archer's abilities and our own experience. Archer is generally quite successful at this sort of thing, usually locating the person or object of his quest rapidly and efficiently, although he may be unable to retrieve him, her or it. The child does not wish to return to the parents, the wife refuses to go back to her husband, and somewhere along the way the case has swerved drastically toward violence–invariably a crime occurs.

As we and Archer discover, things are never as simple as they seem. His initial plot now intersects with another and he is forced to find out more about the case. The Quest of the Archer becomes involved with The Search for the Past. This intersection is no mere artificial escape into meaningless complexity, but a very necessary act. Archer's case has resulted in violence or the potential for violence, his client is endangered or vulnerable, or he may have accidentally uncovered some vital additional evidence; for personal, professional or legal reasons Archer must pursue another plot further than the first. This secondary pattern is by far the richest in problems and possibilities, the most volatile and dangerous in the novels; it is also the personal plot of the man or woman Archer initially investigates. Archer

takes over the plot of Dolly Kinkaid in *The Chill* (1964), of Davy Spanner in *The Instant Enemy* (1968), of Nicholas Chalmers in *The Goodbye Look* (1969), for example, making their attempts to recapture the meaning of some events in the past his own. The Quest of the Archer becomes inseparable from The Search for the Past.

The synchronization of the two plots so powerfully preoccupies Archer that it dominates the rest of the novel, providing the chief source of tension, suspense, urgency and meaning. Not surprisingly this pattern is the one most often noticed by readers and reviewers, provoking the lengthy mystifications of the newspaper and magazine book pages. The Search for the Past is clearly another name for our old friend, the quest for identity, and in this plot we continually encounter a young man or woman looking for his or her true father or mother, true name, true self. We find at the center of Ross Macdonald's complicated novels, as at the center of Dickens' complicated novels, a suffering child. Here we begin to notice the familiar patterns of the Oedipal situation and hear the echoes of Sophocles, Homer, Joyce and Freud. In this plot we witness the cumulative effect of years of suppressed truth or feeling, a generalized, unspecified guilt operating on the lives of all the characters.

This plot, paradoxically, is both the most dynamic and the most static of all; it suggests, incidentally, the curiously static nature of the Archer books in general and indicates the revolutionary departure they make from the tradition of the detective story. In this plot Archer travels significant distances through space, back and forth through all those now familiar California cities, to the Midwest, north to Canada, south to Mexico and so forth. He interviews witnesses to the past: friends, relatives, acquaintances of his client, each of whom contributes his little portion of knowledge. In many cases this plot, too, explodes into violence, and Archer is threatened, beaten or wounded; frequently more deaths occur. The dangers of the detective's personal quest begin to reflect the events of the past. Archer's painful reconstruction of these events begins to obsess him as much as it obsesses the people who have drawn him into it. As he says in *The Chill*, "I had handled cases which opened up gradually like fissures in the firm ground of the present, cleaving far down through the strata of the past.''

The past influences the present so strongly for Archer that he stops acting in the present: the novels stand still as he descends into striations of time and event to achieve some perception of the truth. Though he moves forward in space and becomes an actor in a plot filled with events, he moves backward in time, carrying on a retrogressive plot, repeating and reexperiencing the actions and situations of his clients. Ironically the plot he must recapture has already happened, a chain of events over and done with 15 or 20 or more years before. He finds the links that remain, leading inevitably to the actions that fostered the initial plot. Thus Davy Spanner's insane behavior in *The Instant Enemy* is connected to the horrible death of a man many years before; Dolly Kinkaid's repudiation of her marriage is somehow related not only to a murder she witnessed as a child but also to another murder in the Midwest some years earlier. The completed actions must be analyzed and synthesized in order to discover their relationship and significance.

All along, growing gradually and inexorably out of these two plots, is the third, the process of heightening perception Archer undergoes, The Metamorphic Pattern. Metamorphoses proliferate; things and people keep turning into something or someone else. In *Black Money* Francis Martel turns into Feliz Cervantes, then into Pedro Domingo, regressing from cultured French aristocrat to Panamanian peasant. Putative parents turn into foster or adoptive parents, then back into real ones; murderers become victims, while the ''victims'' turn up alive. Brothers and sisters reveal their true identities; masks are dropped, and disguises and deceptions fall away. An engraved silver box becomes more significant empty than filled with precious objects. A mysterious theft of money becomes the reverse, a spiriting of wealth *into,* rather than out of, a safe. A war hero is revealed as a psychotic weakling; a man's supposed mother turns out to be his wife. A false claimant to a fortune is unmasked as an impostor, then proved to be the man he thought he was impersonating. The literary allusions and suggestions thicken promisingly, betraying further functions that coalesce later–women become wicked stepmothers out of fairy tales, dead men are resurrected, changeling children are restored to their natural parents, sleeping beauties awaken, graves yawn and reveal their hideous secrets.

Perhaps most important in the metamorphic pattern are the metamorphoses of Lew Archer. He discovers that he is changing into the people whose pasts he explores; his compassion draws him into the weary retracing of their previous existence, into re-creating the events that made them what they are. In many books he recognizes and articulates the curious process of the past's effect on him and his cases. In *The Instant Enemy* he sees in a Klee painting an image of his own investigation: ''It showed a man in a geometrical maze, and seemed to show that the man and the maze were continuous with each other.'' In *The Chill* he recognizes the dual nature of time and its importance for his profession; he reads first about Zeno's paradox of the infinite divisibility of space, then about Heraclitus: ''All things flow like a river, he said; nothing abides. Parmenides, on the other hand, believed that nothing ever changed, it only seemed to. Both views appealed to me.'' The books prove the validity of both views. For Archer time has gone, the plots he investigates backward and downward are already completed, but their recurrence engages the whole of his personality and intelligence: time for him is cyclical, repetitive and changeless.

As other people's pasts and plots metamorphose into Archer's, he becomes a participant in the sequence of events, its victim, even its perpetrator. The search for identity becomes his own search; he remembers himself as a lost child, or a young man about to go wrong. (It may be somewhat irreverent here, but Archer's preoccupation with the Oedipal pattern and his tortuous quests for identity may indicate that he himself is of dubious paternity. There are enough allusions to *The Maltese Falcon* in the novels to imply that Lew is the illegitimate son of Sam Spade and Iva Archer, which may also explain Iva's desperation in Hammett's book.) Archer's sympathy becomes an imaginative identification, his reconstruction an immersion in another self. He often arrives at the solution of the problem–*his* problem now–by some flash of irrational and illogical thought, by intuition or dream. In one book he describes this process as "having a Gestalt." In *The Goodbye Look* he has the delusion that he is the young man he is trying to help: "I dreamed that I was Nick and Mrs. Shepherd was my grandmother who used to live with birds in Contra Costa County." He awakens from the dream with the solution to the case, bringing together a mosaic of plots. The dream explains both what really matters about the plots and their curiously static nature. The events and people of long ago are not as important as their configuration, the shape they assume, their relationships with one another. After this particular dream, all relationships untangle and explain themselves, and the dream is projected for everyone in some 20-year-old home movies in which all the characters appear. In *The Goodbye Look*, incidentally, Archer's metamorphosis is so complete that he sleeps with the woman the murderer had loved many years before, thus becoming both victim and murderer.

The dreamlike intuition that ensues from the metamorphic pattern leads inevitably to the climactic revelation of the true identities, the true actions, the real murderers in the novels. Everything has come full circle and no more plots seem possible. We are left instead with a generalized guilt, perhaps more guilt than seems necessary, possible or endurable. The configuration of relationships, bloody, nightmarish and complex, generates sorrow and remorse in everyone, always including Archer and the reader. Lew Archer's final actions constitute the fourth and the final plot, the result of the three that he has experienced. What he discovers and recounts is The Mythic Plot, encompassing all others and simultaneously transforming them into another version of reality. Archer's subtle and complex functions of detective, participant and man of sorrows coalesce in the final plot, not so much a series of actions as a single act.

The single act, closely related to dream, is the act of memory. Lew Archer remembers; he tells us in the book. In the remembering and the telling, he brings together the fragmented past and the disordered present, using the configuration he has discovered to explain the reality he has seen. The telling, of course, occurs after the book's events are completed and all plots now belong to the past. In the recollection and narration Archer integrates the various levels of time, reveals the truth, reconciles discordant elements, redeems

some portion of suffering. He takes a multiple and dismembered series of unrelated actions, discrete units of the past, and a set of unrelated characters, and joins them all together in a unified and harmonious shape–he re-members them.

The remembering and re-membering confer upon the novels the richness of the mythic plot, which has been submerged under all activities and now emerges in retrospect. We now see how Archer's contemplation of the palimpsest of human action yields our realization that the plot is the theme of all the novels. We now can see how the allusions to myth and literature, fairy tale and folklore emphasize the universality of the specific actions and people of the books. We see why *The Goodbye Look*, for example, alternates between two explicitly repeated creation myths–Adam and Eve in the garden and Pandora's box: they provide the universal mythic plot, which states that all men are guilty because of some terrible aboriginal calamity–all men, not just the characters in the book. The mythic plot explains why Ross Macdonald, like Dickens or Faulkner, is so fond of coincidence and ironic complication. The terribly complex human relationships that he demonstrates sooner or later involve everyone. Through blood or sex or guilt or chance, we are all related, all part of the universal configuration. We now know why the Oedipal patterns recur–many of us are parents, after all, and all of us have been children. We all, therefore, suffer the guilt that the novels generate; we know that if Lew Archer had sufficient time and space he would draw us all in and find us all out, somehow, someway. And we would accept the configuration, because the mythic plot forces us to recognize it as the pattern of our own dreams, delusions and nightmares as well as the dreams, delusions and nightmares of the race.

At the risk of seeming laboriously obvious, it may be appropriate to conclude with some of the thematic statement that Ross Macdonald's plots express. All men are guilty and all human actions are connected. The past is never past. The child is father to the man. True reality resides in dreams. And most of all, everyone gets what he deserves, but no one deserves what he gets.

* * * * *

[308]

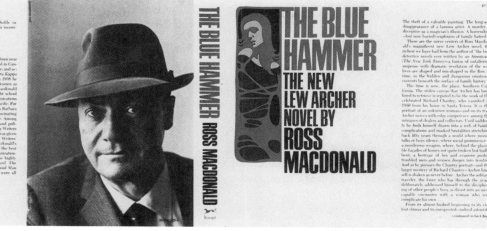

Dust jacket for the final Macdonald novel, published in 1976

ESSAY:
Ross Macdonald, "Down These Streets a Mean Man Must Go," *Antaeus*, 25-26 (Spring/Summer 1977): 211-216.

The title plays on Raymond Chandler's sentence defining his detective-knight-errant: "down these mean streets a man must go. . . ." This essay records Millar's first reading of Hammett.

I once compared the detective story to a welder's mask which enables both writer and reader to handle dangerously hot materials. For even at its least realistic crime fiction reminds us of real things. The world is a treacherous place, it says, where a man must learn to watch his step and guard his rights. It is a difficult place to know; still, both the natural and the human worlds are subject to certain laws which we can understand rationally and make predictions by. Traditional detective fiction offers us the assurance that in spite of all its horrors–the speckled band in Conan Doyle, the dead girl thrust up the chimney in Poe's *Rue Morgue*–the world makes sense and can be understood.

Poe lived out in his short brilliant career the last days of the age of reason and the descent into the maelstrom of the unconscious, where everything revolved at a new angle. It was with a kind of desperation–a desperation we continue to feel–that he held on to rational explanations. The murdered girl in the chimney, Dupin assures us, was only the victim of an animal. But in spite of this explanation the story leaves a residue of horror. The forces of terror and reason remain in unresolved conflict.

In the following century that conflict became the central feature of the detective story. Explaining fears which can't quite be explained away, transforming nightmares into daymares, it helped to quiet the nerves and satisfy the minds of countless readers.

Poe's master Coleridge had written of the Gothic romance, the precursor of the modern detective story:

"As far, therefore, as the story is concerned, the praise which a romance can claim, is simply that of having given pleasure during its perusal. . . . To this praise, however, our author has not entitled himself. The sufferings which he describes are so frightful and intolerable, that we break with abruptness from the delusion and indignantly suspect the man of a species of brutality. . . . Let him work *physical* wonders only, and we will be content to dream with him for a while; but the first *moral* miracle which he attempts, he disgusts and awakens us . . . how beings like ourselves would feel and act . . . our own feelings sufficiently instruct us; and we instantly reject the clumsy fiction that does not harmonize with them."

This is as you may recognize from a review of Lewis's *The Monk* written by Coleridge in 1796,

[309]

the year that he began to compose *The Ancient Mariner*. It is worth quoting not just for its associations but because it can remind us that the Gothic tradition goes back at least as far as the eighteenth century, and its basic rule hasn't changed radically since. The moral life of the characters is the essence of the story, authenticated by the moral life of the reader.

It was not just as a critic that Coleridge was interested in Gothic romance. *The Ancient Mariner* was touched by it, and the unfinished *Christabel* might almost be described as a Gothic novel in verse. Perhaps I am old enough to confess publicly what forty years ago was my secret ambition. When I was a young would-be poet going to school at the University of Western Ontario, I planned to finish *Christabel* and made an attempt which fortunately doesn't survive, indeed it was still-born. With the shocking realization of my limitations, my ambition split into two divergent parts which I have spent most of my life trying to put together again. I migrated to Ann Arbor and wrote a dissertation on the psychological backgrounds of Coleridge's criticism. At the same time I followed my wife's example and began to write mystery stories.

For a long time I was made to feel by my friends and colleagues that these two departments of my mental life, the scholarly and the popular, were rather schizophrenically at odds with each other. Most of my best friends are fiction writers and scholars—most of my enemies, too. The writers viewed my interest in scholarship with suspicion not untinged with superstitious awe. The scholars—with significant exceptions like Marshall McLuhan and Hugh Kenner—considered my fiction writing a form of prostitution out of which they tried to wrestle my soul. But I persisted in my intellectual deviance, trying to stretch my legs to match Chandler's markings, telling myself that down these streets a mean man must go.

It may be timely—I may not have another chance—to offer for the record some further autobiographical fragments and a few conclusions. The connections between the work and the life—other men's as well as my own—have always interested me. It becomes more and more evident that novels, popular or otherwise, are built like Robinson Crusoe's cabin out of the flotsam of the author's past and his makeshift present. A man's fiction, no matter how remote it may seem to be from the realistic or the autobiographical, is very much the record of his particular life. Gradually it may tend to become a substitute for the life, a shadow of the life clinging to the original so closely that (as in Malcolm Lowry's *Under the Volcano*) it becomes hard to tell which is fiction and which is confession.

As a writer grows older more and more of his energy goes to sustain the shadow. He seems to live primarily in order to go on writing, secondarily in order to have something to write about. This double *modus vivendi* is like that of an aging husband and wife each of whom knows what the other is going to say, and it often issues in stretching silences. Then we turn back in memory to the past, where the crucial events and conversations of our lives repeat themselves forever in the hope of being understood and perhaps forgiven.

I was born near San Francisco in 1915. My father and his father were both Scots-Canadian newspaper editors. There are writers and painters in my mother's family. My father left my mother when I was four. To me he ultimately bequeathed his copy of *Walden* and a life insurance policy for two thousand dollars which in Canada, in the thirties, was exactly enough to see me through four years of University.

Before I reached University, looking for something to become in my father's absence, I had become a writer. I think most fiction writers must suffer some degree of alienation, a suppression of the conative by the cognitive which stands like a reflecting window between them and the actual world of satisfactions. We wish to reach and remake that world symbolically, sometimes out of anger and revenge, sometimes out of a humane desire to reclaim it.

When I was eleven I discovered *Oliver Twist* and read that novel with such intense absorption that my mother feared for my health. She took the book away and sent me outside to play hockey. The scene was Kitchener, Ontario, a main source of talent for the National Hockey League. I fell on the ice and got my face cut by the skate of my friend Wilbert Hiller, who not many years later was playing for the New York Rangers. Thus I acquired my wound.

I seem to have got the makings of my bow at the Kitchener Public Library. The librarian, B. Mabel Dunham, was a novelist whose books are still alive though she is not. At least one of her novels was about the migration of the Pennsylvania Dutch to Canada in the nineteenth century. My mother's people, like Miss Dunham's, were Pennsylvania Dutch; I must be the only American crime novelist who got his early ethical training in a Canadian Mennonite Sunday School. I believe that Mabel Dunham's living example, combined with the books both English and American with which she stocked the public library, permitted me to think of becoming a writer. By my middle teens I was a practising crime writer, and my high school classmate and future wife Margaret had begun to write in the Gothic vein, too. I have often wondered why. Perhaps we both felt that with the suppression of the personal and emotional life which afflicted Canada, particularly in those depression years, expressions of the angry self had to come out in devious ways.

What were we angry about? I think it may have been our sense of being provincial in a double sense, in relation to both Great Britain and the United States. My own feeling of distance from the center was deepened by the fact that I had been born in California and was an American citizen by birth. *Civis Romanus sum.*

Popular fiction is not generally thought of as autobiographical–it is considered less a person than a thing–and it is true that the popular conventions offer an apparent escape from both the author's and the reader's lives. But in a deeper sense they can offer the writer a mask for autobiography–a fencer's mask to deflect the cold steel of reality as he struggles with his own Falstaffian shadows. The convention provides means of disguising the auctorial self, but that self reappears on other levels in the forms of other characters, and as the Hamlet's cloud on which the whole thing is projected.

I can think of few more complex critical enterprises than disentangling the mind and life of a first-person detective-story writer from the mask of his detective-narrator. The assumption of the mask is as public as vaudeville but as intensely private as a lyric poem. It is like taking an alias, the alias John Doe or Richard Roe; and it constitutes among other things an act of identification with the people one is writing for. Sam Spade is both Hammett and Hammett's audience, a Janus figure representing a city.

Hammett's books were not in the thirties to be found on the open shelves of the Kitchener Public Library. Neither were the novels of Hemingway, Faulkner, or Flaubert: as I recorded in my own early novel *Blue City*, these masters were kept in a locked cupboard for posterity. But one day in 1930 or 1931 I found *The Maltese Falcon* on the shelf of a lending library in a Kitchener tobacco shop, and I read a good part of it on the spot. It wasn't escape reading. As I stood there absorbing Hammett's novel, the slot machines at the back of the shop were clanking and whirring, and in the billiard room upstairs the perpetual poker game was being played. Like iron filings magnetized by the book in my hands, the secret meanings of the city began to organize themselves around me like a second city.

For the first time that I can remember I was consciously experiencing in my own sensibility the direct meeting of art and contemporary actuality– an experience that popular art at its best exists to provide–and beginning to find a language and a shape for that experience. It was a long time before I got it into writing, even crudely: *Blue City* was written fifteen years later. And it was much later still, long after I had made my way back to California and realized that the work of writers like Hammett and Chandler was as much my heritage as anyone's, that I wrote a detective novel called *The Galton Case*, about the reclamation of a California birthright. I was forty or so, and it was getting very late. I made an all-out effort to bend the bow that Hammett and Chandler, and Mabel Dunham, had strung for me, and to hit the difficult target of my own life.

Most popular writers seem to begin, as I did, by imitating their predecessors. There is a convention to be learned. It keeps the forms of the art alive for both the writer and his readers, endowing both with a common stock of structural shapes and formal possibilities. A popular work like Mrs. Radcliffe's *Mysteries of Udolpho*, which incidentally Coleridge gave a better review than he gave Monk Lewis's book, prepares the ground for a *Northanger Abbey*, possibly even for a *Christabel*.

The story line of Coleridge's unfinished poem, if not its subtle content, had its sources in several popular modes, including the Gothic tales of terror and the ballads, as well as in the terrible dreams that shook Coleridge nightly.

I believe that popular culture is not and need not be at odds with high culture, any more than the rhythms of walking are at odds with the dance. Popular writers learn what they can from the masters; and even the masters may depend on the rather sophisticated audience and the vocabulary of shapes and symbols which popular fiction provides. Without the traditional Gothic novel and its safety net of readers, even Henry James could not have achieved the wire-walking assurance with which he wrote *The Turn of the Screw*. The work which T. S. Eliot considered the next step taken after James by the Anglo-American novel, *The Great Gatsby*, has obvious connections with American crime fiction and the revolution effected in that fiction during the twenties. The skeleton of Fitzgerald's great work, if not its nervous system, is that of a mystery novel.

A functioning popular literature appears to be very useful if not essential to the growth of a higher literature. Chandler's debt to Fitzgerald suggests that the reverse is also true. There is a two-way connection between the very greatest work and the anonymous imaginings of a people.

I don't intend to suggest that popular literature is primarily a matrix for higher forms. Popular fiction, popular art in general, is the very air a civilization breathes. (Air itself is 80 percent nitrogen.) Popular art is the form in which a culture comes to be known by most of its members. It is the carrier and guardian of the spoken language. A book which can be read by everyone, a convention which is widely used and understood in all its variations, holds a civilization together as nothing else can.

It reaffirms our values as they change, and dramatizes the conflicts of those values. It absorbs and domesticates the spoken language, placing it in meaningful context with traditional language, forming new linguistic synapses in the brain and body of the culture. It describes new modes of behavior, new versions of human character, new shades and varieties of good and evil, and implicitly criticizes them. It holds us still and contempla-tive for a moment, caught like potential shoplifters who see their own furtive images in a scanning mirror, and wonder if the store detective is looking.

FOREWORD:

A Collection of Reviews by Ross Macdonald (Northridge, Cal.: Lord John Press, 1979).

Millar wrote book reviews for the San Francisco Chronicle *during 1958-1960, as well as occasional reviews throughout his career. His foreword to this collection is one of his many attempts—in both reminiscence and fiction—to deal with the father who abandoned him.*

On the morning of December 13, 1915, a man who had never seen Scotland sat down at his desk in a California town and wrote a Scots dialect poem in something like the manner of Bobby Burns. The poem began:

December's glaur was thick the morn
that Jock and Nanny's bairn was born.
His name was Kenneth.

Jock was my father John Millar. Nanny was my mother Ann. The bairn of course was I. Having completed the poem, my father took it down the street to the offices of the Los Gatos newspaper and offered it for publication. It was cheerfully accepted. My father and the editor were friends: both were printers as well as writers, and the poem celebrating my birth was soon in print.

My father and mother were forty years old at the time, and had returned from a difficult assignment in the Northwest Territories, on the shores of Great Slave Lake. There my father had started a small government-supported newspaper, and my mother, who was a graduate of Winnipeg General Hospital, set up a nursing station. But they had retreated at least temporarily to California.

Both of their early lives had been intensely active. My father had been a swimmer and wrestler, once winner of the two-mile swim across Colpoys Bay; a man of middle size who could lift a half-ton weight. Before he was out of his teens he was teaching school, and beginning to write. Writing came naturally to him. His father was the founding editor of the local weekly, *The Walkerton Herald*, and a literate Glasgow Scot. But I somehow doubt that my father was wholly at ease with his father.

At any rate he had come west again and taken up some of his earlier interests. Supporting himself as a harbor pilot in and out of Vancouver Harbor, and living with my mother and me in a waterfront hotel, he resumed the pursuits that had in the first place drawn him west. He had long since become familiar with the Indians of Vancouver Island and the mainland, and with the artists (like John Innes) who were painting them. My father's interests ranged into other fields, and focused on the west coast Japanese. According to the family mythology (which in this case seemed to be true), when the young Mackenzie King came out to the coast to study the Japanese and other groups, my father was one of his consultants.

I was on the scene myself in a year or two, and recording fragments of those far-off days. I haven't forgotten the childish embarrassment I suffered when I spilled black ink on a Japanese gentleman's writing pad, but I remember the courtesy he showed me, sixty years ago, on the far edge of my life. Quite suddenly, I began to notice more public events, culminating in the marching and the cheering in the Vancouver streets which signalled the end of the war. One of those days still seems the happiest day of my childhood if not my life. I mean the unforgettable day when my father first took me to sea in a harbor boat, and I stood beside him in the offshore light, with his hands and my hand on the wheel.

Not all of the adventures I shared with my father were serious. He had lost most of his hair by the time I was born, and in my earliest memories of him he was totally bald. He bought a red wig matching his coloring, but soon grew weary of it. I inherited the wig, and the streets of downtown Vancouver were haunted for a while by a three-year-old midget with shaggy red hair.

It was a time of relief for most of the western world, but not for my mother. Though she had lived in large cities like Chicago, she remained at heart an Ontario farmer's daughter. I think she had grown weary of hotels and the changing lives of their occupants, weary of even gentle people like Mrs. Swinkels, who lived just down the hall and sometimes talked of her days as a lady in waiting to the Queen of Holland. Such grandiose myths or memories only set in relief the problems of the present. My father changed place too often,

and spent too much time on what my mother considered his hobbies. He would pass half the morning explaining Indian signs to a casual visitor, or while away the night listening to the Klondike veteran who lived in a basement room of our hotel. The veteran's name was Joe Brewer, and he gave me the hunting knife with which he claimed he had once fought off a grizzly bear. The knife was there to prove it, and I believed him. So did my father, I think. My mother didn't. And when even the Great War had ended, her private war with the two men continued.

Not long after the impromptu marching in the streets that marked the end of the war, my parents separated. My mother took me to her home territory in Ontario, and from then on I lived mostly with her and her people. But throughout my life I remained my father's son, even though I saw him infrequently, sometimes not for years at a time. He grew ill and prematurely old. When he returned from his absences, his decline was underlined, sometimes very sharply, as if he had aged five years in as many weeks. I grew afraid of losing him entirely. But east and west he traveled, still on the trail of a wished-for world where Indians and white men shared the unploughed territories or climbed through the blowing passes to the north. Though my father's life was more adventurous, and less prosperous, I became aware at almost every turn that it was patterned on *his* father's life, just as my own recurrences to the west and north have been patterned on my father's.

His younger sister Margaret had become for a while the center of the family, at least for me. She was a business woman in Manitoba, and for two years she kept me in a Winnipeg boarding school. My father came to visit his sister and me on his last trip out of the far west. He was smiling but uncertain, not only of me and his sister but of the world. I loved him still (though I faulted him perhaps unfairly for leaving me years ago) but I was unable to commit myself to his uncertain life. I was eleven years old, just starting my high school years, and there was nothing I could do for my father except think of him, as I still do, with love and sorrow.

I stayed in the Winnipeg boarding school and spent the weekends with my aunt. She was a generous aunt and it was a good school; I was grateful for their protection. In my second year there, I took some scholastic prizes and spent a lot of time in the gymnasium. My father had finally gone back to his home territory in Ontario, to Walkerton and the Bruce Peninsula where I had spent earlier years with his cousin Rob. If I was inclined to believe in conspiracies, I might have come to believe that someone, perhaps my mother's family, had conspired to keep my father and me apart. But I think it was more blind accident, my father's illness and my childish inability to govern my own life. Still I felt guilty. It seemed that he had left me when I was young and helpless; now I was leaving him in his helpless age. And I wonder if the Bruce Peninsula still fosters these long conspiracies of silent pain.

My father came close to ending his days on a rundown Bruce Peninsula farm with a sick male cousin. My father had lost the power of speech but was still able to write. When I visited him and his cousin he sat smiling up at me, propped by pillows, in the middle of the ruined farm, and showed me what he had been writing. His eyes were alive with it, shining in contrast with the dull dead eyes of his cousin.

The last time I saw my father's living eyes, I was a high school boy in Southern Ontario. He was a patient in a metropolitan hospital in Toronto. He had entirely lost the power of speech, but he could still write.

He wrote me a few lines in a book on his knee.

I wish I could tell you what he wrote to me that day. His writing was so shaky that I couldn't make out the words. But I could see that it was written in rhymed couplets.

INTERVIEW:

Jane S. Bakerman, "A Slightly Stylized Conversation with Ross Macdonald," *Writers' Yearbook (1981)*, pp. 86, 88-89, 111.

In his last published interview Millar emphasized the necessity for a writer to continue probing for the meanings of his material. Kenneth Millar died of Alzheimer's Disease in 1983.

Mystery writer Ross Macdonald is tall, calm and courteous. He values his privacy, avoids talk shows, even uses a pseudonym (his real name is Kenneth Millar). Yet, he enjoys meeting people and doesn't mind being interviewed. "An interview is just a slightly stylized conversation," he tells me. "I like talking. I like conversation."

Macdonald sits quietly at the table in the Santa Barbara beach club cabaña where he has agreed to talk to me. He wears a beige, vaguely Western hat with a wide brim that shades his eyes. As he begins to speak, he looks away, but as his thoughts unfold, he looks back, sometimes from the corner of his eyes, especially when he jokes. At 66, he talks slowly and very softly, carefully thinking through his comments. Genuine communication–in its various forms–is important to him now, and it always has been. "I started writing very young and was meant to write," he says. "The verbal talent, or whatever we call it, is in your genes. Both my father and my mother were writers; also my paternal grandfather. I think it's hereditary. I'm very much what Marshall McLuhan refers to as the print mind. Print has always been terribly important to me. Both my father and my grandfather, I believe, set their own type or were capable of setting their own type. I'd like to draw a comparison between a man setting something up into type and me setting a story up into words."

Macdonald reinforced the family ties to writing when he married Margaret Sturm in 1938. Sturm would later establish herself as a successful mystery writer under the name Margaret Millar. In fact, Macdonald's family influenced his choice of his pen name. When Macdonald entered the detective story field, his wife had already established herself as a mystery writer, so Macdonald decided to use another name to keep his career separate from his wife's. Drawing on his father's name, John Macdonald Millar, he published a book as John Macdonald. That same year, however, John D. Macdonald also published a private eye story. (In fact, John D. Macdonald's mother bought several copies of Millar's book under the impression that it had been written by her son.) "It was just bad luck for me that I started out with a name that another writer really owned. And, of course, it was bad luck for John D. Macdonald's mother!" To sort out all these complications, he wrote for a time as John Ross Macdonald and then finally settled on Ross Macdonald, the name under which he has become famous.

His books, particularly the detective stories, are widely known. *The Moving Target* became the film *Harper*, and he has been honored by the Mystery Writers of America for such works as *The Wycherly Woman* and *The Zebra-Striped Hearse*. In 1973, Macdonald received the MWA's Grand Master award. In England, where he is equally famous, the Crime Writers Association singled out *The Chill* and *The Far Side of the Dollar* for recognition. Many of his books have become bestsellers, and interest, in even his earliest books, remains high. For instance, Bantam recently reissued *Meet Me at the Morgue*, originally published in 1953.

Success Follows Me

The early part of Macdonald's career was an interesting mix of success and successful failures. "I didn't get too much encouragement from editors at the very beginning," he says. "Of course, I was writing for years before I wrote a mystery novel. I had written many different kinds of things: fiction, poetry, book reviews, a column." Finally, he wrote *The Dark Tunnel*, a spy novel, while teaching English at the University of Michigan. It was accepted by Dodd, Mead & Co., the first publisher to see the book. Macdonald wrote a second spy novel while serving in the Navy. That book, *Trouble Follows Me*, was also accepted by Dodd, Mead, and was published in 1946. When he left the Navy, Macdonald joined his wife in Santa Barbara, where he lives today. There, "I wrote what I considered–and consider–my first book of any consequence, and that was *Blue City*." Dodd, Mead didn't like it–"showed no enthusiasm at all," Macdonald recalls. "Anyway, it was the best thing that ever happened to me, because I sent it to Alfred Knopf, who accepted it immediately, and the editor at Dodd, Mead said later [rejecting the book] was the greatest mistake of his professional life as a mystery editor." Macdonald's failure at Dodd, Mead worked out well for him, "because Knopf was where I wanted to be; Knopf was the leading publisher of what might be called literary crime fiction in the United States–with Hammett, Chandler and so on."

Macdonald was in fitting company. His books are intricately plotted and exciting, yet are written with the skill and polish of "the serious writer." As a result, the author's work is tremendously popular with the general public, and is taken seriously by the "establishment" of literary critics. *The Goodbye Look* (1969), for instance, placed Macdonald on the front page of *The New York Times Book Review* and the best-seller list.

This dual recognition pleases both sides of Ross Macdonald. He earned a Ph.D. in English in 1951 (he lists Faulkner, Graham Greene and Fitzgerald among his influences), yet he is a strong proponent of popular fiction: "Writers go back into the popular arts, not out of any desire to slum, but because that's where the new life is coming." Art, he says, "comes up out of a popular form, written for the people, and gradually–or, quite rapidly–it converts itself into art. . . . There are many people who consider themselves superior to popular fiction who actually aren't good enough to write it. A lot of the so-called literary material that young writers produce . . . the sentence finishes itself."

It's one of the few sentences Macdonald doesn't finish, because his speech is generally thoughtful, calm and measured. He talks slowly, and he writes slowly. "I generally produce two or three pages in a session–or, some days, less; some days, a little more. . . . Before I learned how to write slowly, I would write a book in a month, but I gradually learned how to concentrate and put more meaning into my books. There's no great honor in writing fast. I'll plan a book in great detail, spend months or even years, but chapter by chapter and page by page, I don't know what's going to come next. Factual writing is different; factual writing should be organized. But so many happy accidents happen as you are writing fiction, and if you organize too tightly in the beginning, you miss them."

Dreams and Nightmares

By writing slowly and by not overplanning, Macdonald is "conscious of being able to go in different directions at different times." he sees the writing process as "a little bit like riding a surfboard; you have to know how to stay on. You have to sense very much what the direction of the surf is and what the currents are doing, and what the wind is, and whether the shore you're aiming at has rocks on it. There are a lot of things going on at once, influencing the movement of the surfboard or the story, and you have to be aware of them all." The image is a likely one for a man who, until very recent years, enjoyed diving from the high board just a few yards from a Santa Barbara cabaña and who still swims daily in the Pacific. In fact, his cabaña seems like the American Dream come true. The three-walled little room is on the second level in a kind of cabaña complex, a bank of them, which reminds me of a barnswallow house for humans. Painted in brilliant yellow with white accents and housing orange beach furniture (easily movable but solid and comfortable), the shelter speaks of success. But it is the American Dream in more ways than one, for the cabaña's open end overlooks not only the comfortable oceanside pool and a seemingly attractive beach, but also an oil rig, vivid on the horizon.

The duality is appropriate, for Macdonald is both fiction writer *and* environmentalist, and though he has realized his own lifelong dream of making his living by his pen, he has never lost sight of the nightmare–the potential for violence and for environmental as well as personal destruction–which shadows the American Dream. "I was interested in ecology before I knew there was such a word." He has written about ecological questions in both fiction and journalistic pieces. For example, some of the powerful scenes in his novel, *The Underground Man,* take place during a forest fire. For that, he drew on his own experiences with a fire that threatened his home in Santa Barbara.

Santa Barbara, he says, is "the most interesting place in the United States, and I have an idea that California is the front edge now of American civilization. This is in both a good and a bad sense. It's where the future is beginning to happen. And where we can learn, I hope, to improve the future. One obvious thing that we want the future to have in it is a sea clean enough to swim in, and air clean enough to breathe without dying. And it means we're going to *have* to control our use of fuels and other sources of energy.

"We're right up against it here. Here we have the most complete and wonderful possibility–and, right out there on the horizon, oil platforms, and the promise of many, many, many more, a promise which I hope we will persuade them to break."

Pitching In

Macdonald, who got his start writing short stories, has great respect for short fiction: "Certainly, the short story is a major form in American literature, much more so than in English literature. It's *our* form, and I can't think of any other literary form in which so many good things have been done, starting with Hawthorne and coming right down to Flannery O'Connor." Yet, he believes he does his best writing in longer works. "I don't really set any great store by any of my short stories. Most of them were written very rapidly a long time ago, before I learned to write slowly. There are some of us who require a very long windup before we can pitch, and you don't have time for that in a short story."

Not only does he write more slowly now, but he also rewrites more. "I think my work requires more revision as it becomes a little more exploratory, perhaps. I'm talking now about sentences; I'm not talking about whole books. I do a lot of correcting, but I never sit down and rewrite a book."

Macdonald writes from about noon until he gets tired of writing, usually about 4 p.m. "One of the things I do to keep things from leaving completely what I hope is the human scale–I don't use a typewriter. I write in notebooks, by hand, and let my typist use the typewriter." His attention to the "human scale" is another reason he writes slowly. "Quite a few writers have been publicized on the grounds that they've written, oh, dozens or hundreds of books. I'm much more interested in just leaving a personal mark on the paper, and a series of marks that correspond to my own development and aging process."

It's almost as if he wants to set Ross Macdonald himself into type. And in many ways, he has done that by creating Lew Archer, Macdonald's continuing character who first appeared in *Moving Target*. Archer is not the central character of these books, but rather a recurring character; Macdonald doesn't want to "use him up," so Archer has become the focus of narrative action. "I once said, with some degree of truth, that I'm not Archer, but Archer is me. . . . He is primarily a representative of the storyteller." Calling Archer a representative of Macdonald, however, is simplifying the matter. Archer's parentage, like many of Macdonald's creations, is complex and many-faceted.

Macdonald says flatly that Archer is an imitation of James Fenimore Cooper's Natty Bumppo in that both characters are pathfinders, trackers. Their relationships to society are also somewhat similar; they are "outsiders who are inside, in a sense." George Grella, writing in *The New Republic*, has suggested that Lew Archer is the illegitimate son of Sam Spade, hero of Dashiell Hammett's *The Maltese Falcon*, and Iva Archer, the wife of Spade's partner in that book. "It's a great idea," says Macdonald of Grella's suggestion. "He's the legitimate son, legitimate in the sense that I'm Hammett's disciple. When I gave him the name Archer, I didn't recognize that I was tipping my hat to Hammett. I suppose an unconscious compliment is better than a willed one."

Actually, Archer is a combination of the author, the imagined and the observed: "I don't think he behaves terribly differently from several of the good detectives I've known and seen at work. Like Archer, they're not just interested in getting their man; they're interested in the whole picture. They love understanding what's going on, helping people, helping things to happen as they should."

Exaggerated Experiences

Perhaps the attention to "the whole picture" explains the popularity of crime and detective fiction. Macdonald calls it "one of the leading forms of the novel in this particular generation," and he agrees that crime, particularly murder, is a good metaphor for contemporary American society. "Hasn't it historically been true, from Sophocles on down, that crime has been used to focus on the problems of a culture?" In Macdonald's books, for example, readers confront, fictionally, family entanglements, problems facing various social classes, greed and environmental problems. "It seems to me that a commission of crime is an advertisement of weakness and not knowing where to go and what to do. I don't mean to sentimentalize the criminal, either; those conditions are not desirable."

What's more, Macdonald says that events in crime fiction are exaggerations of events all of us ex-perience. "We all have to make life and death judgments. It isn't just those moments involving murder and sudden death; we all have to act as judges in many things. For instance, accepting people or banishing them from our company." In the detective novel, these everyday experiences are pushed to what Macdonald calls their "extreme" form: murder and sudden death. This extreme metaphor is one lure of the genre.

Another lure is elasticity: "I have always been attracted to detective fiction. To one who was aware, as I was, of the underside of city life, detective stories seemed natural. They cover a wide range–the *full* range–from the comic to the tragic. They can be written on a dozen different levels of seriousness. These levels constitute a series of steps on which a beginning writer can gradually move toward increasing power and seriousness, or, if that is his aim, toward a wilder comedy. The field of detective fiction is so wide that it continually opens up to new ideas. It really has no set limit."

One of the directions the detective story has taken has been toward sensationalism. It has moved that way without Macdonald's active participation, however. Terrible events take place in his novels, but the overall impression is one of search rather than sex or violence, and Archer makes himself understood at all levels of society within a rather standard–and sedate–vocabulary. Macdonald says that he abandoned sensationalism before he began developing Archer. Now, "I write the kind of prose which would be destroyed by the gross impact of four-letter words. They would simply shatter the context, which depends on fairly delicate shades of meaning and echoes and references and cross-references. They would just be blown up by these words, though the words *are* legitimate. It's just that my kind of prose doesn't include the possibility of using them."

Macdonald is fascinated by words and how they're used: "I'm terribly interested in the gradations of society, and in expressing the language of various groups." Yet, he realizes his limitations: "I think a lot of my characters talk too much alike. I don't have nearly the range that some writers have."

Macdonald believes that a writer must know about two gradations of society, two cultures, in order to analyze one of them. For instance, "most people in trouble are people caught in between two of those gradations, and in order to explain what the trouble is, you have to define both sides of the pincers, so to speak." He, for instance, has lived in both the United States and Canada, and had, by age 16, lived in 50 different houses. These changes enable him to contrast and evaluate both cultures. Yet, writers don't have to be physically mobile to achieve that objectivity: "You can observe a culture without moving. You can do it through books. There has to be a third dimension, whatever provides it. It can be provided by another language; traditionally, in our culture, people have acquired that third dimension in their education, by studying Latin and Greek. Nowadays, we're doing it by turning to the Orient."

Macdonald rounds out his view of the culture he writes about by talking with detectives and attending trials. "Trials are the best source of, well, reality–or actuality–for a murder mystery writer. And things happen in the trials that you wouldn't *dare* to write about because nobody would believe them. For example, I've seen a witness in a murder case step off the stand after he'd completed his testimony and drop dead."

Macdonald recommends that writers draw from a mix of internal and external influences in writing fiction: "You have to learn to please yourself; you have to learn to slow down, and explore your own nature and your own life, and the life that you observe." What's more, he says, you can't depend only on your genes to get the work done. Nor can you depend on inspiration because inspiration arises out of the work, and not vice versa. "If you're lucky, if you're finding the subject that your imagination really wants to grapple with, it certainly is exhilarating. But you have to keep searching for it in the work as you go. There's no letup; you have to keep searching and inventing right up to the last moment."

INDEX

$106,000 Blood Money (Hammett), 229

31st of February (Symons), 63

Academy (periodical), 73
Adakian, The, 170, 176, 176–177, 240
  Hammett's editorials, 170–175
Adventures of Sam Spade (Hammett), 189, 190, 191
Adventures of the Thin Man (Hammett), 226
"Advertising IS Literature, The" (Hammett), 101, 103
"Advertising Man Writes a Love Letter" (Hammett), 103–104
"After School" (Hammett), 126
After the Thin Man (film), 157, 159
After the Thin Man (Hammett), 213
Afterwords (Macdonald), 260–266
Agee, James, 25
Alexander, Miriam, 206, 216
Alfred A. Knopf Publishers, 81, 138, 190, 193, 207, 221
  releases Hammett, 161
All the King's Men (Warren), 27
Allen, F. L., 37
  letter from Raymond Chandler, 30–31
Altman, Robert, 25
Ambler, Eric, 302, 303
American Magazine, 190
American Mercury, Incorporated, 191
American Scholar, 26
American Tragedy, An (Dreiser), 132
And Now Tomorrow (film), 23
Anderson, Isaac, 146
"Ann Vickers" (Lewis), 146
"Another Perfect Crime" (Hammett), 100–101
Another Thin Man (Hammett), review, 160, 170
Antaeus (periodical), 56–59, 61
Anthony Galton, 263, 264
Arbuckle, Roscoe (Fatty), 142, 212, 224, 237
Archer in Jeopardy (Chandler), 266–269
Arlen, Michael, 23
Armstrong, C., Mischief, 63
Arnstein, Nicky, 212
Asbury, Herbert, reviews Red Harvest, 113–114
Atkinson, Brooks, 286
Atlantic Monthly, 12, 26, 43
"Author of Stories is Sorry He Killed His Book Character" (Hammett), 149

Bacall, Lauren, 18
Bakerman, J. S., interviews Macdonald, 314–318
Balmer, Edwin, 142, 150
Baltimore News-American, 237–238
Baltimore Sun, 238–240

"Barber and His Wife, The" (Hammett), 99
Barzun, Dr. Jaques, 268
Baumgarten, Bernice, 49
  letter from Raymond Chandler, 29
Bazelon, David T., 217
Bedford-Jones, H., 97, 98
Bendix, William, 21
"Ber-Bulu" (Hammett), 98–99
"Big Knock-Over, The" (Hammett), 229
Big Sleep (Chandler), 5, 10, 17, 22, 43, 48–49, 55, 59, 65, 67, 73, 74–75, 75, 81, 254
Big Sleep (film), 23, 25
Black Mask, ix, 5, 22, 38, 72, 74, 75, 83, 86, 96, 104, 127, 190, 193, 194, 228, 229, 244, 248
  contributors, photo, 11
  See also pulp magazines
Black Money (Macdonald), 248, 307
blacklist, and Dashiell Hammett, 237, 238
Blackmail (film), 127
"Blackmailers Don't Shoot" (Chandler), 17, 73, 83
Block, Harry C., edits *Red Harvest*, 108
"Blood Money" (Hammett), 194
Blue City (Macdonald), 246, 255, 258, 262, 311
Blue Dahlia (Chandler), 18, 20–21, 23
  summary of plot and characters, 23–25, 25
Blue Dahlia (Chandler), 6, 18, 57
  reviewed by Bosley Crowther, 20–21
Bogart, Humphrey, 18, 25, 26, 81
Boucher, Anthony, 7,
  reviews Chandler, 31–32
  reviews *The Far Side of the Dollar*, 269
Box, Muriel and Sidney, 25
Boyd, William, 126
Brackett, Leigh, 25, 26
Brandt, Carl, letter from Raymond Chandler, 32
Brasher Dubloon, The (film), 25
Bready, J. H., 238–240
Brickell, Herschel, 146
Brief Stories (D. Hammett), 99
Brockden Brown, Charles, 268
Brooks, Walter R., 142, 190
  reviews *Red Harvest*, 114
Brophy, Brigid, 266
Bruccoli, Matthew J.
  Ross Macdonald, 21–26, 248–249, 252–254, 260
  "Raymond Chandler and Hollywood", 21–26
Buck, Pearl S., 276

Cain, James M., 17, 23, 276
  Cain x3 (reviewed by Ross Macdonald), 269, 271–272, 274
  Chandler comments on, 17
  The Postman Always Rings Twice, 253

California, Southern, culture, 37–38, 38, 39, 70–72, 81–82
Callaghan, Morley, 298, 299
Camus, Albert, 274
Carr, John Dickson, 7, 65
Catcher in the Rye (Salinger), 287
Cerf, Bennett, 161
Chamberlain, John, reviews *The Thin Man*, 147
Chambers's Journal, 7–8
Chandler, Maurice (Raymond Chandler's father), 82
Chandler, Raymond, ix, ix–x
  Archer in Jeopardy, 266–269
  location of archives, 4
  The Big Sleep. See under title
  on James M. Cain, 17
  reviews Cain x3, 269, 271–272, 274
  "Blackmailers Don't Shoot", 17, 73, 83
  Blue Dahlia, 20–21, 23, 57
  Chronicles of Hecate County, 7
  Double Indemnity, 5–6, 23
  Down These Mean Streets, 42
  early life, 4–5, 18, 82–83
  Farewell, My Lovely. See under title
  Five Murderers, 32
  compared to Hemingway, 37
  High Window. See under title
  Lady in the Lake, 17, 18, 25, 31, 43, 73
  use of language, 42–43
  in later life, 43–44
  letters, 4–5, 8–9, 10, 12, 14, 29–34, 36–37 61–65
  Little Sister, 6, 25, 31, 39, 49, 67, 75
  The Long Goodbye. See under title
  Macdonald compared to, 254–260
  marriage, 75, 77, 83
  military service, 5, 82
  on *The Moving Target*, 254
  Murder, My Sweet, 18
  obituary, 65
  as oil executive, 82
  "Oscar Night in Hollywood", 12
  Philip Marlowe. See under Philip Marlowe
  Playback, 23, 67, 73, 77
  poems of, 7–8
  Poodle Springs Story, 77
  published materials, list of, 3, 9–10, 12, 26
  Ross Macdonald compared to, 255–260
  scarlet fever, 4–5
  on screenwriting, 14–15, 17, 18, 21–22, 24
  "Simple Art of Murder", 42, 67
  as social historian, 77–80
  Strangers on a Train, 25
  suicide attempt, 75
  "Twelve Notes on the Mystery Story", 56–59, 61
  "Writers in Hollywood", 21–22
  on writing, 4, 6, 7, 8–9, 29–32, 56–59, 61
  unfinished works, 10, 12
Charteris, Leslie, 17
Chekhov, Anton, 299
Chesterton, G. K., 268
Chill, The (Macdonald), 277, 306

Christie, Agatha, 58, 73
  Murder in a Calais Coach, 56
Chronicles of Hecate County (Chandler), 7
City Streets (Hammett), 127
Civil Rights Congress, 184, 207, 209, 211, 216, 221, 225, 227, 238
  bail fund matter hearing, 196–205, 206
  See also Committee for Free Election, Committee on Election Rights,
  Communism, McCarthy, Smith Act, Un-American Activities
Cleansing of Poisonville (Hammett). See *Red Harvest*.
Clork, Harry, Mr. Dynamite, 157
Cody, Phil, 96, 228
Coleridge, Samuel Taylor, *Rime of the Ancient Mariner*, 274, 309–310
Collier, John, 246
Collier's magazine, 190
Collins, Wilkie, 235, 268
Colodny, Corporal Robert, 169
Commentary Magazine, 217
Committee on Election Rights–1940, 164
Committee on Free Elections, 167
Communism, Communist Party, 26, 27, 162, 165, 188–189, 197, 206, 207, 209, 211, 217, 218, 219, 220, 221, 222, 223, 224, 226, 237, 241
  See also Civil Rights Congress, Committee on Free Elections,
  McCarthy, Smith Act, Un-American Activities Committee
Conan Doyle, Sir Arthur, 17, 41–42, 56, 77, 283, 284, 309
  "A Study in Scarlet", 191
  The Hounds of the Baskervilles, 65
Conrad, Joseph, 101
Continental Op, 191, 193, 194, 195, 206, 214, 215, 216, 229, 237
Cooper, Gary, 126, 127
Cooper, James Fenimore, 67, 224
Coxe, George Harmon, 22
  letter from Raymond Chandler, 29
Crane, 248–249
CRC, See Civil Rights Congress.
Crosland, Alan, 157
Crowther, Bosley, 20–21, 25
  reviews film *Blue Dahlia*, 20–21
Cuppy, Will, 136, 148
Curley, James Michael, 82

da Silva, Howard, 23
Daily Express, 82
Daily Princetonian, 159–160
Daily Worker, 188–189, 227–228
Dain Curse (Hammett), 190, 193, 194, 195, 209, 213, 215, 224, 228, 229, 239
Daly, Carroll John, 22
Dannay, Frederick. See *Ellery Queen*
Dark Tunnel (Macdonald), 246, 297, 298, 315
Dashiell Hammett Omnibus, The (Hammett), 193
David Copperfield (Dickens), 64

Davies, Robertson, 296, 298
Davis, Bette, 166
"Dead Yellow Women" (Hammett), 98–99, 194
"December 1" (Hammett), 205
"Decline and Fall of the Detective Story" (Maugham)
Delilah (Biblical), 99
Depression, Great, 5, 246
Detroit News, 190
Development of the Detective Novel (Murch), 267–269
Dickens, Charles, 215, 235, 268, 306, 308
   David Copperfield, 64
   Oliver Twist, 296
dime novels. See pulp magazines
Dmytryk, Edward, 23
Dodd, Mead Publishers reject Macdonald, 315
Dolan, Josephine Anna (later Josephine Hammett), 88, 89, 215, 227
Dos Passos, John, 217
Double Indemnity (Cain), 269, 271, 272
Double Indemnity (screenplay), 5–6, 23
Douglas, Kirk, 237
Dowling, Doris, 21
"Down These Streets A Mean Man Must Go" (Macdonald), 309
Dreiser, Theodore, 272
   An American Tragedy, 132
drug use in Hammett novels, 215
Dulwich College Preparatory School, 82
Dunham, Mabel, 311
Durham, Philip, *Down These Mean Streets a Man Must Go*, 26, 44, 228
dust jackets, importance of, in marketing, x

Editor, 98
Eisler, Gerhardt, 184, 206, 237
Ellin, Stanley, 302
Elliot, G., 65, 67–72
Equality Publishers, 162
Esquire magazine, 142
Experience (magazine), 100

Far Side of the Dollar (Macdonald), 315
   reviewed by Anthony Boucher, 269
Farewell Murder (Hammett), 194
Farewell My Lovely (film), 25
Farewell, My Lovely (Chandler), 17, 18, 23, 40, 43, 45, 47, 48, 73, 83
   characters of, 40–41
Farrell, 217
Faulkner, William, 22, 26, 138, 215, 268, 308, 311, 315
Fiedler, Leslie, 79
Fisher, Steve, 25
Fitzgerald, F. Scott, x, 20, 22, 246, 249, 288, 299, 315
   The Great Gatsby, 39, 274, 288, 300
Five Murderers (Chandler), 32
five word question, the, 150
Flagg, James Montgomery, 98
Flaubert, Gustave, 263, 311
   Madame Bovary, 263

Flint, R. W., reviews Chandler, 26–27
Ford, Bob, 297
France, Anatole, 97, 101
Francis, J., letter from Raymond Chandler, 63
Franco, General Francisco, 227
Freeling, Nicholas, *In Bloody Murder*, 302
Freeman, Austin, 57, 58
Freud, Sigmund, influence on Ross Macdonald, 260–266, 286, 293. See also Oedipus
Friends of Eddie Coyle (Higgins), 81
"From the Memoirs of a Private Detective" (Hammett), 90–91
Furthman, Jules, 26

Galton Case, The (Macdonald), 248, 282, 283, 286, 295, 297, 311
   plot, 264, 265, 266
   as representation of author's psychological conflicts, 260–267
Gardner, Erle Stanley, 17, 22
Garner, James, 25
G.I. Galley, 174
Gide, Andre, 239
Gilkes, A. H., 83
"Girl Hunt" (Hammett), 158, 212
Glass Key, The (Hammett), 127, 132, 138, 160, 195, 196, 215, 225, 228, 229, 238
   reviews, 136, 142
Gogol, 301
"Golden Age" mystery, 100
"Golden Horseshoe, The" (Hammett), 194, 229
Goldman, William, reviews *The Goodbye Look*, 274–277
Goldwyn, Samuel, 128
Goodbye Look, The (Macdonald), 306, 308, 315
   reviewed by William Goldman, 274–277
Goodrich, Frances, 159, 160, 170
Gores, Joe, 304
Gould, Elliot, 25
Grant, Cary, 33
Graves, Robert, 72–73, 239
Great Gatsby, The (Fitzgerald), 39, 274, 288, 300
Green, Ashbel, 81
Greene, Graham, 78, 315
Greene, Helga, letter from Raymond Chandler, 74
Grella, George, 289, 318
   on Archer novels, 305–308
Grettir the Strong, 253
Grogg, Sam Jr., interviews Ross Macdonald, 288–295
Grosset and Dunlop, 190
Gruber, Frank, 22
Guardian Review, 81
Guessworthy, John, 101

Hackett, Albert, 159, 160, 170
"Hairy One, The" (Hammett), 98–99
Hall, Gus, 221
Halliday, Brett, 23
Hamilton, Hamish, 31, 43
   letters from Raymond Chandler, 36, 74
Hammett, Dashiell, 22, 38, 43, 58, 63, 64, 65, 67, 72, 79,

83, 238, 247, 255, 269, 272, 274, 284, 300, 302–303, 305, 311, 315
Adventures of Sam Spade, 190
"The Advertisement IS Literature", 101
"The Advertising Man Writes a Love Letter", 103–104
"After School", 126
After the Thin Man, 159, 213
and alcohol, 238, 239, 241
"Another Perfect Crime", 100–101
Another Thin Man, review, 160, 170
location of archives, 86
"Author of Stories is Sorry He Killed His Book Character", 149
"Barber and His Wife", 99
"Ber-Bulu", 98–99
"The Big Knock-Over", 229
blacklisted, 237, 238
"Blood Money", 194
Brief Stories, 99
credited with capture of robbers, 93, 96
City Streets, 127
and Civil Rights Congress. See under Civil Rights Congress
and Communist Party. See under Communist Party
Dain Curse. See under title
The Dashiell Hammett Omnibus, 193
Dead Yellow Women, 98–99, 194
death, 225
divorce, 225
drug use in novels, 215
early life, 86–87, 209–210, 227, 239,
editorials in *The Adakian*, 170–175
The Farewell Murder, 194
and FBI, 152
and Ferris wheel case, 212
"From the Memoirs of a Private Detective", 90–91
"Girl Hunt", 158, 212
The Glass Key. See under title.
The Golden Horseshoe, 194, 229
"The Hairy One", 98–99
compared to Hemingway, 235–236, 249
The House in Turk Street, 195
testifies in Warner Brothers suit, 189–190
"$106,000 Blood Money", 229
"In Defence of the Sex Story", 97–98
jailed, 196, 206, 216, 225, 237
testifies before McCarthy Committee, 219–224
Maltese Falcon. See under title
military service, 87, 88, 156, 168, 174–175, 178–179, 179, 182–183, 187–188, 210, 210–211, 227, 240–242
No Orchids for Miss Blandish, 194
novels banned, 226
obituaries, 225–228
writes parody, 101, 103
as Pinkerton Detective. See under Pinkerton Detective.
political activism of, ix. See also Civil Rights Congress, Committee for Free Election,

Communism, McCarthy, Smith Act, Un-American Activities.
publications, list of, 85
"Question's One Answer", 97
Red Harvest. See under title
reviews written by, 122–123, 125
royalties blocked, 224
Sam Spade. See under Sam Spade
taxes delinquent, 230–234
"There Was a Young Man" (unfinished novel), 161
Thin Man. See under title.
Thin Man (film), 149
and tuberculosis, 212, 215, 225
"Watch on the Rhine" (screenplay), 166, 237, 240
women in writing of, 195, 214
"Women, Politics, and Murder", 96, 97, 229
"Zigzags and Treachery", 229
Hammett, R. T. (Dashiell's nephew), 236–237, 237–238
Hammett, Rebecca (Dashiell's sister), 228, 239
Hammett, Richard (Dashiell's brother), 237
hard-boiled style, ix, 22, 248, 254–260, 289
Harker, Herbert, 260
"Harper" (screenplay), 274
Harrington, Joseph, 150, 156
Harvard University, 301
Hawthorne, Nathaniel, 316
Hecht, Ben, 25, 215
Helen Morrison, 23
Hellman, Lillian, 129, 132, 207, 237, 240
    An Unfinished Woman, 238
    Watch on the Rhine, 166, 208
Hemingway, Ernest, 22, 132, 147, 211, 217, 226, 235, 248–249, 288, 299
    Chandler compared to, 37
    Hammett compared to, 227, 235–236, 249
Henderson, D., *Mr. Bowling Buys a Newspaper*, 63
Henry VIII (Shakespeare), 97
Herrmann, David, letter from Ross Macdonald, 247
Higgins, George V., 81–83
    The Friends of Eddie Coyle, 81
High Window (Chandler), 17, 18, 23, 25, 43, 47, 73, 75
Highsmith, Patricia, *Strangers on a Train*, 25, 60
Hitchcock, Alfred, 25
    Shadow of a Doubt, 33
    "Strangers on a Train" (screenplay), 60
Hitler, Adolph, 189, 218
Hitler-Stalin pact, 218
Hogan, Mrs. Robert, letter from Raymond Chandler, 30
Holding, Elizabeth Saxony, *The Innocent Mrs. Duff*, 61, 63
Hoover, J. Edgar, 152
Hounds of the Baskervilles (Conan Doyle), 65
House in Turk Street (Hammett), 195
Houseman, John, 23
    letter from Raymond Chandler, 36
Howard, James, letter from Raymond Chandler, 8–9
Hurlburt, Pearl Eugenie (later Cissy Chandler), 82–83

Ibberson, D. J., letter from Raymond Chandler, 32–34, 35
In Bloody Murder (Freeling), 302
"In Defence of the Sex Story" (Hammett), 97–98
In Short, 175, 178–179
Innes, John, 313
Innocent Mrs. Duff (Saxony Holding), 25, 26
Instant Enemy, The (Macdonald), 306, 307
Inward Journey (Macdonald), 249, 254–260, 355
Ivory Grin, The (Macdonald), 248

James, Francis, 86
Jeffers, Robinson, 215
Jefferson School of Social Science, 218
Jessie Florian, 40, 45, 46, 46–47
Journal of Popular Culture, 288–295
Judge (magazine), 103
Julia (film), 240

Kafka, Franz, 300
Kalb, Bernard, 240–242
Kaufman, Mary, 207
Kierkegaard, *The Sickness Unto Death*, 274
Kibbee, Guy, 129
King Features Syndicate, 155, 158
King, Makenzie, 313
Kitchener, Ontario, 296, 297, 310
Kitchener Collegiate Institute Grumbler, 246
Knopf, Alfred A., 127, 257, 271, 315
    letter from Raymond Chandler, 10
    letter from Ross Macdonald, 254–260
Knopf, Blanche, 107
    letter from Raymond Chandler, 17
Krasner, William, *Walk the Dark Streets*, 63
Kross, Sid, 174–175, 178–179

Ladd, Alan, 21, 23, 25
Lady in the Lake (Chandler), 17, 18, 25, 31, 43
Lake, Veronica, 21, 23, 24–25, 25
Lardner, Ring, 26
Last Tycoon, The (Fitzgerald), 25
Laurence, Margaret, 298
Lawrence, D. H., 194–195
Leacock, Stephen, 246, 296–297, 299
League of American Writers, 218, 227
Lew Archer, ix, 247, 252, 253, 255, 264, 267, 269, 274, 275, 279, 283, 285, 290, 291, 305, 525
    character of, 279, 281, 282, 292–293, 293–294
    relationship to Macdonald, 316–317
Lewis, Sinclair, 239
    Ann Vickers, 146
    The Monk, 309–310
Lid, R. W., reviews Chandler, 37–51, 53, 55–56
    discusses California setting, 37–40
Lindsay Marriott, 40, 45, 46, 46–47
Little Sister, The (Chandler), 6, 25, 31, 39, 49, 67, 75
London, Jack, 97
Long Goodbye, The (Chandler), 25, 37, 38, 43, 49, 50, 55, 67, 73, 77, 79, 83, 301
Los Angeles Times, 10, 205–206, 228–229, 235–237

Lowe, Edmund, 157
Loy, Myrna, 149, 154, 160, 224, 237
Lukas, Paul, 126, 127, 129, 166

McCarten, John, 25
McCarthy, Joseph, Committee, 219, 226, 227, 237
McClellan, John, 222, 223, 238
McCloor, Babe, 212
McCoy, Horace, 22
Macdonald, Ross, x, 22, 260, 312–314
    location of archives, 244
    autobiographical information, 261–262
    Black Money, 248, 307
    Blue City, 246, 255, 311, 315
    compared to Raymond Chandler, 254–260
    The Chill, 277, 306, 307
    The Dark Tunnel, 246, 298, 315
    death, 314
    "Down These Streets a Mean Man Must Go", 309
    early life, 244, 246, 263, 285, 296, 297, 312–314
    The Far Side of the Dollar, 315
    father, 297, 312, 313
    and influence of Sigmund Freud, 260–266
    The Galton Case. See under title.
    The Goodbye Look, 274–277, 306, 308, 315
    on hard-boiled style, 254–260
    as high school teacher, 261
    "In the First Person" Self-Portrait, 249 n. 2
    The Instant Enemy, 306, 307
    interviewed by college students, 282–288
    Inward Journey, 249, 254–260, 355
    The Ivory Grin, 248
    letters, 247, 254
    military service, 246, 253, 261, 300, 315
    The Moving Target, 247, 252, 258
    "Preface to the Galton Case", 260–263
    psychiatric treatment of, 260
    publications, list of, 243–244
    published in high school annual, 249–252
    reviews for *San Francisco Chronicle*, 312–314
    reviews *The Development of the Detective Novel*, 267–269
    social commentary of, 284–285, 289–292, 317, 318
    The Zebra-Striped Hearse, 248
    Three Roads, 246–247
    Trouble Follows Me, 315
    The Underground Man, 277–278, 279, 281, 282, 295, 316
    on use of vernacular, 302–303
    The Way Some People Die, 258
    on writing, 260–263, 288–295, 317–318
McLuhan, Marshall, 298, 299, 314
McManus, John, 25
MacMurray, Fred, 18
McShane, Frank, 81
    The Life of Raymond Chandler, 82
Madame Bovary (Flaubert), 263
magazines, pulp. See pulp magazines, *Black Mask*
Mailer, Norman, 300
Malloy, Doris, *Mr. Dynamite*, 157

Maltese Falcon (Hammett), 22, 72–73, 126, 132, 174, 189, 190, 191, 193, 195, 214–215, 225, 228, 229, 240, 252, 274, 301, 307, 318
Mamoulian, Rouben, 126, 127
marketing, literary, x, 133, 144, 150, 155
Marlowe (film), 25
Marshall, George, 21, 24
Marshall, Josephine (later Josephine Hammett), 227
Matthews, T. S., 148
Maugham, Somerset, 20, 210
    "The Decline and Fall of the Detective Story", 63–65
Measure for Measure (Shakespeare), 97
Melville, Herman, 272
Mencken, H. L., 99–100, 101, 228, 272
Mersereau, John, 266
Metro-Goldwyn-Mayer, 22, 149, 154, 157, 159, 160, 170, 192, 213
Mildred Pierce (Cain), 269, 271, 272
Miles Archer, 253, 274, 301
Millar, Kenneth. See Macdonald, Ross
Millar, Margaret (Ross Macdonald's wife), 246, 269, 311
Miller, Henry, 194–195
Miller, Mary Hammett (Dashiell Hammett's daughter) 227
Mischief (Armstrong), 63
Mitchum, Robert, 25
Monk, The (Lewis), 309–310
Monroe Stahr, 25
Montgomery, George, 25
Moose Malloy, 40
Morgan, Claudia, 226
Morton, Charles, 43
    letter from Raymond Chandler, 12, 14–15, 17, 29–30
Moving Target (Macdonald), 247, 252, 253, 256, 258, 292, 315, 316
    Raymond Chandler comments, 254
Mr. Bowling Buys a Newspaper (Henderson), 63
Mr. Dynamite (Clork and Malloy), 157
Munro, H. H., 82
Murch, A.E., *The Development of the Detective Novel*, 267–269
Murder in a Calais Coach (Christie), 56
Murder, My Sweet (Chandler), 18
Murder, My Sweet (film), 23
"Murders in the Rue Morgue" (Poe), 284
Mystery Writers' Annual, 235–237
Mystery Writers of America, 8
    Ross Macdonald elected President, 269

Name is Archer, The (Macdonald), 259
Nat Turner (Styron), 263
Nathan, George J., 99–100, 228
Nation, 25, 65, 67–72
National Observer, 249 n.1
Natty Bumppo, 247
Ned Beaumont, 63–64, 211, 238
New Candor, The, 143, 145, 150

New Republic, 148, 305–308, 318
New Statesman, 114
New York Evening Journal, 150
New York Evening Post, 125, 190, 210
New York Herald-Tribune, 136, 142, 190
New York Post, 190, 206–219
New York Review of Books, 238
New York Times, 10, 127, 136, 145, 157, 225, 240–242, 286
New York Times Book Review, x, 31–32, 146, 269, 277, 315
New Yorker, 25, 72, 132
Newman, Paul, 256
Nick Carraway, 39
Nick Charles, 146, 154, 156, 159, 160, 170, 191, 211, 214, 226, 239. See also *The Thin Man*
"Nightshade" (Hammett), 220
No Orchids for Miss Blandish (Hammett), 194
Nobel Prize, 276
Nora Charles, 159, 226, 239
Norris, Frank, 67, 247
North American Review, 146
North, Harry, 228
Nugent, Frank S., 157, 159, 160, 170

O'Connor, Flannery, 316
O'Hara, John, 22, 81
Oliver Twist (Dickens), 296
"On The Make" (Hammett), 157
Ontario, Canada, 296
Ormonde, Czenzi, 25
Oscar Night in Hollywood (Chandler), 12
Othello (Shakespeare), 48
Outlook, 190
Outlook and Independent, 101
Oxford English Dictionary, 302

Packard, Frank L., 296
Pagano, Joe, 246
Pageant (magazine), 17
Paramount studio, 14, 22, 126, 157
Parker, Dorothy, 132
parody
    written by Dashiell Hammett, 101, 103
Partisan Review, 26, 27
Pascal, Cissy (later Cissy Chandler), 82–83
Paul, Elliot, 246
Philip Marlowe, ix, 17, 20, 22, 23, 25, 26, 27, 31, 33, 38, 39, 39–40, 41–42, 46–47, 49, 50, 55, 62, 65, 67, 75, 77, 78, 78–79, 252, 253, 255, 301
    character of, 20, 33–34, 36, 36–37, 41
    and marriage, 80
    relationship to Chandler, 44, 44–45
Pilat, Oliver, 206, 206–219
Pinkerton's Detectives and Dashiell Hammett, 86, 90–91, 93–94, 100, 105, 125–126, 142, 193, 210, 212, 216, 224, 225, 227, 229, 237, 239
Piper, Henry Dan, 159–160
Playback (Chandler), 23, 25, 43, 67, 73, 77
PM magazine, 25